The Official (ISC)²®
SSCP® CBK® Reference

Sixth Edition

The Official (ISC)²® SSCP® CBK® Reference

Sixth Edition

MICHAEL S. WILLS, SSCP, CISSP, CAMS

SYBEX®
A Wiley Brand

Acknowledgments

This newly revised sixth edition that you hold in your hands is the culmination of more than a year of effort with the team at (ISC)² that I had the privilege of working with. This Common Book of Knowledge reflects the consensus across that team of the know-how that SSCPs need, on the job, to be part of maintaining the safety, security, integrity, and availability of the information systems we all depend upon.

Where it achieves that objective, and provides you value in the years to come—is a testament to the generosity of everyone on that combined set of project teams in sharing their insights with me. (And where it fails to work well, or work at all, it's my own darned fault.) Countless hours on Zoom and Webex with subject-matter experts like Graham Thornburrow-Dobson, John Warsinksi, Maytal Brooks-Kempler, Laural Hargadon, and Fabio Cerullo sharpened my thinking and focused my writing more toward the operational aspects of cybersecurity and less on the theoretical. A special thank-you too goes out to Kaitlyn Langenbacher, the project owner for those updates at (ISC)², and all of the editors and proofreaders working with her; throughout all of that, the support, questions, and co-creativity they brought made this work a truly joint, collaborative one. I would also like to acknowledge my faculty teammates here at Embry-Riddle Aeronautical University for sharing their frank and candid views throughout many conversations on making this body of knowledge accessible and engaging in the classroom. The ideas and experiences of Drs. Aaron Glassman and Jason Clark have also profoundly affected my approach to what you see before you here in this book.

Since this book needed to speak to troubleshooters, I drew on decades of teaching I'd received from many professionals in the military, in government, and in the private sector about the fine art and brute-force cybernetics of debugging networks, systems, highly secure communications systems, and all of the arcana of controlling space-based systems working many different missions. I've also drawn on years of working with small and medium but otherwise rather down-to-earth business IT systems and what it took to get them back into operations. Where that problem-solving focus comes through clearly and helps you shoot the troubles you have to deal with, I owe a great debt of thanks to those who let me learn how in real time.

Without the tireless support of the editorial team at Wiley/Sybex—especially Jim Minatel and Pete Gaughan—I think I'd still be struggling with unflowing the lessons and reflowing them into reference and troubleshooting memory-joggers. The technical review by Graham Thornburrow-Dobson, as well as by Tara Zeiler and Fabio Cerullo at (ISC)², have all helped make what you have in your hands right now deliver the right content in the best way possible. Tracy Brown, Barath Kumar Rajasekaran, Kim Wimpsett, and the rest of the team of proofreaders and copyeditors made it all look great too! Any remaining mistakes, omissions, or confusing passages that remain are mine and no one else's; let me know please when you find one!

Finally, I wish to thank my wife Nancy. She saved my life and brought me peace. Her strength inspired me to say "yes" one more time when Jim called me, again, about doing this book, and she has kept both of us healthy and happy throughout. We go together, on adventures like writing, and on ones for which we do need to pack a pocket handkerchief.

About the Author

 **Michael S. Wills**, SSCP, CISSP, CAMS, is Assistant Professor of Applied and Innovative Information Technologies at the College of Business, Embry-Riddle Aeronautical University—Worldwide, where he continues his graduate and undergraduate teaching and research in cybersecurity and information assurance.

Mike has also been an advisor on science and technology policy to the UK's Joint Intelligence Committee, Ministry of Justice, and Defense Science and Technology Laboratories, helping them to evolve an operational and policy consensus relating topics from cryptography and virtual worlds, through the burgeoning surveillance society, to the proliferation of weapons of mass disruption (not just "destruction") and their effects on global, regional, national, and personal security. For a time, this had him sometimes known as the UK's nonresident expert on outer space law.

Mike has been supporting the work of (ISC)² by writing, editing, and updating books, study guides, and course materials for both their SSCP and CISSP programs. He wrote the *SSCP Official Study Guide 2nd Edition* in 2019, followed quickly by the *SSCP Official Common Book of Knowledge 5th Edition*. He was lead author for the 2021 update of (ISC)²'s official CISSP and SSCP training materials. Mike has also contributed to several industry roundtables and white papers on digital identity and cyber fraud detection and prevention and has been a panelist and webinar presenter on these and related topics for ACAMS.

Mike earned his BS and MS degrees in computer science, both with minors in electrical engineering, from Illinois Institute of Technology, and his MA in Defence Studies from King's College, London. He is a graduate of the Federal Chief Information Officer program at National Defense University and the Program Manager's Course at Defense Systems Management College.

Mike and his wife Nancy currently call Wexford, Ireland, their home. Living abroad since the end of the last century, they find new perspectives, shared values, and wonderful people wherever they go. As true digital nomads, it's getting time to move again. Where to? They'll find out when they get there.

About the Technical Editor

Graham Thornburrow-Dobson, CISSP, SSCP, is a security consultant and instructor with more than 30 years of experience in IT, with 20 years focused on IT security and related training.

Graham is an authorized (ISC)^2 instructor who has delivered security training to a wide range of security professionals globally via both classroom-based and online training.

Graham has also been supporting the efforts of (ISC)^2 in the continued development of their CISSP, SSCP, and ISSAP programs as both a writer and a technical editor.

Graham currently resides in Lincolnshire, United Kingdom. Graham would add more, but, hey, security!

Contents at a Glance

Contents

Foreword

WELCOME TO THE OFFICIAL *(ISC)² SSCP CBK Reference*! By picking up this book, you have demonstrated your commitment to continuing your professional education and have made the decision to take the next step in your career.

An (ISC)² Systems Security Certified Practitioner (SSCP) credential shows an understanding of and proficiency with the hands-on technical work that is needed in the information security field. The certification is ideal for IT professionals responsible for the hands-on operational security of their organizations' critical assets, including those in positions such as network security engineers, systems administrators and engineers, security analysts, consultants and administrators, database administrators, and network analysts.

It demonstrates that you closely follow best practices, policies, and procedures in accordance with the SSCP Common Body of Knowledge. Whether you are using this guide to supplement your preparation to sit for the exam or you are an existing SSCP member using this as a reference, this book helps to facilitate the practical knowledge you need to assure strong information security for your organization's daily operations.

(ISC)² promotes the development of information security professionals throughout the world. As an SSCP with all the benefits of (ISC)² membership, you will become part of a global network of more than 160,000 certified professionals who are working to inspire a safe and secure cyber world. By becoming a member of (ISC)² you will have also officially committed to ethical conduct that aligns with your position of trust as a cybersecurity professional.

Reflecting the most pertinent issues that security practitioners currently face, along with the best practices for mitigating those issues, *The Official (ISC)² SSCP CBK Reference* offers step-by-step guidance through the seven different domains included in the exam, which are:

- Access Controls
- Security Operations and Administration
- Risk Identification, Monitoring and Analysis
- Incident Response and Recovery

- Cryptography
- Networks and Communications Security
- Systems and Application Security

Drawing from a comprehensive, up-to-date global body of knowledge, this book prepares you to join thousands of practitioners worldwide who have obtained the SSCP. For those with proven technical skills and practical security knowledge, the SSCP certification is the ideal credential. The SSCP confirms the breadth and depth of practical security knowledge expected of those in hands-on operational IT roles. The certification provides industry-leading confirmation of a practitioner's ability to implement, monitor, and administer information security policies and procedures that ensure data confidentiality, integrity, and availability (CIA).

The goal for SSCP credential holders is to achieve the highest standard for cybersecurity expertise—managing multiplatform IT systems while keeping sensitive data secure. This becomes especially crucial in the era of digital transformation, where cybersecurity permeates virtually every data stream. Organizations that can demonstrate world-class cybersecurity capabilities and trusted transaction methods enable customer loyalty and fuel success.

The opportunity has never been greater for dedicated professionals like yourself to carve out a meaningful career and make a difference in their organizations. *The Official (ISC)² SSCP CBK Reference* will be your constant companion in protecting and securing the critical data assets of your organization, and it will serve you for years to come as you progress in your career.

I wish you luck on the exam and success in your next step along your career path.

Best regards,

Clar Rosso

Clar Rosso, CEO, (ISC)²

Introduction

CONGRATULATIONS ON CHOOSING TO become a Systems Security Certified Practitioner (SSCP)! In making this choice, you're signing up to join the professionals who strive to keep our information-based modern world safe, secure, and reliable. SSCPs and other information security professionals help businesses and organizations keep private data *private* and help to ensure that published and public-facing information stays unchanged and unhacked.

Whether you are new to the fields of information security, information assurance, or cybersecurity, or you've been working with these concepts, tools, and ideas for some time now, this book is here to help you grow your knowledge, skills, and abilities as a systems security professional.

Let's see how!

ABOUT THIS BOOK

You're here because you need a ready reference source of ideas, information, knowledge, and experience about information systems security. Users of earlier editions of the CBK describe it as the place to go when you need to look up something about bringing your systems or networks back up and online—when you can't exactly Google it. As a first responder in an information security incident, you may need to rely on what you know and what you've got at hand as you characterize, isolate, and contain an intruder and their malware or other causal agents. This book cannot answer all of the questions you'll have in real time, but it may just remind you of important concepts as well as critical details when you need them. As with any reference work, it can help you think your way through to a solution. By taking key definitions and concepts and *operationalizing* them, showing how they work in practice, this book can enrich the checklists, troubleshooting guides, and task-focused procedures that you may already be using in your work.

The SSCP Seven Domains

This book directly reflects the SSCP Common Body of Knowledge, which is the comprehensive framework that (ISC)² has developed to express what security professionals should have working knowledge of. These domains include theoretical knowledge, industry best practices, and applied skills and techniques. Chapter by chapter, this book takes you through these domains, with major headings within each chapter being your key to finding what you need when you need it. Topics that are covered in more than one domain will be found within sections or subsections in each chapter as appropriate.

This Sixth Edition has been updated to reflect (ISC)²'s Domain Content Outline, released in November 2021. This outline update changed the relative order of the first two domains, but largely kept the topics within each domain the same. Revisions, clarifications, and additions have been made throughout, while a new Appendix brings topics from across those Domains together to provide you assistance with today's thorniest of information security challenges.

(ISC)² is committed to helping members learn, grow, and thrive. The Common Body of Knowledge (CBK) is the comprehensive framework that helps it fulfill this commitment. The CBK includes all the relevant subjects a security professional should be familiar with, including skills, techniques, and best practices. (ISC)² uses the various domains of the CBK to test a certificate candidate's levels of expertise in the most critical aspects of information security. You can see this framework in the SSCP Exam Outline at `https://www.isc2.org/-/media/ISC2/Certifications/Exam-Outlines/2021/SSCP-Exam-Outline-English-Nov-2021.ashx?la=en&hash=ABCB9E34548D2E8170ADA04EAAD3003F5577D3F5`

Successful candidates are competent in the following seven domains:

Domain 1 Security Operations and Administration Identification of information assets and documentation of policies, standards, procedures, and guidelines that ensure confidentiality, integrity, and availability, such as:

1.1 Comply with codes of ethics.

1.2 Understand security concepts.

1.3 Identify and implement security controls.

1.4 Document and maintain functional security controls.

1.5 Participate in asset management lifecycle (hardware, software, and data).

1.6 Participate in change management lifecycle.

1.7 Participate in implementing security awareness and training (e.g., social engineering/phishing).

1.8 Collaborate with physical security operations (e.g., data center assessment, badging).

Domain 2 Access Controls Policies, standards, and procedures that define users (human and nonhuman) as entities with identities that are approved to use an organization's systems and information assets, what they can do, which resources and information they can access, and what operations they can perform on a system, such as:

2.1 Implement and maintain authentication methods.

2.2 Support internetwork trust architectures.

2.3 Participate in the identity management lifecycle.

2.4 Understand and apply access controls.

Domain 3 Risk Identification, Monitoring, and Analysis Risk identification is the review, analysis, and implementation of processes essential to the identification, measurement, and control of loss associated with unplanned adverse events. Monitoring and analysis are determining system implementation and access in accordance with defined IT criteria. This involves collecting information for identification of, and response to, security breaches or events, such as:

3.1 Understand the risk management process.

3.2 Understand legal and regulatory concerns (e.g., jurisdiction, limitations, privacy).

3.3 Participate in security assessment and vulnerability management activities.

3.4 Operate and monitor security platforms (e.g., continuous monitoring).

3.5 Analyze monitoring results.

Domain 4 Incident Response and Recovery Prevent. Detect. Respond. Recover. Incident response and recovery focus on the near real-time actions that must take place if the organization is to survive a cyberattack or other information security incident, get back into operation, and continue as a viable entity. In this domain, the SSCP gains an understanding of how to handle incidents using consistent, applied approaches within a framework of business continuity planning (BCP) and disaster recovery planning (DRP). These approaches are utilized to mitigate damages, recover business operations, and avoid critical business interruption:

4.1 Support incident lifecycle (e.g., National Institute of Standards and Technology [NIST], International Organization for Standardization [ISO]).

4.2 Understand and support forensic investigations.

4.3 Understand and support business continuity plan (BCP) and disaster recovery plan (DRP) activities.

Domain 5 Cryptography The protection of information using techniques that ensure its integrity, confidentiality, authenticity, and nonrepudiation, and the recovery of encrypted information in its original form:

5.1 Understand reasons and requirements for cryptography.

5.2 Apply cryptography concepts.

5.3 Understand and implement secure protocols.

5.4 Understand and support public key infrastructure (PKI) systems.

Domain 6 Network and Communications Security   The network structure, transmission methods and techniques, transport formats, and security measures used to operate both private and public communication networks:

6.1 Understand and apply fundamental concepts of networking.

6.2 Understand network attacks (e.g., distributed denial of service [DDoS], man-in-the-middle [MITM], Domain Name System [DNS] poisoning) and countermeasures (e.g., content delivery networks [CDN]).

6.3 Manage network access controls.

6.4 Manage network security.

6.5 Operate and configure network-based security devices.

6.6 Secure wireless communications.

Domain 7 Systems and Application Security   Countermeasures and prevention techniques for dealing with viruses, worms, logic bombs, Trojan horses, and other related forms of intentionally created damaging code:

7.1 Identify and analyze malicious code and activity.

7.2 Implement and operate endpoint device security.

7.3 Administer Mobile Device Management (MDM).

7.4 Understand and configure cloud security.

7.5 Operate and maintain secure virtual environments.

Appendix: Cross-Domain Challenges   In 2020 and 2021, the world was rocked by the Covid-19 pandemic and a significant increase in the complexity, scale, and severity of cybercrime and cyber attacks on businesses, government services, and critical infrastructures. In response, information security professionals around the globe worked tirelessly to address incident response and recovery. They also worked to improve systems hardening and intrusion detection techniques. Many of the persistent (and pernicious) attack strategies exploit aspects of nearly every topic in every SSCP Domain. Here in the CBK, the appendix offers five sets of strategies that can help security professionals shift the offense-versus-defense struggle more into the defense's favor. These five shifts or *pivots* are:

- Turn the attackers' playbooks against them.
- Cybersecurity hygiene: think small, act small.

- Flip the "data-driven value function."
- Operationalizing security across the immediate and longer term.
- Zero-trust architectures and operations.

The appendix also helps put the challenges of maintaining information security at the interface between an organization's IT systems and its *operational technology (OT)* ones. Since 2019, cyber attacks on process controls, autonomous devices, smart buildings elements, and Internet of Things (IoT) systems have disrupted many organizations. The pressure is on for SSCPs and other information security professionals to better understand the security and safety issues related to how their organization's data actually makes physical actions take place; the appendix provides you some places to start.

Using This Book to Defeat the Cybersecurity Kill Chain

Your employers or clients have entrusted the safety and security of their information systems to you, as one of their on-site information security professionals. Those systems are under constant attack—not just the threat of attack. Each day, the odds are great that somebody is knocking at your electronic front doors, trying the e-window latches on your organization's web pages, and learning about your information systems and how you use them. That's reconnaissance in action, the first step in the cybersecurity kill chain.

As an SSCP you're no doubt aware of the cybersecurity kill chain, as a summary of how advanced persistent threat (APT) actors plan and conduct their attacks against many private and public organizations, their IT infrastructures, and their information assets and systems. Originally developed during the 1990s by applying military planning doctrines of effects-based targeting, this kill chain is similar to the value chain concept used by businesses and public-sector organizations around the world. Both value chains and kill chains start with the objective—the desired end state or result—and work backward, all the way back to choosing the right targets to attack in the first place.[1] Lockheed-Martin first published its cybersecurity kill chain in 2011; the MITRE Corporation, a federally funded research and development corporation (FFRDC), expanded on this in 2018 with its threat-based Adversarial Tactics, Techniques, and Common Knowledge (ATT&CK) framework. ATT&CK takes the kill chain concept down into the tactics, techniques, and procedures used by squad-level and individual soldiers in the field. (Note that in military parlance, planning flows from strategic, through operational, to tactical; but common

---

[1] I had the privilege of developing and teaching some of these evolving concepts at the U.S. National Defense University's School of Information Warfare and Strategy, 1998-2000. At the School, we made extensive use of the "Strategic Information Warfare" series of publications by Roger C. Molander and others at the RAND Corporation, which were exploring this backward chain from desired strategic effect to the "kill effect" required of attacks on information and information systems.

business-speak usage flips the names of the last two steps, looking at business operations as being the point-of-contact steps with customers, and the tactical layer of planning translating strategic objectives into manageable, measurable, value-producing packages of work.) ATT&CK as a framework is shown in Figure I.1, highlighting the two major phases that defenders need to be aware of and engaged with: prestrike planning and the enterprise-level targeted strikes at your systems, your data, and your mission.

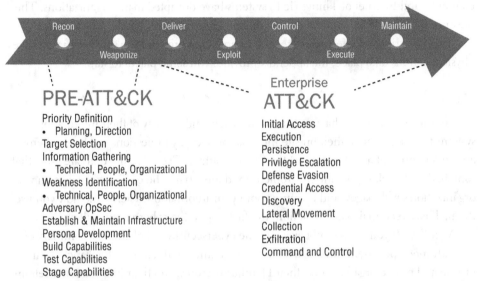

FIGURE I.1 MITRE's ATT&CK cybersecurity kill chain model   © 2018 The MITRE Corporation. This work is reproduced and distributed with the permission of The MITRE Corporation.

MITRE, Lockheed Martin, and others may give slightly different names to the different phases of their kill chain models. For example, MITRE's combines exploitation with installation, while emphasizing the persistent presence of the adversary inside your systems as they maintain their capabilities to quietly wreak havoc and achieve their objectives. The names of the phases aren't important; their underlying flow of ideas is what matters. To date, there does not seem to be any evidence that any given attacker has used exactly one planning model or another. There is abundant evidence, however, that defenders who do not understand these models pay for their ignorance—or, more precisely, their employers and clients do.

Combining these two models gives us eight phases of the life of an APT's kill chain and suggests which domains of knowledge (and therefore which chapters) may be your first ports of call as you plan to detect, prevent, degrade, or defeat the individual tasks that might make up each step in such a kill chain's operation. These are shown in Table I.1.

TABLE I.1 Kill Chain Phases Mapped to Chapters

KILL CHAIN PHASE	ATTACK OPERATIONS	DEFENSIVE OPTIONS
Reconnaissance	All-source intelligence gathering to inform the attack: OSINT, scanning, early intrusion, social engineering	All chapters: enhance overall risk/security posture, awareness, vigilance
Weaponization	Select and prepare access techniques and pathways	Chapters 2, 7
Delivery	Email, USBs, URLs, access control gaps, etc.	Chapters 1, 2, 5, 6, 7
Exploitation	Malware, rootkit exploits, live off the land	Chapters 2, 4, 6, 7
Installation	Backdoors, false or subverted user IDs	Chapters 2, 7
Command & Control	Privilege escalation, credential access; lateral movement; find, fix, select in-system targets	Chapters 1, 2, 4, 6
Execute the Attack	Exfiltrate; corrupt; encrypt for ransom; springboard to other targets	Chapters 4, 5
Maintain Hostile Presence	Continue to exploit target's systems and data; continue hiding one's tracks	Chapters 2, 4, 6, 7

You might be wondering why all chapters seem to apply to the Reconnaissance phase. The key to this is to recognize that the attacker will seek to find all possible sources of information about your organization, its business associates and relationships, its communications patterns, and its IT systems. APTs seek understanding of their targets' business and social networks, the "watering holes" where their people gather to collaborate with others in their trade or market. They'll try to suck up every unencrypted, unprotected, unsecured bit of anything that might be of use to them, as they determine your value to them as a set of exploitable opportunities. As the defender, this is your first clear opportunity to practice what insurance companies call "all-risks coverage" by exerting all possible efforts to identify, prioritize, and control all hazards that your systems and your organization might be exposed to.

The attack execution phase, by contrast, must rely heavily on your organization's ability to detect and respond in real time, or as close to real time as you can manage. Industry-wide, we're not doing too well on this front. It takes businesses and organizations an average of 190 days to *detect* an intrusion into their IT systems, according to research for IBM Security done by the Ponemon Institute in 2021.[2] On average, worldwide, any given

[2] Ponemon Institute LLC, for IBM Security. "2021 Cost of a Data Breach Study: Global Overview." Other sources, particularly business news media in India and Asia, have claimed as high as 220 days for this average, but there is little hard data to support this larger claim. Either way, this is seriously bad news.

business may suffer as much as $3.86 million USD in losses due to a data breach attack. A ransom attack, however, can demand $50 million USD or more in payouts. Those firms that have chosen not to pay off their attackers have reportedly suffered even greater losses. The same research conducted by Ponemon, by the way, demonstrates that having an effective security incident response plan in place, with first responders properly trained and equipped, can save at least $340,000 *per incident*.

As an SSCP, you've got your work cut out for you. Let this book be one of the many sources of knowledge, experience, and information you can count on, before, during, and after intruders start to target your organization's information, its systems, and its very existence.

WHERE DO YOU GO FROM HERE?

The world of information systems security is constantly changing. You need to continually grow your skills and keep up with the latest changes in the ways that businesses and organizations use the Internet and information technologies, as well as how the threat actors continually evolve to find new and different ways to exploit our systems against us. As a digital citizen of the 21st century, staying current—staying on the cutting edge of change, if not sometimes on the bleeding edge of it—is part of how you meet your due care and due diligence responsibilities to your clients, to your employers, and to the larger society around you. As a recognized member of that profession, the world expects you to stay sharp, stay focused, and stay informed.

That journey begins with this book, which provides you with a tangible foundation for your learning, exploration, and discovery. As a resource, this book provides the following strengths:

- It provides *context*. The domain-based structure maps concepts, ideas, problems, and solutions into a comfortable, straightforward framework that should make it easier to find what you need when you need it *and* find it positioned in a proper context. This book grounds you in the fundamental concepts, principles, design standards, and practices that are an invaluable resource.

- It *extends your memory*, as all reference works can do, as it shows you best practices in action, focused on the essentials and, again, in context.

- It provides *clarity* that can help you quickly orient to an issue or situation, while establishing links in your mind's eye to other related or important information.

The SSCP CBK and Your Professional Growth Path

As an international, nonprofit membership association with more than 160,000 members, (ISC)² has worked since its inception in 1989 to serve the needs for standardization and certification in the cybersecurity workplaces around the world. Since then, (ISC)²'s founders and members have been shaping the information security profession and have developed the following information security certifications:

- **Certified Information Systems Security Professional (CISSP):** The CISSP is an experienced professional who holds the most globally recognized standard of achievement in the industry and is the first information security credential to meet the strict conditions of ISO/IEC Standard 17024. The CISSP certification has three concentrations:

  - **Certified Information Systems Security Professional: Information Systems Security Architecture Professional (CISSP: ISSAP):** The CISSP-ISSAP is a chief security architect, analyst, or other professional who designs, builds, and oversees the implementation of network and computer security for an organization. The CISSP-ISSAP may work as an independent consultant or other professional who provides operational guidance and direction to support business strategies.

  - **Certified Information Systems Security Professional: Information Systems Security Engineering Professional (CISSP-ISSEP):** The CISSP-ISSEP can effectively incorporate security into all facets of business operations.

  - **Certified Information Systems Security Professional: Information Systems Security Management Professional (CISSP-ISSMP):** The CISSP-ISSMP is a cybersecurity manager who demonstrates deep management and leadership skills and excels at establishing, presenting, and governing information security programs.

- **Systems Security Certified Practitioner (SSCP):** The SSCP is a high-value practitioner who demonstrates technical skills in implementing, monitoring, and administering IT infrastructure using information security policies and procedures. The SSCP's commitment to continuous learning and practice ensures consistent information assurance.

- **Certified Cloud Security Professional (CCSP):** The CCSP is a globally recognized professional who demonstrates expertise and implements the highest standards in cloud security.

- **Certified Authorization Professional (CAP):** The CAP is a leader in information security and aligns information systems with the risk management framework (RMF). The CAP certification covers the RMF at an extensive level, and it's the only certification under the DoD 8570/DoD 8140 Approved Baseline Certifications that aligns to each of the RMF steps.
- **Certified Secure Software Lifecycle Professional (CSSLP):** The CSSLP is an internationally recognized professional with the ability to incorporate security practices—authentication, authorization, and auditing—into each phase of the software development lifecycle (SDLC).
- **HealthCare Information Security and Privacy Practitioner (HCISPP):** The HCISSP is a skilled practitioner who combines information security with health-care security and privacy best practices and techniques.

Each of these certifications has its own requirements for documented full-time experience in its requisite topic areas.

Newcomers to information security who have not yet had supervised work experience in the topic areas can take and pass the SSCP exam and then become recognized as Associates of (ISC)². Associates then have two years to attain the required experience to become full members of (ISC)².

Maintaining the SSCP Certification

SSCP credentials are maintained in good standing by participating in various activities and gaining continuing professional education credits (CPEs). CPEs are obtained through numerous methods such as reading books, attending seminars, writing papers or articles, teaching classes, attending security conventions, and participating in many other qualifying activities. Visit the (ISC)² website for additional information concerning the definition of CPEs.

Join a Local Chapter

As an SSCP, you've become one of more than 160,000 members worldwide. They, like you, are there to share in the knowledge, experience, and opportunity to help accomplish the goals and objectives of being an information security professional. Nearly 12,500 of your fellow members participate in local area chapters, and (ISC)² has over 140 local chapters around the world. You can find one in your area by visiting www.isc2.org/Chapters.

Being an active part of a local chapter helps you network with your peers as you share knowledge, exchange information about resources, and work on projects together. You can engage in leadership roles and participate in co-sponsored local events with other industry associations. You might write for or speak at (ISC)² events and help support other

$(ISC)^2$ initiatives. You can also be a better part of your local community by participating in local chapter community service outreach projects.

Chapter membership earns you CPE credits and can make you eligible for special discounts on $(ISC)^2$ products and programs.

LET'S GET STARTED!

This book is for you. This is your journey map, your road atlas, and your handbook. Make it work for you.

Choose your own course through it, based on what you need on the job today and every day.

Go for it.

HOW TO CONTACT THE PUBLISHER

If you believe you've found a mistake in this book, please bring it to our attention. At John Wiley & Sons, we understand how important it is to provide our customers with accurate content, but even with our best efforts an error may occur.

In order to submit your possible errata, please email it to our Customer Service Team at wileysupport@wiley.com with the subject line "Possible Book Errata Submission".

Security Operations and Administration

THIS IS WHERE THE planning hits reality; it's in the day to day of information security operations that you see every decision made during the threat assessments and the risk mitigation plans being live-fire tested by your co-workers, customers, legitimate visitors, and threat actors alike. Whether you're an on-shift watch-stander in a security operations center (SOC) or network operations center (NOC) or you work a pattern of normal business hours and days, you'll be exposed to the details of information security in action.

Security operations and administration entail a wide breadth of tasks and functions, and the security professional is expected to have a working familiarity with each of them. This can include maintaining a secure environment for business functions and the physical security of a campus and, specifically, the data center. Throughout your career, you will likely have to oversee and participate in incident response activities, which will include conducting investigations, handling material that may be used as evidence in criminal prosecution and/or civil suits, and performing forensic analysis. The Systems Security Certified Practitioner (SSCP) should also be familiar with common tools for mitigating, detecting, and responding to threats and attacks; this includes knowledge of the importance and use of event logging as a means to enhance security efforts. Another facet the security practitioner may have to manage could be how the organization deals with emergencies, including disaster recovery.

There is a common thread running through all aspects of this topic: supporting business functions by incorporating security policy and practices with normal daily activities. This involves maintaining an accurate and detailed asset inventory, tracking the security posture and readiness of information technology (IT) assets through the use of configuration/change management, and ensuring personnel are trained and given adequate support for their own safety and security.

This chapter will address all these aspects of security operations. The practitioner is advised, however, to not see this as a thorough treatment of all these concepts, each of which could be (and has been) the subject of an entire book (or books) by themselves; for each topic that is unfamiliar, you should look at the following content as an introduction only and pursue a more detailed review of related subject matter.

NOTE   The countries and regions that an organization operates in may have varying, distinct, and at times conflicting legal systems. Beyond considerations of written laws and regulations, the active functioning of court systems and regulatory bodies often has intricate, myriad applications in the real world that extend far beyond how things are codified in written laws. These factors become even more varied and complex when an organization functions in multiple countries and needs to deal with actual scenarios that directly involve international law and the laws of each respective nation. With that in mind, it is always imperative to get the input of a professional legal team to fully understand the legal scope and ramifications of security operations (and basically all operations and responsibilities beyond security as well).

COMPLY WITH CODES OF ETHICS

Your day-to-day journey along the roadmap of security operations and administration must keep one central ideal clearly in focus. Every day that you serve as an information security professional, you make or influence decisions. Every one of those decision moments is an opportunity or a vulnerability; it is a moment in which you can choose to do the technically and ethically correct thing or the expedient thing. Each of those decision moments is a test for you.

Those decisions must be ethically sound; yes, they must be technically correct, cost-effective, and compliant with legal and regulatory requirements, but at their heart they must be *ethical*. Failure to do so puts your professional and personal integrity at risk, as much as it puts your employer's or your clients' reputation and integrity at risk.

Being a security professional requires you to work, act, and think in ways that comply with and support the codes of ethics that are fundamental parts of your workplace, your profession, and your society and culture at large. Those codes of ethics should harmonize with if not *be* the fundamental ethical values and principles you live your life by—if they do not, that internal conflict in values may make it difficult if not impossible to achieve a sense of personal *and* professional integrity! Professional and personal integrity should be wonderfully, mutually self-reinforcing.

Let's first focus on what ethical decision-making means. This provides a context for how you, as an SSCP, comply with and support the (ISC)² Code of Ethics in your daily work and life. We'll see that this is critical to being able to live up to and fulfill the "three dues" of your responsibilities: due care, due diligence, and due process.

Understand, Adhere to, and Promote Professional Ethics

Let's start with what it means to be a professional: It means that society has placed great trust and confidence in you, because you have been willing to take on the responsibility to get things done right. Society trusts in you to know your practice, know its practical limits, and work to make sure that the services you perform meet or exceed the best practices of the profession. This is a legal and an ethical responsibility.

Everything you do requires you to understand the needs of your employers or clients. You listen, observe, gather data, and ask questions; you think about what you've learned, and you come to conclusions. You make recommendations, offer advice, or take action within the scope of your job and responsibilities. Sometimes you take action outside of that scope, going above and beyond the call of those duties. You do this because you are a professional. You would not even think of making those conclusions or taking those actions if they violently conflicted with what known technical standards or recognized best technical practice said was required. You would not knowingly recommend or act to violate the law. Your professional ethics are no different. They are a set of standards that are both constraints and freedoms that you use to inform, shape, and then test your conclusions and decisions with before you act.

As a professional—in any profession—you learned what that profession requires of you through education, training, and on-the-job experience. You learned from teachers, mentors, trainers, and the people working alongside of you. They shared their hard-earned insight and knowledge with you, as their part of promoting the profession you had in common. In doing so they strengthened the practice of the ethics of the profession, as well as the practice of its technical disciplines.

(ISC)² Code of Ethics

(ISC)² provides a Code of Ethics, and to be an SSCP, you agree to abide by it. It is short and simple. It starts with a preamble, which is quoted here in its entirety:

> *The safety and welfare of society and the common good, duty to our princi-*
> *pals, and to each other, requires that we adhere, and be seen to adhere, to*
> *the highest ethical standards of behavior.*
>
> *Therefore, strict adherence to this Code is a condition of certification.*

Let's operationalize that preamble—take it apart, step-by-step, and see what it really asks of us.

- **Safety and welfare of society:** Allowing information systems to come to harm because of the failure of their security systems or controls can lead to damage to property or injury or death of people who were depending upon those systems operating correctly.

- **The common good:** All of us benefit when our critical infrastructures, providing common services that we all depend upon, work correctly and reliably.

- **Duty to our principals:** Our duties to those we regard as leaders, rulers, or our supervisors in any capacity.

- **Our duty to each other:** To our fellow SSCPs, others in our profession, and to others in our neighborhood and society at large.

- **Adhere and be seen to adhere to:** Behave correctly and set the example for others to follow. Be visible in performing your job ethically (in adherence with this code) so that others can have confidence in us as a profession and learn from our example.

The code is equally short, containing just four canons or principles to abide by.

> *Protect society, the common good, necessary public trust and confidence,*
> *and the infrastructure.*
>
> *Act honorably, honestly, justly, responsibly, and legally.*
>
> *Provide diligent and competent service to principals.*
>
> *Advance and protect the profession.*

The canons do more than just restate the preamble's two points. They show you *how* to adhere to the preamble. You must take action to protect what you value; that action should be done with honor, honesty, and with justice as your guide. Due care and due diligence are what you owe to those you work for (including the customers of the businesses that employ us!).

The final canon talks to your continued responsibility to grow as a professional. You are on a never-ending journey of learning and discovery; each day brings an opportunity to make the profession of information security stronger and more effective. You as an SSCP are a member of a worldwide *community of practice*—the informal grouping of people concerned with the safety, security, and reliability of information systems and the information infrastructures of the modern world.

In ancient history, there were only three professions—those of medicine, the military, and the clergy. Each had in its own way the power of life and death of individuals or societies in its hands. Each as a result had a significant burden to be the best at fulfilling the duties of that profession. Individuals felt the calling to fulfill a sense of duty and service, to something larger than themselves, and responded to that calling by becoming a member of a profession.

This, too, is part of being an SSCP. Visit `https://www.isc2.org` for more information.

Organizational Code of Ethics

Most businesses and nonprofit or other types of organizations have a code of ethics that they use to shape their policies and guide them in making decisions, setting goals, and taking actions. They also use these codes of ethics to guide the efforts of their employees, team members, and associates; in many cases, these codes can be the basis of decisions to admonish, discipline, or terminate their relationship with an employee. In most cases, organizational codes of ethics are also extended to the partners, customers, or clients that the organization chooses to do business with. Sometimes expressed as *values* or *statements of principles*, these codes of ethics may be in written form, established as policy directives upon all who work there; sometimes, they are implicitly or tacitly understood as part of the organizational culture or shaped and driven by key personalities in the organization. But just because they aren't written down doesn't mean that an ethical code or framework for that organization doesn't exist.

Fundamentally, these codes of ethics *have the capacity to* balance the conflicting needs of law and regulation with the bottom-line pressure to survive and flourish as an organization. This is the real purpose of an organizational ethical code. Unfortunately, many organizations let the balance go too far toward the bottom-line set of values and take shortcuts; they compromise their ethics, often end up compromising their legal or regulatory responsibilities, and end up applying their codes of ethics loosely if at all. As a case in point, consider that risk management must include the dilemma that sometimes there are more laws and regulations than any business can possibly afford to comply with *and* they all conflict with each other in some way, shape, or form. What's a chief executive or a board of directors to do in such a circumstance?

It's actually quite easy to incorporate professional and personal ethics, along with the organization's own code of ethics, into every decision process you use. Strengths, weaknesses, opportunities, and threats (SWOT) analyses, for example, focus your attention on the strengths, weaknesses, opportunities, and threats that a situation or a problem presents; being true to one's ethics should be a *strength* in such a context, and if it starts to be seen as a weakness or a threat, that's a danger signal you must address or take to management and leadership. Cost/benefits analyses or decision trees present the same opportunity to include what sometimes is called the *New York Times* or the *Guardian* test: How would each possible decision look if it appeared as a headline on such newspapers of record? Closer to home, think about the responses you might get if you asked your parents, family, or closest friends for advice about such thorny problems—or their reactions if *they* heard about it via their social media channels. Make these thoughts a habit; that's part of the *practice* aspect of being a professional.

As the on-scene information security professional, you'll be the one who most likely has the first clear opportunity to look at an IT security posture, policy, control, or action, and challenge any aspects of it that you think might conflict with the organization's code of ethics, the (ISC)² Code of Ethics, or your own personal and professional ethics.

UNDERSTAND SECURITY CONCEPTS

What does it mean to "keep information secure?" What is a good or adequate "security posture?" Let's take questions like these and operationalize them by looking for characteristics or attributes that measure, assess, or reveal the overall security state or condition of our information.

- **Confidentiality:** Limits are placed on who is allowed to view the information, including copying it to another form.
- **Integrity:** The information stays complete and correct when retrieved, displayed, or acted upon.
- **Availability:** The information is presented to the user in a timely manner when required and in a form and format that meets the user's needs.
- **Authenticity:** Only previously approved, known, and trusted users or processes have been able to create, modify, move, or copy the information.
- **Utility:** The content of the information, its form and content, and its presentation or delivery to the user meet the user's needs.
- **Possession or control:** The information is legally owned or held by a known, authorized user, such that the user has authority to exert control over its use, access, modification, or movement.

- **Safety:** The system and its information, by design, do not cause unauthorized harm or damage to others, their property, or their lives.

- **Privacy:** Information that attests to or relates to the identity of a person, or links specific activities to that identity, must be protected from being accessed, viewed, copied, modified, or otherwise used by unauthorized persons or systems.

- **Nonrepudiation:** Users who created, used, viewed, or accessed the information, or shared it with others, cannot later deny that they did so.

- **Transparency:** The information can be reviewed, audited, and made visible or shared with competent authorities for regulatory, legal, or other processes that serve the public good.

Note that these are characteristics of the information itself. Keeping information authentic, for example, levies requirements on all of the business processes and systems that could be used in creating or changing that information or changing anything about the information.

All of these attributes boil down to one thing: *decision assurance.* How much can we trust that the decisions we're about to make are based on reliable, trustworthy information? How confident can we be that the competitive advantage of our trade secrets or the decisions we made in private are still unknown to our competitors or our adversaries? How much can we count on that decision being the right decision, in the legal, moral, or ethical sense of its being correct and in conformance with accepted standards?

Another way to look at attributes like these is to ask about the *quality* of the information. Bad data—data that is incomplete, incorrect, not available, or otherwise untrustworthy— causes monumental losses to businesses around the world; an IBM study reported that in 2017 those losses exceeded $3.1 trillion, which may be more than the total losses to business and society due to information security failures. Paying better attention to a number of those attributes would dramatically improve the reliability and integrity of information used by any organization; as a result, a growing number of information security practitioners are focusing on data quality as something they can contribute to.

Conceptual Models for Information Security

There are any number of frameworks, often represented by their acronyms, which are used throughout the world to talk about information security. All are useful, but some are more useful than others.

- *The CIA triad* (sometimes written as CIA) combines confidentiality, integrity, and availability and dates from work being done in the 1960s to develop theoretical models for information systems security and then implement those technologies into operating systems, applications programs, and communications and network systems.

- *CIANA* combines confidentiality, integrity, availability, nonrepudiation, and authentication. The greater emphasis on nonrepudiation and authentication provides a much stronger foundation for both criminal and civil law to be able to ascertain what actions were taken, by whom, and when, in the context of an incident, dispute, or conflicting claims of ownership or authorship.

- CIANA+PS expands CIANA to include privacy and safety. Cyberattacks in the Ukraine since 2014 and throughout the world from 2017 to present highlight the need for far more robust operational technology (OT) safety and resiliency. At the same time, regulators and legislators continue to raise the standards for protecting privacy-related data about individuals, with over 140 countries having privacy data protection laws in effect.

- *The Parkerian hexad* includes confidentiality, integrity, availability, authenticity, utility, and possession or control.

These frameworks, and many more, have their advocates, their user base, and their value. That said, in the interest of consistency, we'll focus throughout this book on CIANA+PS, as its emphasis on both nonrepudiation and authentication have perhaps the strongest and most obvious connections to the vitally important needs of e-commerce and our e-society to be able to conduct personal activities, private business, and governance activities in ways that are safe, respectful of individual rights, responsible, trustworthy, reliable, and transparent.

It's important to keep in mind that these attributes of systems performance or effectiveness build upon each other to produce the overall degree of trust and confidence we can rightly place on those systems and the information they produce for us. We *rely* on high-reliability systems because their information is correct and complete (high integrity), it's where we need it when we need it (availability), and we know it's been kept safe from unauthorized disclosure (it has authentic confidentiality), while at the same time we have confidence that the only processes or people who've created or modified it are trusted ones. Our whole sense of "can we trust the system and what it's telling us" is a greater conclusion than just the sum of the individual CIANA+PS, Parkerian, or triad attributes.

Let's look further at some of these attributes of information security.

Confidentiality

Often thought of as "keeping secrets," confidentiality is actually about sharing secrets. Confidentiality is both a legal and ethical concept about *privileged communications* or *privileged information*. Privileged information is information you have, own, or create, and that you share with someone else with the agreement that they cannot share that knowledge with anyone else without your consent or without due process in law. You place your trust and confidence in that other person's adherence to that agreement. Relationships between professionals and their clients, such as the doctor-patient or attorney-client ones, are prime examples of this privilege in action. In rare exceptions, courts cannot compel parties in a privileged relationship to violate that privilege and disclose what was shared in confidence.

Confidentiality refers to how much we can trust that the information we're about to use to make a decision with has not been seen by unauthorized people. The term *unauthorized people* generally refers to any person or any group of people who could learn something from our confidential information and then use that new knowledge in ways that would thwart our plans to attain our objectives or cause us other harm.

Confidentiality needs dictate who can read specific information or files or who can download or copy them; this is significantly different from who can modify, create, or delete those files.

One way to think about this is that integrity violations change what *we* think *we* know; confidentiality violations tell others what *we* think is *our* private knowledge.

Business has many categories of information and ideas that it needs to treat as confidential, such as the following:

- Proprietary, or company-owned information, whether or not protected by patent, copyright, or trade secret laws

- Proprietary or confidential information belonging to others but shared with the company under the terms of a nondisclosure agreement (NDA)

- Company private data, which can include business plans, budgets, risk assessments, and even organizational directories and alignments of people to responsibilities

- Data required by law or regulation to be kept private or confidential

- Privacy-related information pertaining to individual employees, customers, prospective customers or employees, or members of the public who contact the firm for any reason

- Customer transaction and business history data, including the company's credit ratings and terms for a given customer

- Customer complaints, service requests, or suggestions for product or service improvements

In many respects, such *business confidential* information either represents the results of investments the organization has already made or provides insight that informs decisions they're about to make; either way, all of this and more represent *competitive advantage* to the company. Letting this information be disclosed to unauthorized persons, *inside or outside* of the right circles within the company, threatens to reduce the value of those investments and the future return on those investments. It could, in the extreme, put the company out of business!

Let's look a bit closer at how to defend such information.

Intellectual Property

Our intellectual property are the ideas that we create and express in tangible, explicit form; in creating them, we create an ownership interest. Legal and ethical frameworks have long recognized that such creativity benefits a society and that such creativity needs to be encouraged and incentivized. Incentives can include financial reward, recognition and acclaim, or a legally protected ownership interest in the expression of that idea and its subsequent use by others. This vested interest was first recognized by Roman law nearly 2,000 years ago. Recognition is a powerful incentive to the creative mind, as the example of the Pythagorean theorem illustrates. It was created long before the concept of patents, rights, or royalties for intellectual property were established, and its creator has certainly been dead for a long time, and yet no ethical person would think to attempt to claim it as their own idea. Having the author's name on the cover of a book or at the masthead of a blog post or article also helps to recognize creativity.

Financial reward for ideas can take many forms, and ideally, such ideas should pay their own way by generating income for the creator of the idea, recouping the expenses they incurred to create it, or both. Sponsorship, grants, or the salary associated with a job can provide this; creators can also be awarded prizes, such as the Nobel Prize, as both recognition and financial rewards.

The best incentive for creativity, especially for corporate-sponsored creativity, is in how that ownership interest in the new idea can be turned into profitable new lines of business or into new products and services.

The vast majority of intellectual property is created in part by the significant investment of private businesses and universities in both basic research and product-focused developmental research. Legal protections for the intellectual property (or IP) thus created serve two main purposes. The first is to provide a limited period of time in which the owner of that IP has a monopoly for the commercial use of that idea and thus a sole claim on any income earned by selling products or providing services based on that idea. These monopolies were created by an edict of the government or the ruling monarchy, with the first being issued by the Doge of Venice in the year 1421. Since then, nation after nation has created patent law as the body of legal structure and regulation for establishing, controlling, and limiting the use of patents. The monopoly granted by a patent is limited in time and may even (based on applicable patent law) be limited in geographic scope or the technical or market reach of the idea. An idea protected by a patent issued in Colombia, for example, may not enjoy the same protection in Asian markets as an idea protected by U.S., U.K., European Union, or Canadian patent law. The second purpose is to publish the idea itself to the marketplace so as to stimulate rapid adoption of the idea, leading to widespread adoption, use, and influence upon the marketplace and upon society. Patents may be *monetized* by selling the rights to the patent or by licensing the use of the patent to another person or business; income from such licensing or sale has long been called the *royalties* from the patent (in recognition that it used to take an act of a king or a queen to make a patent enforceable).

Besides patents and patent law, there exist bodies of law regarding copyrights, trademarks, and trade secrets. Each of these treats the fruits of one's intellectually creative labors differently, and like patent law, these legal and ethical constructs are constantly under review by the courts and the cultures they apply to. Patents protect an idea, a process, or a procedure for accomplishing a practical task. Copyrights protect an artistic expression of an idea, such as a poem, a painting, a photograph, or a written work (such as this book). Trademarks identify an organization or company and its products or services, typically with a symbol, an acronym, a logo, or even a caricature or character (not necessarily of a person). Trade secrets are the unpublished ideas, typically about step-by-step details of a process, or the recipe for a sauce, paint, pigment, alloy, or coating, that a company or individual has developed. Each of these represent a competitive advantage worthy of protection. Note the contrast in these forms, as shown in Table 1.1.

TABLE 1.1 **Forms of Intellectual Property Protection**

LEGAL CONCEPT	PUBLIC DISCLOSURE	MONETIZE BY	COMPROMISE BY
Patent	Mandatory, detailed	License to use	Failure to develop or monetize; failure to defend against infringement
Copyright	Published works	Sell copies	Failure to defend
Trademark	Logos, signs, product stampings	Creates brand awareness in marketplace	Failure to defend
Trade secret	Must be undisclosed	Sell products and services based on its use; can be licensed	Failure to keep secret or defend

The most important aspect of that table for you, as the on-scene information security professional, is the fourth column. Failure to defend and failure to keep secret both require that the owners and licensed or authorized users of a piece of IP must take all reasonable, prudent efforts to keep the ideas and their expression in tangible form safe from infringement. This protection must be firmly in place throughout the entire lifecycle of the idea—from its first rough draft of a sketch on the back of a cocktail napkin through drawings, blueprints, mathematical models, and computer-aided design and manufacturing (CADAM) data sets. All expressions of that idea in written, oral, digital, or physical form must be protected from inadvertent disclosure or deliberate but unauthorized viewing or copying. Breaking this chain of confidentiality can lead to voiding the claim to protection by means of patent, copyright, or trade secret law. In its broadest terms, this means that the organization's information systems must ensure the confidentiality of this information.

Protect IP by Labeling It

Protection of intellectual property must consider three possible exposures to loss: exfiltration, inadvertent disclosure, and failure to aggressively assert one's claims to protection and compensation. Each of these is a failure by the organization's management and leadership to exercise due care and due diligence.

- *Exfiltration* generally occurs in part because decisions have been made to ignore risks, disregard alarm indications, and knowingly operate information systems in insecure ways. (There are cases of data breaches that happen to highly secure systems, hardened to the best possible standards, but these are few and far between.)

- Inadvertent exposure can happen due to carelessness, due to accident, or through faulty design of business processes or information security measures.

- An expression of an idea must, in almost all cases, be labeled or declared as a protected idea; this is how its owner asserts rights against possible infringement. This first assertion of a claim of ownership provides the basis for seeking legal means to stop the infringement, seek damages for lost business, or enter into licensing arrangements with the infringers.

Each of these possible exposures to loss starts with taking proper care of the data in the first place. This requires properly classifying it (in terms of the restrictions on handling, use, storage, or dissemination required), marking or labeling it (in human-readable and machine-readable ways), and then instituting procedures that enforce those restrictions.

Software, Digital Expression, and Copyright

Most software is protected by copyright, although a number of important software products and systems are protected by patents. Regardless of the protection used, it is implemented via a license. Most commercially available software is not actually sold; customers purchase a license to use it, and that license strictly limits that use. This license for use concept also applies to other copyrighted works, such as books, music, movies, or other multimedia products. As a customer, you purchase a license for its use (and pay a few pennies for the DVD, Blu-Ray, or other media it is inscribed upon for your use). In most cases, that license prohibits you from making copies of that work and from giving copies to others to use. Quite often, they are packaged with a copy-protection feature or with features that engage with digital rights management (DRM) software that is increasingly part of modern operating systems, media player software applications, and home and professional entertainment systems. It is interesting to note that, on one hand, digital copyright law authorizes end-user licensees to make suitable copies of a work in the normal course of consuming it—you can make backups, for example, or shift your use of the work to another device or another moment in time. On the other hand, the same laws prohibit you from using any reverse engineering, tools, processes, or programs to defeat, break, side-step, or circumvent such copy protection mechanisms. Some of these laws go further and specify that attempts to defeat any encryption used in these copy protection and rights management processes is a separate crime itself.

These laws are part of why businesses and organizations need to have acceptable use policies in force that control the use of company-provided IT systems to install, use, consume, or modify materials protected by DRM or copy-protect technologies. The employer, after all, can be held liable for damages if they do not exert effective due diligence in this regard and allow employees to misuse their systems in this way.

Copyleft?

By contrast, consider the Creative Commons license, sometimes referred to as a copyleft. The creator of a piece of intellectual property can choose to make it available under a Creative Commons license, which allows anyone to freely use the ideas provided by that license so long as the user attributes the creation of the ideas to the licensor (the owner and issuer of the license). Businesses can choose to share their intellectual property with other businesses, organizations, or individuals by means of licensing arrangements. Copyleft provides the opportunity to widely distribute an idea or a practice and, with some forethought, leads to creating a significant market share for products and services. Pixar Studios, for example, has made RenderMan, its incredibly powerful, industry-leading animation rendering software, available free of charge under a free-to-use license that is a variation of a creative commons license. In March 2019, the National Security Agency made its malware reverse engineering software, called Ghidra, publicly available (and has since issued bug fix releases to it). Both approaches reflect a savvy strategy to influence the ways in which the development of talent, ideas, and other products will happen in their respective marketplaces.

Industrial or Corporate Espionage

Corporations constantly research the capabilities of their competitors to identify new opportunities, technologies, and markets. Market research and all forms of open source intelligence (OSINT) gathering are legal and ethical practices for companies, organizations, and individuals to engage in. Unfortunately, some corporate actors extend their research beyond the usual venue of trade shows and reviewing press releases and seek to conduct surveillance and gather intelligence on their competitors in ways that move along the ethical continuum from appropriate to unethical and, in some cases, into illegal actions. In many legal systems, such activities are known as *espionage*, rather than research or business intelligence, as a way to clearly focus on their potentially criminal nature. (Most nations consider it an illegal violation of their sovereignty to have another nation conduct espionage operations against it; most nations, of course, conduct espionage upon each other regardless.) To complicate things even further, nearly all nations actively encourage their corporate citizens to gather business intelligence information about the overseas markets they do business in, as well as about their foreign or multinational competitors operating in their home territories. The boundary between corporate espionage and national intelligence services has always been a blurry frontier.

When directed against a competitor or a company trying to enter the marketplace, corporate-level espionage activities that might cross over an ethical or legal boundary can include attempts to do the following:

- Establish business relationships to gain federated access to e-business information such as catalogs, price lists, and specifications
- Gather product service or maintenance manuals and data
- Recruit key personnel from the firm, either as new employees or as consultants
- Engaging in competitive, information-seeking arrangements with key suppliers, service vendors, or customers of the target firm
- Probing and penetration efforts against the target's websites and online presence
- Social engineering efforts to gather intelligence data or provide the reconnaissance footprint for subsequent data gathering
- Unauthorized entry or breaking into the target's property, facilities, or systems
- Visiting company facilities or property, ostensibly for business purposes, but as intelligence-gathering

All of the social engineering techniques used by hackers and the whole arsenal of advanced persistent threat (APT) tools and techniques might be used as part of an industrial espionage campaign. Any or all of these techniques can and often are done by third parties, such as hackers (or even adolescents), often through other intermediaries, as a way of maintaining a degree of plausible deniability.

You will probably never know if that probing and scanning hitting your systems today has anything to do with the social engineering attempts by phone or email of a few weeks ago. You'll probably never know if they're related to an industrial espionage attempt, to a ransom or ransomware attack, or as part of an APT's efforts to subvert some of your systems as launching pads for their attacks on other targets. Protect your systems against each such threat vector as if each system does have the defense of the company's intellectual property "crown jewels" as part of its mission. That's what *keeping confidences*, what protecting the confidential, proprietary, or business-private information, comes down to, doesn't it?

Integrity

Integrity, in the common sense of the word, means that something is whole, complete, its parts smoothly joined together. People with high personal integrity are ones whose actions and words consistently demonstrate the same set of ethical principles. Having such integrity, you know you can count on them and trust them to act both in ways they have told you they would and in ways consistent with what they've done before.

When talking about information systems, *integrity* refers to both the information in them and the processes (that are integral to that system) that provide the functions we perform on that information. Both of these—the information and the processes—must be complete, correct, function together correctly, and do so in reliable, repeatable, and deterministic ways for the overall system to have integrity.

When we measure or assess information systems integrity, therefore, we can think of it in several ways.

- **Binary:** Either our information system has integrity or it does not. We can rely upon it or we cannot.

- **Threshold-based:** Our information system has at least a minimum level of systems and information integrity to function reliably but possibly in a degraded way, either with higher than desired (but still acceptable) error rates or at reduced transaction throughput or volume levels.

Note that in all but the simplest of business or organizational architectures, you'll find multiple sets of business logic and therefore business processes that interact with each other throughout overlapping cycles of processing. Some of these *lines of business* can function independently of each other, for a while, so long as the information and information systems that serve that line of business directly are working correctly (that is, have high enough levels of integrity).

- Retail online sales systems have customer-facing processes to inform customers about products, services, and special offers. Their shopping cart systems interact with merchandise catalog databases, as well as with order completion, payment processing, and order fulfillment. Customer sales order processing and fulfillment can occur—with high integrity—even though other systems that update the catalogs to reflect new products or services or bring new vendors and new product lines into the online store are not available.

- Computer-aided manufacturing systems have to control the flow of materials, parts, subassemblies, and finished products on the factory floor, interacting with logistics and warehousing functions on both the input and output sides of the assembly line. These systems are typically not tightly coupled with the functions of other business elements, such as finance, sales and marketing, or personnel management, even though at some point the assembly line grinds to a halt if finance hasn't paid the bills to suppliers in a timely way.

▶▶ REAL WORLD EXAMPLE:
Trustworthiness Is Perceptual

You make a decision to trust in what your systems are telling you. You choose to believe what the test results, the outputs of your monitoring systems, and your dashboards and control consoles are presenting to you as "ground truth," the truth you could observe if you were right there on the ground where the event reported by your systems is taking place. Most of the time, you're safe in doing so.

The operators of Iran's nuclear materials processing plant believed what their control systems were reporting to them, all the while the Stuxnet malware had taken control of both the processing equipment and the monitoring and display systems. Those displays lied to their users, while Stuxnet drove the uranium processing systems to self-destruct.

An APT that gets deep into your system can make your systems lie to you as well. Attackers have long used the techniques of perception management to disguise their actions and mislead their targets' defenders.

Your defense: Find a separate and distinct means for verifying what your systems are telling you. Get out-of-band or out-of-channel and gather data in some other way that is as independent as possible from your mainline systems; use this alternative source intelligence as a sanity check.

Integrity applies to three major elements of any information-centric set of processes: to the people who run and use them, to the data that the people need to use, and to the systems or tools that store, retrieve, manipulate, and share that data. Note, too, that many people in the IT and systems world talk about "what we know" in four very different but strongly related ways, sometimes referred to as D-I-K-W.

- Data consists of the individual facts, observations, or elements of a measurement, such as a person's name or their residential address.

- Information results when you process data in various ways; information is data plus conclusions or inferences.

- Knowledge is a set of broader, more general conclusions or principles that you've derived from lots of information.

- Wisdom is (arguably) the insightful application of knowledge; it is the "a-ha!" moment in which you recognize a new and powerful insight that you can apply to solve problems with or take advantage of a new opportunity—or to resist the temptation to try!

Figure 1.1 illustrates this knowledge pyramid.

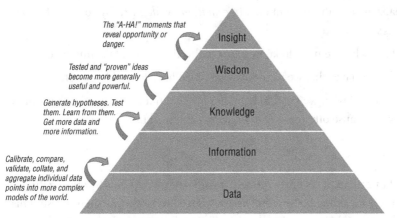

FIGURE 1.1 **The DIKW knowledge pyramid**

Professional opinion in the IT and information systems world is strongly divided about data versus DIKW, with about equal numbers of people holding that they are the same ideas, that they are different, and that the whole debate is unnecessary. As an information security professional, you'll be expected to combine experience, training, and the data you're observing from systems and people in real time to know whether an incident of interest is about to become a security issue, whether your organization uses knowledge management terminology like this or not. This is yet another example of just how many potentially conflicting, fuzzy viewpoints exist in IT and information security.

Availability

Is the data there when we need it in a form we can use?

We make decisions based on information; whether that is new information we have gathered (via our data acquisition systems) or knowledge and information we have in our memory, it's obvious that if the information is not where we need it when we need it, we cannot make as good a decision as we might need.

- The information might be in our files, but if we cannot retrieve it, organize it, and display it in ways that inform the decision, then the information isn't available.

- If the information has been deleted, by accident, sabotage, or systems failure, then it's not available to inform the decision.

Those might seem obvious, and they are. Key to availability requirements is that they specify what information is needed; where it will need to be displayed, presented, or put in front of the decision-makers; and within what span of time the data is both available (displayed to the decision-makers) and meaningful. Yesterday's data may not be what we need to make today's decision.

Note that availability means something different for a system than it does for the information the system produces for us. *Systems availability* is measurable, such as via a percentage of capacity or a throughput rate. *Information availability*, by contrast, tells us one of three things.

- Yes, we have what we need to know to make this decision or take this action.

- No, we do not have what we need to know, so we have to decide blindly.

- We have *some* of what we need to know, and we cannot logically infer that what's missing won't cause our decision to be wrong and lead us to harm.

Accountability

Information and information systems represent significant investments by organizations, and as a result, there's a strong bottom-line financial need to know that such investments are paying off—and that their value is not being diluted due to loss of control of that information (via a data breach or exfiltration) or loss or damage to the data's integrity or utility. Organizations have three functional or operational needs for information regarding accountability. First, they gather information about the *use* of corporate information and IT systems. Then they consolidate, analyze, and audit that usage information. Finally, they use the results of those reviews to inform decision-making. Due diligence needs, for example, are addressed by resource chargeback, which attributes the per-usage costs of information to each internal user organization. Individuals must also be held accountable for their own actions, including their use or misuse of corporate information systems. Surrounding all of this is the need to know whether the organization's information security systems are actually working correctly and that alarms are being properly attended to.

Privacy

Although legal and cultural definitions of privacy abound, we each have an internalized, working idea of what it means to keep something *private*. Fundamentally, this means that when we do something, write something down, or talk with another person, we have a reasonable expectation that what is said and done stays within a space and a place that we can control. We get to choose whom we share our thoughts with or whom we invite into our home. And with this working concept of privacy deep in our minds, we establish circles of trust. The innermost circle, those closest to us, we call our *intimates*; these are the people with whom we mutually share our feelings, ideas, hopes, worries, and dreams. Layer by layer, we add on other members of our extended family, our neighbors, or even people we meet every morning at the bus stop. We know these people to varying degrees, and our trust and confidence in them varies as well. We're willing to let our intimates make value judgments about what we consider to be our private matters or accept criticism from them about such matters; we don't share these with those not in our "inner circle," and we simply not tolerate them (tolerate criticism or judgments) from someone who is not at the same level of trust and regard.

Businesses work the same way. Businesses need to have a reasonable expectation that problems or issues stay within the set of people within the company who need to be aware of them and involved in their resolution. This is in addition to the concept of business confidential or proprietary information—it's the need to take reasonable and prudent measures to keep conversations and tacit knowledge inside the walls of the business and, when applicable, within select circles of people inside the business.

✔ Privacy Is Not Confidentiality

As more and more headline-making data breaches occur, people are demanding greater protection of personally identifiable information (PII) and other information about them as individuals. Increasingly, this is driving governments and information security professionals to see *privacy* as separate and distinct from *confidentiality*. While both involve keeping closely held, limited-distribution information safe from inadvertent disclosure, we're beginning to see that they may each require subtly different approaches to systems design, operation, and management to achieve.

Privacy: In Law, in Practice, in Information Systems

In legal terms, privacy relates to three main principles: restrictions on search and seizure of information and property, self-incrimination, and disclosure of information held by the government to plaintiffs or the public. Many of these legal concepts stem from the idea that government must be restricted from taking arbitrary action against its citizens, or people (human beings or fictitious entities) who are within the jurisdiction of those governments. Laws such as the Fourth and Fifth Amendments to the US Constitution, for example, address the first two, while the Privacy Act of 1974 created restrictions on how government could share with others what it knew about its citizens (and even limited sharing of such information within the government). Medical codes of practice and the laws that reflect them encourage data sharing to help health professionals detect a potential new disease epidemic but also require that personally identifiable information in the clinical data be removed or anonymized to protect individual patients.

The European Union has enacted a series of policies and laws designed to protect individual privacy as businesses and governments exchange data about people, about transactions, and about themselves. The latest of these, the General Data Protection Regulation 2016/679, is a law binding upon all persons, businesses, or organizations doing anything involving the data related to an EU person. GDPR's requirements meant that by May 2018, businesses had to change the ways that they collected, used, stored, and shared information about anyone who contacted them (such as by browsing to their website); they also had to notify such users about the changes and gain their informed consent to such use. Many news and infotainment sites hosted in the United States could not serve EU persons until they implemented changes to become GDPR compliant.

Privacy as a data protection framework, such as GDPR, provides you with specific functional requirements your organization's use of information must comply with; you are a vital part in making that compliance effective and in assuring that such usage can be audited and controlled effectively. If you have doubts as to whether a particular action or an information request is legal or ethical, ask your managers, the organizational legal team, or its ethics advisor (if it has one).

In some jurisdictions and cultures, we speak of an inherent right to privacy; in others, we speak to a requirement that people and organizations protect the information that they gather, use, and maintain when that data is about another person or entity. In both cases, the right or requirement exists to prevent harm to the individual. Loss of control over information about you or about your business can cause you grave if not irreparable harm.

Law at local, national, and international levels continues to evolve. Let's look at a fews.

Universal Declaration of Human Rights

Following World War II, there was a significant renewal and an increased sense of urgency to ensure that governments did not act in an arbitrary manner against citizens. The United Nations drafted the Universal Declaration of Human Rights that set forth these expectations for members. Article 12 states, "No one shall be subjected to arbitrary interference with his privacy, family, home or correspondence, nor to attacks upon his honour and reputation. Everyone has the right to the protection of the law against such interference or attacks."

OECD and Privacy

The Organization for Economic Cooperation and Development (OECD) promotes policies designed to improve the economic and social well-being of people around the world. In 1980, the OECD published "Guidelines on the Protection of Privacy and Transborder Flows of Personal Data" to encourage the adoption of comprehensive privacy protection practices. In 2013, the OECD revised its Privacy Principles to address the wide range of challenges that came about with the explosive growth of information technology. Among other changes, the new guidelines placed greater emphasis on the role of the data controller to establish appropriate privacy practices for their organizations.

✔ OECD Privacy Principles: Basic Principles of National Application

The OECD Privacy Principles are used throughout many international privacy and data protection laws and are also used in many privacy programs and practices. The eight privacy principles are as follows:

1. **Collection Limitation Principle:** This principle states that data that is collected should be obtained by lawful and fair means, that the data subject should be aware of and consent to the collection of the data where appropriate, and that the quantity and type of data should be limited.

2. **Data Quality Principle:** This principle is aimed at the accuracy and completeness of data, whether it is appropriately maintained and updated, and whether the data retained is relevant to the purposes it is used for.

3. **Purpose Specification Principle:** Purpose specification means that the reasons that personal data is collected should be determined before it is collected, rather than after the fact, and that later data reuse is in line with the reason that the data was originally obtained.

4. **Use Limitation Principle Security:** This principle notes that release or disclosure of personal data should be limited to the purposes it was gathered for unless the data subject agrees to the release or it is required by law.

5. **Security Safeguards Principle:** Reasonable security safeguards aimed at preventing loss, disclosure, exposure, use, or destruction of the covered data are the focus of this principle.

6. **Openness Principle:** The principle of openness is intended to ensure that the practices and policies that cover personal data are accessible and that the existence of personal data, what data is collected and stored, and what it is used for should all be disclosed. Openness also requires that the data controller's identity and operating location or residence is openly disclosed.

7. **Individual Participation Principle:** This includes an individual's right to know if their data has been collected and stored and what that data is within a reasonable time and in a reasonable way. In addition, this principle allows the

CONTINUES

> subject to request that the data be corrected, deleted, or otherwise modified as needed. An important element of this principle is the requirement that data controllers must also explain why any denials of these rights are made.
>
> 8. **Accountability Principle:** The final principle makes the data controller accountable for meeting these principles.
>
> The OECD Privacy Guidelines can be found at `www.oecd.org/internet/ieconomy/privacy-guidelines.htm`.

In developing the guidelines, the OECD recognized the need to balance commerce and other legitimate activities with privacy safeguards. Further, the OECD recognizes the tremendous change in the privacy landscape with the adoption of data breach laws, increased corporate accountability, and the development of regional or multilateral privacy frameworks.

Asia-Pacific Economic Cooperation Privacy Framework

The Asia-Pacific Economic Cooperation (APEC) Privacy Framework establishes a set of common data privacy principles for the protection of personally identifiable information as it is transferred across borders. The framework leverages much from the OECD Privacy Guidelines but places greater emphasis on the role of electronic commerce and the importance of organizational accountability. In this framework, once an organization collects personal information, the organization remains accountable for the protection of that data regardless of the location of the data or whether the data was transferred to another party.

The APEC Framework also introduces the concept of proportionality to data breach—that the penalties for inappropriate disclosure should be consistent with the demonstrable harm caused by the disclosure. To facilitate enforcement, the APEC Cross-border Privacy Enforcement Arrangement (CPEA) provides mechanisms for information sharing among APEC members and authorities outside APEC.

It's beyond the scope of this book to go into much depth about any of these particular frameworks, legal systems, or regulatory systems. Regardless, it's important that as an SSCP you become aware of the expectations in law and practice, for the communities that your business serves, in regard to protecting the confidentiality of data you hold about individuals you deal with.

PII and NPI

Many information security professionals are too well aware of personally identifiable information (PII) and the needs in ethics and law to protect its privacy. If you've not worked in the financial services sector, you may not be aware of the much broader category of nonpublished personal information (NPI). The distinction between these two seems simple enough:

- PII is that information that is used to identify, locate, or contact a specific person.
- NPI is all information regarding that person that has not been made public and is not required to be made public.

However, as identity and credential attacks have grown in sophistication, many businesses and government services providers have been forced to expand their use of NPI as part of their additional authentication challenges, when a person tries to initiate a session with them. Your bank, for example, might ask you to confirm or describe some recent transactions against one of your accounts, before they will let a telephone banking consultation session continue. Businesses may issue similar authentication challenges to someone calling in, claiming to be an account representative from a supplier or customer organization.

Three important points about NPI and PII need to be kept in mind:

- **Legal definitions are imprecise and subject to continuous change.** Many different laws, in many jurisdictions, may directly specify what types of information are considered as PII or NPI. Other laws may make broad categorical statements about what is or is not PII or NPI. These laws are updated often and subject to review by the courts in many nations.

- **Doing business in a jurisdiction does not require physical presence there**. If your organization has one customer or supplier in a jurisdiction – possibly even a single prospective such relationship – that government may consider its laws and regulations now apply to you. Ignoring this is a frequent and costly mistake that many businesses make.

- **Persons include companies and organizations as well as natural people.** Businesses and organizations share significant quantities and types of information with each other, much of which they do not wish to have made public. Privacy considerations and the need for information security protections apply here, as well as they do to data about individual people.

It may be safest to treat all data you have about any person you deal with as if it is NPI, unless you can show where it has been made public. You may then need to identify subsets of that NPI, such as health care, education, or PII, as defined by specific laws and regulations, that may need additional protections or may be covered by audit requirements.

Private and Public Places

Part of the concept of privacy is connected to the *reasonable expectation* that other people can see and hear what you are doing, where you are (or are going), and who might be with you. It's easy to see this in examples: Walking along a sidewalk, you have every reason to think that other people can see you, whether they are out on the sidewalk as well, looking out the windows of their homes, offices, or passing vehicles. The converse is that when out on that *public* sidewalk, out in the open spaces of the town or city, you have no reason to believe that you are *not* visible to others. This helps differentiate between *public places* and *private places*.

- Public places are areas or spaces in which anyone and everyone can see, hear, or notice the presence of other people and observe what they are doing, intentionally or unintentionally. There is little to no degree of control as to who can be in a public place. A city park is a public place.

- Private places are areas or spaces in which, by contrast, you as owner (or person responsible for that space) have every reason to believe that you can control who can enter, participate in activities with you (or just be a bystander), observe what you are doing, or hear what you are saying. You choose to share what you do in a private space with the people you choose to allow into that space with you. In law, this is your reasonable expectation of privacy, because it is "your" space; and the people you allow to share that space with you share in that reasonable expectation of privacy.

Your home or residence is perhaps the prime example of what we assume is a private place. Typically, business locations can be considered private in that the owners or managing directors of the business set policies as to whom they will allow into their place of business. Customers might be allowed into the sales floor of a retail establishment but not into the warehouse or service areas, for example. In a business location, however, it is the business owner (or its managing directors) who have the most compelling reasonable expectation of privacy, in law and in practice. Employees, clients, or visitors cannot expect that what they say or do in that business location (or on its IT systems) is private to them and not "in plain sight" to the business. As an employee, you can reasonably expect that your pockets or lunch bag are private to you, but the emails you write or the phone calls you make while on company premises are not necessarily private to you. This is not clear-cut in law or practice, however; courts and legislatures are still working to clarify this.

The pervasive use of the Internet and the web and the convergence of personal information technologies, communications and entertainment, and computing have blurred these lines. Your smart watch or personal fitness tracker uplinks your location and exercise information to a website, and you've set the parameters of that tracker and your web account to share with other users, even ones you don't know personally. Are you doing your workouts today in a public or private place? Is the data your smart watch collects and uploads public or private data?

"Facebook-friendly" is a phrase we increasingly see in corporate policies and codes of conduct these days. The surfing of one's social media posts, and even one's browsing histories, has become a standard and important element of prescreening procedures for job placement, admission to schools or training programs, or acceptance into government or military service. Such private postings on the public web are also becoming routine elements in employment termination actions. The boundary between "public" and "private" keeps moving, and it moves because of the ways we think about the information, not because of the information technologies themselves.

GDPR and other data protection regulations require business leaders, directors, and owners to make clear to customers and employees what data they collect and what they do with it, which in turn implements the separation of that data into public and private data. As an SSCP, you'll probably not make specific determinations as to whether certain kinds of data are public or private; but you should be familiar with your organization's privacy policies and its procedures for carrying out its data protection responsibilities. Many of the information security measures you will help implement, operate, and maintain are vital to keeping the dividing line between public and private data clear and bright.

Privacy versus Security, or Privacy *and* Security

It is interesting to see how the Global War on Terror has transformed attitudes about privacy throughout the Western world. Prior to the 1990s, most Westerners felt quite strongly about their individual rights to privacy; they looked at government surveillance as intrusive and relied upon legal protections to keep it in check. "That's none of your business" was often the response when a nosy neighbor or an overly zealous official tried to probe too far into what citizens considered as private matters. This agenda changed in 2001 and 2002, as national security communities in the United States and its NATO allies complained bitterly that legal constraints on intelligence gathering, information sharing, and search and seizure hampered their efforts to detect and prevent acts of terrorism. "What have you got to hide," instead, became the common response by citizens when other citizens sought to protect the *idea* of privacy.

It is important to realize several key facets of this new legal regime for the 21st century. Fundamentally, it uses the idea that international organized crime, including the threat of terrorism, is the fundamental threat to the citizens of law-abiding nations. These new legal systems require significant information sharing between nations, their national police and law enforcement agencies, and international agencies such as the OECD and Interpol, while also strengthening the ability of these agencies to shield or keep secret their demands for information. This sea change in international governance started with the Uniting and Strengthening America by Providing Appropriate Tools Required to Intercept and Obstruct Terrorism Act of 2001, known as the USA PATRIOT Act. This law created the use of National Security Letters (NSLs) as classified, covert ways to demand information from private businesses. The use of NSLs is overseen by the highly secret Foreign Intelligence Surveillance Court, which had its powers and authorities strengthened by this Act as well. Note that if your boss or a company officer is served with an NSL demanding certain information, they cannot disclose or divulge to *anyone* the fact that they have been served with such a due process demand. International laws regarding disclosure and reporting of financial information, such as bank transactions, invoices and receipts for goods, and property purchases, are also coming under increasing scrutiny by governments.

It's not the purpose of this chapter to frame that debate or argue one way or another about it. It is, however, important that you as an information security specialist within your organization recognize that this debate is not resolved and that many people have strongly held views about it. Those views often clash with legal and regulatory *requirements* and *constraints* regarding monitoring of employee actions in the workplace, the use of company information or information systems by employees (or others), and the need to be responsive to digital discovery requests of any and every kind. Those views and those feelings may translate into actions taken by some end users and managers who are detrimental to the organization, harmful to others, illegal, unethical, or all of these to a degree. Such actions—or the failure to take or effectively perform actions that *are* required—can also compromise the overall information security posture of the organization and are an inherent risk to information security, as well as to the reputation of the organization internally and externally.

Your best defense—and your best strategy for defending your company or your organization—is to do as much as you can to ensure the full measure of CIANA+PS protections, including accountability, for all information and information systems within your areas of responsibilities.

Nonrepudiation

The fundamental design of the earliest internetworking protocols meant that, in many cases, the sender had no concrete proof that the recipient actually received what was sent. Contrast this with postal systems worldwide, which have long used the concept of registered mail to verify to the sender that the recipient or his agent signed for and received the piece of mail on a given date and time. Legal systems have relied for centuries on formally specified ways to *serve process* upon someone. Both of these mechanisms protect the sender's or originator's rights and the recipient's rights: Both parties have a vested interest in not being surprised by claims by the other that something wasn't sent, wasn't done, or wasn't received. This is the basis of the concept of *nonrepudiation*, which is the aspect of a system that prevents a party or user from denying that they took an action, sent a message, or received a message. Nonrepudiation does not say that the recipient *understood* what you sent or that they agreed with it, only that they received it.

NOTE   You can think of nonrepudiation as being similar to submitting your income tax return every year or the many other government-required filings that we all must make no matter where we live or do business. Sometimes, the only way we can keep ourselves from harm is by being able to prove that we sent it in on time and that the government received it on time.

Email systems have been notorious for not providing reliable confirmation of delivery and receipt. Every email system has features built into it that allow senders and server administrators to control whether read receipts or delivery confirmations work reliably or correctly. Email threads can easily be edited to show almost anything in terms of sender and recipient information; attachments to emails can be modified as well. In short, off-the-shelf email systems do not provide anything that a court of law or an employment relations tribunal will accept as proof of what an email user claims it is.

Business cannot function that way. The transition from postal delivery of paper to electronic delivery of transactions brought many of the same requirements for non-repudiation into your web-enabled e-business systems. What e-business and e-commerce did *not* do a very good job of was bringing that same need for nonrepudiation to email.

There are a number of commercial products that act as add-ons, extensions, or major enhancements to email systems that provide end-to-end, legally compliant, evidence-grade proof regarding the sending and receiving of email. A number of national postal systems around the world have started to package these systems as their own government-endorsed email version of registered postal mail. Many industry-facing vertical platforms embed these nonrepudiation features into the ways that they handle transaction processing, rendering reams of fax traffic, uncontrollable emails, or even postal mail largely obsolete.

Systems with high degrees of nonrepudiation are in essence systems that are auditable and that are restricted to users who authenticate themselves prior to each use; they also tend to be systems with strong data integrity, privacy, or confidentiality protection built into them. Using these systems improves the organization's bottom line, while enhancing its reputation for trustworthiness and reliability.

Authentication

This element of the classic CIANA set of information security characteristics brings together many threads from all the others regarding *permission to act*. None of the other attributes of information security can be implemented, managed, or controlled if the system cannot unambiguously identify the person or process that is trying to take an action involving that system and any or all of its elements and then limit or control their actions to an established, restricted set. Note that the word *authentication* is used in two different ways.

- Information is *authenticated* by confirming that all of the metadata about its creation, transmission, and receipt convey that the chain of trust from creator through sender to recipient has not been violated. Authentication of a sent email or file demonstrates that it was created and sent by a known and trusted person or process. This requires that access control as a process grants permission to users or the tasks executing on their behalf to access a system's resources, use them, change them, share them with others, or create new information assets in that system.

- In access control terms, *authentication* validates that the requesting subject (process or user) is who or what they claim that they are and that this identity is known to the system. *Authorization* then allows that authenticated identity to perform a specific set of tasks. Taken together, this is what determines whether you are using someone else's computers or networks with their permission and approval or are trespassing upon their property.

1984 was a watershed year in public law in this regard, for in the Computer Fraud and Abuse Act (CFAA), the U.S. Congress established that entering into the intangible property that is the virtual world inside a computer system, network, or its storage subsystems was an action comparable to entering into a building or onto a piece of land. Entry onto (or into) real, tangible property without permission or authority is criminal trespass. CFAA extended that same concept to unauthorized entry into the virtual worlds of our information systems. Since then, many changes to public law in the United States and a number of other countries have expanded the list of acts considered as crimes, possibly expanding it too much in the eyes of many civil liberties watchdogs. It's important to recognize that almost every computer crime possible has within it a violation of permissions to act or an attempt to fraudulently misrepresent the identity of a person, process, or other information system's element, asset, or component in order to circumvent such restrictions on permitted actions. These authenticity violations are, if you would, the fundamental dishonesty, the lie behind the violation of trust that is at the heart of the crime.

Safety

SUNBURST and other attacks in 2020 and 2021 highlighted how little attention many organizations were paying to the physical control and interaction side of their information systems. Enterprises that did not directly use IT to control manufacturing systems, or command and control vehicles and heavy machinery, believed themselves safe from physical harm, and yet would blithely invest in smart buildings and IoT devices for use in their office environments. They believed that these operational technologies—OT systems that directly cause physical motion or action, or monitor and supervise systems that do—were sufficiently separated from their IT systems, such as their corporate data centers, that there was little danger of a vulnerability on one side of that IT-OT interface from causing harm to systems, data, and people on the other side. That has been shown to be a false hope.

Operational technologies (OT) include industrial control systems (ICS) and the supervisory, control, and data acquisition (SCADA) systems that direct their activities. OT also includes Internet of Things (IoT) devices, autonomous, mobile machines (from custodial devices to chaotic warehouse forklifts), and robots. Most smart city systems, particularly their mass transit, water and sewer, traffic control, and communications management systems are part of the OT world, as are smart building environmental, power, and security management systems at work and in the home. This list of OT use cases grows every day, and in each case, there are data sharing and collaborative control and supervisory linkages with IT systems at many levels. And in most cases, device control involves switching and detecting AC and DC power and signals as part of controlling physical actuators and sensors.

As older OT systems are being phased out, newer systems tend to be making greater use of the Common Industrial Protocol (CIP). This is a feature-rich set of functions that are used within OT architectures to provide management, real-time control, data acquisition, and safety intervention across an architecture. CIP can operate over IP networks, which allows OT regional control workstations to easily interact with organizational IT systems. OT and IT systems both share common problems, such as the challenges of establishing and maintaining a secure supply chain for software, firmware, and hardware updates. Access control problems are quite common; the information security hygiene measures you need to apply to almost every IT systems environment must also be applied to your organization's OT systems, although with different techniques and tools. Integrated visibility—having a SIEM-like insight into the combined IT / OT architecture of your organization—can be achieved, but it's not as straightforward as some vendors may make it seem.

Safety, like security, is an end-to-end responsibility. It's no wonder that some cultures and languages combine both in a single word. For example, in Spanish *seguridad* unifies both safety and security as one integrated concept, need, and mind-set.

Fundamental Security Control Principles

Several control principles must be taken into account when developing, implementing, and monitoring people-focused information security risk mitigation controls. Of these, the three most important are need to know, separation of duties, and least privilege. These basic principles are applied in different ways and with different control mechanisms. However, a solid understanding of the principles is essential to evaluating a control's effectiveness and applicability to a particular circumstance.

Need to Know

Security classification and categorization should be the linch pin that ties together the organization's information security and risk mitigation efforts. It's what separates the highest-leverage proprietary information from the routine, nearly-public-knowledge facts and figures. Information classification schemes drive three major characteristics of your information security operations and administration.

- **Internal boundaries for information control:** Many business processes have "insider knowledge" needed to inform decisions or exert control over risky, hazardous, or sensitive sequences of actions. These can and should be encapsulated with a layer that hides that inside knowledge by allowing controlled "write-up" of inputs and "write-down" of outputs to the points where they interface with other business processes. These boundaries surround data at higher levels, and the trusted processes that can manipulate or see it, from outer, surrounding layers of processes that perforce operate at lower levels of trust. (It's not a coincidence that that sounds like a *threat surface*.)

- **Standards for trust and confidence:** It's only logical to require higher levels of trustworthiness for the people, processes, and systems that deal with our most vital information than we would need for those that handle low-risk information. In most cases, greater costs are incurred to validate hardware, software, vendors, our supply chain, and our people to higher levels of trust and confidence; as with all risk mitigation decisions, cost-effectiveness should be a decision factor. The information classification standards and guide should directly lead to answering the question of how much trustworthiness is enough.

- **Measures of merit for information security processes:** The level of information classification should dictate how we measure or assess the effectiveness of the security measures put in place to protect it.

Taken together these form a powerful set of functional requirements for the design not just of our information security processes but of our business processes as well! But first, we need to translate these into two *control* or *cybernetic* principles.

Least Privilege

Least privilege as a design and operational principle requires that any given system element (people or software-based) has the minimum level of authority and decision-making capability that the specifically assigned task requires, and no more. This means that designers must strictly limit the access to and control over information, by any subject involved in a process or task, to that minimum set of information that is required for that task and no more. Simply put, least privilege implements and enforces need to know.

A few examples illustrate this principle in action.

- A financial disbursements clerk, when generating payments against invoices from suppliers, has to access and use information about each supplier account as well as access his company's bank-related systems to make the payment take place. However, this clerk would not be expected to modify the information about where the payment should be sent, edit the invoice, or alter the amount of the payment. Nor would this clerk be expected to need any information about other employees, such as their payroll information, while generating payments to suppliers.

- A process control system that actively manages a chemical processing system for a paint manufacturer would not normally be expected to access the Internet or have a need to run web searches of any kind.

Each time you encounter a situation in which a person or systems element is doing something in unexpected ways—or where you would not expect that person or element to be present at all—is a red flag. It suggests that a different role, with the right set of privileges, may be a necessary part of a more secure solution.

Least privilege should drive the design of business logic and business processes, shaping and guiding the assignment (and separation) of duties to individual systems and people who accomplish their allocated portions of those overall processes. Driven by the Business Impact Analysis (BIA), the organization should start with those processes that are of highest potential impact to the organization. These processes are usually the ones associated with achieving the highest-priority goals and objectives, plus any others that are fundamental to the basic survival of the organization and its ability to carry on day-to-day business activities.

Separation of Duties

Separation of duties is intrinsically tied to accountability. By breaking important business processes into separate sequences of tasks and assigning these separate sequences to different people, applications, servers or devices, you effectively isolate these information workers with accountability boundaries. It also prevents any one person (or application) from having end-to-end responsibility and control over a sequence of high-risk or highly vulnerable tasks or processes. This is easiest to see in a small, cash-intensive business such as a catering truck or small restaurant.

- The individual server takes orders, serves the food, and hands the bill to the patron, who pays either the server or the cashier; the cash collected goes into the cash drawer, which is also where any change due the patron is taken from.

- The cash register or change drawer is set up and counted by a shift lead or manager and counted again at intervals throughout the shift and at shift change.

- The daily accounting of cash at start, bills to patrons and receipts paid, and cash drawer tallies is reconciled by the accounting manager.

- The accounting manager prepares the daily cash deposit, which is verified by the overall manager.

- The deposit is counted by the bank and verified to match what is claimed on the deposit slip.

This system protects each worker from errors (deliberate or accidental) made by other workers in this cash flow system. It isolates the error-prone (and tempting!) cash stream from other business transactions, such as accounts payable for inventory, utilities, or payroll. With the bank's knowledge of its customer, it may also offer reasonable assurances that this business is not involved in money laundering activities (although this is never foolproof with cash businesses). Thus, separation of duties separates *hazards* or risks from each other; to the best degree possible it precludes any one person, application, system, or server (and thereby the designers, builders, and operators of those systems) from having both responsibility and control over too many hazardous steps in sequence, let alone end to end.

Other examples demonstrate how separation of duties can look in practice.

- Employees in the finance department can access a financial application and create and change transaction records, which in turn generate audit logs, but those end users cannot access the audit logs. Inversely, a security administrator who can access the audit logs cannot create or change transactions in the financial application itself.

- A developer who writes code for a software release can't also be a tester for that same release or be the one who approves or moves that release into the production environment. If a developer put a flaw into that code maliciously, it will be intentionally allowed to pass. If the flaw was introduced accidentally or through ignorance or poor training, there is a chance the developer will just miss it again in testing. Involving a second person in the testing process allows the organization the opportunity to catch the mistake or malicious flaw.

- An emergency has arisen, and an administrator needs to access a superuser account to perform a sensitive task that is far above their normal level of permissions. Authentication to that account requires a specific hardware token, which must be obtained from the shift lead at the SOC. The SOC lead verifies with the administrator's supervisor and/or verifies that there is an outage, incident ticket, or some other valid reason why the superuser token must be used before issuing it, and the token must be returned when the incident is resolved.

While implementing separation of duties, keep a few additional considerations in mind. First, separation of duties must be well-documented in policies and procedures. To complement this, mechanisms for enforcing the separation must be implemented to match the policies and procedures, including access-level authorizations for each task and role. Smaller organizations may have difficulty implementing segregation of duties, but the concept should be applied to the extent possible and logistically practical. Finally, remember that in cases where it is difficult to split the performance of a task, consider compensating controls such as audit trails, monitoring, and management supervision.

Another, similar form of process security is *dual control*. In dual control, two personnel are required to coordinate the same action from separate workstations (which may be a few feet or miles apart) to accomplish a specific task. This is not something reserved to the military's release of nuclear weapons; it is inherent in most cash-handling situations and is a vital part of decisions made by risk management boards, loan approval boards, and many other high-risk or safety-critical situations.

A related concept is *two-person integrity*, where no single person is allowed access or control over a location or asset at any time. Entry into restricted areas, such as data centers or network and communications facilities, might be best secured by dual control or two-person integrity processes, requiring an on-shift supervisor to confirm an entry request within a fraction of a minute.

Separation of duties is often seen as something that introduces inefficiencies, especially in small organizations or within what seem to be simple, well-bounded sequences of processes or tasks. As with any safeguard, senior leadership has to set the risk appetite or threshold level and then choose how to apply that to specific risks.

These types of risk mitigation controls are often put in place to administratively enforce a separation of duties design. By not having one person have such end-to-end responsibility or opportunity, you greatly reduce the exposure to fraud or abuse. In sensitive or hazardous material handling and manufacturing or in banking and casino operations, the work areas where such processes are conducted are often called *no lone zones*, because nobody is allowed to be working in them by themselves. In information systems, auditing, and accounting operations, this is sometimes referred to as a *four-eyes* approach for the same reason. Signing and countersigning steps are often part of these processes; these signatures can be pen and ink or electronic, depending upon the overall security needs. The needs for individual process security should dictate whether steps need both people (or all persons) to perform their tasks in the presence of the others (that is, in a no lone zone) or if they can be done in sequence (as in a four-eyes sign/countersign process).

Safety considerations also should dictate the use of no lone zones in work process design and layout. Commercial air transport regulations have long required two pilots to be on the flight deck during flight operations; hospital operating theaters and emergency rooms have teams of care providers working with patients, as much for quality of care as for reliability of care. Peer review, structured walkthroughs, and other processes are all a way to bring multiple eyes and minds to the process of producing high-quality, highly reliable software.

Note that separation of duties does not presume intent: It will protect the innocent from honest mistakes while increasing the likelihood that those with malicious intent will find it harder, if not impossible, to carry out their nefarious plans (whatever they may be). It limits the exposure to loss or damage that the organization would otherwise face if any component in a vital, sensitive process fails to function properly.

Separation of duties, for example, is an important control process to apply to the various event logs, alarm files, and telemetry information produced by all of your network and systems elements.

Of course, the total costs of implementing, operating, and maintaining such controls must be balanced against the potential impacts or losses associated with those risks. Implementing separation of duties can be difficult in small organizations simply because there are not enough people to perform the separate functions. Nevertheless, separation of duties remains an effective internal control to minimize the likelihood of fraud or malfeasance and reduce the potential for damage or loss due to accident or other non-human causes.

✔ Separation of Duties and Least Privilege: It's Not Just About Your People!

In many business settings, the dual concepts of separation of duties and least privilege are seen as people-centric ideas—after all, far too much painful experience has shown that by placing far too much trust *and power* in one person's hands, temptation, coercion, or frustration can lead to great harm to the business. Industrial process control, transportation, and the military, by contrast, have long known that any decision-making component of a workflow or process can and will fail, leading also to a potential for great harm. Separation of duties means that autopilot software should not (one hopes!) control the main electrical power systems and buses of the aircraft; nor should the bid-ask real-time pricing systems of an electric utility company direct the CPUs, people, and actuators that run its nuclear reactors or turbine-powered generators.

Air gaps between critical sets of duties—gaps into which systems designers insert different people who have assessment and decision authority—become a critical element in designing safe and resilient systems.

Access Control and Need-to-Know

As you should expect, these key control principles of need to know, separation of duties, and least privilege also drive the ways in which you should configure and manage identity management and access control systems, as shown in Chapter 2. Best practices for implementing and managing any IAM system include:

- Create hierarchies of groups of user identities and accounts, with privileges assigned to limit users to the least privileges they require for related tasks and functions.

- Use role-based access control as part of your strategies so that one system or user must explicitly re-authenticate as they change roles to perform more privileged sets of tasks.

- Create nonprivileged user accounts and identities for systems administrators, and others with privileged accounts, and enforce their use for tasks that do not require elevated privileges (such as email or routine web page access).

- Separate groups of user identities and accounts (for people and nonhuman elements of your systems) based on separation of duties.

- Thoroughly examine all installed software, and connections to web or cloud-hosted applications platforms to identify any instances in which apps elevate privileges for nonprivileged users who use such apps or connection. Eliminate such elevation or find ways to explicitly control and restrict it.

Job Rotation and Privilege Creep

Job rotation can be a powerful HR investment strategy that leads to increasing the knowledge and skills of a company's workforce while improving retention of quality personnel, but these are not the concerns of the SSCP. From a security perspective, there are many reasons for creating a job rotation policy. These include reducing risks of both insider and external threats, reducing dependence on a single person (who can become a single point of failure), and increasing resiliency for business continuity and disaster recovery (BCDR) purposes. Banking and investment companies, for example, have used (and have sometimes been required by government regulators or by law) such career-broadening or rotations strategies as part of their loss control and fraud prevention mechanisms.

We cannot overstress the importance of carefully managing what should be the temporary changes in user privileges during such job rotations. Far too often, privilege creep resulting from each job rotation (temporary or permanent) ends up with the user accumulating new sets of privileges with each new task, job, or skills-broadening assignment. Over time, this can lead to an individual having far greater insight into and control over the organization's information assets than should ever be allowed.

In practice, job rotation requires cross-training personnel for various positions and tasks within the organization. This may be within a particular business functional area or discipline, or it might involve a temporary transfer of an employee to other areas within the company. Some of the personnel in the security office, for example, might all be trained on the various roles in that office (such as log analysis, incident response, security training, or systems testing) as an intra-departmental job rotation and then learn more of the company's human resources or product development business via a career-broadening assignment.

Job rotation helps to mitigate insider threats in several ways. It serves as a deterrent for a potentially malicious insider actually committing fraud. In cases where separation of duties would necessitate collusion, job rotation disrupts opportunities for collusion. In cases where a malicious insider has found a way to mishandle data or abuse their access, job rotation disrupts them from doing long-term damage once they've started. The cross-training aspect of job rotation may also aid the overall security effort by reducing the potential for employees/staff to become dissatisfied and possibly become insider threats; skilled personnel appreciate receiving additional training and challenges of new tasks, and increased training opportunities make those personnel more valuable. Increased morale of skilled personnel reduces costs because of turnover and accentuates loyalty to the organization.

Alternatives to job rotation are forced vacation or leave. The logic here is that if a malicious insider is suppressing alarms, changing or erasing audit logs, or conducting any other activity to cover their tracks or support or assist an attack, this activity should be easier to detect if the suspected insider is suddenly forced to stay away from work. During the period of mandatory vacation, that user's account access should be suspended, and a thorough audit/review of their activity should be performed. This is especially important for those users with privileged access. For example, after the U.S. stock market crash and the collapse of its banking systems in 1929, Congressional action established not only such forced vacations but also frequent bank holidays during which banks suspended customer transaction processing while they performed extensive internal systems integrity checks; both mitigated the risks of fraud, embezzlement, and over-extension by the bank or its staff.

Another goal of job rotation is to keep malicious outsiders from being able to learn about your staff over time and trying to target or manipulate them for information or access. Reducing static patterns in personnel taskings and changing access roles repeatedly reduces the opportunity for external actors to subvert particular employees as targets.

Finally, job rotation also greatly improves the resiliency of an organization, essential in successfully executing BCDR actions. During contingency events or disasters, you must assume that some personnel will not be available/capable of performing particular tasks and functions necessary to maintain the organization's critical processes; having other personnel not normally assigned to those functions but trained on how to perform them is a great benefit and vastly increases the likelihood of BCDR response success.

DOCUMENT, IMPLEMENT, AND MAINTAIN FUNCTIONAL SECURITY CONTROLS

Functional security controls implement the risk mitigation decisions that management and leadership have endorsed. The risk assessment and vulnerabilities assessment tasks have led to these decisions; now it's time to make appropriate cost-effective choices about particular controls, thus *operationalizing* those decisions by providing the tools, techniques, systems elements, and procedural step-by-step that the organization's workforce will need as they go about their day-to-day activities.

The organization has already made decisions about which risks to avoid (by not doing business in particular locations or by abandoning particular business processes); it's also recognized some risks must just be accepted as they are, as an unavoidable but still potential cost of doing business. Chapter 3, "Risk Identification, Monitoring, and Analysis" goes into further depth on how information risks are identified and assessed and how organizational leadership makes both strategic, big-picture risk management decisions, as well as planning for risk mitigation and making the resources available to carry out those plans. Management has also transferred what risks it can to other third parties to deal with. What's left are the risks that you and the rest of your organization's security professionals must deal with. You deal with risk using five basic types of controls: deterrent, preventative, detective, corrective, and compensating. Note that there are no hard and fast boundary lines between these types—a fence around the property both deters and prevents attackers from attempting to cross the fence line, while a network intrusion prevention system both detects and attempts to block (or prevent) intrusions on your networks.

Note that this section focuses on *security* controls, which are of course a subset of the larger problem of risk mitigation. From a security controls perspective, you think about these controls as interfering with a human attacker (or their software and hardware minions) who is carrying out an unauthorized intrusion into your information systems or causing damage or disruption to those systems.

Let's take a closer look at each type of control and then examine common issues involved with their implementation, maintenance, and operational use.

Deterrent Controls

Deterrent controls work to dissuade an attacker from initiating or continuing in their efforts to attack your systems, property, information, or people. Their design, deployment, and use should all raise either the perceived costs or risks to an attacker and the actual costs the attacker could face should they choose to persist. Guard dogs off of the leash, free to range around your property (but within a fence line), are an example of a deterrent that offers painful costs to an attacker, while raising the probability of being forcibly detained and subjected to arrest and prosecution as well.

Deterrent controls should provide a variety of capabilities to the security architect by placing barriers (real and perceived) between potential attackers and the systems they defend.

- Visible, tangible barriers, which an attacker can see, sense, or probe, signal that the target is defended.

- This suggests that the barriers are alarmed and monitored, which increases the possibility of an intrusion being detected.

- The barriers suggest to the attacker that greater assets, time, or effort must be expended for their attack to succeed.

- They also suggest that *more* barriers may be encountered, layer upon layer, should the attacker continue in their attempt.

Note the key concept that to be effective, a deterrent control must be visible, observable, and verifiably present to the prospective intruder. It cannot deter an attacker if the attacker doesn't know that it is there! This directly suggests that you're defending against a known group of attackers and that you have some degree of operational threat intelligence data, which you can use in selecting potentially effective deterrent tactics and techniques.

Simple deterrents can be physical controls, such as fences, locked doors and windows, or landscaping and paving that restricts the movement of vehicles and pedestrians onto a protected property or campus. Exterior lighting, including the use of moving spotlights or floodlights, can also provide a deterrent effect. Most physical controls are passive, in that they do not react to an intrusion attempt; active controls would include guard dogs and security controls, for example.

Physically, the architecture of buildings or workspaces make statements about an organization and the work that is performed there. These statements can also be powerful deterrents to would-be attackers. Think about how many modern embassy compounds (and not just the American ones) around the world have been transformed into little fortresses as they've been blast-hardened, surrounded by impact-resisting barrier walls, and armed military personnel or security guards; entry onto such embassy grounds is restricted and tightly controlled in most cases. High technology companies have also made similar architectural deterrent statements with the ways that they design, build, and operate their physical locations. These are definitely not statements of security through obscurity.

Network systems such as firewalls and intrusion detection and prevention systems can act as powerful deterrents by thwarting an attacker's ability to gain meaningful insight via reconnaissance probes or scans. (It's somewhat unfortunate that the line between NIDS and NIPS as product systems has become quite blurred at this point since both apply filtering rules of varying potency to block or restrict traffic from crossing their point of protection.) Well-trained, highly aware *people* throughout your organization are also effective deterrents when they smoothly deflect social engineering attack attempts, perhaps by guiding unknown callers through a well-rehearsed script to filter out the innocent prospective customer, client, or job seeker from the whaler-wannabee.

Preventative Controls

Preventative (or prevention) controls provide two forms of protection to keep your systems from harm by reducing the probability of an occurrence of a risk or, when it starts to occur, by containing it in such a way as to limit the spread of its disruption or damage. Securely locked doors and windows prevent an intruder from unlawfully entering your home, unless they want to elevate their risk by breaking through the locks, the windows, or the doors in question. The design of interior walls, doors, and utility spaces restricts the speed with which fire can spread from room to room, while reducing or blocking the spread of smoke and heat. This suggests that security architects should use prevention (like deterrence) in layers.

Prevention can be active or passive, as with deterrence; the same types of controls used for physical, passive deterrence also bring some prevention with them.

Host-based or network-based firewalls, intrusion detection and prevention systems, and of course identity management and access control systems are the main components of a solid prevention architecture. Layer upon layer, they detect attempts to cross a threat boundary's controlled access points; they test that access attempt against varying sets of criteria and in some cases issue challenges requesting further credentials from the requesting subject. Since all of these systems can and should generate both accounting log information for successfully authenticated attempts, and alerts or alarms for failures, they are deterrent, prevention, and detection systems all at the same time.

Detective Controls

Detective (or detection) controls look for any out-of-limits conditions, such as signatures associated with an intrusion attempt, and then take two fundamental and important actions. First, the detection controls notify operations personnel or higher-level supervisory systems that a problem exists; this is absolutely critical if you are to have any command and control over your systems or any ability to manage an effective response to incidents as and when they occur. Second, the detection controls can (if desired) signal an attacker that you've noticed what they're doing, which leads them to believe you'll be responding to their attack. This may deter them from continuing their efforts.

All intrusion or incident detection systems are subject to error rates. Getting the crossover point set so that your risk of harm or loss due to false acceptance errors is balanced by your ongoing costs of investigating and resolving false rejections (and their concomitant "sky is falling" feeling) is a never-ending process. In fact, the smarter these controls get—and the more that they employ machine learning and predictive analytic capabilities—the more time you'll have to invest in understanding their behavior and tuning it to fit your constantly changing threat landscape and the dynamic nature of your routine business activities.

Physical detection systems can include motion detectors, motion switches on doors and windows, and continuity circuits embedded or built into walls, fences, and other landscaping features. Many such systems can support change detection as well, which can highlight suspicious portions of the systems they surveil to human security monitors for analysis and possible action. Physical systems such as power conditioning, air and environmental conditioning systems, and other aspects of your data center or network operations facilities should be primary sources of alarms that indicate a potential disruption, possibly due to an intrusion, is underway.

Don't forget the end-user element! Properly motivated and trained, having a cadre of end users who can spot something that's not quite right *and* appreciate that management wants to hear about it sooner rather than later can often stymie an attack before it gets too far.

Corrective Controls

Corrective controls provide for the containment, isolation, or restoration of services that have been disrupted for any reason. Uninterruptible power supplies (UPSs) are a good example of this: They isolate or buffer your IT and communications systems from external commercial electrical power providers and in doing so can correct for temporary under-voltage, overvoltage, spikes, noise, or other problems with power before those problems pop circuit breakers or damage equipment. Power problems, incidentally, can also cause equipment to operate in degraded ways that are oftentimes hard to diagnose. Consumer and small business-grade routers, switches, and servers, for example, are prone to odd and intermittent outages for this reason, and the simple expedient of putting them onto an inexpensive battery backup power conditioner or UPS can save hours of fruitless troubleshooting.

Another example of a corrective control in action is when your access control system or a web page design remediates or quarantines a subject's access request when information about that subject and that access request indicates that something is not quite right. Systems can interrogate the subject's endpoint device, for example, to determine whether its operating system, applications, antimalware, or other functions are all properly updated, and if not, route the connection to a remediation server or page that only allows for repair actions to be taken. User subjects can also be challenged to provide further authentication credentials, if something about the time of day, the user's geographic position, or other criteria dictate the need for enhanced vigilance.

Compensating Controls

Compensating controls are put in place when the normal, recommended, or required "best choice" of a risk mitigation control is not available or is unworkable or not affordable or when another approach has been chosen for valid reasons. Depending upon the source of the original requirement for that control, this may or may not be an issue. NIST documents, for example, tend to focus on the risk or threat to protect against, rather than attempting to specify a specific approach. (Best practices, though, often rule out approaches that are no longer useful to consider.) Another example of this can be seen in the Payment Card Industry Data Security Standard (PCI DSS), which specifies stringent security functional or performance standards by which controls must operate, as well as a formalized process for justifying the use of an alternative approach.

PCI DSS gives a good working definition of a compensating control, which can easily apply to other information risk control situations. A compensating control must do the following:

- Meet or exceed the intended level of protection as specified in the original control requirement

- Provide a level of protection that sufficiently offsets or covers the risk that the original control requirement should address

- Must provide greater levels of protection, against the total risk set that the originating or reference standard addresses, than would be achieved by the original control requirement

- Must provide a degree of overall safety and security that is commensurate with the risk of *not* using the recommended or required original standard in whole or in part

This can seem a bit wordy, if not confusing. An example might help. Consider PCI DSS Requirement 3.6.4, as illustrated in a white paper by Robert Schwirtz and Jeff Hall, both at RSM McGladrey. (This paper, which can be found at `https://rsmus.com/pdf/understanding_pci_comp_controls.pdf`, provides good insight into the thinking about compensating controls and how to ensure that a soundly reasoned, well-supported argument is made to justify their use.) This particular requirement specifies that encryption keys must be kept secure. Suppose your system is implemented using a public key cryptography approach such as pretty good privacy (PGP), in which there also is not a centralized certificate authority; there are no keys to keep secure! So, your *compensating* control is the use of a PKI system and the details by which you protect and manage certificates. (Yes, that process involves the use of both parties' private keys, and yes, those have to be kept secure, but these are *not* the keys used to encrypt a PCI DSS transaction. And, yes, it's arguable that the requirement would then apply to keeping the resultant *session keys* secure.)

Another example might be a requirement (in PCI DSS or many other systems requirements specifications) that requires passwords to be of a minimum length and complexity. Using a multifactor authentication system, common sense will tell us, obviates the need for attempts to constrain or dictate user choices of passwords since they are not the sole means of gaining access and privileges.

> ### ✔ Residual Risk Isn't "Compensated For"
>
> In common use, we talk about compensating for something as a way to imply that the original would have been better, but for whatever reason, we are settling for less. You compensate for the absence of a key team member by letting others substitute for them, knowing that your team just won't be as strong or the results as good. That's not what *compensating* means when talking about security and risk controls!
>
> For a control to be a compensating control, there is no additional residual risk just because you've replaced the originally required control approach with something different. And if there is a residual risk, then your compensating control is not the right choice.

The Lifecycle of a Control

As with any systems element and the systems themselves, risk mitigation and security controls have a lifecycle that they progress through, from initial observation and expression of a need through implementation, use, and replacement or retirement. More specifically, that lifecycle might include the following:

- Risk identification and characterization
- Vulnerability assessments, with links to specific risks
- Risk management planning decisions, on a per-risk basis, in terms of what to accept, transfer, treat, or avoid
- Risk mitigation decisions, including specifics as to the chosen controls and the anticipated residual risk after the controls are put into practice
- Success criteria, in operational terms, which indicate whether the control is successfully performing its functions
- Anticipated ongoing costs and efforts to use and maintain a set of controls
- End-user and support team training, including any requalification training, needed to keep the controls operating effectively
- Continuous, ongoing monitoring of operational use of the controls

- Ongoing periodic or random assessment, including penetration testing, aimed at assessing the controls

- Decisions to upgrade, replace, or completely retire a set of controls

As you'll see in Chapter 3, there are a number of information products generated by risk management and risk mitigation planning. Although they may be known by various names or be produced in many different formats, the core set of information includes the business impact analysis, risk assessment, risk mitigation plan, and the change management and baseline documentation for the chosen and implemented controls. These could include vendor-supplied manuals as well as your organization's own functional performance requirements allocated to a particular control.

PARTICIPATE IN ASSET MANAGEMENT

Effective information systems management must achieve three distinctly different goals:

- Are we spending what we need to (and no more) to achieve the right business priorities and objectives?

- Are we using our information systems effectively in ways that help us achieve our objectives?

- Are we maintaining, changing, or upgrading our information systems in effective ways to meet changing conditions and needs?

Those three questions all focus on our information systems architecture, the elements we've brought together to create those systems with, and the business logic by which we use those systems. As we'll see in Chapter 3, having a solid baseline that captures and describes our organization's information systems and IT architecture is the foundation of how we manage those information systems. It's also worthwhile to consider that well-managed systems are often more reliable, resilient, safe and secure; unmanaged systems may be just as trustworthy, but if they are, it's more by luck than by design.

Information systems asset management comprises all of the activities to identify each asset, know and control its location and use, and track modifications, changes, or repairs done to it. Asset management also includes keeping track of any damages or losses that an asset incurs through accident, failures of other systems or business functions, misuse, abuse, or attacks of any kind. Due care and due diligence require asset management to be effective, thorough, and accountable, which in turn require that proper inventory and tracking records be kept and that standards be set for proper usage, routine maintenance and repair, safety, and security. Asset management and configuration management and control go hand in hand as the main processes you should use to keep these important, value-producing assets working well and working for you; they're also crucial to keeping those assets being used by someone else!

ISO 55000 provides extensive guidance for the proper management of physical assets, including buildings, facilities, and infrastructure elements such as electrical power, plumbing, and heating, ventilation, and air conditioning (HVAC) systems. COBIT5, from ISACA (previously known as the Information Systems Audit and Control Association, but now by its acronym only), is another framework of structured guidance for information systems and information asset management, which your organization may already be using.

Broadly speaking, an information systems asset is any element of a system for which it is useful to assess or estimate a value, a cost, and a loss or impact. The value should relate to the gains to the organization that can be realized through effective use of that asset. Costs should reflect all that was spent, including time and effort, to create or acquire, install, use, and maintain the asset. The loss or impact can reflect either the replacement cost, the decrease in value, or some other assessment of how damage, destruction, or degradation of the asset will affect the organization.

Nominally, an asset has one point of management: You manage a single server or you manage a data center, but two data centers integrated via a VPN connection supported by a third party is most likely easier to manage as a set of related assets.

Parts or Assets?

At some point it is easier and more meaningful to track and manage a system as an asset but consider all of the replaceable bits and pieces of it as units or parts. Your network backbone, for example, may consist of high-capacity, redundant routing and switching elements tied together with fiber, cable, WiFi, or other media. As a system, it's useful to track it as an asset, while having a logically distinct inventory of its spare parts.

Asset Inventory

Information systems asset management starts with the asset inventory, which must completely and unambiguously identify every information systems element to be managed as an asset. The inventory should include hardware, firmware, software, virtual machine environments, cloud systems services, databases, websites, and the supporting documentation for end users and maintainers.

Having a current and complete inventory is the absolute bedrock for implementing and monitoring technical security controls.

Robust asset inventory tools and processes will also inform the organization of unauthorized assets. These may be unlicensed copies of software or uncontrolled devices, software, or systems used by employees, clients, or visitors that thus become parts of your system. They may also be elements of an intrusion in progress. Each of these situations could be risks to the overall safety, security, and reliability of your IT systems.

Note that almost any device that can attempt to access your networks or systems is an object to be inventoried, placed under configuration control, and incorporated into your access control systems' databases as an authenticated identity. Failing to tie these three processes together—and keep them tied together—leaves an unnecessary degree of access open to potential intruders.

Inventory Tool/System of Record

Because of the size, complexity, and frequency of the task, an organization should use automated tools to assist in creating and maintaining the asset inventory. The tools should have awareness of all assets in the organization's enterprise and the ability to discover new assets introduced to the environment that have not been properly documented in the inventory. This data comes from either an asset management agent or a client installed on each asset or "baked in" to each system image. It can also be generated with various scanner and sensor tools, or, in the case of hosted or cloud assets, from a data feed or recurring report from the vendor (which may or may not be shared with clients, depending on the terms of their service-level agreements [SLAs] or terms of reference [TORs] with their clients).

An asset inventory tool should have a way to distinguish authorized devices and applications from unauthorized devices and an ability to send alerts when the latter are discovered. The tool should also collect and track individual asset details necessary for reporting, audits, risk management, and incident management. These details need to cover technical specifications, such as the following:

- Hardware
  - Manufacturer
  - Model number
  - Serial number
  - Physical location
  - Number and type of processors
  - Memory size
  - Network interfaces and their MACs and IPs
  - Hostname
  - Hypervisor, operating systems, containers, virtual images running on this device

- Purchase date, warranty information
- Last update dates (firmware, hypervisor, etc.)
- Asset usage metrics
- Software
  - Publisher
  - Version number, service pack/hotfix number, and date of last update
  - Digital signatures on installation packages
  - License information
  - Purchase date
  - Install date

In addition, operational security details should be collected, such as the type of data stored and processed on the asset, the asset classification and special handling requirements, the business processes or missions it supports, and the owner, administrators, end users, or user groups nominally authorized to use it, and their contact information.

There are of course many tools available that do these tasks or portions of these tasks. Most organizations already own many such tools. Consider the following:

- An Active Directory or Lightweight Directory Access Protocol (LDAP) server can provide a large portion of this information.
- Other integrated identity management and access control systems can provide some of this information and can be especially useful in identifying assets that aren't under management but are attached (or attempting to attach themselves) to your systems.
- Vulnerability scanners, configuration scanners, and network mapping tools can find and provide basic information about all the hosts in the organization's IP ranges.
- Tools that manage/track software licenses can perform a large portion of this task.
- Data loss prevention (DLP) solutions typically have a discovery capability that can serve this purpose.

For gaps in their available tools, organizations can and do compensate with manual efforts, spreadsheets, and scripting to pull and tabulate asset data. Dedicated asset inventory tools usually provide this functionality and preclude the need for manual data pulls and tool integration.

Regardless of the tool or combination of tools used, there should be one the organization deems authoritative and final so that it can be referenced throughout the organization. The information in this tool needs to be definitive. This is the data source to trust if there is conflict between what other tools are reporting. This should also be the source used for official reports and other data requests, such as part of an audit.

Process Considerations

Let's now look at some inventory management best practices. First, the organization must define the authoritative inventory list or system of record and define the frequency with which the inventory should be refreshed or updated. In addition to the regular interval inventory updates, it is also a good practice to ensure that the inventory management system is updated, and its administrator notified when assets are installed, removed, or updated/changed in a significant way.

This can be accomplished in a different way for environments that make heavy use of virtualized components, including managed cloud service implementations. In these cases, use of automated tools to seek out, tabulate, and provision assets is often preferable; popular tools include Puppet, Chef, and Ansible.

For on-premises assets, it is often helpful to augment the inventory process with the use of geolocation information/geotags or the use of RFID inventory tags. This can increase the speed and accuracy of locating an asset, especially during an incident when time is critical.

Lifecycle (Hardware, Software, and Data)

Although some legacy systems may *seem* to be lasting forever, it's much more common that information systems assets of every kind have a useful economic life span, beyond which it is just not useful or cost-effective to continue to use it and keep it working. Once past that point, the asset should be disposed of safely, so as to terminate exposing the organization to any risks associated with keeping it or failing to care for it. The typical systems development lifecycle model (SDLC) can be applied to hardware, systems software, applications software, and data in all of its many forms; let's look at this from an asset manager's perspective:

- The requirements phase identifies the key functional and physical performance needs that the system should meet and should link these to the organization's mission, goals, and objectives. When any of these change, the asset manager is one of the stakeholders who evaluates whether the asset is at or past its useful economic life.

- During the design phase, the functional requirements are allocated to individual elements of the design; it's worth considering at this point whether these components of the total system should be tracked as assets by themselves versus tracking the system as a whole or as a single asset.

- Development, integration, and acceptance testing quite often conclude with a list of identified discrepancies that must be tracked and managed. In effect, each open discrepancy at the time of systems acceptance is a lien on the overall value of the system (much as a mortgage or mechanic's lien on your home reduces the equity you would realize from selling your home). Tracking those discrepancies is a form of tracking residual risk.

- Operational use presents an opportunity to appraise the value of the system; finding new uses for it increases its value to the organization as an asset, but if users find better, faster ways to do the same jobs instead, this in effect decreases the value of the asset.

- Maintenance and upgrade actions can extend the useful life of the system while adding to its cost. This is also true for ongoing license payments, whether as per-seat or site-wide licenses for software use.

- Retirement and safe disposal, and the costs associated with these, bring this particular asset's lifecycle and its asset management account to a closed state.

Disposal must deal with the issue of data remanence, which refers to information of any kind remaining in the memory, recording surfaces, physical configuration settings, software, firmware, or other forms. This applies to more than just the familiar disks, tapes, and thumb drives; all hardware devices have many different internal nooks and crannies through which live data flows during use. Old-fashioned cathode ray tube (CRT) displays risked having images burned into their display surfaces. Printers have been known to go to the scrap dealer with fragments of previously printed documents, or impressions on their printing drums and ribbons of what they last printed, still legible and visible. Printed documents may need to be shredded or pulped. As a complication, you may end up having to store these retired assets, at a secure location, while awaiting the time (and money) to have a proper zeroization, purge, or destruction of the element to prevent an unauthorized disclosure from happening.

Hardware Inventory

In many work environments, people and whole workgroups can move around within a large facility. People shift from one workstation to another or to larger (or smaller) spaces in another room or another building; some may even move to a different city or country or travel extensively. Hardware inventory needs to know *logically* and *physically* about each device, be it an endpoint, a server, a peripheral such as a printer or scanner or a removable storage device. Assuming for a moment that no MAC address spoofing or alteration is allowed, the identity of an individual device should remain constant; knowing that it's currently attached via a certain IP address and that it is (or is not) connecting through a VPN is part of knowing *logically* where it is. But…knowing *physically* what desk or tabletop, rack, room, building, or continent it's on (or in) can be problematic. It's prudent to avoid procedurally intensive ways to address this problem, as the German military found out a few years ago. They went from simply allowing their military and civilian staff to just pick up and move their desktop and laptop computers from office to office, as temporary shifts in duties arose, and instituted a work-order process as a way of capturing location information for their asset inventory. This added days of work as each move had to have a form filled in, which was sent to an approvals and dispatch center; then had to have a worker move the equipment; and finally have the form sent back to the user to sign off that the move was now complete. Attribute-based access control (ABAC) may be a smarter solution to such problems, although it may require endpoints that can be trusted to accurately report their physical location without end-user intervention.

I cannot overstress the need to know the physical location for infrastructure elements such as servers, routers, switches, and such, to as detailed a level as possible. Precious time can be wasted during an incident response by having to search for which room, which rack, and which unit or position in the rack is the device that's been sending up alarms (preferably not sending up smoke signals). It's also especially important to note which power distribution panel or circuit breaker box serves each equipment rack or bay and which power conditioning systems feed which distribution panels or breaker boxes.

Software Inventory and Licensing

Software and firmware come in many different forms; almost without question, all of these forms should be under the right combination of configuration control, configuration management, and asset management. Between those three processes, you'll have a very good chance to know that all of your software elements:

- Have been protected from unauthorized changes

- Have had all required changes, patches, and updates correctly applied

- Have had all outstanding discrepancy reports or change requests reviewed and dispositioned by the right set of stakeholders and managers

- Where each element is, physically and logically, how it's being used, and whether or not it is up to date

You'll also know, for each software element, whose intellectual property it is and whether there are license terms associated with that ownership interest. For each license, you'll need to know the detailed terms and conditions that apply and whether they apply to all copies you've installed on any number of devices or to a specific maximum number of devices; the license may also restrict your ability to move an installed copy to another system. The license might be *seat limited* to a specific number of individual users or *capacity limited* to a maximum number of simultaneous users, maximum number of files or records, or other performance ceilings.

Many modern applications programs (and operating systems) facilitate this by using digital signatures in their installation processes so that each installed and licensed copy has a unique identifier that traces to the license identifier or key. Software license inventory management tools can easily poll systems on your network, find copies of the application in question, and interrogate that installation for its license and identifier information. This can also find unlicensed copies of software, which might be legitimate but have yet to activate and register their licenses or might be bootleg or unauthorized copies being used.

Proper software license management and software inventory management can often save money by eliminating duplicate or overlapping licenses, or by restricting usage of a particular app or platform strictly to where it's needed.

Data Storage

Whether you think of it as *data* or *information*, it is either in use, in motion, or being stored somewhere in the information architectures and systems you are keeping safe and secure. Data can be used by endpoints, servers, or the infrastructure itself. Data is in motion when it is being transferred across networks, communications links, or even to and from a storage device temporarily attached to an endpoint computer or smartphone. Data can be stored – be at rest – in endpoint devices, in removable media, and in storage subsystems that are part of an on-premise network or hosted in a public or hybrid cloud. Chapter 7, "Systems and Application Security," will look in greater depth at security issues relating to data storage in the cloud and within your networks and their servers. What remains is the vexing problem of data storage on paper and on removable storage media and devices, and when those storage media and paper documents are being moved around.

Information Lifecycle

Information has a natural lifecycle, but as with most things in the IT world, there are many different models for this lifecycle, with different emphasis placed on different phases of the data's existence. For example, ISO 27002 defines this cycle with five phases: creation, processing, storage, transmission, and deletion/destruction (see Figure 1.2). Other models, such as those built into many systems management platforms such as SAP, may combine creation and use with processing; then add a *retention* phase in which the data is not actively used but cannot be disposed of because of legal, regulatory, or liability reasons; and finally end with a disposal and destruction activity.

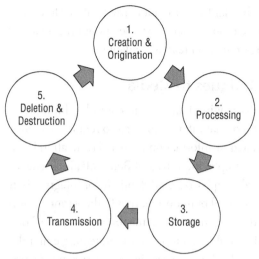

FIGURE 1.2 **ISO 27002 phases**

Security is an important consideration at every phase, but the level of importance can vary, depending on the phase. The formats and media used in the various phases can also affect the security considerations.

Consider, for example, design documents for a new product or technology. When those documents/data are new, they are valuable and actionable, especially if a competitor acquires them. Once the product or technology is in production and is being sold on the market, those same documents could be near the end of their lifecycle. At this point, one could argue that the documents would do less damage in the hands of a competitor, but they still need to be afforded some level of protection, right up to the moment they are destroyed. In this example, even though the creators have benefited from the "rush to market" advantage, the design documents themselves could still contain sensitive data, such as a proprietary production method, which the organization plans to reuse in future products.

There are several important points to take from this example. First, the security impact may vary depending on where the information is in its lifecycle. Next, even though the impact may vary, there can be negative outcomes for the organization at *any* phase. Finally, phase five, the deletion and destruction phase, is important because destruction of unneeded assets reduces the organization's attack surface. Data at the end of its lifecycle only introduces risk, with little to no benefit.

The lifecycle view shows that datasets (or information assets) are constantly going back and forth from storage to use; throughout *that* ever-repeating cycle, your systems designs should protect the information while it is at rest, in use, and in motion. Currently, well-chosen encryption systems can protect data in motion and at rest and by means of digital signatures offer the stored copies protection in time as well. (Chapter 5 goes into this in further detail.) However, thus far there are not many solutions to protect data while it is being used from compromise or loss, since most operations on data and its use by humans needs to have the meaning of the data readily available.

Apply Resource Protection Techniques to Media

Protecting the information on storage media requires that you can control or limit the onward use, copying, or other redistribution of that information; it also requires you to protect your systems from being contaminated by information from a classification level that does not belong on your systems. For example, the Biba and Bell–LaPadula access control models to show how different models emphasize confidentiality or integrity. Both choices can be undone by putting the wrong level of information onto the wrong removable media and then introducing that media into another system. You'll see a variety of standards and practices in use that may place different emphasis on protecting either the information (and its confidentiality, nonrepudiability, or integrity) or the systems (by protecting their integrity, and hence their availability and authenticity).

Before covering the methods for properly managing media, it's important to acknowledge that these methods will vary based on the types of media used. The umbrella term of *media* or *information system media* could mean legacy analog formats, such as hard-copy documents, photos, and microfilm. It could also (more likely) be in reference to a wide range of digital formats, such as external hard drives, floppy disks, diskettes, magnetic tape, memory cards, flash drives, and optical disks such as CDs, DVDs and Blu-Ray disks.

As you might expect, making secure but removable media work requires successfully integrating your security classification schema, your device-level identity management and access control, and the management of all endpoints' capabilities to use removable storage—including on the endpoint itself.

Marking

Handling sensitive or classified information involves everything necessary to meet its protection requirements; handling storage media refers to all processes, be they human, electronic, or mechanical, which are involved in mounting, dismounting, storing, shipping, using, reusing, and ultimately destroying the media. This protection requires a combination of marking the media and establishing and using administrative and logical processes that perform those tasks in controlled, reliable, and auditable ways. The marking achieves nothing without the procedures being understood and used properly!

Marking involves labeling in both human-readable and machine-readable manners so that it is immediately obvious what the highest security classification level of data on that media can be and should be. Humans are known to put "for unclassified use only" disks into drives and then write secret, proprietary, or private data to them, either deliberately as part of an exfiltration attempt or accidentally. The labeling should clearly link to the proper handling procedures for that level of security classification. Done properly, your device-level identity management and access control systems can then use this marking to authenticate the media when it is first mounted and then authorize each attempt to read or write data or metadata to it.

It's strongly recommended that your IT or security teams be the ones who purchase, label, initialize, and inventory storage media used for sensitive, proprietary or other data security classifications your company uses. When teamed with user-facing policy directives, this can significantly reduce the compromise of classified information due to a user forgetting to properly label a piece of media.

✔ Colorize to Classify

Marking media might become complicated, depending on the media used. For instance, it might be possible to include a significant amount of information on the label of a 3.5" floppy disk, but much, much more difficult to put that same information on the label of a USB flash drive that is the size of a thumbnail. Quite often, it's much more effective to use color schemes as a visible part of media security marking, when the media itself can be readily purchased in a range of colors suitable for your organization's security labeling needs. Many media vendors can also prelabel the physical media itself to meet your needs.

Protecting

Consistent with the least privilege and separation of duties concepts discussed previously, your organization should restrict access to and usage of removable media to specifically authorized staff members who need it for their daily duties, based on their specific roles.

To do this, there must be an element of physical protection and storage that is commensurate with the sensitivity and classification of the data on the media. Here are a few examples, illustrating different levels of protection:

- Backup copies of audit logs are kept in a locked desk drawer or cabinet, where the key is available only to administrators who may need to review the logs.

- Signed hard-copy health insurance forms are in a locked file cabinet in a room restricted to HR staff via proximity-badge access.

- An external hard drive with classified data on it is fully encrypted and is in a locked safe in a protected area, accessible only to users with appropriate security clearance and need to know. The encrypted files can be decrypted only on systems that are cleared for using information at that level and then only when being used by a user with matching privileges.

As you can see in the examples, different layers of both physical and logical access control can and should be provided to media to meet your information security needs. There are additional measures to consider, based on the sensitivity and criticality of your media. You may need to create redundant copies of critical media to mitigate accidental damage or loss. Suitable encryption and other techniques can protect the classified data while it is at rest (stored on the media) and in motion between the media and the systems that are processing it (and making it available to users). Remember, too, that all storage media and technologies suffer degradation over time, resulting in data loss. Your data integrity, availability, and retention needs may drive you to establish a media rotation strategy, which periodically moves the files (the in-use set and the backup copies) to new, fresh media. (Data centers have been doing this since the 1960s, as they discovered that reels of magnetic tape quite literally saw bits flaking off when they hung in storage for too long.) Finally, you should treat the collection of all of your sensitive, critical information and the media it is stored on as a library of assets and define formal processes for periodically verifying your inventory of media, for formally authorizing users to check media in and out of the media library, and for leaving an audit trail. These processes should be followed until the media is either sanitized and then downgraded for uncontrolled use (not recommended—it's a false economy!) or destroyed for disposal, using approved equipment and methods in either case.

Transport

Your organization needs to have a defined set of procedures for protecting media when it is transported outside of controlled or restricted areas. These procedures should define the check-in and checkout accountability mechanisms used for transport, as well as the documentation requirements of the transportation activities. You should also explicitly define what information must be captured or logged upon checkout, during transport, and upon check-in of media, which might include details such as who requested the transport and who was responsible for the media during transport.

Any staff or courier transporting media should clearly understand the restrictions applied to the transport (such as approved travel methods, routes) as well as special handling and packaging considerations, based on media type, to protect it from hazards such as moisture, temperature, and magnetic fields. This also includes when, whether, and how encryption should be used during transport. Couriers should also understand your rules on deviations from procedures in the event of unforeseen circumstances encountered during such transport.

Transport procedures should be clear as to when appointed custodians are necessary, who the approved custodians or couriers are, and how to verify identity if external couriers are used. Consideration should also be given to when and how the responsibilities of the custodian can be transferred to another, as well as specific points of contact to whom the media can be transferred at arrival.

Sanitization and Disposal

The topics of media sanitization and disposal overlap and are interrelated. There is a time in the information lifecycle when certain data is no longer needed, and having this data sitting on media for no reason presents an unacceptable risk. If there is no benefit, why accept even the slightest risk that the media could be compromised? At that point, the information must be destroyed by sanitizing or zeroizing the media; the media may be returned to your library as reformatted, empty, but suitable for reuse with information at a security level consistent with the media's marking or destroyed if the media is past its economically useful life as well. So, what are the differences between the two?

The first difference is the reuse scenario. According to NIST 800-53, media should be sanitized "prior to disposal, release out of organizational control, or release for reuse." Disposal of media doesn't acknowledge a need to reuse the media, but sanitization does. Blank, new media might cost $50 to $3,000 or more apiece, so it may be worthwhile to have effective reuse and sanitization strategies in place. With the rapidly increasing capacity and decreasing cost of solid-state drives and flash media, many organizations choose verifiable destruction rather than risk an incomplete sanitization of such media. Destruction can also be done faster and at less cost in most cases.

The next difference is in the methods. The sanitization methods are less physically destructive than disposal methods. For example, sanitizing nondigital media, such as paper documents, is accomplished by removing sensitive pages or entire sections or by redacting or obscuring specific text. In contrast, disposal of paper documents would entail cross-shredding, pulping, or burning the papers entirely. Sanitizing digital media, such as hard drives, would mean overwriting each sector and byte of the drive many times with random characters. (The NSA has been known to call this process *zeroization*, even though it doesn't actually recommend writing nothing but zeros to the media; this would risk a missed block or sector being completely readable.) Disposal of hard drives, in contrast, entails either degaussing the drive, physically abrading or chemically corroding the surface of the disk platters, or breaking the entire drive in a powerful shredder. Even when degaussed or abraded, disposal of sanitized media may be constrained by local laws, including any limitations on the search of trash disposal sites with or without a search warrant.

NOTE   Degaussing does not work on a solid-state drive (SSD) or optical disk.

Another slight difference you can see in the NIST verbiage is that sanitization is often a defense-in-depth approach to precede disposal and augment it as a security control. Imagine, for example, a scenario where a hard drive was not effectively destroyed by the organization's normal disposal method or was, for example, intercepted by a curious or malicious person in the chain of custody. Even if the drive wasn't destroyed but had been previously overwritten many times with random characters, it may still be unreadable, and the sanitization is a good mitigation for the failure in the disposal process.

Having discussed the differences, what are the commonalities between sanitization and disposal? Essentially, everything else. The goal of both sanitization and disposal is to ensure that the data previously on the media is not readable or recoverable. They should both happen according to formal processes that review, approve, document, and verify the sanitization/disposal. In both cases, the methods and tools should be commensurate with the data stored on the media. This also includes the removal of external markings and labels.

For both sanitization and disposal, the sensitivity of the data on the media should drive how rigorously you apply these processes and how thoroughly you control it procedurally. In some cases, also consider that it may be less expensive to apply the more stringent sanitization or disposal method to all media than to spend time separating them.

Both sanitization and disposal use specific tools, whether software tools, grinder, shredder, degausser, etc. These tools need to be periodically tested to ensure they are effective and that the media/remnants cannot be read or restored.

When storing and collecting media *prior* to sanitization or disposal, consider affording additional protection above and beyond normal media classification and marking. If there is a large quantity of nonsensitive information in one place, it can become more sensitive by aggregation.

✔ Media Disposal and Information Retention Must Match

Almost every category of corporate or private-sector sensitive or classified information has to have a *retention strategy* defined for it, as part of keeping the organization compliant with a growing and sometimes bewildering body of law and potentially conflicting stakeholder interests. Make sure that your information library procedures, including the ones for destruction of information and disposal of media, match with those retention requirements. If they don't, you'll need help from senior management and the organization's legal team to find an acceptable solution.

IMPLEMENT SECURITY CONTROLS AND ASSESS COMPLIANCE

Although it seems a bit of an oversimplification to do so, you can characterize the world of information security controls (also known as *risk mitigation controls*) by their mix of physical, technical (or logical), and administrative elements. For example, a perimeter fence is both a physical investment in a control technology and its accompanying procedures for a periodic inspection, including "walking the fence line" by the security patrols and repairing damage by Mother Nature, vandals, or intrusion attempts. Technical or logical controls are the software and data settings, the jumper plugs or control switches, or other device or system configuration features that administrators use to get the software and hardware to implement a security control decision. Windows-based systems, for example, use software-defined data structures called *group policy objects* (GPOs) that apply logical rules to subjects and objects in the system to exert security control over their behavior. Most network devices are *logically* configured by interacting with their GUI, a built-in web page, or a command-line interpreter, to accomplish the technical configuration of that device so that it does its part in carrying out the organization's security policies.

NOTE   It's helpful to remember that a *physical* control interacts *physically* with the subject or object being controlled; technical and logical controls interact with data flows and signals being sent around the system as ways to control the logical behavior of software and hardware.

Chapter 3 will focus on how you choose what mix of physical, logical, and administrative controls to build into your security architecture; here, we'll focus on them after you've installed them and declared them operational.

Regardless of the type of control elements involved, compliance can be measured or assessed by the same set of techniques: review, audit, exercise, and operational evaluation. Help-desk trouble tickets, user complaints or suggestions, the "police blotter" or daily logs kept by your security teams, and many other sources of information should all be subject to review and audit. Performance metrics can also be adopted (preferably in automated ways) that can alert management when controls are not being used effectively, as indicated by increasing rates of incidents, error rates, problem reports, and end-user dissatisfaction with system usability and reliability. Don't forget to keep an eye on customer or client behavior and input: A decline in orders, transactions, or web page hits may be as much about the quality and price of your products as it is about the security (or lack thereof) of your information systems and practices, as seen by your customers.

Technical Controls

In all cases, you should first have an administrative (people-facing) control document, such as a policy statement or a procedure, that provides the justification and the details you need to configure, operate, inspect, and update all of the technical settings that implement the electronic aspects of your security architecture. These include both the networks, servers, and endpoint technologies, such as software Group Policy Objects, parameter files, access control lists, or even jumper and patch panel settings. Also included are the programming, options, and controls for fire and safety alarm systems, motion detectors, entryway alarms, power conditioning, and environmental control systems. (Remember, it was through a maintenance back door in the heating, ventilation, and air conditioning systems that attackers were able to gain entry into Target's systems in 2013.)

Two of the most common technical controls used in many security strategies are related to setting time limits on user activity. *Session timeouts* or *inactivity lockouts* can be implemented on an endpoint device level, on a per-user ID level, or by individual applications platforms, servers, or systems. They force a user to take a positive action to reconnect or renew a login (and go through some or all authentication factor steps) to continue, once their device, session, or use of that resource has been inactive for a specified period of time. This can be frustrating to users when they've come into a system via SSO authentication, gaining initial access to a set of resources and applications at the start of their workday but then having to repeatedly log back in again when they've let individual sessions with specific apps or servers go idle for too long. Session timeouts provide protection against the "lunchtime attack," which got its name from an intruder being able to wander around an office building and find computers unattended but still logged into the system during lunch breaks. Device-level timeouts on company-managed endpoints are typically set for short periods, such as 10 minutes, based on similar reasoning. Specific applications platforms and the portals that your users access them through may need to impose their own timeout periods and choose whether to use timeout warning reminders, based on specific systems security needs.

Another time-based technical control, the merits of which are hotly debated, is *password aging*; this sets a time period (usually measured in days, not minutes) after which a user must change their password. Other password policy settings can limit password reuse as well. Password aging, length, complexity, or other password characteristics should be determined as part of your integrated approach to identity management and access control; proper implementation of multifactor authentication, for example, may provide greater security and ease of use than complex, rapidly aging passwords were once thought to provide.

All of these settings should be subject to formal configuration management and control and documented in some fashion so that an incident response team, network operations staff, or the IT team can quickly refer to them to determine whether the alarms are sounding due to a misconfigured control or because a security incident is occurring.

Physical Controls

Physical controls are things you can touch (or bump into); they are the walls, doors, locks, fences, mantraps, concrete barriers, and their relative placement in your overall physical arrangement of a facility. By themselves, physical security features provide deterrent, prevention, and containment capabilities; to get your money's worth out of them, most organizations add monitoring equipment such as cameras, motion detectors, alarms, and people (and perhaps security canine patrols). As more robots and autonomous mobile devices enter the workplace, physical access controls must be able to cope with their presence and movements. Gluing that all together requires administrative controls in the form of policies, procedures, and control documentation. It also relies upon the human element—the monitors, the watch-standers, and the administrative and technical people who make it work and who use it to secure and protect the organization, its people, its information, and its assets.

> ## ✔ Human Vigilance—Keep It Working *for* You
>
> Whether you consider it part of your physical or administrative control systems, the human element in your security architecture can and should provide significant return on your investment in it, which you can achieve by treating them as professionals. Recruit them as if they matter to you (which they do!). Make sure that initial onboarding and training informs, empowers, and inspires them.
>
> You have a leadership opportunity with everyone involved with security operations, whether you're their supervisor or not. Step up to that challenge, work with them, and lead them as a team to be part of what keeps *everybody's* jobs secure. No matter what functions they perform or whether they stand around-the-clock watches and patrols or only work normal business hours, they can be pivotal to keeping your systems and your company safe—or become some of the weakest links in your chain of security if you ignore them or let others in the organization treat them shabbily.
>
> And if it's your first day on the job, be sure to treat each and every one of them as the helpful, dedicated professional that they are. The paybacks of this strategy can be unlimited.

Physical security architectures usually place high-value assets and systems within multiple, concentric rings of physical perimeters. Entry onto the property might require going past a guard post; checkpoints at the entries to individual buildings on the property would authenticate the individuals attempting to enter and possibly conduct a search of the personal property such as briefcases or backpacks under their control. (Most jurisdictions do consider that owners or managers of private property have the legal right to require that visitors or staff voluntarily allow a search of their person and belongings and deny entry to those who decline to cooperate with such a search.) Once inside, lateral movement within an area or access to high-value areas such as documentation or software libraries, financial operations centers, server and network rooms, or security operations control centers are further restricted, perhaps requiring two-person control as part of authentication procedures. Layer by layer, these cascades of control points *buy time* for the defenders, time in which any errors in authentication can be detected or subsequent attempts by the subject to exceed authorized privileges generate alarm conditions.

Controlled entry systems, such as mantraps and turnstiles, are electromechanical systems at heart. On the one hand, these must interface with some portion of your identity management and access control systems to be effective; on the other hand, they need routine maintenance, as well as remedial maintenance when they fail during use. In most cases, human guards or controllers are present in the immediate vicinity of such control points.

Controlled egress systems may employ the same physical, logical, and administrative tools as used to control entry into and movement within a facility; they bring the added benefit of controlling inventory, equipment, software, or data loss (sometimes called shrinkage by wholesale and retail businesses), by both deterring and preventing unauthorized removals from occurring. This usually requires a degree of search of property as it leaves the controlled area. A growing number of high-technology firms, especially in biotechnology, rigorously enforce controlled egress and search as vital components of protecting their intellectual property and competitive advantage.

Video and audio monitoring systems have become standard elements in most security systems—and all the more so as the costs of fully digital systems have become much more affordable. Even the small office/home office (SOHO) entrepreneur can afford a multicamera, digital video recorder security system, complete with Internet interfaces for remote monitoring. Many security cameras now come with infrared LEDs that provide surreptitious illumination of the scene, which improves monitoring significantly without needing to add visible light floodlighting systems and their power distribution and control elements; note that after keeping the lenses clean, proper lighting is essential for useful image quality.

Inspection and maintenance of physical control systems is vital to continued security. Administratively, there should be no surprises here; if a maintainer or inspector shows up, your on-shift, on-site guards and monitors and the security control force all need to first authenticate their identity and further confirm that they've been properly called out or dispatched to perform a specified set of tasks.

All physical control systems elements should be documented and under formal configuration management and control appropriate to their physical nature. Concrete block exterior walls, for example, should not be subject to having holes drilled or cut into them without proper authorization. The security department might not control or manage all of this documentation or the change management processes for the structural elements of the physical security aspects of your systems; regardless, your organization's security needs suggest how closely the building maintenance teams and the security teams need to work with each other.

Administrative Controls

In most organizations and the cultures they are rooted in, there is a natural hierarchy of guidance and direction, starting with broad, sweeping, and visionary statements that get progressively less motivational as they become more prescriptive. Subsequent layers become *proscriptive*, tending to have as many "thou shalt nots" as they have "shall" statements in them (if not more). Although the names for many of these layers may be different in different settings and cultures, it's still reasonably useful to expect the same basic layers of policies, standards, procedures, baselines, and guidelines.

Policies

Policies are at the heart of what the organization is trying to accomplish. At a high level, policies provide critical instruction to senior executive management to implement measures to achieve external compliance expectations or support the larger strategic vision of the organization. This layer of senior management then promulgates these vision statements down to more tactical and operational managers both as policy statements and in finer-grained direction. As governance documents, the responsibility for creating and maintaining policy rests with the board of directors or other formalized group of senior stakeholders and leaders. As such, policies are one of the ways in which the board demonstrates due care. Boards can and often do delegate or direct that executive or operational management develop these policies and bring them back to the board for review and endorsement.

Policies, relative to other organizational documents, are less likely to change. They provide consistency to the organization's management, allowing the leadership to shape standards and create procedures that achieve the policy end. They should provide management with sufficient flexibility to adapt to new circumstances or technologies without a policy revision.

Mature organizations routinely review their policies within their governance processes. Changing external compliance expectations or shifts in business strategy almost always require changes in statements of policy and vision. Additionally, these same external factors may cause the organization to confront or consider changes to their previously established strategic goals and objectives, which will probably drive more policy changes. The policy review process must address the changing needs of external stakeholders to support predictability in execution of the policies by management.

The use of the term *policy* when implementing security practice in an organization is often confusing. For example, a password policy may, or may not, be of interest to the governing organization—but it certainly would be of interest to the management team! The organization's governance structure would likely express interest in ensuring access controls are present and that the compliance expectations are appropriate to the organization's needs at the policy level and leave to management the decision of how many times a password should be rotated. That management chooses to refer to the outcome of their due diligence as a policy is an organizational decision.

Sometimes referred to as *subpolicies*, these amplifying instructions further set behavior expectations for the organization. Some of the areas that might be addressed include passwords, cryptography, identity management, access control, and a wide range of other topics. The critical distinction is whether the instruction comes from the governance body (making it a policy) or whether it is derived from a higher-level policy by the organization's management.

This broad use of the term *policy* reflects one of the major challenges in our industry. A lack of a common language for information security practice has been repeatedly identified as one of the factors inhibiting the development of a common body of practice in the information security community. It is further complicated in an international environment where translations and cultural differences affect how people perceive information. In addition, the various standards bodies have published specific definitions for information security terms that may have nuanced differences between each other.

And if that's not confusing enough, there are many instances of operating systems configuration settings that are also called *policies*.

Standards

Once the organization has decided what it wants to accomplish, management can start to perform tactical planning and operational activities to carry out the intent of the policies. One tool to support efficient management of resources is the use of standards. Standards simplify management by providing consistency in control. External standards are ones developed outside of the organization, usually by governments or industry association standards-setting bodies such as the IETF or IEEE. These provide the world with a uniform vision, purpose, and set of details about the issues that the standard focuses on. Companies can also generate their own internal standards, which they may choose to make as mandatory on all of their systems. Regardless of where the standards come from, they are downward-directed by management onto lower levels of management and supervision to support the achievement of the organization's strategic goals and are tied directly to the organization's policies. Standards also represent a consensus of best practice, as understood by the body that issues the standard. Standards may also be required as part of legal or regulatory needs or because a contract with a key customer requires the standard to be applied to work performed under that contract.

Private organizations may be required to adopt certain standards to do business in a particular market. For example, if an organization wants a web presence, it has to take into account the standards of the World Wide Web Consortium (W3C) in developing applications.

While standards are a management tool, standards often evolve out of organizational practice. For example, selecting a particular vendor to provide a product may force a standard where none was originally contemplated. De facto standards often evolve inside organizations as different parts of the organization adopt a new technology, not as a conscious management decision.

Well-structured standards provide mechanisms for adaptation to meet local conditions. Through the use of baselines, an organization can shape a standard to better reflect different circumstances. Baselines enable the delegation of decision-making within strict parameters to lower levels of management.

Nevertheless, standards are directive in nature; compliance is not optional. At most, the standard itself and the contractual or legal requirement to abide by it may specify ways in which the application of the standard can be tailored to the task at hand. Organizations that adopt standards may also be required by those standards, by contracts, or by other compliance needs to monitor the successful application of and compliance with those standards.

Procedures

Procedural documents provide highly detailed task-oriented instructions. Procedural documents are useful when a high degree of compliance is necessary and the precise steps to achieve the outcome are not readily apparent to individuals not familiar with the environment.

Management, as part of its diligence responsibilities, enforces organizational procedures through routine oversight and audit. Compliance is not optional, and well-structured organizations track compliance with procedural steps.

In certain environments, procedural compliance is achieved by using various separation-of-duties methods. For example, in cloud environments, an organization might require that every action applied to the cloud environment is performed by using an approved configuration management script, such as a Chef recipe or a Puppet task, while further dictating that the author of a script cannot be the same individual who approves the script.

Note, too, that the word *procedure* is also used by software developers and programming languages to refer to a unit of software, such as a function, a subroutine, or a stored query.

Baselines

Some organizational cultures refer to a tailored version of a standard as a *baseline*. Typically, tailoring of a standard reduces the requirements set by the standard; if additional requirements are needed, it is best practice to put them into some other document, such as a local or internal standard. Once a baseline has been established, any deviation from the baseline should be formally approved through the organization's change management practice. As with standards, baselines establish a compliance expectation.

As a subset of baselines, *security baselines* express the minimum set of security controls necessary to safeguard the information security requirements and properties for a particular configuration. *Scoping guidance* is often published as part of a baseline, defining the range of deviation from the baseline that is acceptable for a particular baseline. Once scoping guidance has been established, then tailoring is performed to apply a particular set of controls to achieve the baseline within the scoping guidance.

The term *baseline* can also refer to a reference set of systems components; the inventory of software installed on a server by the vendor, at the time when the server is first turned on and configured, is an *architectural* baseline.

Guidelines

Guidelines are necessary when an organization determines that some level of flexibility in implementation is necessary to achieve business objectives. Guidelines often rely upon best practices for a particular discipline or are the codification of an organization's experience in a particular area.

Guidelines may be useful when a range of options exist to achieve a particular control objective and it is acceptable to encourage creativity and to experiment to compare the effectiveness of different options. Guidelines may also be useful when the organization's staff has a broad base of experience and a shared vision for an outcome. In that case, the explicit directions of procedures, standards, and baselines may provide too much structure and impede the adoption of more efficient methods.

There are many sources of guidelines for information security practice. Certainly, the CISSP Body of Knowledge is one, as it reflects a broad range of security practices but is not prescriptive inside an organization's information security environment. The ISO/NIST/ITIL frameworks are often leveraged as guidelines; however, they may become policies or standards if the organization has a compliance expectation. Other sources of guidelines include manufacturers' default configurations, industry-specific guidelines, or independent organizations such as the Open Web Application Security Project (OWASP) work in software development.

There is no single, correct answer for the number and breadth of policies, standards, baselines, procedures, and guidelines an organization should have. Different regulatory environments, management expectations, and technology challenges will affect how the organization expresses and achieves its goals.

Periodic Audit and Review

There are two major shortcomings with most human-facing procedural and administrative controls for security and risk mitigation. The first is that in their human-facing form as an end product, they invariably end up being anywhere *but* right at the point of contact between the humans involved and the vulnerable system element the adminis-trative controls are designed to protect. Policies and procedures distributed on paper or as email attachments end up being lost or buried in a desk drawer or folder tree and for-gotten about. Signs and warning placards catch the eye during the first few days or weeks after they've been posted, but after a while, the human mind tunes them out; they're just part of the visual clutter of the background.

Because of these shortcomings, it's good to audit your administrative controls with an eye to separating them into two major categories: those that direct or require a real-time action, such as emergency notification and incident response; and those that provide longer-term guidance for behavior, such as inappropriate or unauthorized use of company-provided assets and resources. That first category represents opportunities for some smart investment to ensure that just the right amount of policy guidance, direction, and constraint is at the right fingertips at the right time.

Audits

Audits are structured reviews that compare a set of security and risk controls, and the systems that they protect, against a controlled administrative baseline. This baseline can include inventories, performance standards, compliance standards and requirements, quality measurements and standards, or process maturity models and standards. Informal audits can be used as part of troubleshooting, to improve organizational knowledge of its own systems, or to gain insight into opportunities for improvement. Informal audits do not require the use of outside auditors who are trained and certified for the type of audit being performed. Formal audits, by contrast, are typically conducted to meet legal, reg-ulatory, or contractual compliance needs, such as those imposed by governments or the organization's finance or insurance providers. Audits produce a report, which is typically addressed to the management or leadership levels of the organization that requested the audit. Although the structure of these reports can vary considerably, they usually include an executive summary of the audit, key findings, issues or discrepancies that need to be resolved, and any recommendations as appropriate.

Audits can place a significant burden on information security operations and support teams. Typically, extensive preparation is required to identify the audit baseline or stan-dards that will be used and ensure that the auditors will be able to access all of the items being audited. Workspaces will need to be provided for the audit team, and the auditors may require special access and privileges to the IT elements being audited. They may also need to have IT systems to use for gathering and organizing audit data and to pro-duce and report their findings.

Exercises and Operational Evaluations

Things change; that is the only constant we have in life. The proficiency and currency of the tacit knowledge within your team changes with time; the threats change how they seek opportunities that meet their needs and how they attempt to exploit them. Your systems change, and sometimes not for the better as they age in place. For these and many other reasons, it's wise to establish a process of exercising and evaluating security and risk mitigation control systems, in as realistic an operational setting as you can manage without unduly disrupting normal business operations. A properly designed and well-considered exercise and operational evaluation plan should gain the support of management and leadership; their guidance and sponsorship are crucial to make time and talent available to plan and conduct such activities. Be sure that each plan closes with a thorough post-event debrief and analysis, producing documented recommendations or action items to finish the job of learning what each exercise or evaluation just finished teaching you and the evaluation team.

PARTICIPATE IN CHANGE MANAGEMENT

Change Management or Configuration Management?

These two terms are quite often confused with each other or used as if they are interchangeable; in point of fact, it depends upon the culture and environment you're in as to which name is best to use. In business and leadership development contexts, change management (and change leadership) involves motivating, guiding, and leading people to change the ways they perceive their work and their systems and then further leading and guiding them toward making changes in those systems and in themselves. In these same contexts, configuration management is about taking a defined set of hardware, software, information, and even people skills and tasks, each of which has its particular collection or configuration of settings, options, parameters, and feature selections, and changing it into the same set of elements with different configuration settings. When you talk about IT change management and what you really mean is changing an IT systems' technical configuration into another configuration, it may be less confusing to talk about this as IT configuration management rather than IT change management. (Fortunately, nobody seems to talk about leading people to behave differently as "reconfiguring" them or managing that growth and development as "configuration managing" the HR assets!)

In an effort to reduce confusion, throughout this book I will refer to decisions about changing the configuration settings of an IT system as *configuration management*. (Change management, in the sense of organizational mission, vision, purpose, and culture, is beyond the scope of this book.)

As with many other topic areas, configuration and change planning and management present opportunities for you to work with the people around you, and with the procedures they already have in place, to understand what meanings they are implying by their use of certain terms. Guide them if you can to clarify, remove ambiguity, and become more aligned with industry-standard terms and meanings.

Configuration management and its partner process configuration control together keep a system and all of its elements managed in a cohesive, controlled way as changes, updates, or repair actions take place. Configuration management is a responsibility of both due care and due diligence and is vital to asset management. It is also a high-payoff set of process investments to make for improved information systems security. Configuration management ensures that the right stakeholders have made informed decisions to make changes, apply patches, or delete elements of your systems; configuration control ensures that those directed changes get made and that no other changes are allowed to take place.

Configuration management has perhaps the largest and most direct impact on an IT system's security posture. Without an active and effective configuration management and configuration control (CM/CC) system in place, your systems are essentially unmanaged and vulnerable. Consider as your starting point that straight from the shipping cartons, the default settings on all of your IT hardware, software, firmware, and data are often unsafe. One simple misconfiguration such as leaving a guest account open can bypass all other security controls. If by chance the new equipment or software you install is set up correctly and has no exploitable vulnerabilities still exposed, without configuration control, subsequent changes to that system and other systems it interacts or coexists with can re-expose those factory default weaknesses. Don't get the wrong impression here — without those factory or vendor default settings in place, you'd never be able to install and get the system up and running the first time. Once you do, of course, change them and lock them down tight.

The record-keeping that is the backbone of a good CM/CC system has another great payoff waiting for you, in the event that disaster strikes and you have to reload a bare-iron backup processing facility (or virgin VMs in the cloud) before you can get back into normal business operations. Those CM/CC records give you a known configuration baseline to use to *verify* that the backup images you loaded are configured, in all details, the way your management processes said they should be—the way your live production systems had been configured just before disaster struck.

Your organization should start by developing a configuration management plan if it does not have one in operation already. A configuration management (CM) plan defines how an organization will manage the configuration of its hardware and software assets. It defines details such as the roles, responsibilities, policies, and procedures that are applicable. A configuration control board (CCB), which ITIL guidance refers to as a change advisory board (CAB), will manage the CM plan. As the CCB is comprised of qualified stakeholders from the organization, they will often be the authors, editors, reviewers, and approvers of the organization's configuration policies and procedures. They will also be tasked with applying and enforcing the CM plan and helping technical administrators adhere to and understand the CM plan. Most importantly, the CCB controls and approves changes throughout the lifecycle of the IT systems, which is why they may also be known as the change control board.

Configuration management and change control focus on the life history of individual configuration items and on sets of configuration items. A configuration item (CI) is one discrete part of an IT system, like a piece of hardware or software, that has configurable settings or parameters and should be under formal configuration control. A baseline configuration is a defined, desired set of configurations for a specific CI (or combine multiple CIs into an IT system), which has been formally reviewed and approved. A baseline configuration is valid for a given point in time and may need to be adjusted over time as software or hardware versions change, new vulnerabilities are discovered, or different usage and needs dictate the need for change. When the baseline configuration needs to change, it should be done only through predefined change control procedures. Deciding what a CI should be is a matter of perspective. Consider as an example that a modern platform system such as Microsoft Office Professional might contain between 5,000 to 10,000 individual files, or about 2 GB of code, configuration data, settings, forms, and templates. To the Microsoft Office developer team, each of those files is a CI. To your company's systems administrators who download licensed distribution kits, configure them, and install them onto dozens or hundreds (or more!) of endpoint systems throughout your company, they may see each new patch version of Office as one CI or see it as thousands of CIs (all those files and all of the patches to them). Fortunately, Microsoft (and many other platform product vendors) provide some pretty extensive maintenance management tools to help you manage their products as deployed systems, rather than as deployed swarms of a huge and unwieldy number of files.

Execute Change Management Process

As the systems security analyst and administrator, your duties may combine or overlap with those of other systems administrators who actually install, manage, and maintain the operating systems, applications, platforms, web pages, and datasets that make up your organization's IT architecture. Without their extensive training and significant experience with those products, it's probably unrealistic for you to try to manage both the security configuration and the product configuration for each installed product. Let's look at a few of the methods and tools used in establishing and managing both kinds of configurations.

Manual configuration is the easiest to understand conceptually — it involves the administrator viewing and changing the configuration settings directly, either by editing a configuration settings data file or by using something like the Windows Registry Editor (regedit). Registry edits (or their equivalents in other operating systems environments) can also be done using batch or script files. Either way, this is a fine-grained, detailed, step-by-step process, which can be useful if you're stepping through various settings to diagnose a problem or as part of an incremental hardening process.

Configuration scanning tools can read the stored data structures used by the operating system and installed programs, extract information from those settings, and in some cases test some of those configuration settings for validity. The resulting list of all of these settings is sometimes called a *configuration enumeration*. NIST maintains a set of Common Configuration Enumerations that have been associated with security issues that are tracked in the National Vulnerability Database (NVD), and more recent versions of configuration scanning tools can help you detect similarities between a CCE and your system's current configuration. The CCE database can then provide you with insights and recommendations, drawn from best practices in the field, as to changes you should make in your systems to improve their overall security.

In the same breath, NIST and others often provide, specify, or recommend systems hardening information as it pertains to a given configuration enumeration. As a result, some professionals refer to the total bundle (the enumerated configuration and its related hardening information) as an *enumeration* or as a *set of hardening standards* for a particular configuration. Since the purpose of having the enumerated configurations in the first place is to collate hardening recommendations with specific configuration items and settings, this is to be expected. If in doubt as to what is meant or included, ask for clarification.

Another useful tool is a configuration change detection tool. It is different than a configuration scanner tool in that instead of asking the IT asset "Are you configured correctly?" it asks, "Did your configuration change?" It takes a snapshot of a given system's configurations, presumably after it was configured correctly and securely. Then, if any of the configurations are changed, it sends an alert to one or more relevant security stakeholders. Vendors are adding additional features and capabilities to both scanner tools and change detection tools, blurring the line between the two. Some tools now do both.

When you want to control how your security tools share data, you can use the Security Content Automation Protocol (SCAP). SCAP is a way for security tools to share data. It is an XML-based protocol that has many subcomponents called *specifications*, including one for CCE. It is a taxonomy for describing configuration requirements, which is essential because of the sheer number of configurations and their nuanced differences.

CCEs are written for, and are grouped by, specific IT products or technology types. The vulnerability equivalent to CCE is the Common Vulnerabilities and Exposures (CVE). CVE is more widely adopted than CCE because the vulnerability scanner market is larger and more mature than the configuration scanner market. In fact, some major vulnerability scanning tool vendors have added CCE (configuration) scanning to their traditional CVE (vulnerability) capabilities. Learn more about CCEs at `https://nvd.nist.gov/config/cce/index`.

In addition to other standards and guides, vendors (especially OS vendors) typically publish secure build outlines for their own products and often make tools available for provisioning and monitoring configurations.

Identify Security Impact

Any proposed change, even applying a patch kit or bug fix to alleviate a security problem, may inadvertently introduce a new vulnerability or a new risk into your systems and your business operations. Change packages should be examined to identify any potential changes to your operational procedures for getting work done with the affected systems and assets. Descriptions of the changes, and in particular the issues or vulnerabilities that are acknowledged as not addressed in the patch or update kit, should also be closely looked at to see if they suggest possible new areas of risks to your operations. If it's practical for you to delay installing the update until other organizations have installed it and operated on it for a short while, you may want to consider this—but only if you have an alternative way to protect your system from exploits targeted at the vulnerabilities the patch or update is going to remediate!

When analysis fails to surface anything to help alleviate your fears of causing more trouble and risk with an update than the fix is trying to eliminate, it may be time for some security-driven testing.

Testing/Implementing Patches, Fixes, and Updates

Chapter 7 goes into more detail on the overall software development process and the concepts behind the software development lifecycle (SDLC) models, both classic and cutting-edge, that are in widespread use today. As the security administrator or team member, you may need to be involved in the overall development process to ensure that any security-relevant issues, perspectives, functional requirements, and insights get incorporated into both the product as it is developed and the management process that keeps that development on track. At some of those test opportunities—which there are more of in a large systems development than there would be for a small, tightly focused patch or update—security may need to be more of an active member of the test team and not just an interested stakeholder and observer. Your experience and insight about what happens when systems fail to be secure can be of great help to test teams as they conduct scenario-based test cases; your knowledge of how the application or system under test *should* be interacting with network and systems security monitoring and incident detection tools may also benefit the post-test analysis activities as well.

It is best and common practice to do security-related testing in an isolated testing environment, safely quarantined off from your live production environments. Virtual machines in tightly secured test and development subnets, and hosts are ideal for this. This contains any problems that the test may otherwise set loose into your production systems or out into the wild. It also allows you to be more aggressive in stressing the system under test than you could otherwise afford to be if testing were conducted on or associated with your live production environment.

You can also adapt penetration testing scenarios and approaches you would otherwise use against your systems hosted in an isolated testing environment, before you've released those new versions of the systems into live production and operational use. Black box, white box, or other forms of penetration testing may be quite useful, depending upon the nature of the changes you're trying to evaluate.

PARTICIPATE IN SECURITY AWARENESS AND TRAINING

In many respects, you, as the on-scene security professional, have the opportunity to influence one of the most critical choices facing your organization, and every organization. Are the people in that organization the strongest element in the defense, security, safety, and resiliency of their information systems, or are these same end users, builders, and maintainers of those systems the weakest link in that defense? This is not an issue of fact; it is a matter of choice. It is a matter of *opinion*. Shape that opinion.

Awareness is where you start shaping opinion, and in doing so, you inspire action—action to learn, action to become, action to change the way tasks get done and problems get set right. You might not be a trained and experienced educator, trainer, or developer of learning paths, course materials, and the tactics to engage your co-workers in making such an awareness campaign succeed. Don't worry about that. What you *can* and *should* do, as part of your professional due care and due diligence responsibilities, is engage with management and leadership at multiple levels to obtain their support and energy in moving in the right direction.

Increasing your co-workers' awareness of information security needs, issues, and opportunities is the first step. They'll then need a combination of the conceptual knowledge and the practical skills to translate that awareness into empowerment, and empowerment into action. Depending upon the lines of business your organization is involved in and the marketplaces or jurisdictions it operates in, there may be any number of risk management frameworks, information security policies and standards, or legal and regulatory requirements regarding effective security awareness, education, and training of your organization's workforce that must be complied with. This is not a cost or a burden; this is an opportunity for small, focused investments of effort to turn the tables on the threat actors and thereby take a significant bite out of the losses that might otherwise put your team out of work and the organization out of business.

Security Awareness Overview

It's easy to see that in almost every organization, no matter how large or small its workforce, no one single person can possess the knowledge, skills, abilities, and attitudes to successfully do all of the jobs that make that organization successful. By the same token, no one information security professional can keep all of the systems and elements of the IT architecture secure *and* plan, develop, and teach the security awareness, education, and training programs the rest of the workforce needs. What any of us *can* do—what *you* can do—is to take a thumbnail sketch of what such programs need to achieve, share this with management and leadership, and assist where you can with the expertise and talent you do have to make that sketch of a plan become reality. Let me offer you some thoughts about this, from my experiences as an educator, trainer, and information security professional.

Let's start with awareness—the informed recognition that a set of topics, ideas, and issues exists *and is important.* Awareness shines a different light on the day-to-day, triggering moments of recognition. Awareness shatters the false myths, the explanations that everybody "knows" but have never tested for validity. Simple but compelling examples can do this; even something as simple as "fake phishing" attack emails that you send to your own workforce can, over time, increase the percentage of that workforce that get better at spotting a possible attack and dealing with it immediately and correctly.

Education explains concepts and links them to awareness. Education can be formal, focused around an identified body of content or aimed at the student attaining a credential of some kind attesting to their accomplishment. Informal education can be just as effective and often is well suited to rapidly evolving situations. Education stimulates thinking and creativity. A short course in root cause analysis can start with getting students to recognize the power of simple, open-ended questions.

Training teaches skills and guides learners in becoming increasingly proficient in applying them to realistic situations. Training activities that use "spotters' guides," for example, can demonstrate packet sniffing and filtering or anti-phishing email screening techniques and then use checklist approaches as the frameworks of labs and exercises to enhance learners' abilities to recognize concepts in action and make informed decisions regarding actions to take.

Competency as the Criterion

It's well worth the investment of time and thought to create a short list of the key information security competencies that different subgroups of your workforce need, if they are going to be able to make real contributions to improving information security for the team as a whole. The larger your organization and the more diverse the individual workgroups are in terms of tasks, context, and the sensitivities of the information they work with, the greater the likelihood that you'll need numerous short lists of such competencies. This is okay; make this manageable by starting with the groups that seem to need even a small step-change in security effectiveness and work with them to identify these core competencies.

By the way, some education and training program professionals will refer to this core competencies approach as a *needs assessment*. The name does not matter; the results do. Both should produce as an outcome a list of tangible, clear statements of what learners need to learn and the standards by which they must be assessed to demonstrate the success of that learning.

It's likely that your company or organization has trainers and human resources developer talent within the HR or personnel department. Find them; get them involved. Get their help in translating these first few sets of core competencies into the next layer of detail: the activities that learners have to perform well at to demonstrate that they've successfully learned that competency to the required degree of rigor. Get them to help you find teaching and learning assets and materials that the company already has; or, get them to help you find other assets. Reuse what you can find, learning from how well it works, before spending the time to develop something custom-made for your situations, people, mission, and needs.

Build a Security Culture, One Awareness Step at a Time

You've successfully engaged others in the company to take on the tasks of selecting or developing the teaching and learning assets, structuring the courses, and finding the right people to act as trainers and teachers. You've got them managing the identification of which employees need what levels of learning, how often they need it, and when they need to get the learning accomplished. As the on-shift or day staff security administrator, that's a great segregation of duties to achieve! Now what?

Walk the hallways of the company's campus or locations; keep your eyes and ears open for signs that awareness, learning, and skills-building are happening. Look for signs of trouble that suggest it isn't working fast enough or well enough. Step into those situations informally and casually, and lead by example and inspire by action and word. Suggest to people in these problematic contexts, be they workers, supervisors, or mid-level managers, that they've got the opportunity to empower themselves, and you can help them.

Too many organizations fall into the administratively simple task of regularly scheduling repetitive training activities. These could be messaging opportunities that strengthen each worker's future with the company by enhancing the organization's survival and success. Instead, they oftentimes turn them into tick-the-box, square-filling exercises in futility. If this is happening in your organization, shine some light on it; help others become aware of the need to turn that messaging around. Quickly.

PARTICIPATE IN PHYSICAL SECURITY OPERATIONS

Information security specialists, such as SSCPs, need to be aware of all threats to the information systems in their care and be able to assist, advise, and take action as required across many functional areas in their organization. If your company is truly cloud-based, with no data center of its own, you've still got threats in the physical domain to contend with. Remember, too, that your attacker could turn out to be an insider who turns against your team for any number of political, financial, emotional, or personal reasons.

Physical Access Control

If the attackers can get to your systems, they've got a chance to be able to get *into* them. This starts in the physical domain, where access includes physical contact at Layer 1 network systems, at the USB ports or memory card slots on your endpoints and other devices. It includes being able to see the blinking LEDs on routers (which blink with each 1 or 0 being sent down the wire), and it includes being bold as brass and just walking into your office spaces as if they're a pizza delivery person or business visitor. And although we've not yet seen it reported, it won't be long now before we do see an attacker using hobbyist-grade UAVs to carry out intrusion attempts.

Chapter 2 will look at the concept of defense in depth, integrating a variety of deterrence, prevention, and detection capabilities to defend the points of entry into your systems. Threat modeling, done during the risk assessment and vulnerability assessment phases (which Chapter 3 examines in more detail), have given you maps of your systems architecture, which show it at the data, control, and management planes as well as in the physical dimension. Start at the outermost perimeter in those four planes and put on your penetration-tester hat to see these control concepts in action.

One major caution: What you are about to do is tantamount to penetration testing, and to keep that testing ethical, you need to first make sure that you're on the right side of law and ethics. Before you take *any* action that might be construed as an attempted penetration of an organization's information systems or properties under their control, gain their owners and senior managers permission *in writing*. Lay out a detailed plan of what you are going to attempt to do, why you propose it as worthwhile, and what you anticipate the disruptions to normal business operations might be. Work with them to specify how you'll monitor and control the penetration test activities and how you'll suspend or terminate them immediately if required. As you learn with each step, err on the side of caution and go back to that management team and ask for their written permission to take the *next* step.

At a minimum, this will keep you out of jail. It will enhance your chances of staying employed. It will also go a long way toward increasing the awareness of the threat and the opportunity that your management and leadership stakeholders have to *do something* about it.

✔ Don't Fail to Imagine

The vast majority of businesses and nonprofit organizations have almost nothing to do with national defense or with international intrigue; their leaders, managers, and owners see themselves as light years away from international terrorist plots or organized crime. And they probably are. Unfortunately, this distance can bring a false sense of security with it, one that turns off their imagination.

In virtually every cyber attack, the target is the *data* that the organization holds. Data about their employees, their customers, or their suppliers; or transaction histories with their partners and their banks. Attackers may have far more reasons for finding value in *your* data than you think.

Without your data, you can't operate. With your data, your attackers can gain in ways you don't have to imagine in order to stop cybercrime in its tracks.

Property Approach

From early reconnaissance and target selection onward, an APT actor will need to see, sense, observe, and probe at your facilities, your people, and your IT systems. You need to balance allowing these contacts for *legitimate* outsiders while not making it too easy for a hostile agent to learn too much. You don't control the Internet any more than you control the physical spaces outside of the property line around the buildings your company occupies, but you can and should consider what you choose to make visible, audible, or otherwise physically observable, for example, via:

- Visual line of sight, depending on the sensitivity of the organization's operations. Line of sight might be obscured by limiting windows in construction, covering windows in sensitive areas, obstructing views with landscaping/formation, or other means.

- Vehicular approach, including roads and driveways toward the property/facilities. For secure facilities, these should deter a straight approach to disallow a drive to build up excessive speed and should include obstacles with bollards, barriers, or retractable tire spikes.

- Movement patterns of your workforce can reveal when they're working a special, important activity that demands a surge of effort, versus a normal routine pattern of arrivals and departures.

In the digital domain, use periodic black-box ethical penetration testing techniques to examine all publicly-facing information that your organization makes available on web pages, via e-commerce or e-business connections, and even in advertising and print media. Port scanning and network mapping also may show you spots where your systems reveal too much about themselves.

Perimeter

At the outer boundary of the property, security controls can be implemented for access control.

- **Fences/walls:** While generally seen as deterrent or preventive controls, fences and walls can also be combined with additional mechanisms to offer detection capabilities.

- **Cameras:** Cameras serve a deterrent purpose but can be combined with monitoring capabilities (such as guards watching a video feed or motion sensors) for detection functions. Know that it's fairly easy for dedicated attackers to separate the cameras that are actually monitored from those that are "perimeter dressing" and most often ignored.

- **Buried lines:** While these serve no deterrent function, underground sensors can be used for intrusion detection within the border of a property.

- **Access control points:** Guard stations or gates can be staffed or equipped with additional mechanisms (card readers, cameras, turnstiles, etc.).

- **Patrols:** Guards (human or canine) can provide deterrent, detective, corrective, and recovery controls.

- **Motion sensors:** There are a variety of technologies that support the organization's ability to surveil the perimeter and any area outside facilities, including the cameras and buried lines, as well as microwave, laser, acoustic, and infrared systems.

- **Lighting:** Well-lit areas serve both deterrent and detective purposes. Continual maintenance of all lighting sources is crucial, as a burned-out or broken bulb can defeat any security benefit the light might provide.

Parking

The most dangerous workplace location is the site where vehicles and pedestrians meet. It is imperative to include sufficient lighting, signage, and conditions (width of right-of-way, crosswalks, etc.) to minimize the possibility of threats to human health and safety. Monitoring is also useful, as parking areas are often locations that are accessible to the public and have been frequently used to stage criminal activity (workplace violence, robbery, rape, murder, etc.).

If the parking structure allows for entry to the facility, this entry should be equipped with access controls, and all entryways should feed to a single reception point within the facility.

Generators and fuel storage, as well as utility access (power lines, water/sewer pipes, etc.), should be protected from vehicular traffic, either with distance or with additional physical obstructions. There must be sufficient access for fuel delivery traffic, but this should be severely limited to reduce risk.

Facility Entrance

In addition to the other entrance controls already mentioned, the entry to the facility might include the following:

- **Reception staff:** This includes guards or administrative personnel who observe people entering and leaving the facility.

- **Logging:** This may be as technologically rudimentary as a sign-in book or combined with sophisticated badging/monitoring capabilities.

- **Flow control:** Turnstiles or other mechanisms ensure only one person at a time can pass, typically only after presenting a credential (such as a badge or biometric element).

Internal Access Controls

In addition to the other access control elements used for maintaining physical control of the workplace environment listed elsewhere in the book, the security practitioner should be familiar with the following:

- **Safes:** Secure containers that can offer protection from unauthorized access, fire, water damage, and, in some cases, chemical contaminants. Both the safe itself and the lock on the safe should be rated by a standards body for specific criteria, according to the particular needs of the organization.

- **Secure processing areas:** Specific areas within the workplace that are set aside, both administratively, technically, and physically, from the rest of the production environment. These are typified by secure entryways, severe limitations on personnel access, hardened structures (walls, no windows, etc.), and electromagnetic shielding. In the U.S. government sphere, these are referred to as *sensitive compartmented information facilities* (SCIFs), although the term has begun to see wider use in nongovernment activities in recent years.

TIP   Can Visitors Spot your Vulnerabilities? "Reconnaissance by walking around" is a time-honored component of many an intrusion; it's even easier nowadays when smartphones can conduct full Wi-Fi surveys. Try it yourself, as part of an ethical penetration test.

The Data Center

As the focal point of the data assets of the organization, the data center is in particular need of protection within the property/facility. The data center also has some specific requirements that make it somewhat different than the rest of the production environment. In addition to the other access controls placed on secure areas within the workplace (discussed earlier in this chapter and in Chapter 5), security of the data center should include consideration of the following factors:

- **Ambient temperature:** IT components generally function better in relatively cold conditions; if the area is too hot, the machines will not function optimally. However, if the area is too cold, it will cause discomfort for personnel.

- **Humidity:** An interior atmosphere that is too dry will increase the potential for electrostatic discharge. An atmosphere that is too damp will increase the potential for development of mold, mildew, and insects.

Standards for maintaining a desirable range of data center environmental conditions should be used to establish targets. One such reference is the ASHRAE Technical Committee 9.9 thermal guidelines for data centers; see http://ecoinfo.cnrs.fr/IMG/pdf/ashrae_2011_thermal_guidelines_data_center.pdf.

The data center should also be designed, constructed, and equipped for resiliency, such that it is resistant to unplanned outages from human error/attack, system/component failure, or natural effects. This is typically accomplished by including a great deal of redundancy within the data center. The use of design standards to achieve a significant level of robustness and resiliency is highly recommended.

The Uptime Institute publishes a multitier standard for use by data center owners in determining and demonstrating their particular requirements and capabilities ("Data Center Site Infrastructure Tier Standard: Topology"; see `https://uptimeinstitute .com/tiers`). The tiers range in purpose and requirements from basic data centers that might be used for archiving or occasional data storage to facilities that support life-critical processes. The CISSP should have a cursory knowledge of the four-tier levels and their descriptions. (For more information, see `https://journal.uptimeinstitute.com/ explaining-uptime-institutes-tier-classification-system/`.)

The standard is free for review/guidance; certification against the standard is performed only by the Uptime Institute and requires payment.

Organizations that receive Uptime Institute tier certification for their data centers can be listed in the Institute's online register: `https://uptimeinstitute.com/TierCertification/ allCertifications.php?page=1&ipp=All`.

Finally, fire poses a significant, common risk to data centers because of the high potential for occurrence and because of the disproportionately heavy impact a data center fire would have on the organization. The selection, design, implementation, maintenance, and use of fire protection and alarm systems can be quite complex, and in many jurisdictions must be undertaken by a properly licensed fire protection engineer. Municipal standards such as building codes also must be taken into account. Insurance providers may also levy strict inspection and compliance constraints on any and all fire protection systems and practices in order to maintain policy coverage. This all goes well beyond what the SSCP can or should attempt to take on.

Service Level Agreements

In the modern IT environment, there are many reasons (not the least of which is cost) for an organization to consider contracting with an external service provider to handle regular operational tasks and functions. To create a contract favorable for both parties in this sort of managed services arrangement, everyone involved must clearly understand what is being requested, what is being provided, what the cost is, and who is responsible for what. This is particularly important in what could be considered the most popular current form of managed services: cloud-managed services. In the majority of cloud-managed service contracts, the cloud provider and customer must determine the expected level of service, and the contract or service level agreement is the element that gives both parties the confidence to expect defined outcomes: assuring the provider that they will receive payment and assuring the customer that the service will meet the customer's needs.

In these cases, you need a formal agreement that defines the roles and responsibility of each party, explicit to the point where it can be easily understood and measured. The common name for this is the service level agreement. However, depending on the services provided, the agreement can go by other names, like *network services agreement*, *interconnection security agreement*, etc. The SLA is part of the overall contract but deals directly with the quantifiable, discrete elements of service delivery.

These are scenarios where an organization might need an SLA:

- Third-party security services
  - Monitoring/scanning
  - Security operations center/response-type services
  - Media courier/media disposal
  - Physical security
- Hosted/cloud
  - Servers
  - Storage
  - Services
- Interconnecting information systems, especially with data feed/pull/push
- Supply chain scenarios

The SLA portion of the contract vehicle is best limited to those elements of the managed service that are routinely provided as part of continual operational requirements; the SLA is not the optimum place for including contingency requirements (such as BCDR tasks) or for anything that cannot be distilled into a numeric value.

Specific Terms and Metrics

To be effective (and enforceable), an SLA must use clear and unambiguous language to specify its terms and conditions for all services that each party brings to the contract. Key performance indicators or other quality of service metrics should also be defined in the SLA, along with explanations as to how they are measured, computed, and reported. Without this, there is no basis for measuring or knowing whether a provider is providing the agreed level of service.

Amazon Web Services (AWS), a well-known cloud service provider, uses a standard SLA for their Elastic Cloud Compute (EC2) services, which you can review at https://aws.amazon.com/ec2/sla/. Among other items, it specifies a server uptime metric:

- If your servers enjoy anything above 99.99 percent uptime, AWS has met its SLA.

- If your servers have anywhere between 99.00 and 99.99 percent uptime for the month, you will get a 10 percent discount on the service fee for that period.
- For anything less than 99.00 percent, you will get a 30 percent discount for your hosting for that month.

This is a good example not only because the metrics and terms are clear but also because it is clear about what happens in the event of noncompliance with the SLA. The contracting manager (in conjunction with the organization's IT department) must determine whether the price reduction would realistically offset the loss in productivity a service outage would cause; if the cost of the outage outweighs the benefit of the rebate/discount, the SLA is insufficient for the customer's needs.

Mechanism for Monitoring Service

It is not enough, however, just to understand the terms of the SLA. You also need a mechanism with which to monitor and measure whether the service provided matches the level specified in the SLA.

To continue with the previous example of AWS, visit `https://status.aws.amazon.com/`. You will initially see a dashboard similar to Figure 1.3. The horizontal rows represent the AWS regions. If you look at the corresponding region where your servers are hosted, you can see whether they are having, or have had, any degradation of service or outages.

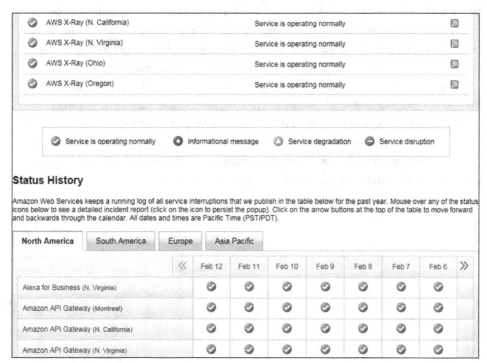

FIGURE 1.3 **AWS dashboard**

While this dashboard can be used to inform the customer as to the efficacy of the service overall, it might not provide, by itself, the level of assurance the customer desires; the information is necessarily coming from the provider, and the provider has a vested interest in the outcomes of the data (i.e., getting paid) and so is inherently biased. For such SLA elements, the customer may prefer some third-party validation of the service/data to feel confident that the reporting mechanism adequately reflects the actual level of service provided/received.

SUMMARY

It's in the day-to-day details that you have the greatest opportunity to thwart an attacker from gaining meaningful insights about your information systems and then leveraging those insights to attempt an intrusion. It's in the day to day that you mentally, virtually, and physically patrol your perimeters, layer by layer, and stay in touch with the sensors and preventers that are working to keep things safe and secure. It's hard to keep a paranoid edge to your awareness; it's hard to avoid being lulled into a no-news-is-good-news complacency. One built-in advantage you have is that in a properly planned and executed security posture, the list of things you need to check up on is almost limitless: Boredom should never be your problem! Get curious, and stay curious, as you check with the badge readers and the other AAA elements of your access control technologies. Review what the security information logging and analysis systems are trying to tell you. Touch base with the help-desk people, with visitor control, and with all of the human elements that make your security strong—or break it, if left ignored and uncared for.

Making information security into something that works effectively every day, every hour, is an operational and administrative task. It needs you to manage it by physically and virtually walking around. Think like a hacker; turn that thinking into ideas for ethical penetration testing, even if only on paper or sitting around a conference table with people from other functional areas in your organization. Hear what they say, and help them grow the security culture you all need to enjoy and be safe in.

Access Controls

IDENTITY MANAGEMENT AND ACCESS control are two sides of the same coin. Attacks on your systems happen because there are exploitable vulnerabilities in your systems that allow the attacker to bypass your identity authentication and access control processes. Once inside your systems, other access control failures (be they physical, logical, or administrative) allow the attacker to exfiltrate data, corrupt your systems, or use your systems as the launching pad for attacks on other parties' systems.

Unfortunately, most intrusions are not discovered until months after attackers have already taken copies of your data and left your systems. If you've kept good records of all access and connection attempts, you may be able to identify what data has been lost or changed; if not, you'll probably not learn about the data breach until your lost data is found somewhere on the Dark Web.

This chapter provides you a detailed, operationalized guide to implementing and benefiting from an integrated identity management and access control system and process. In doing so, it makes extensive use of confidentiality, integrity, availability, nonrepudiation, authorization, privacy, and safety (CIANA+PS) as a way to focus our attention on the total set of an organization's information security needs. CIANA+PS starts, of course, with the CIA triad of confidentiality, integrity, and authentication, as is addressed in Chapter 1. This total set of attributes focuses our attention on the vital importance to business (and in law) of having highly reliable, auditable, and verifiable control of access to information assets and the systems that support them.

The CIANA+PS set of needs illustrates why information security and assurance is much more than just cybersecurity. Cybersecurity focuses intently upon the information technology aspects of keeping computers, networks, data centers, and endpoints safe, secure, and reliable. That focus on the technologies of the information infrastructure is important; it does not, however, provide much assistance in designing business processes for cross-organization collaboration that provide the appropriate assurance to each party that their knowledge, information, and data are safe and secure. Information assurance is about information risk management, which Chapter 3, "Risk Identification, Monitoring, and Analysis," will address in more detail. Chapter 3 will also emphasize the use of physical, logical, and administrative means by which vulnerabilities are mitigated. Maintaining and operating those information assurance processes almost invariably requires a significant degree of attention to the human-facing procedural details, many of which are involved in how information systems and the IT they rely upon are managed; this is addressed in Chapter 1, "Security Operations and Administration," as well as in Chapter 7, "Systems and Application Security."

This chapter, however, deals almost exclusively with the *logical* means of implementing identity management and access control. These logical means will involve management making decisions that establish organizational and local policies and procedures, which will be addressed here in context, but I'll leave the physical restriction of access to computing and communications hardware to Chapter 7.

ACCESS CONTROL CONCEPTS

Access control is all about subjects and objects (see Figure 2.1). Simply put, *subjects* try to perform an action upon an object; that action can be reading it, changing it, executing it (if the object is a software program), or doing anything to the object. *Subjects* can be anything that is requesting access to or attempting to access anything in a system, whether data, metadata, or another process, for whatever purpose. Subjects can be people, software processes, devices, or services being provided by other web-based systems. *Subjects* are trying to do something to or with the *object* of their desire. *Objects* can be collections of information, or the processes, devices, or people who have that information and act as gatekeepers to it. This subject-object relationship is fundamental to your understanding of access control. It is a one-way relationship: objects do not "do anything" to a subject. Don't be fooled into thinking that two subjects, interacting with each other, is a special case of a bidirectional access control relationship. It is simpler, more accurate, and much more useful to see this as two one-way subject-object relationships. It's also critical to see that every task is a chain of these two-way access control relationships. It's clearer to see this as two one-way trust relationships as well.

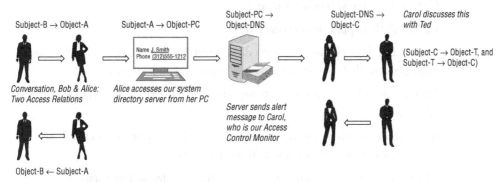

FIGURE 2.1 **Subjects and objects**

As an example, consider the access control system itself as an *object*. It is a lucrative target for attackers who want to get past its protections and into the soft underbellies of the information assets, networks, and people behind its protective moat. In that light, hearing these functions referred to as *data center gatekeepers* makes a lot of sense. Yet the access control system is a *subject* that makes use of its own access control tables and of the information provided to it by requesting subjects. (You, at sign-on, are a subject providing a bundle of credential information as an object to that access control process.)

Subjects and Objects

The first notion you have to come to grips with is just how many millions of objects can exist within even a small office/home office (SOHO) local area network (LAN) environment; scale this up to a large cloud-hosted data center operation and you could be dealing with billions and billions of objects. Even at the small end of this scale, the sheer number of objects involved dictates the need for efficient processes and effective, automated solutions to carry out most of the work that an access control system has to perform. For example, a typical SOHO LAN environment with an ISP-provided modem, a Wi-Fi router, and peer-to-peer file and resource sharing across a half-dozen devices on that LAN might have the following types of objects as part of that LAN system:

- Each hardware device; its onboard firmware, configuration parameters, or device settings; and its external physical connections to other devices
- Power conditioning and distribution equipment and cabling, such as a UPS
- The file systems on each storage device, on each computer, and on each subtree and each file within each subtree
- All of the removable storage devices and media, such as USB drives, DVDs, or CDs used for backup or working storage
- Each installed application on each device
- Each defined user identity on each device and the authentication information that goes with that user identity, such as username and password
- Each person who is a user or is attempting to be a user (whether as *guest* or otherwise)
- Accounts at all online resources used by people in this organization and the access information associated with those accounts
- The random access memory (RAM) in each computer, as free memory
- The RAM in each computer allocated to each running application, process, process thread, or other software element
- The communications interfaces to the ISP, plain old telephone service, or other media

Wi-Fi is a registered trademark of the Wi-Fi Alliance, the nonprofit organization that promotes wireless connectivity, certifies products as conforming to their standards for interoperability. The name does not stand for anything; in particular, it does not mean "wireless fidelity," even though a number of websites say that it does.

Note that third item: on a typical Windows 10 laptop with 330GB of files and installed software on a 500GB drive, that's *only* half a million files—and *each* of those, as well as each of the 100,000 or so folders in that directory space, is an *object*. Those USB drives, and any cloud-based file storage, could add similar amounts of objects for each computer; mobile phones using the Wi-Fi might not have quite so many objects on them to worry about. A conservative upper bound might be 10 million objects.

What might the population of *subjects* be, in this same SOHO office?

- Each human, including visitors, clients, family, or even the janitorial crew
- Each user ID for each human
- Each hardware device, including each removable disk
- Each mobile device each human might bring into the SOHO physical location with them
- Each *executing* application, process, process thread, or other software element that the operating system (of the device it's on) can grant CPU time to
- Any software processes running elsewhere on the Internet, which establish or can establish connections to objects on any of the SOHO LAN systems

That same Windows 10 laptop, by the way, shows 8 apps, 107 background processes, 101 Windows processes, and 305 services currently able to run—loaded in memory, available to Windows to dispatch to execute, and almost every one of them connected by Windows to events so that hardware actions (such as moving a mouse) or software actions (such as an Internet Control Message Protocol packet) hitting a system's network interface card will wake them up and let them run. That's 521 pieces of *executing* code. And as if to add insult to injury, the one live human who is using that laptop has caused 90 *user identities* to be currently active. Many of these are associated with installed services, but each is yet another subject in its own right.

Subjects and objects have *identities* by which they are known to the systems that they participate in. For identity management and access control to work effectively, these identities need to be unique—that there is a one-to-one correspondence between a subject and its identity (or identifying information). Human names fail this uniqueness need more often than not; thus, we have to end up assigning some kind of identification key or value to each new human entity that comes into our identity management system's purview. Hardware identities, such as the media access control (MAC) addresses, are reasonably unique, but they can be locally altered and spoofed. You'll look at this *identity proofing* problem in more detail later in the "Proofing" section.

Privileges: What Subjects Can Do with Objects

The next key ingredient to access control is to define the privileges that subjects can have with respect to objects. A privilege is a type of action that the subject can perform upon the subject, such as:

- Read data from the object.
- Write data into the object.
- Delete the object.
- Read or inspect metadata associated with the object.
- Modify the metadata associated with the object.
- Load the object into memory and execute it as a program.
- Extend or alter the system resources (such as storage space) allocated to the object.
- Copy the object from one location to another.
- Move the object from one location to another.
- Read or inspect the security data associated with the object.
- Modify the security data associated with the object.
- Verify the existence of the object.

It is true that some of those privileges can be thought of as aggregates of others: Copying a file requires one to be able to read it, as well as create another instance of it someplace else; moving a file further requires the privilege of deleting the file after it has been copied. Verifying that a file is in fact on a given storage device requires read access to another object (the device's directory structure), as well as interpretation of metadata about the object. It is also true that not all commercial operating systems or access control systems provide this level of granularity. Organizations need to look at their information security classification needs as part of deciding how to establish privileges and relate them to subjects and to objects to make effective use of access control as part of their information security posture.

The privilege of being able to confirm or deny the existence of an object within a given system is frequently used for user logon systems, in which a failure of a subject to provide a valid user ID and password should not result in confirmation that the user ID is legitimate. Some operating systems, such as Windows, also implement features that can hide certain classes of files (by file type or location) from certain classes of users, both to declutter a user's view of folder trees and to protect systems resources from prying eyes. Organizations with more stringent (higher) security needs often make extensive use of this privilege to deny reconnaissance attempts to discover the presence of lucrative information assets, to infer knowledge about processes within the system, or to gain insight into a possible pathway to other objects.

This brings me to define identity management as the set of processes that are used to create identities within a system, provision those identities across all elements of the system as required, assign and manage privileges to those identities, revoke privileges, and finally retire or delete an identity once it is no longer needed. Access control uses this information about identities and privileges as its standards by which to adjudicate each access request or attempt.

However, before you can learn about identity management, you need to look at how the security classification of the various information assets should drive the way you use access control to deliver those various levels of protection.

Data Classification, Categorization, and Access Control

Next, let's talk layers. No, not layers in the TCP/IP or OSI 7-layer reference model sense! Instead, you need to look at how permissions layer onto each other, level by level, much as those protocols grow in capability layer by layer.

Information risk management should start by classifying the many different kinds of information your organization uses, in terms of the degree of impacts resulting from any security compromise. In short, the greater the threat to the existence of the company, the higher the *security classification level* of that information. The lowest level of such protection is often called unclassified, or suitable for public release. It's the information in press releases or in content on public-facing web pages. Employees are not restricted from disclosing this information to almost anyone who asks. Privacy-related data, company proprietary, pre-procurement sensitive, and even client-specific proprietary data are often treated as separate classification levels today.

Categorization then groups information assets (the information, not the systems that process them) of similar security classifications together. This facilitates common control strategies for assets in the same category.

A good demonstration of classification and categorization at work can be seen in the Computer Emergency Readiness Team (US-CERT)'s Traffic Light Protocol (TLP), shown in Figure 2.2. The TLP is a schema for identifying how information can or cannot be shared among the members of the US-CERT community. It can be seen at www.us-cert.gov/tlp and appears in Figure 2.1. It exists to make sharing sensitive or private information easier to manage so that this community can balance the risks of damage to the reputation, business, or privacy of the source against the needs for better, more effective national response to computer emergency events.

Color	When should it be used?	How may it be shared?
TLP:RED Not for disclosure, restricted to participants only.	Sources may use TLP:RED when information cannot be effectively acted upon by additional parties, and could lead to impacts on a party's privacy, reputation, or operations if misused.	Recipients may not share TLP:RED information with any parties outside of the specific exchange, meeting, or conversation in which it was originally disclosed. In the context of a meeting, for example, TLP:RED information is limited to those present at the meeting. In most circumstances, TLP:RED should be exchanged verbally or in person.
TLP:AMBER Limited disclosure, restricted to participants' organizations.	Sources may use TLP:AMBER when information requires support to be effectively acted upon, yet carries risks to privacy, reputation, or operations if shared outside of the organizations involved.	Recipients may only share TLP:AMBER information with members of their own organization, and with clients or customers who need to know the information to protect themselves or prevent further harm. **Sources are at liberty to specify additional intended limits of the sharing: these must be adhered to.**
TLP:GREEN Limited disclosure, restricted to the community.	Sources may use TLP:GREEN when information is useful for the awareness of all participating organizations as well as with peers within the broader community or sector.	Recipients may share TLP:GREEN information with peers and partner organizations within their sector or community, but not via publicly accessible channels. Information in this category can be circulated widely within a particular community. TLP:GREEN information may not be released outside of the community.
TLP:WHITE Disclosure is not limited.	Sources may use TLP:WHITE when information carries minimal or no foreseeable risk of misuse, in accordance with applicable rules and procedures for public release.	Subject to standard copyright rules, TLP:WHITE information may be distributed without restriction.

FIGURE 2.2 US-CERT Traffic Light Protocol for information classification and handling

Note how TLP defines both the conditions for use of information classified at the different TLP levels as well as any restrictions on how a recipient of TLP-classified information can then share that information with others.

Each company or organization has to determine its own information security classification needs and devise a structure of categories that support and achieve those needs. They all have two properties in common, however, which are called the *read-up* and *write-down* problems.

- Reading up refers to a subject granted access at one level of the data classification stack, which then attempts to read information contained in objects classified at higher levels.

- Writing down refers to a subject granted access at one level that attempts to write or pass data classified at that level to a subject or object classified at a lower level.

Shoulder-surfing is a simple illustration of the read-up problem, because it can allow an unauthorized person to masquerade as an otherwise legitimate user. A more interesting example of the read-up problem was seen in many login or sign-on systems, which would first check the login ID and, if that was correctly defined or known to the system, then solicit and check the password. This design inadvertently confirms the login ID is legitimate; compare this to designs that take both pieces of login information and return "username or password unknown or in error" if the input fails to be authenticated.

Writing classified or proprietary information to a thumb drive and then giving that thumb drive to an outsider illustrates the write-down problem. Write-down also can happen if a storage device is not properly zeroized or randomized prior to its removal from the system for maintenance or disposal.

Having defined subjects and objects, let's put those read-up and write-down problems into a more manageable context by looking at privileges or capabilities. Depending on whom you talk with, a subject is granted or defined to have permission to perform certain functions on certain objects. The backup task (as subject) can read and copy a file and update its metadata to show the date and time of the most recent backup, but it does not (or should not) have permission to modify the *contents* of the file in question, for example. Systems administrators and security specialists determine broad categories of these permissions and the rules by which new identities are allocated some permissions and denied others.

Access Control via Formal Security Models

Let's take a closer look at CIANA+PS, in particular the two key components of confidentiality and integrity. Figure 2.3 illustrates a database server containing proprietary information and an instance of a software process that is running at a level not approved for proprietary information. (This might be because of the person using the process, the physical location or the system that the process is running on, or any number of other reasons.) Both the server and the process act as subjects *and* objects in their different attempts to request or perform read and write operations to the other. As an SSCP, you'll need to be well acquainted with how these two different models approach confidentiality and integrity.

- Protecting confidentiality requires that you prevent attempts by the process to read the data from the server, but you also must prevent the server from attempting to write data to the process. You can, however, allow the server to read data inside the process associated with it. You can also allow the process to write its data, at a lower classification level, up into the server. This keeps the proprietary information safe from disclosure, while it assumes that the process running at a lower security level can be trusted to write valid data up to the server.

- Protecting integrity by contrast requires just the opposite: You must prevent attempts by a process running at a lower security level from writing into the data of a server running at a higher security level.

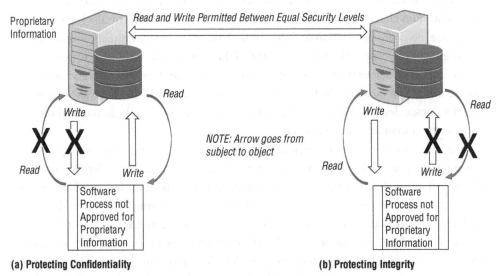

(a) Protecting Confidentiality   **(b) Protecting Integrity**

FIGURE 2.3 **Bell–LaPadula (a) versus Biba access control models (b)**

The first model is the Bell–LaPadula model, which was developed by David Bell and Leonard LaPadula for the Department of Defense in the 1970s as a fundamental element of providing secure systems capable of handling multiple levels of security classification. Bell–LaPadula emphasized protecting the confidentiality of information—that information in a system running at a higher security classification level must be prevented from leaking out into systems running at lower classification levels. Shown in Figure 2.3(a), Bell–LaPadula defines these controls as follows:

- The simple security property (SS) requires that a subject may not read information at a higher sensitivity (i.e., no "read up").

- The * (star) security property requires that a subject may not write information into an object that is at a lower sensitivity level (no "write-down").

Another property is the *discretionary security property*, which requires that systems implementing Bell–LaPadula protections must use an access matrix to enforce discretionary access control.

Remember that in the examples in Figure 2.3, the process is both subject and object and so is the server! This makes it easier to see that the higher-level subject can freely read from (or be written into) a lower-level process; this does not expose the sensitive information to something (or someone) with no legitimate need to know. Secrets stay in the server.

Data integrity, on the other hand, isn't preserved by Bell–LaPadula; clearly, the lower-security-level process could disrupt operations at the proprietary level by altering data that it cannot read. The other important model, developed some years after Bell–LaPadula, was expressly designed to prevent this. Its developer, Kenneth Biba, emphasized data integrity over confidentiality; quite often the nonmilitary business world is more concerned about preventing unauthorized modification of data by untrusted processes than it is about protecting the confidentiality of information. Figure 2.3(b) illustrates Biba's approach.

- The simple integrity property requires that a subject cannot read from an object that is at a lower level of security sensitivity (no "read-down").

- The * (star) integrity property requires that a subject cannot write to an object at a higher security level (no "write-up").

Quarantine of files or messages suspected of containing malware payloads offers a clear example of the need for the "no-read-down" policy for integrity protection. Working your way down the levels of security, you might see that "business vital proprietary," privacy-related, and other information would be much more sensitive (and need greater *integrity* protection) than newly arrived but unfiltered and unprocessed email traffic. Blocking a process that uses privacy-related data from reading from the quarantined traffic could be hazardous! Once the email has been scanned and found to be free from malware, other processes can determine whether its content is to be elevated (written up) *by some trusted process* to the higher level of privacy-related information.

As you might imagine, a number of other access models have been created to cope with the apparent and real conflicts between protecting confidentiality and assuring the integrity of data. Biba and Bell–LaPadula show up quite frequently in many situations. Other formal models you may not encounter as often include the following:

- The Clark–Wilson model considers three things together as a set: the subject, the object, and the kind of transaction the subject is requesting to perform upon the object. Clark–Wilson requires a matrix that allows only transaction types against objects to be performed by a limited set of trusted subjects.

- The Brewer and Nash model, sometimes called the Chinese Wall model, considers the subject's recent history, as well as the role(s) the subject is fulfilling, as part of how it allows or denies access to objects.

- Noninterference models, such as Gogun–Meseguer, use security domains (sets of subjects) such that members in one domain cannot interfere with (interact with) members in "another domain."

- The Graham–Denning model also uses a matrix to define allowable boundaries or sets of actions involved with the secure creation, deletion, and control of subjects, and the ability to control assignment of access rights.

All of these models provide the foundational theories or concepts behind which access control systems and technologies are designed and operate. Let's now take a look at other aspects of how you need to think about *implementing* and *managing* access control.

✔ **Star or Simple? Which Way?**

Biba and Bell–LaPadula define properties (sometimes called *axioms, principles,* or *rules*) that can easily be confused with each other if you don't look at the next word in the property name. Always ask "What are we protecting?" and let that need for confidentiality or integrity tell you which directions you can read or write in!

IMPLEMENT AND MAINTAIN AUTHENTICATION METHODS

Authentication is the process of verifying that the *factors* or identity credentials presented by a subject actually match with what the identity management system has already established and approved. (Later sections in this chapter will address how these different functions—identity management, authentication, authorization, and accounting—can be hosted in different server architectures to meet the organization's needs in a cost-effective way.) When the identity management function provisions a newly created identity, it also creates or initializes the set of identity credentials, such as username and password, for that subject to use once the identity itself is provisioned across the systems that the subject has been granted use of.

Note that in common practice, the username is by definition the identity by which that subject is known within the system; the rest of the information created and provisioned by the identity management process, which is then used during access authentication and authorization, is known as the *credentials*. Some credentials, such as passwords, may also become *factors* and are presented as part of access authentication.

As with any process, authentication can be prone to errors. Type 1 errors, also called false negative errors, occur when an otherwise legitimate subject is denied access; this is an incorrect or false rejection of the subject. Type 2 errors, also called false positive errors, give the "green light" to a subject to proceed in their attempt to access the system or object in question. These false acceptances are the greater security worry, as they potentially are allowing an intruder into your systems. You'll look at these errors and how to manage their rate of occurrence several times in this chapter. Note that many IT professionals refer to these directly as *false rejection* or *false acceptance* errors and avoid the possible confusion of types, positive and negative.

Single-Factor/Multifactor Authentication

Authentication is the first step in controlling what subjects (people, processes, or hardware) can access any portion of your systems. As you think about authentication, keep in mind that there are three sometimes competing needs to address. Human subjects need to get work done; their identity, and the parameters and attributes associated with that identity, need to be kept safe and secure; and the information assets that are the very reasons for your system to exist in the first place need to be kept safe and secure. Each of those needs requires its own dose of CIANA+PS sauce; each will need a different mix of those security ingredients, tailored to your organization's needs and its approach to information risk.

Traditionally, the issue of single-factor versus multifactor authentication has been discussed in terms of human end users as access control subjects. With more autonomous and semi-autonomous systems becoming part of our networks—or becoming *users* of your networks—it's probably time to reconsider this in more general terms. It's time to focus on subjects *regardless* of whether they are people, robots, IoT devices, or processes, of *any* level of complexity, as having identities that must be authenticated prior to allowing them to connect to our systems and networks. If our security needs require multifactor authentication for one class or type of entity, we take on great risk for any other class of entity for which we only require single factor authentication.

Authentication of human user access attempts has traditionally been based on one or more of three authentication factors.

- **Type I:** Something you know, such as a username or password
- **Type II:** Something you have, usually a hardware device, a machine-readable identity card, or a smart card or key fob
- **Type III:** Something you are, such as a physical characteristic that does not change over time

Two additional factors (not, so far, named Type IV and Type V) have been gaining more widespread use in the marketplace: "something you do" and "somewhere you are," which relate to specific behavioral patterns associated with you as a subject.

These factors can be applied alone or in combination with each other as both a deterrent against intrusion or reconnaissance attempts and as a way to reduce the overall rate of Type 2 (false acceptance) errors. Single-factor authentication involves the use of only one of these three factors to carry out the authentication process being requested. Multifactor authentication requires the subject to present two or more such factors for sequential authentication. Successfully passing the gate of each factor's test increases the confidence that the subject is in fact whom (or what) it claims to be. Of course, the more factors you want to use for authentication, the more effort it will take to create and provision them, update them, and otherwise manage and maintain them. When it comes to any factor used for authentication, do remember that human users forget things, lose things, misplace things, and sometimes willfully violate administrative policies and allow other people to use those things and thereby have access to systems. The use of multifactor authentication by itself won't necessarily address these human frailties. The chosen authentication factor technology must also support rapid revocation of a factor when it is lost or compromised; and in some cases, you may also need to provide *recovery* of a factor, such as a passphrase or other information the user should know and remember when it is lost, forgotten, or garbled in use.

Regardless of the choice of factors used, at some point your security protocols need to deal with locking a user out from further access attempts (also known as a *false rejection* error). A user who fails to authenticate properly after a small number of attempts (typically three to five attempts) is locked out and may have to either wait a certain amount of time or contact the systems help desk and request a reset of their access credentials. Although false rejections cause you to spend extra effort to resolve and potentially waste otherwise productive time for your users, they are far less worrisome than *false acceptance* errors, which occur when an attacker manages to spoof a set of identification and authentication credentials and is accepted by your system and granted access. The frequency with which both of these types of errors occur is an important security diagnostic you should monitor, if not treat as an alarm condition.

Figure 2.4 shows one statistic you will often see cited in vendor material about biometric devices. The crossover error rate (CER) is the number that results when the device is adjusted to provide equal false acceptance (false positive or Type II) and false rejection (false negative or type 1) error rates in your environment. This is also referred to as an equal error rate (EER). All other things being equal, the device with the lower CER or EER may be demonstrating a greater intrinsic accuracy and yield you less wasted effort spent on false rejects and lower your risk of allowing an intrusion (a false acceptance) to occur. Since most systems see tens of thousands of access attempts per day, it's important and meaningful to look at the *rate* that these errors occur as indicators of whether you've got your access control system tuned properly.

In selecting, tuning, and deploying any access control methods, including biometric technologies, it is critical to choose the tolerance for false positive and false negative error rates to meet your risk tolerance. Let's look at some numbers:

- The false rejection rate (FRR) is the ratio of false rejection errors to valid authentications. If 1,000 attempts to authenticate result in two rejections of legitimate users, the FRR is .002, or .2 percent.

- The false acceptance rate (FAR) is the ratio of false acceptance errors to valid authentications. If, in 1,000 attempts to authenticate, two impostors are erroneously allowed in, the FAR is .002, or .2 percent.

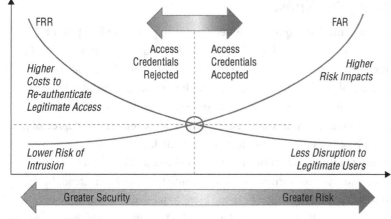

FIGURE 2.4 **Crossover error rate**

You can see in this figure that the costs associated with implementing more rigorous access authentication techniques, such as multifactor biometric technologies, do buy you lower false acceptance rates (that is, spending more money moves your operational point to the left on that graph). False rejections cause you to spend extra effort to validate that a legitimate but rejected user should in fact be allowed to have access. If your circumstances and risk appetite suggest that you can tolerate the increased risk by spending less, then, by all means, move toward the right side of the graph and be willing to accept a greater likelihood of an intrusion while minimizing the disruptions to legitimate users (and increased costs of legitimate work).

Be aware that it is false reasoning to associate a lower cost with the right edge of this graph: You "win" on this trade space only if your systems are never penetrated in ways that inflict great impact via a data breach or ransom attack or that cause other losses. As Bob Lockhart pointed out at `https://www.tractica.com/biometrics/in-biometrics-which-error-rate-matters/`, most real-world applications of access control have to operate well on the left side of this graph.

Note, too, that regardless of which type or types of authentication factors your systems use, you also need to support these with administrative, logical, and physical processes for revocation of existing credentials, replacement of credentials that have been lost or stolen, and reissue or revalidation of credentials as part of periodic review of access privileges. This is covered in more depth later in this chapter.

Let's look at these factors in some depth and each one's strengths and weaknesses when used as a single-factor authentication of a subject claiming to be a legitimate human user on your systems. (You'll learn about device authentication in more detail in Chapter 6, "Network and Communications Security.")

Type I: Something You Know

Everyone who has used a modern computer system is familiar with the first type of authentication factor, "something you know." Common forms of this authentication factor include passwords, passphrases, personal identification numbers (PINs), and security questions. Some systems also ask users to authenticate themselves by confirming recent activity on the system, such as the last three transactions on a bank account. All of these forms assume that human memory and willpower can provide a reasonable degree of protection for the chosen type of "secret knowledge" used as the factor.

Note that the more complex and secure you try to make your Type 1 factor implementations, the more you risk transforming into something the user *has* instead, by making the temptation to write it down somewhere too great to pass up. By the same token, a password manager such as LastPass is another device (albeit a software one) being used as the source of the authentication factor, rather than the human being's own memory. That said, current practice treats the use of password or passphrase managers as being part of the Type I authentication factor process and problem set.

Passwords

Almost every month, the news media publish a story about another data breach in which usernames and passwords were accessed, corrupted, or copied by the attackers. The damages suffered by individual users in such incidents can be both traumatic and financially crippling; the damage to the targeted business can be enough to put it out of business, and in extreme cases, its directors can suffer time in jail.

Passwords are by far the most commonly used authentication mechanism and perhaps the one most prone to self-inflicted vulnerabilities when users:

- Choose trivial or easily cracked passwords.
- Forget their passwords.
- Fail to keep them safe and secure.
- Share them with others (whether those others are trusted systems users or not).
- Reuse the same password on multiple systems, websites, and accounts.
- Reuse the same password, or a simple transform of it, when asked by the system to change it.
- Leave passwords set to the default values set by the vendor or manufacturer.
- Store passwords on paper or in unprotected files kept on the systems or websites that they use.

In many cases, the use of password policies that require the use of special characters, numbers, and mixed case have contributed to these vulnerabilities, as many users find it difficult to create strong passwords in 12 to 16 characters or less that comply with such requirements. Requirements for frequent password changes also add to user frustration, which leads to some of the poor password security hygiene habits described in the previous list.

At some point, the chosen length of a password causes the user to shift into thinking of it as a passphrase instead.

✔ Classical Password Policies—and Pitfalls

Human beings just aren't good at creating a seemingly random, *short* string of text that makes for a strong password, in other words, one that is hard to guess but also easy for the user to remember. Despite this, many early ideas about password security became institutionalized, as reflected by their presence as security policy options in nearly all modern operating systems. These include the following:

- Complexity, which is usually interpreted as a mix of letters, symbols, and numbers used to transform a correctly spelled word into a secure password

- Minimum length, which may be as short as eight characters or more commonly 12 to 16 characters

- Reuse limitations, prohibiting the reuse of any of the last three to five passwords

- Prohibitions on commonly used words, such as names of days or months, names of sports teams, popular expressions, or other words in a restricted dictionary

One problem with these policies is that these policies may end up leading users to create passwords that are easy for password-cracking algorithms to crack, even if they are too complex for the average human to guess at. Consider a password like "@u28&iza710n," which a single CPU password cracker might need 200 years to crack, primarily because it's a few short transformations away from the word *authorization*. Switching the order of the front and back halves of that string do improve its strength—to about 76,000 years of single-CPU work factor. But in doing so, it's made the password harder to remember.

Another problem with all of these policies is that they assume a common human understanding of what makes a chosen string of text, complete with special characters and misspellings, be a nonobvious choice for a password. The experts don't agree; how, then, can a billion users guess correctly on this? This leads to the incredible range of different password policy requirements that typical users see across the many websites and systems they interact with every day.

CONTINUES

The stronger we attempt to make our password policies, the greater the frustration for our end users; and experience tells us that frustrated end users will find ways to cheat on the system and in doing so weaken its security.

And no matter how complex we make our passwords (or passphrases), chances are that if they are easy for us as a user to use, they're also vulnerable to a quick peek from a shoulder-surfer. That quick peek doesn't have to capture the entire phrase—just enough of it to help a puzzle-freak combine their intuition, their open source knowledge of you and your personal history and habits, and the job or system you're working with to be able to feed some smart guesses into their favorite cracking tool.

Complexity rules also run the risk of creating a false sense of security for administrators, users, and organizational senior leadership alike. More often than not, complexity rules that humans can use to select and use passwords can easily be broken by modern cracking tools, especially ones that draw upon zombie botnets to provide massive boosts to their computational capabilities.

Passwords are useful as a first authentication step—but they should never be the one and only step.

Password managers are software tools that provide users with a one-stop way to store, manage, and use all of their access credentials across many different platforms, systems, and websites. Password managers typically are used as browser extensions, providing automatic fill-in of the user's credentials when the browser navigates to a web page known to the password manager. They typically encrypt the stored user ID and password/passphrase information in a local file (sometimes called a *vault*). They can also be used to store and manage local device login information, such as the usernames, IP or MAC addresses, and passwords for a small office/home office (SOHO) router or modem or for other devices on the user's local area network. A single set of access credentials, typically an email address and a password, enables the password manager's vault system to interact with user login prompts. Password managers also provide users with a variety of security-enhancing features, such as automatic creation of unique, strong passwords for each login, routine testing of password strength and age, and multifactor authentication of the user when they attempt to access or use the password manager's vault.

It is important to distinguish the use of a password manager by an individual from single sign-on (SSO) access to your systems. Single sign-on does not depend upon each application, platform, or system within your architecture having a password defined for a user to access it. SSO is discussed in more detail later in the "Single Sign-On" section.

Using a password manager system can provide greater security for an individual user, and organizations that need their users to routinely access systems outside of the organization may find it worthwhile to look at corporate implementation strategies for them. They can, however, lead to two novel and potentially catastrophic security failures, if not configured and used properly.

- The first case, in which all passwords would be compromised, occurs when the central repository for the user's passwords is breached. This can happen either if the master password is guessed by an attacker on the user's system (the one your organization manages) or if the password manager vendor's central repository is breached. This should not be possible if proper encryption techniques are used in either case to protect the repository information while in use, at rest, and in motion; that said, it is a significant risk that must be addressed.

- Password managers entail another, much simpler risk, too, which is the possibility that the user might forget the master password. Eventual recovery might be possible, depending on the brand of password management software, but some operational disruption would be certain. This also requires users (individual or corporate) to repose great trust in their password management system vendor, the recovery agent, or both.

✔ Stay Current on Best Password Practices

In 2017, the U.S. National Institute of Standards and Technology (NIST) has updated its password and passphrase policy recommendations. (See https://pages.nist .gov/800-63-3/sp800-63-3.html.) Based on many years of industry experience and with input from security researchers and academics alike, NIST's new recommendations overturn many of password policies that have been in widespread use for decades. For example, NIST no longer recommends requiring a periodic reset of user passwords, as this tends to promote poorer password hygiene among users. NIST also recommends against classical ideas of password complexity for the same reason. Many of these recommendations are reflected in this chapter; study them and see how they can be put to use to improve your organization's security posture.

Passphrases

Since about 2016, more and more voices in the information security community have recommended the use of strong passphrases instead of passwords, primarily as a way to avoid all of the inherent failings of humans and human organizations to make effective use of more complex passwords. (One of the industry pundits who first advocated complex passwords actually offered a bit of an apology for doing so, as he acknowledged his change of heart on this topic.) A passphrase is a longer string of characters that ideally is both meaningful and memorable to its user and creator but is not easily inferred by others based on public knowledge about that individual. It should also not be a direct quote (with or without spaces and punctuation) from a published work. For example, if I am a well-known fan of J. R. R. Tolkien's body of fantasy works, a passphrase such as "inawholeindagroundlovedahobbit" might be too easy for someone to deduce based on my interests. (If I am anything but a fan of fantasy, by contrast, it just might be a start on a good passphrase.) Some of the best passphrases are made by combining four or five totally unrelated words together, with the occasional shift of letter case or a substitution of vowels with numbers. "Strongch33z3janerator," for example, might start with "strong phrase generator" and be tweaked by the user into a phrase that might withstand attack for 35 quintillion years, according to www.howsecureismypassword.net (but don't use it as is because it's been published). Adding a few extra characters to a passphrase, such as tacking on a four-digit number to its end, does nothing for its overall hardness. Do be aware that many systems have length limits on the input fields for passwords (or passphrases) and advise users to stay within those lengths.

Several key benefits come from using passphrases instead of classic but complex passwords:

- Users find them easier to create and remember, without relying on publicly available knowledge about them as a person.

- Longer passphrases exponentially increase the search space that a password cracker has to operate in, requiring much larger dictionaries or rainbow tables as well as far more CPU cycles.

- Passphrases actually make it easier for users to creatively use numbers, case shifts, and special characters as part of their phrase than they can in much shorter passwords.

Security practitioners are also recommending that with proper use, passphrases do not benefit from being changed periodically.

Passphrases, of course, are prone to being written down and to being reused on more than one system that the user has access to. Using a password manager application can help with these risks.

✔ Salt What You Know Before You Hash It

All but the most rudimentary legacy systems actually store a hash of a user's password, passphrase, or other Type I factor value; if an attacker exfiltrates a copy of the stored hash of the factor, they face a computationally infeasible (or tremendous brute force) burden of trying to unhash that back into its original plaintext form. This hash function should be applied at the endpoint device at which the user enters the factor so that only the hash is transmitted to the access control system.

Secure hash functions can be made much more secure by appending a pseudorandomly generated *salt value* to the input plaintext version of the factor before hashing it. Secure frameworks and systems tools make it easier for systems administrators to add salt to their hash function use and provide many powerful ways to select and manage salts.

There is no practical reason why the plaintext version of a Type I factor has to be stored in your system—anywhere.

Security Questions

Security questions are often used as an additional Type I factor during authentication. These often use a preset list of security questions that users must answer during account provisioning or after a password is forgotten. Typically, the system hashes the answers entered by the user (ideally at the user's endpoint device!) and stores the hashed answers in a table associated with the user ID. A very few systems treat the answer to a security question in ways that allow the user to vary the way that they enter it (such as with fewer blank spaces or in a different mix of upper and lowercase); while this may make "passing this quiz" easier on the user, it also reduces the security of the system overall and would not therefore be a recommended approach.

At each login or access attempt, the user is asked to provide answers to a certain number of these questions. Retry logic might allow two incorrect responses to a set of five randomly chosen questions, for example, before the user must contact the help desk for assistance and verification of their identity.

In many respects, security questions are just another set of passwords, and they suffer from all of the shortcomings and risks that passwords do. Users have been prone to take screenshots of the questions and answers as they first establish them and then store that file in an unprotected way on their system, for example. (You don't do that, do you?)

In practice, most security questions reflect open source information (often called OSINT) about the subject—that is, information that is published or public-facing—which can be used to deduce both correct and incorrect answers to traditional security questions. Users can, of course, establish incorrect answers for these questions when the account is being provisioned, but those wrong answers still have to be memorable.

Because of this, NIST has dropped security questions from its list of policy recommendations for user authentication. It might be argued that security questions can be used as part of a password reset dialog process; this might make life for your users easier at the risk of making it easier for an attacker to gain access.

Personal Identification Numbers or Memorable Information

Personal identification numbers are another example of a "what you know" factor in use. Frequently, you see PINs used as a second authentication factor when using a credit card, debit card, or other form of automated teller machine (ATM) card to access banking and financial services. PINs typically are from four to eight digits in length, and as with all factors depending upon human memory, they may be easily deduced using publicly available knowledge about the PIN's legitimate user. It also doesn't take that much machine time to crack a four-digit PIN, or even an eight-digit PIN; the search space is just too small. However, most ATMs and other systems using PINs will set limits on how many times the wrong PIN can be entered before locking the card out of that device.

A variation on the PIN is the use of a user-specified string of memorable information; the access control system then asks the user to provide a few individual characters from this string, rather than the whole value itself. Again, this has all the risks of presenting a very small search space to an attacker and might not actually make things easier for your legitimate users in the process.

Recent Access History

Another technique, often used by banks and financial institutions, is to prompt the user for additional information pertaining to recent activities associated with their user ID or account. Banks might ask about the last five deposits, for example, while an insurance provider might ask for particular information regarding a recent claim that the (purported) user had submitted. Some secure systems also have displayed information regarding the last access attempt (failed or successful) made by the user and then asked for additional information as part of confirmation of the user's authenticity.

Conceptually, this is asking for information that the legitimate user should know, but in practice, it often ends up with the user having to access the systems themselves or their off-board (paper) records of system activity in order to answer the questions correctly.

In any event, use of such information only establishes that the person trying to access the system *now* already has enjoyed access to it previously, which does not help separate legitimate user access attempts from an attempted identity theft.

Escrow, Recovery, and Reset

Let's face it: Every choice of Type I factor is at risk of being forgotten by a user, and this includes the master password or passphrase for a password manager! There are basically two options available that you as a systems security administrator need to consider as you plan ahead to deal with this human forgetfulness. Both require procedures that ensure that the user asking for recovery of a password in escrow is in fact the user whose identity was proofed and is part of your identity management record-keeping systems.

- **Password reset:** This is merely an immediate action taken by the administrator to require a new password or passphrase at the next user login attempt. Most of us have had far too many experiences with using password reset functions, because of either forgetfulness or system policies about period reset.

- **Password escrow:** This option provides for the storage of an encrypted (not hashed) form of the password in a physically and logically separate space. You also have to pay attention to the choice of encryption used, so as to protect against *that* key being compromised or lost. Regardless of whether your organization manages this escrow activity or has contracted it out to a password manager and recovery service, password escrow requires a level of trust and confidence at least as great as the most sensitive or confidential information in your systems.

Users will ask about having their password "recovered," which is tantamount to running your own password cracker on it for them. You'll probably have to explain to them that if the password system is going to do its job of keeping the systems secure, it therefore shouldn't be something that can be easily cracked.

Type II: Something You Have

The second type of authentication factor is "something you have," meaning a physical object of some kind. Physical keys, passes, and tokens have been used throughout history for this, with each form of pass becoming obsolete, impractical, or both over time. Consider how many hotels have replaced the nonelectronic locks on the doors to guest rooms with electronic locks that read the key cards generated by the front desk when a guest checks in. Physical access control factors provide additional information during the authentication process, information that you would not normally know. For example, a smart card or electronic ID card contains a chip, which contains firmware and data that interact with the authentication process.

Smart Cards

Machine-readable *smart cards* or digital ID cards have been becoming more common-place during the last two decades. Much of this was spurred on by the U.S. government, and this drove the creation of NIST guidelines and standards for physical access control systems (PACSs). Standards describing two different cards, the common access card (CAC) and the personal identity verification (PIV), have been developed for their use, and they support high-volume mass production of the blank cards that are then initialized as part of the identity provisioning process by the using organizations. Each card type uses an embedded chip to store digital certificates and information about the identity of the person the card has been issued to, which is then used as part of the access authentication. These cards are not foolproof and can be prone to radio frequency crosstalk that in some cases can render the card inoperable. Within many U.S. government organizations, for example, CACs are used not only for face-to-face verification of identity but as part of access control to computer and communications systems and for entry to restricted or controlled areas. Many private companies use one or the other card as part of their physical access control for data centers or other high-value assets. CAC and PIV cards may be used with magnetic stripe readers, with OCR readers, or in some cases with near-field communications (NFC) RF readers.

NOTE In the United States, Federal Information Processing Standard Publication 201 (FIPS 201, Parts I and II), developed by the National Institute of Standards and Technology, provides current standards and technical details related to using physical access control systems (PACSs) and the associated CAC or PIV cards as part of an authentication system. See https://csrc.nist.gov/publications/detail/fips/201/2/final.

Note that in the European Union's Genera Data Protection Regulation (GDPR), which went into effect in 2018, there are additional requirements about how data can be collected from humans during the identity verification process, how that data can be compared to data in other sources, and what if any of that data can be retained by the data processor without explicit consent of the user.

Because electronic ID cards like the CAC and PIV are intended for mass production and because millions of mass-produced cards make an alluring target for attackers, it is critical for researchers and practitioners alike to keep abreast of vulnerability concerns with these and similar devices. For example, an alarming report by two Czech scientists in 2014 about a "highly theoretical" vulnerability in Estonian CAC ID cards led to an investigation identifying a manufacturing error requiring 15 cards to be canceled immediately. After further investigation, the Estonian software was rewritten to compensate for the problem. (For more information, see, for example, https://news.postimees .ee/4236857/id-card-tip-from-czech-scientists.) While the fundamental technology appears sound and the cards practical, you can expect many more vulnerabilities and alarms in the future as these hardware-based devices, impossible to perfect and resistant (in their current forms) to patching, proliferate in number and increase in importance in our careers and in our everyday life.

Security Tokens

Security tokens such as key fobs are small electronic devices that can be used as part of physical facilities access control or as part of a user login and authentication process. The simplest form of such a token or key fob uses NFC readers to detect the presence of the fob and validate its use as part of granting access through external or internal doors. The provisioning process can tailor the access privileges for each fob for the individual user — for example, allowing guests to freely enter or exit through some doors, but not through others, and only during business hours plus or minus a small margin.

Another common use of a security token is to provide users with an additional identification factor to be used during authentication. Some of these security tokens use an onboard pseudorandom number generator, which is initialized with a seed during provisioning; the same seed is used by a matching generator function in the access control system, which means that the token and the access control system generate the same sequence of numbers as they are repeatedly used. In effect, this provides a limitless one-time pad of secret keys, which can then be used by the chosen authentication protocol. These tokens can either be synchronous, with both the token device and the host access control system moving to the next one-time pad value at controlled time intervals; or asynchronous, which usually requires the user to push a button or activate the token to have it generate and display the next key value in the sequence. Asynchronous token systems often use a login counter value in both the token and the host as part of their synchronization and error detection processes. In either case, users typically must bring the security token physically to the provisioning facility if the token gets out of sync or no longer functions properly. The result of using the security token either can be an additional authentication step or can be appended or prepended to the normal "what you know" password or passphrase and then submitted (suitably hashed, one hopes) to the server for validation.

Security tokens are frequently implemented via mobile device apps. Such so-called soft tokens can provide the same functionality as the physical hard token-based systems do but often can provide important additional benefits. Deployment of multifactor authentication using soft tokens can be a significant cost savings and—with the right mobile device management (MDM) systems approach—be easier to administer. More importantly, such an integrated management of soft tokens and the devices they are associated with allows for more real-time response when a device is reported or suspected to be missing, lost, or stolen (or if its user's privileges are being suspended for other reasons).

Although adding "something you have" to the security stack of authentication is generally sound practice, physical items such as smart card, badges, and tokens can be lost or stolen. Security architectures, policies, and procedures should take this possibility into account and deal with notification and revocation in the wake of such events.

Another concept related to soft tokens is that of an authenticator. Sometimes used synonymously with soft token, the term can also refer to a special onetime code sent to a pre-vetted smartphone. Such authenticators are sometimes invoked in the middle of a login sequence—for example, when a login is attempted by a device unfamiliar to the authentication service. In this case, the code, when read from the phone and typed into the login software, provides a separate, out-of-channel means (such as a separate email to an address on file) of authenticating the request.

Still more complex authenticator schemes involve a challenge-and-response method, whereby the login sequence displays a "challenge." The user then types the challenge string into an authenticator app on the phone, the app displays a response (often a string of digits), and the user relays the response string back into the challenging software to complete that extra stage of authentication. Amazon, Google, and many Microsoft websites routinely provide this additional challenge-response means as part of authenticating a subject before they can modify their account profiles, for example.

Type III: Something You Are

Human memory has limitations as a reliable, unique, and secure authentication factor. Physical characteristics of a human being, however, remain reasonably constant over time and are not prone to being lost, stolen, or counterfeited in quite the same way that Type I or Type II authentication factors can be. *Biometric identification systems* make real-time measurements of a select set of physical characteristics of a person, which an authentication process can then compare with measurement data taken during the provisioning process.

Using personal recognition as part of an identity verification process is nothing new. Human beings have identified each other by face and by voice for millennia. Footprints have helped to implicate or rule out criminal suspects for centuries. Fingerprints have been acceptable as evidence in a court of law since 1910, and the use of human DNA in criminal proceedings became accepted in 1988. In all cases, it was the development of automated measurement, characterization, storage, comparison, and retrieval systems to make any of these or other biometric identification means become practical and affordable.

Biometric methods offer a wide range of choices for the security architect, each with different degrees of reliability, practicality, and cost considerations. End-user acceptance and ease-of-use factors may also need to be taken into account, as well as any legal or cultural constraints (real or perceived) pertaining to a particular biometric method. These methods can be either static methods, which characterize the subject at a particular moment in time, or behavioral methods, which measure the subject as they perform a sequence of actions.

Static biometric methods include the following:

Body Weight   Measuring a subject's body weight provides a simple, noninvasive, and oftentimes affordable second authentication factor. Although an individual's body weight does vary seasonally, with age, and with health and fitness conditions, day by day these variations are slight. Simple body weight biometric systems compare one moment's weight measurement with the value established during identity provisioning; more advanced systems trend measurements across recent history and flag anomalous changes as potentially worthy of investigation prior to granting access. Weight measurement is often used in high-security environments, in conjunction with mantrap, turnstile, or other single-person entry and exit control techniques (for example, when a second person tries to "tailgate" through a mantrap with the subject). Weight measurement devices can easily be built into the floors or floor coverings in entry vestibules or corridors, where they can be an unobtrusive, often-unnoticed component of physical area access control processes.

Fingerprint   More than 100 years of experience supports our use of fingerprints as reliable and repeatable forms of identification. Fingerprint recognition technologies now are built into many consumer-grade smartphones, phablets, laptops, and other devices. Fingerprint scanning and verification is routinely done as part of immigration (and emigration) checks at airports and other border control points. The complexities of the science of fingerprint measurement, characterization, and matching have been commoditized at this point, although individual scanning units can need frequent cleaning or wipe-down between users.

Palm Print   Palm prints are at least as old as fingerprints as an authentication method and may actually be older. The larger surface area makes possible more detailed differentiation, and palm prints do have some technical advantages over fingerprints. Still, palm prints have never been as popular for everyday authentication. Today, two relatively new technologies have brought the palm back into the mainstream as an authentication element. Palm vein recognition is a biometric method that uses near-infrared illumination to see (and record for comparison) subcutaneous vascular patterns, which are the pattern of blood vessels beneath the skin that is unique to each individual. Palm scans are fast, passive, and painless. Perhaps because palm vein recognition may seem more invasive, some people placing their hand onto a scanner would prefer the alternate older approaches of palm topography and hand geometry.

In these methods, features of the hand such as finger and palm length and width (and perhaps the ridges of the palm) are scanned, recorded, and compared. In the one-hand geometry method, you would be asked to place your palm on a flat metal plate.

The plate has small round metal stanchions sticking up out of it; they are there to guide your placement so that the stanchions are nestled up against the places where the webbing of your fingers come together. With your palm properly placed, the device can register an image of your hand and develop a set of measurements sufficient to authenticate you in the future.

Iris or Retina Scan   Biometric measurements of the eye proceed similarly. The iris is the colorful part of the eye that surrounds the pupil, which is the dark circle in the middle. Gradations of color and patterns of light and dark are distinctive for any individual. These colors and these patterns persist throughout a lifetime, with little change due to age or illness, making the iris one of the most reliable forms of biometric measurement.

Biometric scans using the retina are even more individualistic than those of the iris. The retina, a thin segment of light-sensitive tissue at the back of the eye, contains both arteries and veins. The structure of the inner retinal vasculature is unique to each human eye, differing even for identical twins. It can be recorded for biometric use by means of infrared light. To acquire a good picture of the back of the eye, it is necessary for the individual being measured to place their eye directly up against a viewpiece similar to that of a microscope; some people find this experience physically or psychologically uncomfortable. Another drawback of retinal scans is that the appearance of the retina can be affected by diseases of the eye such as glaucoma and cataracts or even the progression of diseases such as diabetes.

Facial Recognition   Facial recognition uses measurements of the external geometry of the face, such as the positions, sizes, and relative orientations of the eye sockets, nose, mouth, chin, and ears, as its basis for comparison, typically using visible light measurements. It can also use infrared measurements to identify and map the subcutaneous (below the skin) blood vessels and structures. All of this data about the subject is first collected during identity provisioning and then measured again as part of authentication. Minor changes in facial hair, skin tone or tan, health, and even the changes due to aging can be accommodated by the measurement and comparison technologies now widely in use.

New Factor Type: Something You Do

Two broad applications of user security behavior analysis are part of the current security landscape, although one is much more well-developed than the other at the time of this writing. The first is the use of behavioral patterns, primarily ones associated with simple motions or actions, as additional authentication factors used with access control systems. Voice print identification, signature and handwriting dynamics, and keystroke dynamics are all available in the marketplace today. The second is the use of behavioral analytics to monitor ongoing user behavior to assess whether a legitimate subject is behaving in abnormal ways. Changes in behavior might be a precursor or indicator of a possible security incident. Employees can be under stress because of health or family concerns, which can lead to making mistakes or choosing wrong courses of action. In other instances, disgruntled employees might experience dissatisfaction and stress that builds to a tipping point and they react. Employees can also be vulnerable to coercion, extortion, or other threats. Some of these stresses (but not all) may show in biometric identification readings. Others may show in larger patterns of behavior, such as patterns of applications use, data accesses, or interactions in the workplace. Behavioral analytics as a form of predictive intelligence is a hot topic in security research and analytics research worldwide and could be a game-changing technology in the very near term.

Behavioral biometric methods are good examples of "something you do" rather than "something you are," in that they all relate to measuring actions you take over time. The most frequently used forms of behavioral biometrics include the following:

Voice Print   Voice print authentication systems typically work by capturing a digital recording of a subject speaking one of several prompted phrases and then comparing that to a recording of the subject speaking the same phrase during the identity provisioning process. Digital signal processing techniques are constantly improving the ability of these systems to deal with minor illness, slight changes in cadence or tone, or ambient conditions while still providing acceptable rates of false match or false reject errors.

Signature or Handwriting Dynamics   Handwriting dynamics measures the speed and direction of the pen or stylus tip as a subject writes their signature or a standardized short phrase; in some instances, a pressure-sensitive pad and stylus can also gather useful data on how forcefully the subject presses the stylus into the pad. Without these measurements, digital signature or handwriting analysis reduces to more classical graphological analysis techniques, which can with good reliably distinguish authentic handwriting samples from clever forgeries or detect indications that the writer is under stress.

Keystroke Dynamics   Keystroke dynamics can also be used for biometric purposes. In this application, the characteristics of key presses—dwell time, for example, and the pauses between and after certain key combinations—can be recorded and registered as belonging to the legitimate user, for later comparison. As with signature dynamics, keystroke analysis verges on a new dimension of biometric security. It represents, perhaps, "something you do" as opposed to "something you are."

Considerations When Using Biometric Methods

Regardless of the specific technology that is used, biometric techniques all involve the same stages of preparation as any other authentication method. First, the user must be enrolled, and the characteristics that will be used for authentication are captured and recorded as part of the registration process. This creates a reference profile to which comparisons can be made. Preparations must be made for the secure storage of reference profiles and their retrieval in a timely way. A method must be available to verify, promptly and within specified accuracy limits, whether a person claiming an identity should be authenticated. A final requirement is a secure method of updating the reference profile when the characteristics to be compared change (due to age or illness, for example) or revoking the reference profile when it is no longer needed, has expired, or can no longer be trusted to be accurate.

Let the specific information security and risk mitigation needs of each system and situation dictate how you specify, design, configure, and maintain your choice of biometric access authentication technologies. Situations that involve high levels of risk to life and limb, such as safety of aircraft flight or medical laboratory information systems in a major hospital, demand that you tolerate extremely low false acceptance rates, and as a result, you'll have to ensure that users and other team members appreciate the risks and the concomitant need for more extreme security measures.

If, on the other hand, you are responsible for adjusting the office badge reader at a newspaper office, you will want to consider trying to keep the false rejection rate reasonably low—if only to avoid reading flaming editorials complaining about how security has run amok in modern society.

In selecting a set of biometric tools for authentication, it is certainly important to be aware of the error rates. There is more to be considered, though, besides the accuracy and reproducibility of a potential biometric technique.

First, of course, you want the measurements taken to be unique to an individual. While many (not all—think body weight) biometric tools will succumb to impersonation by an identical twin, uniqueness of the measure is important. After all, depending on the precise nature of the tool, you may find yourself with a degraded reading. Fingerprints can smudge, voice recordings may have a lot of background noise, and poor lighting or infrared interference may cloud a photographic record. A good biometric will have the attribute that the copy to be compared to the registered base will vary minimally and predictably as it degrades in quality.

Consider, too, that it is not only the measurement taken for comparison that may be degraded. Fingers, palms, and faces may be scarred by accident (or, alas, intentionally). Aging, illness, and injury must all be anticipated and compensated for. Sometimes, this may include having to redo the reference measurements.

Another factor to consider is the accessibility of the part of the body that must be registered. It is not a coincidence that fingers, at the end of our extensible arms, were employed as the first widely used biometric.

Further, one wants biometric measurements to be noninvasive, passive, and safe. Individuals to be vetted will vary in general health; in dexterity; in their ability to see and hear; in their alertness and the ability to follow instructions; and in their physical and psychological tolerance to being prodded, scanned by various rays, or enclosed in an examination compartment. Many individuals will be concerned about electromagnetic irradiation. Some women to be authenticated by your biometric device may be pregnant at the time or may become pregnant later. All of these individual conditions should be anticipated and respected with due concern for the examined individual's health, well-being, privacy, dignity, and legal rights.

As with all security measures, when selecting a biometric for deployment in your enterprise, you must consider the cumulative costs of setting up the system, registering each person, taking each measurement such as a fingerprint, and storing and retrieving the candidates' measurements.

Note that biometric sensors can produce data that indicates the subject may be suffering from a variety of illnesses, injuries, substance abuse, or other medical conditions. Depending upon the technologies you're using, the data you collect may cross the fuzzy boundary between what is personally identifying information (PII), nonpublished personal information (NPI), and protected healthcare information (PHI). Each category, of course, comes with its own compliance and regulatory requirements for data protection. As medical technologists discover even more ways to use noninvasive sensing to learn more about the condition of their patients, this frontier between identification and medical data will only become more complex to navigate.

Finally, be sure to consider the likelihood and effectiveness of antibiometric tactics by potential attackers.

If you are using facial recognition, attackers might wear masks.

If you rely on fingerprints, you had better anticipate and test the effectiveness of fake finger casts made out of silicone, rubber, or even ordinary wood glue. Japan's National Institute of Informatics even found that fingerprints can be copied by a digital camera from 10 feet away and then easily reproduced with simple technology. Depending on just how low you need to drive down the false acceptance rate, you might want to select a vendor for fingerprint sensors that can supply "liveness detection," sensing temperature, pulse, and even body capacitance as a means of detecting fake fingers.

In the age of 3D printers, security architects need to think creatively about the technology relied upon by their biometric tools.

New Factor Type: Somewhere You Are

For some time now, access control systems have been able to check whether the IP address, origin URL, or information about the physical location of the subject is in fact within allowable limits. These constraint checks are usually expressed as attributes as part of an attribute-based access control system. Some systems can even use a soft token app to interrogate the location services within many smartphones, phablets, and laptops, and return that location information to the access control system to see whether the user-subject is where they are authorized, expected, or claim to actually be. Many mobile phone systems already provide this as part of their processing of calls to emergency service numbers, making GPS or other high-accuracy location information available to service dispatchers within seconds of a call being placed to their systems. Extending this to more mundane, nonemergency circumstances is worth considering if your organization needs to restrict access privileges or take other actions based on where you (and your soft token device) happen to be connecting or initiating an access attempt from.

Accountability

Accounting, you recall, is one of the "big three" functions of access control (the other two are authentication and authorization). Having strong, effective accountability as part of your information systems architecture supports three main objectives that most (if not all) organizations need to achieve.

- **Resource utilization, monitoring, and chargeback:** In all but the smallest of SOHO environments, organizations need to plan and budget for IT resource usage by the organization. Budgets can and should allocate resources not only to departments or work units but also to objectives, goals, projects, and initiatives. Once a budget has allocated IT resource use in this way, accounting functions track actual usage so management can control usage and investigate budget variances (usage over or under predicted and budgeted amounts). In this way, resource usage accounting can also identify the need to scale or resize the organization's IT resources in more deliberate ways.

- **Individual accountability:** By providing detailed records of each individual's accesses to systems resources, management has an informed basis upon which they can hold individuals responsible for their actions and decisions. This type of digital forensic evidence can play a vital role in supporting any corrective actions management needs to take, such as counseling or admonishing an employee; it also can support litigation if required.

- **Information security monitoring, analysis, and incident characterization and response:** At each step of the access control process, detailed information can and should be generated about: which subjects, under what conditions, attempted what kind of accesses to which objects; what decisions were made as to granting or denying access; and what outcomes if any resulted from these access attempts. Authentication or authorization rejects can send alarms to systems security reporting and monitoring functions, including to the watch-standers in the security operations center (SOC) or network operations center (NOC). Accounting information can provide the diagnostic and forensics data that may be needed in analyzing and characterizing the event, as well as supporting decisions about containment and other required responses. Accounting data as part of access control also can provide important trending data, which may reveal whether the access control system is doing its job effectively enough to provide the required level of security and protection. After a security incident, this data may also help identify changes to sensitivity settings, constraints and conditions, or alarm filtering levels as part of providing better protection before the next incident occurs.

Taken together, this means that the data your accounting functions generate must be reliable and verifiable as to its accuracy and completeness. Data that cannot unambiguously identify the subject or subjects in question and precisely identify the actions they took or attempted to take are of little value to the troubleshooter or the litigator.

You must also take actions to protect the accounting data and related information in various systems or applications log files from inadvertent or deliberate damage, alteration, or loss. This not only protects the chain of custody of such data as forensics evidence but also provides another opportunity for early detection of an intrusion or unauthorized access or usage attempt. For example, by routing all security-related event notifications and supporting data to a separate logging agent, which is protected by separate and distinct administrator credentials, you both protect the log data while providing another source of alarms if some other process (a subject), even one with systems administrator, root, or other elevated privileges, attempts to access that data. It's also good to keep in mind that unplanned system restarts can sometimes be part of attempts to obscure an attacker's actions, including their attempts to cover their tracks by altering log files.

It is worthwhile to consider all of your security-related information as high-value, high-payoff assets—ones where the losses to the organization if they are compromised, destroyed, or lost is far greater than the modest investments to properly gather, isolate, and protect this data. Don't let your log files overwrite themselves too quickly. Instead, work with your security experts and your legal team to set an effective data retention policy for this data and then implement this in your security information management practices and procedures.

Having said all of that, it's worth remembering that each month seems to bring news of even more sophisticated attack mechanisms being used by the black hats; in many cases, rootkits and other stratagems can alter the reality of your systems while keeping your perceptions of them largely intact. When all else fails, having "golden image" backup copies from which you can reinstall *everything*, from the bare metal up, may be your only safe and sane path back to normal, trustworthy operations.

Single Sign-On

Single sign-on (SSO) was the first outgrowth of needing to allow one user identity with one set of authenticated credentials to access multiple, disparate systems to meet organizational needs. SSO is almost taken for granted in the IT world—cloud-based service providers that do not support an SSO capability often find that they are missing a competitive advantage without it. On one hand, critics observe that if the authentication servers are not working properly (or aren't available), then the SSO request fails, and the user can do nothing. This may prompt some organizations to ensure that each major business platform they depend on has its own sign-on capability, supported by a copy of the central authentication server and its repository. SSO implementations also require the SSO server to internally store the authenticated credentials and reformat or repackage them to meet the differing needs of each platform or application as required. Because of this, SSO is sometimes called *reduced sign-on*.

SSO is an implementation of the federated identity concept, which focuses around four basic services: authentication, authorization, user attribute exchange, and user management. Authentication and authorization are the same familiar faces access control concepts. User attribute exchange provides a mapping of an authenticated and authorized user's identity into attributes or parameters that meet the unique needs of the different platforms, servers, and applications in your systems. This aspect of a federated identity management system also helps reduce redundancy by keeping one central edition of user data (such as their first and last names).

Multiple implementations of SSO are possible, using a variety of protocols and supporting software, including:

- Kerberos-based ticket granting ticket (TGT) systems
- Active Directory (which must be hosted on at least one system running Microsoft Windows Server)

- Smart card based
- Integrated Windows Authentication
- SAML-based systems

A variety of protocols support SSO, such as Open ID Connect, Facebook Connect, SAML, and the Microsoft Account (which used to be known as Passport). A variety of frameworks can make implementing SSO for your organization less painful.

Device Authentication

Remember, devices are *subjects* in access control terms; therefore, whenever a device attempts to establish a connection with your networks or with a system, your organization's information security requirements should dictate how rigorously that device must authenticate its identity and then how your systems will authorize it to take whatever actions (such as accesses to objects) it attempts to do.

Device identity should be established with a combination of hardware, firmware, and software characteristics; this allows your systems to confirm that not only is the device itself known to your authentication system, but its firmware, systems-level software, and applications are all at or above the required update or patch level. Other information, such as the human user or organizational identity associated with that device, might also be something that authentication and authorization functions check and verify. Be aware that all of this information, starting with hardware-level IDs such as the media access control (MAC) address, can be spoofed or altered; choose your mix of authentication factors for devices with this in mind.

Chapter 6 will look into controlling and monitoring device access to your systems in greater depth, while Chapter 7 will provide insights on improving data security. Both are necessary parts of your defense against a business-killing data exfiltration *before* it occurs.

✔ Removable Media: A Mixed Blessing or Only a Curse?

There are days when it seems that our modern e-commerce world cannot live without a thumb drive or other USB storage device—yet with thumb drive storage capacities now coming in terabyte-sized chunks, the prospects of massive data exfiltration should be just as scary as the threat of removable media as a vector for introducing malware to your systems.

Think carefully as to whether the convenience of letting users connect any USB storage device they want to any aspect of your systems infrastructure is worth the risk.

Federated Access

Federated identity management systems provide mechanisms for sharing identity and access information, which makes identity and access portable, allowing properly authorized subjects to access otherwise separate and distinct security domains. Federated access uses open standards, such as the OASIS Security Assertion Markup Language (SAML), and technologies such as OAuth, OpenID, various security token approaches, web service specifications, Windows Identity Foundation, and others. Federated access systems typically use web-based SSO for user access (which is not to be confused with SSO within an organization's systems). Just as individual platform or system access is logically a subset of SSO, SSO is a subset of federated access. SSO, properly implemented, eases the administrative burden for systems administrators, makes end users' lives simpler, and significantly enhances systems security (and its auditability).

One outgrowth of federated identity and access management (IAM) approaches has been to emphasize the need for better, more reliable ways for entities to be able to assert their identity as a part of an e-business transaction or operation. Work to develop an identity assurance framework is ongoing, and there are efforts in the United States, United Kingdom, and a few other nations to develop standards and reference models to support this.

There are two related, but different, approaches to SSO, which are federated identity management (FIM) and delegated identity management (DIM). Federated identity management provides ways for users to supply any credentials they choose that are compatible with the particular website and the authentication services behind it. For example, an OpenID account can be used with any service that implements the OpenID service. Delegated identity management, on the other hand, transfers responsibility for authentication to a third party. Facebook Connect is an example. If you have ever been offered a chance to "authenticate through Facebook," you have seen delegated authentication in action. Both approaches allow you to authenticate once and then conduct a session using applications across several cooperating enterprises. A user can log into one enterprise and then be able to employ resources in a second, affiliated network without additional authentication or applying a second credential.

These two approaches offer a good way to enforce multifactor authentication across many applications. Both methods scale well and extend cleanly into cloud environments.

One important design element is that each of these two authentication schemes rely on mutual trust. The user's credentials are stored with an "identity provider" accessible on the connected networks or the cloud. When the user logs into a service (for example, a security as a service or identity as a service [IDaaS] application), the service provider puts its trust in the identity provider. These trust relationships mean effectively that the compromise of one significant element of the service chain can lead to the compromise of all connected systems that trust that identity.

One facet of this arrangement that amplifies operational security considerably is that it is no longer necessary to de-authorize a compromised account or persona non grata user on every individual system or application for which they are authorized. A user can be de-authorized once with immediate effect everywhere on all of the systems using this distributed method.

An implementer of federated identity management has plenty of technical choices. They can use Security Assertion Markup Language (SAML) or even plain XML to transmit authorization messages among partners. Other options include using OAuth, OpenID, and even security tokens or PKI. Various combinations are possible; for example, WS-Federation is an Identity Federation specification developed by a group of companies, part of the Web Services Security framework. WS-Federation has mechanisms for brokering information on identities, identity attributes, and authentication itself.

Using SAML for Federated Identity Management

Security Assertion Markup Language (SAML) is an XML-based way of tagging identities and assertions about identities to provide federated identity management and use. SAML, as a modern open standard defined by the Organization for the Advancement of Structured Information Systems (OASIS), consists of four main components: assertions, protocols, bindings, and profiles. It also establishes three main roles as part of the identity and access management process.

In its simplest application within Identity and Access Management, SAML provides a formal mechanism and format for one entity to assure a second entity about the identity of a third, usually a human being. These three SAML roles include the following:

- **Identity provider (IdP):** This is the first entity. It makes an assertion about another identity, based on information it has. This information might have just been obtained, say by querying the user for a username/password pair.

- **Service provider (SP):** This entity is the relying party that is being asked to provide its service or resource, based on the assurance provided by the IdP.

- **Subject or principal:** This entity is the subject of the assertion, usually a person, who is in some sense being vouched for.

The four primary components of SAML are as follows:

- **Assertions:** In a SAML assertion, an identity provider makes one or more statements about a subject (also known as the *principal*—usually, a user) that the relying party can use to make access control decisions. The statement vouches for the authentication of the subject (perhaps providing details in an *authentication statement*) and may provide one or more *attribute statements*, describing the subject by means of name-value pairs. The assertion may also specify, in an *authorization decision statement*, conditions under which the principal is permitted to perform certain actions on a given resource.

- **Protocols:** SAML protocols describe how information is to be exchanged between, or consumed by, SAML entities. These rules specify the format and content of several types of SAML exchanges, especially *queries* between entities. For example, SAML version 1.1 provides for queries concerning the kind of authentication, attribute, and authorization information contained in assertions. Additional protocols, added in SAML 2.0, include the Artifact Resolution Protocol, a Name Identifier Management Protocol, and Single Logout Protocol.

- **Bindings:** SAML *bindings* specify how to encapsulate the various SAML protocols in various types of messages. Since SAML 2.0, these bindings have described how to include queries, for example, not only in SOAP envelopes but also in HTTP POST and GET exchanges (among others).

- **Profiles:** SAML bindings, protocols, and assertions can be pulled together to make a *profile*, a set of definitions and instructions for a specified use case. SAML 2.0, for instance, makes available five different profiles for single sign-on use cases: Enhanced Client or Proxy (ECP), Identity Provider Discovery, Name Identifier Management, Single Logout, and Web Browser SSO. Several other profiles are available in SAML 2.0. There are third-party profiles, too, such as the OASIS WS-Security SAML Token Profile.

SAML assertions themselves do not provide authentication of the user or principal. Your choice of access controls to implement, and how rigorously to apply those controls, establishes how your system authenticates subjects (be they users, processes, or hardware devices) in real time. This is covered in more detail in the "Implement Access Controls" section later in this chapter.

NOTE For more information about SAML, its roles and components, and their formats, see "Security Assertion Markup Language (SAML) V2.0 Technical Overview, OASIS Committee Draft 02," at https://wiki.oasis-open.org/security/Saml2TechOverview.

SUPPORT INTERNETWORK TRUST ARCHITECTURES

In general terms, trust between two or more parties requires agreement as to what set of ideas, subjects, or actions the trust will involve (the *trust domain*), the obligations each party promises to fulfill with respect to that trust domain, and the protocols by which the parties interact with each other to establish trust, confer trust upon other parties, or withdraw or revoke trust as circumstances may dictate. Trust architectures, therefore, consist of trust relationships, the elements or systems in the trust domain, and the protocols for conferring, confirming, managing, and revoking trust between parties.

In internetworking terms, a trust framework is the set of protocols and standards that provide automated ways to create, manage, and use trust relationships between servers and clients. Trust architectures are the design concepts and ideas by which organizations identify their needs for technical and administrative implementation of trust frameworks as part of their broader organizational information security posture.

Trust Relationships (One-Way, Two-Way, Transitive)

One of the key considerations in federating access between or across systems is the way that trust relationships do or do not transfer. One example might be a humanitarian relief operation that involves a number of nonprofit, nongovernmental organizations (NGOs) from different countries, sharing a consolidated planning, coordination, and information system platform operated by a major aid agency. Some of the NGOs might trust aid agency employees with shared access to their information systems; others might not. There might also be local organizations, working with some of the NGOs, who are not known to the international aid agency; even host nation government agencies might be part of this puzzle. The aid agency might want to grant only a limited set of accesses to some of the NGOs and their staff and maybe no access at all to a few of the NGOs. This demonstrates several types of trust relationships.

- One-way trust relationships exist where organization A trusts its users and trusts the users of organization B, but while B trusts its own people as users, it does not fully trust the users in organization A and must limit their access to B's systems and information resources.

- Two-way trust relationships exist when both organizations have the same level of trust in all of the users in the other's domain. This does not have to be as high a level of trust as what they repose in their own people but just a symmetric or matching degree of trust.

- Transitive trust relationships happen when organization A trusts organization B, organization B trusts C, and then in effect organization A trusts C.

Note how transitive relationships establish a *chain of trust*, with the *trust anchor* being the one at the root or start of that set of relationships. In the previous example, C has in effect delegated its trust authority to B, and B then provides its assurance of trustworthiness to A. As you'll see in a moment, these third-party connections can provide two different approaches to authentication and trustworthiness, known as *hierarchical* or *web trust relationships*.

As the complexity of the relationships between organizations, their systems and platforms, and the domains of user subjects (and objects) associated with those platforms increase, trust relationships can start to matrix together sometimes in convoluted ways. This could quickly overwhelm efforts by each organization's systems administrators to manage locally. Federated approaches to identity and access management are not by themselves simple, but they can be easier to manage, especially when the social or organizational context and trust relationships are straightforward. Federated systems also allow for much quicker, cleaner disconnects, such as when the relief operation ends or when one agency's systems are found to be less secure than can be tolerated by others in the federation.

Solutions to situations like this might contain elements of the following:

- Advanced firewall technologies
- Gateways and proxies as interface control points
- VLANs and restricted VLANs
- Public access zones
- Extranets for data center access
- Extensive Authentication Protocol (EAP)
- Using allowed list management to restrict execution of applications, with application visibility and control functions to monitor and enforce these policies
- Multifactor authentication of subjects
- Behavior and posture monitoring, such as enforcing device update status and using remediation or quarantine to enforce updates or limit access
- Network segmentation to include zero trust architectures where required

Let's take a closer look at some of these trust architectures and frameworks.

Extranet

An extranet is a virtual extension to an organization's intranet (internal LAN) system, which allows outside organizations to have a greater degree of collaboration, information sharing, and use of information and systems of both organizations. For example, a parts wholesaler might use an extranet to share wholesale catalogs, or filtered portions thereof, with specific sets of key customers or suppliers. Extranets typically look to provide application-layer shared access and may do this as part of a service-oriented architecture (SOA) approach. Extranets may also see extensive use of electronic data interchange (EDI) protocols, which facilitate automated exchange of substantial volumes of information such as parts lists, inventories, or catalogs. Prior to the widespread adoption of VPN technologies, organizations needed significant investment in additional hardware, network systems, software, and personnel to design, deploy, maintain, and keep their extranets secure. In many industries, the use of industry-focused applications provided as a service (SaaS or PaaS cloud models, for example) can take on much of the implementation and support burden of a traditional extranet. As with any network access, careful attention to identity management and access control is a must!

Note that the prefix *extra* usually means "outside of," or beyond a known boundary or perimeter. In some respects, having a demilitarized zone (DMZ) as part of your network provides this boundary point. If external users still must be defined in your access control systems and provide valid credentials to gain access, then that DMZ (or a portion thereof) is an extranet. If the general web-crawling public can access it, then it's a public-facing DMZ. In either case, an extranet or a DMZ is usually logical and physical segments of your organizational internet, usually isolated by routers from other segments (such as those inside the DMZ).

As an aside, compare these concepts with that of an *intranet*, which is an internet segment logically restricted to users who are members of the organization (that is, *insiders*).

Intranets, like extranets, are often part of VPN systems and can provide secure infrastructures for collaboration and information sharing for authorized users.

Third-Party Connections

Third-party trust relationships usually involve three parties (people or organizations): a content user, a content owner, and a certifying authority that can attest that the content in question being sent by the content owner to the content user is authentic. Note that the certificate authority has no real role in verifying that the content is what the content user *needs* to accomplish their purpose or objective—only that the content the user receives is exactly and completely what the content owner provided. Identity management uses this concept in somewhat different ways than access control, encryption, digital signature, and other information security systems usually do, as a quick look will reveal.

During identity proofing (the first step in establishing a new identity for a subject or user), your organization needs to obtain authoritative evidence that the applicant is whom and what they claim to be. Documentation that attests to a person's identity is often issued by a government or corporate entity, but in this day and age when almost anyone can make a convincing official-looking but fake document, you need ways to authenticate the *documents* that are presented. In almost all countries, national law establishes a hierarchy of authorities who can authenticate a document, either because they were the issuing authority or because they can otherwise confirm its legitimacy. In the United States, notary publics can *notarize* many types of documents; in other countries, similar functions may be done by notarios, by solicitors, or by the local or national government itself. These are examples of human-to-human certificate authorities who support two other parties in establishing trust. (On the international level, a process known as *apostille* is used by agencies of one nation's government to attest to the authenticity of documents they generate, which a person then provides to an agency of another nation's government. This usually requires layers of authentication in the source country, as well as layers of verification and confirmation in the receiving country.)

As you'll see in Chapter 5, "Cryptography," most of our modern information security depends upon the use of digital certificates, which are a fundamental part of our public key infrastructure (PKI). These are issued by a certificate authority and assert that the person (human or organizational entity) named on the certificate matches the public key that the certificate contains. Chapter 5 will also address hierarchies of trust and webs of trust, in the context of the use of digital certificates.

In both cases, the process is similar. A certificate authority establishes itself in the marketplace, and others (content owners) come to it to obtain a credential, token, or certificate that they can provide to a content user as proof of the content owner's trust-worthiness. Content users can then challenge the content by requesting a verification or authentication service from the certificate authority. Certificates issued by a certificate authority can, in some circumstances, in effect delegate authority to a subordinate.

Zero Trust Architectures

In late 2020 the information security profession began a major paradigm shift away from focusing on defense in depth and its association with trust but verify (or verify at initial access, then trust until end of session) as the dominant metaphor. *Zero trust* as a set of concepts focuses instead on protecting data assets first and foremost. NIST published its SP 800-207 Zero Trust Architecture (ZTA) as a reference and guide in August 2020; a number of vendors have begun providing implementation roadmaps that use this, and in May 2021, the US Defense Information Systems Agency published its zero trust ref-erence architecture. All of these represent snapshots in time of a rapidly evolving set of concepts, ideas, strategies, and tactics.

NIST SP 800-207 describes a ZTA as one that demonstrates the following design tenets:

- Data and computing services are treated as resources to be managed and protected.

- All communications are secured regardless of network (or physical) locations; trust is not implied by where on the network it originates.

- Resource access is granted on a per-session basis, with requestor trustworthiness being evaluated with each access request, and granted with least privileges.

- Dynamic policies based on observable behavior dictate access control decisions.

- Integrity and security posture of all owned and associated assets is measured and monitored by the system's owners and administrators.

- Strict enforcement of authentication and authorization, including on a continu-ing basis, is required for all access attempts.

- Systems owners and administrators continuously monitor systems, network infra-structures, communications, and asset security posture, and use this information to continually improve security posture.

As an individual person, you are an *entity*; you then use multiple *identities*, which are the dataset that an organization or its systems creates and uses to bind to your assertion as an entity of who (or what) it is to the sets of privileges that organization chooses to grant to you. Systems like just in time identity provisioning and identity as a service require us to keep the concepts of entities and identities separate and distinct. Logging into your systems at work involves multiple entities—you, the endpoint device you're using, the applications you're using, each of which are part of fulfilling your purpose for accessing the system. Traditional views of identity management treated entities and human user identities as separate problems; zero trust architectures and systems like user and entity behavioral analytics (UEBA) bring them back closer together.

PARTICIPATE IN THE IDENTITY MANAGEMENT LIFECYCLE

Traditionally, identity management has only been thought of in terms of human users. With the publication of the Open ID 2.0 standard, it's clear that identity management has to embrace both human users (the traditional subjects of access control and identity management) and nonhuman users such as the devices people use, autonomous mobile systems, IoT devices, bots, and other software entities. As of this writing, we do not have an "entity **and** identity" management lifecycle, but this will have to change as more organizations go towards zero trust architectures and their need to identify, track, and model the behavior of all entities, human or non, that are attempting to access their resources.

Identity management is often described as a set of major functions, such as provisioning, review, and revocation. These actually involve a number of more fine-grained tasks at the detailed level, by which systems administrators do the following:

- Create a new identity.
- Determine which systems and assets that identity should have access privileges to.
- Determine what authentication factors, including what security tokens or devices (company-owned, employee-owned or BYOD, or a mix of both) will be used for access and for work-related functions.
- Provision that identity into those systems.
- Review those privileges as circumstances, on-the-job duties and responsibilities, or business needs evolve.
- Add, modify, or revoke some or all privileges as required.
- Suspend or revoke an identity.
- Delete the identity from active systems.

From this list, you can see that creating and provisioning an identity creates the data that drives your authentication and authorization processes; accounting then links this new identity to the transaction-level history of access attempts and their results. Accounting data is then used during privilege review.

Previous sections in this chapter have looked at authentication in greater detail. Let's look further at some of the other identity management tasks and processes.

Authorization

Every access attempt by a subject should test that subject's identity in two ways: first, by authentication of that identity, and second, by testing what the subject wants to do to see whether it is authorized to do so. Prior to the first access attempt, administrators must decide which permissions or privileges to grant to an identity and whether additional constraints or conditions apply to those permissions. The results of those decisions are stored in access control tables or access control lists in the access control database.

Authorization systems use one or more of the concepts known as *access control models*. These models, such as role-based, subject-based, or attribute-based, translate your information security choices about information classification, and the relative importance of integrity versus confidentiality (think Bell–LaPadula versus Biba), into which technologies you choose and their implementation details. These models were examined in some detail in the "Access Control via Formal Security Models" section. You'll need that conceptual foundation as you look to the "Implement Access Controls" section later in this chapter for more practical guidance.

✔ How Useful Is Your Identity Management and Access Control System?

Whatever identity management and access control scheme you select, you will need to ensure that it has the following attributes:

- **Fast in operation:** Logic that is involved in every decision on the network must be crisp. Keep in mind that, usually, simpler principles lead to faster execution.

- **Scalable:** Whether you need to control hundreds of assets or billions, you will want to use the same basic approach. Most enterprises, especially successful ones, grow and change and sprawl and spurt. You do not want your access scheme to hinder growth.

- **Comprehensive:** It is not always possible to subsume all of an enterprise's assets under a single identity or access management scheme. You may not be able to ensure that each employee and consultant and advisor in every department can be given a username and appropriate access regardless of when they join the company and what it is they do. Strive, however, for the minimal number of arrangements that is possible to achieve in managing assets and identities.

- **Maintainable:** Your organization will change. In a big company, divisions may be added, product groups may be invented, or an entire business arm may be broken up. Even in a small enterprise, individual contributors will be reassigned, and reporting relationships will change. You want an identity scheme that will power through any such changes and not require that someone changes their internal email address or even their username because of a transfer or promotion.

- **Adaptable:** Ideally, the same scheme and decision factors should be capable of controlling access on individual computer systems, within a wholly owned data center, in a globe-circling cloud environment, or (more realistically) in all of these environments and more simultaneously.

- **Just (and justifiable):** Authorization decisions need to be justifiable in the eyes of those who are denied as well as those who are granted permission. Arbitrary decisions, or decisions that can reasonably be criticized as discriminatory or frivolous, will at the least drain energy away from security as they are defended.

- **Comprehensible:** Do not underrate the advantage of being able to explain the reasoning behind the identity and access management scheme you have selected. Management, vendors, board members or advisors, and many curious and sometimes frustrated employees will want to know how names and access roles are determined and what policy and infrastructure is carrying out access decisions.

Proofing

Provisioning starts with the initial claim of identity and a request to create a set of credentials for that identity; typically, a responsible manager in the organization must approve requests to provision new identities. (This demonstrates separation of duties by preventing the same IT provisioning clerk from creating new identities surreptitiously.) Key to this step is identity proofing, which separately validates that the evidence of identity as submitted by the applicant is truthful, authoritative, and current. Such evidence might include the following:

- Identity cards or papers, such as government-issued ID cards, passports, or birth certificates. You validate against third-party identity systems (which should draw directly from databases supporting those government ID processes).

- Citizenship, permanent resident, or right to reside and work status, as pertains to the country in which the applicant will perform work-related functions for you. You'll validate this via official channels or third parties who can access that data for you.

- Personal employment history data, which you validate via credit histories or direct contact with those employers.

- Residential address information, supported by applicant-provided utility bills, leases, or deeds, which you validate via issuing parties or agencies.

- Personal and professional references, which you validate via contact.

- Legal, criminal, or other court system records. (Your human resources management screening functions often have a "block-crimes" list, which they use to preclude hiring someone with such convictions as a way of limiting the company's exposure to risks. Note that the old-fashioned concept of a "crime of moral turpitude" can include such acts as making false statements to government officials, which might be a valid indicator of a personal integrity risk.)

- Open source information via social media websites, web searches, news media, and so on.

Whether your organization uses a few of these proofing techniques or all of them or adds even more to the proofing process should be driven by two things: the overall risk management process and how that drives the requirements for personnel integrity and reliability.

All of that results in the first decision to hire the individual in question and for what duties; this leads to the decisions as to what information assets they'll need to use and what information or business processes they'll need to execute to perform those duties. This should lead in fairly straightforward ways to which systems, platforms, and server-provided services the individual will need access to and what mix of privileges they'll need on each of those systems or platforms.

Provisioning/Deprovisioning

Having made the decision to create a new identity and having decided what privileges it will have associated with it, it's time to actually provision it. Provisioning is the process of implementing the management decisions about a subject's identity and the privileges associated with it into the logical, physical, and administrative aspects of the access control functions throughout all of the systems this identity will require (and be allowed) access to and use of. (Note that I separate proofing from provisioning here for clarity.) Depending upon your overall systems architecture, this "push" of a new identity, and all subsequent updates to it, might be simple and straightforward or complex and time-consuming.

- Typical SOHO-style architectures that do not use an integrated identity management and access control set of technologies will require creating the new identity and provision its access privileges on each system, endpoint, or platform the user needs access to. This might include creating the username and credentials on each Windows, Mac, or Linux workstation and endpoint device and then creating similar credentials on each network-attached storage system, website, or cloud-hosted storage, database, or applications platform that the employee will use. Every one of these systems, sites, and platforms will need to be "touched" or updated every time this user's privileges are modified, revoked, or suspended.

- Integrated identity and access management (IAM) systems can reduce this to a single creation/update task and then push this information to all connected systems. Systems, platforms, and apps that support the organization's single sign-on access process are also updated with a single push, whether for the initial provisioning or for updates.

Note that the IAM/SSO "single push" process is not instantaneous. Depending upon the scale and complexity of your information architecture, it can take minutes or hours for every server, every platform, every applications suite, and every affected endpoint to process the update. (Globe-spanning organizations, even ones of 500 people or fewer, can often see this take half a day or more.) Creation and update of identities can and should be a deliberate process, and "next business day" availability is quite often acceptable. However, systems administrators need to be able to support rapid updates to meet urgent and compelling needs, either to grant new identities new privileges or to revoke or suspend them.

Deprovisioning is the process of temporarily or permanently revoking both the privileges associated with an identity and the identity itself. Typically, deprovisioning is done in a series of steps that disable (but do not remove) privileges and accounts and then remove them completely. As with provisioning, this is either a straightforward, single "unpush" kind of action supported by your integrated identity and access management system or a laborious system-by-system, app-by-app, site-by-site effort. Since many deprovisioning actions are related to situations involving an employee being disciplined or terminated from employment, two special considerations should apply.

- The employee's work unit managers or directors, the human resources management team, and the information systems security specialists should coordinate informing the employee of their change of status and the deprovisioning itself. This is necessary to prevent a disgruntled employee from inflicting damage to systems or exfiltrating data from them.

- The deprovisioning should be something that can be done rapidly, across all systems, and in ways that can be readily confirmed or validated.

When it comes to the identities you manage for the people in your systems, nothing is forever; every such identity you create and provision will at some point need to be modified, suspended, and then ultimately removed. Whether this commonsense notion holds for the identities associated with devices remains to be seen.

✔ Revoking vs. Deleting an Identity

It's vital that you keep these two concepts separate and distinct. Think of all of the information associated with a typical user, such as:

- Their identity itself and the supporting information that was used to initially create it

- Files created, modified, or maintained by them on company systems, whether for personal use, business use, or both

- Records containing information about that identity or user, which were created in other files in the company's systems; these might be payroll, training, personnel management, or workflow control settings

- Metadata, systems event logs, and other information that attests to what information the user has accessed, used, modified, or attempted to access

- Emails sent or received by the user or with message text pertaining to that user

- Archive or backup copies of those files, records, metadata, or systems that contain it

Revoking the identity blocks it from further access but changes no other data pertaining to that identity, no matter where it might be stored in your systems. *Deleting* that identity could mean a catastrophic loss of information, if the company ever has to answer a digital discovery request (about a wrongful termination, for example).

Identity and Access Maintenance

Three major activities—account access review, auditing, and enforcement—should be part of the ongoing monitoring and assessment of the health, status, and effective operation of any identity management and access control system. As you might expect, the particular CIANA+PS needs of your organization should drive how rigorous and extensive these efforts are—and what you do when you discover indications that something about a particular identity, its privileges, and the actions taken in its name reveals.

Let's start with account review. In the case of human users who have identities in your systems, this review should encompass two sets of data being reviewed by the right team of information risk managers from IT, human resources management, functional area supervisors or division managers, and possibly your legal team.

- **Identity data review:** Individual employees of almost any organization will go through any number of changes in their jobs as well as in their personal lives. Some of these changes are probably reflected in the organization's human resources (HR) or payroll functions; these systems do not, as a general rule, automatically notify IT security departments or the integrated IAM system that a change has occurred. Changes in marital status, significant changes in credit score or indebtedness, or legal actions (such as lawsuits, divorces, child custody actions, or criminal matters) might all be events in any person's life. The key question, though, is whether your security needs dictate such a high degree of personnel integrity and reliability that changes of these types are warning signs of greater risk levels regarding the affected employee.

- **Privilege and access review:** Regardless of changes in personal circumstances, all of your employees who have access to organizational IT systems and information assets should have a periodic review of those access privileges in the context of their *current* job or duties.

Note that in both cases, employment law and regulations may establish constraints or conditions as to how these sorts of reviews are done, how frequently they can be done, or whether changes in conditions outside of job-related functional requirements provide reasonable grounds for such a review. Your organization's HR and legal teams, as well as your compliance officer (or department), should take the lead on ensuring this is done properly. In any event, your organization should create and use detailed, specific procedures for these reviews, that specify what data to gather and how it is evaluated in the context of such a review. Procedures should also provide for an employee appeal process—quite often bad data or poorly validated data has either granted or denied access and privileges in both incorrect and damaging ways.

Other factors to balance when establishing such review processes should include:

- How frequently employees change jobs, in ways that may require changes in access privileges

- The pace of change, generally speaking, across your organization (or its individual but larger business units)

- The burden that such reviews place on administrative, IT, and other staff within the organization

- The direct and indirect costs of such reviews

After all, these reviews are a *safeguard*—they are an administrative control that is attempting to mitigate the risk of privilege abuse leading to an information security incident and the loss or damage that results from it. In all things, seek a cost-effective balance.

Account access review should consider two broad categories of accounts: users and systems. Let's take a closer look at each.

User Access Review

All accounts associated with a human user of your systems should be subject to review on a periodic basis and special reviews when circumstances warrant it. For the most part, these will be user-level accounts and not systems accounts that are restricted to systems processes to use. (You'll learn about those next.) Whether you control access by enforcing rules or interpreting the various roles of the user, you must periodically review the access privileges accorded to each user (or system or software entity). The period of the review should be set by policy and strictly enforced by well-documented processes. Many organizations review the access of each user once per year.

Your user access review process should include, at a minimum, the following:

- All of the accounts created for the user or the accounts to which the user has been granted access
- All of the computers this user can connect to, use, or log into
- All of the databases this user can read from or write to
- All of the applications this user can use
- All of the websites controlled by your enterprise that the user can visit and whether the user can log in, change things on the site, or merely read from it
- What sorts of data this user can see or change
- The times of day or days of the week all of these things may be done
- The geographical locations—and logical places on the enterprise network or in the cloud—from which all of these things may be done

Many of the most serious computer breaches in history have been the result of access rights left in place after a user changed assignments or left the company. Leftover accounts and no-longer-needed access are like land mines in your network. Defuse them with periodic substantive access review.

System Account Access Review

More often than not, software and devices are acting in their own name (so to speak) as subjects in your systems and have user IDs created for them. Database systems, systems belonging to partners in your federated access environment, storage subsystems, and even individual endpoint devices are just some examples of devices and their installed software and firmware that might have user IDs; if they do, then their accounts should be subject to review. Underneath all of that "user-level" devices-as-users activity, though, you'll find an ever-increasing number of operating systems and support functions, each with its own user ID and privileged account, which are automatically invoked as part of routine systems operation and use. In effect, invoking such a function causes a login-like event to happen for that function's user ID; or, if it's a continuously logged-in user ID, the function "wakes up" the process thread related to that user ID, and it starts requesting other systems functions to take action as needed to get its job done. Often used for housekeeping purposes such as backups, disk management, or the general gathering and analysis of monitoring and log data, these accounts usually have elevated privileges that grant access to special devices or system files.

It's therefore a very good practice to check the access accounting information for these system-level user IDs as well. Ideally, you would check system by system for every computer, every security device on your network, and every database—in fact, every technical entity—to see which software and systems can do any of these things:

- Connect
- Read
- Write
- Move
- Delete
- Verify the presence and state of health of the device on the system
- Start or stop
- Read or change access settings
- Read or change any other configuration settings
- Perform privileged actions, or act as a system administrator

Such checks are time-consuming and even in a modest-sized network must be automated in order for a comprehensive scan to be practical. As with so many security measures, you may find it necessary to prioritize which systems (and which system accounts) are reviewed.

Auditing

It may seem strange to separate *account reviews* from *account auditing*. Reviews have as their focus the task of identifying any cases of privilege creep or the retention of privileges no longer required for that user ID to perform its currently assigned set of functions, tasks, or duties. Reviews may be periodic or based on known changes in circumstances, such as a change of jobs or changes in the software and systems themselves. Reviews are more often than not performed internally by the organization and its own people, using internally generated procedures and measurement or assessment standards. By contrast, audits are used to generate an evidence-grade record of behavior on the part of one or more user IDs, either as part of troubleshooting a problem, investigating an incident, or building a forensics case to support a legal or administrative corrective action. Audits are often required (by law or by insurance or financial services regulations) to be done by outside auditors who may have to meet various certification standards, producing audit findings and reports that are authoritative.

Note that in many organizations it's common to refer to a special, circumstances-driven review of a particular user account or set of accounts as an *informal audit*. This often happens when there is sufficient grounds to worry that an employee or a group of employees may be acting in ways that violate inappropriate systems use policies or that their accounts (rather than they themselves) have been hijacked by others.

Whether it's a review or an audit, formal or informal, it's good practice to get the requesting management or leadership team's clear statement of the purpose and expectations regarding this examination of the data from the third A in AAA.

Enforcement

At some point, the review or audit findings (or other decisions made by management) will direct that a particular user ID needs to be brought back under control, by either a reduction in privileges, a temporary suspension, or a revocation. All of these actions are part of *deprovisioning*, as discussed in the previous "Provisioning/Deprovisioning" section.

Entitlement

The word *entitlement* has two meanings within an information systems security concept: a personal one and a systems one. Both are important and relevant to you as the access control and identity management systems administrator; you're the one who has to broker the first set of ideas into the second set of physical, logical, and administrative controls and their use.

On the personal front, some employees will believe that because of who and what they are, they have some kind of overarching right to have access to systems and privileges on those systems. In many cases, this is a legitimate and logical conclusion they've reached: If I am hired to lead a software development team, I have a reasonable expectation that I can see into all of the software units, support files, log files, and such, that are the work of all the people assigned to my team and to the projects I'm responsible for. In other cases, a newly appointed senior manager might believe (perhaps based on perceptions and emotions rather than logic) that their position somehow grants them this *uber*-authority. In either case, the strong principle of *separation of duties* should be able to sort through, function by function, what privileges the person actually requires on which systems, platforms, or applications to do their assigned duties. This is the basis of principle of *least privilege*.

On the technical front, entitlement refers to the ways in which user IDs are constructed, assigned privileges, and managed.

As an illustration, consider the seemingly simple task of installing a new application on a Windows-based desktop or laptop computer. As part of its own self-defense mechanisms, Windows uses a specific identity called the *trusted installer* to perform this task; no other identity can actually perform the set of steps associated with installing and registering an application. As an out-of-the-shrink-wrap user of my new Windows 10 laptop, each attempt I make to install an app causes the User Account Control functions to intercede, seeking my conscious affirmation and permission to continue. On my company-provided system, Group Policy Objects (GPOs) have been configured in the system by the sysadmins to require that a software allowed and blocked list management to restrict execution system intercepts any such attempt. This happens on both machines even though my user account is an Administrator account. Thus, my Windows machines have internally applied a separation of duties concept in the way that user IDs are constructed and the ways in which systems policies (via GPOs) are set to restrict each ID to just what it should be authorized to do, and no more. Note how the use of allowed and blocked lists is implementing both positive and negative security control measures. Each attempt by one ID to ask another to do a restricted task on its behalf is defined as a *security event* and is logged for later troubleshooting; security events can also be treated as real-time alarm conditions, and in many cases, *they should be*.

✔ Are You Positive?

Using allowed list management for controlling software execution is a powerful defense against most of the malware infection vectors by prohibiting any software to execute if it is not on a controlled list of previously-approved tasks. If your organization is not using it, it's only a matter of time before you'll wish you had been. See Chapter 7 for more details.

Manage by Groups, Not by Individual Accounts

Modern operating systems such as Windows 10 or Apple's macOS Mojave provide many built-in features that encourage systems administrators (and sole proprietor end users of SOHO systems) to structure their user IDs into groups and arrange those groups in hierarchies. This again implements separation of duties by means of separately entitling a group of like user IDs with the same set of privileges.

The hierarchy starts with separating IDs into major systems groups: root or superuser, trusted installer, security administrator, user account manager, device manager, and so on. Servers and platforms should form another group, which might also include things like print servers, archival storage systems, or backup/restore platforms.

Your systems administrators (you included!) should recognize and support the need for this. Separate the different job functions and duties that your network administrators, database administrators, and security operations specialists must perform into different user account ID groups; set privileges *derived from those official duties* for each group; and then create each new user ID within a group for each systems administrator so that this unique user ID inherits the privileges from the group it belongs to.

Now the hard part: your ordinary, everyday users. Systems vendors recognize that the retail buyer of a laptop, desktop, or other endpoint device is a "company of one" and needs to have administrative privileges upon the first power-on boot of their new investment. This is also true of organizational purchases, of course. The "company of one," however, often ends up with that default user account, created with administrative privileges by the original equipment manufacturer (OEM), being used for day-to-day routine operations. Larger organizations, or just ones with a more astute sense of information security, may need to manage subsets of users with separate but overlapping privileges. Retail stores, restaurants, or even banks, for example, might need to create and manage user subgroups such as:

- A severely restricted user group for their customer-facing retail sales and service people

- Another group for customer service managers, who might have authorities to override transaction limits or errors or perform lookup operations across a customer's transaction history as part of their duties

- A different set of privileges for accounting systems operators that would allow them to process transactions but not initiate or modify them; their managers might be in another user group, which has those specific privileges associated with it

- And so on

Note that depending upon the business systems, platforms, and technologies involved, this might require user account provisioning at the operating system level, on specific servers or websites, or within specific applications platforms.

Consider a whaling attack, in which a company's chief financial officer receives an email purportedly from his chief executive officer; he knows that she is traveling and working on trying to put together a new, significant deal for the company. The email says, "It's urgent that you wire transfer $15,000 to our new partners' account to bring this deal home. Do that now, please! The account details are...." Separation of duties by means of user IDs should require that although the CFO might be an *approval* authority on such a transfer of funds that it's actually a disbursement clerk who performs this action; furthermore, when such a transfer exceeds a certain amount or when other suspicious activity conditions are met, the transfer might take multiple interactions, even by the CEO, before the system will allow the clerk to initiate the transfer with the company's bank systems. (Effective use of an attribute-based access control system can significantly lower the risk that even your smart, savvy CFO, a lower-level accounts manager, or even the disbursement clerk might fall for such a whaling attack.)

Managing entitlements by groups of users is far simpler to do than trying to create individual user IDs as "groups of one" and do it account by account. In almost all cases, situations that seem to suggest otherwise might be best handled by role-based user accounts—by requiring that disbursements clerk in the whaling example do a separate re-authentication as they shift from being a "routine transaction handler" *as a role they are fulfilling* into being a "high-value transaction handler" instead.

Manage Devices in Groups, Too

Two powerful ideas come together when you think about managing access control for groups of devices rather than one by one.

- Trusted classes or groups of devices should serve business functions and have the privileges those devices (and their onboard firmware and software) need in order to fulfill those functions.

- Nefarious or untrustworthy devices can easily masquerade as other types of devices, as part of an attempted intrusion into your systems.

Applying these principles would lead us to doubt the legitimacy of a printer, for example, trying to create or modify the security settings on a user or process ID or to raise alarms when an intrusion detection system is trying to access the company's employee or payroll database. As with people-based identities, device-based identities can be spoofed, and legitimate known devices previously deemed to be trustworthy can be misused (deliberately or accidentally). A lost or stolen smartphone illustrates the need for device-level access control.

This is not just an endpoint problem! Poorly secured systems and their Wi-Fi access points can end up allowing an intruder device to spoof itself as the Dynamic Host Control Protocol (DHCP) server for that LAN segment; you shouldn't normally consider service providers such as DHCP as endpoint functions, so over-focusing your security efforts on just the endpoints may not help you much in such cases.

Identity and Access Management Systems

There are several prominent methods for authentication in use today, ranging from getting a simple username/password pair to the use of multifactor authentication to the most complex of modern centralized methods. Some of these methods, such as RADIUS, may seem to be legacy systems, but they are alive and well in the marketplace. Infrastructures that are substantially based on Linux or Unix often use a combination of Kerberos and Lightweight Directory Access Protocol (LDAP). Microsoft-centric infrastructures almost invariably use Microsoft's Active Directory. All of these products and systems, to a greater or lesser degree, are platform- and OS-agnostic, supporting almost any device or network system that can work with their respective protocols. Almost all of them use the X.500 Directory Access Protocol or variations of it.

Remote authentication dial-in user service (RADIUS) originated in the early 1990s as a method of authenticating dial-up customers and has seen much use in support of classical remote access. A RADIUS server, when queried by a client supplying candidate login credentials, can reply with either an Access-Accept message, an Access-Reject, or an Access-Challenge. With this lightweight structure, RADIUS can conduct fast and simple authentications when possible or move on to multifactor authentication and even challenge-response dialogs when those are required. RADIUS can also support extensions, such as the Extensible Authentication Protocol (EAP); it also provides support for roaming users and devices.

The Terminal Access Controller Access Control System (TACACS, pronounced "tack-axe") grew out of early Department of Defense network needs for automating the authentication of remote users. By 1984, it started to see widespread use in Unix-based server systems; Cisco Systems began supporting it and later developed a proprietary version that it called Extended TACACS (XTACACS) in 1990. Neither of these was an open standard. Although they have largely been replaced by other approaches, you may see them still being used on older systems.

TACACS+ was an entirely new protocol based on some of the concepts in TACACS. Developed by the Department of Defense and then later enhanced, refined, and marketed by Cisco Systems, TACACS+ splits the authentication, authorization, and accounting into separate functions. This provides systems administrators with a greater degree of control over and visibility into each of these processes. It uses TCP to provide a higher-quality connection, and it also provides encryption of its packets to and from the TACACS+ server. It can define policies based on user type, role, location, device type, time of day, or other parameters. It integrates well with Microsoft's Active Directory or with LDAP systems, which means it provides key functionality for single sign-on capabilities. TACACS+ also provides greater command logging and central management features, making it well suited for systems administrators to use to meet the AAA needs of their networks.

LDAP is a directory service based on the X.500 Directory Access Protocol standard developed by the International Telecommunications Union Technical Standardization sector (known as ITU-T). It was designed to take advantage of the IP protocol suite, which evolved after the adoption of the X.500 Directory Access Protocol. LDAP is often compared to an old-fashioned telephone directory. An LDAP server contains information about users in a directory tree, and clients query it to get details. Large enterprises maintain replicated LDAP servers at various points across the enterprise to facilitate quick response.

Each entry in an LDAP directory tree is a collection of information about an object, pointed to by a unique identifier called a distinguished name (DN). The DN represents the complete path in the tree to the desired entry. A set of named component parts called attributes hold the data for that entry. Various user attributes are typically stored in LDAP directories, including telephone numbers, physical addresses, postal addresses, and email addresses.

LDAP can also be used to authenticate user credentials by an LDAP command called *bind*. In the simplest case, bind checks the entered candidate password against the userPassword attribute (receiving either a success code or the error Invalid credentials).

Microsoft's ubiquitous Active Directory (AD), developed for Windows domain networks, uses LDAP versions 2 and 3. Active Directory is a proprietary directory service, which is part of the Windows Server technology base; while this means it must be deployed on a Windows Server platform, AD can support networks with virtually any mix of device types and operating systems. A server running Active Directory Domain Services (AD DS), called a domain controller, authenticates users and authorizes actions, verifying their credentials and defining their access rights. Active Directory Domain Services provide structured hierarchical data storage for users, printers, and services, as well as support for locating and working with those objects.

On a larger, multinetwork or multi-enterprise playing field, Active Directory Federation Services (AD FS) can allow the sharing of information between trusted business partners. AD FS can provide single sign-on to federated partners just as other federated identity management systems can.

Two more modern protocols are commonly used together to provide authentication services. OAuth 2.0 and OpenID Connect offer a related but competing approach to SAML.

OpenID Connect is an implementation of the authorization framework OAuth 2.0, facilitating the communication of attribute and authentication information. Whereas SAML specifically relays requests from a website, OpenID Connect can work to effect authentication with either a website or mobile application as the requester.

An OpenID Connect (OIDC) authentication sequence requires the selection of an OpenID identify provider. Once the IdP is known, OIDC operates as an authentication layer on top of the OAuth 2.0 protocol, allowing the relying party to request and receive information about the user from the IdP.

OAuth 2.0 is itself an authorization protocol. Using it, a client application can request access to a protected resource from the entity that owns that resource. The request goes to an authorization server, which must authenticate the resource owner, validate the request, obtain authorization from the resource owner, and then relay an authorization token to the resource server that hosts the protected resource.

In the OIDC authentication implementation, the relying party (RP) is an OAuth 2.0 application requesting an ID token from an OpenID Connect Provider (OP). The fields in the token will contain data ("claims") about both the user (called the subject, or sub, and known by a locally unique identifier) and the timing (both the "issued at" time, or iat, and the expiration time, exp) of the authentication event. Also, the ID token will contain the issuer identifier (iss) of the OP and the client identifier (audience, or aud) registered for the RP at the issuer. Additionally, the claims can contain more information about the user, such as first_name, last_name, and so on. One way to view this extension of OAuth 2.0 is that OpenID Connect effectively allows an application to request authorization to authenticate a user.

IMPLEMENT ACCESS CONTROLS

Two more major decisions need to be made before you can effectively design and implement an integrated access control strategy. Each reflects in many ways the decision-making and risk tolerance culture of your organization, while coping with the physical realities of its information infrastructures. The first choice is whether to implement a centralized or decentralized access control system.

- Centralized access control is implemented using one system to provide all identity management and access control mechanisms across the organization. This system is the one-stop-shopping point for all access control decisions; every request from every subject, throughout the organization, comes to this central system for authentication, authorization, and accounting. Whether this system is a cloud-hosted service or operates using a single local server or a set of servers is not the issue; the organization's logical space of subjects and objects is not partitioned or segmented (even if the organization has many LAN segments, uses VPNs, or is geographically spread about the globe) for access control decision-making. In many respects, implementing centralized access control systems can be more complex, but use of systems such as Kerberos, RADIUS, TACACS, or Active Directory can make the effort less painful. Centralized access control can provide greater payoffs for large organizations, particularly ones with complex and dispersed IT infrastructures. For example, updating the access control database to reflect changes (temporary or permanent) in user privileges is done once and pushed out by the centralized system to all affected systems elements.

- Decentralized access control segments the organization's total set of subjects and objects (its access control problem) into partitions, with an access control system and its servers for each such partition. Partitioning of the access control space may reflect geographic, mission, product or market, or other characteristics of the organization and its systems. The individual access control systems (one per partition) have to coordinate with each other to ensure that changes are replicated globally across the organization. Windows Workgroups are examples of decentralized access control systems, in which each individual computer (as a member of the workgroup) makes its own access control decisions, based on its own local policy settings. Decentralized access control is often seen in applications or platforms built around database engines, in which the application, platform, or database uses its own access control logic and database for authentication, authorization, and accounting. Allowing each workgroup, platform, or application to bring its own access control mechanisms to the party, so to speak, can be simple to implement and simple to add each new platform or application to the organization's IT architecture; but over time, the maintenance and update of all of those disparate access control databases can become a nightmare.

Mandatory vs. Discretionary Access Control

The next major choice that needs to be made reflects whether the organization is delegating the fine-grained, file-by-file access control and security policy implementation details to individual users or local managers or is retaining (or enforcing) more global policy decisions with its access control implementation.

- Mandatory access control (MAC) denies individual users (subjects) the capability to determine the security characteristics of files, applications, folders, or other objects within their IT workspaces. Users cannot make arbitrary decisions, for example, to share a folder tree if that sharing privilege has not been previously granted to them. This implements the mandatory security policies as defined previously and results in highly secure systems.

- Discretionary access control (DAC) allows individual users to determine the security characteristics of objects, such as files, folders, or even entire systems, within their IT workspaces. This is perhaps the most common access control implementation methodology, as it comes built in to nearly every modern operating system available for servers and endpoint devices. Typically, these systems provide users with the ability to grant or deny the privileges to read, write (or create), modify, read and execute, list contents of a folder, share, extend, view other metadata associated with the object, and modify other such metadata.

The choices of centralized versus decentralized architectures, and whether to use mandatory, discretionary, or nondiscretionary access control as a global policy are important decisions that must be made before you can start implementing your IAM project. You've also got to make another set of decisions regarding the specific roles, tasks, or responsibilities that individual users or groups of users must fulfill, and correlate that with your organization's information classification guide. Combining those two sets of information informs your choice of access control models: Do your security needs dictate a role-based access control, for example, or can you safely operate with something simpler such as subject-based or object-based control? And with *that* decision in hand, you can then start putting AAA servers in place, configuring their services, and loading up their control information. *Now*, you can start provisioning user accounts.

✔ "Built-In" Solutions?

Almost every device on your organization's networks (and remember, a device can be both subject and object) has an operating system and other software (or firmware) installed on it. For example, Microsoft Windows operating systems provide policy objects, which are software and data constructs that the administrators use to enable, disable, or tune specific features and functions that the OS provides to users. Such policies can be set at the machine, system, application, user, or device level, or for groups of those types of subjects. Policy objects can enforce administrative policies such as password complexity, renewal frequency, allowable number of retries, and lockout upon repeated failed attempts. Many Linux distributions, and as well as Apple's operating systems, have similar functions built into the OS. All devices ship from the factory with most such policy objects set to "wide open," you might say, allowing the new owner to be the fully authorized systems administrator they need to be when they first boot up the device. As administrator/owners, you're highly encouraged to use other built-in features, such as user account definitions and controls, to create "regular" or "normal" user accounts for routine, day-to-day work. You then have the option of tailoring other policy objects to achieve the mix of functionality and security you need.

Role-Based

Role-based access control (RBAC) grants specific privileges to subjects regarding specific objects or classes of objects based on the duties or tasks a person (or process) is required to fulfill. Several key factors should influence the ways that role-based privileges are assigned.

- *Separation of duties* takes a business process that might logically be performed by one subject and breaks it down into subprocesses, each of which is allocated to a different, separate subject to perform. This provides a way of compartmentalizing the risk to information security. For example, retail sales activities will authorize a salesclerk to accept cash payments from customers, put the cash in their sales drawer, and issue change as required to the customer. The salesclerk cannot initially load the drawer with cash (for making change) from the vault or sign off the cash in the drawer as correct when turning the drawer in at the end of their shift. The cash manager on duty performs these functions, and the independent counts done by salesclerk and cash manager help identify who was responsible for any errors.

■ *Need to know*, and therefore need to access, should limit a subject's access to information objects strictly to those necessary to perform the tasks defined as part of their assigned duties, and no more.

Duration, scope, or extent of the role should consider the time period (or periods) the role is valid on and any restrictions as to devices, locations, or factors that limit the role. Most businesses, for example, do not routinely approve high-value payments to others after business hours or normally consider authorizing these when submitted (via their approved apps) from a device at an IP address in a country with which the company has no business involvement or interests. Note that these types of attributes can be associated with the subject (such as role-based), the object, or the conditions in the system and network at the time of the request.

Role-based access has one strategic *administrative* weakness: *privilege creep*. This unnecessary accumulation of privileges or the retention of privileges no longer strictly required for the performance of one's duties can put the organization and the individual employee at considerable risk. Quality people take on broader responsibilities to help the organization meet new challenges and new opportunities; and yet, as duties they previously performed are picked up by other team members or as they move to other departments or functions, they often retain the access privileges their former jobs required. To contain privilege creep, organizations should review each employee's access privileges in the light of their currently assigned duties, not only when those duties change (even temporarily!) but also on a routine, periodic basis.

Attribute-Based

Attribute-based access control (ABAC) systems combine multiple characteristics (or attributes) about a subject, an object, or the environment to authorize or restrict access. ABAC uses Boolean logic statements to build as complex a set of rules to cover each situation as the business logic and its information security needs dictate. A simple example might be the case of a web page designer who has limited privileges to upload new web pages into a beta test site in an extranet authorized for the company's community of beta testers but is denied (because of their role) access to update pages on the production site. Then, when the company prepares to move the new pages into production, they may need the designer's help in doing so and thus (temporarily) require the designer's ability to access the production environment. Although this could be done by a temporary change in the designer's subject-based RBAC access privileges, it may be clearer and easier to implement with a logical statement, as shown here:

```
IF (it's time for move to production) AND (designer-X) is a member of
(production support team Y) THEN (grant access to a, b, c...)
```

Attribute-based access control can become quite complex, but its power to tailor access to exactly what a situation requires is often worth the effort. As a result, it is sometimes known as *externalized*, *dynamic*, *fine-grained*, or *policy-based* access control or authorization management.

Subject-Based

Subject-based access control looks at characteristics of the subject that are not normally expected to change over time. For example, a print server (as a subject) should be expected to have access to the printers, to the queue of print jobs, and to other related information assets (such as the LAN segment or VLAN where the printers are attached); you would not normally expect a print server to access payroll databases directly! As to human subjects, these characteristics might be related to age, their information security clearance level, or their physical or administrative place in the organization. For example, a middle school student might very well need separate roles defined as a student, a library intern, or a software developer in a computer science class, but because of their age, in most jurisdictions they cannot sign contracts. The web pages or apps that the school district uses to hire people or contract with consultants or vendors, therefore, should be off-limits to such a student.

Object-Based

Object-based access control uses characteristics of each object or each class of objects to determine what types of access requests will be granted. The simplest example of this is found in many file systems, where objects such as individual files or folders can be declared as read-only. More powerful OS file structures allow a more granular approach, where a file folder can be declared to have a set of attributes based on classes of users attempting to read, write, extend, execute, or delete the object. Those attributes can be further defined to be inherited by each object inside that folder, or otherwise associated with it, and this inheritance should happen with every new instance of a file or object placed or created in that folder.

SUMMARY

You might say that there are two kinds of organizations in this world: those with thoughtful, deliberate, and effective information security plans and processes already in effect when an information security event occurs and those that realize the need for those security processes *after* their first major security breach has disrupted their business. Ideally, your organization is more of the former and less of the latter. In either case, the information risk assessment leads to an information classification policy that dictates how *types* or *groups* of users need to use information assets to get vital business processes accomplished. That mapping of the confidentiality, integrity, availability, nonrepudiation, and authentication aspects of information security needs to groups of users (or types of roles and functions users can take on) is the starting point for identity management and access control, as you've seen throughout this chapter.

Those CIANA+PS attributes guide your work in creating and managing the process by which identities are created for people and processes and by which privileges are assigned that allow (or deny) these identities the capabilities to do things with the information assets you're charged with protecting. You've seen how this involves creating and maintaining trust relationships that allow different access control strategies and techniques to be put in place. These are the nuts and bolts of the systems that achieve the authentication, authorization, and accounting functions—the "big AAA"—that are the heart and soul of identity management and access control.

Identities and access control, privileges and actions, subjects and objects—they're all different perspectives upon the same underlying and important needs.

Risk Identification, Monitoring, and Analysis

INFORMATION SECURITY IS ABOUT controlling and managing risk to information, information systems, and the people, processes, and technologies that support them and make use of them. Most information security risks involve events that can disrupt the smooth functioning of the business processes used by a company, an organization, or even an individual person. Since all systems are imperfect, and all organizations never have enough time or resources to fix every problem, risk management processes are used to identify risks, select and prioritize those that must be dealt with soonest, and implement risk mitigations that control or limit the possibility of the risk event's occurrence and the damage it can inflict when (not if) it occurs. Risk management also requires ongoing monitoring and assessment of both the real-world context of risks that the organization operates in, and the success or failure of the risk mitigations that management has chosen to implement.

Information risk management operationalizes the information security needs of the organization, expressed in terms of the need to preserve the confidentiality, integrity, availability, nonrepudiation, authentication, privacy, and safety aspects of the information and the organizational decisions that make use of it. It does this by using a variety of assessment strategies and processes to relate risks to vulnerabilities, and vulnerabilities to effective control or mitigation approaches.

At the heart of information security risk management is the prompt detection, characterization, and response to a potential security event. Setting the right alarm thresholds is as important as identifying the people who will receive those alarms and respond to them, as well as equipping those people with the tools and resources they'll need to contain the incident and restore the organization's IT systems back to working order. Those resources include timely senior leadership and management decisions to support the response, escalating it if need be.

DEFEATING THE KILL CHAIN ONE SKIRMISH AT A TIME

It's often been said that the attackers have to get lucky only once, whereas the defenders have to be lucky every moment of every day. When it comes to *advanced persistent threats (APTs)*, which pose potentially the most damaging attacks to our information systems, another, more operationally useful rule applies. Recall that APTs are threat actors who spend months, maybe even years, in their efforts to exploit target systems and organizations in the pursuit of the threat actors' goals and objectives. APTs quite often use low and slow attack patterns that avoid detection by many network and systems security sensor technologies; once they gain access, they often live off the land and use the built-in capabilities of the target system's OS and applications to achieve their purposes. APTs often subcontract out much of their work to other players to do for them, both as a layer of protection for their own identity and as a way of gaining additional attack capabilities. This means that APTs plan and conduct their attacks using what's called a robust *kill chain*, the sequence of steps they go through as they discover, reconnoiter, characterize, infiltrate, gain control, and further identify resources to attack within the system; make their "target kill" by copying, exfiltrating, or destroying the data and systems of their choice; and then cover their tracks and leave.

The bad news is that it's more than likely that your organization or business is already under the baleful gaze of more than just one APT bad actor; you might also be subject to open source intelligence gathering, active reconnaissance probes, or social engineering attempts being conducted by some of the agents and subtier players in the threat space that APTS often use (much like subcontractors) to carry out steps in an APT's kill chain.

Crowded, busy marketplaces provide many targets for APTs; so, naturally, many such threat actors are probably considering some of the same targets as their next opportunities to strike. For you and your company, this means that on any given day, you're probably in the crosshairs of multiple APTs and their teammates in various stages of their own unique kill chains, each pursuing their own, probably different, objectives. Taken together, there may be thousands, if not hundreds of thousands, of APTs out there in the wild, each seeking its own dominance, power, and gain. The millions of information systems owned and operated by businesses and organizations worldwide are their hunting grounds. Yours included.

The good news is that there are many field-proven information risk management and mitigation strategies and tactics that you can use to help your company or organization adapt and survive in the face of such hostile action and continue to flourish despite the worst the APTs can do to you. These frameworks and the specific risk mitigation controls should be tailored to the confidentiality, integrity, availability, nonrepudiation, authentication, privacy and safety (CIANA+PS) needs of your specific organization. With them, you can first deter, prevent, and avoid attacks. Then you can detect the ones that get past that first set of barriers and characterize them in terms of real-time risks to your systems. You then take steps to contain the damage they're capable of causing and help the organization recover from the attack and get back up on its feet.

You probably will not do battle with an APT directly; you and your team won't have the luxury (if we can call it that!) of trying to design to defend against a particular APT and thwart their attempts to seek their objectives at your expense. Instead, you'll wage your defensive campaign one skirmish at a time, never knowing who the ultimate attacker is or what their objectives are vis-à-vis your systems and your information. You'll deflect or defeat one scouting party as you strengthen one perimeter; you'll detect and block a probe from somewhere else that is attempting to gain entry into and persistent access to your systems. You'll find where an illicit user ID has made itself part of your system, and you'll contain it, quarantine it, and ultimately block its attempts to expand its presence inside your operations. As you continually work with your systems' designers and maintainers, you'll help them find ways to tighten down a barrier *here* or mitigate a vulnerability *there*. Step by step, you strengthen your information security posture—and, if you're lucky, all without knowing that one or many APTs have had you in their sights.

But in order to have such good luck, you've got to have a layered, integrated, and proactive information systems defense in place and operating; and your best approach for establishing such a security posture is to consciously choose which information and decision risks to manage, which ones to mitigate, and what to do when a risk starts to become an event. That's what this chapter is all about.

Identity Theft as an APT Tactical Weapon

Since 2011, energy production and distribution systems in North America and Western Europe have been under attack from what can only be described as a large, sophisticated, advanced persistent threat actor team. Known as Dragonfly 2.0, this attack depended heavily on fraudulent IDs and misuse of legitimate IDs created in systems owned and operated by utility companies, engineering and machinery support contractors, and the fuels industries that provide the feedstocks for the nuclear, petroleum, coal, and gas-fired generation of electricity. The Dragonfly 2.0 team wove a complex web of attacks against multiple private and public organizations as they gathered information, obtained access, and created fake IDs as precursor steps to gaining *more* access and control. For example, reports issued by NIST and Symantec make mention of "hostile email campaigns" that attempted to lure legitimate email subscribers in these organizations to respond to fictitious holiday parties.

Blackouts and brownouts in various energy distribution systems, such as those suffered in Ukraine in 2015 and 2016, have been traced to cyberattacks linked to Dragonfly 2.0 and its teams of attackers. Data losses to various companies and organizations in the energy sector are still being assessed.

You can read Symantec's report at `www.symantec.com/blogs/threat-intelligence/dragonfly-energy-sector-cyber-attacks`.

Why should security practitioners put so much emphasis on APTs and their use of the kill chain? In virtually every major data breach in the past decade, the attack pattern was *low and slow*: sequences of small-scale efforts designed not to cause alarm, each of which gathered information or enabled the attacker to take control of a target system. More low and slow attacks launched from that first target against *other* target systems. This springboard or stepping-stone attack pattern is both a deliberate strategy to further obscure the ultimate source of the attack and an opportunistic effort to find more exploitable, useful information assets along the way. They continually conduct reconnaissance efforts and continually grow their sense of the exploitable nature of their chosen targets. Then they gain access, typically creating false identities in the target systems. Finally, with all command, control, and hacking capabilities in place, the attack begins in earnest to exfiltrate sensitive, private, or otherwise valuable data out of the target's systems.

This same pattern of events shows itself, with many variations, in ransom attacks, in sabotage, and in disruption of business systems. It's a part of attacks seen in late 2018 and early 2019 against newspaper publishers and nickel ore refining and processing industries. In any of these attacks, detecting, disrupting, or blocking any step along the attacker's kill chain might very well have been enough to derail that kill chain and motivate the attacker to move on to another, less well-protected and potentially more lucrative target.

Preparation and planning are your keys to survival; without them, you cannot operationally defeat your attacker's kill chain. Previous chapters examined the day-to-day operational details of information security operations and administration; now, let's step back and see how to organize, plan, and implement risk management and mitigation programs that deliver what your people need day-to-day to keep their information and information systems safe, secure, reliable, and resilient. We'll also look in some depth at what information to gather and analyze so as to inform management and leadership when critical, urgent decisions about information security must be made, especially if indicators of an incident must be escalated for immediate, business-saving actions to take place.

Kill Chains: Reviewing the Basics

Many businesses, nonprofits, and even government agencies use the concept of the *value chain*, which models how they create value in the products or services they provide to their customers (whether internal or external). The value chain brings together the sequence of major activities, the infrastructures that support them, and the key resources that those activities need to transform each input into an output. The value chain focuses the attention of process designers, managers, and workers alike on the outputs *and* the outcomes that result from each activity. Critical to thinking about the value chain is that each major step provides the organization with a chance to improve the end-to-end experience by reducing costs, reducing waste, scrap, or rework, and by improving the quality of each output and outcome along the way. Value chains extend well beyond the walls of the organization itself, as they take in the efforts of suppliers, vendors, partners, and even the actions and intentions of regulators and other government activities.

Even when a company's value chain is extended beyond its own boundaries, the company *owns* that value chain—in the sense that they are completely responsible for the outcomes of the decisions they make and the actions they take. The company has end-to-end due care and due diligence responsibility for each value chain they operate. They have to appreciate that every step along each of their value chains is an opportunity for something to go wrong, as much as it is an opportunity to achieve greatness. A key input could be delayed or fail to meet the required specifications for quality or quantity. Skilled labor might not be available when we need it; critical information might be missing, incomplete, or inaccurate.

Ten years ago, you didn't hear too many information systems security practitioners talking about the *kill chain*. In 2014, the U.S. Congress was briefed on the kill chain involved in the Target data breach of 2013, which you can (and should!) read about at `https://www.commerce.senate.gov/public/_cache/files/` `24d3c229-4f2f-405d-b8db-a3a67f183883/23E30AA955B5C00FE57CFD709621592C` `.2014-0325-target-kill-chain-analysis.pdf`. Today, it's almost a survival necessity that you know about kill chains, how they function, and what you can do about them.

Whether we're talking about military action or cybersecurity, the "kill chain" as a plan of action is in effect choosing to be the sum total of all of those things that can go wrong in the target's value chain systems. Using a kill chain does not defeat the target with overwhelming force. Instead, the attacker out-thinks the target by meticulously studying the target as a system of systems and by spotting its inherent vulnerabilities and its critical dependencies on inputs or intermediate results; then it finds the shortest, simplest, lowest-cost pathway to triggering those vulnerabilities and letting them help defeat the target. Much like any military planner, an APT plans their attack with an eye to defeating, degrading, distracting, or denying the effectiveness of the target's intrusion deterrence, prevention, detection, and containment systems. They've further got to plan to apply those same "four Ds" to get around, over, or through any other security features, procedures, and policies that the target is counting on as part of its defenses. The cyber-security defensive value chain must effectively combine physical, logical, and administrative security and vulnerability mitigation controls; in similar fashion, the APT actor considers which of these controls must be sidestepped, misdirected, spoofed, or ignored, as they pursue their plans to gain entry, attain the command and control of portions of the target's systems that will serve their needs, and carry out their attack. (In that regard, it might be said that APT actors and security professionals are both following a similar risk management framework.)

Figure 3.1 shows a generalized model of an APT's kill chain, which is derived in part from the previously mentioned Senate committee report.

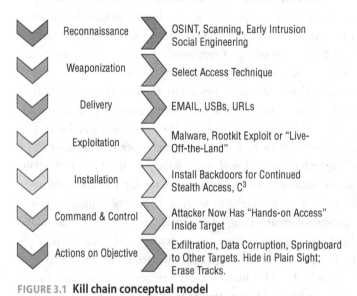

Reconnaissance	OSINT, Scanning, Early Intrusion Social Engineering
Weaponization	Select Access Technique
Delivery	EMAIL, USBs, URLs
Exploitation	Malware, Rootkit Exploit or "Live-Off-the-Land"
Installation	Install Backdoors for Continued Stealth Access, C^3
Command & Control	Attacker Now Has "Hands-on Access" Inside Target
Actions on Objective	Exfiltration, Data Corruption, Springboard to Other Targets. Hide in Plain Sight; Erase Tracks.

FIGURE 3.1 **Kill chain conceptual model**

One important distinction should be obvious: as a defender, you help own, operate, and protect your *value chains*, while all of those would-be attackers own their *kill chains*.

With that as a starting point, you can see that an information systems kill chain is the total set of actions, plans, tasks, and resources used by an advanced persistent threat to do the following:

- Identify potential target information systems that suit their objectives.
- Gain access to those targets, and establish command and control over portions of those targets' systems.
- Use that command and control to carry out further tasks in support of achieving their objectives.

How do APTs apply this kill chain in practice? In broad general terms, APT actors may take many actions as part of their kill chains, as they:

- Survey the marketplaces for potential opportunities to achieve an outcome that supports their objectives.
- Gather intelligence data about potential targets, building an initial profile on each target.
- Use that intelligence to inform the way they conduct probes against selected targets, building up fingerprints of the target's systems and potentially exploitable vulnerabilities.
- Conduct initial intrusions on selected targets and their systems, gathering more technical intelligence.
- Establish some form of command and control presence on the target systems.
- Elevate privilege to enable a broader, deeper search for exploitable information assets in the target's systems and networks.
- Conduct further reconnaissance to discover internetworked systems that may be worth reconnaissance or exploitation.
- Begin the exploitation of the selected information assets: Exfiltrate the data, disrupt or degrade the targeted information processes, and so on.
- Complete the exploitation activities.
- Obfuscate or destroy evidence of their activities in the target's system.
- Disconnect from the target.

The more complex, pernicious APTs will use multiple target systems as proxies in their kill chains, using one target's systems to become a platform from which they can run reconnaissance and exploitation against other targets. In the Target breach, the attackers entered Target's payment processing systems utilizing a maintenance back door left in place by Target's heating, ventilation, and air conditioning (HVAC) contractors, as shown in Figure 3.2, which is from the previously mentioned Senate report. Defeating an

APT's kill chain requires you to think about breaking each step in the process, in as many ways as you can—and in ways that you can continually monitor, detect, and recognize as being part of an attack in progress. (Target's information security team, by contrast, failed to heed and understand the alarms that their own network security systems were generating; and Target's mid-level managers also failed to escalate these alarms to senior management, thus further delaying their ability to respond.)

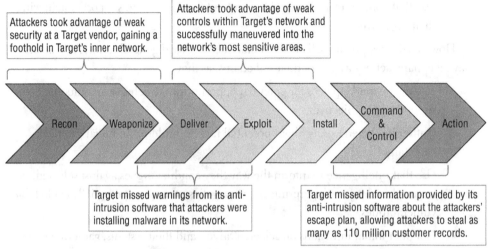

FIGURE 3.2 **Target 2013 data breach kill chain**

✔ Avoid Stereotyping the APTs

APTs can be almost any kind of organized effort to achieve some set of objectives by means of extracting value from your information systems. That value might come from the information they can access, exfiltrate, and sell or trade to other threat actors, or it might come from disrupting your business processes or the work of key people on your team.

APTs have been seen as parts of campaigns waged by organized crime, terrorist organizations, political and social activist campaigners, national governments, and even private businesses. The APT threat actors, or the people whom they work with or for, have motives that range from purely mercenary to ideological, from seeking power to seeking revenge.

APT threat actors and the campaigns that they attempt to run may be of almost any size, scale, and complexity. And they're quite willing to use any system, no matter how small, personal or business, if it can be a stepping-stone to completing a step in their kill chain.

Including yours.

Events vs. Incidents

A typical business information system, such as a corporate data center and the networks that make it available to authorized users, might suffer millions of hits each day from unknown and unauthorized Internet addresses. Some of these are merely events—something routine that has happened, such as an innocent ping or ICMP packet attempting to make contact. Others might be part of information security incidents. You obviously cannot spend human security analyst time on each of those events; you've got to filter it down to perhaps a few dozen or more each day that *might* be something worthy of further analysis and investigation. This brings us to define an event of interest as something that happens that might be an indicator (or a precursor) of one or more events that might impact your information's systems security. An event of interest may or may not be a warning of a computer security incident in the making, or even the first stages of such an incident.

But what is a computer security incident? Several definitions by NIST, ITIL, and the IETF[1] suggest that computer security incidents are events involving a target information system in ways that:

- Are unplanned

- Are disruptive

- Are hostile, malicious, or harmful in intent

- Compromise the confidentiality, integrity, availability, authenticity, or other security characteristics of the affected information systems

- Willfully violate the system owners' policies for acceptable use, security, or access

The unplanned shutdown of your on-premises mail server, as an example, might have been caused by a thunderstorm-induced electrical power transient or by an accidental unplugging of its power supply and conditioning equipment. Your vulnerability assessment might have discovered these vulnerabilities and made recommendations as to how to reduce their potential for disruption. But if neither weather nor hardware-level accident caused the shutdown, you have to determine whether it was a software or systems design problem that caused the crash or a vulnerability that was exploited by a person or persons unknown.

Another challenge that is becoming more acute is to differentiate phishing attacks from innocent requests for information. An individual caller to your main business phone number, seeking contact information in your IT team, might be an honest and innocent

---

[1] NIST is the National Institute of Standards and Technologies, IETF is the Internet Engineering Task Force, and the Information Technology Information Library has been known simply as ITIL since 2013.

inquiry (perhaps from an SSCP looking for a job!). However, if a number of such innocent inquiries across many days have attempted to map out your entire organization's structure, complete with individual names, phone numbers, and email addresses, it's quite likely that your organization is the object of some hostile party's reconnaissance efforts.

It's at this point that you realize that you need some information systems risk management.

UNDERSTAND THE RISK MANAGEMENT PROCESS

Risk is about a *possible* occurrence of an event that leads to loss, harm, or disruption. Individuals and organizations face risk and are confronted by its possibilities of impact, in four basic ways, as Figure 3.2 illustrates. Three observations are important here—so important that they are worth considering as rules in and of themselves.

- **Rule 1:** All things will end. Systems will fail; parts will wear out. People will get sick, quit, die, or change their minds. Information will never be complete or absolutely accurate or true.

- **Rule 2:** The best you can do in the face of rule 1 is spend money, time, and effort making *some* things more robust and resilient at the expense of others and thus trading off the risk of one kind of failure for another.

- **Rule 3:** There's nothing you can do to avoid rule 1 and rule 2.

One of the difficulties we face as information systems security professionals is that simple terms, such as *risk*, have so many different "official" definitions, which seem to vary in degree more than they do in substance. For example:

- ISO Guide 73:2009, "Risk Management – Vocabulary," defines risk as "the effect of uncertainty on objectives."

- Federal Information Processing Standard FIPS 200 defines risk as "the level of impact on organizational operations (including mission, functions, image, or reputation), organizational assets, or individuals resulting from the operation of an information system given the potential impact of a threat and the likelihood of that threat occurring."

- (ISC)² defines risk as "the possibility of damage or harm and the likelihood that damage or harm will be realized."

NIST's Computer Security Resource Center online glossary offers 29 different definitions of *risk*, many of which have significant overlap with each other, while pointing at various other NIST, ISO, IEC, and FIPS publications as their sources. It's worthwhile to note the unique contributions of some of these definitions.

- Relative impact that an exploited vulnerability would have to a user's environment (note that this is not necessarily restricted to a digital or virtual environment)

- A measure of the extent to which an entity or individual is threatened by a potential circumstance or event

- The potential for impact to organizational operations, mission, functions, reputation or image, assets, investments, individuals, other organizations, and the nation (Impacts to "other nations" are not explicitly called out in any of these definitions.)

- The highest acceptable probability for an inauthentic message to pass the decryption-verification process

- Adverse impacts to critical infrastructure(s) or to systems that are paramount to continuity of government operations

Much like the debate over C-I-A versus CIANA (or CIANA+PS), there is probably only one way to decide which definition of risk is right for you: what works best for your organization, its objectives, and its tolerance for disruption?

As you might imagine, risk management has at least as many hotly debated definitions as does risk itself. For our purposes, let's focus on the common denominator and define risk management as the set of decision processes used to identify and assess risks; make plans to treat, control, or mitigate risks; and exercise continuous due care and due diligence over the chosen risk treatment, control, and mitigation approaches. This definition attempts to embrace all risks facing modern organizations—not just IT infrastructure risks—and focuses on how you monitor, measure, or assess how good (or bad) a job you're doing at dealing with the risks you've identified. As a definition, it goes well with our working definition of risk as the possibility of a disruptive event's occurrence and the expected measure of the impacts that event could have upon you if the event in question actually takes place.

✔ Who Owns Risk Management?

For almost all organizations, the most senior leaders and managers are the ones who have full responsibility for all risk management and risk mitigation plans, programs, and activities that the organization carries out. These people have the ultimate due care and due diligence responsibility. In law and in practice, they can be held liable for damages and may even be found criminally negligent or in violation of the law, and face personal consequences for the mistakes in information security that happened on their watch.

CONTINUES

Clearly, those senior leaders (be they board members or C-suite office holders) need the technically sound, business-based insights, analysis, and advice from everyone in the organization. Organizations depend upon their chains of supervision, control, and management to provide a broad base of support to important decisions, such as those involving risk management. But it is these senior leaders who make the final decisions.

Your organization will have its own culture and practices for delegating responsibility and authority, which may change over time. As an information security professional, you may have some of that delegated to you. Nonetheless, it's not until you're sitting in one of those "chief's" offices—as the chief risk manager, chief information security officer, or chief information officer—that *you* have the responsibility to lead and direct risk management for the organization.

Risk management consists of a number of overlapping and mutually reinforcing processes, which can and should be iteratively and continuously applied.

- Understanding, characterizing, and managing the critical infrastructures, systems, people, assets, and processes that your organization depends upon for its success— and its existence. This includes the information processes, information systems, IT architectures, production systems and facilities; it includes managing and controlling changes to those systems, architectures, and processes.

- Understanding and characterizing the threats common to your organization's lines of business, marketplace, region, technologies, or regulatory jurisdiction.

- Identifying, characterizing, and assessing in terms of probabilities of occurrence and their expected impacts.

- Analyzing the underlying vulnerabilities inherent in the systems and processes your organization depends upon.

- Applying the organization's risk tolerance (or *risk appetite*) to identified vulnerabilities so as to prioritize risk mitigation efforts.

- Choosing and implementing risk mitigation strategies and controls.

- Continuously monitoring the operational use of those controls.

- Detecting conditions that suggest risk mitigation may have failed to thwart an intrusion or attack.

- Responding to an intrusion or attack.

We'll look at each of these in greater detail throughout this chapter. It's worth noting that because of the iterative, cross-fertilizing, and mutually supportive nature of every aspect of risk management, mitigation, monitoring, and assessment, there's probably no one right best order to do these steps in. Risk management frameworks (see the "Risk Management Frameworks" section) do offer some great "clean-slate" ways to start your organization's journey toward robust and effective management of its information and decision risks, and sometimes a clean start (or restart) of such planning and management activities makes sense. You're just as likely to find that bits and pieces of your organization already have some individual risk management projects underway; if so, don't sweat getting things done in the right order. Just go find these islands of risk management, get to know the people working on them, and help orchestrate their efforts into greater harmony and greater security.

Fortunately, you and your organization are not alone in this. National governments, international agencies, industry associations, and academic and research institutes have developed considerable reference libraries regarding observed vulnerabilities, exploits against them, and defensive techniques. Many local or regional areas or specific marketplaces have a variety of communities of practitioners who share insight, advice, and current threat intelligence. Public-private partnership groups, such as InfraGard (`https://infragard.org`) and the Electronic Crimes Task Force (ECTF), provide "safe harbor" meeting venues for private industry, law enforcement, and national security to learn with each other. (In the United States, InfraGard is sponsored by the Federal Bureau of Investigation, and the U.S. Secret Service hosts the ECTF; multinational ECTF chapters, such as the European ECTF, operate in similar ways.)

Let's look in some detail at the various processes involved in risk management; then you'll see how different risk management frameworks can give your organization an overall policy, process, and accountability structure to make risk *manageable*.

Risk Visibility and Reporting

In any risk management situation, risks need to be *visible* to analysts and managers in order to make them manageable. This means that as the process of risk and vulnerability assessment identifies a risk, characterizes it, and assesses it, all of this information about the risk is made available in useful, actionable ways. As risks are identified (or demonstrated to exist because a security incident or compromise occurs), the right levels of management need to be informed. Incident response procedures are put into action because of such risk reporting. *Risk reporting* mechanisms must provide an accountable, verifiable set of procedures and channels by which the right information about risks is provided to the right people, inside and outside of the organization, as a part of making management and mitigation decisions about it.

Risk reporting to those outside of the organization is usually confined to trusted channels and is anonymized to a significant degree. Businesses have long shared information about workplace health and safety risks—and their associated risk reduction and hazard control practices—with their insurers and with industry or trade associations so that others in that group can learn from the shared experience, without disclosing to the world that any given company is exposed to a specific vulnerability.

In the same vein, companies share information pertaining to known or suspected threats and threat actors. Businesses that operate in high-risk neighborhoods or regions, for example, share threat and risk insights with local law enforcement, with other government agencies, and of course with their insurance carriers. Such information sharing helps all parties take more informed actions to cope with potential or ongoing threat activities from organized crime, gang activities, or civil unrest. These threats could manifest themselves in physical or Internet-based attempts to intrude into business operations, to disrupt IT systems, or as concerted social engineering and propaganda campaigns.

Let's look at each of these processes in some detail.

Risk Register

Every organization or business needs to be building a *risk register*, a central repository or knowledge bank of the risks that have been identified in their business and business process systems. This register should be a living document, constantly refreshed as the company moves from risk identification through mitigation to the "new normal" of operations after instituting risk controls or countermeasures. It should be routinely updated with each newly discovered risk or vulnerability and certainly as part of the lessons-learned process after an incident response. For each risk in your risk register, it can be valuable to keep track of information regarding the following:

- The name or other identification of the risk
- How and when the risk was discovered
- Links or references to reports in common vulnerabilities and exploitations databases
- The root causes or vulnerabilities the risk is related to
- The objectives, outcomes, or goals that the risk can impact
- Systems, processes, and procedures potentially impacted or disrupted by the risk
- Versions, update levels, or patches related to the discovery or activation of the risk
- Updates, patches, or replacement versions of systems or components that (seemed to) eliminate the risk
- Test conditions or procedures that verify the existence of the risk
- Trigger conditions or root-cause analysis findings regarding the risk
- Decisions as to whether to accept, transfer, treat, or avoid the risk
- Decisions as to mitigation or treatment, controls put in place to do so, and residual risk if any

- Costs incurred as a result of attempting to mitigate or treat the risk

- Impacts or costs incurred upon occurrence of the risk as an event

- After-action reports or assessments for incidents in which the risk played a major or contributing role

- Recovery efforts, or considerations for recovery, pertaining to the risk

- Indicators or precursors pertaining to the risk

Your organization's risk register should be treated as a highly confidential, closely held, or proprietary set of information. In the wrong hands, it provides a ready-made targeting plan that an APT or other hacker can use to intrude into your systems, disrupt your operations, hold your data for ransom, or exfiltrate it and sell it on to others. Even your more unscrupulous business competitors (or a disgruntled employee) could use it to cripple or kill your business, or at least drive it out of their marketplaces. As you grow the risk register by linking vulnerabilities, root-cause analyses, CVE data, and risk mitigation plans together, your need to protect this information becomes even more acute.

There are probably as many formats and structures for a risk register as there are organizations creating them. Numerous spreadsheet templates can be found on the Internet, some of which attempt to guide users in meeting the expectations of various national, state, or local government risk management frameworks, standards, or best practices. If your organization doesn't have a risk register now, start creating one! You can always add more fields to each risk (more columns to the spreadsheet) as your understanding of your systems and their risks grows in both breadth and depth. It's also a matter of experience and judgment to decide how deeply to decompose higher-level risks into finer and finer detail. One rule of thumb might be that if an entry in your risk register doesn't tell you how to fix it, prevent it, or control it, maybe it's in need of further analysis.

The risk register is an example of making tacit knowledge explicit; it captures in tangible form the observations your team members and other co-workers make during the discovery of or confrontation with a risk. It can be a significant effort to gather this knowledge and transform it into an explicit, reusable form, whether before, during, or after an information security incident. Failing to do so leaves your organization held hostage to human memory. Sadly, any number of organizations fail to document these painful lessons learned in any practical, useful way, and as a result, they keep re-learning them with each new incident.

Threat Intelligence Sharing

Threat intelligence is both a set of information and the processes by which that information is obtained. Threat intelligence describes the nature of a particular category or instance of a threat actor and characterizes its potential capabilities, motives, and means while assessing the likelihood of action by the threat in the near term. Current threat intelligence, focused on your organization and the marketplaces it operates in, should play an important part in your efforts to keep the organization and its information systems safe and secure. Information security threat intelligence is gathered by national security and law enforcement agencies, by cybersecurity and information security researchers, and by countless practitioners around the world. In most cases, the data that is gathered is reported and shared in a variety of databases, websites, journals, blogs, conferences, and symposia. (Obviously, data gathered during an investigation that may lead to criminal prosecution or national security actions is kept secret for as long as necessary.)

As the nature of advanced persistent threat actors continues to evolve, much of the intelligence data we have available to us comes from efforts to explore sanctuary areas, such as the Dark Web, in which these actors can share information, find resources, contract with others to perform services, and profit from their activities. These websites and servers are in areas of the IP address space not indexed by search engines and usually available on an invitation-only basis, depending upon referrals from others already known in these spaces. For most of us cyber-defenders, it's too great a personal and professional risk to enter into these areas and seek intelligence information; it usually requires purchasing contraband or agreeing to provide illegal services to gain entry. However, many law enforcement, national security, and researchers recognized by such authorities do surf these dark pages. They share what they can in a variety of channels, such as InfraGard and ECTF meetings; it gets digested and made available to the rest of us in various blogs, postings, symposia, and conference workshops. Another great resource is the Computer Society of the Institute of Electrical and Electronics Engineers, which sponsors many activities, such as their Center for Secure Design. See `https://cybersecurity.ieee.org/center-for-secure-design/` for ideas and information that might help your business or organization.

Many local universities and community colleges work hand in hand with government and industry to achieve excellence in cybersecurity education and training for people of all ages, backgrounds, and professions. Threat intelligence regarding your local community (physically local or virtually/Internet local) is often available in these or similar communities of practice, focused or drawing upon companies and like-minded groups working in those areas.

Be advised, too, that a growing number of social activist groups have been adding elements of hacking and related means to their bags of disruptive tactics. You might not be able to imagine how their cause might be furthered by penetrating into the systems you defend; others in your local threat and vulnerability intelligence sharing community of practice, however, might offer you some tangible, actionable insights.

CVSS: Sharing Vulnerability and Risk Insight

Most newly discovered vulnerabilities in operating systems, firmware, applications, or networking and communications systems are quickly but confidentially reported to the vendors or manufacturers of such systems; they are reported to various national and international vulnerabilities and exposures database systems after the vendors or manufacturers have had an opportunity to resolve them or patch around them. Systems such as Mitre's common vulnerabilities and exposures (CVE) system or NIST's National Vulnerability Database are valuable, publicly available resources that you can draw upon as you assess the vulnerabilities in your organization's systems and processes. Many of these make use of the Common Vulnerability Scoring System (CVSS), which is an open industry standard for assessing a wide variety of vulnerabilities in information and communications systems. CVSS makes use of the CIA triad of security needs by providing guidelines for making quantitative assessments of a particular vulnerability's overall score. (Its data model does not directly reflect nonrepudiation, authentication, privacy, or safety.) Scores run from 0 to 10, with 10 being the most severe of the CVSS scores. Although the details are beyond the scope of this book, it's good to be familiar with the approach CVSS uses—you may find it useful in planning and conducting your own vulnerability assessments.

As you can see at `https://nvd.nist.gov/vuln-metrics/cvss`, CVSS consists of three areas of concern.

- Base metrics, which assess qualities intrinsic to a particular vulnerability. These look at the nature of the attack, the attack's complexity, and the impacts to confidentiality, integrity, and availability.

- Temporal metrics, which characterize how a vulnerability changes over time. These consider whether exploits are available in the wild and what level of remediation exists; it also considers the level of confidence in the reporting about this vulnerability and exploits related to it.

- Environmental metrics, which assess dependencies on particular implementations or systems environments. These include assessments of collateral damage, what percent of systems in use might be vulnerable, and the severity of impact of an exploit (ranging from minimal to catastrophic).

Each of these uses a simple scoring process—impact assessment, for example, defines four values from Low to High (and "not applicable or not defined"). Using CVSS is as simple as making these assessments and totaling up the values.

Many nations conduct or sponsor similar efforts to collect and publish information about system vulnerabilities that are commonly found in commercial-off-the-shelf (COTS) IT systems and elements or that result from common design or system production weaknesses. In the United Kingdom, common vulnerabilities information and reporting are provided by the Government Communications Headquarters (GCHQ, which is roughly equivalent to the U.S. National Security Agency); find this and more at the National Cyber Security Centre at www.ncsc.gov.uk.

Note that during reconnaissance, hostile threat actors use CVE and CVSS information to help them find, characterize, and then plan their attacks. (And there is growing evidence that the black hats exploit this public domain, open source treasure trove of information to a far greater extent than we white hats do.) The benefits we gain as a community of practice by sharing such information outweighs the risks that threat actors can be successful in exploiting it against our systems *if* we do the rest of our jobs with due care and due diligence. That said, do not add insult to injury by *not* looking at CVE or CVSS data as part of your own vulnerability efforts!

✔ Start with the CVE?

Given the incredible number of new businesses and organizations that start operating each year, it's probably no surprise that many of them open their doors, their Internet connection, and their web presence without first having done a thorough information security analysis and vulnerabilities assessment. In this case, the chances are good that their information architecture grows and changes almost daily. Starting with CVE data for the commercial off-the-shelf systems they're using may be a prudent risk mitigation first step.

One risk in this strategy (or, perhaps, more fairly a *lack* of a strategy) is that the organization can get complacent; it can grow to ignore the vulnerabilities it has already built into its business logic and processes, particularly via its locally grown glueware or people-centric processes. As another risk, that may encourage putting off any real data quality analysis efforts, which increase the likelihood of a self-inflicted garbage-in, garbage-out series of wasted efforts, lost work, and lost opportunities.

It's also worth reminding the owner-operators of a startup business that CVE data cannot protect them against the zero-day exploit; making extra effort to institute more effective access control using multifactor authentication and a data classification guide for its people to use is worth doing early and reviewing often.

If you're part of a larger, more established organization that does not have a solid information security risk management and mitigation posture, starting with the CVE data and hardening what you can find is still a prudent thing to do—while you're also gathering the data and the management and leadership support to a proper information security risk assessment.

Risk Management Concepts

Risk management is a decision-making process that must fit within the culture and context of the organization. The context includes the realities of the marketplaces that the business operates in, as well as the legal, regulatory, and financial constraints and characteristics of those marketplaces. Context also includes the perceptions that senior leaders and decision-makers in the organization may hold about those realities; as in all things human, perception is often more powerful and more real than on-the-ground reality. The culture of the organization includes its formal and informal decision-making styles, lines of communication, and lines of power and influence. Culture is often determined by the personalities and preferences of the organization's founders or its current key stakeholders. While much of the context is written down in tangible form, that is not true of the cultural setting for risk management.

Both culture and context determine the risk tolerance or risk appetite of the organization, which attempts to express or sum up the degree of willingness of the organization to maintain business operations in the face of certain types of risks. One organization might have near-zero tolerance for politically or ethically corrupt situations or for operating in jurisdictions where worker health and safety protections are nonexistent or ineffective; another, competing organization, might believe that the business gains are worth the risk to their reputation or that by being a part of such a marketplace they can exert effort to improve these conditions.

Perhaps a simpler example of risk tolerance is seen in many small businesses whose stakeholders simply do not believe that their company or their information systems offer an attractive target to any serious hackers—much less to advanced persistent threats, organized crime, or terrorists. With such beliefs in place, management might have a low tolerance for business disruptions caused by power outages or unreliable systems but be totally accepting (or willing to completely ignore) the risks of intrusion, data breach, ransom attacks, or of their own systems being hijacked and used as stepping-stones in attacks on other target systems. In such circumstances, you may have to translate those loftier-sounding, international security–related threat cases into more local, tangible terms—such as the threat of a disgruntled employee or dissatisfied customer—to make a cost-effective argument to invest in additional information security measures.

Information Security: Cost Center or Profit Center?

As the on-site information security specialist, you may often have the opportunity to help make the *business case* for an increased investment in information security systems, risk controls, training, or other process improvements. This can sometimes be an uphill battle. In many businesses, there's an old-fashioned idea about viewing departments, processes, and activities as either *cost centers* or *profit centers*—either they add value to the company's bottom line, via its products and services, or they add costs. As an example, consider insurance policies (you have them on your car, perhaps your home or furnishings, and maybe even upon your life), which cost you a pre-established premium each year while paying off in case an insured risk event occurs. Information security investments are often viewed as an insurance-like cost activity—they don't return any value each day or each month, right?

Let's challenge that assertion. Information security investments, I assert, add value to the company (or the nonprofit organization) in many ways, no matter what sector your business operates in, its size, or its maturity as an organization. They bring a net positive return on their investment, when you consider how they enhance revenues, strengthen reputation, and avoid, contain, or eliminate losses.

First, let's consider how good information security hygiene and practice adds value during routine, ongoing business operations.

- By building a reputation for protecting your customers' and suppliers' private data that has positive effects on retaining good customers, you increase customer activity (and revenues) and increase customer retention. This lowers marketing costs, particularly those involved in capturing new customers.

- This reputation for secure handling of information also strengthens relationships with suppliers, vendors, and strategic partners. This can lead to reduced costs for supplies and services and may also lead to expanded opportunities to co-market or cross-market your products and services.

- By contrast, as more and more business moves to e-business, many simply won't want to do business with a company known for leaking information like a sieve—or they'll do so only at premium prices.

- All businesses are subject to some form of compliance reporting; having solid, secure information systems that transparently and demonstrably meet your CIANA+PS needs show auditors that you're exercising due diligence and due care.

- Investment and financial services providers are increasingly demanding to see the results of information security audits, including ethical penetration testing, before they will commit to favorable financing terms, banking arrangements, or insurance premiums.

That list (which is not complete) shows just some of the positive contributions that effective information security programs and systems can make, as they enhance ongoing revenues and reduce or avoid ongoing costs. Information security adds value. Over time it pays its own way. If your organization cannot see it as a profit center, it's at least a cost *containment* center.

Next, think about the unthinkable: What happens if a major information security incident occurs? What are the worst-case outcomes that can happen if your customers' data is stolen and sold on the Dark Web or your proprietary business process and intellectual property information is leaked? What happens if ransom attacks freeze your ongoing manufacturing, materials management, sales, and service processes, and your company is dead in the water until you pay up?

- Industry experience suggests that the average cost impact of a ransom or ransomware attack is at least $500,000 U.S. dollars; this is only going to increase.

- Customer data breaches can cost millions of dollars in lost revenues and restitution.

- Prosecution, personal and civil liability actions, and other legal and regulatory penalties divert significant senior management time and effort from managing the business to resolving these issues; jail time for company officials is a distinct possibility.

- Reputational damage alone can drive customers and partners away.

- Fines, remediation costs, and loss of business can significantly disrupt a large business and might even force smaller ones into bankruptcy.

In short, a major information security incident can completely reverse the cost savings and value enhancements shown in that first list.

✔ Paybacks via Cost Avoidance

Security professionals often have problems persuading mid-level and senior management to increase spending on information security—and this uphill battle is halfway lost by calling it *spending*, rather than *cost avoidance*.

Nobody expects an information security department to show a profit; after all, it has no direct revenues of its own to offset its expenses. Even in nonprofit or government organizations, having your work unit or department characterized as a *cost center* frames your work as a necessary evil—it's unavoidable, like paying taxes, but should be kept to an absolute minimum. You need to turn this business paradigm around by showing how your risk mitigation recommendations *defer* or *avoid* costs.

For example, take all of your quantitative risk assessment information and project a five-year budget of losses incurred if all of those risks occur at their worst-case frequency of occurrence. That total impact is the cost that your mitigation efforts, your investments in safeguards, needs to whittle down to a tolerable size. Putting the organization's information security needs into business terms is crucial to gaining the leadership's understanding and support of them.

Next, let's consider what happens when the stakeholders or shareholders want to sell the business (perhaps to fund their retirement or to provide the cash to pursue other goals). Strong market value and the systems that protect and enhance it reduce the merger and acquisition risk, the risk that prospective buyers of the company will perceive it as having fragile, risky processes or systems or that its assets are in much worse shape than the owners claim they are. Due diligence is fundamentally about protecting and enhancing the value of the organization, which has a tangible or book value component and an intangible or good will component. Book value reflects the organization's assets (including its intellectual property), its market share and position, its revenues, its costs, and its portfolio of risks and risk management processes. The intangible components of value reflect all of the many elements that go into reputation, which can range from credit scores, compliance audit reports, and perceptions in the marketplace. The maturity of its business logic and processes also plays an important part in this valuation of the organization (these may show up in both the tangible and intangible valuations).

If you're working in a small business, its creator and owner may already be working toward an *exit strategy*, their plan for how they reap their ultimate reward for many years of work, sweat, toil, and tears; or, they might be working just to make this month's bottom line better and better and have no time or energy to worry about the future of the business. Either way, the owner's duties of due care and due diligence—and your own—demand that you work to protect and enhance the value of the company, its business processes, and its business relationships, by means of the money, time, and effort you invest in sound information security practices.

How Do We Look at Risk?

Many of the ways that we look at risk are conditioned by other business or personal choices that have already been made. Financially, we're preconditioned to think about what we spend or invest as we purchase, lease, or create an *asset*, such as an assembly line, a data center, or a data warehouse full of customer transactions, product sales, marketing, and related information. Operationally, we think in terms of processes that we use to accomplish work-related tasks. Strategically, we think in terms of goals and objectives we want to achieve—but ideally we remember the reasons that we thought those goals and objectives were worth attaining, which means we think about the outcomes we achieve by accomplishing a goal. (When you're up to your armpits in alligators, as the old saying goes, do you remember why draining the swamp was an important thing to do?) And if we are cybersecurity professionals or insurance providers or risk managers, we think about the dangers or risks that threaten to disrupt our plans, reduce the effectiveness (and value) of our assets, and derail our best-laid processes; in other words, we think about the threats to our business or the places our business is vulnerable to attack or accident.

These four perspectives, based on assets, processes, outcomes, or vulnerabilities and threats, are all correct and useful; no one is the best to use in addressing your risk management and risk mitigation needs. Some textbooks, risk management frameworks, and organizations emphasize one over the others (and may even not realize that the others exist); don't let this deceive you. As a risk management professional, you need to be comfortable perceiving the risks to your organization and its systems from all four perspectives.

Note, too, that on the one hand, these are perspectives or points of view; on the other hand, they each can be the basis of estimate, the foundation or starting point of a chain of decisions and calculations about the value of an asset. All quantitative estimates of risk or value have to start somewhere, as a simple example will illustrate. Suppose your company decides to purchase a new engineering workstation computer for your product designer to use. The purchase price, including all accessories, shipping, installation, and so on, establishes its initial acquisition cost to the company; that is its *basis* in accounting terms. This number can be the starting point for spreading the cost of the asset over its economically useful life (that is, depreciating it) or as part of break-even calculations.

NOTE Incidentally, accountants and risk managers pronounce *bases*, the plural of *basis*, as "bay-seez," with both vowels long, rather than "bay-sez," short "e," as in "the bases are loaded" in baseball.

All estimates are predictions about the various possible outcomes resulting from a set of choices. In the previous example, the purchase price of that computer established its cost basis; now, you've got to start making assumptions about the future choices that could affect its economically useful life. You'll have to make assumptions about how intensely it is used throughout a typical day, across each week; you'll estimate (that is, *guess*) how frequently power surges or other environmental changes might contribute to wear and tear and about how well (or how poorly) it will be maintained. Sometimes, modeling all of these possible decisions on a decision tree, with each branch weighted with your guesses of the likelihood (or probability) of choosing that path, provides a way of calculating a probability-weighted *expected value*. This, too, is just another prediction. But as long as you make similar predictions, using similar weighting factors and rules about how to choose probabilities among various outcomes, your overall estimates will be *comparable* with each other. That's no guarantee that they are more correct, just that you've been fair and consistent in making these estimates. (Many organizations look to standardized cost modeling rules, which may vary industry by industry, as a way of applying one simple set of factors to a class of assets: All office computers might be assumed to have a three-year useful life, with their cost basis declining to zero at the end of that three years. That's neither more right nor more wrong than any other set of assumptions to use when making such estimates; it's just different.)

One way to consider these four perspectives on risk is to build up an Ishikawa or fishbone diagram, which shows the journey from start to desired finish as supported by the assets, processes, resources, or systems needed for that journey, and how risks, threats, or problems can disrupt your use of those vital inputs or degrade their contributions to that journey. Figure 3.3 illustrates this concept.

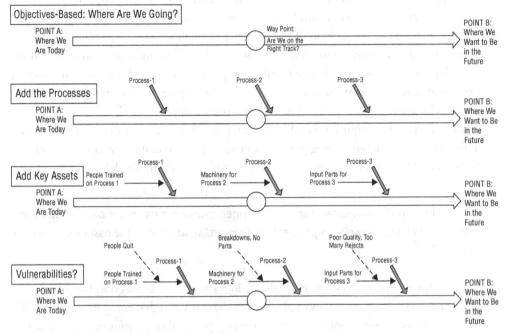

FIGURE 3.3 **Four bases of risk, viewed together**

Let's look in more detail at each of these perspectives or bases of risk.

Outcomes-Based Risk

This perspective on risk focuses on the overarching *objective*—the purpose or intent behind the actions that organizations take. Outcomes are the goal-serving conditions that are created or maintained as a result of accomplishing a series of tasks to fulfill those objectives. Your income tax return, along with all of the payments that you might owe your government, is a set of *outputs* produced by you and your tax accountant; the act of filing it and paying on time achieves an *outcome*, a goal that is important or valuable to you in fulfilling an *objective*. This might at a minimum be because it will keep you from being investigated or prosecuted for tax evasion; it might also be because you believe in doing your civic duty, which includes paying your taxes. The alarms generated by your intrusion detection or prevention systems (IDSs or IPSs) are the *outputs* of these systems; your decision to escalate to management and activate the incident response procedures is an *outcome* that logically followed from that set of outputs (and many other preceding outputs that in part preconditioned and prepared you to interpret the IDS and IPS alarms and make your decision).

Outcomes-based risk assessment looks at the ultimate value to be gained by the organization when it achieves that outcome. Investing in a new product line to be sold in a newly developed market has, as its outcome, an estimated financial return on investment (or RIO). Risks associated with the plans for developing that product, promoting and positioning it within that market, selling it, and providing after-sales customer service and support are all factors that inject uncertainty into that estimate — risks decrease the anticipated ROI, in effect multiplying it by a decreased probability of success. Organizations with strongly held senses of purpose, mission, or goals, or that have invested significant time, money, and effort in attempting to achieve new objectives, may prefer to use outcomes-based risk assessment.

Process-Based Risk

Organizations describe, model, and control the ways they get work done by defining their business logic as sequences of tasks, including conditional logic that enforces constraints, chooses options, or carries out other decision-making actions based on all of the factors specified by that business logic. Many organizations model this business logic in data models and data dictionaries and use systems such as workflow control and management or enterprise resource management (ERP) to implement and manage the use of that business logic. Individually and collectively these sequences or sets of *business processes* are what transform inputs — materials, information, labor, and energy — into *outputs* such as products, subassemblies, proposals, or software source code files. Business processes usually are *instrumented* to produce auxiliary outputs, such as key performance indicators, alarms, or other measurements, which users and managers can use to confirm correct operation of the process or to identify and resolve problems that arise. The absence of required inputs or the failure of a process step along a critical path within the overall process can cause the whole process to fail; this failure can cascade throughout the organization, and in the absence of appropriate backups, safeguards or fail-safes, the entire organization can grind to a halt.

Organizations that focus on continually refining and improving their business processes, perhaps even by using a capabilities maturity modeling methodology, may emphasize the use of process-based risk assessment. The failure of critical processes to achieve overall levels of product quality, for example, might be the reason that customers are no longer staying with the organization. While this negative outcome (and the associated outcome of declining revenues and profits) is of course important, the process-oriented focus can more immediately associate cause with effect in decision-makers' minds.

Asset-Based Risk

Broadly speaking, an asset is anything that the organization (or the individual) has, owns, uses, or produces as part of its efforts to achieve some of its goals and objectives. Buildings, machinery, or money on deposit in a bank are examples of hard, *tangible assets*. The people in your organization (including you!) are also tangible assets (you can be counted, touched, moved, or even fired). The knowledge that is recorded in the business logic of your business processes, your reputation in the marketplace, the intellectual property that you own as patents or trade secrets, and every bit of information that you own or use are examples of soft, *intangible assets*. (Intellectual property is the idea, not the paper it is written on.) Assets are the tools you use to perform the steps in your business processes; without these tools, without assets, the best business logic by itself cannot accomplish anything. It needs a place to work, inputs to work *on*, and people, energy, and information to achieve its required outputs.

Many textbooks on information risk management start with *information assets*—the information you gather, process and use, and the business logic or systems you use in doing that—and *information technology assets*—the computers, networks, servers, and cloud services in which that information moves, resides, and is used. The unstated assumption is that if the information asset or IT asset exists, it must therefore be important to the company or organization, and therefore, the possibility of loss or damage to that asset is a risk worth managing. This assumption may or may not still hold true. Assets also lose value over time, reflecting their decreasing usefulness, ongoing wear and tear, obsolescence, or increasing costs of maintenance and ownership. A good example of an obsolete IT asset would be a mainframe computer purchased by a university in the early 1970s for its campus computer center, perhaps at a cost of over a million dollars. By the 1990s, the growth in personal computing and network capabilities meant that students, faculty, and staff needed far more capabilities than that mainframe computer center could provide, and by 2015, it was probably far outpaced by the capabilities in a single smartphone connected to the World Wide Web and its cloud-based service provider systems. Similarly, an obsolete information asset might be the paper records of business transactions regarding products the company no longer sells, services, or supports. At some point, the *law of diminishing returns* says that it costs more to keep it and use it than the value you receive or generate in doing so.

It's also worth noting that many risk management frameworks seem to favor using information assets or IT assets as the basis of risk assessment; look carefully, and you may find that they actually suggest that this is just one important and useful way to manage information systems risk, but not the only one. Assets, after all, should be kept and protected because they are *useful*, not just because you've spent a lot of money to acquire and keep them.

Threat-Based (or Vulnerability-Based) Risk

These are two sides of the same coin really. *Threat actors* (natural or human) are things that can cause damage, disruption, and lead to loss. *Vulnerabilities* are weaknesses within systems, processes, assets, and so forth, that are points of potential failure. When (not if) they fail, they result in damage, disruption, and loss. Typically, threats or threat actors exploit (make use of) vulnerabilities. Threats can be natural (such as storms or earthquakes), accidental (failures of processes or systems due to unintentional actions or normal wear and tear, causing a component to fail), or deliberate actions taken by humans or instigated by humans. Such intentional attackers have purposes, goals, or objectives they seek to accomplish; Mother Nature or a careless worker do not intend to cause disruption, damage, or loss.

Ransom attacks are an important, urgent, and compelling case in point. Unlike ransomware attacks, which require injection of malware into the target system to install and activate software to encrypt files or entire storage subsystems, a ransom attack "lives off the land" by taking advantage of inherent system weaknesses to gain access; the attacker then uses built-in systems capabilities to schedule the encryption of files or storage subsystems, all without the use of any malware. This threat is real, and it's a rare organization that can prove it is invulnerable to it. Prudent threat-based risk assessment, therefore, starts with this attack plan and assesses how your systems are configured, managed, used, and monitored as part of determining just how exposed your company is to this risk.

It's perhaps natural to combine the threat-based and vulnerability-based views into one perspective, since they both end up looking at vulnerabilities to see what impacts can disrupt an organization's information systems. The key question that the threat-based perspective asks, at least for human threat actors, is *why*. What is the motive? What's the possible advantage the attacker can gain if they exploit this vulnerability? What overall gains might an attacker achieve by an attack on our information systems at all? Many small businesses (and some quite large ones) do not realize that a successful incursion into their systems by an attacker may only be a step in that attacker's larger plan for disruption, damage, or harm to others. By thinking for a moment like the attacker, you might identify critical assets that the attacker might really be seeking to attack; or, you might identify critical outcomes that an attacker might want to disrupt for ideological, political, emotional, or business reasons.

Note that whether you call this a *threat-based* or *vulnerability-based* approach or perspective, you end up taking much the same action: You identify the vulnerabilities on the critical path to your high-priority objectives and then decide what to do about them in the face of a possible threat becoming a reality and turning into an incident.

Impact Assessments

Your organization will make choices as to whether to pursue an outcomes-based, asset-based, process-based, or threat-based assessment process, or to blend them all together in one way or another. Some of these choices might already have been made if your organization has chosen (and perhaps tailored) a formal risk management framework to guide its processes with. (You'll look at these in greater depth in the "Risk Management Frameworks" section.) The priorities of what to examine for potential impact, and in what order, should be set for you by senior leadership and management, which is expressed in the business impact analysis (BIA). One more choice remains, and that is whether to do a quantitative assessment, a qualitative assessment, or a mix of both.

Impact assessments for information systems must be guided by some kind of information security classification guide, something that associates broad categories of information types with an expectation of the degree of damage the organization would suffer if any aspect of that information's CIANA+PS security was compromised. For example, nonrepudiation and authentication requirements for payment approval for invoices drive processing and business logic design, in ways that limit or contain impacts and losses due to mistakes or fraud. This relates (or should relate) to the classification level for such information. (False invoicing scams, by the way, are amounting to billions of dollars in losses to businesses worldwide, as of 2021).

The process of making an impact assessment seems simple enough.

1. You start by identifying a risk (an undesirable outcome) that might occur.
2. Next, you link that risk to the various processes, systems, assets, or people-facing procedures that it impacts. This set of elements, end to end, is a critical path: Successful attainment of the goal depends upon all elements in that path working correctly. The risk event occurs when one of them doesn't perform correctly and completely.
3. Then, you examine each element in that chain to see if you can determine the trigger, or the root cause, that would allow the risk to occur. It might be an inherent vulnerability that can be exploited; it might be an accident or an act of Nature.
4. Given that, you estimate how frequently this risk might occur.

Now you have a better picture of what can be lost or damaged because of the occurrence of a risk event. This might mean that critical decision support information is destroyed, degraded, or delayed, or that a competitive advantage is degraded or lost because of disclosure of proprietary data. It might mean that a process or system is rendered inoperable and that repairs or other actions are needed to get it back into normal operating condition.

Risk analysis is a complex undertaking and often involves trying to sort out what can cause a risk (which is a statement of probability about an event) to become an incident. Root-cause analysis looks to find what the underlying vulnerability or mechanism of failure is that leads to the incident. By contrast, proximate cause analysis asks, "What was the last thing that happened that caused the risk to occur?" (This is sometimes called the "last clear opportunity to prevent" the incident, a term that insurance underwriters and their lawyers often use.) Proximate cause can reveal opportunities to put in back-stops or safety controls, which are additional features that reduce the impact of the risk from spreading to other downstream elements in the chain of processes. Commercial airlines, for example, scrupulously check passenger manifests and baggage check-in manifests; they will remove baggage from the aircraft if they cannot validate that the passenger who checked it in actually boarded, and is still on board, the aircraft, as a last clear opportunity to thwart an attempt to place a bomb onboard the aircraft. Multifactor user authentication and repeated authorization checks on actions that users attempt to take demonstrate the same layered implementation of last clear opportunity to prevent.

You've learned about a number of examples of risks becoming incidents; for each you've identified an outcome of that risk, which describes what might happen. This forms part of the *basis of estimate* with which you can make two kinds of *risk assessments*: quantitative and qualitative.

Quantitative Risk Assessment: Risk by the Numbers

Quantitative assessments use simple techniques (such as counting possible occurrences or estimating how often they might occur) along with estimates of the typical cost of each loss.

- **Single loss expectancy (SLE):** Usually measured in monetary terms, SLE is the total cost one can reasonably expect should the risk event occur. It includes immediate and delayed costs, direct and indirect costs, costs of repairs, and restoration. In some circumstances, it also includes lost opportunity costs or lost revenues due to customers needing or choosing to go elsewhere.

- **Annual rate of occurrence (ARO):** ARO is an estimate of how often during a single year this event could reasonably be expected to occur.

- **Annual loss expectancy (ALE):** ALE is the total expected losses for a given year and is determined by multiplying the SLE by the ARO.

- **Safeguard value:** This is the estimated cost to implement and operate the chosen risk mitigation control. You cannot know this until we've chosen a risk control or countermeasure and an implementation plan for it.

Other numbers associated with risk assessment relate to how the business or organization deals with time when its systems, processes, and people are not available to do business. This "downtime" can often be expressed as a mean (or average) allowable downtime or a maximum downtime. Times to repair or restore minimum functionality and times to get everything back to normal are also some of the numbers the SSCP will need to deal with. Other commonly used quantitative assessments are:

- The *maximum acceptable outage (MAO)* is the maximum time that a business process or task cannot be performed without causing intolerable disruption or damage to the business. Sometimes referred to as the *maximum tolerable outage (MTO)* or the *maximum tolerable period of disruption (MTPOD)*, determining this maximum outage time starts with first identifying *mission-critical outcomes*. These outcomes, by definition, are vital to the ongoing success (and survival!) of the organization; thus, the processes, resources, systems, and no doubt people they require to properly function become *mission-critical resources*. If only *one* element of a mission-critical process is unavailable and no immediate substitute or work-around is at hand, then the MAO clock starts ticking.

- The *mean time to repair (MTTR)*, or *mean time to restore*, reflects your average experience in doing whatever it takes to get the failed system, component, or process repaired or replaced. The MTTR must include time to get suitable staff on scene who can diagnose the failure, identify the right repair or restoration needed, and draw from parts or replacement components on hand to effect repairs. MTTR calculations should also include time to verify that the repair has been done correctly *and that the repaired system works correctly*. This last requirement is critically important—it does no good at all to swap out parts and say that something is fixed if you cannot assure management and users that the repaired system is now working the way it needs to in order to fulfill mission requirements.

These types of quantitative assessments help the organization understand what a risk can do when it occurs (and becomes an incident) and what it will take to get back to normal operations and clean up the mess it caused. One more important question remains: How long to repair and restore is too long? Two more "magic numbers" shed light on this question.

- The *recovery time objective (RTO)* is the amount of time in which system functionality or ability to perform the business process must be back in operation. Note that the RTO must be less than or equal to the MAO (if not, there's an error in somebody's thinking). As an *objective*, RTO asks systems designers, builders, maintainers, and operators to strive for a better, faster result. But be careful what you ask for; demanding too rapid an RTO can cause more harm than it deflects by driving the organization to spend far more than makes bottom-line sense.

- The *recovery point objective (RPO)* measures the data loss that is tolerable to the organization, typically expressed in terms of how much data needs to be loaded from backup systems in order to bring the operational system back up to where it needs to be. For example, an airline ticketing and reservations system takes every customer request as a transaction, copies the transactions into log files, and processes the transactions (which causes updates to their databases). Once that's done, the transaction is considered completed. If the database is backed up in its entirety once a week, let's say, if the database crashes five days after the last backup, then that backup is reloaded, and then five days' worth of transactions must be reapplied to the database to bring it up to where customers, aircrew, airport staff, and airplanes expect it to be. Careful consideration of an RPO allows the organization to balance costs of routine backups with time spent reapplying transactions to get back into business.

Figure 3.4 illustrates a typical risk event occurrence. It shows how the ebb and flow of normal work can get corrupted, then lost completely, and then must be re-accomplished, as you detect and recover from an incident. You'll note that it shows an undetermined time period elapsing between the actual damage inflicted by an incident—the intruder has started exfiltrating data, corrupting transactions, or introducing false data into your systems, possibly installing more trapdoors—and the time you actually detect the incident has occurred or is still ongoing. The major stages of risk response are shown as overlapping processes. Note that MTTR, RTO, and MAO are not necessarily equal. (They'd hardly ever be in the real world.)

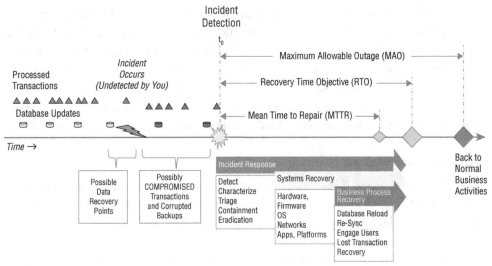

FIGURE 3.4 **Risk timeline**

Where is the RPO? Take a look "left of bang," left of the incident *detection* time (sometimes called t_0, or the reference time from which *you* measure durations), and look at the database update and transaction in the "possible data recovery points" group. Management needs to determine how far back to go to reload an incremental database update, then reaccomplish known good transactions, and *then* reaccomplish suspect transactions from independent, verifiably good transaction logs. This logic establishes the RPO. The further back in time you have to fall back, the more work you reaccomplish.

It used to be that we thought that RPO times close to the incident reference time were sufficient; and for non-APT-induced incidents, such as systems crashes, power outages, etc., this may be sound reasoning. But if that intruder has been in your systems for weeks or months, you'll probably need a different strategy to approach your RPO.

Chapter 4, "Incident Response and Recovery," goes into greater depth on the end-to-end process of business continuity planning. It's important that you realize these numbers play three critical roles in your integrated, proactive information defense efforts. All of these quantitative assessments (plus the qualitative ones as well) help you:

- Establish the "pain points" that lead to information security requirements that can be measured, assessed, implemented, and verified.

- Shape and guide the organization's thinking about risk mitigation control strategies, tactics, and operations, and keep this thinking within cost-effective bounds.

- Dictate key business continuity planning needs and drive the way incident response activities must be planned, managed, and performed.

One final thought about the "magic numbers" is worth considering. The organization's leadership has its stakeholders' personal and professional fortunes and futures in their hands. Exercising due diligence *requires* that management and leadership be able to show, by the numbers, that they've fulfilled that obligation and brought it back from the brink of irreparable harm when disaster strikes. Those stakeholders—the organization's investors, customers, neighbors, and workers—need to trust in the leadership and management team's ability to meet the bottom line every day. Solid, well-substantiated numbers like these help the stakeholders trust, but verify, that their team is doing their job.

Qualitative Risk Assessment

Qualitative assessments focus on an inherent quality, aspect, or characteristic of the risk as it relates to the outcome(s) of a risk occurrence. "Loss of business" could be losing a few customers, losing many customers, or closing the doors and going out of business entirely!

So, which assessment strategy works best? The answer is *both*. Some risk situations may present us with things we can count, measure, or make educated guesses about in numerical terms, but many do not. Some situations clearly identify *existential threats* to the organization (the occurrence of the threat puts the organization completely out of business); again, many situations are not as clear-cut. Senior leadership and organizational stakeholders find both qualitative and quantitative assessments useful and revealing.

Qualitative assessment of information is most often used as the basis of an *information classification system*, which labels broad categories of data to indicate the range of possible harm or impact. Most of us are familiar with such systems through their use by military and national security communities. Such simple hierarchical information classification systems often start with "Unclassified" and move up through "For Official Use Only," "Confidential," "Secret," and "Top Secret" as their way of broadly outlining how severely the nation would be impacted if the information was disclosed, stolen, or otherwise compromised. Yet even these cannot stay simple for long.

Business and the military have another aspect of data categorization in common: the concept of *need to know*. Need to know limits who has access to read, use, or modify data based on whether their job functions require them to do so. Thus, a school's purchasing department staff members have a need to know about suppliers, prices, specific purchases, and so forth, but they do not need to know any of the PII pertaining to students, faculty, or other staff members. Need-to-know leads to *compartmentalization of information* approaches, which create procedural boundaries (administrative controls) around such sets of information.

Threat Modeling

Threat modeling provides an overall process and management approach organizations can use as they identify possible threats, categorize them in various ways, and analyze and assess both these categories and specific threats. This analysis should shed light on the nature and severity of the threat; the systems, assets, processes, or outcomes it endangers; and offer insights into ways to deter, detect, defeat, or degrade the effectiveness of the threat. While primarily focused on the IT infrastructure and information systems aspects of overall risk management, it has great potential payoff for all aspects of threat-based risk assessment and management. Its roots, in fact, can be found in centuries of physical systems and architecture design practices developed to protect physical plant, high-value assets, and personnel from loss, harm, or injury due to deliberate actions (which are still very much a part of overall risk management today!).

Threat modeling can be proactive or reactive; it can be done as a key part of the analysis and design phase of a new systems project's lifecycle, or it can be done (long) after the systems, products, or infrastructures are in place and have become central to an organization's business logic and life. Since it's impossible to identify all threats and vulnerabilities early in the lifecycle of a new system, threat modeling is (or should be) a major component of ongoing systems security support.

As the nature, pervasiveness and impact of the APT threat continues to evolve, many organizations are finding that their initial focus on confidentiality, integrity, and availability may not go far enough to meet their business risk management needs. Increasingly, they are placing greater importance on their needs for nonrepudiation, authentication, and privacy as part of their information security posture. Data quality, too, is becoming much more important, as businesses come to grips with the near-runaway costs of rework, lost opportunity, and compliance failures caused by poor data quality control. Your organization should always tailor its use of frameworks and methodologies, such as threat modeling, with its overall and current information security needs in mind.

In recent years, greater emphasis has been placed on the need for an overall secure software development lifecycle approach; many of these methodologies integrate threat modeling and risk mitigation controls into different aspects of their end-to-end approach. Additionally, specific industries are paying greater attention to threat modeling in specific and overall secure systems development methodologies in general. If your organization operates in one of these markets, these may have a bearing on how your organization can benefit from (or must use) threat modeling as a part of its risk management and mitigation processes. Chapter 7, "Systems and Application Security" will look at secure software development lifecycle approaches in greater depth; for now, let's focus on the three main threat modeling approaches commonly in use.

- **Attacker-centric:** This threat modeling approach works well when organizations can characterize the types of attackers who are most likely to inflict the greatest damage to the organization and its objectives; it's not well suited to dealing with the broad universe of attackers, motivations, means, and abilities. Even so, it can be quite illuminating to narrow your threat modeling scope to consider a specific set of attacker types, in conjunction with asset-centric or systems-centric approaches. Financial institutions, for example, often focus on specific internal attacker types (such as embezzlers), while credit card payment processors focus on external attackers to protect against fraud. Nontechnical professionals can often contribute to this type of threat modeling by capturing and analyzing the means, methods, and motivations of the attackers to build a profile (or persona) of an attacker.

- **Asset-centric:** As opposed to an attacker-centric approach, an asset-centric threat model identifies the assets of value first. It's important to realize that the same asset may have a dramatically different value to the organization than it would to different types of attackers. The means by which the asset is managed, manipulated, used, and stored are then evaluated to identify how an attacker might compromise the asset. Many compliance regimes focus on protection of an asset (e.g., protected health information under HIPAA, personally identifiable information under the General Data Protection Regulation [GDPR], or the Primary Account Number under PCI-DSS), so this approach is helpful when establishing or verifying compliance. Tools that support asset-centric analysis include classification and categorization of information, which identifies information that is sensitive to disclosure, and the importance of the information to the organization's business processes. As is done with the attacker-centric model, organizations typically maintain an inventory or library process to identify those assets of value.

■ **System or software-centric:** In this approach, the system is represented as a set of interconnected processes, often using data flow diagrams (DFDs) as a key visualization and analysis tool, which often reveal threat surfaces or trust boundaries that exist (or should exist) between groups of systems components or elements. Analysts can then further identify the channels that cross such surfaces or boundaries and determine whether sufficient control and detection is in place to protect each such crossing point. This approach can also help identify covert channels, which use system functions in ways unintended by their designers, often in combination, to allow information or signals to cross a threat surface or trust boundary. This approach is often called *systems-of-systems-centric* when organizations must examine the threats to a combination of infrastructure, applications, platforms, and services elements.

It's possible that the greatest risk that small and medium-sized businesses and non-profit organizations face, as they attempt to apply threat modeling to their information architectures, is that of the failure of imagination. It can be quite hard for people in such organizations to imagine that their data or business processes are worthy of an attacker's time or attention; it's hard for them to see what an attacker might have to gain by copying or corrupting their data. It's at this point that your awareness of many different attack methodologies may help inform (and inspire) the threat modeling process.

There are many different threat modeling methodologies. Some of the most widely used are SDL, STRIDE, NIST 800-154, PASTA, and OCTAVE, each of which is explored next.

Secure Development Lifecycle and STRIDE

Over the years, Microsoft has evolved its thinking and its processes for developing software in ways that make for more secure, reliable, and resilient applications and systems by design, rather than being overly dependent upon seemingly never-ending "testing" being done by customers, users, and hackers after the product has been deployed. Various methodologies, such as STRIDE and SD3+C, have been published by Microsoft as their concepts have grown. Although the names have changed, the original motto of "secure by design, secure by default, and secure in deployment and communication" (SD3+C) continue to be the unifying strategies in Microsoft's approach and methods.

STRIDE, or spoofing, tampering, repudiation, information disclosure, denial of service, and elevation of privilege, provides a checklist and a set of touchpoints by which security analysts can characterize threats and vulnerabilities. As a methodology, it can be applied to applications, operating systems, networks and communications systems, and even human-intensive business processes. These are still at the core of Microsoft's current secure development lifecycle (SDL) thinking, but it must be noted that SDL focuses intensely on the roles of managers and decision-makers in planning, supporting, and carrying out an end-to-end secure software and systems development and deployment lifecycle, rather than just considering specific classes of threats or controls. Check out `https://www.microsoft.com/en-us/securityengineering/sdl/practices` for current information, ideas, and tools on SDL.

NIST 800-154 Data-Centric Threat Modeling

In 2016, NIST placed for public comment a threat modeling approach centered on protecting high-value data. This approach is known as NIST 800-154, "Data-Centric Threat Modeling." It explicitly rejects that best-practice approaches are sufficient to protect sensitive information, as best practice is too general and would overlook controls specifically tailored to meet the protection of the sensitive asset. In this model, the analysis of the risk proceeds through four major steps.

1. **Identify and characterize the system and data of interest.** The data and information should be defined narrowly to a particular logical set of data on a single host or small group of hosts. Then the information is characterized, taking into account the authorized locations for the data within the system, how the information moves within the system between authorized locations, and the security objectives for the data using the CIA, CIANA, or CIANA+PS construct. This characterization should recognize that not all of the objectives are of equal importance for any particular data set. At this point, you've identified the people and process that are authorized to access the data within the context of the security objectives.

2. **Identify and select the attack vectors to be included in the model.** Identify potential attack vectors and then prioritize those that meet the likelihood and consequence criteria established for the data or system.

3. **Characterize the security controls for mitigating the attack vectors.** Identify the security control alterations that would address the risk and are reasonably feasible to accomplish. Next, for each selected control alteration, estimate the effectiveness of the control on the attack vector. Finally, estimate the negative consequences of the control, taking into account issues such as cost, functionality, usability, and performance.

4. **Analyze the threat model.** Taking into account the characteristics documented in the previous steps, evaluate the controls to identify which controls give an acceptable level of risk reduction while minimizing the negative impacts of the control.

PASTA

The Process for Attack Simulation and Threat Analysis (PASTA), as the full name implies, is an attacker-centric modeling approach, but the outputs of the model are focused on protecting the organization's assets. Its seven-step process aligns business objectives, technical requirements, and compliance expectations to identify threats and attack patterns. These are then prioritized through a scoring system. The results can then be analyzed to determine which security controls can be applied to reduce the risk to an acceptable level. Advocates for this approach argue that the integration of business concerns in the process takes the threat modeling activity from a technical exercise to a process more suited to assessing business risk.

OCTAVE

Operationally Critical Threat, Asset, and Vulnerability Evaluation (OCTAVE) is an approach for managing information security risks developed at the Software Engineering Institute (SEI). While the overall OCTAVE approach encompasses more than threat modeling, asset-based threat modeling is at the core of the process. In its current form, OCTAVE Allegro breaks down into a set of four phases.

1. Establish drivers, where the organization develops risk measurement criteria that are consistent with organizational drivers.

2. Profile assets, where the assets that are the focus of the risk assessment are identified and profiled, and the assets' containers are identified.

3. Identify threats, where threats to the assets—in the context of their containers—are identified and documented through a structured process.

4. Identify and mitigate risks, where risks are identified and analyzed based on threat information, and mitigation strategies are developed to address those risks.

As compared with previous versions of OCTAVE, Allegro simplifies the collection of data, improves focus on risk mitigation strategies, and provides a simple quantitative model (as opposed to the qualitative approaches previously emphasized). Proponents argue this makes the model easier to understand and use, simplifying training and increasing the likelihood that the approach will be consistently adopted as a risk method inside organizations.

Other Models

Other threat modeling methodologies include the following:

- TRIKE is an open source threat modeling approach and tool.

- Construct a platform for Risk Analysis of Security Critical Systems (CORAS), also open source, relies heavily on UML as the front end for visualizing the threats.

- Visual, Agile, and Simple Threat Modeling (VAST) is a proprietary approach that leverages Agile concepts.

Business Impact Analysis

The business impact analysis (BIA, also sometimes called the business impact assessment) should start with the prioritized strategic objectives and goals of the organization, linking the potential impacts of risks to these prioritized objectives. The BIA is the way in which senior management and leadership document their decisions about which categories of risks to deal with first and which ones can wait to be mitigated; it lays out commitments to spend money, time, talent, and management attention and direction on specific sets of risks. The BIA is thus part of the strategic and high tactical risk management process and a vitally important output product of that risk management process.

Note that prioritizing the risks is not as simple as ranking them in total expected dollar loss to the organization, even though common sense and experience may suggest these often go hand in hand. Consider the plight of Volkswagen America, which has suffered significant loss in market share and damage to its reputation after it was discovered that key decision-makers approved the falsifying of data that it had to report to regulators in the United States and the European Union. It might be exceedingly hard to quantify another reputational risk that the company might face, while at the same time the company (and its parent) might be facing other risks in the Asian markets that can be quantified. Which is the greater risk, the (hypothetical) millions of dollars involved in the Asian markets or another major reputational risk in the EU and North American markets? That decision belongs to senior management and leadership; the BIA and the plans built upon it should reflect that decision and direct efforts to carry it out.

> ### ✔ Compliance as a Risk to Manage?
>
> We might think that laws, regulations, and contractual terms are non-negotiable burdens that organizations and their leadership and management teams must comply with. After all, in many cases, the penalties for not complying with them can be quite severe! Take note, however: One commonly held viewpoint says that laws, regulations, and even contract terms are *risks* that confront the company, and like all risks, managers should choose which terms or constraints to accept, transfer to others, treat (that is, implement effective responses to the constraint), avoid, or ignore.
>
> An insurance claims processing company, for example, might choose to cut corners on protecting patient and care provider data, which public law (HIPAA in the United States, GDPR and others in the European Union) requires be protected. The risk of a data breach, they argue, is transferred (along with its impacts and losses) to the individual patients or care providers; at most, any fines the company receives are passed along in higher costs to the insurance carriers, clinicians, and patients. The (ISC)² Code of Ethics would consider

There is no one right, best format for a BIA; instead, each organization must determine what its BIA needs to capture and how it has to present it to achieve a mix of purposes.

- BIAs should inform, guide, and shape risk management decisions by senior leadership.

- BIAs should provide the insight to choose a balanced, prudent mix of risk mitigation tactics and techniques.

- BIAs should guide the organization in accepting residual risk to goals, objectives, processes, or assets in areas where this is appropriate.

- BIAs may be required to meet external stakeholder needs, such as for insurance, financial, regulatory, or other compliance purposes.

You must recognize one more important requirement at this point: to be effective, a BIA must be *kept up to date*. The BIA must reflect today's set of concerns, priorities, assets, and processes; it must reflect today's understanding of threats and vulnerabilities. Outdated information in a BIA could at best lead to wasted expenditures and efforts on risk mitigation; at worst, it could lead to failures to mitigate, prevent, or contain risks that could lead to serious damage, injury, or death, or possibly put the organization out of business completely. Gone should be the days when an annual, routine review and update cycle of the BIA is considered sufficient.

At its heart, making a BIA is pretty simple: You identify what's important, estimate how often it might fail, and estimate the costs to you of those failures. You then rank those possible impacts in terms of which basis for risk best suits your organization, be that outcomes, processes, assets, or vulnerabilities. For all but the simplest and smallest of organizations, however, the amount of information that has to be gathered, analyzed, organized, assessed, and then brought together in the BIA can be overwhelming. The BIA is one of the most critical steps in the information risk management process; it's also perhaps the most iterative, the most open to reconsideration as things change, and the most in need of being kept alive, current, and useful.

Risk Management Frameworks

A *risk management framework (RMF)* is a set of concepts, tools, processes, and techniques that help you organize information about risk. As you're no doubt aware, the job of managing risks to your information is a set of many jobs, layered together. More than that, it's a set of jobs that changes and evolves with time as the organization, its mission, and the threats it faces evolve.

Let's start by taking a quick look at NIST Special Publication 800-37 Rev. 2, "Risk Management Framework for Information Systems and Organizations: A System Life Cycle Approach for Security and Privacy." Published in late 2020, this RMF establishes a broad, overarching perspective on what it calls the fundamentals of information systems risk management. Organizational leadership and management must address these areas of concern:

1. Organization-wide risk management
2. Information security and privacy
3. System and system elements
4. Control allocation
5. Security and privacy posture
6. Supply chain risk management

You can see that there's an expressed top-down priority or sequence here. It makes little sense to worry about your IT supply chain (which might be a source of malware-infested hardware, software, and services) if leadership and stakeholders have not first come to a consensus about risks and risk management at the broader, strategic level. (You should also note that in NIST's eyes, the big-to-little picture goes from strategic, through operational, and then to tactical, which is how many in government and the military think of these levels. Business around the world, though, sees it as strategic, to tactical, to day-to-day operations.)

The RMF goes on by specifying seven major phases (which it calls *steps*) of activities for information risk management:

1. Prepare
2. Categorize
3. Select
4. Implement
5. Assess
6. Authorize
7. Monitor

It is tempting to think of these as step-by-step sets of activities—for example, once all risks have been categorized, you then start selecting which are the most urgent and compelling to make mitigation decisions about. Real-world experience shows us, though, that each step in the process reveals things that may challenge the assumptions we just finished making, causing us to reevaluate what we thought we knew or decided in that previous step. It is perhaps more useful to think of these steps as overlapping sets of attitudes and outlooks that frame and guide how overlapping sets of people within the organization do the data gathering, inspection, analysis, problem-solving, and then implementation of the chosen risk controls.

Although NIST publications are directive in nature for U.S. government systems and indirectly provide strong guidance to the IT security market in the United States and elsewhere, many other information risk management frameworks are in widespread use around the world. For example, the International Organization for Standardization publishes ISO Standard 31000:2018, "Risk Management Guidelines," in which the same concepts are arranged in a slightly different fashion. First, it suggests that three main tasks must be done (and in broad terms, done in the order shown):

1. Scope, context, criteria
2. Risk assessment, consisting of risk identification, risk analysis, risk evaluation
3. Risk treatment

Three additional, broader functions support or surround these central risk mitigation tasks.

4. Recording and reporting
5. Monitoring and review
6. Communication and consultation

As you can see in Figure 3.5, the ISO RMF also conveys a sense that, on the one hand, there is a sequence of major activities, but on the other hand, these major steps or phases are closely overlapping.

FIGURE 3.5 **ISO 31000 RMF**

✔ Standards: Not Just for the Compliant

Your organization may not have to comply with these RMFs or any of the standards and guidelines published by ISO, NIST, or other standards bodies. That's fine.

Instead...treat these standards as your opportunity to avoid repeating the painful mistakes that led to these standards in their current form?

ISO Standard 31000:2018 is based on a set of eight principles that drive the development of a risk framework. That framework, in turn, structures the processes for implementing risk management. Continual process improvement is an essential component of the ISO 31000 process. The ISO 31000 principles characterize an effective risk management framework that creates and protects organizational value through structured processes.

- **Proportionate:** The framework should be customized and proportionate to the organization and the level of risk.

- **Aligned:** The appropriate and timely involvement of stakeholders is necessary.

- **Comprehensive:** A structured and comprehensive approach is required.

- **Embedded:** Risk management is an integral part of all organizational activities.

- **Dynamic:** Risk management anticipates, detects, acknowledges, and responds to changes.

- **Best available information:** Risk management explicitly considers any limitations of available information.

- **Inclusive:** Human and cultural factors influence all aspects of risk management.

- **Continual improvement:** Risk management is continually improved through learning and experience.

To assist organizations in implementing the ISO 31000 standard, ISO 31004, "Risk Management-Guidance for the Implementation of ISO 31000," was published to provide a structured approach to transition their existing risk management practices to be consistent with ISO 31000 and consistent with the individual characteristics and demands of the implementing organization.

While the 31000-series addresses general risk, information security practices are addressed in the ISO 27000 series. The use of the ISO/IEC Guide 73 allows for a common language, but ISO/IEC 27005:2018, "Information technology – Security techniques – Information Security Risk Management," gives detail and structure to the information security risks by defining the context for information security risk decision-making. This context includes definition of the organization's risk tolerance, compliance expectations, and the preferred approaches for assessment and treatment of risk.

ISO 27005 does not directly provide a risk assessment process. Rather, it provides inputs to, and gets outputs from, the risk assessment practice used by the organization. In this framework, the assessment process may be performed in either a quantitative or qualitative manner but done consistently so that prioritization can be performed. ISO 27005 further emphasizes the need for communication with stakeholders and for processes that continuously monitor for changes in the risk environment.

The ISO standards have seen broad adoption, in part because of the broad international process in the development of the standards. Further, the standards themselves, while constantly under review, connect to other standards managed within the ISO. This enables organizations to adopt those standards that are appropriate for their business and provides a more holistic view of organizations' compliance activities.

It's wise to bear in mind that each major section of these RMFs gives rise to more detailed guidance, instruction, and "lessons-learned" advice. For example, NIST Special Publication 800-61 Rev. 2, "Computer Security Incident Handling Guide," looks more in-depth at what happens when an information risk actually occurs and becomes an incident. Its phases of Preparation, Detection, Analysis, Containment, Eradication, Recovery, and Post-Incident Activities parallel those found in the RMF, which looks at the larger picture of information risk management.

A number of other frameworks have been developed to identify and evaluate risk, suited to the unique needs of different industries and processes. Individually, these frameworks address assessment, control, monitoring, and audit of information systems in different ways, but all strive to provide internal controls to bring risk to an acceptable level.

Regardless of the framework, to effectively address risk in an organization, standard processes to evaluate the risks of operation of information systems must take into account the changing threat environment, the potential and actual vulnerabilities of systems, the likelihood that the risk will occur, and the consequence to the organization should that risk become manifest.

From a governance perspective, the selection of a framework should create a controls environment that is as follows:

- **Consistent:** A governance program must be consistent in how information security and privacy is approached and applied.

- **Measurable:** The governance program must provide a way to determine progress and set goals. Most control frameworks contain an assessment standard or procedure to determine compliance and in some cases risk as well.

- **Standardized:** As with measurable, a controls framework should rely on standardization so results from one organization or part of an organization can be compared in a meaningful way.

- **Comprehensive:** The selected framework should cover the minimum legal and regulatory requirements of an organization and be extensible to accommodate additional organization-specific requirements.

- **Modular:** A modular framework is more likely to withstand the changes of an organization as only the controls or requirements needing modification are reviewed and updated.

There are dozens of different risk management frameworks. While many of the frameworks address specific industry or organizational requirements, the information security professional should be aware of the broad characteristics of the more common frameworks.

Comprehensive Frameworks

Many frameworks have been developed to address risk in different contexts. Many of these are general in nature, while others are limited to a single industry or business practice. Organizations use comprehensive frameworks to take advantage of the consistency and breadth offered by the framework. This simplifies a wide range of challenges, including a consistent evaluation of performance, the conduct of audits for compliance, and the standardization of training the workforce in the activities and processes of a particular methodology.

NIST Cybersecurity Framework

Many people have found formal RMFs and related standards to be far too complex to apply to their business logic in meaningful ways. Recognizing this, NIST published in 2021 its Cyber Security Framework, available at `https://www.nist.gov/cyberframework`. It simplifies the risk management process, focusing it on five task areas (Identify, Protect, Detect, Respond, and Recover). It provides other tools and resources, such as standards, best practices, and guidelines, written in plainer, non-bureaucratic language and structure, to help businesses and government activities take on cybersecurity risk management in an incremental manner. ISO and ENISA (the EU Agency for Cybersecurity) have taken similar approaches, reflecting the need to enable and empower more widespread adoption and implementation of better cybersecurity practices across all marketplaces and industries.

U.S. Federal Information Processing Standards

NIST also publishes the Federal Information Processing Standards (FIPS), which are mandated for all federal computer systems, with the exception of certain national security systems that are governed by a different set of standards. Authorized under a series of related laws, the FIPS address a range of interoperability and security practices for which there are no acceptable industry standards or solutions.

Three NIST standards link classification and categorization to security baselines. FIPS 199, "Standards for Security Categorization of Federal Information and Information Systems," requires agencies to perform information security classification and categorization; this of course needs a comprehensive systems inventory to be complete. FIPS 200, "Minimum Security Requirements for Federal Information and Information Systems," then uses a "high-water mark" approach to select security controls from

17 sets of security controls, the details of which can be found in NIST Special Publication 800-53, "Recommended Security Controls for Federal Information Systems." Correct implementation and ongoing monitoring contribute to certifying that the controls are correctly implemented and achieving required results, which (depending upon the organization and its mission) may be necessary for initial and ongoing formal authorization for operational use of the system and its controls.

While focused on the computing activities of the U.S. government, the NIST standards and guidelines have had a pervasive effect on the security community because of their broad scope, their availability in the public domain, and the inclusion of industry, academic, and other standards organizations in the development of the standards. Further, the NIST standards often set the expectations for security practice that are placed on regulated industries. This is most clearly shown in the Health Information Privacy and Portability legislation, where healthcare organizations must demonstrate their controls align with the NIST security practice.

Committee of Sponsoring Organizations

The Committee of Sponsoring Organizations of the Treadway Commission (known as COSO) is a U.S. private organization created in 1985 to help combat corporate fraud. It provides a comprehensive, organizational-level view of risk management. Its framework, "Enterprise Risk Management—Integrating with Strategy and Performance," recognizes that the pursuit of any organizational objectives incurs some level of risk, and good governance must accompany risk decisions.

Based on five components, the framework captures the responsibilities of governance to provide risk oversight and set an appropriate tone for ethical, responsible conduct.

The complementary "Internal Control—Integrated Framework" extends the COSO practice to the organization's internal control environment. The three objectives (operations, reporting, and compliance) are evaluated against five components: control environment, risk assessment, control activities, information and communication, and monitoring activities. The objectives and the components are further evaluated within the context of the organizational structure. Ultimately, the system of internal control requires that each of these components be present and operating together to bring the risk of operations to an acceptable level.

In short, the framework provides a high-level set of tools to establish consistency in the process in the identification and management of risks to acceptable levels.

The COSO organization originally came about to address weaknesses in the financial reporting environment that allowed fraud and other criminal activities to occur without detection, exposing financial organizations to considerable risk. While the framework evolved out of the need for better internal control in the financial services industry, the framework is now broadly applied to corporations operating in a wide variety of industries. As a result, it is not designed to address industry-specific issues. Further, the breadth of the framework requires management at all levels to apply considerable judgment in its implementation.

ITIL

ITIL, formerly known as the IT Infrastructure Library, was developed over the course of 30 years to address the service delivery challenges with information technology. Emphasizing continuous process improvement, ITIL provides a service management framework, of which risk management is an integrated element.

The ITIL framework is organized into five volumes that define 26 processes.

- **Volume 1:** Service Strategy seeks to understand organizational objectives and customer needs.

- **Volume 2:** Service Design turns the service strategy into a plan for delivering the business objectives.

- **Volume 3:** Service Transition develops and improves capabilities for introducing new services into supported environments.

- **Volume 4:** Service Operation includes processes that manage services in supported environments.

- **Volume 5:** Continual Service Improvement achieves services incremental and large-scale improvements.

The ITIL Framework has been substantially incorporated into other standards, notably ISO 20000, "Information technology – Service management," and has strongly influenced the development of ISACA's COBIT framework and others.

ITIL does not directly address risk management as a separate process. However, its emphasis on continuous improvement, which consists of leveraging metrics to identify out-of-specification activities and processes to address information security management systems, availability, and incident and event management, clearly incorporates the concepts of an enterprise risk management process. Indeed, if the goal of risk management is to reduce uncertainty, the ITIL framework emphasizes the importance of predictability in the processes.

COBIT and RiskIT

In the late 1990s the audit community in the United States and Canada recognized there was a significant gap between information technology governance and the larger organizational management structures. Consequently, information technology activities were often misaligned with corporate goals, and risks were not comprehensively addressed by the control structure's risk or consistently reflected in financial reporting. To address this gap, the Information Systems Audit and Control Association (ISACA) developed a framework through which the information technology activities of an organization could be assessed.

The Control Objectives for Information and Related Technologies (COBIT) framework differentiates processes into either Governance of Enterprise IT (five processes) or Management of Enterprise IT (32 processes). Each process has a set of objectives, inputs, key activities and outputs, and measures to evaluate performance against the objectives. As the framework is closely aligned with other management frameworks and tools (ISO20000, ISO27001, ITIL, Prince 2, SOX, TOGAF), it has gained wide acceptance as an encompassing framework for managing the delivery of information technology.

Based on the ISACA COBIT IT governance framework, the RiskIT framework provides a structure for the identification, evaluation, and monitoring of information technology risk. This simplifies the integration of IT risk into the larger organization enterprise risk management (ERM) activities.

Unlike the more generic risk management frameworks of COSO and ISO 31000 and the industry-specific risk structures of PCI-DSS or HITRUST, RiskIT fills the middle ground of generic IT risk. The framework consists of three domains—risk governance, risk evaluation, and risk response—each of which has three processes. The framework then details the key activities within each process and identifies organizational responsibilities, information flows between processes, and process performance management activities. Additional detail on how to implement the framework and link it to other organizational management practices is contained in the RiskIT Practitioner Guide.

Industry-Specific Risk Frameworks

Many industries have unique compliance expectations. This may be the result of requirements to meet the security expectations from multiple different regulatory entities or because of unique business processes. Some of these industry-specific frameworks are described next.

Health Information Trust Alliance Common Security Framework

The Health Information Trust Alliance Common Security Framework (HITRUST CSF) was developed to address the overlapping regulatory environment in which many healthcare providers operate. Taking into account both risk-based and compliance-based considerations, the HITRUST CSF normalizes the many requirements while providing an auditable framework for the evaluation of the security environment. In many ways, the HITRUST CSF is a "framework of frameworks."

North American Electric Reliability Corporation Critical Infrastructure Protection

The responsibility for protecting the electrical power grid in North America falls on the individual bulk electrical system (BES) operators. However, as the systems are interconnected, a failure of one operator to secure their environment may leave weaknesses that could affect the delivery of power throughout the continent. Over the past two decades, the North American Electric Reliability Corporation Critical Infrastructure Protection (NERC CIP) published a set of standards designed to enforce good cybersecurity practice and provide an auditable framework for compliance. This framework has been influenced by the NIST standard but is a standalone framework specific to the power industry.

ISA-99 and ISA/IEC 62443

The International Society of Automation has developed a series of standards to address the unique needs of the industrial process control environment. Organized into four groups, 13 different standards provide a policy, operational, and technical framework to increase the resilience of the industrial controls environment.

Industrial process control applications provide clear examples of the competing interests at work in the application of the CIA Triad to systems which, if they fail, might endanger thousands of lives and destroy assets worth millions of dollars. Availability – seen as the continued safe functioning of the manufacturing or other physical process – directly impacted the bottom line of the company; safety considerations were often seen as injecting costs, and often were not added unless dictated by regulators or insurers. Protecting the confidentiality of information used in these systems was usually not a concern but protecting the integrity and availability of the information was. One of the major motivations in the development of the ISA/IEC 62443 body of standards for industrial automation and control systems was to provide an appropriate emphasis on all aspects of the security challenge.

Payment Card Industry Data Security Standard

The PCI Security Standards Council (PCI SSC) developed the PCI-DSS standard to define a set of minimum controls to protect payment card transactions. Developed in response to increasing levels of credit card fraud, the PCI-DSS standard has undergone several modifications to increase the level of protection offered to customers. The current version of the standard, 3.2.1, identifies six goals with 12 high-level requirements that merchants are contractually obligated to meet. Figure 3.6 illustrates these goals and their respective PCI DSS requirements. The level of compliance is dependent on the volume of transactions processed by the merchant. Failing to meet the requirements can result in fines levied by the credit card processor.

PCI-DSS Goals and Requirements	
Goals	PCI DSS Requirements
Goal 1: Build and Maintain a Secure Network	1. Install and maintain a firewall configuration to protect cardholder data
	2. Do not use vendor-supplied defaults for system passwords and other security parameters
Goal 2: Protect Cardholder Data	3. Protect stored cardholder data
	4. Encrypt transmission of cardholder data across open, public networks
Goal 3: Maintain a Vulnerability Management Program	5. Use and regularly update anti-virus software or programs
	6. Develop and maintain secure systems and applications
Goal 4: Implement Strong Access Control Measures	7. Restrict access to cardholder data by business need-to-know
	8. Assign a unique ID to each person with computer access
	9. Restrict physical access to cardholder data
Goal 5: Regularly Monitor and Test Networks	10. Track and monitor all access to network resources and cardholder data
	11. Regularly test security systems and processes
Goal 6: Maintain an Information Security Policy	12. Maintain a policy that addresses information security for employees and contractors

FIGURE 3.6 **PCI-DSS goals and requirements**

The PCI SSC also has published standards for PIN entry devices, point-to-point encryption (P2PE), token service providers, and software applications (PA-DSS).

Risk Treatment

Having identified, characterized, and assessed the possible impacts of a particular risk, it's time to make some strategic, tactical, and operational choices regarding what if anything to do about it.

Strategic choices stem directly from senior leadership's risk appetite or risk tolerance and in many cases reflect the external context the organization is in. These choices are whether to accept, transfer, remediate or mitigate, avoid, eliminate, or ignore the risk.

Ethical or political considerations, for example, may dictate that a particular risk simply must be avoided, even if that means choosing to not operate where that risk is present. Existing systems may prove to be too costly to mitigate (repair or remediate) the vulnerabilities related to the risk, while completely replacing those systems with new ones that do not face that risk will no doubt take time to achieve; this may lead to temporarily accepting the risk as a fact of business life.

Risks, you recall, can be strategic, tactical, or operational in terms of their impacts to the organization. It's tempting to conclude, therefore, that the strategic risks should be owned (be decided about) by senior leadership and management, with tactical risks (that affect the near-term planning horizons) managed by mid-level management. The remaining day-to-day operational risks may rightly be owned and managed by line-level managers and supervisors. Be careful this delegation decision should be made explicitly, by senior leadership and management, and directed in the organization's approved risk management plan. To do otherwise could degenerate into risk management by assuming that somebody else has got that particular risk under control.

Let's look more closely at each of these choices.

Accept

This risk treatment strategy means you simply decide to do nothing about the risk. You recognize it is there, but you make a conscious decision to do nothing differently to reduce the likelihood of occurrence or the prospects of negative impact. This is also known as being *self-insuring*—you assume that what you save on paying risk treatment costs (or insurance premiums) will exceed the annual loss expectancy over the number of years you choose to self-insure or accept this risk.

It can also be the case when facing a risk, the impacts of which could conceivably kill the organization or put it out of business completely; but the best estimates available suggest that there are no practical or affordable ways to contain, mitigate, or avoid this risk. So, senior leaders must grit their teeth and carry on with business as usual, thus accepting the risk but choosing to do nothing about it. Other risks quite commonly accepted without much analysis are ones that involve negligible damages, very low probabilities of occurrence, or both. As a result, it's just not prudent to spend money, time, and effort to do anything about such risks, including over-analyzing them.

Note that accepting a risk is not "taking a gamble" or betting that the risks won't ever materialize. That would be *ignoring* the risk. For many years, most businesses, nonprofit organizations, and government offices throughout the United States and Europe, for example, blithely ignored the risk that an "active shooter" incident could occur on their premises; and in many respects, they may have been right to do so. Recent experience, alas, has motivated many organizations to gather the data, do the analysis, and make a more informed decision as to how to manage this risk to meet their needs. Many early adopters of IoT devices were ignorant of the lack of even minimal security features in these systems and have only recently started to understand the technologies, identify the risks inherent in their use, and begin to formulate risk management and mitigation strategies.

Note also the need to distinguish between accepting a risk and accepting the use of a compensating control to address the risk. The first is a choice to do nothing; the second is to choose to do something else to control or contain the risk, rather than use the control strategy recommended or required by standards, regulations, or contractual agreements.

Share or Transfer

Transferring or *sharing* a risk means that rather than spend our own money, time, and effort to reduce, contain, or eliminate the risk, and to recover from its impacts, we assign all or some of the risk to someone else; they then carry the responsibility of repairing or restoring our systems and processes, and perhaps reimburse us for lost business, in exchange for our payment to them of some kind of premium. In nearly all cases, this will leave some residual risk still in your organization's span of control and responsibility, hence ISO's preference to refer to *sharing* rather than *transferring* a risk. A large data center operations facility, for example, might share (with various third parties) its risks of having its customers' business operations disrupted in a number of ways.

- Another data center or a cloud services provider might be used to provide partial, incremental, or transaction-level backup or mirroring, either as part of a load-sharing arrangement or as a hot backup. The operation, maintenance, and risk management of that cloud services provider's systems is their responsibility (thus transferring a large portion of the risk of the redundant, backup systems not leading to prompt and complete recovery to the cloud services provider).

- Security assessments, including internal and external ethical penetration testers, may be covered by liability insurance, which would financially protect the company (and the individual testers) in the event that a test goes horribly wrong, crashing the data center, disrupting customer work in progress, or leaving the systems and customers vulnerable to attack.

- The risk that fire at the data center could significantly damage equipment or injure or kill any people on-site is transferred by a combination of an insurance policy, and by relying on local emergency responders, the fire department, and even the city planners who required the builders to install water mains and fire hydrants throughout your neighborhood. Typically, this transfer happens as a consequence of local law or municipal ordinances. The data center's owners paid for this risk to be assumed by the city and the fire department as part of their property taxes, as part of their business taxes, and perhaps even via a part of the purchase price (or lease costs) on the property.

In almost all cases, transferring a risk is about transforming the risk into something somebody else can deal with for you. You save the money, time, and effort you might have spent to deal with the risk yourself and instead pay others to assume the risk and deal with it for you; they also reimburse you (partially or completely) for consequential losses you suffer because of the risk.

Remediate or Mitigate (also Known as Reduce or Treat)

Simply put, this means you find and fix the vulnerabilities to the best degree that you can; failing that, you put in place other processes that shield, protect, augment, or bridge around the vulnerabilities. Most of the time this is *remedial* action—you are repairing something that either wore out during normal use, was not designed and built to be used the way you've been using it, or was designed and built incorrectly in the first place. You are applying a remedy, either total or partial, for something that went wrong.

Do not confuse taking remedial action to mitigate or treat a risk with making the repairs to a failed system itself. Mitigating the risk is something you aim to do *before* a failure occurs, not after! Such remediation or mitigation measures might therefore include the following:

- Designing acceptable levels of redundancy into systems so that when components or elements fail, critical business processes continue to function correctly and safely

- Designing acceptable "fail-safe" or graceful degradation features into systems so that when something fails, a cascade of failures leading to a disaster cannot occur

- Identifying acceptable amounts of downtime (or service disruption levels) and using these times to dictate design for services that detect and identify the failure, correct it, and restore full service to normal levels

- Prepositioning backup or alternate operations capabilities so that critical business functions can go on (perhaps at a reduced capacity or quality)

- Identifying acceptable amounts of time by which all systems and processes must be restored to normal levels of performance, throughput, quality, or other measures of merit

It's useful to distinguish between fixing the vulnerable element in your systems and adding a possibly redundant safeguard or alternate capability. Updating a software package to the latest revision level brings a reasonable assurance that the security fixes contained in that revision have been dealt with; those vulnerabilities have been eliminated or reduced to negligible residual risks. Providing uninterruptible power supplies or power conditioning equipment may eliminate or greatly reduce the intermittent outages that plague some network, communications, and computing systems, but they do so by making up for shortcomings in the quality and reliability of the commercial power system or the overall power distribution and conditioning systems in your facility. Either approach can be cost-effective, based on your specific risk situation and security needs.

> ## ✔ When in Doubt, What's the Requirement Say?
>
> Common sense might dictate simple solutions such as physical locks on the doors to the server room or installing uninterruptible power supplies on critical systems. However, common sense usually cannot tell you the *performance criteria* that you should use to choose those locks or how much you should spend on those UPSs. Those numbers come from having first done the analysis to determine what the real needs are and then estimating the costs to purchase, install, verify, operate, and maintain the risk mitigation controls.
>
> The written information security requirements documents, such as your BIA and the risk assessment that flows from it, should capture what you need to know in order to decide whether your chosen risk control is cost-effective.

Avoid or Eliminate

It's important to distinguish between these two related ways of treating risks. Risk avoidance usually requires that you abandon a vulnerable business process, activity, or location, so that the risk no longer applies to your ongoing operations. You eliminate a risk by replacing, repairing, or reengineering the vulnerable process and the systems and components it depends upon. You're still achieving the outputs and outcomes that were originally exposed to the risk. Risk purists might argue that eliminating a risk in this way is the same as remediating it; the net result is the same.

In either case, you achieve zero residual risk by spending money, time, and effort (either the costs incurred to abandon the risk-prone process, activity, or location, or the costs incurred to eliminate the risk).

Recast

Most risk treatments won't deal with 100 percent of a given risk; there will be some *residual risk* left over. You recast the risk by writing a new description of the residual risks, in the context of the systems or elements affected by them. This gives management and leadership a clearer picture of what the current risk posture (that is, the posture *after* you've implemented and verified the chosen risk mitigations and controls) really is. This recast statement of the risk should be reflected in updates to the BIA and the risk register so that subsequent assessments and mitigation planning have the most current and complete baseline to work from.

Residual Risk

This is the risk that's left over, unmitigated, after you have applied a selected risk treatment or control. For example, consider the risk of data exfiltration from a system. Improving the access control system to require multifactor authentication may significantly reduce the risk of an unauthorized user (an intruder) being able to access the data, copy it, prepare it for extraction, and extract the copies from your system. This will not prevent an insider from performing an exfiltration, so this remains as a residual data exfiltration risk. Improved attribute-based access control, along with more frequent privilege review, may reduce the insider threat risk further. Protecting the data at rest and in motion via encryption may reduce it as well. Adding administrative and logical controls to prevent or tightly control the use of live data in software testing, or even using recent backups of the production database in software testing, might also reduce the risk of exfiltration. (This also illustrates how oftentimes you must decompose an overall risk into the separate possible root causes that could allow it to occur and deal with those one by one to achieve a balance of risk and cost.)

Risk Treatment Controls

As you saw in Chapter 1, "Security Operations and Administration," risk treatments or controls are often categorized as to whether they are primarily physical, logical, or administrative in their essence. Since almost everything we do in modern organizations requires an audit trail, almost every control will have some administrative elements associated with it. But a guard dog is fundamentally a physical security control, even if its handler should be following written procedures and guidelines in putting that dog to work. Physical locks on doors need the paperwork (or e-records) that authorize their initial keying, while accounting for keys issued to and retrieved from staff members. Despite that bit of complexity, let's take a closer look. Getting value for money invested in each of these classes of controls means choosing the right control for the right job, installing or otherwise putting it into operational use, and then ensuring that they're being properly used, maintained, and monitored, as you saw in previous chapters.

Physical Controls

Physical controls are combinations of hardware, software, electrical, and electronic mechanisms that, taken together, prevent, delay, or deter somebody or something from physically crossing the threat surface around a set of system components we need to protect. Large-scale architectural features, such as the design of buildings, their location in an overall facility, surrounding roads, driveways, fences, perimeter lighting, and so forth, are visible, real, and largely static elements of our physical control systems. You must also consider where within the building to put high-value assets, such as server rooms, wiring closets, network and communication provider points of presence, routers and Wi-Fi hotspots, library and file rooms, and so on. Layers of physical control barriers, suitably equipped with detection and control systems, can both detect unauthorized access attempts and block their further progress into our "safe spaces" within the threat surface.

Network and communications wiring, cables, and fibers are also physical system components that need some degree of physical protection. Some organizations require them to be run through steel pipes that are installed in such a way as to make it impractical or nearly impossible to uncouple a section of pipe to surreptitiously tap into the cables or fibers. Segmenting communications, network, and even power distribution systems also provides a physical degree of isolation and redundancy, which may be important to an organization's CIANA+PS needs.

Note the important link here to other kinds of controls. Physical locks require physical keys; multifactor authentication requires logical and physical systems; both require "people power" to create and then run the policies and procedures (the administrative controls) that glue it all together and keep all of the parts safe, secure, and yet available when needed.

Logical (or Technical) Controls

Here is where we use software and the parameter files or databases that direct that software to implement and enforce policies and procedures that we've administratively decided are important and necessary. It can be a bit confusing that a "policy" can be both a human-facing set of rules, guidelines, or instructions, and a set of software features and their related control settings. Many modern operating systems, and identity-as-a-service provisioning systems, refer to these internal implementations of rules and features as policy objects, for example. So we write our administrative "acceptable use" policy document and use it to train our users so that they know what is proper and what is not; our systems administrators then "teach" it to the operating system by setting parameters and invoking features that implement the software side of that human-facing policy.

Administrative Controls

In general terms, anything that human organizations write, state, say, or imply that dictates how the humans in that organization should do business (and also what they should *not* do) can be considered an administrative control. As you saw in Chapter 1, administrative controls such as policy documents, procedures, process instructions, training materials, and many other forms of information all are intended to guide, inform, shape, and control the way that people act on the job (and to some extent, too, how they behave *off* the job!).

Administrative controls are typically the easiest to create—but sometimes, because they require the sign-off of very senior leadership, they can be ironically the most difficult to update in some organizational cultures. It usually requires a strong sense of the underlying business logic to create good administrative controls.

Such controls can be used to inform, teach, train, or otherwise reinforce more security-conscious behavior and action.

Choosing a Control

For any particular risk mitigation need, an organization may face a bewildering variety of competing alternative solutions, methods, and choices. Do we build the new software fix in-house or get a vendor to provide it? Is there a turn-key hardware/software system that will address a lot of our needs, or are we better off doing it internally one risk at a time? Choosing the right mix of controls should also take users into account.

Build and Maintain User Engagement with Risk Controls

Selecting and implementing risk controls must include new or modified end-user awareness and training. Far too many simple systems upgrades have gone wrong because the designers, builders, and testers failed to consider what the changes would mean to the people who need to use the new system effectively to get work done. Addressing end-user needs for new awareness, refresher training, or new training regarding new or modified security controls can be a double win for the organization. The first payoff is that it gets them engaged with the ideas behind the change; when users understand the purpose and intent, they can better relate it to their own jobs and their own particular needs. Building upon this, working with the end users to develop new teaching and training materials and then helping users become familiar with the changes leads to their being comfortable and competent with their use. This can greatly increase the chances of this change being successfully adopted.

Many organizations are implementing security controls with a just-in-time approach. This can range from building advisories right into workflows and playbooks for common user tasks, to redesigning problem-prone applications to more successfully guide users to make the better, more secure choice between alternatives. Verizon UK, for example, did this by first gathering data on which apps (and which processes in those apps) were most frequently involved in fraud or other security violations, and then selectively redesigning those troublesome spots to be more effective, resilient, and secure. Just-in-time security approaches give users the security help they need at the moment that they need it, rather than weeks later during a post-incident debrief.

One important example is that of defending your organization against phishing attacks (of all kinds), which becomes more urgent and compelling with each new headline about a data breach or systems intrusion. All employees have important roles to play in making this defense effective and seamless. Initial user training can create awareness;

specific job-related task training can highlight possible ways that the new user's position and duties are exposed to the threat and familiarize them with required or recommended ways of dealing with it. "Phishing tests," which you conduct that directly target members of your workforce, can reinforce specific elements of that training, while sharpening users' abilities to spot the bait and not rise to it. (These tests also generate useful metrics for you.) Adding additional risk controls, which simplify the ways that employees report phishing attempts (or vishing attempts via telephone or voicemail), both engage users as part of the solution while providing you with additional threat intelligence.

The key to keeping users engaged with risk management and risk mitigation controls is simple: Align their own, individual interests with the interests the controls are supporting, protecting, or securing. Help them see, day by day, that their work is more meaningful, more productive, and more *valued* by management and leadership, because each of them is a valued part of protecting everybody's effort. Share the integrity.

PERFORM SECURITY ASSESSMENT ACTIVITIES

Security assessment is both a broad, categorical term that encompasses many tasks, and a specific, detailed type of activity itself. These activities include the following:

- Security testing verifies that a risk mitigation or security control is functioning correctly, particularly in the face of systems and procedural updates, changes in business logic and the marketplace, and changes in the threat environment.

- Security assessments are comprehensive, structured reviews of the security and risk mitigation characteristics of a deployed system, infrastructure, application, platform, or other tested environment.

- Security audits are formal assessments, conducted by qualified and certified third-party independent auditors, which principally demonstrate that the organization's systems are in compliance with the legal, regulatory, contractual, or standards-based requirements that the audit focuses on.

Risk assessments are often updated, or completely redone, as part of security assessments. This is particularly true when the perceived changes in the external threat environment suggest that it's time to challenge the assumptions underneath the existing security and risk mitigation controls and systems.

Do not confuse these assessments with ongoing monitoring of your systems. Monitoring involves the routine inspection, review, and analysis of data that systems diagnostics, error and alarm indicators, and log files are making available to your security team, network administrators, systems administrators, and IT support staff. Monitoring is the day-to-day exercise of due diligence; it is the constant vigilance component of your security posture. Detection of a possible security incident, or a precursor, indicator, or indicator of compromise, is part of monitoring your systems and reporting what that monitoring tells you to responsible managers and leaders in the organization. Security assessment, by contrast, is intended to answer a structured set of questions that reveal whether your systems, your security posture, your procedures, and your people are doing what's required to meet or exceed your organization's overall information security and risk mitigation needs.

Depending upon the size and complexity of your organization, its activities, and its information systems, you may find that formal assessment, testing, and audit activities are planned throughout the year. Two facts drawn from current experience argue for a busy, frequent, and dynamic assessment schedule.

- The average ransomware or ransom attack on businesses causes at least half a million U.S. dollars in losses.

- It takes on average more than 200 days for organizations to detect that their systems have suffered a hostile intrusion; often, this discovery is not made until after valuable data that has been exfiltrated is being sold on the Dark Web, when it is too late to prevent the loss.

> ## ✔ Attackers Are Outspending You on *Their* Assessments!
>
> Some sources suggest that as of early 2019, organized crime spends as much as 80 percent more on cyber-attack technologies than businesses, on average, spend on cyber defense. Since the birth of the cybercrime era, attackers have been thoroughly exploiting the same common vulnerability data and using the same scanning and analysis tools that cyber defenders should be using but often fail to take advantage of.
>
> Isn't it time you stopped giving away this advantage to the attackers?

Security Assessment Workflow Management

Many organizations use a security assessment workflow process to identify, schedule, manage, and integrate all of their formal and informal testing, auditing, assessment, analysis, and reporting tasks. Additionally, organizations that adopt a vulnerability-focused security management approach also benefit from instituting workflow processes that plan, schedule, and account for activities involved in vulnerability management.

Workflow management systems, in general, eliminate or greatly reduce the risk that high-value processes might be left to ad hoc activities, taken on because they sound like "good ideas." Many times, these ad hoc collections of processes become inextricably bound up with one or two key people, and no one else in the organization—including managers and senior leaders—understands why they're worth spending time and resources on. As with any other risk reduction effort, security assessment must be managed, if it is to be accountable. Unmanaged security activities, especially assessments, can achieve proper levels of due care and due diligence only by means of blind luck. (An unmanaged exercise in accountability ought to sound like a contradiction in terms. It is.)

Your organization's security assessment workflow management ought to integrate or harmonize with several other workflow management processes (and their plans and schedules).

- IT schedules for systems upgrades, routine updates, maintenance, and decommissioning of systems elements.
- Planned migrations to new applications platforms or cloud services.
- Planned launch of new products and the IT support (such as web pages, database back-end servers, etc.) that empower them. Such launches routinely include significant public relations efforts to increase brand awareness, create interest, and stimulate demand; these also catch the attention of the attacker communities as they continually seek new targets of opportunity.
- Anticipated major changes, upgrades, or migrations, and their internal schedules for requirements analysis and design (get your security sensitivities addressed early and often!).
- Expansion of business activities to new or larger spaces and locations, requiring changes to or expansion of infrastructures, networks, access control, and security processes.

The information security team does not own all of those schedules, of course; having a greater awareness of what the business or the organization is doing and how the contexts and markets it is part of are changing should be part of your security assessment workflow thinking.

The bottom line of your security assessment workflow management process should be that you can clearly identify:

- Which vulnerabilities you've found
- Which ones the organization decided to fix
- Which systems or components have been updated to (theoretically) remediate or mitigate that vulnerability
- Which systems and components still need to be fixed
- When those fixes are scheduled (or promised) to be carried out

Many security information and event management systems use a variety of dashboards to present this workflow information in summary form; drill-down capabilities then let security operations and analysis staff, or senior management, learn more about which particular systems, network segments, or parts of the overall organization are most affected by outstanding vulnerabilities.

TIP   Your ongoing security assessments should always take the opportunity to assess the entire set of information risk controls—be they physical, logical, or administrative in nature.

Participate in Security Testing

Security testing is a set of evaluation activities that attempt to validate that the system under test meets or exceeds all (or a designated subset) of the functional and nonfunctional security requirements allocated to that system. This testing and evaluation can be driven in two basic ways.

- Requirements-driven testing starts with written or otherwise acknowledged security requirements and uses agreed-to test plans, test procedures, test cases, and analysis tasks to force the system to reveal to what degree it fulfills the requirements. This testing process uses the systems requirements specifications (SRS), or similar documentation, as the starting point from which test plans, procedures, test data, etc., are developed. Requirements are allocated to test cases (some requirements may be allocated to multiple test cases). Post-test analysis tells the users (and their managers and leaders) how well or how poorly the system meets their needs; in the case of security testing, this provides insight as to specific information security risks that the organization will face if they continue to use the system with known deficiencies demonstrated by the testing. By comparison, systems development testing, including integration and acceptance testing, is fundamentally a requirements-driven test process.

- Operational test and evaluation (OT&E) identifies a set of operationally realistic scenarios that model the use of the system, while observing its behavior to assess whether it meets security requirements or not. Scenarios may model normal business use or be geared to evaluate various stressing cases. Security testing will often use scenarios that simulate internal or external threat actors attacking the organization by means of attacking the systems under test.

Requirements-driven testing is often part of a systems development acceptance process—it measures how well the developer met the requirements as specified in their contract, statement of work, or system requirements specifications. It is usually conducted by the developer, although end users quite often are active participants in test planning, have roles within test teams, and are part of post-test analysis activities.

OT&E, by contrast, usually involves the as-deployed system, including the end-user organization's own people, the procedures that they use as part of their business processes, and their tacit knowledge about the business logic, the system, and the rest of the larger context of their work.

Black-Box, White-Box, or Gray-Box Testing

All testing involves several different sets of people, each of whom may or may not have the same breadth and depth of knowledge about the system under test. In the case of OT&E, recall that the system under test *includes* the normal crew of end users, operators, and their supervisors and managers. This gives rise to three definitions about testing (based on traditional use of these terms in the physical sciences and philosophy):

- Opaque (or black) box testing treats the system (inside the box) as something that is known only at its specified external interfaces and by its behavior that can be observed from the outside. The test team has no knowledge about the design, construction, or interior functionality of the system; they only gain knowledge by running test activities and drawing logical inferences about the interior nature of the system.
- Transparent, white-box, or crystal-box testing provides the test team with full knowledge of the system under test; its internal design and expected behavior are fully known by the test team.
- Gray box (or *partly obscured*) testing provides the test team with some, but not all, of the internal knowledge of the system under test.

When conducting most forms of OT&E, and particularly when conducting ethical penetration and other security testing activities, these monochromatic terms also refer to just how much knowledge the system under test, including its people and managers, have with regards to the planned or ongoing test activities.

- Opaque box operational testing shields knowledge of the planned or ongoing testing from the people and organizational units that are the focus of the evaluation or testing. This is sometimes called zero-knowledge testing.
- Transparent box operational testing informs the people and organizational units of the planned and ongoing testing and the existence and identities of the test team.
- Gray box operational testing provides the people who are part of the system with some, but not all, awareness of the planned and ongoing test activities.

A common example of white-box operational testing is when network or security administrators conduct probes, port scans, or network mapping activities against their own systems and networks. As a routine, periodic (but ideally not regularly scheduled) assessment activity, these can be invaluable in discovering unauthorized changes that might reveal an intruder's presence in your systems.

Look or Touch?

It may seem a fine line to draw, but there is a line between *testing* and *assessing*. Examining the log files from systems, packets that you've set sniffers to capture, or reviewing the AAA data from your access control systems is not attempting to inject data into or interact with the systems you're observing. Testing, by contrast, involves your taking actions that attempt to change the behavior of the system so that you can observe whether it behaves properly or not.

In black- or gray-box security testing, it is vital to have key processes in place and people identified within the organization who can act as "cutouts" or backstops when issues arise. Ethical penetration testers often are required to attempt to enter the physical workplace as part of test activities, but you don't want them placed under arrest if employees happen to identify them as an intruder. You also don't want other suspicious or unusual events, not caused by the security testing, to be ignored or dismissed as if they are just part of the ongoing testing.

All of these issues, and others, need to be thoroughly examined and brought under management control as a part of the test planning process.

Vulnerability Scanning

Part of your routine assessment of your systems security posture should include the same kinds of scanning techniques your attackers will use as they seek vulnerabilities to exploit against you. Vulnerability scanning should be an automated set of tasks, which generate alerts to the security team when out-of-limits conditions are detected, so as to focus your inspection and analysis to the most likely exploitable vulnerabilities. Four main categories of scanning should be part of your approach.

- Discovery scanning does not actively probe the systems it finds on your networks; it does not directly identify vulnerabilities in that regard. Discovery scanning also can (and should) generate network maps, allowing you to identify new and potentially unauthorized devices, or devices that have been physically relocated but aren't supposed to be mobile. For more than 20 years, the information security community (and the hackers) have used NMAP, an open source network mapping tool, as a mainstay of their network discovery scanning efforts.

- Note that as with any testing tool, test results can be false—either a false positive report of something that isn't a vulnerability or a false negative report that misses an actual, exploitable vulnerability. It is of course the false negatives that intruders are trying to find; you and the IT security team may consider time spent resolving false positive errors as wasted effort. As with access control, this is a tough balancing act, and there is no guaranteed safe "sweet spot" on the graph of error rates. Nessus, QualysGuard, NeXpose, and OpenVAS are some of the many choices in vulnerability scanning systems available to you, either as open source, as freeware, or as fully supported commercial products.

■ Web vulnerability scanning tries to discover exploitable flaws in your web applications, web hosting frameworks, other front-end elements, and the back-end database servers and programs that are all part of the web app itself. As with other vulnerability scanning approaches, they use databases of known vulnerabilities; quite often, the same tool you used to conduct network vulnerability scanning, such as Nessus, can also help you do web application vulnerability scanning.

■ Database vulnerability scanning looks for vulnerabilities both in the databases themselves (such as in stored queries, access control settings, and data validation logic) as well as in the web apps that connect to the database. Sql-map is an open source database vulnerability scanner that is in widespread use by white hats to examine database-centric applications for potential vulnerabilities. It does take a working knowledge of Structured Query Language (SQL), as well as the database design detailing all of its tables, relationships, keys, fields, and stored procedures, to use tools like Sql-map effectively.

✔ **Scanners Can't Protect You Against Zero-Day Exploits**

By definition, a zero-day exploit is one that hasn't been reported to a vulnerability and exposures sharing and reporting system; as a result, automated vulnerability scanners of any kind really cannot find them in your system. Other techniques, such as code inspection, penetration testing, or security-focused software testing, may help you find them before the attackers do.

Adding a Security Emphasis to OT&E

Operational testing and evaluation (OT&E) verifies or assesses that an as-built system, including its operational procedures and external interfaces, provides the capabilities that end users need to be able to accomplish everyday work (including successful handling of contingencies, special cases, and errors, so long as these were part of the use cases that drove the design and development). It is not acceptance testing—it does not check off each functional and nonfunctional requirement as satisfied or deficient; instead, OT&E is based on scenarios that have varying levels of operational realism in their flow of activities, test input data, and the conditions to be verified upon completion. OT&E evaluates, or at least provides insight about, the readiness of the people elements of the system under test as much as it does the hardware, software, data, and communications capabilities. Quite often, OT&E discovers that the tacit knowledge of the end users and operators is not effectively captured in the system specifications or operational procedures; this can also reflect that business needs and the real world have moved on from the time the requirements were specified and design and development began. OT&E events usually run in separate test environments, with some degree of isolation from production systems and data, and can run from hours to days in nonstop duration.

This same lag between what the requirements asked the systems to do and what its users know (tacitly) that they actually *do* with the system can be a mixed blessing when you look to include OT&E activities as part of security assessment and testing. It's quite likely, too, that your security team's knowledge of the threats and vulnerabilities has also continued to evolve. For everyone, OT&E activities can and should be a great learning (and knowledge management) experience.

OT&E provides a great opportunity to look for ways to operationally assess specific security concerns in a realistic setting. It is white-box testing primarily; the test team, planners, users, and security personnel are all aware of the test and have as perfect knowledge about the system and the scenarios as possible.

Ethical Penetration Testing

Ethical penetration testing involves running attacks against your own systems; you (or, more correctly, your organization) contractually spell out what tests to accomplish, what objectives to attempt to achieve, and what limitations, constraints, and special conditions apply to every aspect of the ethical penetration testing process. Emphasis must be placed on that first word—*ethical*—because the people planning, conducting, and reporting on these tests work for your organization, either as direct employees or via contracts. Their loyalties must be with your organization; they have to be your "white hats for hire" because you are trusting them with your most vital business secrets: knowledge of the vulnerabilities in your security posture.

Ethical penetration testing, therefore, depends upon the trust relationship between testers and the target organization; it depends upon the integrity of those testers, including their absolute adherence to contract terms or statements of work regarding your need to have them protect the confidentiality of all information about your systems and your processes that they gather, observe, learn, or evaluate as part of the testing. Ethical penetration testing also depends upon a legally binding written agreement that grants specific permissions to the test team to attempt to penetrate your facilities, your systems, attempt deceptions (such as social engineering), plant false data, malware, or take actions that change the state of your systems. In most jurisdictions around the world, it is illegal to perform such actions without the express consent of the owners or responsible managers of the systems in question—so this contract or agreement is all that keeps your ethical penetration testers out of jail for doing what you've asked them to do!

(This is not a good time to save some money by hiring convicted former hackers simply because they seem to know their technical stuff without some very powerful and enforceable legal assurances that your testers will turn over all copies of all data about your systems and retain absolutely nothing about them once testing and reporting is completed.)

Even with such contracts in place or detailed, written permission in hand, things can always go wrong during any kind of testing, especially during penetration testing. Such tests are attempting to do what an advanced persistent threat would do if it was attacking your systems. Test activities could inadvertently crash your systems, corrupt data, degrade throughput, or otherwise disrupt your normal business operations; if things go horribly wrong, the actions the penetration testers are taking could jump from your systems out into the wild and in effect springboard their attack onto some third party systems—whose owners or managers no doubt have *not* signed your penetration test plan and contract.

It's beyond the scope of this book to delve further into ethical penetration testing. One good resource is Chapter 6 of *Grey Hat Hacking, 5th Edition*,[2] which provides an excellent overview of penetration testing from the insider's perspective. It also makes the point that penetration testing, as with other security assessments, should confirm what is working properly as much as it should find vulnerabilities that need correction (whether you knew about them before but hadn't done anything about them yet or not).

✔ Pen Testing and Moral Hazards

We normally think of the *ethical* in ethical penetration testing as describing the pen tester's honesty, integrity, and ultimately their professional dedication to their client. Pen testing by its nature is trying to break your systems; it's trying to find exploitable

CONTINUES

[2] Allen Harper, Daniel Regalado, Ryan Linn, Stephen Sims, Branko Spasojevic, Linda Martinez, Michael Baucom, Chris Eagle, and Shon Harris (2018). *Gray Hat Hacking: The Ethical Hacker's Handbook, Fifth Edition*. McGraw-Hill Education. ISBN-13: 978-1260108415.

weaknesses, and oftentimes this involves placing your people under the microscope of the pen test. For the test results to be meaningful, you need your people to act as if everything is normal; they should respond to strange events (which might be test injects) as they have been trained to. The testing is evaluating the effectiveness of that training and how well it really equips your end users to do their bit in keeping your systems secure.

Security testing of any kind can quickly lose its value to your organization, if the workforce perceives it as nothing more than a tool to weed out workers who need to be moved to less sensitive jobs or out of the organization completely.

Security testing is a legitimate and necessary means to assess training effectiveness, people effectiveness, and systems functionality, as they all contribute to organizational security and success. These must be harmonized with keeping your workforce engaged with security and avoid having them see it as a thinly disguised reduction in staffing levels.

Assessment-Driven Training

Whether your assessment results indicate findings (of problems to fix) or good findings (celebrating the things the organization is doing well), each set of assessment results is an opportunity to improve the effectiveness of the human element in your information security system of systems. Problems or recommendations for corrective actions are typically exploited as opportunities to identify the procedural elements that could be improved, as well as possibly identifying the need for refresher training, deeper skills development training, or a more effective engagement strategy with some or all of your end users.

The good news—the good findings—are the gold that you share with your end users. It's the opportunity to share with them the "wins" over the various security threats that the total organization team has achieved; it's a time to celebrate their wins over the APTs, offer meaningful appreciation, and seek their input on other ways to improve the overall security posture. Sadly, many organizations are so focused on threat and risk avoidance that they fail to reap the additional benefits of sharing successes with the workforce that made it possible. (It does require that assessment analysts make the effort to identify these good findings in their overall assessment reports; one might argue that this is an ethical burden that these analysts share with management.)

Post-assessment debriefs to your end-user groups that were affected by or involved with the assessment can be both revealing and motivating. Questions and discussions can identify potential areas of misunderstanding about security needs, policies, and controls, or highlight opportunities to better prepare, inform, and train users in their use of these controls. Each such bit of dialogue, along with more informal conversations that you and your other team members have with end users, is an opportunity to further empower your end users as teammates; it can help them to be more intentional and more purposeful in their own security hygiene efforts.

Be sure to invite end users to post-assessment debriefs and discuss both findings and good findings with them.

Design and Validate Assessment, Test, and Audit Strategies

Projects require creating a methodology and scope for the project, and security assessment and audit efforts are no different. Management must determine the scope and targets of the assessment, including what systems, services, policies, procedures, and practices will be reviewed, and what standard, framework, or methodology the organization will select or create as the foundation of the assessment.

Commonly used industry frameworks include the following:

- NIST SP 800-53r4, "Assessing Security and Privacy Controls in Federal Information Systems and Organizations."

- NIST SP 800-115, "Technical Guide to Information Security Testing and Assessment." This is an important information source for you, as it provides an in-depth explanation of information systems testing, penetration testing, assessment, analysis, and reporting.

- ISO 18045, "Information technology – Security techniques – Methodology for IT security evaluation," and the related ISO for controls ISO/IEC 27002, "Information Technology – Security Techniques – Code of practice for information security controls."

- ISO 15408, "Information Technology – Security Techniques – Evaluation criteria for IT security," also known as the Common Criteria.

Although NIST standards may appear U.S.-centric at first glance, they are used as a reference for organizations throughout the world if there is not another national, international, or contractual standard those organizations must meet. In addition to these broad standards, specific standards like the ISA/IEC 62443 series of standards for industrial automation and control systems may be used where appropriate.

Using a standard methodology or framework allows consistency between assessments, allowing comparisons over time and between groups or divisions. In many cases, organizations will conduct their own internal assessments using industry standards as part of their security operations efforts, and by doing so, they are prepared for third-party or internal audits that are based on those standards.

In addition to choosing the standard and methodology, it is important to understand that audits can be conducted as internal audits using the organization's own staff or as external audits using third-party auditors. In addition, audits of third parties like cloud service providers can be conducted. Third-party audits most often use external auditors, rather than your organization's own staff.

Once the high-level goals and scope have been set and the assessment standard and methodology have been determined, assessors need to determine further details of what they will examine. Detailed scoping questions may include the following:

- What portions of the network and which hosts will be tested?
- Will auditing include a review of user files and logs?
- Is susceptibility of staff to social engineering being tested?
- Are confidentiality, integrity, and availability in scope?
- Are there any privacy concerns regarding the audit and data it collects?
- Will processes, standards, and documentation be reviewed?
- Are employees and adherence to standards being examined?
- Are third-party service providers, cloud vendors, or other organizations part of the assessment?

Other aspects of security are also important. A complete assessment should include answers to these questions:

- Are architectural designs documented with data flows and other details matching the published design?
- Are things designed securely from the beginning of the design process?
- Is change management practiced?
- Does a configuration management database exist?
- Are assets tracked?
- Are regular vulnerability scans, and maybe even penetration tests, conducted?
- Are policies, procedures, and standards adhered to?
- Is the organization following industry-recognized best practices?

Budget and time constraints can make it impossible to test everything, so management must determine what will be included while balancing their assessment needs against their available resources.

Once the goals, scope, and methodology have been determined, the assessment team must be selected. The team may consist of the company's own staff, or external personnel may be retained. Factors that can aid in determining which option to select can include industry regulations and requirements, budget, goals, scope, and the expertise required for the assessment.

With the team selected, a plan should be created to identify how to meet the assessment's goals in a timely manner and within the budget constraints set forth by management. With the plan in place, the assessment can be conducted. This phase should generate significant documentation on how the assessment target complies or fails to comply with expectations. Any exceptions and noncompliance must be documented. Once the assessment activities are completed, the results can be compiled and reported to management.

Upon receipt of the completed report, management can create an action plan to address the issues found during the audit. For instance, a timeframe can be set for installing missing patches and updates on hosts, or a training plan can be created to address process issues identified during the assessment.

Interpretation and Reporting of Scanning and Testing Results

Your security assessment workflow doesn't stop when the tests are done and the scans are complete. In many respects, this is when the hardest task begins: analyzing and assessing what those tests and scans have told you and trying to determine what they mean with respect to your security posture, a particular set of security or risk controls, or a potential threat.

NIST 800-115 provides succinct but potent guidance on this subject when it says that (in the context of security assessment and testing) the purpose of analysis is to identify false positives, identify and categorize vulnerabilities, and determine (if possible) the underlying cause(s) of the vulnerabilities that have been detected. Once that analysis is complete, you can then make informed judgments as to whether each vulnerability represents a risk to avoid, accept, transfer, or treat. You're also in a more informed position to recommend risk treatment approaches, some of which may need further analysis and study to determine costs, implementation strategies, and anticipated payback periods.

Root-cause analysis (RCA) is a simple but powerful technique to apply here, as you're struggling to reduce e-mountains of test data into actionable intelligence and reporting for your senior managers and leaders. RCA is essentially asking "why?" over and over again, until you've chased back through proximate causes and contributing factors to find the essential best opportunity to resolve the problem.

NIST 800-115 identifies a variety of categories of root or contributing (proximate) causes of vulnerabilities.[3]

- Insufficient patch management, such as failing to apply patches in a timely fashion or failing to apply patches to all vulnerable systems.
- Insufficient threat management, including outdated antivirus signatures, ineffective spam filtering, and firewall rulesets that do not enforce the organization's security policy.

[3] NIST 800-115, 2008, pg 58.

- Lack of security baselines, such as inconsistent security configuration settings on similar systems.
- Poor integration of security into the system development life cycle, such as missing or unsatisfied security requirements and vulnerabilities in organization-developed application code.
- Security architecture weaknesses, such as security technologies not being properly integrated into the infrastructure (e.g., poor placement, insufficient coverage, or outdated technologies), or poor placement of systems that increases their risk of compromise.
- Inadequate incident response procedures, such as delayed responses to penetration testing activities. Inadequate training, both for end users (e.g., failure to recognize social engineering and phishing attacks, deployment of rogue wireless access points) and for network and system administrators (e.g., deployment of weakly secured systems, poor security maintenance).
- Lack of security policies or policy enforcement (e.g., open ports, active services, unsecured protocols, rogue hosts, weak passwords).

As you do your analysis, characterize your conclusions into two broad sets: findings and good findings. On the one hand, findings are the recommendations you're making for corrective action; they identify problems, deficiencies, hazards, or vulnerabilities that need prompt attention. Your analysis may or may not provide enough insight to recommend a particular approach to resolving the finding, but that's not immediately important. Getting management's attention on the findings should be the priority. On the other hand, *good* findings are the positive acknowledgment that previously instituted security controls and procedures are working properly and that the investment of time, money, and people power in creating, installing, using, maintaining, and monitoring these controls is paying off. Management and leadership need to hear this as well. (Ethical penetration testers often make good use of this analysis and reporting tactic; it helps keep things in perspective.)

Remediation Validation

So, you found a risk or a vulnerability, and you decided to fix it; you've put some kind of control in place that in theory or by design is supposed to eliminate the risk or reduce it to a more acceptable level. Perhaps part of that remediation includes improving the affected component's ability to detect and generate alarms concerning precursors or indicators of possible attempts to attack the component. Common sense dictates that before turning that risk control and the new versions of the affected systems or applications over to end users, some type of regression testing and acceptance testing must be carried out. Two formal test processes, often conducted together, are used to validate that risk remediation actions do what is required without introducing other disruptions into the system. Security acceptance testing validates that the risk control effectively does what is required by the risk mitigation plan and that any residual risks are less than or equal to what was anticipated (and approved by management) in that plan. Regression testing establishes confidence that the changes to the component (the fix to the identified problem or vulnerability) did not break other required functions; the fix didn't introduce other errors into the system.

Unfortunately, it's all too common to discover that security acceptance testing (or regression testing) has identified additional items of risk or levels of residual risk that go beyond what was anticipated when the decision was made to apply the particular mitigation technique in question. At this point, the appropriate levels of management and leadership need to be engaged; it is their responsibility to decide whether to accept this changed risk posture and migrate the control into production systems for operational use or to continue to accept the risk as originally understood while "going back to the drawing board" for a better fix to the vulnerability and its root cause.

Audit Finding Remediation

In almost all cases, audit findings present your organization with a set of deficiencies that must be resolved within a specified period of time. Depending upon the nature and severity of the findings and the audit standards themselves, your business might be disbarred (blocked) from continuing to engage in those types of business operations until you can prove that the deficiencies have been remediated successfully. This might require the offending systems and procedures be subjected to a follow-on audit or third-party inspection. Less severe audit findings might allow your organization to provisionally continue to operate the affected systems but perhaps with additional temporary safeguards (such as increased monitoring and inspection) or other types of compensating controls until the remediation can be successfully demonstrated.

Naturally, this suggests that finishing the problem-solving analysis regarding each audit finding, identifying and scoping the cost-effective remediation options, and successfully implementing management's chosen risk control are key to staying in the good graces of your auditors and the regulatory authorities they represent.

As with any other risk control, your implementation planning for controls related to audit findings should contain a healthy dose of regression and acceptance testing. It should also have clearly defined decision points for management and leadership to sign off on the as-tested fix and commit to having it moved into production systems and use. The final audit findings closure report package should also contain the relevant configuration management and change control records pertaining to the systems elements affected by the finding and its remediation; don't forget to include operational procedures in this too!

Manage the Architectures: Asset Management and Configuration Control

Think back to how much work it was to discover, understand, and document the information architecture that the organization uses and then the IT architectures that support that business logic and data. Chances are that during your discovery phase, you realized that a lot of elements of both architectures could be changed or replaced by local work unit managers, group leaders, or division directors, all with very little if any coordination with any other departments. If that's the case, you and the IT director, or the chief information security officer and the CIO, may have an uphill battle on your hands as you try to convince everyone that proper stewardship does require more central, coordinated change management and control than the company is accustomed to.

The definitions of these three management processes are important to keep in mind:

- *Asset management* is the process of identifying everything that could be a key or valuable asset and adding it to an inventory system that tracks information about its acquisition costs, its direct users, its physical (or logical) location, and any relevant licensing or contract details. Asset management also includes processes to periodically verify that "tagged property" (items that have been added to the formal inventory) is still in the company's possession and has not disappeared, been lost, or been stolen. It also includes procedures to make changes to an asset's location, use, or disposition.

- *Configuration management* is the process by which the organization decides what changes in controlled systems baselines will be made, when to implement them, and the verification and acceptance needs that the change and business conditions dictate as necessary and prudent. Change management decisions are usually made by a configuration management board, and that board may require impact assessments as part of a proposed change.

- *Configuration control* is the process of regulating changes so that only authorized changes to controlled systems baselines can be made. Configuration control implements what the configuration management process decides and prevents unauthorized changes. Configuration control also provides audit capabilities that can verify that the contents of the controlled baseline in use today are in fact what they should be.

What's at Risk with Uncontrolled and Unmanaged Baselines?

As a member of your company's information security team, consider asking (or looking yourself for the answers to!) the following kinds of questions:

- How do you know when a new device, such as a computer, phone, packet sniffer, etc., has been attached to your systems or networks?

- How do you know that one of your devices has "gone missing," possibly with a lot of sensitive data on it?
- How do you know that someone has changed the operating system, updated the firmware, or updated the applications that are on your end users' systems?
- How do you know that an update or recommended set of security patches, provided by the systems vendor or your own IT department, has actually been implemented across all of the machines that need it?
- How do you know that end users have received updated training to make good use of these updated systems?

This list should remind you of the list of NIST 800-115's list of root causes of vulnerabilities that you examined in the "Interpretation and Reporting of Scanning and Testing Results" section. If you're unable to get good answers to any of these kinds of questions, from policy and procedural directives, from your managers, or from your own investigations, you may be working in an environment that is ripe for disaster.

Auditing Controlled Baselines

To be effective, any management system or process must collect and record the data used to make decisions about changes to the systems being managed; they must also include ways to audit those records against reality. For most business systems, you need to consider three different kinds of baselines: recently archived, current operational, and ongoing development. Audits against these baselines should be able to verify that:

- The recently archived baseline is available for fallback operations if that becomes necessary. If this happens, you also need to have an audited list of what changes (including security fixes) are included in it and which documented deficiencies are still part of that baseline.
- The current operational baseline has been tested and verified to contain proper implementation of the changes, including security fixes, which were designated for inclusion in it.
- The next ongoing development baseline has the set of prioritized changes and security fixes included in its work plan and verification and test plan.

Audits of configuration management and control systems should be able to verify that the requirements and design documentation, source code files, builds and control systems files, and all other data sets necessary to build, test, and deploy the baseline contain authorized content and changes only.

This was covered in more depth in Chapter 1.

OPERATE AND MAINTAIN MONITORING SYSTEMS

Traditional approaches to security process data collection involved solution-specific logging and data capture, sometimes paired with a central SIEM or other security management device. As organizational IT infrastructure and systems have become more complex, security process data has also increased in complexity and scope. As the pace of change of your systems, your business needs, and the threat environment continue to accelerate, this piecemeal approach to monitoring applications, systems, infrastructures, and endpoints is no longer workable.

NOTE Extending your security monitoring systems to include OT systems, such as smart buildings, ICS, SCADA, or IoT, has its own challenges, which are covered in the Appendix.

Information security continuous monitoring (ISCM) is a holistic strategy to improve and address security. ISCM is designed to align facets of the organization including the people, the processes, and the technologies that make up the IT infrastructure, networks, systems, core applications, and endpoints. As with any security initiative, it begins with senior management buy-in. The most effective security programs consistently have upper management support. This creates an environment where the policies, the budget, and the vision for the company all include security as a cornerstone of the company's success.

Implementing a continuous information security monitoring capability should improve your ability to do the following:

- Monitor all systems.
- Understand threats to the organization.
- Assess security controls.
- Collect, correlate, and analyze security data.
- Communicate security status.
- Actively manage risk.

A number of NIST publications, and others, provide planning and implementation guidance for bringing ISCM into action within your organization. Even if you're not in the U.S. Federal systems marketplace, you may find these provide a good place to start:

- NIST SP800-137, "Information Security Continuous Monitoring (ISCM) for Federal Information Systems and Organizations" (https://csrc.nist.gov/publications/detail/sp/800-137/final).
- Cloud Security Alliance STAR level 3 provides continuous monitoring-based certification (https://cloudsecurityalliance.org/star/continuous/).

- The FedRAMP Continuous Monitoring Strategy Guide (`https://www.fedramp.gov/assets/resources/documents/CSP_Continuous_Monitoring_Strategy_Guide.pdf`).

Most of these show a similar set of tasks that organizations must accomplish as they plan for, implement, and reap the benefits of an effective ISCM strategy.

- Define the strategy based on the organization's risk tolerance.
- Formally establish an ISCM program by selecting metrics.
- Implement the program and collect the necessary data, ideally via automation.
- Analyze and report findings, and determine the appropriate action.
- Respond to the findings based on the analysis and use standard options such as risk mitigation, risk transference, risk avoidance, or risk acceptance.
- Plan strategy and programs as needed to continually increase insight and visibility into the organization's information systems.

✔ **ISCM Is a Strategy; SIEM Is Just One Tool**

Don't confuse the overall tasks you need to get done with the marketing copy describing a tool you may want to consider using. Security incident and event management (SIEM) systems have become increasingly popular over the last few years; be cautious, however, as you consider them for a place in your overall security toolkit. Your best bet is to focus first on what jobs the organization needs to get done and how those jobs need to be managed, scheduled, and coordinated, as well as how the people doing them need to be held accountable for producing on-time, on-target results. Once you understand that flow of work and the metrics such as key performance indicators (KPIs) or key risk indicators (KRIs) that you'll manage it all with, you'll be better able to shop for vendor-supplied security information management and analysis tools.

It's prudent to approach an ISCM project in a step-by-step fashion; each step along the way, as that task list suggests, offers the opportunity for the organization to learn much more about its information systems architectures and the types of data their systems *can* generate. With experience, your strategies for applying continuous monitoring as a vital part of your overall information security posture will continue to evolve.

ICSM has become increasingly complex as organizations spread their operations into hosted and cloud environments and as they need to integrate third parties into their data-gathering processes. Successful ICSM now needs to provide methods to interconnect legacy ICSM processes with third-party systems and data feeds. Be mindful, too, that compliance regimes (and their auditors) are becoming increasingly more aware of the benefits of a sound ICSM strategy and will be looking to see how your organization is putting one into practice.

Let's take a closer look at elements of an ICSM program; you may already have many of these in place (as part of "traditional" or legacy monitoring strategies).

Events of Interest

Broadly speaking, an event of interest is something that happens (or is still ongoing) that may have a possible information systems security implication or impact to it. It does not have to be an ongoing attack in and of itself to be "of interest" to your security operations center or other IT security team members. Vulnerability assessments, threat assessments, and operational experience with your IT infrastructures, systems, and applications should help you identify the categories of events that you want to have humans (or machine learning systems) spend more time and effort analyzing to determine if they are a warning sign of an impending attack or an attack in progress. Root-cause analysis should help you track back to the triggering events that may lead to a series of other events that culminate in the event of interest that you want to be alarmed about. (Recall that by definition an event *changes* something in your system.)

Let's start with the three broad categories of events or indicators that you'll need to deal with. Think of each as a step in a triage process: the further along this list you go, the greater the likelihood that your systems are in fact under attack and that you need to take immediate action.

First, let's look at precursor events. A *precursor* is a signal or observable characteristic of the occurrence of an event; the event itself is not an attack but might indicate that an attack could happen in the future. Let's look at a few common examples to illustrate this concept:

- Server or other logs that indicate a vulnerability scanner has been used against a system

- An announcement of a newly found vulnerability by a systems or applications vendor, an information security service, or a reputable vulnerabilities and exploits reporting service that might relate to your systems or platforms

- Media coverage of events that put your organization's reputation at risk (deservedly or not)

- Email, phone calls, or postal mail threatening an attack on your organization, your systems, your staff, or those doing business with you

- Increasingly hostile or angry content in social media postings regarding customer service failures by your company
- Anonymous complaints in employee-facing suggestion boxes, ombudsman communications channels, or even graffiti in the restrooms or lounge areas

Genuine precursors—ones that give you actionable intelligence—are quite rare. They are often akin to the "travel security advisory codes" used by many national governments. They rarely provide enough insight that something specific is about to take place. The best you can do when you see such potential precursors is to pay closer attention to your indicators and warnings systems, perhaps by opening up the filters a bit more. In doing so, you're willing to accept more false positive alarms and spend more time and effort to assess them as the price to pay that a false negative (a genuine attack spoofing its way into your systems) is overlooked. You might also consider altering your security posture in ways that might increase protection for critical systems, perhaps at the cost of reduced throughput due to additional access control processing.

An *indicator* is a sign, signal, or observable characteristic of the occurrence of an event that an information security incident may have occurred or may be occurring right now. Common examples of indicators include:

- Network intrusion detectors generate an alert when input buffer overflows might indicate attempts to inject SQL or other script commands into a web page or database server.
- Antivirus software detects that a device, such as an endpoint or removable media, has a suspected infection on it.
- Systems administrators, or automated search tools, notice filenames containing unusual or unprintable characters in them.
- Access control systems notice a device attempting to connect, which does not have required software or malware definition updates applied to it.
- A host or an endpoint device does an unplanned restart.
- A new or unmanaged host or endpoint attempts to join the network.
- A host or an endpoint device notices a change to a configuration-controlled element in its baseline configuration.
- An applications platform logs multiple failed login attempts, seemingly from an unfamiliar system or IP address.
- Email systems and administrators notice an increase in the number of bounced, refused, or quarantined emails with suspicious content or ones with unknown addressees.
- Unusual deviations in network traffic flows or systems loading are observed.

One type of indicator worth special attention is called an indicator of compromise (IOC), which is an observable artifact with high confidence signals that an information system has been compromised or is in the process of being compromised. Such artifacts might include recognizable malware signatures, attempts to access IP addresses or URLs known or suspected to be of hostile or compromising intent, or domain names associated with known or suspected botnet control servers. The information security community is working to standardize the format and structure of IOC information to aid in rapid dissemination and automated use by security systems.

As you'll see in Chapter 4, the fact that detection is a war of numbers is both a blessing and a curse; in many cases, even the first few "low and slow" steps in an attack may create dozens or hundreds of indicators, each of which may, if you're lucky, contain information that correlates them all into a suspicious pattern. Of course, you're probably dealing with millions of events to correlate, assess, screen, filter, and dig through to find those few needles in that field of haystacks.

There's strong value in also characterizing events of interest in terms of whether they are anomalies, intrusions, unauthorized changes, or event types you are doing extra monitoring of to meet compliance needs. Let's take a closer look.

Anomalies

In general terms, an anomaly is any event that is out of the ordinary, irregular, or not quite normal. Endpoint systems that freeze for a few seconds and then seem to come back to life with no harm done are anomalies. Timeouts, or time synchronization mismatches between devices on your network, may also be anomalies. Failures of disk drives to respond correctly to read, write, or positioning commands may be indicators of incipient hardware failures, or of contention for that device from multiple process threads. In short, until you know something odd has occurred and that its "oddness" has passed your filter and you've decided it's worth investigating, you probably won't know the anomaly occurred or whether it was significant (as an event of interest) until you gather up all of the log data for the affected systems and analyze it.

There are some anomalous events that ought to be considered as suspicious, perhaps even triggering immediate alarms to security analysts and watch officers. Unscheduled systems reboots or restarts, or re-initializations of modems, routers, switches, or servers, usually indicate either that there's an unmanaged software or firmware update process going on, that a hung application has tempted a user into a reboot as a workaround, or that an intruder is trying to cover their tracks. It's not that our systems are so bug-free that they never hang, never need a user-initiated reboot, or never crash and restart themselves; it's that each time this happens, your security monitoring systems should know about it in a timely manner, and if conditions warrant, send up an alarm to your human security analysts.

Intrusions

Intrusions occur because something happens that allows an intruder to bypass either the access control systems you've put in place or your expectations for how well those systems are defending you against an intrusion. Let's recap some of the ways intruders can gain access to your systems:

- You've left the factory default usernames and passwords set on anything, even guest access.
- Your network communications devices, especially wireless access points, are physically accessible and can be manually triggered to install a bogus firmware update.
- Your chosen identity authentication approaches have exploitable vulnerabilities in them.
- A user's login credentials have been compromised, exposed, intercepted, or copied.
- An otherwise trustworthy employee becomes a disgruntled employee or has been coerced or incentivized to betray that trust.
- A social engineering attacker discovers sufficient information to be able to impersonate a legitimate user.
- An endpoint device has been lost, stolen, or otherwise left untended long enough for attackers to crack its contents and gain access information.
- An attacker can find or access an endpoint device which an authorized user has left logged in, even if only for a few minutes.
- Keystroke loggers or other endpoint surveillance technologies permit an attacker to illicitly copy a legitimate user's access credentials.
- And so on.

Other chapters in this book offer ways to harden these entry points into your systems; when those hardening techniques fail, and they will, what do you do to detect an intrusion while it is taking place, rather than waiting until a third party (such as law enforcement) informs you that you've been the victim of a data breach?

Your organization's security needs should dictate how strenuously you need to work to detect intrusions (which by definition are an unauthorized and unacceptable entry by a subject, in access control terms, into any aspect of your systems); detection and response will be covered in Chapter 4.

Unauthorized Changes

Configuration management and configuration control must be a high priority for your organization. Let's face it: If your organization does not use any type of formalized configuration management and change control, it's difficult if not impossible to spot a change to your systems, hardware, networks, applications, or data in the first place, much less decide that it is an unauthorized change.

Security policy is your next line of defense: administrative policies should establish acceptable use; set limits or establish procedures for controlling user-provided software, data, device, and infrastructure use; and establish programs to monitor and ensure compliance.

Automated and semi-automated tools and utilities can help significantly in detecting and isolating unauthorized changes:

- Many operating systems and commercial software products now use digital signatures on individual files and provide auditing tools that can verify that all the required files for a specific version have been installed.

- Software blocked listing, typically done with antimalware systems, can identify known or suspected malicious code, code fragments, or associated files.

- Software allowed listing tools can block installation of any application not on the accepted, approved lists.

- Network scanning and mapping can find devices that may not belong, have been moved to a different location in the system, or have been modified from previous known good configurations.

It may be that some or all of your information systems elements are not under effective configuration management and control (or may even be operating with minimal access control protections). This can happen during mergers and acquisitions or when acquiring or setting up interfaces with special-purpose (but perhaps outdated) systems. Techniques and approaches covered in other chapters, notably Chapter 1, should be considered as input to your plan to bring such potentially hazardous systems under control and then into your overall IT architecture.

Compliance Monitoring Events

Two types of events can be considered as compliance monitoring events by their nature: those that directly trace to a compliance standard and thus need to be accounted for when they occur, and events artificially triggered (that is, not as part of routine business operations nor as part of a hostile intrusion) as part of compliance demonstrations.

Many compliance standards and regulations are becoming much more specific in terms of the types of events that have to be logged, analyzed, and reported on as part of their compliance regime. This has led to the development of a growing number of systems and services that provide what is sometimes called *real-time compliance monitoring*. These typically use a data mart or data warehouse infrastructure into which all relevant systems, applications, and device logs are updated in real time or near real time. Analysis tools, including but not limited to machine learning tools, examine this data to detect whether events have occurred that exceed predefined limits or constraint conditions.

Many of these systems try to bridge the conceptual gap between externally imposed compliance regimes (imposed by law, regulation, contract, or standards) and the detail-level physical, logical, and administrative implementation of those compliance requirements. Quite often, organizations have found that more senior, policy-focused individuals are responsible for translating contracts, standards, or regulations into organizational administrative plans, programs, and policies, while more technically focused IT experts are implementing controls and monitoring their use.

The other type of compliance events might be seen when compliance standards require the use of deliberately crafted events, data injects, or other activities as part of verification and validation that the system meets the compliance requirements. Two types of these you might encounter are synthetic transactions and real user monitoring events.

Synthetic Transactions

Monitoring frequently needs to involve more than simple log reviews and analysis to provide a comprehensive view of infrastructure and systems. The ability to determine whether a system or application is responding properly to actual transactions, regardless of whether they are simulated or performed by real users, is an important part of a monitoring infrastructure. Understanding how a system or application performs and how that performance impacts users as well as underlying infrastructure components is critical to management of systems for organizations that want a view that goes deeper than whether their systems are up or down or under a high or low load. Two major types of transaction monitoring are performed to do this: synthetic transactions and real user monitoring.

Synthetic transactions are actions run against monitored objects to see how the system responds. The transaction may emulate a client connecting to a website and submitting a form or viewing the catalog of items on a web page, which pulls the information from a database. Synthetic transactions can confirm the system is working as expected and that alerts and monitoring are functioning properly.

Synthetic transactions are commonly used with databases, websites, and applications. They can be automated, which reduces the workload carried by administrators. For instance, synthetic transactions can ensure that the web servers are working properly and responding to client requests. If an error is returned during the transaction, an alert can be generated that notifies responsible personnel. Therefore, instead of a customer complaining that the site is down, IT can proactively respond to the alert and remedy the issue, while impacting fewer customers. Synthetic transactions can also measure response times to issues, allowing staff to proactively respond and remediate slowdowns or mimic user behavior when evaluating newly deployed services, prior to deploying the service to production.

Synthetic transactions can be used for several functions, including the following:

- **Application monitoring:** Is an application responsive, and does it respond to queries and input as expected?

- **Service monitoring:** Is a selected service responding to requests in a timely manner, such as a website or file server?

- **Database monitoring:** Are back-end databases online and responsive?

- **TCP port monitoring:** Are the expected ports for an application or service open, listening, and accepting connections?

- **Network services:** Are the DNS and DHCP servers responding to queries? Is the domain controller authenticating users?

Real User Monitoring

Real user monitoring (RUM) is another method to monitor the environment. Instead of creating automated transactions and interactions with an application, the developer or analyst monitors actual users interacting with the application, gathering information based on actual user activity. Real user monitoring is superior to synthetic transactions when actual user activity is desired. Real people will interact with an application in a variety of ways that synthetic transactions cannot emulate because real user interactions are harder to anticipate. However, RUM can also generate much more information for analysis, much of which is spurious since it will not be specifically targeted at what the monitoring process is intended to review. This can slow down the analysis process or make it difficult to isolate the cause of performance problems or other issues. In addition, RUM can be a source of privacy concerns because of the collection of user data that may include personally identifiable information, usage patterns, or other details.

Synthetic transactions can emulate certain behaviors on a scheduled basis, including actions that a real user may not perform regularly or predictably. If a rarely used element of an application needs testing and observation, a synthetic transaction is an excellent option, whereas the developer or analyst may have to wait for an extended amount of time to view the transaction when using RUM.

By using a blend of synthetic transactions and real user monitoring, the effectiveness of an organization's testing and monitoring strategy can be significantly improved. Downtime can be reduced because staff is alerted more quickly when issues arise. Application availability can be monitored around the clock without human intervention. Compliance with service level agreements can also be accurately determined. The benefits of using both types of monitoring merits consideration.

Logging

Logs are generated by most systems, devices, applications, and other elements of an organization's infrastructure. They can be used to track changes, actions taken by users, service states and performance, and a host of other purposes. These events can indicate security issues and highlight the effectiveness of security controls that are in place. Assessments and audits rely on log artifacts to provide data about past events and changes and to indicate whether there are ongoing security issues, misconfigurations, or abuse issues. Security control testing also relies on logs including those from security devices and security management systems.

The wide variety of logs, as well as the volume of log entries that can be generated by even a simple infrastructure, means that logs can be challenging to manage. Logs can capture a significant amount of information and can quickly become overwhelming in volume. They should be configured with industry best practices in mind, including implementing centralized collection, validation using hashing tools, and automated analysis of logs. Distinct log aggregation systems provide a secure second copy, while allowing centralization and analysis. In many organizations, a properly configured security information and event management (SIEM) system is particularly useful as part of both assessment and audit processes and can help make assessment efforts easier by allowing reporting and searches. Even when centralized logging and log management systems are deployed, security practitioners must strike a balance between capturing useful information and capturing too much information.

✔ CIANA+PS Applies to Log Files Too!

Maintaining log integrity is a critical part of an organization's logging practice. If logs cannot be trusted, then auditing, incident response, and even day-to-day operations are all at risk since log data is often used in each of those tasks. Thus, organizations need to assess the integrity of their logs as well as their existence, content, and relevance to their purpose.

Logs should have proper permissions set on them, they should be hashed to ensure that they are not changed, a secure copy should be available in a separate secure location if the logs are important or require a high level of integrity, and of course any changes that impact the logs themselves should be logged!

Assessing log integrity involves validating that the logs are being properly captured, that they cannot be changed by unauthorized individuals or accounts, and that changes to the logs are properly recorded and alerted on as appropriate. This means that auditors and security assessors cannot simply stop when they see a log file that contains the information they expect it to. Instead, technical and administrative procedures around the logs themselves need to be validated as part of a complete assessment process.

Assessments and audits need to look at more than just whether logs are captured and their content. In fact, assessments that consider log reviews look at items including the following:

- What logs are captured?
- How is log integrity ensured? Are log entries hashed and validated?
- Are the systems and applications that generate logs properly configured?
- Do logging systems use a centralized time synchronization service?
- How long are logs retained for, and does that retention time period meet legal, business, or contractual requirements?
- How are the logs reviewed, and by whom?
- Is automated reporting or alarming set up and effective?
- Is there ongoing evidence of active log review, such as a sign-off process?
- Are logs rotated or destroyed on a regular basis?
- Who has access to logs?
- Do logs contain sensitive information such as passwords, keys, or data that should not be exposed via logs to avoid data leakage?

Policies and procedures for log management should be documented and aligned to standards. ISO 27001 and ISO27002 both provide basic guidance on logging, and NIST provides SP 800-92, "Guide to Computer Security Log Management." Since logging is driven by business needs, infrastructure and system design, and the organization's functional and security requirements, specific organizational practices and standards need to be created and their implementation regularly assessed.

Source Systems

On the one hand, nearly every device, software package, application, and platform or service that is part of your systems should be considered as a data source for your continuous monitoring and analysis efforts. But without some logical structure or sense of purpose to your gathering of sources, you're liable to drown in petabytes of data and not learn much in the process.

On the other hand, it might be tempting to argue that you should use a prioritized approach, starting with your highest-valued information assets or your highest-priority business processes and the platforms, systems, and other elements that support them. Note the danger in such a viewpoint: It assumes that your attackers will use your most important "crown jewels" of your systems as their entry points and the places from which they'll execute their attack. In many respects, you have to face this as an "all-risks" approach, as insurance underwriters refer to it.

There is some benefit in applying a purposeful or intentional perspective as you look at your laundry list of possible data sources. If you're trying to define an "operational normal" and establish a security baseline for anomaly detection, for example, you might need to tailor what you log on which devices or systems differently, than if you're trying to look at dealing with specific categories of risk events.

No matter how you look at it, you're talking large volumes of data, which require smart filtering and analysis tools to help you make sense of it quickly enough to make risk containment decisions before it's too late.

✔ Data Collection and Processing: Probably Cheaper Than Disaster Recovery

In some IT circles, people are known to say that disk space is cheap as a way of saying that the alternatives tend to be far, far more costly in the long run. A Dell EMC survey, reported by Johnny Wu at Searchdatabackup.techtarget.com in March 2019, suggests that the average impact to businesses of 20 hours of downtime can exceed half a million dollars; losing 2.13 TB of data can double that average impact. Compare that with the budget you'd need to capture *all* log and event data and have sufficiently high-throughput analysis capabilities to make sense of it in near real time, and you've got the makings of your business case argument for greater IT security investment.

This is also part of the argument for moving to SIEM and SOAR (security orchestration, automation, and response) systems or services. These can provide smarter ways to gather operational security insights—and detect security incidents more quickly—than the traditional filtering-the-logs approach could ever support.

For *all* data sources, be they hardware, software, or firmware, part of your infrastructure or a guest endpoint, you should strongly consider making current health and status data something that you request, capture, and log. This data would nominally reflect the current identity and version of the hardware, software, and firmware, showing in particular the latest (or a complete list) of the patches applied. It would include antimalware, access control rule sets, or other security-specific dataset versions and update histories. Get this data every time a subject connects to your systems; consider turning on health and status-related access control features like quarantines or remediation servers, to prevent out-of-date and out-of-touch endpoints from possibly contaminating your infrastructures. And of course, log everything about such accesses!

In doing this, and in routinely checking on this health information periodically throughout the day, you're looking for any indicators of compromise that signal that one of your otherwise trusted subjects has been possibly corrupted by malware.

Depending upon the security needs of your organization, you may need to approach the continuous monitoring, log data analysis, and reporting set of problems with the same sensibilities you might apply to investigating an incident or crime scene. The data you can gather from an incident or crime scene is *dirty*; it is incomplete, or it may have been inadvertently or deliberately corrupted by people and events at the scene or by first responders. So, you focus first on what looks to be a known signature of an event of interest and then look for multiple pieces of corroborating evidence. Your strongest corroboration comes from evidence gathered by dissimilar processes or from different systems (or elements of the incident scene); thus, it's got to walk, talk, and swim like a duck, rather than just be seen to walk by three different people, for you to sound the alarm that a duck has intruded into your systems.

Let's look at the obvious lists in a bit more detail; note that a given device or software element may fit in more than one category.

On-Premises Servers and Services

Almost all server systems available today have a significant number of logging features built in, both as troubleshooting aids and as part of providing accountability for access control and other security features. Services are engaged by users via applications (such as Windows Explorer or their web browser), which use applications program interfaces or systems interfaces to make service requests to the operating system and server routines; more often than not, these require a temporary elevation of privilege for that execution thread. All of those transactions—requests, acknowledge or rejection, service performance, completion, or error conditions encountered—can generate log entries; many can be set to generate other events that route alarm signals to designated process IDs or other destinations. Key logs to look for include the following:

- The server security log will show successful and unsuccessful logins, attempts to elevate privilege, and connection requests to resources. Depending upon the operating system and server system in use and your own customization of it, this log may also keep track of attempts to open, close, write, delete, or modify the metadata associated with files.

- The access control system logs should be considered as a "mother lode" of rich and valuable data.

- Systems logs on each server keep track of device-level issues, such as requests, errors, or failures encountered in attempting to mount or dismount removable, fixed, or virtual storage volumes. Operating system shutdown and restart requests,

OS-level updates, hibernation, and even processor power level settings are reflected here.

- Directory services, including workstation, endpoint, and system-level directory services (such as Microsoft Active Directory or other X.500 directory services), can be tailored to log virtually everything associated with entities known to these systems as they attempt to access other entities.

- Single sign-on (SSO) activities should be fully logged and included on your shopping lists as a quality data source.

- File replication services, journaling services, and other storage subsystems services log or journal a significant amount of information. This is done to greatly enhance the survivability of data in the event of device-level, server, or application problems (it's what makes NTFS or EFS a far more reliable and better-performing file system than good old FAT, for example). These logs and journals are great sources of data when hunting for a possible exfiltration in the works.

- DNS servers can provide extensive logs of all attempts to resolve names, IP addresses, flush or update caches, and the like.

- Virtual machine managers or hypervisors should be logging the creation, modification, activation, and termination of VMs.

- DHCP services should log when new leases are issued or expire or devices connect or disconnect.

- Print servers should log jobs queued, their sources, destination printer, and completion or error status of each job.

- Fax servers (yes, many business still use fax traffic, even if over the Internet) should log all traffic in and out.

- Smart copiers and scanners should log usage, user IDs, and destination files if applicable.

- Email servers should log connection requests, spoof attempts or other junk mail filtered at the server, attempts to violate quality or security settings (such as maximum attachment sizes), and the use of keyword-triggered services such as encryption of outbound traffic or restriction of traffic based on keywords in the header or message body.

Applications and Platforms

What started out decades ago as a great troubleshooting and diagnostic capability has come of age, as most applications programs and integrated platform solutions provide extensive logging features as part of ensuring auditable security for the apps themselves and for user data stored by or managed by the app. Many apps and platforms also do their own localized versions of access control and accounting, which supports change management and control, advanced collaboration features such as co-authoring and revision management, and of course security auditing and control. Some things to look for include the following:

- User-level data, such as profiles, can and should be logged, as changes may reveal that a legitimate user's identity has been spoofed or pirated.

- Document-, file-, or dataset-level logging can reveal patterns of access that might be part of an exfiltration, a covert path, or other unauthorized access.

- Integrated applications platforms, particularly ones built around a core database engine, often have their own built-in features for defining user identities, assigning and managing identity-based privileges, and accounting for access attempts, successes, and failures.

- Application crash logs might reveal attacks against the application.

- Other application log data can highlight abnormal patterns of applications usage.

- Application-managed data backup, recovery, and restoration should all be creating log events.

External Servers and Services

Your organization may have migrated or originally hosted much of its business logic in cloud-hosted solutions, using a variety of cloud service models. Unless these have been done "on the cheap," there should be extensive event logging information available about these services, the identities of subjects (users or processes) making access attempts to them, and other information. If you're using an integrated security continuous monitoring (ISCM) product or system, you should explore how to best automate the transfer of such data from your cloud systems provider into your ISCM system (which, for many good reasons based on reliability, availability, and integrity, may very well be cloud hosted itself).

Other services that might provide rich security data sources and logs, nominally external to your in-house infrastructure and not directly owned or managed by your team, might include:

- IDaaS and other identity management solutions

- Services provided via federated access arrangements

- Data movement (upload and download, replication, etc.) across an external interface to such service providers

- Hot, warm, and cold backup site service providers

- Off-site data archiving services

Workstations and Endpoints

All endpoint devices that are allowed to have any type of access arrangements into your systems should, by definition and by policy, be considered as part of your systems; thus, they should be subject to some degree of your security management, supervision, and control. You'll look at endpoint security in greater detail in Chapter 7, and endpoint device access control will be addressed in Chapter 6. That said, consider gathering up the following kinds of data from each endpoint every time it connects:

- Health check data (current levels of patches, malware definitions, rule sets, etc., as appropriate); require this data at initial connect and query it throughout their connected day, and use automated tools to detect changes that might be worthy of an alarm.

- Local account login and logoff.

- Device-level reboots.

- Application installations or updates.

- Security events, such as elevation of user privilege or invoking trusted superuser or administrative IDs.

- File services events, such as creation, deletion, movement, and replication.

- USB or removable storage mounts, dismounts, and use.

- Other USB device type connections.

- Bluetooth, Wi-Fi, or other connection-related events.

- Applications use, modification, and diagnostics logs.

- IP address associated with the device.

- Changes to roaming, user, or device-level profiles.

Network Infrastructure Devices

All of the modems, routers, switches, gateways, firewalls, IDS or IPS, and other network security devices and systems that make up your networks and communications infrastructures should be as smart as possible and should be logging what happens to them and through them.

- Administrator logins and logouts to the device itself

- Reboots, resets, loss of power or similar events

- Connections established to other services (such as DHCP and DNS)

- Health check information

- Data transfers in and out of the device

- Configuration changes of any kind

- Attempts to access restricted domains, IP addresses, applications, or services

- Attempts to circumvent expired certificates

- Dial-in connection attempts from caller IDs outside of your normal, accepted ranges (that is, if you still have real POTS-supported dial-in connections available!)

Some of these classes of data, and others not in this list, may be found in the services and servers that provide the support (such as managing certificates, identities, or encryption services).

IoT Devices

The first generations of Internet of Things (IoT) devices have not been known to have much in the way of security features, even to the level of an ability to change the factory-default username, password, or IP address. If your company is allowing such "artificial stupidity" to connect to your systems, this could be a significant hazard and is worthy of extra effort to control the risks these could be exposing the organization to. (See Chapter 7 and the Appendix for more information.)

If your IoT or other robot devices can provide any of the types of security-related log or event information such as what you'd require for other types of endpoints, by all means include them as data sources for analysis and monitoring.

Legal and Regulatory Concerns

Chapter 1 highlighted many of the significant changes in international and national laws that dictate information security requirements upon organizations that operate within their jurisdictions. And for all but the most local of organizations, most businesses and nonprofits find themselves operating within multiple jurisdictions: Their actions and information, as well as their customers and suppliers, cross multiple frontiers. As a result, you may find that multiple sets of laws and regulations establish constraints on your ability to monitor your information systems, collect specific information on user activities, and share that data (and with whom) as you store, collate, analyze, and assess it. There is often a sense of damned-if-you-do to all of this: You may violate a compliance requirement if you do collect and exploit such information in the pursuit of better systems security, but you may violate another constraint if you do not.

Almost all audit processes require that critical findings be supported by an audit trail that supports the pedigree (or life history) of each piece of information that is pertinent to that finding. This requires that data cleansing efforts, for example, cannot lose sight of the original form of the data, errors and omissions included, as it was originally introduced into your systems (and from whence it came). Auditors must be able to walk back each step in the data processing, transformation, use, and cleansing processes that have seen, touched, or modified that data. In short, audit standards dictate very much the same type of chain of custody of information—of all kinds—that forensics investigations require.

From one point of view, the information systems industries and their customers have brought this upon themselves. They've produced and use systems that roughly two out of three senior leaders and managers do not trust, according to surveys in 2016 by CapGemini and EMC, and in 2018 by KPMG International; they produce systems that seemingly cannot keep private data private nor prevent intruders from enjoying nearly seven months of undetected freedom to explore, exploit, exfiltrate, and sometimes destructively disrupt businesses that depend upon them. At the same time, organized crime continues to increase its use of cybercrime to pursue its various agendas.

Governments and regulators, insurers and financial services providers, and shareholders have responded to these many threats by imposing increasingly stringent compliance regimes upon public and private organizations and their use of information systems. Yet seemingly across the board, senior leadership and management in many businesses consider that the fines imposed by regulators or the courts are just another risk of doing business; their costs are passed on to customers, shareholders, or perhaps to workers if the company must downsize. Regulators and legislatures are beginning to say "enough is enough," and we are seeing increasing efforts by these officials to respond to data breaches and information security incidents by imposing penalties and jail time on the highest-ranking individual decision-makers found to be negligent in their duties of due care and due diligence.

It's beyond the scope of this book to attempt to summarize the many legal and regulatory regimes you might need to be familiar with. Your organization's operating locations and where your customers, partners, and suppliers are will also make the legal compliance picture more complex. Translating the legal, regulatory, and public policy complexities into organizational policies takes some considerable education and expertise, along with sound legal advice. As the on-scene information security practitioner, be sure to ask the organization's legal and compliance officers what compliance, regulatory, or other limitations and requirements constrain or limit your ability to monitor, assess, and report on information security-related events of interest affecting your systems. Let the organization's attorneys and compliance officers or experts chart your course through this minefield for you.

ANALYZE MONITORING RESULTS

Ongoing and continuous monitoring should be seen as fulfilling two very important roles. First, it's part of your real-time systems security alarm system; the combination of controls, filters, and reporting processes are providing your on-shift watch standers in your security or network operations centers with tipoffs to possible events of interest. These positive signals (that is, an alarm condition has been detected) may be true indications of a security incident or false positives; either way, they need analytic and investigative attention to determine what type of response if any is required.

The second function that the analysis of monitoring data should fulfill is the hunt for the false negative—the events in which an intruder spoofed your systems with falsified credentials or found an exploitable vulnerability in your access control system's logic and control settings.

In either case, analysis of monitoring data can provide important insight into potential vulnerabilities within your systems. And it all starts with knowing your baselines. The term *baseline* can refer to any of three different concepts when we use it in an IT or information security context.

An architectural baseline is an inventory or configuration management list of all of the subsystems, elements, procedures, or components that make up a particular system. From most abstract to most detailed, these are:

- An information architecture baseline captures what organizations need to know in order to get work done, as they use, create, and share information.

- An information systems architecture baseline provides the "how-to" of an information architecture by describing the workflows and processes used by an organization and its people in terms of the information they know, learn, and create.

- An information technology architecture baseline identifies all the hardware, software, firmware, communications and networks, and procedural elements that comprise a system, detailed to the specific version, update, patch, and other configuration-controlled changes that have been applied to it. This baseline description also should include the physical and logical location or deployment details about each element.

We typically see asset-based risk management needing to focus on the IT architecture as the foundational level; but even an asset purist has to link each asset back up with the organizational priorities and objectives, and these are often captured in process-oriented or outcomes-oriented terms—which the other two baselines capture and make meaningful.

Chapter 1 examined the tailored application of a standard, or a set of required or desired performance characteristics, as a *baseline*. As a subset of baselines, security baselines express the minimum set of security controls necessary to safeguard the information security requirements and properties for a particular configuration. Scoping guidance is often published as part of a baseline, defining the range of deviation from the baseline that is acceptable for a particular baseline. This scoping guidance should interact with configuration management and control processes to ensure that the directed set of security performance characteristics are in fact properly installed and configured in the physical, logical, and administrative controls that support them.

The third use of baselines in information security contexts refers to a behavioral baseline, which combines a description of a required set of activities with the observable characteristics that the supporting systems should demonstrate; these characteristics act as confirmation that the system is performing the required activities correctly. Many times, these are expressed as confirmation-based checklists: You prepare to land an aircraft by following a checklist that dictates flap, engine power, landing gear, landing lights, and other aircraft configuration settings, and you verify readiness to land by checking the indicators associated with each of these devices (and many more).

The next section will explore how you can put these concepts to work to enhance your information security posture.

Security Baselines and Anomalies

As you saw in the "Source Systems" section, you've got many rich veins of data to mine that can give you near-real time descriptions of the behavior of your IT systems and infrastructures. Assuming these IT systems and infrastructures are properly described, documented, and under effective configuration management and configuration control, you're ready for the next step: identifying the *desired* baseline behavior sets and gathering the measurements and signatures data that your systems throw off when they're acting properly within a given behavioral baseline.

Let's use as an illustration a hypothetical industrial process control environment, such as a natural gas-fired electric power generation and distribution system. Furthermore, let's look at just one critical subsystem in that environment: the real-time pricing system that networks with many different electric power wholesale distributor networks, using a bid-ask-sell system (as any commodity exchange does) to determine how much electricity to generate and sell to which distributor. This process is the real business backbone of national and regional electric power grids, such as the North American or European grid system.

NOTE   Enron's manipulation of demand and pricing information, via the network of real-time bid-ask-sell systems used by public utilities across North America, led to the brownouts and rolling blackouts that affected customers in California in 2000 and 2001. Nothing went wrong with the power generation and distribution systems—just the marketplaces that bought and sold power in bulk. Accidents of data configuration caused a similar cascade of brownouts in Australia in the mid-1990s; it is rumored that Russian interference caused similar problems for Estonia in 2007.

This bid-ask-buy system might be modeled as having the following major behavioral conditions or states:

- Development, test, and pre-deployment
- Transition from pre-deployment to operational use
- Normal demand cycles, based on North American seasonal weather patterns
- Disrupted demand cycles, due to major storms
- Distribution network failures (weather, accidents, or other events that disrupt high voltage bulk power distribution)
- Emergency shutdown of generating stations or key power distribution substations

This list isn't comprehensive. Many permutations exist for various circumstances.

Define the Behavioral Baselines

For each of those behavioral sets, analysts who know the systems inside and out need to go through the architectures and identify what they would expect to see in observable terms for key elements of the system. The bulk price of electricity (dollars per megawatt-hour [mwh] in North America, Euros per mwh in Europe) would be a gross level indicator of how the overall system is behaving, but it's not fine-grained enough to tell you why the system is misbehaving. For each of those behavioral states (and many, many more), picture a set of "test points" that you could clip a logic probe, a protocol sniffer, or a special-purpose diagnostic indicator to, and make lots of measurements over time. If the system behaved "normally" while you gathered all of those measurements, then you have a behavioral fingerprint of the system for that mode of operational use.

Behavioral baselines can be tightly localized in scope, such as at the individual customer or individual end user level. Attribute-based access control, for example, is based on the premise that an organization can sufficiently characterize the work style, movement patterns, and other behaviors of its chief financial officer, as a way of protecting itself from that CFO being a target of a whaling attack.

Your systems, the tools you're using, and your ability to manage and exploit all of this data will shape your strategies and implementation choices. It's beyond our scope here to go into much detail about this, save to say that *something* has got to merge all of that data, each stream of which is probably in a different format, together into a useful data mart or data warehouse that you can mine and analyze.

You'll no doubt want to apply various filters, data smoothing and cleansing, and verification tools, as you preprocess this data. Be mindful of the fact that you're dealing with primary source evidence as you do this; protect that audit trail or the chain of custody as you carry out these manipulations, and preserve your ability to walk back and show who authorized and performed which data transformations where, when, and why. Successful detection and response to an incident, and survival of the post-response litigation that might follow, may depend upon this bit of pedigree protection.

Finding the Anomalies

Think about your systems environments, within your organization, as they exist right now, today. Some obvious candidates for anomalies to look for in your data should come to mind.

- Internal IP addresses, user IDs, and devices (MAC addresses or subject IDs) that aren't predefined and known to your access control moat dragons

- Large, inexplicable swings in performance metrics, such as traffic levels on internal network segments, your external connections, or the rate of help-desk ticket creation or user complaints

- Multiple failures by antimalware systems to work effectively or need intervention to restart

- Multiple attempts to log into accounts (perhaps a "replay attack" being conducted)

- Logins outside of normal business hours

- Dramatic changes in outbound traffic, especially from database, mail, or multimedia servers (Are you being exfiltrated, perhaps?)

- Numerous hits on your firewalls from countries, regions, or other address ranges that are outside of your normal business patterns

- Too many attempts by an internal workstation to connect to internal hosts, or external services, in ways that exceed "normal" expectations

Some of those anomalies might be useful precursors to pay attention to; others, such as changes in traffic and loading, are probably high-priority emergency alarm signals!

Start with that list; peel that behavioral onion down further, layer by layer, and identify other possible anomalies to look for.

Do You Allow or Block Behaviors?

By its very name, *behavioral anomaly detection* suggests that you can define what "business normal" (or *acceptable*) is and is not. Too tightly defined and you risk your positive and negative control approach being little more than signature recognition, templating, or profiling. To avoid this, a mix of AI and ML techniques may help you set the balance between positive and negative control approaches.

Visualizations, Metrics, and Trends

If the abiding purpose of doing analysis is to inform and shape decisions, then the format and manner of how you present your findings and support those findings with your data is critical to success. This is especially true when you look at visualizations, dashboards, and other aggregate representations of security-related data, especially when you're using single-value metrics as your measures of merit, fit, or safety.

Consider for a moment a typical security dashboard metric that displays the percentage of endpoint systems that have been updated with a critical security patch during the last 48 hours. A midsize organization of 5,000 employees scattered across four countries might have 10,000 to 15,000 endpoint devices in use, either company-owned and managed, employee-owned and managed, or any combination thereof. Even if your "green" reporting threshold is as high as 99 percent, that means that as many as 150 endpoint devices are still providing a welcome mat to an exploit that the patch was supposed to lock down. Seen that way, a key risk indicator might not be as meaningful on a dashboard as you might think.

Dashboard-style indicators are well suited to comparing a metric that changes over time against a required or desired trend line for that metric. Color, blink animations, or other visual cues are also useful when a clip level for the metric can be set to transform the metric into an alarm indicator. Geolocating indicators on a dashboard (including what we might call logical net-location or workspace-location, to show health and status or alarm indicators plotted on a logical network segment map or within or across physical facilities) can also help orient troubleshooters, responders, and managers to an evolving situation.

Rolling timeline displays that can show a selected set of measurements as they change over time can also be quite useful; sometimes the human brain's ability to correlate how different systems characteristics change over the same time period can trigger a sense that something might be going wrong.

Industrial process control environments have had to cope with these problems for over a century; many innovative and highly effective data representation, visualization, and analysis techniques have been developed to keep physical systems working safely and effectively. Much of what we see in information security dashboards borrows from this tradition.

Of course, there are some compliance requirements that dictate certain metrics, data, and other information be displayed together, correlated in certain ways, or trended in other ways. It may take some quiet contemplation to ferret out what key questions these required formats are actually trying to answer; that might be worth the effort, especially if your management and leadership keep asking for better explanations of the compliance reporting.

Event Data Analysis

Let's get purposeful and intentional here: why do you need to analyze all of this data? You need to do it to help people make decisions in real time—decisions about incipient incidents, about incidents that have already happened that we've just found out about, or about what to do to prevent the next incident from happening, or at least reduce its impacts. That's the only reason you gather event or anomaly or other data and analyze it every which way you can: to inform and shape decision-making.

Combine that for a moment with the survey findings mentioned earlier—that roughly two out of three senior executives and managers do not trust the data from their own systems, and you begin to see the real analysis challenge.

Simply put: What questions are you trying to answer?

If your organization does not already have a well-developed set of plans, policies, and procedures that strongly and closely couple analysis with information security–related decision-making, then filling that void might be a good place to start. Try a thought experiment or two: Put yourself in each decision-maker's shoes, and write down the key decision that has to be made—one that you know is necessary and logical and *must* be made soon. Focus on action-related decisions, such as "call in the police," "notify the government that we've suffered a major data breach," or "scrap our current security information and event management system and replace it with something better." Another good set of decision points to ponder might be the escalation check points or triage levels in your incident response procedures, which require you to determine how severe an incident seems to be, or might become, as a litmus test for how far up the management chain to escalate and notify key decision-makers. For each of those decisions, analyze it; write down four or five questions that you'd need the answers to, to make that decision yourself.

Do your analysis plans, programs, procedures, and tools help you answer those questions?

If they do, test and assess those analysis processes using real data and decisions. If not, sanity check the questions and decisions with others in your team (such as your supervisor or team chief) or with others in the organization that you have a good working relationship with. If after that the questions still seem relevant to the decision that has to be made, it may be time to reexamine the analysis processes *and* their expressed or implied assumptions about what data to collect, how often, and what to do with it.

This is a good time to go back to your security testing, assessment, and analysis workflow and the management systems you use with it. Are those processes set up to support you in getting the answers that decision-makers need? Or are they "merely" responding to compliance reporting requirements?

While you're doing that, keep thinking up security-related questions that you think are important, urgent, and compelling—the sort of questions that *you* would ask if you were running the company. The more of those you find that don't quite seem to fit with your workflows and analysis procedures, the more that either your intuition is faulty or the workflows and procedures need help urgently.

Other sections in this chapter have already looked at aspects of the overall analysis of security information and event-related data, which I won't go through again here.

Document and Communicate Findings

There are three basic use cases for how and why you report findings based on your monitoring, surveillance, testing, assessment, and observations that you gather as a security professional "just by walking around." The first is the ad hoc query, the question from a manager, leader, or a co-worker, which may or may not have a bearing you're aware of on a decision that needs to be urgently made. As with the question itself, the format and content of your reply may be very ad hoc and informal. The second use case is that of the routine and required reporting of information, results, observations, conclusions, and recommendations. Formats, expected content, and even the decision logic you use in coming to required conclusions and recommendations may be well structured for you in advance, although there's probably more room for you to think outside of the box on those conclusions and recommendations than you might believe.

Those first two use cases don't really involve *escalation*, which is defined as the urgent notification to higher levels of management, leadership, or command that something has been observed or is happening that may require their urgent attention. Escalation procedures may require a link-by-link climb up the chain of command, or it may require directly engaging with designated officials at higher levels when appropriate. Escalation separates this third data analysis and reporting use case from the previous two: When analysis results dictate that a decision needs to be made *now*, or at least very quickly, escalation is in order.

Kipling's six wise men[4] can be helpful to you in formulating the report, finding, or recommendation that you're about to launch up to higher headquarters. What has happened? Where did it happen, and which systems or elements of your organization are involved in it? Why do you believe this to be the case? When did it happen (or is it still happening now)? How did it happen? Who or what in your organization or your objectives is endangered, is impacted, may be harmed, or likely won't be able to conduct normal operations because of this? And what do you recommend we do, and how quickly, in response to this news flash?

Your organization's escalation procedures should detail those sorts of essential elements of information that your target audience needs to know; if they don't, write your own checklist-style format guide that prompts you in addressing each key point. If you're not in a real-time escalation firefight, take the time to get a second opinion, or a sanity check from your boss, and include those views into your checklist. Share it with other team members, just in case they have to use it in real time.

SUMMARY

By this point you've seen three vitally important concepts come together to shape, if not dictate, what you must achieve with your risk management and risk mitigation plans, programs, and actions. The first is that your organization faces a unique set of risks and challenges, and given its own goals, objectives, and appetite for risk, it must choose its own set of risk management and mitigation strategies, tactics, and operational measures and controls. The second is that the advanced persistent threat actors you face probably know your systems better than you do and are spending more effort and resources in learning to exploit vulnerabilities in your systems than you're able to spend in finding and fixing them. The third painful lesson of this chapter is that you'll need more data and more analysis tools, which you'll use nonstop, 24/7, to maintain constant vigilance as you seek precursors and indicators of behavioral anomalies that might suggest that your systems are under attack.

Or have already been attacked.

You've got a lot of opportunity to improve, as one sad statistic indicates. Each year, the cybersecurity industry average for how long it takes for businesses to notice that an intruder is in their e-midst keeps going up; as of May 2021, this time to detect still stands at more than 220 days worldwide.

---

[4] Whether you call it *root cause analysis* or *applying the scientific method*, Kipling suggested that you just keep asking simple open-ended questions until you have enough insight to form explanations you can test against what you've observed.

Incident Response and Recovery

THIS CHAPTER FOCUSES YOUR attention in the here and now by applying the kill chain concept operationally. You'll start by assuming that multiple attacks, each in its own different phase of its own unique kill chain, are happening *right now*. You'll also assume that other systems anomalies, which might be accidents or design flaws raising their bad-news heads, are also occurring in the midst of your day by day, moment by moment watch-standing activities. You'll make it part of your checklist-driven approach to defending your systems and the information that keeps your organization alive and flourishing. This is all about translating all of the decisions you made during risk management and mitigation planning and all of the actions you took in implementing your chosen risk and security control tactics into real-time operational use. In Chapter 3, "Risk Identification, Monitoring, and Analysis" you used the concept of the *kill chain* to identify high-impact risks and link them to exploitable vulnerabilities in your systems, processes, and data; you then used those insights to decide what and how to harden which high-leverage elements of those systems so that your business could *stay* in business in the face of risk. You saw how a single advanced persistent threat (APT) actor might go through a complex, dynamic, ever-evolving sequence of steps as they attempt to attack your systems. This led to planning, preparing, testing, assessing, and monitoring your systems so that you could defeat multiple, overlapping patterns of hostile action, from multiple APTs, one skirmish at a time.

It's time to dive deeper into getting your organization ready to detect an information security incident, respond to it, recover from it, and continue to learn to respond better as a result of its rough teaching. In some respects, that means that the *preparation* portions of this chapter will seem as if they speak to you in the past tense—they offer advice and ideas about what you *should* have done to prepare better—while the respond and investigate portions focus more on actions you'll need to do in real time. You'll need to think and act in three different, overlapping time frames, as you deal with pre-event readiness, real-time hands-on response, and post-incident analysis and learning. You'll also see how to incorporate the human elements in your information systems into real-time detection, characterization, and response.

Although there are as many incident response frameworks as there are risk management ones (as you saw in Chapter 3), let's focus our attention here in this chapter on NIST SP 800-61 as a point of departure. Nearly all of these standards and frameworks call for organizations to create some form of an incident response team, which then acts as the focal point for real-time decision-making and action during an information security incident and its immediate aftermath. Senior leadership and management designate this team, equip it, train its people, and provide it with the visibility and connectivity it needs to detect and respond in ways that just might keep the company in business. No matter what you call it—a computer emergency response team (CERT), a computer security incident response team (CSIRT), or any other name—it's your last clear line of defense in real time.

What do you do if your organization doesn't have an established incident response team? Let's jump right in, do some focused preparation, and improve your operational information security posture so that you can detect, identify, contain, eradicate, and restore after the next anomaly.

SUPPORT THE INCIDENT LIFECYCLE

Before diving into the lifecycle of an information security incident, let's start by defining an incident as the occurrence of an event that the systems' owners or users consider as both unplanned and disruptive. Incidents can be hostile, accidental, or natural in origin.

- Incidents that are deliberately triggered or caused are defined as *hostile* events, whether the systems owners know or understand their attacker's motives or not. Hostile events almost always involve attackers who exploit vulnerabilities in the target organization's information systems, IT architecture, and social and administrative processes and culture.

- Incidents that are caused by accident or acts of nature are not, by definition, hostile; they are still unplanned and disruptive to normal business operations.

Unmanaged systems, as Chapter 3 asserted, are the most vulnerable to exploitation or accidental disruption. You bring such systems under management using risk management frameworks, configuration management, change control, and information security controls. Each of these involves a planning process; taken together, this planning should have identified those risks that must be considered as urgent, compelling, or of sufficient potential impact that you need to know immediately when such a risk event is occurring. Thus, information risk management sets the stage for incident management and response by establishing the alarm conditions you need to watch for and respond to.

It's important at the outset to recognize that such risk events can fall into several broad types, loosely based on how your organization needs to respond.

- *Ongoing attempts to penetrate, gain access, or misuse systems resources and assets* have long been the principle focus of incident response concepts and frameworks. By focusing on real-time urgency of detection, characterization, and response, systems security planners and systems owners hope to limit the damage from such an event. This event response paradigm uses a triage approach to determine when and how to escalate the alarm to appropriate levels of senior leadership.

- *Ransom attacks* of any kind are also real-time emergencies that demand an immediate response; since ransom attacks (using ransomware or built-in systems capabilities) often involve sophisticated encryption of systems resources, databases, and information assets, it's often vitally important that the right expert talent be tasked in real time to assist.

- *Rude awakenings* are as good a name as any to refer to those events in which you happen to discover—or are told by a third party—that your systems were breached weeks or even months ago and that your valuable and confidential or proprietary data had been exfiltrated and sold on the Dark Web or other marketplaces. In too many cases, businesses and organizations are discovering (or being informed about) such exfiltrations long after the incident itself has ended. Since it's taking many companies over seven months to detect an intrusion into their systems, the opportunity to *prevent* impacts is long gone. In such events, emphasis shifts from technical responses to an incident to coping with customer claims for losses or damages, defense against litigation, or charges of criminal negligence. *Anomalies* can be any kind of event that occurs without much warning, such as a server crash, an internal network segment suffering from too much traffic or too little throughput, or almost any other kind of odd event. Until you've gathered data and analyzed or characterized them, you don't really know if an anomaly is caused by a hardware failure, a software bug, a user error, bad data, nature, the enemy, or a combination of all of these.

It's important to realize that *events* and *incidents* are two related yet different terms. In management and leadership terms, it may not matter much whether it was an *event* or an *incident* that caused the organization to suffer disruption, damage, or losses; as security planners, however, it's useful to have some commonly understood terms to help deal with them when they occur. Let's review a few key terms as they pertain to information security incidents by stepping through the sequence in which you'd see them in action as an incident unfolds. An event is something that happens; it is either a physical or logical activity. Events cause something to change state, value, or condition; they are observable, although you have to know what to look for and how to look for it to notice that an event has occurred. Events may be discrete, single occurrences, or they may be made up of many distinct events.

- Many events can be safely disregarded. Events of interest are some types of events or some events that occur under certain conditions, which may be suggestive of a security-related incident in progress or that already occurred. These are worthy of further analysis, data collection, and characterization.

- Precursors are events, usually occurring outside of your systems, that might be an early warning of an information security incident. Political or social unrest, gang activities, or protests against your organization, its business, or national origin might all be suggesting that your physical facilities, systems, web presence, and people might soon be under attack by various individuals or groups. Much like traveler's security advisories or other threat condition warnings, however, most precursors are hard to translate into specific indicators you can act upon.

- By contrast, an indicator is an event that more clearly signals an information security incident is happening or is about to happen.

- An indicator of compromise is a signal from an event that shows your systems have been penetrated, attacked, or compromised in some way. These are (or should be) clear and unambiguous alarms to your security operations team, network operations team, or computer emergency response teams that an incident is occurring now. These alarms are often generated by your anti-malware, software blocked or allowed list control, access control, intrusion detection and prevention systems, or other systems health and status monitoring systems.

■ An information security incident is declared to have occurred, or is in progress, when alarm data generated via monitoring, analysis, and characterization activities strongly suggests that such is the case. You sound the alarm and start to execute your incident response plans. Note that an information security incident (often referred to just as an incident) is typically a set of multiple, related events that together can or will affect the confidentiality, integrity, availability, authenticity, or other security characteristics of your information system.

Figure 4.1 shows these ideas in the context of several key decisions that the security operations center (SOC), the network operations center (NOC), and senior management have to make. It starts with filtering a combination of open source intelligence, more focused threat intelligence, and your own observations to develop a sense of what types of precursors (if any) might be anticipated in the near term and what they might mean. At most, these might lead you to change the sensitivity settings on your various automated monitoring and detection systems or provide additional, focused guidance to your security team members. Hardware, software, and people systems will be producing a variety of indicators, as they observe events happening throughout the day; an event triage process should be used to consistently assess each event of interest, determine the first best appropriate response, and dispatch that event and the assessment findings to the right response team and process. In an ideal world, only a few of those will be indicators of compromise—but when (not if) these occur, the SOC team needs to swing into immediate action. Other events of interest may or may not be a security incident but may very well indicate a failure in other risk mitigation controls.

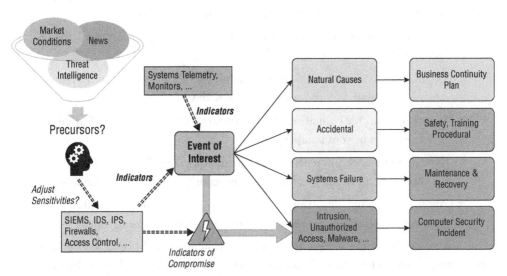

FIGURE 4.1 **Triage: from precursors to incident response**

Note that in each case, the possibility for false positive and false negative outcomes exists: your detectors, filters, and analysis tools will sound false positive alarms when nothing harmful is happening, while failing to sound the alarm when a real event of interest is in progress or already happened.

It's also important to note that those definitions of events, precursors, indicators, and incidents are not limited to just the IT components or infrastructures your organization depends upon. It is *vitally important* to recognize that attackers know from experience that social engineering attacks—such as phishing and vishing—are effective, low-cost, and low-risk ways to penetrate your organization and pave the way toward having unrestricted and undetected access to your information assets. As you think about incident response, be sure to include responding to potential social engineering attacks as well! (As of this writing, only a very few organizations have any processes in place that systematically detect and assess human-to-human contacts as possible social engineering attack attempts; as late as May 2019, even the U.S. government was only starting to consider establishing capabilities to detect possible propaganda, social engineering, or "false news" influencing attacks on the nation, regardless of their source.)

Precursors might be found in a variety of sources.

- Server or other logs that indicate a vulnerability scanner has been used against a system
- Missing or modified systems and security logs
- An announcement of a newly found vulnerability by a systems or applications vendor, information security service, or reputable vulnerabilities and exploits reporting service that might relate to your systems or platforms
- Media coverage of events that put your organization's reputation at risk (deservedly or not)
- Email, phone calls, or postal mail threatening attack on your organization, your systems, your staff, or those doing business with you
- Increasingly hostile or angry content in social media postings regarding customer service failures by your company
- Threat intelligence you receive or a "threat temperature" reading shared with you via your participation in local information security communities of practice
- Anonymous complaints in employee-facing suggestion boxes, ombudsman communications channels, or even graffiti in the restrooms or lounge areas

One of your best systems security monitoring techniques might be called *vigilance by walking around*. The nature of your organization and how its people and chains of command or leadership are both physically and logically arranged may make this easier or harder to do; what's important is that SOC team members be known and recognized as trusted brokers of informal observations about the current security climate and posture and how changes in the "business normal" operations tempo might be causing changes in that security posture or indicating that something *isn't* exactly normal.

It's worth focusing a moment on accidental incidents, which are triggered by your own authorized end users. The root cause of these accidents may be inadequate or ineffective training, gaps in policies and procedures, or simply because the end user in question cannot effectively perform the required tasks despite the training you've provided to them. Useful statistics regarding the frequency of such accidental incidents and their impact are hard to come by, although one indicator is the estimate of lost work and productivity due to poor quality or incomplete data. In 2018, IBM estimated these losses as exceeding $3.1 trillion worldwide; clearly, some portion of that is in part due to accidental misuse of information systems by one's own trusted employees. Your own staff can be accidentally contributing to both your false positive and false negative security alarm rates.

Think like a Responder

Take each step of this chapter from the perspective of someone working in your company's security operations center. It doesn't matter if your organization does not have a physically separate SOC or an officially designated set of people who are the SOC team complete with its leaders and responders. It does not matter if your "normal" IT department or team handles all of the network operations, IT security tasks, and help-desk-like anomaly investigation, response, and escalation processes. Think as if you run the SOC. Own that SOC as a mental set of resources, frameworks, and responsibilities. Take off your planner and architect's hats and start thinking in the near real time. "Job one" of the SOC is to alert management and leadership to situations and conditions that may require urgent or immediate decisions that can keep the business operating—or ensure its survival—in the face of information security risk events.

If your organization already does have an security operations center (SOC) or has otherwise formally designated SOC-like roles and responsibilities, that's good news! Grab a copy of their procedures, their training, and their resourcing plans, and use them as a starting point and checklist as you put this chapter to work for you.

Many organizations will formally define the team of responders who are called into action when an information systems security incident or other information systems emergency occurs. Known by names such as computer emergency response team (CERT), computer incident response team (CIRT), or computer security incident response team (CSIRT), these teams are called into action by the SOC's alerts to management that an urgent situation is in progress. (I'll use CSIRT throughout this chapter to refer to any such team of incident responders.) The SOC does not own either of these teams (usually), and unless the incident is small in scope and can quickly be handled by the SOC team, most incidents are turned over to the CERT or CSIRT for ongoing response activities. So again, in the spirit of putting this chapter to work for *you*, it's time to think and act as if you own the CERT or CSIRT too. During an actual incident, you might be called upon to perform many tasks that start as SOC responsibilities but transition to the on-scene management, direction, and control of the CSIRT.

Physical, Logical, and Administrative Surfaces

Keep in mind that your organization and its information systems present a combined set of physical, logical, and administrative attack or hazard surfaces, places where hostile action, accident, or natural causes can attempt to inflict disruption, damage, or loss upon the organization and its objectives. By the same token, these three surfaces present you, their defender, with powerful opportunities to observe, gather data, make decisions, and respond. Events that might be security incidents in the making can and do happen at all three of these surfaces, and the more complex and pernicious attacks combine physical, logical, and administrative actions throughout their kill chain.

Think of the physical, logical, and administrative surfaces as comparable to the data plane, control plane, and management plane of your networks: each layer or plane presents opportunities to attacker and defender alike. And since you already know your own systems architectures and understand all of these views of them, you should be several steps ahead of your potential adversaries.

Incident Response: Measures of Merit

"If you can't measure it, you can't manage it." This bit of commonsense management wisdom should focus our thinking on what might be the most important question this chapter can help you answer: how do you know you're getting better at incident response?

In many information security professional circles, discussion about this question focuses on what may be the three most vitally important metrics.

- Mean time to detect (MTTD)
- Mean time to respond (MTTR)
- Mean time to eradicate (MTTE)

The MTTD story is not an encouraging one; in 2017, research by the Ponemon Institute for IBM Security showed it had fallen from 201 days to 191 days, but since then, many sources report it is now pushing upward of 220 days to detect an intrusion. (Ponemon's report can be found at `https://www.ibm.com/downloads/cas/ZYKLN2E3`.) MTTR was last reported in 2017 as 66 days; that's nearly 10 months to detect and *contain* an intrusion. Industry average mean time to eradicate estimates are hard to come by; even if MTTE is in the 30- to 60-day range, you still have a serious problem on the front end of this timeline. All of these estimates vary widely across regions and industries.

Note the metric that isn't in this conversation: *mean time to repair or remediate*. The issue here is that depending upon the impacts of an incident, organizations might take days, months, or even years to "recover enough" to consider themselves more or less back to normal. It's also worth considering the number of organizations that get put out of business by a serious information security incident (and what number do you put in to represent the time to repair when you go out of business?). Perhaps, too, it's worth noting that the repairs and remediation are not usually the responsibility of the information security specialists; it's the rest of the management and leadership team that have to make the hard choices about what to repair, and on what kind of timeline, and then get the money, people, and other resources lined up to achieve that desired remediation target.

Your job is to find ways to make the MTTD and MTTR for your organization drive toward immediate. In a 2015 summit report for SANS Institute, Christopher Petersen notes that most organizations already have, on their own networks and systems, all of the threat intelligence data that they need to provide much more timely indications and warnings of an intrusion or incident in the making. That I&W problem—finding the right indications and translating them into useful, actionable warnings—is probably where smart investments can produce high-leverage returns by reducing those metrics *and* by giving you more focused, actionable alarms about threats becoming incidents. (Petersen's report can be found at `https://www.sans.org/cyber-security-summit/archives/file/summit-archive-1493840823.pdf`.)

The Lifecycle of a Security Incident

Traditionally, the incident response lifecycle consists of six major phases of activity: preparation, detection, containment, eradication, recovery, and post-incident analysis and improvement. Chapter 3 put this cycle in the context of the planning decisions that senior management must make, which start with translating risk appetite into measurements such as maximum allowable outage time limits. Figure 4.2 builds on Chapter 3's use of quantitative risk assessment time frames to put these major phases of incident response activity in context.

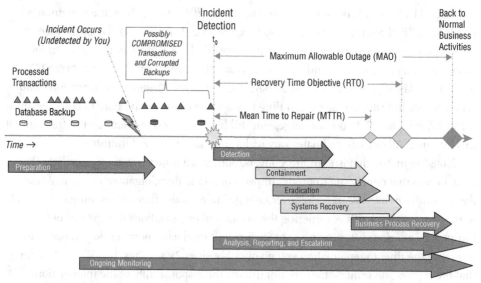

FIGURE 4.2 Incident response lifecycle

It's important to realize that, as Figure 4.2 shows, there are no hard and fast boundary points between these large phases of activity. Similarly, within each major phase of activities there's an ebb and flow of effort, as you shift focus and effort from subtask to subtask or from issue to issue. It is during detection, for example, that you go from sifting through signals to declaring an information security incident alarm, by way of recognizing an event or series of events and subjecting them to further analysis. Notice, too, that the cyclical, backward-chaining, or iterative nature of incident response isn't shown in gory detail on this flow. (Imagine, if you will, multiple APTs at various stages in their kill chains, as they separately attempt to reconnoiter, penetrate, take command, and exploit your systems against you. You need to detect each skirmish-level attack attempt and deal with it, capturing what that experience has taught you into your ongoing efforts to detect and respond to other activities.) Finally, too, it's important to realize that sometimes there is a lot of just plain *waiting* involved, whether waiting on resources to be available, training to be completed, or (shudder!) for an incident to occur.

What's also not explicitly shown in Figure 4.2 is the never-ending cycles of learning that the SOC team and the organization as a whole must engage with throughout. Initial assumptions are made during initial preparation and during each incident response. Those assumptions get tested (often to the breaking point) by reality; the organization either learns from watching those assumptions fail or continues to be vulnerable to repeated attacks that exploit those flawed assumptions.

Let's get into the details using a checklist borrowed from NIST SP 800-61 rev 2 as the road map.

Preparation

Getting prepared to respond to incidents starts with planning; then, of course, you must gain management's commitment to provide the people, funding, tools, connectivity, and management support necessary to achieve the goals of that plan. One useful approach is to start with an incident handling checklist as your "shopping list" of milestones in that plan. NIST's Incident Handling Checklist, shown in Figure 4.3, is a useful place to start. It is designed to be used in real time, incident by incident, reminding your watch-standers and first responders of key steps to perform, data to gather, or decisions to make, phase by phase, as they respond to an unauthorized penetration or other attack. You can use this same checklist as your template to plan and prepare with, by adding columns that prompt you (as preparation planner) to:

- Estimate how long it will take to accomplish each task.
- Identify needed resources, such as digital forensics workbenches, security information and event monitoring and analysis tools, workspaces, or people.
- Identify key decision points, which provide management with critical insights into your readiness preparation.
- Record the accomplishment of each preparation task, along with any action items or open discrepancies.

	Action	Completed
	Detection and Analysis	
1.	Determine whether an incident has occurred	
1.1	Analyze the precursors and indicators	
1.2	Look for correlating information	
1.3	Perform research (e.g., search engines, knowledge base)	
1.4	As soon as the handler believes an incident has occurred, begin documenting the investigation and gathering evidence	
2.	Prioritize handling the incident based on the relevant factors (functional impact, information impact, recoverability effort, etc.)	
3.	Report the incident to the appropriate internal personnel and external organizations	
	Containment, Eradication, and Recovery	
4.	Acquire, preserve, secure, and document evidence	
5.	Contain the incident	
6.	Eradicate the incident	
6.1	Identify and mitigate all vulnerabilities that were exploited	
6.2	Remove malware, inappropriate materials, and other components	
6.3	If more affected hosts are discovered (e.g., new malware infections), repeat the Detection and Analysis steps (1.1, 1.2) to identify all other affected hosts, then contain (5) and eradicate (6) the incident for them	
7.	Recover from the incident	
7.1	Return affected systems to an operationally ready state	
7.2	Confirm that the affected systems are functioning normally	
7.3	If necessary, implement additional monitoring to look for future related activity	
	Post-Incident Activity	
8.	Create a follow-up report	
9.	Hold a lessons learned meeting (mandatory for major incidents, optional otherwise)	

FIGURE 4.3 **NIST incident handling checklist** SOURCE: NIST SP800-61 REV. 2

At each step in the checklist, ask these six questions: who and what do you need; where do you need it; by when; why; how are you going to get it in place, on time; and how will you measure or demonstrate that you've successfully completed this step in the checklist?

One key question to ask, step-by-step in the checklist, is whether an administrative control such as a policy, procedure, or guideline needs to be issued in support of that step. Written administrative documents are either directive, instructional, or advisory in nature; all are important, but the policy documents provide the best opportunity for personnel accountability. Policies set the constraints and expectations on employee behavior and direct affected employees to comply with them; they also provide the legal framework for disciplinary action, changes in job duties, or loss of a job altogether for employees who cannot or will not comply.

NIST breaks its checklist down into three broad categories; these may be useful as guideposts when you consider the current incident response capabilities and state of the practice within your organization. This checklist-focused planning process is also useful to use when auditing or assessing your current incident detection and response capabilities and practices—simply add to it, row by row, as you discover significant gaps in your end-to-end ability to prepare for, detect, contain, eradicate, recover from, and learn from incidents of all types.

The same checklist that you use to develop your preparation plan can and should be used to plan and conduct your response team initial training, as well as ongoing refresher or proficiency training. Clearly, if there's a task on your checklist that you've *not* trained someone to do (or that you cannot identify who's responsible for getting that task done), you've found a gap.

Tests and Exercises

Exercise these preparation processes throughout their planning, development, and operational deployment life. Simple tabletop exercises, either with responsible managers or "stand-ins" taking their functional place at the exercise table, are valuable and inexpensive ways to find misunderstandings and opportunities for miscommunication. As you put a response team in place and equip it with systems, tools, and procedures, include them in the scope of these exercises. The most important part of these exercises is the debrief activity, in which you invite and encourage dialogue, questions, concerns, and complaints to come forward. Resist the temptation to analyze, assess, or judge such inputs during the debrief itself—instead, make sure that exercise participants can see the value you place on their frank and open sharing with you. Analyze it all later and then develop appropriate ways to reflect the results of that analysis back to exercise participants and their managers.

Ethical penetration testing is the penultimate test and evaluation of your ongoing incident detection and response capabilities. Chapter 3 looked at this in some depth; it's worth recalling here that in many businesses, standards or contractual obligations require ethical penetration testing, independent audit, and internal assessments as major components of an ongoing due diligence effort.

Note, too, that this preparation checklist should help you identify key performance or risk management metrics by which you can assess how well you're doing, both with preparation and with ongoing response activities. Ideally, you should be able to link these metrics to other key performance indicators or process maturity indicators used throughout your organization. This may also offer opportunities to assess successful incident response preparation and ongoing operational capabilities in cost avoidance terms, as well as link them to other strategic and tactical goals of the organization.

Taken all at once, that looks like a *lot* of preparation! And it is! Yet much of what's needed by your incident response team, if they're going to be well prepared, comes right from the architectural assessments, your vulnerability assessments, and your risk mitigation implementation activities. Other key information comes from your overall approach to managing and maintaining configuration control over your information systems and your IT infrastructure. And you should already be carrying out good "IT hygiene" and safety and security measures, such as clock synchronization, event logging, testing, and so forth. The "new" effort is in creating the team, defining its tasks, writing them up in procedural form, and then using those procedures as an active part of your ongoing training, readiness, and operational evaluation of your overall information security posture.

One last point to keep in mind is that, as in all things, you should start small and simple. You cannot start from having zero detection and response capability and get prepared for every risk the first time around. Growing and maintaining an effective information security incident response capability should be an iterative learning experience. Start by identifying the risks that have management worried the most, and prepare to be able to detect and respond to these first. From that planning and readiness activity, learn what you can do better the next time, as you take on successively more and more of the risks identified, assessed, and prioritized in your company's risk register. Keeping your organization's information systems healthy and their immune system—your incident response capabilities—strong and effective is an ongoing part of business life. It stops only when the organization ceases to exist.

Incident Response Team: Roles and Structures

Unless you're in a very small organization and as the SSCP you wear all of the hats of network and systems administration, security, and incident response, your organization will need to formally designate a team of people who have the "watch-standing" duty of a real-time incident response team. This team might be called a *computer emergency response team (CERT)*. CERTs can also be known as computer incident response teams, as cyber incident response teams (both using the CIRT acronym), or as computer security incident response teams (CSIRTs). For ease of reference, let's call ours a CSIRT for the remainder of this chapter. (Note that CERTs tend to have a broader charter, responding whether systems are put out of action by acts of nature, accidents, or hostile attackers. CERTs, too, tend to be more involved with broader disaster recovery efforts than a team focused primarily on security-related incidents.)

Your organization's risk appetite and its specific CIANA+PS needs should determine whether this CSIRT provides around-the-clock, on-site support, or supports on a rapid-response, on-call basis after business hours. These needs will also help determine whether the incident response team should be a separate and distinct group of people or be part of preexisting groups in your IT, systems, or network departments. Some organizations see strong value in segregating the day-to-day network operations jobs of the network operations center from the time-critical security and incident response tasks of a security operations center; others leave NOC and SOC functions combined within one set of responders.

Whether your organization calls them a CSIRT or a SOC, or they're just a subset of the IT department's staff, there are a number of key functions that this incident response team should perform. We'll look at them in more detail in subsequent sections, but by way of introduction, they are as follows:

Serve as a Single Point of Contact for Incident Response   Having a single point of contact between the incident and the organization makes incident command, control, and communication much more effective. This should include the following:

- Focusing reporting and rumor control with users and managers regarding suspicious events, systems anomalies, or other security concerns
- Coordinating responses and dispatching or calling in additional resources as needed
- Escalating computer security incident reports to senior managers and leadership
- Coordinating with other security teams (such as physical security) and with local police, fire, and rescue departments as required

Take Control of the Incident and the Scene   Taking control of the incident, as an event that's taking place in real time, is vital. Without somebody taking immediate control of the incident and where it's taking place, you risk bad decisions placing people, property, information, or the business at greater risk of harm or loss than they already are. Taking control of the incident scene protects information about the incident, where it happened, and how it happened. This preserves physical and digital evidence that may be critical to determining how the incident began, how it progressed, and what happened as it spread. This information is vital to both problem analysis and recovery efforts and legal investigations of fault, liability, or unlawful activity.

- Response procedures should specify the chain of command relationships and designate who (by position, title, or name) is the "on-scene commander," so to speak. Incident situations can be stressful, and often you're dealing with incomplete information. Even the simplest of decisions needs to be clearly made and communicated to those who need to carry it out; committees usually cannot do this well in real time.
- Clearly defined escalation paths and procedures, with by-name contact information (and designated alternate points of contact), provide ways to keep key stakeholders informed and engaged as an incident evolves.

- The scene itself and the systems, information, and even the rooms or buildings themselves represent investments that the organization has made. Due care requires that the incident response team minimize further damage to the organization's property or the property of others that may be involved in the incident scene.

Investigate, Analyze, and Assess the Incident   This is where all of your skills as a troubleshooter, an investigator, or just being good at making "informed guesses" start to pay off. Gather data; ask questions; dig for information.

Escalate, Report to, and Engage with Leadership   Once they've determined that a security-related incident might in fact be happening, the team needs to promptly escalate this to senior leadership and management. This may involve a judgment call on the response team chief's part, as preplanned incident checklists and procedures cannot anticipate everything that might go wrong. Experience dictates that it's best to err on the side of caution and report or escalate to higher management and leadership.

Keep a Running Incident Response Log   The incident response team should keep accurate logs of what happened, what decisions got made (and by whom), and what actions were taken. Logging should also build a time-ordered catalog of event artifacts—files, other outputs, or physical changes to systems, for example. This time history of the event, as it unfolds, is also vital to understanding the event, mitigating, or taking remedial action to prevent its reoccurrence. Logs and the catalogs of artifacts that go with them are an important part of establishing the chain of custody of evidence (digital or other) in support of any subsequent forensic investigation.

Coordinate with External Parties   External parties can include systems vendors and maintainers, service bureaus or cloud-hosting service providers, outside organizations that have shared access to information systems (such as extranets or federated access privileges), and others whose own information and information systems may be put at risk by this incident as it unfolds. By acting as the organization's focal point for coordination with external parties, the team can keep those partners properly informed, reduce risk to their systems and information, and make better use of technical, security, and other support those parties may be able to provide.

✔ **Before You Share Incident Information, Get Senior Leadership's Buy-In**

In almost all cases, you'll need senior leadership and management to make the real-time decisions regarding what information about an incident should be shared with outside organizations. Note, too, that your internal CSIRT or SOC should *not* be the liaison with the news media!

Contain the Incident   Prevent it from infecting, disrupting, or gaining access to any other elements of your systems or networks, as well as preventing it from using your systems as launchpads to attack other external systems.

Eradicate the Incident   Remove, quarantine, or otherwise eliminate all elements of the attack from your systems.

Recover from the Incident   Restore systems to their pre-attack state by resetting and reloading network systems, routers, servers, and so forth, as required. Finally, inform management that the systems should be back up and ready for operational use by end users.

Document What You've Learned   Capture everything possible regarding systems deficiencies, vulnerabilities, or procedural errors that contributed to the incident taking place for subsequent mitigation or remediation. Review your incident response procedures for what worked and what didn't, and update accordingly.

Incident Response Priorities

No matter how your organization breaks up the incident response management process into a series of steps or how they are assigned to different individuals or teams within the organization, the incident response team must keep firmly three basic priorities in mind.

The first one is easy: *the safety of people comes first*. Nothing you are going to try to accomplish is more important than protecting people from injury or death. It does not matter whether those people are your co-workers on the incident response team, other staff members at the site of the incident, or even people who might have been responsible for causing the incident, your first priority is preventing harm from coming to any of them—yourself included! Your organization should have standing policies and procedures that dictate how calls for assistance to local fire, police, or emergency medical services should be made; these should be part of your incident response procedures. Legal as well as ethical responsibilities set this as the number-one priority.

WARNING   Throughout every phase of an incident response, the safety of people is always priority one. *After* any issues involving the safety of people have been dealt with, you can deal with the often-conflicting needs to understand what happened versus getting things back up and running quickly.

Priority number two is not so simple to identify. One of the most difficult challenges facing an organization that's found itself in the midst of a computer security incident is whether to prioritize getting back into normal business operations or supporting a digital forensics investigation that may establish responsibility, guilt, or liability for the incident and resultant loss and damages. This is not a decision that the on-scene response team leader makes! Simply put, the longer it takes to secure the scene and gather and protect evidence (such as memory dumps, systems images, disk images, log files, etc.), the longer it takes to restore systems to their normal business configurations and get users back to doing productive work. This is not a binary, either-or decision—it is something that the incident response team and senior leaders need to keep a constant watch over throughout all phases of incident response.

Increasingly, we see that government regulators, civic watchdog groups, shareholders, and the courts are becoming impatient with senior management teams that fail in their due diligence. This impatience is translating into legal and market action that can and will bring self-inflicted damage—negligence, in other words—home to roost where it belongs. The reasonable fear of that should lead to tasking all members of the IT organization, including their information security specialists, with developing greater proficiency at being able to protect and preserve the digital evidence related to an incident, while getting the systems and business processes promptly restored to normal operations.

Detection, Analysis, and Escalation

First and foremost, remember why you're on the SOC: to enable your organization's senior leadership and management to make *informed* decisions about emergency or urgent actions to take to protect the organization from loss or impact. The SOC doesn't unilaterally decide to activate a backup alternate operations location or halt business operations; what it must do instead is *escalate* the event and the need for an urgent decision to previously designated responsible managers and leaders—or to the next rung in the reporting chain in their absence. Your SOC roles and responsibilities will provide you with clear guidance on what issues to escalate and to whom; your procedures should also clearly define what you must *do* in real time and how to escalate the fact of taking those actions to your responsible managers and leaders.

Next, remember that you're not only leading the technical charge to protect your organization's information systems and get them back into action, but you're also a vital part of protecting its *legal* capabilities to respond and recover. Those legal responses will in all probability depend upon evidence that points to who is responsible and in what capacity; your actions during containment, eradication, and recovery can significantly enhance your organization's legal abilities to respond or all but erase them.

Watching for Kill Chains in Action

Let's take a closer look at the kill chain concept shown in Figure 4.4, which was introduced in Chapter 3, and look more closely at the kinds of *outputs* your SOC team members need if they are to detect, characterize, and respond to a security incident or an intrusion promptly.

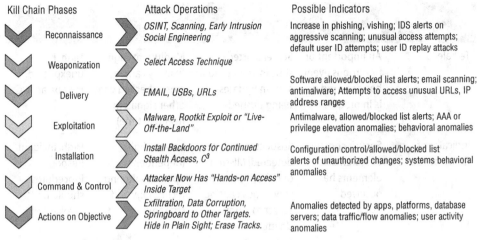

Kill Chain Phases	Attack Operations	Possible Indicators
Reconnaissance	OSINT, Scanning, Early Intrusion Social Engineering	Increase in phishing, vishing; IDS alerts on aggressive scanning; unusual access attempts; default user ID attempts; user ID replay attacks
Weaponization	Select Access Technique	
Delivery	EMAIL, USBs, URLs	Software allowed/blocked list alerts; email scanning; antimalware; Attempts to access unusual URLs, IP address ranges
Exploitation	Malware, Rootkit Exploit or "Live-Off-the-Land"	Antimalware, allowed/blocked list alerts; AAA or privilege elevation anomalies; behavioral anomalies
Installation	Install Backdoors for Continued Stealth Access, C³	Configuration control/allowed/blocked list alerts of unauthorized changes; systems behavioral anomalies
Command & Control	Attacker Now Has "Hands-on Access" Inside Target	
Actions on Objective	Exfiltration, Data Corruption, Springboard to Other Targets. Hide in Plain Sight; Erase Tracks.	Anomalies detected by apps, platforms, database servers; data traffic/flow anomalies; user activity anomalies

FIGURE 4.4 **Indicators of a kill chain in action**

Any kind of surveillance, monitoring, or control system can produce a number of different types of *signals*, which are the observable results of an event having taken place. Table 4.1 illustrates some of these types of signals and the types of events they might be associated with.

TABLE 4.1 **Indicators, Alarms, and IOCs**

SIGNAL TYPE	MEANING	EXAMPLES OF CAUSES	DEGREE OF CONFIDENCE	URGENCY
Precursor	Suggests that a security-related event might occur in the near future	Local area social/political unrest; government threat condition warnings	Low	Low
Indicator	Change of state in a designated systems element	Server successful reboot; User privilege elevation; file deletion	Moderate (can be forensically verified)	Depends upon security alert needs
Alarm	Systems element conditions out of limits, or critical events have occurred	Server halt; ISP connection fails to respond; switchover to backup power	Medium to High (usually can be cross-checked with other signals in near real time)	High: Corrective Actions may be needed immediately

CONTINUES

SIGNAL TYPE	MEANING	EXAMPLES OF CAUSES	DEGREE OF CONFIDENCE	URGENCY
Telltale	An important or hazardous event has occurred or is in progress	Server started shutdown or reboot; system updates being pushed	Medium to High (usually can be cross-checked with other signals in near real time)	High: If unexpected, may be an IOC
Indicator of Compromise	Security posture of systems or elements has occurred	Suspected malware detected; Missing or corrupt security/ server logs causing server to stop; Unauthorized attempts at privilege elevation	Low to High (dependent upon monitoring technology and strategy)	High: Incident Response Procedures should be invoked

Of the five types of signals in Table 4.1, only two—precursors and indicators of compromise—are presumed to be related to some kind of information security event of interest.

Indicators, telltales, and alarms by design are calling attention to an event that *someone* ought to pay attention to, but it will take further investigation and analysis to determine whether the signal is crying out for a repair team, a security response, or a simple acknowledgment of its occurrence. *Telltales* are a case in point: such signals are generally associated with significant changes in the status, state, or health of the system or of major subsystems and elements, and they are often related to complex sequences of events. They also are generally accepted as high-confidence, unambiguous evidence that the event they are related to has happened. A scheduled push of access control data, security policy settings, or a software update might generate a telltale signal to the SOC so that the on-shift crew is aware that this event has started. Progress indicators may be sent to the SOC team as this task progresses, and a final telltale would indicate successful completion. They can then verify that this is a planned, authorized event, and if it is not, they can take appropriate action to correct it. Similarly, indicators and alarms can be calling attention to equipment or systems malfunctions regardless of their root cause.

By contrast, indicators of compromise (IOCs), which should definitely be high on your priority list of security concerns, are typically generated by specific systems-security-monitoring technologies, such as an anti-malware or an intrusion detection and prevention system. Some of these indicators may be clear, unambiguous, and irrefutable. Immediate incident response action should be taken for these types of indicators. Other IOCs may be of lower confidence, requiring additional investigation or analysis before the SOC can declare that a compromise event may in fact be taking place and invoke the incident response procedures to characterize, contain, and respond to it. Precursors may come from threat information sharing communities or even from the news media, and they generally do not convey sufficient information or confidence to act upon. Where do these signals come from? Think about the monitoring and assessment capabilities that you have set up and the data sources that drive them. Chapter 3 provided you with shopping lists of systems, servers, platforms, applications, and devices that can provide you with rich sources of status, state, health, and alarm indications data. With Figure 4.4 in mind, ask yourself: *which* of our systems elements might be trying to tell me that something's gone wrong with it? Start this by focusing on the types of events that steps in an attacker's kill chain might be trying to accomplish, such as:

- Input buffer overflows that indicate attempts to inject SQL or other script commands into a web page or database server.

- Antivirus software detects that a device, such as an endpoint or removable media, has a suspected infection on it.

- Systems administrators, or automated search tools, notice filenames containing unusual or unprintable characters in them.

- Access control systems notice a device attempting to connect, which does not have required software or malware definition updates applied to it.

- A host, server, or endpoint device does an unplanned restart.

- A new or unmanaged host or endpoint attempts to join the network.

- A host or an endpoint device notices a change to a configuration-controlled element in its baseline configuration.

- An application platform logs multiple failed login attempts, seemingly from an unfamiliar system or IP address.

- Email systems and administrators notice an increase in the number of bounced, refused, or quarantined emails with suspicious content or ones with unknown addressees.

- Unusual deviations in network traffic flows or systems loading are observed.

If events of those types do not correlate with administrative information—if they are not planned and approved configuration changes (that might result in restarts of systems) or are not the legitimate actions of known, authorized subjects—then you have an *event of interest* on your hands.

Now, step back from that set of events, and ask what indicators (or alarms) should be observable and reported to your SOC to help you recognize that a possible security incident is happening. Figure 4.4 illustrated some possible indicator events; think these through for your systems to help you determine your needs for event-specific alarms.

In some cases, your desired tell-tale sign is only going to surface from analysis, and potentially deep analysis at that. A data exfiltration attack, for instance, might be using a series of bogus or compromised accounts to initially clone copies of its desired data assets and then fragment, encrypt, and package them for transmission outside of your systems. Each of these steps could be done record by record (if the attacker is that patient); traffic pattern anomaly recognition might not find it for you in such cases. Only a thorough review, account by account, of *everything* it has been doing lately might find this for you.

It's often assumed that the incident response process cannot begin until an incident is detected; the types of risk events examined at the start of this chapter highlight a potentially devastating counter-example, however, with incidents that you become aware of only when someone outside of your organization tells you about them. Even then, investigating what *has* happened is still quite similar to detecting that something *is* happening: you have to wade through a tremendous number of event-level signals to find the real indicators worth worrying about.

Let's consider some of the near-real-time aspects of constant vigilance.

Filtering to Detect: How Many Signals?

Each day, most large organizations that have extensive web presences may see tens of millions of IP packets arrive at the front doors of their web servers or their Internet points of presence. The vast majority of these, perhaps as many as 90 percent of them, are both innocent in purpose and routine in nature: they are part of the background of traffic that is the Internet and the Web keeping itself alive, its clocks and caches synchronized, and its traffic flowing normally. Of that remaining million packets, which are the ones to worry about? Firewall, router, and IPS/IDS access control rules, behavioral anomaly rules, and other filters might further reduce that to 10,000 or so suspicious inbound events in a 24-hour day. Similar rules, tools, and filters looking at outbound traffic might produce a similar-sized set of events. Even so, 20,000+ events is far too many for human analysts to wade through.

It's at this point that it's worthwhile to consider what some security specialists call the two false beliefs about continuous monitoring: it is neither all data from all measurement devices nor in real time.

■ Monitoring every sensor in your system and capturing every measurable event that flows through a node in your network—or even just at its edges, where it interfaces with the Internet—could produce terabytes of data every day. It is impractical, if not impossible, to attempt to capture all of that data, every moment, from every node, box, interconnection point, firewall, gateway, switch, or router. Your access control system would bog down if it attempted to capture everything about every access attempt. You push the filtering, the down-selecting of data, out as far toward the edge as you can, within the capabilities of each systems element and your risk profile. The local device may keep hours, or even days of log data on it; your overall systems architecture and your assessment of your risk profile should help you choose how much log data to import from which devices, how often, and where to put it for safe keeping and later analysis. As a result, your SIEM, IDS, IPS, or other analyst workstation tools have a smaller, more manageable set of data that they can begin to correlate in time, logical space (such as a network segment), or physical space (a building, floor, or zone within your facilities, or even a geographic location). Correlations can also be done against blocked and allowed lists for IP addresses, geographic locations, URLs, or other items pertinent to your risk profile.

■ Monitoring results—the outputs that tell you an alarm condition has been met— are not available instantly. Analysis activities take time: time to get the data, time to analyze it, and time to interpret and assess it. If analysis is conducted continuously, it might be able to generate alarms within handfuls of seconds, or maybe a few minutes, of the occurrence of an event of interest or an indicator of compromise. On the other hand, if the analysis tasks are set to run periodically, perhaps every hour or once per day, their outcomes are naturally lagging behind the events in question. Analysis tasks that ask for distant monitoring devices to forward large log files may also be subject to additional delays.

There are some obvious, painful trade-offs that confront you as a security systems architect in all of this. Measure or monitor too small a set of indicators or log and keep too little data and both your real-time and after-action analysis efforts can be severely limited. This probably results in an increasing rate of false negative errors—and intruders being granted access to your systems. Measure too much, keep too much, and analyze too much, and your false positive error rate goes up, causing you to spend too much analysis effort and waste too much time for legitimate users who were erroneously denied access.

Again, go back to that kill chain model as a set of guideposts: if you assume that multiple attackers are attempting to get at your systems every hour of every day, with each attacker taking different actions in different phases of their own conceptual kill chain, then what no-kidding, bottom-line alarm information do you need to *notice* that something unauthorized is going on? You'll then dive deeper into the data to understand that anomaly better and to characterize it as maintenance gone bad, an accident, or as an attack; you'll also then be on more informed ground as you take your next steps in the response cycle.

Tuning your security monitoring and response systems is a never-ending challenge. Business conditions change about as often as the threats evolve. In many organizations, management does not have the confidence to shut down part of their business just because the machine learning and behavioral modeling systems in the next-generation firewalls or NIPS have signaled an indicator of compromise. As business processes become more tightly integrated and as transaction volumes increase, managers may also believe that recovering from an incident is less disruptive than shutting down a business process on the likelihood that it has been compromised. In such conditions, management will look to its SOC team for clarity. It's up to you to convey to management why you are as confident in that IOC as you are and therefore why your recommended course of action makes the most sense.

Human Observation and Reporting

Sadly, one of the most valuable sources of information in many organizations goes under-utilized. Members of your workforce, at their endpoints and in their workspaces, see, hear, or notice things that are unusual; yet the processes we establish for them to report such problems, and your own processes for triage, correlation, and analysis of them, are often less than effective. Employees may report theft of a company-owned endpoint device, such as a laptop or smartphone, in a reasonably timely manner; loss of such a device or of an employee-owned endpoint device might not get noticed or reported for days. Phishing and vishing attack attempts are often not reported; most training programs teach employees to just delete them and go on with their work. (A few but noteworthy exceptions can be found, such as when organizations not only self-test their workers with fake phishing attacks, actively monitoring employees as their bait-spotting skills improve but also engage employees in other ways as part of the social engineering defense team.)

Leadership and management can change this; with the right set of administrative controls, they can and should create and nurture the security culture that encourages each person in the workplace to maintain a watchful but helpful presence and to take an active role in protecting everyone's job and livelihood. Sometimes, all it takes is a simple process change to transform a painfully inadequate complaint process into a beneficial detection, data capture, and reporting opportunity.

Correlation

As in many other forms of risk management, it's necessary to correlate data of different types, gathered by different measurement or monitoring systems, in order to determine whether an event of interest has actually occurred. A server's system log file might show a shutdown and restart sequence; but until you correlate this with human activity logs, you won't know if this was malware-induced, a deliberate but unauthorized human action, or part of a scheduled software maintenance activity. Traffic monitoring data might suggest that a user's endpoint device is involved in a suspected data exfiltration activity;

correlating that endpoint's anti-malware or software allowed/blocked list systems logs, along with outbound connection attempts, might help you separate malware-induced from insider-perpetrated events.

SIEMs, IDS, or IPS capabilities can automate a great deal of the data gathering and correlation needed to identify potential events like these; they can also be programmed to route selected subsets of such events to human analysis for further triage.

Manufacturing, robotic warehouse, or other environments heavily dependent upon industrial control systems (ICS) or other supervisory control and data acquisition (SCADA) systems present yet another layer of correlation challenges and opportunities. SCADA and ICS technologies are often implemented in companies via contracts that tie specific revision levels of hardware, operating systems, and applications together; vendors often do not support frequent updates or release patch kits, and contracts may actually void vendor support guarantees if end-user clients patch the systems themselves. While this may protect the assembly line or the process systems under control from self-inflicted disruption or downtime, it does mean that other administrative, people-intensive means may be necessary to maintain appropriate vigilance. Security analysts supporting such environments might have to translate CVE data into human-observable terms, for example; for some exploitable vulnerabilities, this might involve specific, focused training for factory floor workers, supervisors, and process control technicians as well as for security operations team members.

Organizations with significant investments in physical security measures, such as motion detectors, video monitoring, and internal foot traffic monitoring systems, may also find it challenging to correlate data between these systems and the SIEMs, IDS, and IPS that monitor their IT backbone and systems. The same is true from data taken from internal environmental control systems or from fire and other safety monitoring systems.

Security Event Triage

Another high payoff that you can achieve by applying the kill chain concept in reverse is to see that not every information security incident *is* an emergency but that any event could *become* an emergency without proper attention. The threat intelligence and modeling communities provide useful insights that suggest that certain types of attack vectors quite often correlate to different phases in the cybersecurity kill chain. This assessment is based in large part on whether such an attack vector can immediately lead to information loss or compromise or to the disruption of critical business functions. Table 4.2 summarizes the views of NIST, MITRE, AT&T Business, and others, which taken together suggest (not dictate) that some types of incidents need more of an incident response than others.

TABLE 4.2 Security Events and Response Priorities

INCIDENT TYPE	KILL CHAIN STAGES	PRIORITY/ URGENCY	RESPONSES
Port scanning	Reconnaissance and Probing	Low	Most can be ignored, unless IP/region is suspect, and scanning is frequent and intensive
False Rejects	All Stages	Low	Gather data for longer-term analytics
Malware Infection	Delivery and Attack	Low to Medium	Contain and eradicate, scan rest of systems for signatures related to this IOC
DDOS	Exploitation and Installation	High	Immediately reconfigure web servers to protect against floods; coordinate with your ISPs or cloud provider
Unauthorized Access	Exploitation and Installation	Medium to High	Investigate; analyze access attempts; isolate/restrict access to high value data or systems
Unauthorized Privilege Escalation	Exploitation and Installation	High	Investigate; analyze access attempts; isolate/restrict access to high value data or systems
Insider Breach	System Compromise	High	Identify accounts involved; monitor; contain or control, especially for access to high-value data or systems
Destructive Attack	System Compromise	High	Contain; gather forensic information; inspect backups prior to restoring from them

Ransom or ransomware attacks illustrate the thinking behind building a severity index based on how close to "payday" the attacker is on their kill chain. These are of course potentially highly destructive attacks on your systems. If you discover that parts of your system are showing signs that a ransom attack is underway (such as files starting to be unavailable to user processes because they have been encrypted by the attacker), this calls for *immediate* action. Working backward along the kill chain, that ransom attacker may have had to use a malware payload as part of gaining access to your systems and to then elevate privileges as required to map out the file systems, prepare encryption scripts, and mask their intrusion into systems. On the other hand, unless you have threat intelligence to identify IP address ranges to be wary of, you probably can't learn anything useful about an impending attack just because your ports are being scanned. Seeing such scanning taking place is a great signal to you to verify that you've got proper security measures in place.

Conducting a rapid triage based on the type of event is a critical step in making a first characterization of the incident at hand. By developing such triage priority tables and procedures beforehand, you can also guide the SOC team on what additional data (if any) to gather to use as part of the assessment they'll need to report to management.

Declaring an Incident: Alarm!

At some point during the initial evaluation of the event of interest, your watch-standers need to come to a decision: is this an information security *incident* that is ongoing, developing, or in the making? Is it indicative of an incident that has already occurred (and completed its dirty deeds)? Or is it just a set of interesting observations but not worthy of elevated concern or the application of emergency response capabilities?

As you prepare and plan for incident response, you should be able to identify or characterize ways in which these declarations of an alarm condition can be made in real time by the people who are on duty when it is first noticed. You may also have to simply rely on the experience and judgment of your watch-standers and their knowledge of your "business normal" conditions for your information systems.

Raising the alarm over an information security incident should be a deliberate, thoughtful, and purposeful decision, for it will quite likely lead to loss of productivity as response measures start to isolate systems, subsystems, or network segments, and as platforms and services are suspended or shut down as part of containment efforts. Senior managers, too, will have to set aside some of what they are investing their time and attention on, as they come up to speed on what your first responders or CERT team leader is reporting to them.

It should not, however, be something that is just assumed to have been communicated by the actions of members of your CERT or IT teams. It should be clear and unambiguous about what your team knows has happened and as to what they don't yet know about the incident. A cautious warning, coupled with "still under investigation," is appropriate. And if your existing SOC processes and procedures or your alert notification and escalation processes don't define this clearly enough, that's a clear sign of an opportunity to improve!

Log It!

Your SOC processes must provide for making and updating its own log files as it starts the incident response process. These logs form an important element in your situational awareness of the incident, especially if it is a complex or time-consuming one to assess, characterize, and respond to. An old-fashioned paper log book can be a great thing to use, in the event of an emergency response; keep track of each alarm, each decision, and each response; log each escalation to senior management, and of course log their contacts with the SOC as they seek information or provide direction to you. Log contacts from users or outsiders, especially from outsiders requesting information or updates about your systems status and your organization's ability to function properly. In most cases, these calls will be from affected users, partners, or others; but other such queries might be from the news media, from government regulators, or even from the attackers themselves using an alias as they seek real-time battle damage assessment insight.

Logbooks are absolutely vital when dealing with any incident that spans a normal work shift boundary; and since almost any reasonably complete effort at post-event debrief and process or systems improvement (and further risk mitigation) will no doubt run into subsequent days, use your log books. Manually generated logs have a distinct advantage that should not be missed out on: they encourage free-format capture of the thoughts, observations, or questions that the SOC team comes up with, in a format that is easy to record and time stamp.

TIP   *Logs* are usually the files that are generated automatically by elements of your IT infrastructure or its security systems. A *logbook*, by contrast, is the contemporaneous record kept by a human being, annotating step by step each activity performed or decision taken during a security incident. Procedures can and should dictate what information to include in the logbook, as well as encouraging the human observer to think about what is going on and make note of that in the logbook.

It's useful if multiple team members keep their own informal notes as they work through the incident response; that said, you need to ensure that there is one official team chief's log book, with clearly defined expectations and procedures for what gets logged, by whom, and when. Reconciling different observations between individual, informal logs and the official logbook is important but may be one of those tasks that you as team chief have to postpone till after the incident response is complete.

Your meticulous record-keeping during an incident response is also a critical component of protecting the chain of custody of an information that might become evidence in any subsequent forensic investigation. This applies to your informal notes as well. Whether you take those notes with pen and paper, a smartphone, or any other device, that information pertains to the incident. It should be immediately put into custody and protected as any other potential evidence would be.

✔ Visually Mapping an Incident

When our systems are all up and running, various dashboard displays can help SOC team members visualize the current status, state, and health of the systems in their care. When the networks go down or critical servers go offline, the team still can gain advantage from having such visualizations handy—even if they need to be done on a whiteboard or other not-so-smart technologies. Diagramming the affected systems elements and being able to quickly update each element's status as you work through containment, eradication, and recovery can be a powerful way to keep the incident response in perspective.

Once your SIEM or other online dashboard systems come back to life *and* you've determined that they are trustworthy, they can and should help you in the ongoing analysis, characterization, containment, eradication, and recovery tasks—once you know you can rely upon them and be sure they're not providing battle damage assessment intelligence to your attackers, of course!

Containment

Containment and eradication are the next major task areas that the CSIRT needs to take on and accomplish. As you can imagine, the nature of the specific incident or attack in question all but defines the containment and eradication tactics, techniques, and procedures you'll need to bring to bear to keep the mess from spreading and to clean up the mess itself.

These two steps are also the ones that could have the greatest impact on the success of any subsequent forensic investigation. Take advantage of the time you have right now, while you're not in the middle of an incident response action, to make sure that your organization has the forensic aspect of containment and eradication thoughtfully considered in its plans. Those plans should address questions such as:

- How does forensic triage relate to incident severity level (or security incident triage) with respect to this incident?

- How does the SOC team determine whether a system component (a server, endpoint, network device, or other) can be isolated without corrupting information in it that may be evidence the investigation needs?

- Are there *forensic triage procedures* in place to determine which systems components must be restored to operational condition as quickly as possible and therefore need to have forensic information collected from them during the incident response? (The rest, presumably, can stay contained or idle until further forensic triage efforts can determine which ones need to be imaged and which ones can be released back to operational use.)

- Are the SOC team or incident responders trained and equipped to conduct forensic triage efforts as part of containment and eradication?

More formally, *containment* is the process of identifying the affected or infected systems elements, whether hardware, software, communications systems, or data, and isolating them from the rest of your systems to prevent the disruption-causing agent from affecting the rest of your systems or other systems external to your own. Pay careful attention to the need not only to isolate the *causal agent*, be that malware or an unauthorized user ID with superuser privileges, but also to keep the damage from spreading to other systems. As an example, consider a denial-of-service (DoS) attack that's started on your systems at one local branch office and its subnets and is using malware payloads to spread itself throughout your systems. You may be able to filter any outbound traffic from that system to keep the malware itself from spreading, but until you've thoroughly cleansed all hosts within that local set of subnets, each of *them* could be suborned into DoS attacks on other hosts inside your system or out on the Internet.

Some typical containment tactics might include the following:

- Logically or physically disconnecting systems from the network or network segments from the rest of the infrastructure

- Disconnecting key servers (logically or physically), such as Domain Name System (DNS), Dynamic Host Configuration Protocol (DHCP), or access control systems

- Disconnecting your internal networks from your ISP at *all* points of presence

- Disabling Wi-Fi or other wireless and remote login and access

- Disabling outgoing and incoming connections to known services, applications, platforms, sites, or services

- Disabling outgoing and incoming connections to *all* external services, services, applications, platforms, sites, or services

- Disconnecting from any extranets or VPNs

- Disconnecting some or all external partners and user domains from any federated access to your systems

- Disabling internal users, processes, or applications, either in functional or logical groups or by physical or network locations

Take another close look at your data sources for monitoring and alarm information. Quite often, attack vectors are trying to cover their tracks by modifying, erasing, or otherwise making log files and indicator data unavailable to the SOC. As the alarms begin to sound, keeping your event data sources clean and pristine needs to be high on the SOC's internal priority watch-and-protect lists.

A familiar term should come to mind as you read this list: *quarantine*. In general, that's what containment is all about. Suspect elements of your system are *quarantined* off from the rest of the system, which certainly can prevent damage from spreading. It also can isolate a suspected causal agent, allowing you a somewhat safer environment in which to examine it, perhaps even identify it, and track down all of its pieces and parts. As a result, containment and eradication often blur into each other as interrelated tasks rather than remain as distinctly different phases of activity.

This gives us another term worthy of a definition: a *causal agent* is a software process, a data object, a hardware element, a human-performed procedure, or any combination of those that perform the actions on the targeted systems that constitute the incident, attack, or disruption. Malware payloads, their control and parameter files, and their carriers are examples of causal agents. Bogus user IDs, hardware sniffer devices, or systems on your network that have already been suborned by an attacker are examples of causal agents. As you might suspect, the more sophisticated APT kill chains may use multiple methods to get into your systems and in doing so leave multiple bits of stuff behind to help them achieve their objectives each time they come on in.

Check your SOC's processes and procedures as to when and how you should escalate or notify management regarding containment activities. Don't lose sight of the need to keep the organization informed and patient.

Before you conclude your containment efforts and begin eradication (or other recovery actions), make sure you've made protected copies of affected systems, as required, for evidence; ensure that you properly log all evidence to establish and protect its chain of custody.

Eradication

It's sometimes difficult to separate containment from eradication, since in many cases, the tools and processes you use to contain a causal agent (such as a malware infection or an unauthorized user ID) provide a one-step contain-and-eradicate. One vital distinction is to remember the need for evidence to support any follow-on forensics investigation: containment, by itself, should not alter information that might be needed as evidence, whereas eradication certainly will! Eradication is the process of identifying and then removing every instance of the causal agent and its associated files, executables, and so forth, from all elements of your system. For example, a malware infection would require you to thoroughly scrub every CPU's memory, as well as all file storage systems (local and in the clouds), to ensure you had found and removed all copies of the malware and any associated files, data, or code fragments. You'd also have to do this for all backup media for all of those systems to ensure you'd looked everywhere, removed the malware and its components, and clobbered or zeroized the space they were occupying in whatever storage media you found them on. Depending on the nature of the causal agent, the incident, and the storage technologies involved, you may need to do a full low-level reformat of the media and completely initialize its directory structures to ensure that eradication has been successfully completed.

✔ Don't Let Eradication Become a Self-Inflicted Attack

Far too many times, incident responders eradicate too much information from too many systems, servers, and endpoints. This can cause two different disastrous effects.

■ Eradicate too many files from too many systems or endpoint, and you may do worse damage than the attacker was trying to inflict. You delay getting business operations back to normal and may cause more data loss than the attack would have done.

■ Eradicate too soon or without proper containment and evidence capture, and you compromise or negate any attempts to conduct a follow-on forensic investigation of the incident.

Treat your eradication tools as if they are scalpels; use them to surgically remove just what needs to be removed.

Eradication is where two priorities potentially collide: getting back into business naturally conflicts with being able to know and prove who or what was responsible for the disruption in the first place. Eradicating malware from infected systems does, at one level, destroy evidence of the malware's presence there. Anti-malware systems usually provide extensive logging capabilities, which may be sufficient to meet evidentiary needs. This is something that should of course have been examined and decided upon during risk management, mitigation, and incident response planning and preparation activities, but there may be incidents where this decision has to be made in real time. If that's the case, get senior leadership or management's concurrence first, if at all possible! The incident response team must make note of these circumstances and management's authorization to proceed in the formal incident response team log files.

Eradication should result in a formal declaration that the system, a segment or subsystem, or a particular host, server, or communications device has been inspected and verified to be free from any remnants of the causal agent. This declaration is the signal that recovery of that element or subsystem can begin.

It's beyond the scope of this book to get into the many different techniques your incident response team may need to use as part of containment and eradication—quite frankly, there are just far too many potential causal agents out there in the wild, and more are being created daily. It's important to have a working sense of how detection and identification provided you the starting point for your containment, and then your eradication, of the threat. Your best bet may be to think even more like an attacker would and continue to get training, education, and experience in ethical penetration techniques, including reverse engineering of malware, as part of staying current and effective as an SSCP.

Recovery

Recovery is the process by which the organization's IT infrastructure, applications, data, and workflows are reestablished and declared operational. In an ideal world, recovery starts when the eradication phase is complete and when the hardware, networks, and other systems elements are declared safe to restore to their required "normal" state. The ideal recovery process brings all elements of the system back to the moment in time just before the incident started to inflict damage or disruption to your systems. When recovery is complete, end users should be able to log back in and start working again, just as if they'd last logged off at the end of a normal set of work-related tasks.

It's important to stress that every step of a recovery process must be *validated* as correctly performed and complete. This may need nothing more than using some simple tools to check status, state, and health information, or using preselected test suites of software and procedures to determine whether the system or element in question is behaving as it should be. It's also worth noting that the more complex a system is, the more it may need to have a specific order in which subsystems, elements, and servers are reinitialized as part of an overall recovery and restart process.

With that in mind, let's look at this step-by-step, in general terms:

Eradication Complete   Ideally, this is a formal declaration by the CSIRT that the systems elements in question have been verified to be free of any instances of the causal agent (malware, illicit user IDs, corrupted or falsified data, etc.).

Restore from "Bare Metal" to Working OS   Servers, hosts, endpoints, and many network devices should be reset to a known good set of initial software, firmware, and control parameters. In many cases, the IT department has made standard image sets that it uses to do a full initial load of new hardware of the same type. This should include setting up systems or device administrator identities, passwords, or other access control parameters. At the end of this task, the device meets your organization's security and operational policy requirements and can now have applications, data, and end users restored to it.

Ensure All OS Updates and Patches Are Installed Correctly   It's critical to ensure that the reloaded operating systems have all the required operational, functional, and security updates and patches correctly applied to them as a part of systems recovery efforts. Some organizations build and maintain a master or *golden image* of each operating system for each type of device and ensure that this golden image is routinely updated in accordance with configuration management and control decisions. Reloading systems from these golden images thus brings with it all current approved updates and patches. Otherwise, you will have to restore from the last known good distribution kit or systems image and then apply all patches and updates.

A special set of system restoration assessment tests should be developed (prior to being in the midst of an incident response) and used to verify that each reloaded system does in fact have its operating system correctly and completely restored.

Restore Applications as Well as Links to Applications, Platforms, and Servers on Your Network   Many endpoint devices in your systems will need locally installed applications, such as email clients, productivity tools, or even multifactor access control tools, as part of normal operations. These will need to be reinstalled from pristine distribution kits if they were not in the standard image used to reload the OS. This set of steps also includes reloading the connections to servers, services, and application platforms on your organization's networks (including extranets). This step should also verify that all updates and patches to applications have been installed correctly.

Restore Access to Resources via Federated Access Controls and Resources Beyond Your Security Perimeter on the Internet   This step may require coordination with these external resource operators, particularly if your containment activities had to temporarily disable such access.

At this point, the systems and infrastructure are ready for normal operations. Aren't they?

Data Recovery

Remember that the IT systems and the information architecture exists because the organization's business logic needs to gather, create, make use of, and produce information to support decisions and action. Restoring the data plane of the total IT architecture is the next step that must be taken before declaring the system "ready for business" again.

> ✔ **Backups: They Exist Only When You Plan for Business Continuity**
>
> When you're in the midst of responding to an information security incident, you do *not* want to discover that you have no backups of the business-critical software systems, databases, or other information resources. It's also not the time to discover you have no backups of encryption keys used to protect those backups or archival copies. Yes, the CSIRT is the *primary customer* of these backups, but somebody else had to have planned and specified how to generate them, how often to make updated backups, and how they should be stored, kept safe, and yet be available when urgently needed.

Business continuity planning is the broad functional area that should address these needs, which is covered in greater detail in the "Understand and Support Business Continuity Plan and Disaster Recovery Plan Activities" section in this chapter. As to the CSIRT, please note that your own *preparation* phase should have found either where the backups are kept and how to know which ones to use…or discovered that nobody's actually making any backups in the first place!

In most cases, incident recovery will include restoring databases and storage systems *content* to the last known good configuration. This requires, of course, that the organization has a routine process in place for making backups of all of their operational data. Those backups might be:

- Complete copies of every data item in every record in every database and file
- Incremental or partial copies, which copy a subset of records or files on a regular basis
- Differential, update, or change copies, which consist of records, fields, or files changed since a particular time
- Transaction logs, which are chronologically ordered sets of input data

Restoring all databases and filesystems to their "ready for business as usual" state may take the combined efforts of the incident response team, database administrators, application support programmers, and others in the IT department. Key end users may also need to be part of this process, particularly as they are probably best suited to verifying that the systems *and* the data are all back to normal.

For example, a small wholesale distributor might use a backup strategy that takes a full copy of their databases once per week and then a differential backup at the end of every business day. Individual transactions (reflecting customer orders, payments to vendors, inventory changes, etc.) would be reflected in the transaction logs kept for their specific applications or by their end users. In the event that their database has been corrupted by an attacker (or a serious systems malfunction), they'd need to restore the last complete backup copy and then apply the daily differential backups for each day since that backup copy had been made. Finally, they'd have to step through each transaction again, either using built-in applications functions that recover transactions from saved log files or by hand.

Now, that distributor is ready to start working on new transactions, reflecting new business. Their CSIRT's response to the incident is over, and they move on to the post-incident activities I'll cover in just a moment.

Post-Recovery: Notification and Monitoring

One of the last tasks that the incident response team has is to ensure that end users, functional managers, and senior leaders and managers in the organization know that the recovery operations are now complete. It is important to note that the response team notifies responsible management and leadership that systems are ready for normal operational use; management and leadership then decide to move the organization from "incident response" back to normal business operations. The CSIRT does not make this decision nor own the responsibilities that go with it—the management team does!

Once the CSIRT has given this "ready to relaunch" signal to management and management decides to move in that direction, three separate communications need to take place.

- **Back in business:** This notice gives the green light to the organization to get back into normal business operations. Each department or functional division of the organization may have a different approach to this, based on their business logic and processes. This is particularly true as to how each department addresses any work lost during the overall downtime. Synchronization of efforts across departments and between lines of business may require extensive coordination, depending upon the incident and its impacts.

- **Proceed with caution:** Users and their managers should be extra vigilant as they start to use the systems, applications, and data once again. They may want to start with load-balancing constraints in place so that processes can be closely monitored as they start up slowly and then throttle up to the normal pace of business.

- **Get the word out:** Senior leaders and managers should help make sure that key external stakeholders, partners, and others are properly informed about the successful recovery operation. They may also need to meet legal and regulatory obligations and keep government officials, shareholders or investors, customers, and the general public properly informed. This is also a great opportunity for leadership and management, from the top down to the first-rung supervisors, to help ensure that every member of the team can be confident in the post-recovery state of the organization.

At this point the incident response team's real-time sense of urgency can relax; they've met the challenges of this latest information security incident to confront their organization. Now it's time to take a deep breath, relax, and *capture their lessons learned*.

While remaining vigilant for the *next* incident, of course.

Lessons Learned; Implementation of New Countermeasures

Figure 4.2, you recall, suggests but does not explicitly show the web of cross-connections that are the *opportunities* for you and your teammates to learn from the painful lessons of the experiences you gain, moment by moment, in dealing with an information systems security incident. As the SOC team and the CSIRT focused on the details of further characterizing the incident, containing it, eradicating as necessary, and recovering all systems back to normal, those teams learned important lessons. Perhaps some procedures were found to be incomplete; tools and processes were found to be inadequate or had significant room for improvement to make them more effective and reliable to use. Logging, record-keeping, and the gathering of evidence might have shown that your chain of custody processes need improvement, if you're going to help the organization make its bullet-proof case really bullet-proof, based on that evidence and its associated records. People-to-people communication skills, processes, or protocols might not have worked very well.

No lesson is too small to make note of, capture, and then consider as part of your continuing process of improvement. Nor should you push this lessons-learning too far off into the future. Yes, the textbook portrayals of the incident response lifecycle can suggest that it's *after* the incident is over that you begin the process of debriefing the responders, capturing the ideas and problems, prioritizing which to deal with first, and getting those fixes or improvements into production. This does not need to be a "Monday-morning quarterbacking" exercise of trying to second-guess what happened in Sunday's game. Instead, reality and experience suggest several reasons why immediately starting to implement the lessons your *current* response experiences are teaching you is sound practice.

- **Incidents may have long dwell times:** APTs using a sophisticated kill chain strategy may take months to go from their first attempts to infiltrate your systems to finally departing your systems (if they leave at all); you'll need to respond to such an attack over weeks or months as well.

- **Attacks by different threat actors may overlap in time and space:** As you respond to one element of one APT's kill chain, you may discover that other unwanted guests are attempting to capture your systems' resources and capabilities to use for their own ends.

- **Let different teams work in parallel across the incident response lifecycle:** In all but the smallest of organizations, the on-shift watch-standing SOC teams and incident response team members are not the only ones who can (or should) be working on developing, implementing, and testing new or improved information risk mitigation and security controls. Usually, too, there are subtly different skill sets needed to analyze and assess requirements, select and implement new controls, and operationalize them via administrative, procedural, and training efforts, versus those needed for on-scene incident response.

- **Some fixes, improvements, or changes can and should be quick and easy, so do them:** You have no real reason to wait; if you've got the people time or other assets you need to make some of these fixes *right now*, while the need for them and the pertinent details are fresh in your mind, do it before the next incident arrives.

Go back to that NIST checklist in Figure 4.3; the lessons learned process, be it done after the incident response or during it, can use this same kind of checklist approach. Preparation planning identified assets that you believed would increase your chance of successfully surviving an incident and recovering from it. The reality of an incident has tested the assumptions you made regarding each of those readiness items. In light of that, re-evaluate each item; write down the list of changes, improvements, repairs, or the justification to outright replace that asset, based on what you've just learned in the "live-fire" testing event (the incident) you've just been through. Then get management and leadership to start resolving each action item on that list you've just created.

Third-Party Considerations

Today, with public/private hybrid environments and those that lean heavily on outsourced or third-party services, it is imperative to include them in your incident management program's policies, plans, and procedures. Security teams should be reviewing their third parties as part of their overall risk management strategy; it is also important to make sure they align with your incident management program. This detailed coordination should start *before* selecting and contracting with any such third-party services provider or strategic partner, by identifying the total set of services, information exchanges, coordination, and collaboration activities required by that relationship. Your organization, after all, is totally responsible for every step, every nuance, and every detail of every process that is part of how you do business; delegating some of those responsibilities and actions to third parties does not relieve your team of their due diligence and due care burdens. Once your team has identified everything that needs a particular third-party type of support relationship, your organization can then negotiate with that third party from a more informed and confident position. After the contracts are signed, it can be extremely difficult (and expensive) to renegotiate aspects of that relationship or to attempt to add forgotten or overlooked items. You certainly do not want to be trying to negotiate for exchanges of log files or other forensic data while you're in the middle of responding to an information security incident.

It's important to recognize the demonstrated ability of APTs to use multiple targets of opportunity to ultimately strike at the target that supports their main objective. Along the way, these attacks—as in the Target data breach in 2013—involve using service providers that have existing business relationships with the APT's ultimate target. Third-party considerations for information security incidents reach far beyond your cloud services providers or strategic partners that are part of your SSO-enabled federated systems. Every organization you do business with, including your customers, is a potential player in your next information security incident response. This should be carefully considered during the planning phases, as you develop both your incident response plans and procedures and identify where your third parties can and should be stronger parts of your overall *shared* security posture.

✔ Real-Time Notification and Coordination: Set These Up *Before* the First Incident

One of the most critical service levels that must be coordinated prior to signing a service contract involves *responsiveness* to a suspected information security incident. Your SLA or TOR with that third party must clearly spell out how quickly each party must notify the other and what real-time communications and coordination channels, facilities, or processes must be used when either party suspects or has detected such an incident. The SLA should also address whether that notification and communication must occur *regardless* of whether the detecting party has probable cause to believe that the other party is at risk (or is contributing to the incident) or not.

The ideal, of course, is a real-time secure voice and data collaboration channel between your organization's SOC points of contact and their opposite numbers within the service provider. At the other end of the spectrum are response channels that are based on submitting trouble tickets or emails to the provider, in the hope that *your* sense of urgency will convey to them and elicit a prompt response. Email exchanges are not, in general, effective ways to contain and resolve an information security incident involving a third-party relationship.

Timely coordination and effective collaboration with each third party can be expensive; but with the average data breach or security incident costing their targets upward of $500,000 each, at some point it's worth paying more for the level of services your business really needs and deserves.

Coordination and collaboration continue throughout the entire lifecycle of the relationship with any third-party services provider, whether they provide cloud services, website hosting, off-site data storage and archiving, data recovery, systems maintenance, logistics support, or data and systems disposal and destruction. This covers phases such as the following:

- **Pre-incident**
  - **Prediction:** All service provider relationships should define the real-time and near-real-time telemetry data that needs to be exchanged for both parties to be able to meaningfully detect possible information security incidents in the making. Based on each partner's needs, this might also include behavioral information to support advanced threat detection systems or other trending and performance data. Both parties have a vested interest in improving each other's capabilities in keeping their joint threat surface safe, secure, and useful after all.
  - **Detection:** Does the third party warn of any incidents or take actions to minimize the probability and/or impact of a security incident? This answer can depend greatly with third parties, and it is important to understand how the third party prevents breaches and how they document and provide their customers with security reviews and audits.
- **During the incident**
  - **Notification:** Your incident response procedures must include timely notification to potentially affected third parties, especially those providing services that may be involved in the incident. Your team should also have clearly identified points of contacts to receive incident notifications from third parties (including ones that have no third party standing with you, such as someone surfing your website who detects something suspicious).
  - **Assessment:** Some incidents may be strictly internal, not involving any third-party services or information; for those that do involve one or more third-party relationships, a collaborative assessment process can bring each party's knowledge of their own systems and data to the incident at hand.
  - **Response:** Once an incident is believed to involve third-party systems and services, coordination *before* action is crucial to keeping both organizations and their systems on the safest of paths to recovery. Just as you risk disrupting your own business by too aggressively attempting to contain and eradicate a threat actor's causal agents or in disabling accounts they may be using, so too your business can be derailed if one of your third parties overreacts to an incident. You don't want to help the attacker by cascading the damages to *your* systems into those of your third parties, and vice versa.
- **Post-incident**
  - **Recovery and reporting:** Recovery timelines must be in sync with both internal and external parties as a delay from one could result in damages or

fees. A hosting company that fails to recover a database or application could have severe financial impacts to the organization. It is therefore important to develop relationships with the people who receive notifications and how customers are notified. Reporting of vulnerabilities from third parties in a timely matter must take place and be incorporated with internal vulnerability management programs.

- **After action:** The security team should work with third parties to evaluate how an incident may have happened and what steps can be taken to further prevent a reoccurrence. The security practitioner should regularly evaluate, address, and verify remediation of weaknesses and deficiencies with the third-party providers.

- **During a forensic investigation**
  - At some point in an incident response process, your organization's management and leadership may decide to institute a forensic investigation, either formally or informally. Such investigations may require that third parties be notified that an investigation is underway and that they are requested to protect all information involved with the event; or they may be served with digital discovery motions. In almost all cases, the forensic investigations teams (yours and that of your third parties) and the respective managers and legal counsel will have to take charge of coordinating this with any third parties that are a party to the incident.

The involvement of third parties, both upstream and downstream, is vitally important in incident response, as they may affect explicit and crucial aspects in the sequence of response actions.

UNDERSTAND AND SUPPORT FORENSIC INVESTIGATIONS

A risk event occurs, and the organization suffers its resulting impacts and losses; the organization now needs to determine how the incident occurred, who has what portion of responsibility for it, and what corrective actions to take as part of a longer-term business plan. Ideally, these decisions are based on reliable, credible evidence; that evidence is chained together in a series of logical, well-reasoned steps to argue conclusively what happened, who did it, and what should be done next. Forensics is the science of using evidence to construct logically valid arguments; forensics investigators generate hypotheses (or possible explanations) regarding the event and then look for evidence that confirms or denies each hypothesis. All of this supports the need for management and leadership to make informed, fact-based decisions regarding the incident and its after-math. Gathered together, the body of evidence; the applicable laws, policies, regulations, or administrative controls; and the logical arguments and their conclusion are called the *findings* of a forensic investigation.

In the world of information systems security, there are many reasons to perform an investigation, and there are many scenarios that may require one, such as in response to a crime, a violation of policy, or a significant IT outage/incident. (An interruption of service or malfunction may indicate something beyond routine equipment failure or user error.) Organizations today are faced with an almost nonstop demand for authoritative, reliable, accurate, and complete disclosures of information, and in most cases, the penalties for making or filing false, incomplete, or deliberately misleading statements or findings can be quite severe. Some of these demands include the following:

- Digital discovery motions, issued by a court, demanding disclosure of specified records to the court or to a designated recipient
- Legal briefs to a court on pending or ongoing criminal or civil actions
- Legal briefs and discovery disclosures to government regulators, auditors, or inspectors
- Digital discovery or other legal briefs to labor tribunals, the courts, or others involved in adjudicating, arbitrating, or mediating a civil dispute involving the organization
- Information filings in support of insurance claims
- Compliance filings required by health, safety, or financial regulatory authorities
- Information disclosure and reporting required by contracts with partners, suppliers, vendors, subcontractors, or strategically important customers
- Disclosures in support of contract negotiations
- Investigations to determine causes of systems failures, unsafe operational behavior, or incorrect operation

In short, every aspect of the CIANA+PS stack of information security needs—including privacy and safety considerations—may require an unimpeachable forensic investigation to support a decision to take an urgent and compelling action in its regard.

Key to the success of any investigation is preserving the integrity of the evidence. Incident scenes are *dirty*; they contain some useful objects, bits of information, and clues to the event you're investigating, all thrown against a real-world canvas that is incredibly rich with almost totally irrelevant items. The evidence that *is* in the scene will be incomplete; your guesswork (your hypotheses) will attempt to bridge over the gaps in the evidence, while you systematically filter out the stuff that's not relevant and meaningful to the questions you're investigating. Nevertheless, you must constantly preserve the evidence in exactly the condition you found it in; if you change it in any way, you really cannot rely on it as you build your argument about who did what and why. We'll look at this in more detail in "The Chain of Custody" section.

Legal and Ethical Principles

The complexities of the law at home, much less abroad, dictate that you call in the lawyers early and often throughout your incident response lifecycle. Regardless, there are a few key legal and ethical ideas you should have a solid understanding of as you conduct all of your tasks as an information security specialist.

Chapter 1, "Security Operations and Administration," established the broadly accepted legal and ethical principles behind CIANA+PS, the core information security requirements of confidentiality, integrity, availability, nonrepudiation, authentication, privacy, and safety. Each of these directly links to the common business ethical requirements of due care and due diligence (which many nations have embodied in their criminal and civil laws). Chapter 1 also linked these ideas to the (ISC)² Code of Ethics and to your professional obligations to supporting that code. Taken together, those concepts (CIANA, privacy, safety, due care, and due diligence) should be a sufficient set of foundational elements for you to build your incident response processes upon.

Most legal systems do impose constraints and duties upon everyone involved in an incident scene, whether as participants, bystanders, responders, or owners or managers of the property or location in question. Societies value being able to establish that something happened and further to show who had responsibility for what happened; they need to be able to demonstrate that laws were broken (or complied with) and be able to unemotionally assess what injuries, deaths, damage to property, or other losses resulted from an incident. In almost all societies, *evidence* is required to establish those conclusions; therefore, it's in everyone's interest that evidence at the scene be preserved and protected as best as possible. But societies do recognize that first responders may, in emergency situations, have higher priorities to attend to than the preservation of evidence. Firefighters responding to a structure fire in your data center will not, of course, be worrying about saving the digital contents of your servers or the media, documents, and files kept in your records center; their priority is ensuring the safety of life by controlling the fire, containing it, and ideally extinguishing (eradicating) it.

For the rest of us, the nonemergency and non-life-saving first responders and incident investigators, we share in the legal obligation to ensure that the incident scene be preserved as best as possible so that it can tell its own story; the evidence in that scene needs to be protected from loss, damage, or corruption (be that deliberate or accidental) so that any investigation of that incident will come to an unimpeachable and irrefutable conclusion. By controlling, preserving, and protecting the scene, we limit or prevent loss, damage, or corruption of evidence; this is due care in action. Establishing and maintaining a chain of custody for evidence related to that scene is the accountability proof that *we* need, as responders and investigators, to show that we fulfilled our due diligence responsibilities.

Chapter 1 also examined various legal and ethical concepts regarding the rights that individuals and organizations have against unwarranted search of their belongings (including their information and record-keeping systems) and their rights to privacy of their persons, places, and actions. These legal and ethical rights form a set of constraints on how you and an incident response team can search an incident scene, question people who are or may have been involved in the incident, and attempt to search the property under the control of such persons. They can constrain how you establish internal, perimeter, and external surveillance systems; they can also limit or dictate what you can or must do with surveillance data, such as video or audio recordings these systems collect. Different legal systems have different processes that control how you can give access to such surveillance information to others, such as to national or local government agencies, law enforcement, insurance adjusters, and investigators, or even to others in your management and leadership chain. Thus, it's vital that you get your organization's legal team involved as you develop these aspects of your incident response procedures; gain their approval before you put your teammates in jeopardy by tasking them to carry out those procedures.

Logistics Support to Investigations

Digital forensics is a game of large numbers: the total number of objects to examine can easily exceed one million or more when you consider every file, file header, date and time stamp, location information, and the data in the file itself. It's imperative that the investigators use efficient forensics tool sets, often integrated as a *forensic workstation*, as their investigative infrastructure. When you combine this with the need to preserve and protect such evidence with a strong chain of custody procedures, you can quickly imagine that an investigative team is going to have some specific needs from your organization for facilities and administrative support.

- Separate workspaces, which the investigative team can secure or lock when they are not present. These should be considered as restricted access spaces, and other organizational employees (even senior managers or leaders) must be prevented from attempting to access them without express permission from the investigators. (This supports chain of custody integrity.) Larger or more technically savvy organizations (which as lucrative targets may attract multiple attack attempts per year) may see the need to establish separate *clean room* facilities to support forensic investigations.

- Access to your systems, information storage and documentation libraries, administrative procedures, policies, and guidelines.

- Access to your networks and systems.

- Access to your people.

Depending upon your organization's physical locations, you may also need to provide routine access (such as special visitor badges), reserved parking, or otherwise expedite the ways in which the team can bring in their own forensic analysis, evidence collection, and related equipment and supplies.

It's also wise to designate someone in the organization as the principle point of contact for investigators to come to when special support needs or issues arise. This point of contact can then broker the issues within the organization and get the right resources marshalled to resolve them; or, if need be, get the right managers and leaders to meet with the investigators to seek a common understanding and a way forward.

Evidence Handling

"Evidence collection and handling" can have a broad range of meaning, much of which is beyond the normal duties of an SSCP. Organizations need evidence to support criminal prosecution of attackers and malicious insiders. Evidence informs the choices organizations make during incident response, during recovery, and in remediation, repair, or upgrades of systems and processes after an incident. Evidence also establishes whether the organization fulfilled its due care and due diligence responsibilities in the event of an information security incident or a data breach. Evidence also aids in lawsuits brought in civil court.

There is a tendency for information systems professionals to hear "evidence" and think only about *digital* evidence; this is hard to understand, since as an information *security* professional you also have to make the right choices about physical and administrative risk mitigation and security controls, as well as logical (that is, software-implemented digital) controls. You'll need to use a combination of physical, logical, and administrative evidence to prove to your managers that your physical access control systems, for example, are working correctly. Thus, it's important and relevant to think about all forms of evidence when you consider the collection, protection, and use of evidence pertaining to an incident scene.

As the on-scene SSCP, you might have to assist in gathering and protecting evidence related to a security incident. This evidence could be in many forms:

- Physical IT-related evidence, such as computers, USB or other media, paper documentation, cables, or other hardware devices.

- Physical evidence about the scene itself, such as damaged doors on secured cabinets.

- Images or descriptions of physical evidence, such as a video or photograph of a portion of the incident scene, or video recordings showing the movement of people, vehicles, or other objects in and around the scene.

- Documentary evidence, which can be any log, recording, notes, or papers that describe or attest to something at the scene. A book found at the scene is a physical piece of evidence; your personal notes made during the incident response are your description or documentation of what you believe transpired.

- Digital evidence, such as files, directory structures, memory dumps, disk images, packet trace histories, log files, or extracts from databases.

- Testimony given by any person regarding the incident, either in direct (in person) form, as a recording, or as a transcript.

Everybody who has any role in responding to an incident will become involved with items of evidence such as these. Typical information security incidents may have actions taking place in many different physical and virtual locations, which of course complicates the whole process of identifying who is a "first responder," which incident response teams have responsibility over which portions of this dispersed scene-of-scenes, and what it means to have one person take control of "the" scene. For starters, let's consider a simpler scene, confined to one building, such as a data center at your company's main operating location.

It's useful to think about evidence collection, protection, and analysis from the organizational perspective of the end game: what does the evidence need to do *for* the organization, when it take its case to court or uses the findings of an investigation to take a controversial internal action? Generally speaking, the total set of evidence you put together as the findings of your investigation needs to be the following:

- **Be accurate:** The evidence and documentation must not vary, deviate, or conflict with other evidence or contain any errors. Inaccurate evidence can be disputed or dismissed.

- **Be authentic:** Evidence should not deviate from the truth and relevant facts. In addition to harming your side's opportunity for a favorable court decision, inauthentic evidence may be construed as deceiving the court, which is itself a crime.

- **Be complete:** Both sides of a court case will be allowed to review and dispute all evidence provided by the other side; you will be required to share any and all data related to the case, regardless of whether that data supports your side. Even evidence that does not demonstrate your intended outcomes must be shared with the opposing side to give the court an opportunity to make a fair, informed, and objective decision. Furthermore, as with deception, failure to disclose all evidence in a legal matter may have financial and even criminal consequences.

- **Be convincing:** Regardless of the type of court, the purpose of the case is to determine which side's narrative is more believable, as supported by testimony and evidence. You will try to convince the court your story is more believable, while disputing your opponent's side; the adversary will be doing the same. The evidence you present should support your story, and your story should be reasonably demonstrated by the evidence.

- **Be admissible:** There are many kinds of evidence that are admissible in court and only a few that aren't; some are admissible only after a ruling by the court and discussion/review by opposing counsel (such as expert testimony). Be sure to understand the rules of evidence that are applicable in your jurisdiction to know which evidence will be admissible.

In all matters of evidence, it is absolutely imperative to consult with legal counsel to ensure your efforts are suitable for the court.

✔ Data Cleaning at a Crime Scene?

One of the enduring myths in our industry is the belief that original content will be rendered inadmissible as evidence if it is modified in any way; this is simply not a black-and-white issue. Ideally, the evidence should be unaltered as you collect, preserve, and analyze it; this "gold standard" of evidence, when supported by an unimpeachable set of chain of custody records, is worth striving for.

What do you do when multiple pieces of evidence still do not paint a complete picture or contradict each other? In many cases, *data cleaning* provides an audit-proof approach to find other sources of data (such as official records databases) that can be used to fill in the gaps or resolve conflicts.

"Would you clean a crime scene?" asks Robin Farshadfar, general manager at EastNets Holdings Ltd, a financial integrity and payment solutions provider. Instead, she admonishes us to "let the data stay dirty" by building a *new* record or file that combines the new corrections *on top of* the original data—but avoids changing the original if at all possible. Keep a change log of each bit that is changed; be able to trace back to the sources you used for the new or replacement data; build your argument that each change is correct. Spare no details in doing this!

Sometimes you cannot; destructive testing, or even the nature of the evidence collection process itself, may unavoidably make changes to the evidence. As storage devices become smarter and smarter, it's becoming harder to work around their onboard journaling and data integrity processes as you try to extract a copy of the data from the device. When this happens, take detailed notes of every step you take; build that audit trail step by step.

That chain of argument — that audit trail — and your chain of custody records for the original evidence *and* all of the data you use in cleaning the evidence is what your case will rest upon.

Controlling and Preserving the Scene

In his memoirs, Colin Powell remarked that the U.S. Army used to teach its young officers that when they come to a new location and they determine that they are the senior ranking person there, that they first take charge of the scene by identifying all personnel who are there (military and civilian) and inventorying all assets at the location (whether or not owned by the Army). This is still sound advice!

Treat the incident scene as if it is a physical, logical, and administrative baseline that you must bring under change management and control. First, you inventory what's there; second, you use the authority granted to you as a first responder or incident response team lead, and your incident response procedures, to guide you in asserting *change ownership* over the scene and everything in it. You do this for several important reasons.

- To limit further loss or damage to property, or injury to persons, from whatever cause

- To control the response process so that systems, equipment, or business processes can be safely and controllably brought to a known halt, hazards (malware, smoke, or intruders) can be contained, and their damaging effects prevented from spreading

- To protect and preserve the objects and information contained in the scene as possible evidence

One further benefit of controlling and preserving the scene is that you can assist senior management and leadership in balancing the conflicting needs to understand what happened, prevent it from happening again, pursue claims against responsible parties, and get back into business operations as normal. Each of those legitimate needs pushes or pulls on the responders with different senses of urgency; as the on-scene change control owner, you can to the best extent possible ensure that senior leaders make those priority calls and that people on scene act to achieve them.

As with any change control process, the *record-keeping* that you do as you control and preserve the scene is vitally important. Take notes. Time-tag each note, whether in your smartphone, your incident responder's ruggedized laptop, or your paper pocket notebook; keep track of what happened, who did it, on whose authority did they do it, when they did it, and what resulted from their actions.

The Chain of Custody

In legal terms, the chain of custody is the change control process and the change control record-keeping that is used to identify, preserve, store, and control access to and use of pieces of evidence. The evidence custodian is the person (or agency) who has the responsibility and authority to protect the evidence and maintain records of any attempts to access, move, modify, delete, or destroy such evidence.

The chain of custody can easily be seen by looking at the lifecycle of a piece of evidence related to an information security incident scene. Such a lifecycle model can consist of steps such as the following:

- **Creation:** Someone or something does something in or at the incident scene that creates something new or modifies something that is already part of the scene.

This may happen well in advance of the start of the incident; other times, evidence is created or changed by the actions that take place during the incident. (A log file that was created the day before the incident and that was not modified during the incident might be useful evidence that indicates that the logging function had been bypassed or disabled.)

- **Recognition and identification:** Someone responding to or investigating the incident determines that an object or set of information might be relevant and material evidence.

- **Taking possession or custody of the evidence item:** This starts the chain of custody and establishes the first set of information about that piece of evidence that needs to be captured and recorded.

- **Cataloging:** Each item of evidence is uniquely identified in an evidence log.

- **Protection, preservation, or control:** At this step, change control is exerted; no one should be permitted to access, touch, view, change, or move the evidence item without proper authorization and without the evidence custodian (the keeper of the chain of custody records) granting permission and access to do so. The evidence item is either preserved on scene (for example, by restricting access to the scene by others) or removed from the scene and placed in secure storage. For digital evidence, this may involve making a complete or partial copy of the physical or logical media that the digital information is on.

- **Analysis:** Many different analysis tasks might need to be performed using various pieces of evidence. Analysis tests can be broadly classified as *destructive* or *nondestructive*, based on whether the tests irreversibly alter the piece of evidence. Most digital evidence analysis tasks can and should be performed on a copy of the evidence item, rather than on the original, as a precaution.

- **Reporting:** The analysis findings are collated and put into summary form, presenting the arguments, their step-by-step results, and the ultimate bottom-line conclusion of the investigation.

- **Transfer:** Evidence may be transferred to other facilities, agencies, or organizations. Transfers may be directed by a court order or by other law enforcement action; the organization holding the evidence and its investigators may also determine that a more effective analysis, or better protection for the evidence, may be obtained by transferring it to another facility.

- **Retention:** After the investigation is complete, evidence is usually retained (and protected) for a number of years, which protects the organization and all parties if appeals or counter-actions are initiated that need to re-examine an item of evidence.

- **Destruction or disposal:** At some point, the findings of the investigation have been accepted as final, all appeals have been exhausted or their time frames have expired, and the data can be disposed of in accordance with applicable data retention and destruction policies.

The first important question that comes up about any and every piece of evidence is whether that evidence itself is credible; is it reasonable to believe that the item of evidence is what it seems to be and claims to be? (That ought to sound familiar; think about what the identity proofing and authentication steps in access control must accomplish.) That lifecycle view of a piece of evidence reveals just how many opportunities there are for someone to accidentally or deliberately change, destroy, or lose a piece of evidence. That *possibility* alone means that someone can *impeach* that piece of evidence, by claiming that the person who had custody of the evidence cannot prove that the evidence item has not been altered in any way by anyone. The chain of custody is the sequence of records kept, step-by-step, for each piece of evidence. Who gathered it? What did they do with it? How and where was it stored? Was the storage facility secure enough that no one could gain access to evidence and alter or remove it without being detected?

This chain of custody continues during the analysis process. Each analyst must sign out a piece of evidence, must record every movement of that evidence, every analysis task that is performed on it, what changes if any of that analysis made to the evidence, and what they did with the evidence at the end of their test. (It is hoped that they *returned* the evidence to the evidence storage facility and logged it back into custody.) Custody records must also capture the details of any copies made (digital or otherwise). Once made, a copy of an evidence item must also be subject to chain of custody record-keeping (imagine the havoc that could result from findings based on a false or altered copy of an important bit of evidence).

Evidence Collection

Your organization will most likely need to collect a variety of physical, administrative, and logical or digital evidence in the course of responding to an incident and supporting a forensic investigation into its cause. In almost all cases, the organization will be better protected if it uses trained, expert forensic investigators to conduct all aspects of evidence collection, preservation, and analysis. You should, however, become familiar with the processes such evidence collection may use and appreciate what your role might be in supporting such expert investigators. Standards such as ISO 27037, "Information technology – Security techniques – Guidelines for identification, collection, acquisition and preservation of digital evidence" (`https://www.iso.org/standard/44381.html`), can provide great insight into what you and your organization need to do to be prepared to call in the experts and support them to achieve *your* investigative needs.

During the preparation phase, the organization should identify candidate investigator teams and establish at least a preliminary working relationship with them. This can help the organization establish on-call or urgent support relationships with investigators and analysts with the proper training, expertise, and tools to perform digital forensics. These investigators can be internal employees, external contractors, or a combination of both. These decisions should take into consideration response time, data classification, and sensitivity.

The ideal forensic team should be made up of people with diverse skillsets, including knowledge of networking principles and protocols, a wide range of security products, and network-based threats and attack vectors. Skillsets should overlap between team members, and cross-training should be encouraged so that no one member is the only person with a particular skill.

Other teams within the organization should be available to support forensic activities. This should have top-down support through policy, and the forensic team should feel enabled to approach members of management, the legal team, human resources, auditors, IT, and physical security staff. Working together, the cross-functional forensic team should have a broad set of skills, capabilities, tools, techniques, and understanding of procedures.

Tools

Digital forensic analysts need an assortment of tools to collect and examine data. Different tools are necessary to be able to collect and examine both volatile and nonvolatile data; to capture information from media, software, and hardware; and to craft meaningful reports from all the data collected and created during analysis. There are, for example, many types of file viewers necessary to view files that have different formats, extensions, or compression types. Investigating systems based on Microsoft Windows technologies will benefit from a variety of third-party tools, such as registry, event log, and virtual disk analysis utilities, which provide analysts with new ways to view and navigate these complex data structures, and investigate changes made to them that might relate to the incident at hand. Debugging tools allow analysts to get more details than default reports or logs will include. Decompilers, reverse assemblers, and binary analysis tools allow analysts to look inside executable programs, at the code level, to find anomalies and malicious code. *Reverse engineering* tools and systems provide for complex, powerful, integrated capabilities to take executable (binary) files apart and identify in human-readable terms the patterns of instructions that they're made of. Many of these reverse engineering suites support communities of practitioners, which allows the power of many, many pairs of eyes to help your investigators identify oddities implanted in your code or potential malware they've found on your system. There are also dedicated tools to extract data from a database. Analysts also use specialized tools to analyze mobile devices for file changes and to find deleted files and messages.

A drive imaging tool is critical to the forensic process. These come in different forms, such as a dedicated workstation, small appliance, or software, but the function is to make an exact copy of a drive or piece of media. Some versions require the physical removal of the drive or media and attachment to the imaging tool, which is called a *dead copy*. Other imaging tools can interface via transfer cables, FireWire technology, network media, and so on, to capture "live" images or copies, meaning that the image is taken while the device is running.

A write blocker is another valuable tool used in forensic investigation. It can be either an appliance or a software tool. It does just what its names says: it prevents any new data from being written to the drive or media and prevents data from being overwritten during analysis of the drive/media. This is useful to reduce the possibility of introducing unintended modifications to the original data.

It is also useful to have a hashing tool to create digests for integrity purposes. A message digest is the output of a hash function, creating a unique representation of the exact value of a given set of data. If the data changes, even in a minor way (even by one character), the entire digest changes; in this way, an investigator can be sure that the original data collected as evidence is the same data that was analyzed and is the same data provided as evidence to the court and opposing parties. Two common algorithms for creating message digests are Secure Hash Algorithm 1 (SHA-1) and Message Digest 5 (MD5). Many popular forensic tools incorporate automatic hashing/integrity checks.

Network traffic is also an important aspect of digital forensics. Capturing traffic from a sniffer, packet analysis tool, or network threat detection tool provides live session data. Log files are also a critical element of analyzing the network aspects of a forensic investigation. Log files are found in many locations, including servers, firewalls, intrusion detection systems/intrusion prevention systems, and routers and can provide significant insight into the events that transpired over networks.

Finally, a video screen capture tool can be valuable for analysis purposes. The ability to capture real-time video can be used to document the steps taken on a forensic workstation, for example. It proves that the analysts are performing the steps they claimed and performing them consistently and in accordance with the written forensic procedures. It can also help with documenting and reporting afterward.

Not all tools are created equally, and there are a wide variety of both open source and commercial tools. It is essential that the selection of tools be made in consultation with the organization's legal counsel, who can provide guidance on which particular tools would provide admissible evidence.

Triage and Evidence?

Applying a triage process to the gathering and processing of evidence might seem a self-contradicting proposition: don't you risk throwing away the very nugget of evidence you need to reveal the real root cause, the real threat actor, and prove your case? The problem, however, is that it's quite likely that you and your forensic investigation team face a literal data deluge, and you won't have the time or resources to gather and examine everything you'll encounter at an incident scene. Terabyte-sized USB drives are commonplace; cloud infrastructures routinely deal in blobs (binary large objects) of storage that can exceed petabytes in size. The challenge to the investigator almost becomes what evidence *not* to capture, take custody of, catalog, and then analyze. The apparent nature of the incident, your systems architecture, and the size and complexity of your organizational structure may provide some guidance to help you and the investigators avoid needlessly copying and preserving huge amounts of data—or be too stingy in what you choose to gather as evidence and potentially throw away too many "smoking guns" without realizing it.

Forensic triage is a rapidly growing practice within the digital forensic community. As you might expect from its name, this process involves the investigative team quickly examining each computer system, other object, or other set of information at the scene and prioritizing it for further examination. If a system, object, or information asset ranks high in that triage priority, it is taken into custody; if it clearly has no material bearing on the case, it can be released to the organization for further eradication, restoration, and normal business use. Items that fall in between the urgent and the probably useless should also be taken into custody, but analysis on these may have to wait until investigative resources are available. Such triage decisions do have something of the nature of a self-fulfilling prophecy to them: if you think you're looking for an embezzler, you'll probably not choose to run search tools on employee or visitor laptops that might suggest they were used to exfiltrate your database, install malware, or buy and sell pornography or pirated videos. (Note, too, that in jurisdictions that require search to be specific, with or without a search warrant, you usually cannot examine a system for *any* evidence of *any* possible crime.) A variety of forensic analysis workstation products now make managing forensic triage easier. Again, your organization's unique risk profile should be your guide; let it focus your attention to the higher-priority threats you face and then develop forensic triage strategies to help you respond to them more efficiently.

Some investigators argue that this is actually *digital triage* and not *forensic triage*, as there's actually no real analysis of the evidence items performed as part of the prioritization process. It's arguably true that calling it *forensic triage* can be appropriate only if the process adheres to all of the rules of evidence and forensic investigative process for the legal jurisdiction in question.

A variety of process models or lifecycles for digital triage have been published, and they do seem to have several important phases in common.

- Planning and preparation looks to organizing, training, and equipping the investigative teams with the tools, techniques, and procedures needed to apply triage principles to an investigation. This should match the preparation activities to a selected range of incident types.

■ Live digital triage focuses on prioritizing the capture of volatile data, such as in-memory data, mobile device memories, or the content of control tables in networks and communications devices.

■ Post-mortem triage addresses the prioritization of evidence collection from non-volatile memories or from other physical sources.

You might also consider whether your organization should prepare for digital triage and investigations based on broad categories of types of crimes or incidents. General personal crimes, for example, require a different investigative and evidence-gathering approach than high-tech corporate crimes do (one typically does not need extensive forensic accounting capabilities to investigate an employee suspected of using work-related IT assets for viewing or selling pornography). There's a lot to learn from the ongoing debates in digital or forensic triage; while learning, focus on what your business impact analysis (BIA) has identified as the high-impact, high-priority risks or threats that face your organization, and apply a bit of winnowing—a bit of triage thinking—to how you'd prepare, respond to, and investigate such incidents.

Techniques and Procedures

The previous sections addressed the skills and tools the forensic team should have. This section discusses the techniques your team should follow. What are the goals and actions of effective analysts as they proceed through investigations?

■ **Start with a standard process:** Analysts should follow a predefined process for collecting data. For example, ISO has standards for the capture, analysis, and interpretation of digital forensic evidence; these include standards 27041, 27042, 27043, and 27050. NIST also publishes NIST SP 800-86, "Guide to Integrating Forensic Techniques into Incident Response," which is free to download as are all NIST publications. Much has changed at the technical level since this publication came out in 2006, but its overall emphasis on process, and how incident response and forensic investigation can and should be mutually supportive, remains an important source of guidance.

■ **Define priorities:** An organization has three possible priorities when responding to an incident: returning to normal operations as fast as possible, minimizing damage, and preserving detailed information about what occurred. These priorities are, necessarily, conflicting: a fast recovery will reduce opportunities to collect evidence, taking time to collect evidence may lead to more damage, and so forth. The organization needs to determine which order to address these priorities, in both the general (what does the policy say?) and the specific (what should we do for this incident?).

- **Identify data sources:** Before a team can begin investigating in earnest, analysts need to define what data they are looking for and all possible sources for that data. Consideration needs to be given as to the flow of certain data and all the places where it is stored and processed. Are copies made along the way? Is the data mirrored off-site or to the cloud for backup? What kind of event logs or notifications are triggered in the process? What devices will this data travel through? At this point, the analysts also need to discover the physical location of the components that store and process the data and who the administrators are for those components. Logging and monitoring are essential for analysis purposes. If logging and monitoring settings are configured at too low a verbosity, some of the important sources of data for the investigators will be missing. The correct level of detail for log collection needs to be determined long before an investigation needs to take place, if at all possible. Long-term storage requirements (and retention policies) for such log data must also be identified and be made an integral part of the organization's overall data archiving, protection, and control plans, policies, and procedures.

- **Make a data collection plan:** The analysts should make a plan addressing how the data will be collected, including the priority and the order in which it should be collected. This should prioritize data of higher value and volatility first to avoid the chance that a machine could be turned off or data could be overwritten.

- **Capture volatile data:** Analysts need to be able to gather volatile data, such as data stored in RAM, which will disappear after the device is powered off, or data at high risk of being overwritten or corrupted by new data. There are risks associated with capturing live data, such as file modification during collection, or affecting the service or performance of the machine from which data is being taken. The organization needs to discuss and document in advance whether and when to accept these risks and capture live data. Analysts should be equipped with special tools for gathering live data and understand how each tool might alter the system during collection. The concept of scheduling collection actions based on possible data loss is often referred to as *order of volatility*; the most volatile data should be collected first.

- **Collect nonvolatile data:** As we discussed in the preceding tools section, an imaging tool is used to copy the contents of a drive. If the image is going to be used for a criminal case or disciplinary actions, it should be a bit-level image, not a logical backup, because it includes the slack space and possible data remnants. A write blocker should be employed to protect the image or data from being changed.

The method used to shut down the target machine must be discussed and decided in advance. Each operating system (OS) has multiple methods for shutdown, and they have different behaviors and effects on the data.

- **Capture time details:** It is essential to know when files were created, accessed, or last changed. These must be preserved for the investigation. Based on the OS, the time formats and method for attributing timestamps to files will vary. Going back to the differing uses of bit-level images and logical backups, this is another aspect of digital forensics where a bit-level image must be used in important investigations. This is because bit-level imaging will not alter the timestamps, but logical backup could, for example, change the original date and time the file was created to the date and time the logical backup was performed. The analysts collecting the data need to account for and document inaccuracies in timestamps, such as if the system clock was wrong and/or not connected to a network time source or if they suspect the attacker altered the timestamps. Inaccurate timestamps can hinder the investigation and hurt the credibility of the evidence.

- **Preserve and verify file integrity:** There are many steps and actions that can preserve and verify file integrity. We've already discussed some of them, such as using a write-blocker during the imaging process, calculating and comparing the message digests of drives and files, and using copies of drives or files for analysis, instead of the originals. A chain of custody should be clearly defined in advance and followed closely to preempt any claims of mishandling evidence. This includes using proper chain of custody forms and sealing evidence taken with evidence tape, evidence bags, and other tamper-proofing packaging.

- **Look for deleted or hidden data:** Deleted, overwritten, or hidden files can provide essential clues to an investigation. Deleted files or remnants can often be recovered from slack space using dedicated recovery applications. Files can be found in hidden system folders or folders that an intruder might have created and then marked as "hidden." Actors might also hide files "in plain sight" by changing the filename and/or changing the file extension, such as changing `virusnamehere.exe` to an innocuous and even boring name like `warranty.txt`. Because the name and extension are so easy to change, even for end users with limited permissions, analysts should inspect file headers and not take the extensions at face value.

- **Look at the big picture:** For example, a failed attempt by an attacker to access a server might leave their *digital footprints* in many places. Such data might be captured in a firewall traffic log, a server OS event log, or an authentication server log, as well as by an intrusion detection system or security information and event management (SIEM) alert. If one action can leave a trail in five places, the analyst must consider this fact in reverse. If the analyst starts working from one or two log entries, are there three or four other places or other pieces of information they haven't seen yet? Would those facts affect how they interpret the few things they currently know? They should seek the other pieces before forming conclusions. Another point to consider is that some monitoring tools operate according to simple rules, such as "event log A + event log B = incident C." In a situation like this, the tool, such as a SIEM tool, is often correct in its conclusion. In an investigation, however, the analyst should verify this type of information. They should look at each event log separately and make their own conclusion about what those things mean together. The logs in this example are more immediate; direct information and the incident alerts from the SIEM tool are derivative and secondhand and have injected an additional layer of inference and decision-making, which may or may not be correct.

- **Make no leaps:** Analysts should use a conservative, fact-based approach in the final analysis and reporting stages. Do not come into an incident investigation (whether an initial event assessment or a full-blown forensic process) with preconceived notions as to how it happened, who did what, and what the "final" results or outcomes of the incident are. Either there is enough data to draw a given conclusion or there is not and no conclusion can be drawn. The data cannot be "almost conclusive" or "point to" being conclusive.

Forensics in the Cloud

Managed cloud computing services pose several challenges for forensic investigation and analysis. Both the technological implementation of cloud computing and the contractual nature of managed services complicate the investigator's ability to perform the actions and use the tools just described. It is important for the security professional to understand the unique characteristics of cloud computing that can make forensic activities difficult to accomplish.

- **Virtualization:** Cloud computing is typified by the use of virtual machines in software *containers* running on various (and constantly changing) host devices. Often, it is difficult, if not impossible, to know the exact physical machine that any given virtual machine might be "on" at any given moment, and virtual machines, when "shut down," are migrated to other devices for storage, in the form of files. This makes forensic examination and establishing a chain of custody extremely difficult. Proving the state and content of any given virtual machine (or the data on it) takes much more effort and will require a much longer set of logs (thus introducing more doubt to the evidence, and thus the case).

- **Access:** Depending on the vendor, the service model, and the cloud deployment model, the cloud customer may have difficulty acquiring and analyzing evidence for a legal case because the customer may not own the hardware/software on which the customer's data resides and therefore may not have administrative access to those systems and the logging data they contain. Furthermore, all the ancillary sources that often provide useful investigatory data (such as network devices, SIEM solutions, data loss prevention tools, firewalls, IDS/intrusion prevention system [IPS] tools, etc.) may also not be under the customer's control, and access to their data may be extremely restricted.

- **Jurisdiction:** The larger cloud vendors often have data centers geographically spread across state, regional, or international boundaries; users and customers making transactions on the cloud can be located anywhere in the world. This creates many legal and procedural challenges and may significantly affect how evidence is collected and utilized.

- **Tools/techniques:** The technologies and ownership of managed cloud computing may hinder the use of common forensic tools; specific or customized tools may be necessary to capture and analyze digital evidence taken from/existing in the cloud.

Because there are so many variables involved in each of these aspects, it is difficult to dictate a specific approach to cloud forensics. However, some professional and governmental organizations are developing standards for this purpose. For instance, the Cloud Security Alliance (a partner of (ISC)², the organization producing this book and the progenitor of the SSCP Common Body of Knowledge) has created instructions for how to use the ISO forensics standard (ISO 27037) in a cloud environment (`https://cloudsecurityalliance.org/download/ mapping-the-forensic-standard-isoiec-27037-to-cloud-computing/`). They've also created a capability maturity model for cloud forensics (`https:// cloudsecurityalliance.org/download/cloud-forensics-capability-model/`). Both should be on your reading list as you prepare to support forensic investigations as part of your incident response activities.

Finally, there is one principle that can be recommended regardless of all other variables and conditions in a cloud-managed services arrangement: start with what it says in the contract. The cloud vendor and customer should have already reached an explicit agreement, in writing, as to how incident investigation and evidentiary collection and analysis will be performed and executed, before the managed service commences. This contract, and the service level agreements (SLAs) or terms of reference (TORs) that are included in it by reference, forms the legally binding agreement between the organization and the cloud services provider. Be absolutely sure that you involve the organization's legal advisors *before* you start any forensic investigation that might spread into such cloud services!

UNDERSTAND AND SUPPORT BUSINESS CONTINUITY PLAN AND DISASTER RECOVERY PLAN ACTIVITIES

In Chapter 3, you looked in depth at how organizations manage and mitigate risks of all kinds; as an information security professional, you may not deal with all aspects of all risks. However, you do need to be aware and perhaps involved with how your organization prepares to cope with natural disasters, local political unrest, riots, or other events that are not directly related to information security but can still severely disrupt the organization's ongoing business operations. Here in Chapter 4, we've also looked at incidents in general and in greater detail at information systems security incidents along withhow to respond to them.

Let's put the incident response concepts shown in Figure 4.1 into the larger context of the various plans and processes organizations need to develop, prepare for, and execute. Figure 4.5 shows a spectrum of disruption that faces most any organization, ranging from anomalies in systems behavior all the way up through disasters—events whose scale of disruption can literally put the business out of business. Figure 4.5 suggests a few ideas worth considering.

- Failing to properly contain the impacts of an incident, recover from its impacts, or restore normal business operations can cascade into more serious incidents that can threaten the survival of the organization.

- Failure of a plan, such as a BCP or DRP, does not necessary mean that the plan was poorly written or carried out—some events can still overwhelm even the best-laid plans organizations try to make.

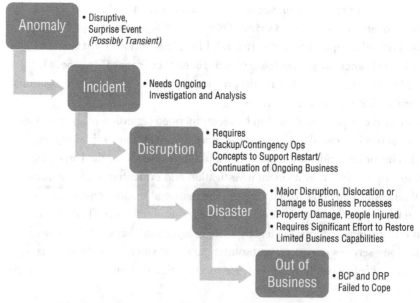

Anomaly
- Disruptive, Surprise Event (*Possibly Transient*)

Incident
- Needs Ongoing Investigation and Analysis

Disruption
- Requires Backup/Contingency Ops Concepts to Support Restart/ Continuation of Ongoing Business

Disaster
- Major Disruption, Dislocation or Damage to Business Processes
- Property Damage, People Injured
- Requires Significant Effort to Restore Limited Business Capabilities

Out of Business
- BCP and DRP Failed to Cope

FIGURE 4.5 **The descent from anomaly to organizational death**

Emergency Response Plans and Procedures

Figure 4.5 also suggests that each type of incident may need to call upon one or more type of response capability. Prudence, if not due care, suggests that organizations plan for many different types of incident response. In broad topical terms, these plans are shown in Figure 4.6. Your own organization may refer to these planning processes by different names and may even put all of this planning activity into one process; it may also split some of these task areas apart. Key to successful risk management planning (which this is all about) is that the plans are suited to the risk environment and context that *your* organization faces; your plans should be tailored to meet that environment, as they should also meet your risk tolerance, the culture of your organization, and its surrounding context. Each of these plans should be driven by the BIA; more to the point, due care requires that your organization be effective at this spectrum of business continuity planning. The bottom-line goal of this planning—and of all of these plans taken together—is that if your organization wants to stay in business, it has to survive if it is to thrive.

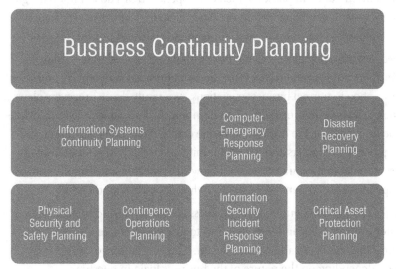

FIGURE 4.6 **Continuity of operations planning and supporting planning processes**

It's safe to conclude that each of the types of plans shown in Figure 4.6 has a different set of champions within your organization, since each type of plan must draw upon knowledge and experience with different aspects of the organization's operations, resource planning, budgeting, and decision-making. While a chief risk officer (CRO) may have overall responsibility for all of these planning processes, it's that set of champions on each plan that will do the leadership and management work of transforming their plan into an operationally prepared capability to respond. Senior leadership, including the CRO, challenges and leads the overall effort to achieve business continuity readiness; mid-level management and knowledge workers throughout the organization both turn the plans into reality and are often the ones who execute those plans when an incident takes place.

Each of these layers of planning is (or should be) driven by the business impact analysis, which took the results of the risk assessment process to produce a prioritized approach to which risks, leading to which impacts to the organization, were the most important, urgent, or compelling to protect against. (Note that *important, urgent,* and *compelling* do address different decision criteria about responding to risks.) Let's take a brief look in more detail at each of these planning processes and the plans they produce.

- *Business continuity planning* considers how to keep core business logic and processes operating safely and reliably in the face of disruptive incidents; it also looks at how to restore these core processes after they have been disrupted. The *business continuity plans (BCPs)* that are produced are at the "high tactical" level; they use the strategic plans of the organization as context to take the prioritized core business processes (as defined by the BIA), specifying the tasks needed to recover from such a disruption. This includes all phases of incident response. BCPs do not normally go into the step-by-step operational details necessary to achieve effective preparation, response, or recovery; they rely on other, subordinate plans and procedures to do so.

- *Disaster recovery planning* must concern itself with significant loss of life, injury to people, damage to organizational assets (or the property or assets of others), and significant disruption to normal business operations. As a result, disaster recovery plans (DRPs) look to ways to prevent a disruption from turning into panic or hysteria, while at the same time meeting the organization's due care and due diligence responsibilities to keep both stakeholders and the community informed. DRPs, for example, often must consider that organizational cash flow will probably suffer significantly as business operations are suspended, or greatly reduced, perhaps for months.

- *Contingency operations planning* takes business continuity considerations a few steps further by examining and selecting how to provide alternate means of getting business operations up and running again. This can embrace a variety of approaches, depending on the nature of the business logic in question.

  - Alternate work locations for employees to use
  - Alternate communications systems, internal and external, to keep employees, stakeholders, customers, or partners in touch, informed, and engaged
  - Information backup, archive, and restore capabilities, whether for physical backup of information and key documents or digital backups
  - Alternate processing capabilities
  - Alternate storage, support, and logistics processes
  - Temporary staffing, financial, and other key considerations

- *Critical asset protection planning* looks at the protection required for strategic, high-value, or high-risk assets in order to prevent significant loss of value, utility, or availability of these assets to serve the organization's needs. As you saw in Chapter 3, these can be people, intellectual property, databases, assembly lines, or almost anything that is hard to replace and almost impossible to carry on business without.

- *Physical security and safety planning* focuses on preventing unauthorized physical access to the organization's premises, property, systems, and people; it focuses on fire, environmental, or other hazards that might cause injury or death, property damage, or otherwise reduce the value of the organization and its ability to function. It works to identify safety hazards and reduce accidents.

Finally, we as SSCPs come back to the *information security incident response planning* processes, as shown in the "Preparation" section of this chapter. That planning process rightly focuses your attention on detecting IT and information systems events (or anomalies) that might be security incidents in the making, characterizing them, notifying appropriate organizational managers and leaders, and working through containment, eradication, and recovery tasks as you respond to such incidents.

The conclusion is inescapable: planning is what keeps you prepared so that you can respond, but your planning has to be multifaceted and allow you to look at your organization, your operations, your information architectures, and your risks across the whole spectrum of business strategic, tactical, and operational concerns and details.

It's important to make a distinction here between *plans* and *planning. Plans* are sets of tasks, objectives, resources, constraints, schedules, and success criteria, brought together in a coherent way to show you what you need to do and how you do it to achieve a set of goals. Planning is a process—an activity that people do to gather all of that information, understand it, and put it to use. Planning is *iterative*; you do it over and over again, and each time through, you learn more about the objectives, the tasks, and the constraints; you learn more about what "success" (or "failure") really means in the context of the planning you're doing. In the worst of all worlds, plans become documents that sit on shelves; they are taken down every year, dusted off, thumbed through, and put back on the shelf with minor updates perhaps. These plans are not living documents; they are *useless*. Plans that people use every day *become* living documents through use; they stay alive, current, and *real*, because the people served by those plans take each step of those plans and develop detailed procedures that they then use on the job to accomplish the intent of the plan.

In a real sense, the planning you'll do to meet the CIANA+PS needs of your organization or business does not and should not end until that organization or business does. Ongoing, continuous planning is in touch with what the knowledge workers and *knowledge-seeking* workers on your team are doing, every day, in every aspect of their jobs.

Interim or Alternate Processing Strategies

When disruption or disaster strikes, your organization is faced with a stark but simple choice: either activate some kind of alternate capability to conduct business processes with or have employees, customers, suppliers, and stakeholders stand around and wait until you have your original (primary) processing capabilities back in operation. Management and leadership frame this choice by setting the *maximum allowable outage (MAO)* time; the shorter that time period is, the greater the need for backup, alternate processing capabilities, and the greater the need for those alternate capabilities to be on "hot standby," ready to swing into action instantly. It's worth a moment to think about what *interim* and *alternate* generally mean in this context.

- Interim processing tends to be thought of as addressing a short-term need, perhaps for less than a day; it normally does not involve the relocation of other business assets, people, or communications links; customers and suppliers are not faced with a temporary change of address or a new location to go to in order to do business with your organization.

- Alternate processing tends to involve a longer-term need, such as when a fire or natural disaster makes your primary business location (or your data center) unusable for weeks or months. Customers, suppliers, employees, and critical business assets need to move to the new location and orient their interactions around it.

Translating that MAO into a processing strategy requires that you shift your thinking for a moment to the *business processes* that your organization uses across its full spectrum of operations. How do these fail when data, communications, processing capabilities, or other critical resources, are not available or have become corrupted or unreliable? Business continuity planning should identify these, ranked in order of their criticality to the survival and continued operation of the organization. This leads to some process-based definitions of systems failure that are most useful for planning for interim or alternate processing.

- **Disaster (or complete disruption):** Most or all of the critical business processes needed for minimum safe operation of the business cannot function.

- **Interruption:** One or more business processes are not able to function for a relatively short period of time.

- **Partial disruption:** Some critical business processes cannot function, but others can continue to operate, perhaps with degraded capability or for a limited period of time.

- **Minor disruption:** A few critical business processes cannot function, but the majority of routine functions can operate with no or minimal impact for some period of time.

Most retail sales businesses, for example, can continue to meet customer needs even though their back-office human resources, accounts payable, or strategic planning functions are disrupted. Similarly, a manufacturer can continue to operate their assembly line without those back-office business functions. Both types of business, however, will start to run into obstacles if they cannot pay their suppliers, process payments from customers, or meet payroll and tax payment obligations. Segmenting your overall business processing workloads in this way (guided of course by the logic in your BCP) should allow you to make cost-effective choices for interim or alternate processing capabilities.

The BCP should also identify which functions are tied to physical locations and which are not. This may also require separating the command, control, and management functions (the automation) from the physical systems themselves. Interim or alternate processing needs to provide some designated subset of the normal set of data acquisition, processing, storage, retrieval, computation, display, and communication services that the business processes depend upon.

Taken all together, this suggests that several strategies may be used by your organization, depending upon its business activities and overall needs for security, reliability, safety, and robustness.

- Edge computing pushes the data acquisition, processing, and command and control of devices as close to the point of action as possible. For example, self-driving vehicles cannot rely on a distant command and control function because of communications latency, potential link failures or interruptions, and the volume of data acquired by the vehicle sensors and used in real time to navigate, avoid hazards, or deal with emergency conditions. Patient care, manufacturing and process control, traffic control, and many integrated logistics functions are making use of edge computing. In these cases, the endpoint systems can operate for some time without the central management system being available; and the failure of one endpoint to function does not usually cascade into failures of other endpoints.

- Mirrored or parallel processing uses two nearly identical data processing systems, physically separated from each other; each transaction or operation is performed simultaneously on both systems, and both centers' underlying databases are updated in parallel and should always be in sync with each other.

- Hot backup provides for physically separated, nearly identical data processing centers as well; the backup center, however, is not mirroring every transaction or operation in real time but is refreshed with periodic incremental database updates (taken as incremental backups on the primary system). The primary system keeps a log file of transactions or operations that occur between such updates; at most, these updates (or *delta transactions*, as they're sometimes called) will have to be repeated on the hot backup system before it can be fully up-to-date with the state of the business.

- Cold backup provides for a minimal set of capabilities at an alternate processing location. This usually consists of having similar IT systems installed and reasonably prompt access to off-site data archival storage. It may take some time to bring operations personnel, current backups, and other critical resources to the cold backup site, start it up, and bring its databases up to date, before business operations can resume.

- Warm backup refers to alternate backup processing capability that is anywhere between cold and hot in terms of responsiveness.

NOTE   Hot, warm, and cold backups are often said to take place at hot, warm, and cold site locations. These temperature terms have some versatility and are applied logically in a variety of ways.

Each of these strategies brings with it some hard choices, as you must trade costs, time, availability of talent, and loss of business opportunity to get different levels of availability. Each brings with it a set of choices about levels of graceful degradation that you'll want to consider, as well as choices you'll need to make regarding fail-safe behavior.

- Fail-safe design and operation ensures that systems failures or disruptions cannot cause part or all of the system to operate in ways that can cause injury or death, or damage information, property, or the system itself. Rapidly shutting down a chemical processing facility, for example, might cause pressure vessels or pipes to overheat (or get too cold), leading to a rupture, explosion, or fire; fail safe design ensures that a pre-planned emergency shutdown operation can be performed instead.

- Graceful degradation is a design and operational characteristic that allows a system to lose or shut down functions in ways that can limit the impact of a disruption. Typically, this provides users and operators with time to safely isolate activities and then use normal shutdown processes to halt those operations. Graceful degradation relies on fail safe design.

Cloud computing delivers any of these alternate or interim processing capabilities, by means of what your organization contracts with the cloud services provider to deliver. Most major cloud services providers, such as Microsoft, Amazon, or Google, can at the flip of a virtual switch provide your organization with fully mirrored backup capabilities running in data centers on different continents, or any degree of hot, warm, or cold backup. Moving business functions into the cloud does not change the overall set of strategic, tactical, and operational choices your organization must make—it only affects how much money the organization must invest up front (to buy or lease its own equipment, and hire its own people), what its recurring costs are, and how much of the technical details of managing the alternate processing capabilities it wants to outsource.

NOTE Interim or alternate processing capabilities can provide significant mitigation strategies against accident, acts of nature, ransom attacks, or even malware attacks. They have little payoff, however, when it comes to data exfiltration risks, especially those involving live-off-the-land tactics. Conceivably, if you detect an intruder before they've started to copy, packetize, and exfiltrate data, an alternate processing capability (even a set of virtual machines) might make a suitable honeynet to isolate the intruder in while you restore systems from known intruder-free golden backups. But once you're told that your data is for sale on the Dark Web, it may be difficult to impossible to determine when the intrusion started and therefore how far back to attempt to recover from and restore to normal.

Restoration Planning

Recovery operations bring a minimum acceptable set of capabilities back into operation and thereby deliver a minimum acceptable set of business services to the organization, its customers, and other stakeholders. Management and leadership define this minimum set of acceptable services as part of the business continuity planning process; as with all plans, the reality of any given incident may require tailoring expectations and needs to what's practical and achievable. *Restoration*, by contrast, brings back the full and complete set of capabilities and services that would be considered "business normal" for the organization. These are not just IT systems–related terms. Both recovery and restoration include actions to ensure that related data, connectivity, and human procedural capabilities are also brought back to being operationally available and useful.

A third possibility exists, which applies in situations where the impact of the incident (or disaster) is significant enough that returning to "normal" business operations at that location, with the same business processes, would be too difficult, time-consuming, or exorbitantly expensive. In this case, the organization needs to build toward a *new business normal*, which may involve new or significantly reengineered business processes, along with the systems and infrastructures to enable and support them. A simple example would be when fire destroys the office of a small business, including its on-premises SOHO LAN system, data storage, and paper records. Migrating this business to a cloud-based platform service model might make a great deal of technical and business sense; using an application platform may require some changes to existing business processes, which might in turn catalyze the owners' thinking in ways that reveal new business opportunities. In more extreme cases, the disaster may make it emotionally, financially, or politically difficult if not impossible to go back to the same location and restart the business at all.

The decision to return to normal operating conditions has its own set of risks that must be recognized and managed. Resuming normal operations too early, particularly at the original or primary operating location, may put people and assets at risk if containment of the causal agent(s), damages at the site, and secondary disruptions related to the incident still present hazards or risks to contend with. Conversely, a delay in returning to normal operations might incur additional unnecessary expense and maybe even additional losses. Key personnel, for example, may emotionally (not logically) react to a disaster or severe disruption by needing to seek greater job security elsewhere. Payroll obligations must be met during an outage; employment law may not allow for temporary layoffs of employees in such circumstances, and this may constrain the organization to paying its employees, or terminating them, if they cannot be put to useful work. Customers may feel the need to take their business elsewhere; investors may lose confidence in the company and its management team; share prices may start to suffer. These, of course, are management's issues to worry about; what they'll need from you and the rest of the information security team is the reassurance during incident response and, afterward, that the information they are getting *about* the organization's systems, and the information *from* those systems, is reliable enough to base those decisions on.

Recovery and restoration planning are important opportunities for security professionals to advise, guide, and, if need be, lead the planning team toward effective ways to protect the organization's information, assets, people, and reputation. Security's viewpoints and experience should be involved as BCP and DRP policies are formulated, as those policies are turned into procedures and guidelines and as implementation programs are developed and put into action. From an information systems security perspective, you'll be the experts to advise on the step-by-step of the recovery and restoration processes so that the right security controls are put back in place, configured, and activated at the right point in the recovery and restoration of each part of the organization's IT infrastructure and its systems, servers, and endpoints. A significant amount of sensitive and important data is in motion during recovery and restoration operations—moving from archival and backup storage facilities and media, being reformatted, being reloaded into its proper operational places, and then validated as ready for use. Each step of that process is an opportunity for mistakes (or malfeasance) to cause more harm.

Every step of the recovery and restoration processes—in fact, every step of business continuity and disaster recovery activities, from planning to post-op—is an opportunity to learn from experience. It's also important to learn from the experiences of other organizations as they have gone through responding to and recovering from incidents, disruptions, and disasters. This cross-fertilization of experience and ideas can be something your company pursues with its strategic partners or members of its trade or industry association; as an SSCP, you have many opportunities within (ISC)² and beyond to do the same. Listen to the people involved with each step, seek their views and impressions, and resist the temptation to explain, solve, or seem to judge what they are saying. Take their candor at face value, go back to your workspaces, and translate those observations into the two favorite lists of the ethical hacker: findings and *good findings*. Findings are the observations of what didn't work right; either the plan was not sufficient or the steps were not executed according to plan. Good findings are observations of what worked correctly and effectively. These are good news! Celebrate them with the team, and with management and leadership. No matter how small the incident was, recovering from it brought stress, worry, aggravation, and lost work with it as part of its impacts. Good findings can be a powerful and inexpensive way to help re-invigorate a tired and worn-out team.

Backup and Redundancy Implementation

Perhaps the most important element in providing for safe, secure, and reliable data backup is the *process* by which you manage, account for, and control the ways that backups are made, stored, validated, used, and retired. If that sounds like another lifecycle model or another configuration management and configuration control opportunity, you're right! It's trivially easy for the smallest of organizations to benefit from many different free or inexpensive cloud-based data backup services, such as OneDrive, Dropbox, or iDrive. Very inexpensive RAID disk systems provide multiterabyte mirroring, striping, and recovery capabilities that bring hardware redundancy to the SOHO LAN user. These same controller and software technologies, when combined with very large arrays of high performance, high-reliability disk drives, are the backbones of modern data center and cloud-hosted storage systems.

Managing the Data Backup Process

All data backup operations involve the same simple steps: first, make a copy of the files; then, move the copy to another location or device for safekeeping (sometimes called the *backing store*). Restoration then involves getting the copy from safe storage and reloading it onto the original target machine, its replacement, or onto another machine for parallel or shared use by another user. Keeping track of what's been backed up, when, where the backup copy is, and knowing when and how to reload which systems from the backups is the heart of the data backup management problem. These simple concepts apply whether your operational systems and backing store are on-premises, in a public or hybrid cloud, or totally within a single cloud service provider's system. (Just because you host your data in the cloud to begin with does not mean you don't need to back it up. Someplace else, preferably.)

Management challenges common to all backup and restore strategies include the following:

- What data was selected and scheduled for a routine backup? Was the backup performed successfully?

- Are backups validated in some way to ensure that they can be reloaded onto the source system or a replacement target system?

- What prevents malware or other software-induced corruption of your source system's files from being propagated into your backup copies?

- Do you have (or need) to know when backups have been partially or completely restored to a system, and if so, by whom?

- What prevents unauthorized access to, copying, or other use of backup data sets?

Managing all of those backup copies, archive copies, and the media they are stored upon is an exercise in *metadata management*. At its heart, backup management needs to have:

- Ways to define sets of files to be backed up (and possibly restored) as logical sets

- A system for creating, dispatching, monitoring, controlling, and verifying backup jobs

- A system for creating, dispatching, monitoring, controlling, and verifying restore jobs, either partial or complete

- Error recovery capabilities (useful when backup jobs get interrupted, or when files cannot be accessed, read, or written to)

- Access control and accounting commensurate with the security needs of the organization, as applied to backup data

It's ideal that your backup management system use a catalog database to capture and keep metadata information on every file that's part of your backup operations. This metadata should tell the full life story of the file, which at a minimum should include:

- Its initial creation, including date, time, system location, and creating user ID or process ID

- Data security classification, handling restrictions, or other security parameters and constraints assigned to the file at creation

- Each subsequent alternation of the file, including date, time, system location, user ID or process ID

- Each copy of the file, to any other media, and whether the copy was for backup, archive, or other operational use

For each archival media set (be that a tape cartridge, disk, NAS, or cloud storage blob), your catalog should also track each time the data has been downloaded (or restored) to a location.

Many backup, archive, and restore management systems provide extensive capabilities to allow systems administrators and security administrators a wide range of control over how data is backed up, shared, restored, and used throughout their organization's information infrastructure. In many ways, the task of managing a data backup and restore capability has merged with that of managing the data in a data center.

Even the smallest of SOHO shops can benefit from a sensible data backup and restore management capability. This starts by first making decisions about what data to protect from catastrophe and outlining some simple procedures to define backup sets and backup processes. Next, choose an appropriate set of technologies, including the management dashboard or functionality that you need. Gone *should be* the days of backups done on seven removable disks, one per day, with six being daily incremental backups and the seventh being a complete backup, all managed by the stick-on labels on the disks themselves. Even the smallest of businesses deserves better.

One significant advantage of a cloud-based backup management system is that no matter what happens to your primary operating location and systems, all you need are your access credentials to get to the tools that you'll use to *manage* the data recovery portion of your incident response plan.

Platform and Database Backup

Application platforms and most database applications have their own built-in data backup, restore, and synchronization capabilities. These are quite often used to define and manage incremental, differential, or transaction-level backup operations, as well as managing complete backups of the data involved with that platform or database. This often provides important capabilities to manage the reload of portions of the data, such as individual transactions, or to back out (logically remove) transactions that are deemed suspect for any reason. Using built-in platform and database capabilities to manage their own data backup and restore does add a layer of complexity to your overall planning, but it's probably worth the effort in terms of data integrity.

Once you've solved the management problem, it's time to consider how you want to implement what degree of redundancy in your backup operations.

Storage Redundancy

In one sense, redundancy and backup are the same concept to enhance data availability and integrity. Both use multiple storage devices (such as disk drives) to which multiple copies of a file, directory structure, or database extent are written. Redundant storage technologies, such as redundant array of independent disks (RAID), write those copies at the same time; when retrieved, all copies of the data are read back at the same time, compared (by the storage controller) to provide error checking and correcting before the data is passed to the compute task and processor that needs it. Backup operations take a file, disk image, or database that is already written to storage media and copy it to a different storage device; depending upon the nature of the backup, both the original and the copy may then be compared as part of error checking and correction.

Redundant storage using RAID technologies provides a number of different options or RAID levels to consider to meet your needs. These include:

- **RAID 0, block-level striping:** Distributes the data across multiple drives. This increases the read and write speed (performance), but it also increases the risk of drive failure since the loss of any one of the drives will make the data unusable.

- **RAID 1, mirroring:** Copies the data to two or more drives so that the loss of a single drive would not mean the loss of the data.

- **RAID 2, bit-level striping:** Manages bit-level striping with error correction. This is not commercially viable because computational overhead exceeds performance benefits.

- **RAID 3, byte-level striping with parity bits:** Stripes data across multiple drives. Parity bits are created that would allow the data to be rebuilt in the event of a single drive failure.

- **RAID 4, block-level striping with parity bits:** Stripes data at a block level. Parity bits are created that would allow the data to be rebuilt in the event of a drive failure.

- **RAID 5, block-level striping with interleaved parity:** Stripes data at a block level. Parity bits are created and distributed among all drives. This would allow the data to be rebuilt in the event of a drive failure.

- **RAID 6, block-level striping with duplicate interleaved parity:** Stripes data at a block level. Parity bits are created that are distributed among all drives. This would allow the data to be rebuilt in the event multiple drives fail.

- **RAID 1+0 and 0+1, a combination of mirroring and striping:** Mirrors the stripes or stripes the mirrored data (the order of operations is different). These are the most expensive options but the best for both performance and reliability.

Backup Protection at Rest and in Motion

Protecting your data while at rest while it is in backup or archive storage systems or location may be required to meet your organization's full set of CIANA+PS information security needs. This may involve using encrypting file systems, digitally signing files, folders, or other container structures. Security may also require or be enhanced by using secure links or connections to protect the data while in motion from source system to backup storage. These same security needs may dictate that any RAID storage devices or systems you use encrypt the stripes or blocks of files as they are written to physically separate disk drives. When (not *if*) an individual disk drive fails, it can simply be scrapped if all of the data on it, including its directory structures, were encrypted; if no encryption is used, somebody has to attempt to randomize or sanitize that drive to ensure that no exploitable information can be recovered from it. Almost all cloud hosting services encrypt each customer's data separately and then bulk encrypt what gets written to each physical disk. They spend a little more CPU time doing encryption and decryption, but this simplifies their maintenance activities while buying them a lot of litigation insurance against a data breach or data loss affecting multiple customers. The same strategy is easy to implement, and highly recommended, for in-house data centers. Chapter 5, "Cryptography," will go into this in more detail.

Backup technologies can involve cloud storage, network-attached storage (NAS), or removable storage devices. It's strongly worth considering RAID technologies for any on-premises NAS or removable storage use.

Data Recovery and Restoration

Your incident response team has all the hardware, operating systems, and network elements of your IT infrastructure back up and running; you're now about to reload data, either directly from archive or backup media or by restarting applications platforms and database systems servers and letting those software systems manage their own data reload. Several possibilities face you at this point:

1. Your archive and backup data exist where your backup management records say that they should, and they can be successfully read and used to reload the systems with.

2. Although you can find and access the backup media, parts or all of it cannot be read or loaded without errors.

3. You have no data backups available to load from.

4. The storage technologies on the systems disrupted by the impact had to be completely sanitized and reformatted as part of containment, eradication, and restoration.

Case 1 is the ideal, of course; it does not come free, and it does require both initial investment and ongoing costs to continually make backups, validate them, and manage them. Case 2 does happen, and as a worst-case situation, you may need to use data recovery tools to scan the storage devices on your systems to see whether you can identify original files, recover them, rebuild directory structures, and then get back into business. Cases 3 and 4, despite the difference in their causes, present your management with a hard choice: either the end users create a new "fresh start" in the data plane and then begin new business operations from that point forward or they exhume paper or other business records from archive, re-create the past transaction history in the systems' data files and databases, and then build a "fresh start" on top of that foundation.

Although these may seem somewhat extreme, experience shows us that most organizations face similar data recovery choices despite their best efforts at pre-planning and arranging for data backup or archive operations.

The skills, tools, and techniques you'll need for recovering data from a crashed or partially corrupted disk drive or storage subsystem are almost the same that you'd need when conducting a forensic analysis of it. Data carving is the name given to the art and science of scanning areas of storage to find partial files, file headers, and other data, and attempting to reassemble those pieces into logically complete files. It's a bit like reverse engineering what's stored on the drive(s) and is logically similar to trying to reverse engineer, decompile, or disassemble executable program files. Sometimes all that is needed is to physically mount the offending disk drive on a system running a different operating system (e.g., mount a Windows NTFS drive on a Linux machine) as a way to work around errors induced into the directory structures by the source operating system's misbehavior during the incident. Other tools, such as RecoverMyFiles, can quickly deal with terabyte-sized disks and locate almost all recoverable files; these tools provide powerful capabilities to manage this recovery process, including extensive logging and reporting functions.

When you finally get to the happy landing of the previously described case (1) and can load backup or archive data directly into your systems, you're just about done. Ideally, the same management tools, application platforms, or database systems you used to create and manage the backups and archive copies are being used to manage and verify the reload.

Three special considerations during data reload (whether by restoring from backups or recovering from damaged media) should come to mind at this point.

■ **Preventing reinfection from malware:** It's a good chance that a backup copy might have a specimen of malware on it that was unknown to your anti-malware scanner when the copy was made; scan all restore media using the latest malware definition and signature files that you can get hold of to reduce this risk.

■ **Prevent reloading of corrupted data files:** Files that are malware-free but contain contradictory, illogical, or erroneous data could cause critical business processes to produce errors, hazardous outputs, or crash. Consider ways to scan or validate that all critical applications data files are logically correct before reloading them.

■ **Intruder user IDs, device IDs, or other subject-related data:** At some point in the recovery of your systems, you may have to reload data into the access control system, which conceivably could be vulnerable to having bogus user IDs, device IDs, or attribute data loaded into it as if it were trustworthy data. The access control technologies you use may determine whether this is a significant or near-zero risk and may provide ways to mitigate that risk.

The nature of your systems and your information architecture will in large part determine whether you must reload all data for all applications before you can validate that the incident response and recovery is complete or whether you can do this by location, by function, by application, or by sets of business processes. Incident response and business continuity planning should consider this and provide structured guidance, which the reality of each incident will then test. Patience is hard to hold on to at this point, unfortunately, as it can seem hard for business unit managers to separate "we're almost there" from "we're ready to go back to business." Regardless, your incident response process should invoke some kind of integrity checking at this point: just because you have everything reloaded, restarted, and running, and all of the data is there, doesn't necessarily mean it's all *working correctly*. Subsets of routine operational test and evaluation (OT&E) test scenarios may offer well-understood and proven benchmarks to use at this point.

Training and Awareness

Once the business continuity and disaster recovery plans have been written, they must be communicated to the entire staff of the organization. Although some people who have specific responsibilities during a crisis will need more advanced training, everyone should be provided an awareness of the organization's plans and how they should react in a crisis.

At high-risk locations, crisis awareness should be provided to all personnel at the time they enter the site. This will ensure that everyone on the site knows how to recognize an emergency situation and how they should respond. All personnel should be familiarized with safety and occupant evacuation plans at the time of hiring and then provided with annual reminders. These awareness sessions will advise staff on evacuation plans and procedures, specify meeting points, declare who is in charge during a crisis, and advise on how to report a crisis or suspicious activity.

Other personnel may require training in the use of tools or procedures such as chemical suits, system recovery procedures, crowd control, team management, evidence preservation, incident analysis, and damage estimation.

Since staff often change roles within the organization, it can be necessary to retrain staff and reorganize recovery teams on a periodic basis.

Personnel training for BCDR activities should be in concert with plan testing, which is discussed in the following section.

Testing and Drills

It may seem odd to have a strong focus on testing and assessment of your information security practices embedded here in a chapter on incident response; if so, think of this as boiling this chapter down to the question of what your readiness to respond actually is. Other chapters will look at security testing and assessment in the context of risk mitigation and controls (Chapter 3) and the protections put in place for your networks and communications (Chapter 6), systems applications, and data (Chapter 7, "Systems and Application Security"). Here, let's use testing, exercises, drills, assessments, inspections, and audits as part of how confident you and your managers can be in your end-to-end incident response capabilities and the people who deliver them day in and day out.

Three different approaches can be used to build confidence in your organization's incident response capabilities; each brings different issues to light while providing a different way to assess overall response readiness. In some organizational and systems cultures, these three words have distinct meanings; in others, they are used interchangeably. The distinctions are useful to keep in mind.

- Testing validates that a system can or does deliver the functional or performance requirements allocated to it. Tests can include the operational procedures and the people who would normally use these systems during routine business operations; tests can also be performed against controlled test scenarios and be conducted by test teams.

- Exercises provide controlled, safe ways for the people and procedural components of systems to use those systems in realistic scenarios that reflect portions of normal operations. Exercises are often the major component in training programs, as they can focus on building skills and proficiency through practice.

- Drills are similar to exercises and tend to use a smaller set of activities in their specified scenario than an exercise might. Drills can be used to provide a simulation of reality, often without notice to end users (or building occupants).

The use of testing, assessment, exercises, and drills in information security has expanded greatly in the last decade and has borrowed many additional concepts from the world of military security and intelligence activities.

- Penetration testing (more properly known as *ethical penetration testing*) is a broad category of activities intended to see your systems from the adversary's point of view; the *pen testers* attempt to challenge the security effectiveness of your organization and its systems to help the organization uncover exploitable weaknesses.

- War games can be a form of testing, exercises, drills, or penetration testing; many war games start with a given scenario or problem set (such as "Can we detect a data breach before it's too late?") and build the scenario to drive toward that assessment. Other war games can focus instead on personnel proficiency, which is at its heart an assessment of what people have been trained to do and how effective that training was in building knowledge and skills.

- Red team/blue team exercises are a form of war gaming or ethical penetration testing. A broad set of rules of engagement (ROE), constraints, and conditions is established; the red team (the attackers) can then do anything they want within those constraints and ROE, to attempt to "capture the flag," exfiltrate the crown jewels of your data, or otherwise achieve objectives set by the red team and the organization. The blue team (the defenders) is usually not told that such a test is taking place; these are no-notice activities, with the conscious intent of having an independent attacker realistically test the organization's defenses.

✔ Why Red and Blue?

Colors have long been associated with nations; and in the 1920s, U.S. Army planners, fearful of the power of Britain's Royal Navy, developed what became known as the Color Plans. War Plan Red assumed that the United States would go to war with the British Empire (remember the red coats worn by the British Army up until World War I?). Other color plans looked at other scenarios. After the end of WW II, heightened fears of a U.S.-Soviet nuclear war led to the United States creating a series of war games called Blue Flag (with controlled scenarios, primarily to evaluate doctrine) and Red Flag (in which the aggressor squadrons modeled the best that the United States knew about Soviet military doctrine).

Americans tend, therefore, to always label the aggressors as the *red team*. However, I was told by the commander of the National Training Center, Fort Irwin, California, that

CONTINUES

during a visit in the late 1980s by Soviet military leaders, one of them remarked that in his country they use the red team/blue team paradigm as well. "But in our country," he went on," the red team are the *good guys."*

I don't know if there are any cultures in which the "black hats" are known to be the good guys; if there are, please let me know.

One further set of color schemes to keep in mind about all of these kinds of events describes the level of knowledge or awareness that participants, especially the attackers, aggressors, or pen testers, have about the organization, its systems, its security measures, and its problems.

- Black-box testing, or zero-knowledge testing, denies the testers any inside knowledge of how the system works, its design, and its operational characteristics. Testers can only learn about the system under test by observing it, probing it, or interacting with it; they can also exploit open source intelligence (OSINT) by seeking publicly available knowledge about the target, such as published filings with government regulators, news coverage, employee social media postings, and the like. Black-box testing is adversarial testing in every sense of the word.

- White-box testing, or full-knowledge testing, shares everything that the systems builders, operators, and owners know about their system with the testers. This is cooperative testing and is most often seen in development and acceptance testing.

- Gray-box testing involves any level of sharing of information between the extremes of zero sharing and full sharing.

This brings us to one more color of testing: purple team testing is a red team/blue team test that is structured to encourage and rely upon active cooperation and communication between the aggressors and the defenders.

Tests, evaluations, exercises, and drills should all be planned events that are managed and conducted by an evaluation, test, or exercise director. Each of these activities has an objective it is trying to achieve; the test or exercise director has to be able to decide in real time if the continued conduct of the activity is on track to demonstrating or achieving that objective or if the issues discovered so far dictate that the activity be suspended or terminated. The test or exercise director must also be able to terminate the activity if other real-world business or environmental circumstances dictate the need to do so. (For example, a *real* severe weather warning may dictate that personnel not essential to a minimum and safe level of business operations be sent home or sent to take shelter, which would probably require terminating a test, exercise, or drill activity.) The test director is also the single face and point of contact to other organizational managers and leaders.

Tests should be part of your ongoing process to validate that your various incident response plans still provide the capabilities you require. They can measure, assess, or demonstrate that functions can be performed and that specific response or recovery actions can be accomplished within the time allotted to them. They can also provide powerful ways to develop and train staff, familiarize them with their roles in carrying out the various plans, and help them bring their role together with those of other team members. Incremental or spiral test strategies help grow team capabilities while they find flaws in the initial concepts, procedures, or processes; this also provides the opportunity for continuously improving your incident response processes.

Test Environments

Testing on your live production system is inherently risky; if something goes wrong, the test activity can interrupt your normal business processing, corrupt it, and in a worst case start a cascade of errors that damages your relationships with key customers or suppliers. Tests that involve the use of malware, such as ethical penetration testing (in any color and shade of gray) could conceivably fail in ways that spread that weaponized malware across your Internet connection to other unsuspecting systems, with concomitant legal repercussions for your organization. Despite these risks, the payoff to organizations from testing in the live environment is significant; this dictates that extraordinary precautions be taken and that the test be closely supervised by the test director, who can pull the plug and terminate the test before things go too far wrong.

Many organizations have separate software and systems test environments (which may merely be a separate set of virtual machines and containers) that they use for development and acceptance testing, operator training, and software remediation testing. These can be easily and safely adapted or replicated for security testing; in fact, it is more than prudent to first perform any test activities in a virtual sandbox environment before you take that same attack scenario into your live production settings.

Tests, exercises, and drills can also involve external players, such as emergency services providers, strategic partners, vendors, or customers, and other members of your federated systems community. Outside observers, such as independent auditors or security professionals, may also be of value to your test approach. In some cases, regulations may require that specific kinds of security-related testing be conducted by specially trained and certified independent testers or auditors; these regulations may specify whether this testing can be done in a test environment or whether it must be done in the live production systems.

At the completion of every test, a debriefing session should be held to review the results of the test and examine ways to improve the plans and mentor staff. The results of the test should be compared against the initial objectives. The examination of the plans following a test should also involve the auditors and the business units to ensure that the plans are aligned with the business priorities and strategy. Debriefing can be conducted immediately after the test in what is sometimes known as a *hot debrief*, when the activities of the test are still fresh in everyone's mind, but this can also run the risk of some of the tension and stress of the test affecting a person's response and perception. A debrief at a later date (preferably within a week) may allow the participants more time to reflect and analyze the test and thereby provide more detailed objective feedback. This can be done through a survey or a formal workshop.

A variety of test strategies and approaches should be considered, as you build your incident response capabilities and assess their effectiveness and readiness.

Read-Through or Tabletop Assessment

The most basic level of business continuity and disaster recovery testing is a simple read-through of the plan. This review should be done by the manager or liaison from each business unit and the emergency planner coordinator on (at least) an annual basis to ensure the plan is up-to-date and reflects business priorities. Each manager should be required to review and approve the plan for their department and provide updates where required.

The manager of each business unit should verify contact information, validate priorities and key personnel, and verify that all of their staff is familiar with the business continuity procedures.

The tabletop exercise accentuates the read-through. The response participants (those with roles in crisis management/response) meet together, along with a moderator, and role-play a response to a simulated contingency situation using the response plan as a guide/resource. This is the least expensive/intrusive form of test/exercise and is used to validate the utility of the plan and familiarize participants with their respective roles.

Walk-Through

A walk-through builds on the concept of the tabletop/read-through, adding the simulation of response activities at actual locations where response actions will be performed. In a tabletop exercise, a participant might say, "I go to the wire closet and flip a switch," whereas, in a walk-through, the participant will actually go to the wire closet, point to the switch, and say, "I flip this switch." The action, at this level of exercise, is only simulated, but the locations are mapped to the activity, and participants are familiarized with specific areas and hardware. In some cases, a test like this may be based on an actual scenario to test the response process and create a realistic setting for the test to be conducted in. A test like this may follow the actual timelines of the scenario or jump ahead to a later point in the scenario to test specific conditions or activities.

Simulation or Drill

Simulations, in general, use a predefined scenario and set of input actions to drive a limited or constrained copy or version of a system (including its human and procedural components) to make decisions and take action. Using a copy of the production system in a virtual environment and operating it with a test team is an example of a simulation. A drill, by contrast, may use the same scenario but is executing on the production system or in the actual workplace and affects the pace of activity of end users, operators, and others in the workplace. Drills can be conducted with advance notice to all parties concerned or run as no-notice events; fire drills and other disaster preparedness drills are often done both ways.

Parallel

Parallel tests are useful and usually involve fully duplicated systems or operational locations. For example, an organization that has a mirrored hot site may run that site in parallel to the primary location once a month, or an organization with a subscription to a commercial hot site may load its data onto the hot site and run its operation at that site once or twice per year. This allows the systems and operations to be tested at the recovery site without impacting normal business operations, which continue to operate at the normal or primary location. Another example is restoring data backup media in a test environment to determine whether the backup can be accessed in a specific time frame (whether the media is on-site or off-site), whether the restoration procedures are sufficiently detailed and clear, and whether the backup data is complete and accurate.

This type of test often finds errors that are not easy to find during other types of tests. Examples of this include access permissions set incorrectly, missing files, incorrect configurations, outdated or unpatched applications, and licensing issues.

Full Interruption

A full interruption test presents the highest level of risk to an organization. It is designed to test the plan or a portion of the plan in a live scenario and requires the participation of many team members. This type of test may inject an intentional failure into the process to ensure that staff and recovery systems operate correctly. An example of this is where a telecommunications company is required to demonstrate to regulators that the telephone system can continue to operate in the absence of commercial power. For this test, the telecom company has to cut over to batteries and diesel backups for several hours once per year. Such tests always introduce a level of stress and uncertainty since it is common that some part of the failover process will not operate correctly on the day of the test. It is noteworthy that these companies will do a parallel test of their power backups monthly but a full interruption only once per year. A full interruption test should be conducted only when other, less risky tests have been completed and only with the approval of senior management.

CIANA+PS AT LAYER 8 AND ABOVE

Although the OSI reference model technically has only seven layers, ever since it was first being drafted, there were any number of authors (including Michael Gregg, in his 2006 classic *Hack the Stack*) who referred to the people-facing administrative, policy, training, and procedural stuff as layer 8. (Pundits have also pointed out additional layers, such as Money, Political, and Dogmatic, but for simplicity of analysis, SSCPs can lump those all into the "people layer.") Layer 8 by that name probably won't appear on any official standards document, but regardless, vulnerabilities, exploitations, and countermeasures involving how people configure, control, manage, use, misuse, mismanage, and miscon-figure their IT systems no doubt will. Figure 4.7 illustrates this concept, and much like Figure 4.6, it too shows many process-focused aspects of running a business or organiza-tion that intermesh with each other. Note that just as every layer within the OSI protocol stack defines and enables interactions with the outside world, so too does every protocol or business architectural element on Figure 4.7. The surrounding layers might be immediate customers, suppliers, and clients; next comes the overall marketplace and maybe the soci-ety or dominant culture in the nation or region in which the organization does business. This layer-by-layer view of interaction can be a powerful way to look at both the power and value of information at, within, or across a layer, as well as a tool that SSCPs can use to think about threats and vulnerabilities within those higher layers of the *uber*-stack.

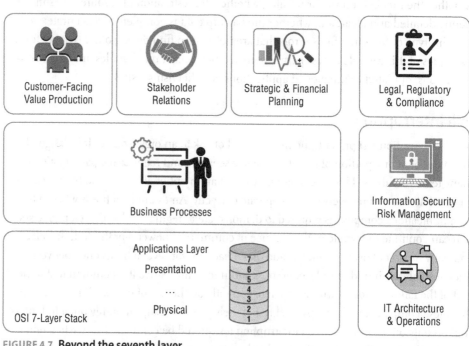

FIGURE 4.7 Beyond the seventh layer

Collaborative workspaces are an excellent case in point of this. The design and manufacturing of the Boeing 767 aircraft family involves hundreds of design, manufacturing, and supply businesses, all working together with a dozen or more major airlines and air cargo operators, collaborating digitally to bring the ideas through design to reality and then into day-to-day sustained air transport operations. At layer 7 of the OSI stack, there were multiple application programs and platforms used to provide the IT infrastructure needed for this project. The information security rules that all players in the B767 design space had to abide by might see implementation using many physical and logical control technologies across layers 1 through 7, yet with all of the administrative controls being implemented out in "people space" and with the interorganizational contractual, business process, and cultural spaces all in layer 8.

To date, sadly, a number of IT security professionals have constrained their gaze to layer 7 and below. The results? Missed opportunities to better serve the information security needs of their organizations. One irony of this is that almost by definition, all administrative controls are instantiated, implemented, and used (and abused or ignored) beyond layer 7.

Let's take a closer look at those next layers.

It *Is* a Dangerous World Out There

If we were to redraw Figure 4.7, we might be able to see that the *people* element of an organization makes up a great deal of its outermost threat surface. Even the digital or physical connections our businesses make with others are, in one sense, surrounded by a layer of people-facing, people-powered processes that create them, operate them, maintain them, and sometimes abuse or misuse them. You can see this reflected in the dark humor of the security services of many nations: before the computer age, they'd joke that if your guards, secretaries, or janitors owned better cars, houses, or boats than you did, you might want to look into who *else* is paying them and why. By the 1980s, we'd added communications and cryptologic technical and administrative people to that list of "the usual suspects." A decade later, our sysadmins and database administrators joined this pool of people to really watch more closely. And like all apocryphal stories, these still missed seeing the real evolution of the threat actor's approaches to social engineering.

The goal of any *social engineering* process is to gain access to *insider information*—information that is normally not made public or disclosed to outsiders, for whatever reason. With such insider information, an outsider can potentially take actions that help them gain their own objectives at greatly reduced costs to themselves, while quite likely damaging the organization, its employees, its customers, its stakeholders, or its community. In Chapter 3 you saw how one classical and useful approach to keeping insider information *inside* involves creating an information security classification process; the more damaging that disclosure, corruption, or loss of this information can cause to the company, the greater the need to protect it. This is a good start, but it's only a start. Social engineering attacks have proven quite effective at sweeping up many different pieces of unclassified information, even that which is publicly available, and analyzing it to deduce the possible existence of an exploitable vulnerability.

Social engineering works because people in general want to be well regarded by other people; we want to be helpful, courteous, and friendly, because we want other people to behave in those ways toward us. (We're wired that way inside.) But we also are wired to protect our group, be that our home and family, our clan, or any other social grouping we belong to. So, at the same time that we're open and trusting, we are hesitant, wary, and maybe a bit untrusting or skeptical. Social engineering attacks try to establish one bit of common ground with a target, one element on which further conversation and engagement can take place; over time, the target begins to trust the attacker. The honest sales professional, the doctor, and the government inspector use such techniques to get the people they're working with to let down their guard and be more open and more sharing with information. Parents do this with their children and teachers with their students. It's human to do so. So, naturally, we as humans are very susceptible to being manipulated by the smooth-talking stranger with hostile intent.

Consider how phishing attacks have evolved in just the last 10 or 15 years.

- *Phishing attacks* tended to use email spam to "shotgun blast" attractive lures into the inboxes of perhaps thousands of email users at a time; the emails either would carry malware payloads themselves or would tempt recipients to follow a URL, which would then expose their systems to hostile reconnaissance, malware, or other attacks. The other major use of phishing attacks is to identity theft or compromise; by offering to transfer an inheritance or a bank's excess profit to the addressee, the attacker tempts the target to reveal personally identifiable information (PII), which the attacker can then sell or use as another step in an advanced persistent attack's kill chain. The attacker can also use this PII to defraud the addressee, banks, merchants, or others by masquerading as the addressee to access bank accounts and credit information, for example.

- *Spear phishing* attacks focused on individual email recipients or very select, targeted groups of individuals, and in true social engineering style, they'd try to suggest that some degree of affinity, identification, or relationship already existed in order to wear down the target's natural hesitation to trusting an otherwise unknown person or organization. Spear phishing attacks often were aimed at lower-level personnel in large organizations—people who by themselves can't or don't do great things or wield great authority and power inside the company but who may know or have access to some *little* bit of information or power the attacker can make use of. The most typical spear phishing attack would be an email sent to a worker in the finance department, claiming to be from the company's chief executive. "I'm traveling in (someplace far away), and to make this deal happen, I need you to wire some large amount of money to this name, address, bank name, account, etc.," such phishing attacks would say. Amazingly, an embarrassingly large number of small, medium, and large companies have fallen for these attacks and lost their money in the process.

- *Whaling attacks*, by contrast, aim at key individuals in an organization. The chief financial officer (CFO) of a company might get an email claiming to be from their chief executive officer (CEO), which says much the same thing: "If we're going to make this special deal happen, I need you to send this payment now!" CFOs rarely write checks or make payments themselves—so they'd forward these whaling attack emails on to their financial payments clerks, who'd just do what the CFO told them to do. (One of my friends is the CEO of a small technology company, and he related the story of how such an attack was attempted against his company recently, and the low-level payments clerk in that kill chain was the only one who said, "Wait a minute, this email doesn't look right…," which got the CEO involved in the nick of time.)

- *Vishing, Smishing, and fraudulent texting* target consumers, employees, and executives alike via any and every short text messaging system they might be using. These can present the unwary device user with drive-by download traps that lead to identity (or account) compromise or worse, packaged with bogus messages about travel arrangements, parcels being delivered, or even vaccination or other medical test results.

- *Catphishing* involves the creation of an entirely fictitious persona; this "person" then strikes up what seems to be a legitimate personal or professional relationship with people within its operator's target set. Catphishing originated within the online dating communities, but we've seen several notorious examples so far of its use in attack strategies that do not involve romance.

This list could go on and on; we've already had more than enough examples of advanced persistent threat operations that create phony companies or organizations, staffed with nonexistent people, as part of their reconnaissance and attack strategies.

Notice that by shifting from phishing to more sophisticated spear phishing, whaling, or even catphishing attacks, attackers have to do far more social engineering, in more subtle ways, to gather the intelligence data about their prospective target, its people, and its internal processes. Of course, the potential payoff to the attacker often justifies the greater up-front reconnaissance efforts.

This all should suggest that if we can provide for more *trustworthy* interpersonal inter-action and communication, we could go a long way toward establishing and maintaining a greater security posture at these additional layers of our organization's information architecture. Much of this will depend on your organization, its decision-making culture and managerial style, its risk tolerance, and its mission or strategic sense of purpose. Similar to how we look at incident detection and its requirements for timely and far-ranging monitoring and analysis (as discussed in this chapter's "Support the Incident Lifecycle" section), we're looking for ways to find precursors and indicators that some kind of recon-naissance probe or attack is in the works. For example, separation of duties can be used to identify "need to know" boundaries; queries by people not directly involved in those duties, whether insiders or not, should be considered as possible precursor signals. This can aid in key asset protection, security for critical business processes, or even the pro-tection of information about the movement or availability of key personnel. Penetration testing or exercises that focus on social engineering attack vectors might also help discover previously unknown vulnerabilities or identify important ways that improved (or different) staff education and training can help "phishing-proof" your organization.

People Power and Business Continuity

There's a lot of great advice out there in the marketplace and on the Internet as to why organizations need to teach their people how to help protect *their own jobs* by protecting critical information about the company. As an SSCP, you can help the organization select or create the right education, training, and evaluation processes and tools for this. A survival tip: use the separation of duties principle to identify groups or teams of people whose job responsibilities suggest the need for specific, focused information protection skills at the people-to-people level.

That's an important thought; this is not about multifactor identification or physical control of the movement of people throughout the business's office spaces or work areas. This is also *not* trying to convert your open, honest, trusting, and helpful team members into suspicious, surly, standoffish "moat dragons" either! All you need to do is get each of them to add one key concept to their mental map of the workplace: trust, but verify. Our network engineers need to build our systems in as much of a zero-trust architectural way as the business needs and can afford, but the most flexible, responsive, surprise-tolerant, and "abnormality-detecting" link in our security chain needs to stay trusting if it's going to deliver the agility that resilient organizations require. They just need to have routine, simple, safe, reliable, and efficient ways to verify that what somebody seemingly is asking them to do, share, or divulge is a legitimate request from a trustworthy person or organization.

Without needing to dive too deeply into organizational psychology and culture, as SSCPs we ought to be able to help our organizations set such processes in place and keep them simple, current, and useful. This won't stop every social engineering attack—but then again, no risk control will stop every threat that's targeted against it either. And as organizations find greater value and power in actually sharing more information about themselves with far larger sets of outsiders—even *publishing* it—the collection of information "crown jewels" that need to be protected may, over time, get smaller. That smaller set of valuable nuggets of information may be both easier to protect from inadvertent disclosure, but may also become much more of an attractive target.

SUMMARY

Incident response can be summarized by using the rule of threes.

First, you've seen that there are three measures of merit that should dominate your thinking when it comes to information security incidents. The mean time to detect an incident can no longer remain in the over-100-day neighborhood if businesses and organizations are going to survive. SSCPs have got to find ways to bring that number down, at least into the double-digit range if not into the bounds of a single week. The mean time to respond is currently hovering around 60 days; this, too, speaks horribly about the security industry's best practices as not being effective in characterizing an intrusion and containing it. And while there's not much data published regarding the mean time to eradicate an intrusion (with or without its malware elements), there's no doubt room for significant improvement on this front as well.

Second, incident responders cannot see their job as being in only one phase of the incident response lifecycle at any given day or time. While one incident is being contained, others are probably already in progress, undetected and unrecognized. Your awareness has to embrace the past, present and enable you to look into the near-term future; your ability to learn from the now has to become the most powerful edge you have over your adversaries.

Third, you've seen that the success or failure of your organization boils down to the people, the processes, and the technologies that are put in place to reduce the information security threats to your organization to a survivable, acceptable minimum. Lessons can and should be learned by applying process maturity models to the ways in which you help organize, train, equip, and prepare your fellow incident response team members to provide constant vigilance and on-time response. Doing so can strengthen your arguments as you seek management's support for focused investments in new technologies, in re-engineered and improved processes, and in the people who will make or break your organization's security posture in the long run.

Fourth (for we are not limited to three uses of the rule of threes), organizations must look at incident response from the strategic, operational, and tactical perspectives. These three different viewpoints should be harmonized continuously. It's not just one department, such as IT security, that has the total responsibility for keeping the organization's information safe, secure, private, and available. Marketing, public relations, budget and finance, sales, manufacturing, customer relations, the product or service development, and every other function in the organization have *people* whose day-to-day job tasks embody opportunities to keep critical information safe and secure…or let it leak out into the gaze of an attacker.

Incident response is where the rubber hits the road; it's where we as SSCPs earn our stripes, earn our pay, every day.

CHAPTER 5

Cryptography

CRYPTOGRAPHY IS THE ART and science of "secret writing" and has been used for thousands of years to provide its users with some degree of protection for their messages, documents, and other information. Today, it is the backbone of our e-business e-society—without pervasive, nonstop use of cryptography as an infrastructure, online banking, international business, personal communications, defense, and national security would be far more difficult (and far less profitable!) to conduct. Cryptography provides powerful ways to prove that a document or a file is what it claims to be and keep it secret and safe. It authenticates people and organizations as well. The transparency, reliability, and integrity of information are all enhanced by smart use of cryptographic systems and techniques. Criminals, too, make use of it; there was no practical way to keep cryptography secret and make it the province of princes and presidents only. In fact, the only thing you *can* keep secret about your cryptographic systems are your keys, and they don't stay secret for long either!

This chapter takes you through the hands-on details of the building blocks of modern cryptographic systems; these systems are a fascinating hybrid of classical techniques and cutting-edge algorithms and technologies.

You'll gain an appreciation for the "hard" math that drives cryptosystem designs and the somewhat easier math of how the basics of encryption work. So much of modern encryption comes together in our public key infrastructure, and this chapter will help you bring all these threads together in practical ways that you can apply in your business, professional, or personal quests for CIANA+TAPS—confidentiality, integrity, availability, nonrepudiation, authentication, transparency, auditability, privacy, and safety, as aspects of your information security needs.

There's an oversimplification that many information systems users, and their managers, often fall prey to—the belief that if you just "sprinkle a little crypto dust" over your systems, you can almost magically make them totally secure. It's natural perhaps to think this way, since cryptography seems to be pervasive; it's everywhere we look. Following this approach can be expensive and probably won't work very well. You'll see in this chapter that there are some high-leverage applications of cryptography that are well understood and should be part of your systems architecture today. The heart of these applications are the secure protocols, such as public key encryption, that make up the bulwark of our information security defenses today.

UNDERSTAND FUNDAMENTAL CONCEPTS OF CRYPTOGRAPHY

In simple terms, cryptography embraces everything involved with protecting the meaning (or contents) of a message or a file by means of manipulations performed on that meaning. Some cryptographic techniques transform that meaning—that plaintext input—into something that is as meaningless as possible to someone else; only those people or processes that can unlock (decrypt) that ciphertext can recover its original meaning and intent. Other cryptographic techniques produce a unique ciphertext that cannot be decrypted to reveal its associated meaning; these one-way *hash functions* prove incredibly useful in digital signatures, file or message integrity and authenticity verification, and many other security-enhancing ways. Cryptographic techniques can be applied to digital signals as well as to analog signals. In many respects the math is the same: an algorithm is used to define how to transform plaintext into ciphertext; that algorithm uses a key, and some control variables, to make the output ciphertext unique. An inverse of that algorithm, along with a key and the control variables, allow the recovery of plaintext from the ciphertext. (We call it *text* whether the signal being encrypted and decrypted is an analog or digital one.) We won't look at analog cryptography any further, as it's beyond the jobs that most SSCPs perform; just be aware that up until the 1980s it was the backbone of many secure communications systems for national security systems, including secure voice telephony and radio links, and still has important uses today.

The math of digital encryption is either simple or far more complicated depending upon the security needed. Symmetric encryption uses simple transformation and substitution to encrypt and decrypt. Symmetric encryption is fast; it's a workhorse of our systems, but its real weakness is its use of the same key to encrypt and decrypt. Asymmetric algorithms, by contrast, use complex algebraic functions to combine plaintext, key, and control variables to produce the ciphertext, and an inverse and equally complex algorithm to decrypt the plaintext. These algorithms use different keys for encryption and decryption, and it's considered computationally infeasible to compute the decryption key from the encryption key alone. Asymmetric encryption is compute-intensive, using tremendous numbers of CPU cycles to encrypt or decrypt a message; but, it's incredibly secure. If you're wondering which to use and when, the answer most likely is a mix of both.

Properly used, cryptography brings many capabilities to the information systems designer, builder, user, and owner.

- **Confidentiality:** Protect the meaning of information and restrict its use to authorized users.
- **Utility:** Map very large sets of possible messages, values, or data items to much smaller, more useful sets.
- **Uniqueness:** Generate and manage identifiers for use in access control and privilege management systems.
- **Identity:** Validate that a person or process is who and what they claim to be (also known as authentication).
- **Privacy:** Ensure that information related to the identity of a person or process is kept confidential, and its integrity is maintained throughout.
- **Nonrepudiation:** Provide ways to sign messages, documents, and even software executables so that recipients can be assured of their authenticity.
- **Integrity:** Ensure that the content of the information has not been changed in any way except by authorized, trustworthy processes.
- **Authorization:** Validate that messages, data, subjects, processes, or objects have been granted the privileges or rights to perform the actions they are attempting to execute.

Cryptographic techniques can be used to protect data at rest, in motion, and in use; in doing so, they also can protect data *through time*, by providing ways to protect data in long-term storage from being exposed to decryption and compromise. Whether this *forward secrecy* is perfect or imperfect depends primarily upon the choice of algorithms and keys, as you'll see in this chapter. Because of its powerful capabilities to ensure the integrity of information while enforcing access control policies and privileges regarding that data, cryptographic systems can make significant improvements in the reliability, availability, resilience, and safe operation of almost any information system.

This distinction between data that we must protect and data that is always "in the clear" is important. For example, the name of a business (like IBM or Microsoft) would always be cleartext (able to be read and recognized) on websites.

Note that you'll often see these terms—and many other information security terms—written in hyphenated form, as single words, or as compound nouns. This minor inconsistency can show up across many different documentation products in your organization. Don't let it throw you.

As an SSCP, be aware of how the other information security team members in your organization may use these terms…with or without a hyphen.

Building Blocks of Digital Cryptographic Systems

Let's first take a closer look at some of these fundamental concepts of cryptography in action; then, in subsequent sections, we can look at the details you'll need to be aware of, or make use of, as you incorporate such cryptographic techniques into systems you're trying to keep secure.

Digital systems represent all information as a series of numbers (and these numbers are ultimately a series of binary digits, 1s and 0s); by contrast, analog systems represent information as a continuously variable physical value. When you make a voice-over-IP (VoIP) call, the sender's speech (and background sounds) must be transformed from the digital form sent over the Internet into acoustic waves in the air that your ears can detect and process; the signal fed into that acoustic device (the headphone) is an analog electrical wave. (Protecting your VoIP conversations requires that you consider protecting the digital data in motion, at rest in recorded versions such as .mp3 files, and in use, by protecting both the digital and analog presentation of the call.) There are many ways to encrypt and decrypt analog signals which we won't go into here, since they're beyond what most of us in computing and networking ever encounter.

Cryptographic Algorithms: The Basics

A *cryptographic algorithm* defines or specifies a series of steps—some mathematical, some logical, some grouping or ungrouping of symbols, or other kinds of operations—that must be applied, in the specified sequence, to achieve the required operation of the system. Think of the algorithm as the total set of "swap rules" that you need to use, *and the correct order to apply those rules in*, to make the cryptographic system work properly. (Note, too, that I sometimes use *cryptographic algorithm* and *encryption algorithm* as interchangeable terms, even though a *decryption* algorithm is part of the same system too.)

We mentioned before that the basic processes of substitution and permutation (also called *transposition*) can be repetitively or iteratively applied in a given cryptographic process. The *number of rounds* that an algorithm iterates over is a measure of this repetition. A combination of hardware and software features can implement this repetition. In many cases, these algorithms require a set of control parameters, such as seeds, salts, keys, block size, and cycle or chain (iteration) values. Both sender and (intended) receiver must agree to use a mutually consistent set of algorithms and control parameters if they are to successfully use cryptographic processes to send and receive information.

Encryption and decryption processes can suffer from what we call a *collision*, which can render them unusable. This can occur if one of the following happens:

- Two different plaintext phrases should not map (encrypt) to the same ciphertext phrase; otherwise, you lose the difference in meaning between the two plaintext inputs.

- Two different ciphertext phrases should not map (decrypt) to the same plaintext phrase; otherwise, you have no idea which plaintext meaning was intended.

Substitution and permutation are done in a series of steps to help make the encryption harder to break. Different cryptographic algorithms define these operations in unique ways and then go on to specify the order in which these combinations of substitutions and permutations is to be performed. Two broad classes of encryption algorithms, symmetric and asymmetric, make up the backbone of our cryptographic infrastructures.

Symmetric vs. Asymmetric Encryption

Both symmetric and asymmetric algorithms depend heavily on advanced mathematical concepts drawn from set theory, group theory, and number theory. These algorithms treat their input plaintext as a set of numbers—not as characters, phrases in a human language, images, or even executable machine language. As a result, the same algorithm, when used with the same keys and cryptovariable settings, will demonstrate the same cryptographic strength regardless of the type of data used as input plaintext.

✔ Cryptovariables Are Not Keys

Nearly all cryptographic systems consist of an algorithm plus a variety of processes that are used to initialize the system, break the input plaintext down into groups of symbols, manage the flow of plaintext and ciphertext through the systems, and control other operational aspects of the system overall. Example cryptovariables might be the seed or salt values, block size, or what bytes to use in padding blocks out to their required length.

These control parameters are *not* the encryption or decryption keys themselves, although in some cryptosystems, the values of these cryptovariables are considered part of the total set of *keying materials* that are distributed by the key distribution and management processes used with that system.

Symmetric algorithms were the first to find extensive use in electronic and electromechanical form, notably in the cipher machines used throughout the first half of the 20th century. These algorithms perform relatively simple operations on each element of the plaintext input (bit, byte, or block), but they do a substantial number of them in combination and iteration to achieve some surprisingly powerful encryption results. By arranging the plaintext into blocks, and those blocks into two-dimensional matrices, *permutation* can swap rows, columns, or both in various blocks of an input plaintext. Substitution can also use these rows or columns (or whole blocks) as input values to functions that further obscure the meaning of the plaintext. Symmetric algorithms use the same key for encryption and decryption, or a simple transformation of one into the other. Symmetric algorithms usually must work on fixed-length blocks, and thus the last block will be padded to the block length specified by the controlling cryptovariables.

In addition to overall cryptographic strength (measured by resistance to attacks or the work factor or time required for a successful brute-force attack), the speed of processing is a major requirement for an effective symmetric algorithm. As a result, many hardware and software implementations will take the explicit iteration expressed as loops in the algorithm's design and implement them in sequentially repeated blocks of code, hardware, or both. Symmetric encryption provides straightforward ways to protect large sets of data, whether in motion, at rest, or in use. However, this protection fundamentally rests upon the strategy used to choose and manage the encryption keys used with the chosen algorithm.

Asymmetric encryption does not use the same key for encryption and decryption; in fact, its cryptographic strength and utility derives from the fact that it is almost impossible to determine the decryption key from the algorithm alone, the encryption key itself, and the ciphertext it produces. It relies on so-called *trapdoor functions* that are relatively easy and straightforward to compute in one direction (for encryption), but their logical inverse is difficult if not impossible to compute in the other direction.

Asymmetric encryption came into practical use as a way of addressing three inherent problems with the widespread use of symmetric encryption: key distribution and management, improved security, and the management of trust relationships. These three sets of concepts are so interrelated that in many respects, it's hard to explain one of these big sets of ideas without using the other two to do so!

Figure 5.1 summarizes the modern families of cryptographic algorithms by types, mathematical algorithms, and use. It also gives a quick round-up of the various protocols used in the public key infrastructure and in key management in general. As an SSCP, you're going to need to be on a first-name basis with most if not all of the items shown on this "family tree." Throughout this chapter we'll use members of each branch of this tree to demonstrate important concepts and provide relevant details.

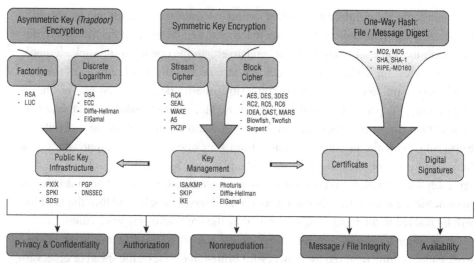

FIGURE 5.1 **Crypto family tree**

Cryptographic Keys

Cryptographic keys are a set of data that the encryption algorithm combines with the input plaintext to produce the encrypted, protected output—the ciphertext. Many different processes have been used over the centuries to produce encryption and decryption keys for use with a particular encryption algorithm or process.

- Published books, such as a specific edition of Shakespeare's *Romeo and Juliet*, *Caesar's Commentaries*, or even holy scriptures can provide a lookup table for either substitution or permutation operations. Bob, for example, could use such a book to encrypt a message by starting on a pre-agreed page, substituting the first letter in his plaintext for the first letter of the first line on the page. Carol would decrypt his message by using the same print edition of the book and go to the same pre-agreed page.

- *One-time pads* are a variation of using published books (and predate the invention of movable type). The key generator writes out a series of key words or phrases, one per sheet of paper, and makes only one copy of this set of sheets. Carol encrypts her message using the first sheet in the one-time pad *and then destroys that sheet.* Alice decrypts the ciphertext she receives from Carol using that same sheet and then destroys that sheet.

- *Pseudorandom numbers* of various length are also commonly used as keys. Senders and recipients each have a copy of the same pseudorandom number generator algorithm, which uses a seed value to start with. A sequence of pseudorandom numbers from such an algorithm provides either a one-time pad of encryption keys or a keystream for stream cipher use.

- Hardware random and pseudorandom number generators, combined with software functions, can also generate keys or keystreams. The latest of these use quantum computing technologies to generate unique keystreams.

In theory and in practice, the one-time pad encryption process is the only truly unbreakable system—when it is used correctly. Well-designed and properly used one-time systems have still resisted attempts to crack them, decades later. In fact, there are products available today that use quantum effects to generate gigabit-length key streams as one-time pads, burned into read-once memory devices, which are distributed to the two parties via bonded, trusted couriers. Once all the bits of that key have been used, the parties must buy new keys. Attempts to read the key values consumes them. Session keys are a form of one-time key system, but they aren't a one-time *pad* key distribution approach.

If the algorithm is known to our adversaries (and probably published in an information security, mathematics, or cryptography journal anyway), how is it that the *key* provides us the security we need? Cryptologic *key strength* is a way to measure or estimate how much effort would be required to break (that is, illicitly decrypt) a cleartext message encrypted by a given algorithm using such a key. In most cases, this is directly related to the key size, defined as how many bits make up a key. Another way to think of this is that the key strength determines the size of the *key space*—the total number of values that such a key can take on. Thus, an 8-bit key can represent the decimal numbers 0 through 255, which means that an 8-bit key space has 256 unique values in it. Secure Socket Layer (SSL) protocol, for example, uses a 256-bit key as its session key (to encrypt and decrypt all exchanges of information during a session), which would mean that someone trying to brute-force crack your session would need to try 2^{256} possible values (that's a 78-digit base-10 number) of a key to decrypt packets they've sniffed from your session. With one million zombie botnet computers each trying a million key values per second, that still needs 10^{59} *years* to go through all values. (If you're thinking of precomputing all such values, how many petabytes might such a "rainbow table" take up?)

Key distribution and management become the biggest challenges in running almost any cryptographic system. Keying material is a term that collectively refers to all materials and information that govern how keys are generated and distributed to users in a cryptographic system and how those users validate that the keys are legitimate. *Key management* processes govern how long a key can be used and what users and systems managers must do if a key has been compromised (by falling into the wrong hands or by a published cryptanalysis demonstrating how easily such keys can be guessed). *Key distribution* describes how newly generated keys are issued to each legitimate user, along with any updates to the rules for their period of use and their safe disposal.

Key distribution follows the same topological considerations as networks do; point-to-point, star, and full-mesh models express how many users of a cryptographic system need to share keys if they are to communicate with each other and under what rules for sharing of protected information. Consider these three typical topologies from a key distribution and management perspective. The simple one-time pad system connects only two users; only one pair of pads is needed. Most real-world needs for secure communication require much larger sets of users, however. For a given set of n users, the star topology requires n pairs of keys to keep traffic between each user and the central site secure and private—from all other users as well as from outsiders. A full-mesh system requires $[n \times (n-1)]$ sets of keys to provide unique and secure communication for each pair of users on this mesh.

Exploitable vulnerabilities will exist in whatever choices you make regarding key generation, distribution, management, and use. Examining these vulnerabilities can also reveal ways that you as the security architect can mitigate the risks that they raise; this is covered in some detail later in this section by addressing cryptanalysis attacks and other attacks on the encryption elements of your information security posture. You'll also look closely at a number of countermeasures you can use to mitigate these risks.

✔ "The Enemy Knows Your System!"

Mathematician and information theorist Claude Shannon's maxim rather bluntly restates Dutch cryptographer Auguste Kerckhoffs's principle from 1883. Whether by burglary, spies, analysis, or just dumb luck, Kerckhoffs first summed up the growing sense of mathematicians and cryptographers by saying that the secrecy of the messages—the real secrets you want to protect—cannot depend on keeping your cryptographic system and its algorithms and protocols secret. The one thing that determines whether your secrets are safe is the cryptographic key that you use and its strength and secrecy. If this key can be guessed, reversed-engineered from analysis of your ciphertext, stolen, or otherwise compromised, your secrets become known to the attacker.

Shannon's maxim dictates that key management provides the highest return on our investments in keeping our secrets safe and secure; and the problems and pitfalls of key management lead us just as inexorably to using the right mix of hybrid encryption systems.

Protocols and Modules

The term *cryptographic protocols* can refer to two different sets of processes and techniques. The first is the use of cryptography itself in the operation of a cryptographic system, which typically can refer to key management and key distribution techniques. The second usage refers to the use of cryptographic systems and techniques to solve a particular problem. Secure email, for example, can be achieved in a variety of ways using different protocols, each of which uses different cryptographic techniques. We'll look at these more closely later in this chapter.

A *cryptographic module*, according to Federal Information Processing Standards (FIPS) publication 140, is any combination of hardware, firmware, or software that implements cryptographic functions. What's interesting about FIPS 140 is that it directly addresses the security of an information systems supply chain with respect to the underlying supply chain of its cryptographic elements. To earn certification as a cryptographic module, vendors must submit their works to the Cryptographic Module Validation Program (CMVP) for testing.

Notice that a vital element of encryption and decryption is that the original meaning of the plaintext message is returned to us—encrypting, transmitting, and then decrypting it did not change its meaning or content. The ciphertext version of information can be used as a signature of sorts—a separate verification of the authenticity or validity of the plaintext version of the message. Digital signatures use encryption techniques to provide this separate validation of the content of the message, file, or information they are associated with.

This brings us to a *cryptographic system*, which is the sum total of all the elements we need to make a specific application of cryptography be part of our information systems. It includes the algorithm for encrypting and decrypting our information; the control parameters, keys, and procedural information necessary to use the algorithm correctly; and any other specialized support hardware, software, or procedures necessary to make a complete solution.

✔ Sets and Functions

The simple concepts of sets and functions make cryptography the powerful concept that it is. As an SSCP, you should have a solid, intuitive grasp of both. The good news? As a human being, your brain is already 90 percent of the way to where you need to go!

Sets provide for grouping of objects or items based on characteristics that they have in common. It's quite common to represent sets as Venn diagrams, using nested or

CONTINUES

overlapping shapes (they don't always have to be circles). In the following figure, part (a) shows an example of proper subsets—one set is entirely contained within the one "outside" it—and of subsets, where not all members of one set are part of another (they simply overlap). Part (b) of the figure shows a group of people who've earned one or more computer security-related certifications; many only hold one, some hold two, and a few hold all three, as shown in the overlapping regions. If a subset contains all elements of another subset, it is called an improper subset.

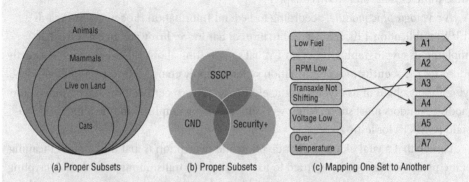

(a) Proper Subsets   (b) Proper Subsets   (c) Mapping One Set to Another

Functions are mathematical constructs that apply a given set of operations to a set of input values, producing an output value as the result. We write this as:

$f(x) = y$ or $f(x) \rightarrow y$

The second form, written as a production function, shows that by applying the function f to the value x, we *produce* the value y.

Note that for any given value of x there can be only one y as a result.

For example, a simple cryptographic substation might be written as $f(x) = mod(xor(x, keypart), b)$, where b is the number base for the modulo function, x is the input plaintext, and *key* is the portion of the key to exclusive-or with x. Cryptographic permutation might be written as $f(x_1 x_2 x_3 \ldots x_8) = x_8 \ldots x_3 x_2 x_1$, which transposes an 8-symbol input plaintext into its reverse order as ciphertext.

One powerful application of functions is to consider them as mapping one set to another. The previous function says that the set of all values of x is mapped to the set y. This is shown in part (c) of the figure, which shows how a list of out-of-limit conditions is mapped to a list of alarms. (This looks like a table lookup function.) If you wanted any of a set of conditions to trigger the same alarm, you wouldn't use a function; you'd end up with something like the "check engine" light in automobiles, which loses more meaning than it conveys!

> Not all mappings have to map every element of the source set into the destination set, nor do they use every element in the destination; some of these pairs (x,y) are just undefined. For example, the division function $f(x) = y/x$ is undefined when $x = 0$ but not when $y = 0$.

Cryptography, Cryptology, or ?

There are many different names for very different aspects of how we study, think about, use, and try to crack "secret writing" systems. Some caution is advised, and as an SSCP you need to understand the context you're in to make sure you're using the right terms for the right sets of ideas.

For example, as Wikipedia and many others point out, many people, agencies, and academics use the terms *cryptography* and *cryptology* interchangeably, as if they mean the same things. Within the U.S. military and intelligence communities and those of many NATO nations, however, these terms have definite meanings.

- Cryptography refers specifically to the use and practice of cryptographic techniques.
- Cryptanalysis refers to the study of vulnerabilities (theoretical or practical) in cryptographic algorithms and systems and the use of exploits against those vulnerabilities to break such systems.
- Cryptology refers to the combined study of cryptography (the secret writing) and cryptanalysis (trying to break other people's secret writing systems or find weaknesses in your own).
- Cryptolinguistics, however, refers to translating between human languages to produce useful information, insight, or actionable intelligence (and has little to do with cryptography).

You may also find that other ways of hiding messages in plain sight, such as steganography, are sometimes included in discussions of cryptography or cryptology.

Note, though, that cryptograms are not part of this field of study or practice—they are games, like logic puzzles, which present ciphers as challenges to those who want something more than a crossword puzzle to play with.

Hostile cyberattackers, ethical penetration testers, and systems designers and builders alike conduct all of these various kinds of cryptography-related activities.

Hashing

Hashing is considered a form of one-way cryptography: you can hash a plaintext value into its hash value form, but you cannot "de-hash" the hash value to derive the original plaintext value, no matter what math you try to use. This provides a way to take a very large set of expressions (such as messages, names, or values) and map them down to a much smaller set of values. Hash algorithms transform the original input plaintext, sometimes called the long key, into a hash value, hash key, or short key, where the long keys can be drawn from some arbitrarily large set of values (such as personal names) and the short key or hash key needs to fit within a more constrained space. The hash key, also called the hash, the hash value, the hash sum, or other term, is then used in place of the long key as a pointer value, an index, or an identifier.

Two main properties of hash functions are similar to those of a good encryption function.

- The hash function must be one way: there should be no computationally feasible way to take a hash value and back-compute or derive the long key from which it was produced.

- The hash function must produce unique values for all possible inputs; it should be computationally infeasible to have two valid long keys as input that produce the same hash value as a result of applying the hash function.

Compare these two requirements with the two main requirements for any kind of encryption system, as shown in Figure 5.2. Hashing and encryption must be one-to-one *mappings* or *functions*—no two input values can produce the same output value. But encryption *must* be able to decrypt the ciphertext back into one and only one plaintext (the identical one you started with!); if it can't, you're hashing, aren't you?

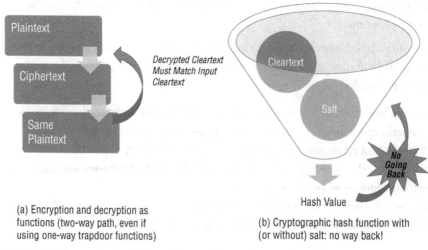

(a) Encryption and decryption as functions (two-way path, even if using one-way trapdoor functions)

(b) Cryptographic hash function with (or without) salt: no way back!

FIGURE 5.2 **Comparing hashing and encryption as functions**

As with encryption algorithms, hash algorithms need to deal with collisions (situations where two different long key inputs can hash to the same hash value). These are typically addressed with additional processing stages to detect and resolve the collision.

Some of the most powerful uses of hashing include the following:

- **Anonymization of user (subject) IDs and credentials:** This is often done locally on the client, with the hash value being transmitted to the server, where hashed values are stored for comparison and authentication. User ID, password, and other factor information is typically hashed as separate values.

- **Error detection and integrity checking for files, messages, or data blocks:** The hash is computed when the file is stored and travels with the file. Each time the file is used, a user function recomputes the hash and compares; a change of even a single bit in the file will produce a mismatching hash value. These are sometimes called *digital fingerprints* or *checksums* when used to detect (and possibly correct) errors in file storage or transmission.

- **Efficient table (or database) lookup:** Compressing or collapsing a large, sparse set of possible values (such as personal names) into a smaller but unique set of lookup key values makes the search space much smaller. Personal names, for example, might be written with any of the 26 Latin alphabet characters and a handful of punctuation marks and could be as long as 50 or 60 characters; they may have culturally or ethically dependent letter frequencies (vowels in Polynesian names versus certain consonants in Eastern European ones). One practical hash might produce an 8-byte hash value to compress this space. As each name is encountered, it is hashed, and the table is searched to see if it already has been entered into the table; if not, it's entered in. Indexing schemes used for files, databases, and other applications often make use of hashes this way.

- **Secure message digests or hashes:** These provide ways to authenticate both the contents of a file and its originator's identity.

A number of published standards define secure hash functions for use in various kinds of information security systems. The SHA series of Secure Hash Algorithms, published by the NSA, is one such series; the original SHA-0 and SHA-1 standards have been shown to be vulnerable to collision attacks and are being disbanded for use with SSL and its successor TLS.

Hashes used for indexing and lookup functions may not need to be as secure as those used in secure message digests, digital signatures, or other high-integrity applications. The greater the need for a secure hash, the more important it is to have a reliable source of random or pseudorandom numbers to seed or salt that hash algorithm with.

✔ Pseudorandom and Determinism

The science of probability gives us a strong definition of what we mean by "random." A random event is one whose outcome cannot be determined in advance with 100 percent certainty. Flipping a "perfect" coin or rolling a "perfect" pair of dice is a good example—in which "perfect" means that no one has tampered with the coin or the dice and the way that they are flipped, rolled, or tossed offers no means of controlling where they land and come to rest with the desired outcome showing. One hundred perfect tosses of a perfect coin will produce 100 random outcomes ("heads" or "tails") for that sequence of 100 events. But despite our intuition as gamblers and humans, the fact that 100 "heads" have been flipped in a row has no bearing whatsoever on what the outcome of the next flip will be as long as we are perfectly flipping a perfect coin. So, the sequence of outcomes is said to have a random distribution of values—any one value has the same likelihood of occurring at any place in the sequence.

In computing, it is difficult to compute purely random numbers via software alone. Specialized hardware can, for example, trigger a signal when a cosmic ray hits a detector, and these natural events are pretty close to being perfectly randomly distributed over time. The beauty of computing is that once you write an algorithm, it is deterministic—given the same input and series of events, it always produces the same result. (Think what it would mean if computers were not deterministic!)

If we look at a very large set of numbers, we can calculate the degree of statistical randomness that set represents. There are lots of ways to do this, which are (blissfully!) well beyond the scope of what SSCPs need in the day-to-day of their jobs. If we use a deterministic algorithm to produce this set of numbers, using a seed value as a key input, we call such sets of numbers pseudorandom: the set as a whole exhibits statistical randomness, but given the nth value of the sequence and knowing the algorithm and the seed, the next element of the sequence—the $(n + 1)th$ value—can be determined. (You can visualize this by imagining what happens when you drop a family-sized container of popcorn across your dark blue living room carpet. It's incredibly difficult to precompute and predict where each bit of popcorn will end up; but look at the patterns. A spray pattern would reveal that you threw the container across the room while standing in one location; other patterns might indicate a stiff breeze was coming in through the windows or the doorway or that you lofted the container upward rather than waved it about in a side-to-side way. A purely random popcorn spill would not have any patterns you could detect.)

Modern operating systems use such pseudorandom number generators for many purposes, some of which involve the encryption of identity and access control information.

In 2007, it was shown that the CryptGenRandom function in Windows 2000 was not so random after all, which led to exploitable vulnerabilities in a lot of services (such as Secure Sockets Layer) when supported by Windows 2000. The math behind this claim is challenging, but the same pseudorandom number generator was part of Windows XP and Vista.

Entropy is a measure of the randomness of a system; this term comes from thermodynamics and has crossed over into software engineering, computer science, and of course cryptography. A simple web search on *entropy and cryptography* will give you a taste of how rich this vein of ideas is.

Salting

One exploitable weakness of hashing is that the stored hash value tables are vulnerable to an attacker precomputing such values themselves; such a *rainbow table* can then be used in a brute-force (all values) or selectively focused attack to attempt to force a match leading to a false positive authentication, for example. Let's look at password protection via hashing as an example. The goals of such protection, as they apply to the use of hashing, would be that:

- An attacker is unlikely to be able to determine the original password from the hashed value.

- An attacker is unlikely to be able to generate a random string of characters that will hash to the same value as the original password (known as a collision).

However, simply hashing the password down into a shorter hash value creates an exploitable vulnerability if the password has been reused, is used by another user, or consists of common words. Simple comparisons with captured hash tables or hash values intercepted via packet sniffing could provide a sufficient set of samples that would facilitate such an attack. This is particularly true if the hash function in question is one that has widespread use on many systems (as most hash functions do).

By using a secret *salt* value added to the input long key to initialize the calculations, the defenders in effect increase the attacker's rainbow tables to impractical sizes. The salt value is typically a random (well, pseudorandom) value that is included with the input long key; if the hash algorithm is dealing with a 256-byte long key, a two-byte salt value effectively has the algorithm work on long keys that are 258 bytes long. That two bytes may not sound like much, but it is a 65,535-fold increase (2^{16}) of the number of rainbow table values that the attacker must precompute and compare.

You can see why combining a random salt with lengthy pass phrases can be a significant security improvement. Using and storing different salt values for each protected credential and determining when and how to change salt values are some of the tricks that defenders can do to make it harder for attackers to find, scrape, harvest, guess, or otherwise work around the salt.

Note that brute-force attacks, such as credential replay ones, have a strong possibility of gaining knowledge of the salt. Once the attacker takes the salt and tries different possible passwords in an attempt to obtain a match, it's more likely the attacker will succeed with matching to hash tables. If the user has chosen a simple or short password, then it matters little which hashing algorithm the security architect has chosen. But if the password is reasonably complex, then the security of the hash will depend on how computationally difficult the hashing algorithm is. For example, Microsoft used an overly simple hashing algorithm in NT LAN Manager (NTLM), and it was possible, using multiple GPU boards, to generate 350 billion password hashes per second, enabling an attacker to try every possible eight-character password in less than seven hours. LinkedIn used a more secure algorithm, SHA-1, to secure its users' passwords, but when its password database was breached, high-powered password-cracking machines using multiple GPUs were able to break 90 percent of the 6.5 million passwords leaked.

Such multiple GPU systems are approaching, if not exceeding, the processing power of many commercial supercomputers, if only for a narrow niche of applications. (Supercomputers still have the massive edge over the GPU clusters in terms of overall data throughput and are still required for manipulating massive data sets.) The costs of ownership of such GPU systems continue to plummet, making them more affordable to a much larger number of adversary cryptanalysts. As a result, and at the risk of oversimplifying, it makes it quite feasible to precompute massive rainbow tables for a given algorithm, against which one captured hashed password can be checked; a match indicates a corresponding password or passphrase. Jeremi Gosney's research, published in 2012, suggests for example that such an NTLM rainbow table might be able to help crack a given password hash in six hours of run time, whereas a hash generated with a different algorithm such as bcrypt might take 3,300 years to crack. There's also been a phenomenal (but predictable) growth in the number of online forums and resources that share both precomputed rainbow tables and services that exploit them.

The rapidly declining cost of cloud computing, particularly with functional or serverless computing models, continues to challenge our thinking about how infeasible and unaffordable such offline back-computation attacks against hash functions and encryption algorithms actually will be in the very near future. Thus, key sizes need to keep increasing and algorithms need to keep improving if we are to continue to enjoy strong but affordable cryptographic hashing for the masses.

The question then becomes: what *is* an appropriate cryptographic hash function? Appropriate sources of current information on cryptographic algorithms, key and salt lengths, and iteration counts (for password hashing) include the Password Hashing

Competition (`https://password-hashing.net/`) and the U.S. National Institute of Standards and Technology (NIST).

Symmetric Block and Stream Ciphers

Let's start with how our cryptographic systems process units of plaintext, whether that unit be a bit, byte, character, block, file, or even an entire storage volume. Early *character* cipher systems took each character of plaintext and applied substitutions to it, transposed it with other characters, and then repeated these processes in a number of *rounds* of processing, all based on the algorithm and its controlling *cryptovariables*. This gave rise to two additional cipher systems, *block* and *stream*, which are the two types of *symmetric encryption algorithms* in common use, which we'll look at in some depth. The extensive development of block and stream cipher algorithms, systems, and technologies predate the birth of asymmetric algorithms by almost a hundred years, and for many very good reasons symmetric block and stream cipher systems are the backbone of our secure information systems today.

> ✔ **Stream vs. Streaming**
>
> Be careful to keep stream ciphers and streaming services separate and distinct in your mind and in your security planning. Streaming services provide large data volumes, such as multimedia, at normal real-time playback rates for users to enjoy and may or may not use flow control, error correction, retransmission, or other features normally associated with file transfers. A variety of protocols are used in supporting these, as you'll see in Chapter 6, "Network and Communications Security." Some streaming services even use block ciphers. Stream ciphers are used in ways that are often associated with streaming services, but the two do not have to go hand in hand.

Block Cipher Basics

Block ciphers take the input plaintext and break it into a fixed-length series of symbols (a block) and then encrypt and decrypt the block as if it was a single symbol. A block of 64 bits (8 eight-bit bytes) can be thought of as a 64-digit binary number, which is what the encryption algorithm would then work on. Block ciphers typically need to pad the last block of a fixed-length plaintext message (such as a file or an email) so that each block has the required length. Block ciphers are used both with symmetric and asymmetric encryption algorithms and keys; in the asymmetric case, the entire padded block is treated as a number, which then has some algebraic function applied to it, such as raising it to a power, to produce the resultant ciphertext.

As cryptographic engineers began building more and more complex systems, they modularized different functions into easily replicated hardware and software elements. Substitution is implemented in S-boxes, for example, while P-boxes perform permutation. Figure 5.3 shows a notional substitution operation (an S-box that does a table lookup), while Figure 5.4 shows a P-box that implements one particular transposition of its eight different input lines.

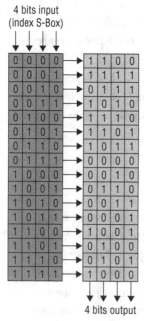

FIGURE 5.3 **Notional S-box**

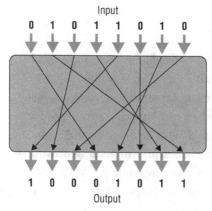

FIGURE 5.4 **Notional P-box**

Many algorithms will split the input to each round of processing into pieces, such as a left half and a right half, and process them separately and recombine at the end of each round. Note that different algorithms will have their own unique definitions of what its S-boxes or P-boxes must perform (XOR, at least, is still an XOR). The Data Encryption Standard (DES) algorithm, which uses a 16-round Feistel network, is an example of rounds of S-Boxes and P-Boxes layered together. Figure 5.5 shows a notional Feistel network being used in encryption and decryption, and as you follow the flow through both processes, you'll get a clearer sense of what cryptographers mean when they talk about iterating the permutations and substitutions.

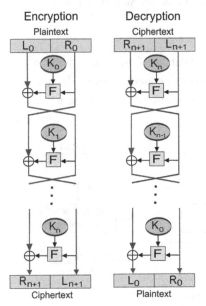

FIGURE 5.5 **Feistel encryption and decryption (notional)**

Feistel networks or Feistel ciphers are named after Horst Feistel, a German-born cryptographer who designed block ciphers for the U.S. Air Force and IBM. Feistel's passion was developing a cipher with repeating iterations or rounds. The use of S-boxes and P-boxes to create a repeating, often reversible structure, makes for a more easily wired or coded implementation that can be used to process a stream of text. DES is one example of a Feistel cipher construction. (AES, by contrast, is *not* a Feistel network.) Learn more about how the Feistel cipher process works during encryption and decryption at:
`https://www.tutorialspoint.com/cryptography/feistel_block_cipher.htm`.

Block ciphers present some interesting problems and opportunities worth examining for a moment—padding, chaining and feedback, and optimization strategies such as the Electronic Code Book approach.

Padding and Block Ciphers

All block ciphers work on fixed-length blocks of plaintext (on one block at a time, of course), and these blocks must be padded out to the fixed block size that the algorithm is designed to use. This can be done by adding bytes (or bits) to the end of the short blocks, along with a counter value that indicates how much padding was used. Note how during decryption the last byte of the message block is examined to determine how many padding bytes have been added. If the plaintext is a multiple of the block size, then a final block that just contains padding must have been added. The padding bytes that have been added will thus need to be removed. Padding is not without its own risks, such as the Padding Oracle Attack described later in the "Side-Channel Attacks" section.

Cipher Block and Feedback Chaining

With Cipher Block Chaining (CBC), the first block of data is XORed with a block of random data called the *initialization vector* (IV). Every subsequent block of plaintext is XORed with the previous block of ciphertext before being encrypted. (See Figure 5.6.)

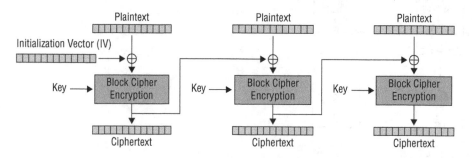

Cipher Block Chaining (CBC) Mode Encryption

FIGURE 5.6 **CBC mode**

With Cipher Feedback (CFB) mode, the IV is encrypted and then XORed with the first block of the plaintext, producing the first block of ciphertext. Then that block of ciphertext is encrypted, and the result is XORed with the next block of plaintext, producing the next block of ciphertext. (See Figure 5.7.)

Because with both CBC and CFB the encryption of block P_{n+1} depends on the encryption of block P_n, neither mode is amenable to the parallel encryption of data. Both modes can, however, be decrypted in parallel.

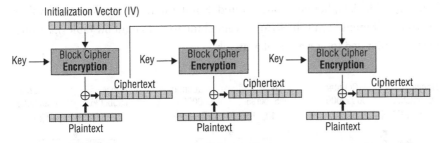

Cipher Feedback (CFB) Mode Encryption

FIGURE 5.7 **CFB mode**

The main differences between CBC and CFB are as follows:

- With CBC, a one-bit change in the IV will result in the same change in the same bit in the first block of decrypted ciphertext. Depending on the application, this could permit an attacker who can tamper with the IV to introduce changes to the first block of the message. This means with CBC it is necessary to ensure the integrity of the IV.

- With CFB, a one-bit change in the IV will result in random errors in the decrypted message and thus is not a method of effectively tampering with the message.

- With CBC, the decryption of messages requires the use of the block cipher in decryption mode. With CFB, the block cipher is used in the encryption mode for both encryption and decryption, which can result in a simpler implementation. Their benefit comes from being structured in a way that is reversible or nearly reversible. For a mathematical view on how the reversibility trait is achieved, read this technical walk-through: `http://cryptowiki.net/index.php?title=Generalized_Feistel_networks`. For a presented discussion of an eight-round Feistel cipher, this video is recommended: `https://www.youtube.com/watch?v=3kr6DbulIVc`.

The problem with both modes is that encryption cannot be parallelized, which affects speed and throughput, and random access is complicated by the need to decrypt block C_{n-1} before one can decrypt the desired block Cn.

Another mode called *counter* or CTR mode addresses this problem by not using previous blocks of the plaintext (CBC) or ciphertext (CFB) in producing the ciphertext. (See Figure 5.8.) By using an IV combined with a counter value, one can both parallelize the encryption process as well as decrypt a single block of the ciphertext. You'll note that Figure 5.8 includes a nonce value. That unique, randomly generated value is inserted into each block cipher encryption round. Similar to how a random "salt" value is used to ensure different hash values (to prevent comparing to rainbow tables), a nonce is unique and is intended to prevent replay attacks.

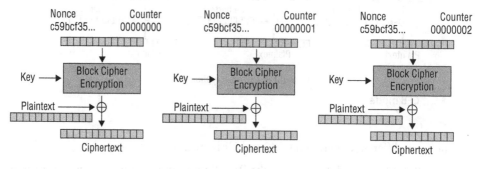

Counter (CTR) Mode Encryption

FIGURE 5.8 **CTR mode**

With all of the modes other than ECB, you need an initialization vector (IV), which either must be communicated to the receiver, or the message must be prefixed by a throw-away block of data (since decryption of an CBC or CFB stream of data without knowing the IV will only cause problems for the first block).

The IV need not be secret (it can be transmitted in plaintext along with the ciphertext), but it must be unpredictable. If an attacker can predict the next IV that will be used and is able to launch a chosen plaintext attack, then that may enable launching a dictionary attack on the ciphertext.

Electronic Code Book

Once the message has been padded to be an exact multiple of the cipher's block size, it can be encrypted. The easiest, obvious, and least secure method (for longer messages) is the Electronic Code Book (ECB) mode of operation. In this mode, each block of plaintext is processed independently by the cipher. And each block is processed or encrypted using the same key.

Using the same key to encrypt each block brings both a significant advantage and disadvantage. Using the same key greatly simplifies the process. The disadvantage is, while it may be adequate for messages that are no greater than the block size, a serious weakness develops for longer messages as identical blocks of plaintext will produce identical blocks of ciphertext. An example of this weakness can be seen in Figure 5.9, where the graphic is encrypted using ECB, using a comparatively small block size. While each block is adequately encrypted, the process is repeated so often to encrypt the entire graphic that the overall picture is actually recognizable.

Original Image   Encrypted Using ECB Mode

FIGURE 5.9 **ECB with small block size weaknesses showing**

Even in situations in which the data to be encrypted is the same or smaller than the block size (e.g., a numeric field in a database), use of ECB may be ill-advised if revealing that different rows of the table have the same value might compromise confidentiality. As a trivial example, if one were to use ECB to encrypt the birthdate field, then one could easily determine all the people in the database born on the same day, and if one could determine the birthdate of one of those individuals, you would know the birthdate of all (with the same encrypted birthdate).

The advantage of ECB, apart from its simplicity, is that encryption can be done in parallel (i.e., divided up across multiple processors), and so can decryption. Consequently, an error in one block does not affect subsequent blocks.

✔ Block Ciphers: Symmetric *and* Asymmetric?

Don't get confused—just because many of the standard, widely accepted block cipher algorithms such as AES use symmetric encryption does not mean that all block encryption is done symmetrically. Many asymmetric encryption algorithms use padded blocks, with sizes specified by their cryptovariables, as their unit of encryption.

Table 5.1 provides a quick overview of some of the block ciphers you'll frequently encounter or hear about. It indicates the type, block sizes, key sizes, and number of rounds (or iterations) that the algorithm defines.

TABLE 5.1 Overview of Block Ciphers

BLOCK CIPHER	TYPE	BLOCK SIZE (n), BITS	KEY SIZE (k), BITS	ROUNDS
DES	Symmetric	64	56	16
AES-128	Symmetric	128	128	10
AES-192	Symmetric	128	192	12
AES-256	Symmetric	128	256	14
Blowfish	Symmetric	64	32 to 448 (some to 576)	16
Twofish	Symmetric	128	128, 192 or 256	16
IDEA	Symmetric	64	128	8.5
CAST-128 / CAST5	Symmetric	64	40 to 128	12 or 16
CAST-256	Symmetric	128	128, 160, 192, 224, or 256	48
RSA	Asymmetric	1024, 2048 typical	1,024 to 4,096 typical	1
Digital signature algorithm (DSA)	Asymmetric	Based on choice of hash function	1024, 2048, or 3072	1

Prior to the 1970s, there were no publicly available encryption systems of any market significance. In fact, U.S. law at the time still reflected post World War I sentiment that only the government should be able to transmit messages in codes. Building on a seminal paper published by Claude Shannon in 1949, commercial, government, and academic researchers around the globe began developing the next generation of complex, powerful block encryption algorithms. The explosive growth of computing in the 1960s and 1970s, the shift of public telephony to digital technologies, and even the birth of the hacking and hobbyist communities came together to make the demand for commercially available encryption systems seem like too good a business opportunity to pass up. Thus was born the first public competition for a new encryption standard.

Data Encryption Standard and Triple

The Data Encryption Standard (DES) was, and still is, quite controversial. It was the first published and open competition by the U.S. government for a new symmetric-key block encryption algorithm. Some reviewers alleged that NSA had inserted elements into the design (its "S-box" circuits) to allow DES-encrypted traffic to be decrypted by NSA without needing the original encryption key; others, in turn, insisted these S-boxes were there to defeat still other backdoors built into DES. To date, no one has been able to convincingly confirm or deny these fears, and the disclosure of many NSA secrets by Edward Snowden only reheated this simmering controversy. There were many arguments about the key length as well; IBM originally proposed using 64-bit keys, which were downsized at NSA's insistence to 56 bits. (The key actually remains 64 bits in length, but since 8 bits are used for parity checking, the effective key length is still 56 bits.) DES was made a U.S. Federal Information Processing Standard in 1977, despite much outcry within the community that it was insecure right from the start.

DES used 16 rounds of processing, and its design reflects the capabilities of 1970s-era hardware. (This was the era of the first 8-bit microprocessors, and most minicomputer architectures had only a 16-bit address space.)

Although many people argued whether DES was in fact secure or insecure, the Electronic Frontier Foundation (EFF) spent $250,000 to build a custom "DES Cracking Machine" to prove their point. Its 29 circuit boards hosted 64 custom application-specific integrated circuit chips (ASICs), with the whole assemblage controlled by a single personal computer. At more than 90 billion key tests per second, it would take about nine days to brute-force test the entire 56-bit DES key space, with typical cracks happening in one to two days. At about the same time, another machine, the Cost Optimized Parallel COdeBreaker or COPACABANA, hit comparable cracking speeds but at substantially lower cost.

Significant work was done to try to tighten up DES, including the Triple DES standard published in 1999, which in effect applied three super-iterations of the basic DES algorithm. But it remained unsecure, and DES in all forms was finally withdrawn as a U.S. government standard in 2002 when it was superseded by AES.

DES remains important, not because it is no longer secure but because in the opinion of academics, industry, and government experts it stimulated the explosive growth in the study of cryptography by those who had no connections at all to the military and intelligence communities and their cryptographers. Even today it is still worth studying as you begin to understand cryptography, cryptanalysis, and common attack strategies.

Advanced Encryption Standard

Throughout the 1980s and 1990s work continued to find a replacement for DES, and in November 2001 the U.S. government published FIPS 197 describing the Advanced Encryption Standard (AES). AES is also a symmetric block encryption algorithm but one that is much more secure in design and implementation than DES or 3DES proved to be. The open competition that NSA had sponsored reviewed a number of promising designs, and the Rijndael (pronounced "rhine-dahl") algorithm by Vincent Rijmen and Joan Daeman was the clear winner. It is the first and still the only publicly available cipher that is approved by NSA for use on government classified information up through Top Secret, when it is used as part of an NSA-approved cryptographic module.

AES uses a fixed block size of 128 bits and provided a number of possible key sizes, which were directly related to the number of rounds of processing used, as shown in

Table 5.1. AES follows the design principles of a substitution-permutation network, which in some respects looks like a pretty straightforward application of substitutions, permutations, XORs, and matrix manipulations. AES is not, however, a Feistel network (which is also a permutation-substitution design concept). AES uses the principles of finite field arithmetic to manipulate its arrays of bytes, known as the *state* of the algorithm. (These states can have a varying number of columns but are always four rows of bytes.) Yet despite this apparent simplicity, it has withstood a number of very ambitious attacks and is still a primary standard of choice by security architects and savvy users.

Internally, the AES algorithm goes through four major phases of processing:

- Key expansion, in which keys for a given round of processing are derived from the cipher key using the Rijndael key schedule, which uses a set of round constants to generate a unique 128-bit round key block for each round (along with one extra round key block).

- Initial round key addition, which does a bitwise XOR of the state and the round key.

- An additional set of 9, 11, or 13 rounds, depending upon key length, which combine byte substitution, row shifting, and column mixing, culminating in another XOR of the final state and the round key.

- A final round consisting of byte substitution, row shifting, and round key addition.

A number of optimization techniques are included in the basic AES design, which allow implementation decisions to trade memory space for processing time, for example.

As usual, the cryptography community has produced a quite lucid set of pages on AES, which you can find starting at `https://en.wikipedia.org/wiki/Advanced_Encryption_Standard`.

Until May 2009, the only known successful attacks on AES were *side-channel attacks*, which rely on observing possible data leaks that reveal internal characteristics of the implemented cryptosystem (such as heat, vibration, power fluctuations, or noise on signal or power connections), rather than attacks on the mathematics of the cipher itself. As of the Snowden disclosures in 2013, there were still no known practical attacks against a properly implemented AES system using 256-bit keys.

Blowfish and Twofish

These algorithms were both developed by Bruce Schneier as part of his work to find a stronger replacement for DES. Twofish, derived from Blowfish's design, was one of the five finalist designs in the AES competition; when that competition chose the Rijndael algorithm, Schneier placed the reference implementation of the designs of Blowfish and Twofish into the public domain. They've been widely incorporated into a wide variety of commercial and open source cryptographic systems and products, with Twofish being one of the few ciphers included in the OpenPGP standard (RFC 4880) by the Internet Engineering Task Force. They both are Feistel substitution-permutation designs, and thus far, the only successful attack has been the SWEET32 or "birthday attack," in an HTTPS context, which was able to recover plaintext from ciphertext for ciphers using a 64-bit block size. As a result, the GnuPG project recommended that so long as Blowfish is not used on files larger than 4 GB in size, it should still be secure.

OpenPGP and GnuPG are both part of what can only be called the public service aspect of the ethics-based cryptographic community of researchers, designers, and users. This community firmly believes that all of us need alternatives to the systems provided to us by governments or large multinational corporations. The intersection of very big business interests and governments' natural drives for control can, this community warns us, have us becoming too dependent upon systems that only are secure *against us*. (As an international banker acquaintance of mine puts it, the Bank Secrecy Acts of various nations are about one-way secrets: banks keeping secrets from their customers.) The commercial and open source successes of GnuPG, OpenPGP, PGP, and GPG are in part a testament to the credibility of these warnings.

International Data Encryption Algorithm

The International Data Encryption Algorithm (IDEA) was first proposed by James Massey and Xuijia Lai in 1991 and was at that time intended as a proposed replacement for DES. It is a symmetric block cipher using a 64-bit block size and 128-bit keys. It consists of eight rounds of bitwise XORs, addition module 2^{16}, and multiplication modulo $2^{16} + 1$; a "half-round" provides an output transformation and swap. Thus far there have been no published linear or algebraic weaknesses demonstrated in the IDEA design, and the only successful attacks thus far (in 2012) demonstrated an effective reduction in cryptographic strength of about two bits (roughly equivalent to reducing the key from 128 to 126 bits, or roughly from 3.4×10^{38} to 8.5×10^{37} as a measure of the time required to crack it). Practically speaking, this does not reduce the security of the IDEA algorithm in use, if properly implemented.

Part of that concern about proper implementation regards what are called *weak keys*, that is, keys that have long repeating stretches of 0 or 1 bits. While there's still debate in cryptologist circles as to the real risks of weak keys, there are a number of practical mitigations—including using IDEA as part of a hybrid system that co-generates a one-time session key.

Although originally protected by a number of patents, IDEA became freely available as a reference design in 2011. MediaCrypt AG, in Zurich, Switzerland, has been working to make commercial versions of it, notably IDEA NXT, available and has been positioning it as the successor to IDEA. IDEA NXT supports block sizes of 64 or 128 bits and key sizes of 128 or 256 bits.

CAST

Carlisle Adams and Stafford Tavares created the CAST family of ciphers, with CAST-128 first made available in 1996. (Bruce Schneier has reported that although the name represents its creators' initials, they meant it to "conjure up images of randomness,"as in the casting of the dice.) These are Feistel networks with large S-boxes that make use of what are called *bent functions* (the name suggests functions that are different from all others in Boolean logic), along with a mix of key-dependent rotations, modular arithmetic, and XOR operations. Entrust, Inc., of Dallas, Texas, holds patents on the CAST design procedure, but CAST-128 itself is available worldwide on a royalty-free basis for both commercial and noncommercial use. CAST-256 (also called CAST6) was published in 1998. As of 2012, the last published results show a theoretical cryptanalysis attack against a 28-round CAST-256 design, which would take $2^{246.9}$ in time to complete; to date, no known successful attacks against CAST-256 have taken place.

PGP, OpenPGP, and GnuPG

These three cryptographic systems—for they are more than just an algorithm or a protocol—have their origins in the social and legal debate over whether private citizens should have both legal and ethical rights to use strong encryption in their private lives. The security services of national governments have long fought against this concept, as you can see in the history of many encryption algorithms and protocols to date. This social agenda is still felt by many to be vitally important today, when many national governments are using cloud-hosted data mining systems combined with mass surveillance to pursue their own agendas. Whether you agree with those agendas in whole or in part is not the issue; the underlying operational security needs and issues are.

The "PGP family" (if I can call these three related but separate systems that) implement an alternative to the hierarchy of trust that the Public Key Infrastructure (PKI) has provided us all. PKI and its certificate authentication system is a *monoculture*, a single ecosystem, the PGP family advocates rightly point out. As the mass market backbone of trust, it is all that we have. If it fails—if it can be corrupted or subverted by anyone—we are all at risk. An alternative is necessary for survival, these advocates claim. The PGP family implements nonhierarchical ways of asserting trust, managing public key exchanges, and providing for user storage and protection of their private keys. (See the "Web of Trust" section later in this chapter for more on these concepts.)

The good news about PGP et al. is that when used correctly it provides comparable levels of security to that provided by traditional PKI and its algorithms. The encryption algorithms used in PGP and its follow-on systems have proven exceptionally difficult to break; notorious examples include attempts by various law enforcement agencies to break PGP-encrypted emails and files. While some successful cracks by law enforcement have been reported, there seems to be some question as to whether they broke the encryption algorithms per se, brute-forced a weak password, or used side-channel attacks on the device in question (such as a BlackBerry or other smartphone) itself.

This gets to what may be the heart of the controversy. Opponents of PGP, OpenPGP, and GnuPGP state that these systems are technically challenging to use; they simply do not scale well into consumer-friendly products and service offerings. While PGP plugins are readily available for most email systems, this sidesteps the issues of certificate generation and management, certificate revocation, and user protection and use of private keys. Bruce Schneier referred to this as "Giving Up on PGP" in 2016[1]; Thaddeus T. Grugq expresses this by proclaiming "I am here to liberate you from PGP" with its emphasis on knowing many "arcane obscure weird commands" in order to use it safely and effectively.[2] A more reasoned approach is posted at AT&T Security's Alienvault site, in which the author (CryptoCypher, a student and intern no less) points out that if you do not understand your own operational security needs *first*, you may actually complicate your own risk posture by diving into PGP use.[3] This advice no doubt applies equally to using mainstream encryption products and services.

While many in industry and research are advising users to "dump PGP," there are also a growing number of voices to the contrary. It is clear that some elements in the marketplace recognize the risk of having all of one's security eggs placed in one basket. Some are also looking at blockchain technologies as a smarter way to make webs of trust more scalable and useful. Some of these voices view the mainstream product offerings as focused too intensely on scaling into the corporate and enterprise user base, with little concern for how individual netizens need to ensure their own information security needs are met. Many of these netizens do see the CIANA+PS model in very different terms than the monoculture does after all.

Watch this space. There are good reasons why PGP, OpenPGP, and GPG haven't gone away yet, in which case they may represent opportunities to be understood and seized.

Stream Ciphers

Stream ciphers are symmetric encryption processes that work on a single byte (sometimes even a single bit) of plaintext at a time, but they use a pseudorandom string (or keystream) of cipher digits to encrypt the input plaintext with. Stream ciphers typically

[1] Bruce Schneier, Dec 16, 2016. "Giving Up on PGP." Available at `https://www.schneier.com/blog/archives/2016/12/giving_up_on_pg.html`

[2] Thaddeus T. Grugq, , Aug 23, 2017. "The Zen of PGP." Available at `https://medium.com/@thegrugq/the-zen-of-pgp-6f55d44657dd`

[3] CryptoCypher, Jan 24, 2019. "PGP Encryption Software: What is it and How Does it Work?" Available at `https://www.alienvault.com/blogs/security-essentials/explain-pgp-encryption-an-operational-introduction`

use simple operations, such as exclusive-or, to encrypt each bit or byte. (Exclusive-or, written as *xor* and using the symbol ⊕, is true if either input is true but not both; think of it as binary 1+1= 0, and ignore the carry to the 2's place.) These operations run very fast (perhaps each encryption taking a few nanoseconds). Figure 5.10 shows the basic concept of a stream cipher, where the plaintext flows through the cipher function as a stream, is encrypted byte by byte (or bit by bit) with a corresponding piece of the key-stream, producing the resulting stream of ciphertext. Decryption, *using the same key*, is the reverse of this process.

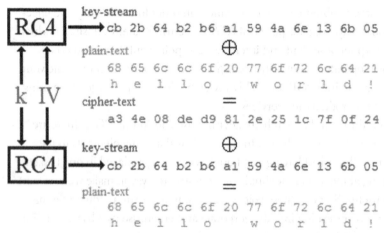

FIGURE 5.10 **RC4 stream cipher**   Posted by *Polynomial* at https://security.stackexchange.com/questions/17434/how-does-wep-wireless-security-work, used under a Creative Commons with Attribution license

The classical one-time pad cipher, which had its random keys written one per page on a pad of paper, has been proven by experience and mathematical analysis to be the only truly unbreakable cipher system; this approach loosely inspired the design of stream cipher systems. However, using a stream cipher to protect any potentially unlimited-length plaintext input requires that the keystream be truly random across its entire use with that plaintext, which makes it somewhat impractical to exchange and keep the keystreams secret. Instead, special hardware or software *keystream generators* take a fixed-length key, typically 128 bits in length, and use it as an input, along with other cryptovariables, to continuously generate the keystream. As a symmetric cipher, the same 128-bit key is used for encryption and decryption; key distribution and management, as with any symmetric cipher, become the most important elements in preserving the security of the overall system. In most implementations, keystream generators produce pseudorandom keystreams, as opposed to truly random ones. Thus, it is quite possible for a stream cipher system to become insecure with use. Figure 5.10 shows how the RC4 stream cipher does this; note the key k and the initialization vector IV are actually combined outside of the RC4 algorithm box itself. (More on this in a moment.)

Stream ciphers by design can work on any length of input plaintext. The keystream generator is a function (implemented in hardware, software, or both) that uses a seed value (the encryption key itself) as input, producing encryption values to be combined with each bit or byte of the input plaintext. Stream ciphers like RC4 found widespread use in mobile communications systems such as cell phones, Wi-Fi™ and others, in which the plaintext input is often of unbounded length and is quite bursty in nature (that is, it is produced in sets of data of unpredictable size separated by unpredictably short or long periods of no signal on the link). Both of these characteristics argued against block encryption approaches with their need to pad blocks (and possibly pad larger groups of blocks) for efficient encryption and decryption. Such bursty communications systems have many applications that call for encryption to provide security, as we'll see in Chapter 6. These all call for fast encryption using little CPU processing power, or the use of dedicated hardware such as field programmable gate arrays (FPGAs).

Practical stream ciphers use a fixed-length key to encrypt messages of variable length. Some ciphers can be broken if the attacker comes into possession of enough ciphertexts that have been encrypted with the same key. Changing the key periodically so that the amount of ciphertext produced with each unique key is limited can increase the security of the cipher.

Stream ciphers are divided into two types: synchronous and self-synchronizing.

- Synchronous ciphers require the sender and receiver to remain in perfect synchronization in order to decrypt the stream. Should characters (bits) be added or dropped from the stream, the decryption will fail from that point on. The receiver needs to be able to detect the loss of synchronization and either try various offsets to resynchronize or wait for a distinctive marker inserted by the sender to enable the receiver to resync.

- Self-synchronizing stream ciphers, as the name implies, have the property that after at most N characters (N being a property of the particular self-synchronizing stream cipher), the receiver will automatically recover from dropped or added characters in the ciphertext stream. While an obvious advantage in situations in which data can be dropped or added to the ciphertext stream, self-synchronizing ciphers suffer from the problem that should a character be corrupted, the error will propagate, affecting up to the next N characters. With a synchronous cipher, a single-character error in the ciphertext will result in only a single-character error in the decrypted plaintext.

Other key aspects of stream cipher designs include a mix of linear-feedback shift registers, nonlinear combining functions, clock-controlled generators, and filter generators.

As with any cipher, its strengths and weaknesses both derive from and affect how you use it. It is impractical to have a keystream that never repeats itself; otherwise, previously transmitted portions of your cipherstream could be subjected to cryptanalysis to identify repeating patterns, which might lead to a potential decryption. Suppose, instead, that you specify a repeat period of 2^{32} bits; this sounds like a lot, but it's a keystream of 4 GB in size. If you're transmitting at a reasonable rate of 8MBPS (which would provide acceptable streaming video or audio, such as from a UAV back to its base station), then that keystream needs to be repeated every half hour. Depending upon your operational security needs, this may or may not be acceptable.

Key to the operation of many stream ciphers is their use of an *initialization vector* (*IV*), which is used along with the encryption key to start up the keystream generator function in some algorithms. RC4, one of the more widely used streaming ciphers, does not use an initialization vector; if applications demand such an IV, then it must be combined with the encryption key externally to the RC4 module itself. (Initialization vectors do seem quite similar to the concept of a session key, which is used in asymmetric encryption systems to generate a *nonce*, a value used only once, as the symmetric encryption and decryption key.) RC4 had other design flaws, which many implementations such as WEP failed to bridge around, making them easy to break.

Table 5.2 summarizes important stream ciphers and provides a peek at the evolution and use of these ciphers.

TABLE 5.2 **Common Stream Ciphers**

CIPHER	CREATION DATE	INITIAL APPLICATION	HARDWARE OR SOFTWARE	KEY LENGTH	INITIALIZATION	ROUNDS	ATTACKS
A5/1, A5/2	1989	GSM cell phone	Software	54 (64 in 2G phone systems)	22 (in 2G phone systems)	1	Known Plaintext
RC4	1987	WEP, WPA	Both	8–2048 (usually 40–256)	None; must be combined with key if required	1	Weak key, initial byte attacks; known plaintext
Salsa20 / Cha-Cha20	Pre-2004	Replacement for RC4 in TLS, OpenSSH	Both	256	64-bit nonce + 64-bit stream position IV	20	As of 2015, none published

It is interesting to compare the controversies around the development of different stream ciphers with the DES history. In both cases, U.S. government perspectives on national security and encryption attempted to make early algorithms—DES or A5/1, A5/2, and RC4—easily breakable by government. Acrimonious disagreement with some NATO allies, such as Germany, pointed out that the closer one was to the Iron Curtain, the stronger one needs to protect one's own communications. As with DES, compromises on design and key length were finally reached; in the meantime, cryptanalysis capabilities outpaced the supposedly secure compromise designs in short order.

As we look at the short history of stream cipher applications, one might be tempted to think that the stream cipher is dead. In many demanding use cases, block ciphers that are part of hybrid systems seem to be replacing them; in others, the stream cipher depends upon a block cipher as a vital part of its keystream generation process. It is true that either basic cell phone service is not encrypted at all, or it is provided with bare-bones and not terribly secure encryption as a basic service in many locations around the world. However, it's prudent to withhold judgment on this question, at least until after putting both stream and block ciphers into the context of secure protocols and the use cases they support. It's also prudent to keep in mind that the onboard processing power, speed, and memory capacity of cell phone chip designs have grown almost astronomically in the short time since GSM2 services were becoming widespread. That processing power and speed enables devices to host far more effective encryption algorithms. This will be explored further in this chapter and in Chapter 6.

Let's take a closer look at a few of these stream ciphers.

A5/1, A5/2

A5/1 and its deliberately weakened stepchild A5/2 were developed in the late 1980s when some Western nations believed that their dominance of cell phone communications markets would remain unchanged for some time. The Berlin Wall had not fallen, yet, and worries about the Soviet Union still dominated government and international business thinking alike. The GSM cell phone system was becoming more widely used in Western Europe but was not considered for use outside of that marketplace at that point in time.

In that context, the arguments reported by security researcher Ross Anderson in 1994 make sense. NATO signals intelligence officials, according to Anderson, argued over whether GSM calls ought to be deliberately made easy to decrypt to plaintext voice or not. One outcome of this was the deliberate weakening of the A5/1 algorithm to produce A5/2 and then later A5/3 variants.

Without getting too much into the cryptanalytic details, it's important to note that this family of ciphers has suffered many different types of attacks. Some of these, such as the Universities of Bochum and Kiel's COPACABANA field programmable gate array (FPGA) cryptographic accelerator, or Karsten Nohl's and Sascha Krißler's use of 12

Nvidia GeForce graphics processors, are reminiscent of EFF's hardware-based attacks on DES some years earlier.

Finally, you do have to consider that documents released to the public by Edward Snowden in 2013 show that the NSA can easily decrypt cell phone traffic encrypted with A5/1.

RC4

Rivest Cipher 4, developed by Ron Rivest of RSA Security in 1987, was initially protected as a trade secret by RSA Security; but in 1994 it was leaked anonymously to the Cipherpunks mailing list and soon became known widely across the Internet cryptanalysis communities (both hostile and friendly). It was originally designed to support wireless encryption, applications in which its efficient, small implementation (hardware or software) and speed made it an ideal solution. It was an important element of the Wired Equivalent Privacy (WEP) algorithm for IEEE 802.11 wireless networking and then later in Wi-Fi™ Protected Access (WPA). Its use in SSL and then later in TLS ended in 2015, when its inherent weaknesses no longer allowed these protocols to be secure in any real sense. RC4 proved vulnerable to a number of attacks, many of which were enabled by lack of attention to detail by various implementations (such as those that did not use a strong message authentication code or tag).

RC4 is no longer recommended for use.

Salsa20/ChaCha20

These two closely related ciphers, designed by Daniel J. Bernstein, are proving remarkably secure and popular in hardware and software implementations. Not protected by patent, Bernstein has also released several different implementations optimized for common architectures to the public domain. Salsa20 was selected as a finalist in the EU's ECRYPT competition, which is discussed later in the "EU ECRYPT" section. ChaCha20 has been adopted by Google, along with another of Bernstein's ciphers (the Poly1305 message authentication code) as a replacement for RC4 in TLS; this strengthens Google's port of Chrome, for example, into its Android operating systems for mobile devices. ChaCha20 has also been adopted as part of the arc4random random number generator, used in the NetBSD, OpenBSD, and FreeBSD implementations of Unix. Dragonfly BSD also uses ChaCha20, and from version 8.4 onward, the Linux kernel uses it as part of the /dev/urandom device.

In May 2015, the IETF published an implementation reference for ChaCha20 in RFC 7539, which did include some modifications to Bernstein's original design. The RFC does point out these modifications may limit effectively secure use to a maximum message length of 256 GB (which we used to think was incredibly large!) and suggests that the original Bernstein design be used if this is insufficient, such as for full disk volume encryption. The IEFT has also proposed, in RFC 7634, the use of ChaCha20 as a standard for Internet Key Exchange (IKE) use and IPsec.

EU ECRYPT

In 2004, the European Union launched its ECRYPT initiative. This European Network of Excellence in Cryptology was a four-year effort to stimulate collaboration across the EU cryptologic communities and to encourage research in five core areas. These "virtual laboratories," as the core areas were also known, and their EU-designated acronyms or monikers were as follows:

- Symmetric key algorithms (STVL)
- Public key algorithms (AZTEC)
- Protocols (PROVILAB)
- Secure and efficient implementations (VAMPIRE)
- Digital watermarking (WAVILA)

Many different collaborative projects were started as part of the ECRYPT effort, and some useful results were achieved. eSTREAM, for example, was part of the STVL portfolio and was in fact a follow-on to the earlier NESSIE project, which failed to find any useful and secure new stream ciphers. Disappointed but not defeated, the EU's researchers reorganized and relaunched eSTREAM, which has indeed surfaced some strong contenders (such as Salsa20) for a next generation of secure stream ciphers. The New European Initiative for Signatures, Integrity, and Encryption (NESSIE) ran from 2000 to 2003. It embraced block and stream ciphers, public key encryption, message authentication, hashing, digital signatures, and identification schemes.

The EU maintains archive pages on both eCRYPT and NESSIE, and you'll find reviews, discussions, and analyses of their work throughout the online cryptographic communities.

Asymmetric Encryption

It's hard to speak of asymmetric encryption without also speaking about shared key generation as well as key management and distribution issues. After all, the original work that led to our modern public key infrastructure was created as if in one burst of interrelated ideas, all inspired by the need to eliminate or mitigate a bundle of known risks:

- Eliminate the need to precompute, distribute, and manage keys, and you eliminate much of the risk in any cryptographic system.
- Eliminate the need for sender and recipient to trust a third party—the key manager—or trust each other, and you can eliminate other significant risks to secure communication.

■ Eliminate the ability to back-compute a decryption key (that is, find the same symmetric encryption key) associated with a set of ciphertext, and you start to provide real forward secrecy.

As if by flashes of insight, the same set of mathematical ideas applies to eliminating or mitigating all of these risks. They also brought with them powerful capabilities to provide strong nonrepudiation (or message authentication). As a result, from the first published paper, asymmetric cryptography has been associated with terms such as *public key*, *private key*, *generator*, *shared key generation*, and *session key*.

At this point, we'll separate out the details of some of the more well-known asymmetric algorithms; then, in the upcoming sections, at the protocols that make use of them. The "Understand Public Key Infrastructure Systems" section of this chapter will bring all of this together in the context of key management.

Asymmetric encryption refers to the use of different algorithms for encryption and decryption, which each use different keys. Both will use the same cryptovariables, which might include a seed value or parameter that both encryption and decryption algorithms need. What makes this asymmetry so powerfully secure—and what delivers an asymmetric advantage to the security architect and users of it—is that if those algorithms are chosen correctly, the iron laws of mathematics dictate that it is highly unlikely that an attacker can decrypt the ciphertext encrypted by an asymmetric algorithm, even if they have the encryption key itself, and all of the other cryptovariables. The only way that such a ciphertext can be decrypted is if the recipient (or interceptor) has the corresponding decryption key. This mathematical limit is known in cryptanalysis circles as the computational infeasibility of reversing the encryption to solve for the decryption key in any practical amount of time. The first publications about these functions and their use in cryptography referred to them as *trapdoor functions*, since it is easy to fall down through an open trap door but rather challenging to fall up through it.

Forward Secrecy

By itself, any form of symmetric encryption by itself has always been vulnerable to revealing the content of encrypted messages or files once an attacker had broken the key. This would often force users to hope that *when* (not *if*) their keys were compromised or broken, they had already fully enjoyed the value of the secrets protected in their encrypted files or messages; those secrets could then be made publicly available at little or no harm or loss to their originators and users. More often than not, such hope was folly. On the other hand, if those messages had been encrypted with a true one-time pad and that pad was destroyed after use, then only the holder of the other copy of the pad could decrypt those messages, even if that was not until years later. *Session keys*, generated and used in hybrid encryption systems, provide such *forward secrecy*, so long as the session keys are destroyed immediately upon the end of the session. (Recall that if I send you a file via such an encrypted process and you store it—but don't decrypt it—you can decrypt it later only if you still have that session key handy. The pseudorandom nature of the way in which good session keys get generated should prevent you or anyone else from decrypting the file without it.) Since a well-designed hybrid system distributes the session key using asymmetric encryption, then by definition there is nothing an eavesdropper can glean from intercepted traffic that can lead to being able to decrypt intercepted ciphertext, even if the originally used keys are later compromised.

A variation on forward secrecy known as *weak forward secrecy* describes the situation where the sender and recipient private keys are compromised. This does not affect the secrecy of the previously generated session keys, but it might allow an attacker to masquerade as the party whose keys have been compromised.

As with any cryptosystem, it takes a set of protocols to make the most of this asymmetric advantage, and we'll look at these in the upcoming sections. First, however, let's look at the basic math (and keep it somewhat basic as we do so). Then let's look at some of the asymmetric algorithms in widespread use, in chronological order rather than any other.

Note the difficulty of using asymmetric encryption systems to protect archival copies of data at rest: at some point in this process, you have to separately store the session keys used in that encryption, or you'll never be able to retrieve the data from the archive. To date, the best approach to this is investing in a hardware security module (HSM) and wisely using its multifactor, shared-secrets architecture to enforce your backup and restore teams to segregate their duties.

Discrete Logarithm Problems

The first broad category of trapdoor functions and the ones first described in the paper by Whitfield Diffie and Martin Hellman (who based their work on concepts developed by Ralph Merkle) capitalized on the problem of computing discrete logarithms. For any given number base b (such as 2, e, or 10), the logarithm is the value of the exponent that b must be raised to in order to produce the required result a. Functionally, that's written as:

$$\log_b(a) = x \text{ such that } b^x = a$$

Except for a few examples, it is computationally difficult to compute discrete logarithms for any particular value a, when a is a member of a particular type of group or set. The details of how you choose such a set of values for a, b, and x, and how you put them to work in a cryptographic system, are all part of each protocol's unique approach.

Diffie-Hellman-Merkle, Elliptical Curve, ElGamal, and the Digital Signature Algorithm are all examples of discrete logarithm-based trapdoor functions at work.

Factoring Problems

The second broad category of asymmetric algorithms involves factoring extremely large semiprime numbers. A *semiprime* number is the product of two prime numbers: 5 and 7 are prime, so 35 is a semi-prime; 3 and 3 are primes, so 9 is a semi-prime; and so on. Calculating a semiprime from two times is a simple, single multiplication. But given a large number such as 33,782, it takes a lot more CPU time and a more complex algorithm to determine whether it is a semiprime or not and, if it is, what its two prime factors are. (It's not, by the way. But its nearest neighbor, 33,783, is.) When such candidate semi-prime numbers have hundreds of digits, the amount of computer time necessary to test it (regardless of how efficient your numerical approach) can become astronomical; even with rooms full of today's GPU-based bitcoin cryptocurrency mining systems, it can be no better than brute force or dumb luck to determine which two prime factors produce a given result. (In 2009, it was reported that factoring a 232-digit number required 1,500 processor years to complete; the large semiprimes in use today typically have in excess of 600 digits.) Thus, the two prime factors and the semiprime that results from them become elements in our encryption and decryption system.

Rivest-Shamir-Adleman (RSA) and LUC are examples of trapdoor algorithms based on factoring very large numbers involving semiprimes.

Diffie-Hellman-Merkle

It's difficult to focus on Diffie-Hellman (or Diffie-Hellman-Merkle, to be precise) as an algorithm without putting it in the context of shared key generation, particularly between two parties who have no shared prior knowledge of each other nor any basis upon which to trust in a shared communications process with each other. Each party must somehow prove their identity—that is, demonstrate that they are who they assert that they are—before they can jointly authorize each other to participate in the session that's about to take place. One important distinction must be recognized at the start: key exchange is not about exchanging secret information between the parties; rather, it is about *creating* a shared key to use for subsequent encrypted sharing of secrets. Furthermore, it's important to realize that the "public" part of public key exchange is that you can quite literally *publish* parts of that key exchange without compromising the security of the encryption it supports. Whitfield Diffie and Martin Hellman, in a 1976 article published in *IEEE Transactions on Information Theory*, first showed that public key exchange requires the use of what they called *trapdoor functions*—a class of mathematical problems that are easy to do in one direction (like falling through the trapdoor in the floor) but extremely difficult if not impossible to do in the other direction. Their work leaned heavily on concepts developed by their friend Ralph Merkle, who was not a co-author on their paper; later, in 2002, Hellman suggested that their work be referred to using all three of their names. Twenty-one years later, the Government Communications Headquarters (GCHQ), the British counterpart to the National Security Agency in the United States, revealed that in 1969, three of their employees had developed similar concepts demonstrating the practicality of a public key cryptographic system. U.S. Patent 4,200,770 was issued in 1977, citing Diffie, Hellman, and Merkle as inventors, and describing the reference implementation of their algorithm and approach; it is now expired.

Diffie, Hellman, and Merkle described their system using what's known as a multiplicative group of integers, modulo p, where the modulus p is a large prime number, and g, the *generator* value, is also another large prime. Choosing these values appropriately allows for a resulting shared secret (later known as the *session key*) to be in the range between 1 and $p - 1$. P and g are both publicly available. What happens next depends upon the two (or more) parties choosing other values, which will be used as exponents in computing the shared secret value.

Let's start with a simple illustration. Suppose Bob and Carol want to establish their own encrypted Internet connection with each other. Here's what happens:

1. Bob and Carol choose a suitable trapdoor function; they choose the key parameters that they will use. What they agree on can be shared in open, unsecured email with each other.

2. Carol chooses her private key and keeps it secret; she uses the trapdoor function to calculate her public key, which she sends to Bob. (Anyone can see her public key. More on this in a moment.) Bob, too, chooses a private key and uses the same trapdoor function to calculate his public key and sends that to Carol.

3. Carol applies the trapdoor function to Bob's public key, using her own private key; call the result the session key. Carol keeps this secret; she doesn't have to send it to Bob, and she shouldn't!

4. Bob applies the same trapdoor function to Carol's public key, using his own private key. This produces the same session key by the magic of the mathematics of the chosen trapdoor function. (The proof is left to the mathematically inclined reader.)

5. Carol and Bob now share a new secret, the session key. This key can be used with an appropriate (and agreed to) symmetric encryption algorithm so that Bob and Carol can exchange information with each other and keep others from being able to read it.

This is shown with *small* values for all numbers in Figure 5.11.

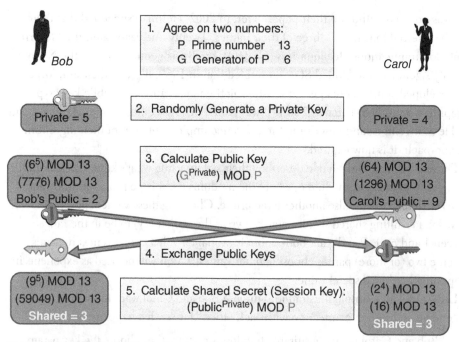

FIGURE 5.11 **Diffie-Hellman-Merkle shared key generation (conceptual)**

What about Eve, sitting along the sidelines of this conversation? Suppose Eve is, well, eavesdropping on Bob and Carol's key exchange; she somehow is trapping packets going back and forth and recognizes that they've agreed to an algorithm and its control parameters; she recognizes the exchange of Bob's and Carol's public keys for what they are. As long as Eve does not have a secret key that participated in the computation of the session key, she does not have anything that lets her read the traffic that Bob and Carol encrypt with the session key. Eve is left to using brute-force, side channel, or other attacks to attempt to break the session encryption.

Ted, on the other hand, is someone Bob and Carol want to include in a three-way secure conversation (still keeping Eve out in the cold, of course). The process previously shown in steps 1 through 5 can easily be expanded to include three or more parties who share the choices about algorithms and parameters, who then compute their own public keys and share them; they then use everybody else's public keys to compute their own copy of the session key.

Obviously, this simplified description of the Diffie-Hellman key exchange process has some vulnerabilities. It doesn't actually authenticate that Bob is Bob, or Carol is Carol, thus tempting Ted to be the "man in the middle" who masquerades to be the other party from the initial handshake and key generation through to the end of the session. The choice of trapdoor function, and the control values for it, can also present exploitable vulnerabilities. But in its simplest form, this is where the public key infrastructure (PKI) got its start.

Building a public key infrastructure starts with the algorithms used to generate the shared secret keys used to establish trustworthy communications. Those algorithms have to be implemented in some combination of software and hardware, which are then made available to users to incorporate into their systems or use as standalone messaging apps. These apps themselves and the software and hardware distribution channels (wholesale, retail, original equipment manufacturer (OEM), or other) all have to be part of a network of trust relationships if two end users are going to trust in such apps to protect their communication with each other. Thus, the problem of building a public key infrastructure must also embrace the problem of trusted software (and hardware) distribution and update. This will be explored further in the "Understand Public Key Infrastructure Systems" section of this chapter.

RSA

Immediately after Diffie and Hellman published their article in 1976, two MIT computer scientists, Ron Rivest and Adi Shamir, teamed with MIT mathematician Leonard Adleman and set out to create a suitable trapdoor or one-way function for use in a public key exchange process. These three focused on both an algorithm (based on modular exponentiation) as well as on a process by which users could authenticate themselves, hence eliminating the risk of the man-in-the-middle attack. As is typical in the scientific and technical literature, they named the algorithm after themselves (thus the acronym RSA). The three authors founded RSA Security, Inc., in 1982, and MIT was granted a U.S. Patent in 1983 that used the RSA algorithm. Prior publication in 1973 by Clifford Cocks in the United Kingdom of very similar concepts precluded patenting RSA in other countries, and had that publication by Cocks been known, it would have invalidated even the U.S. patent (it was not disclosed by GCHQ until 1997). RSA later released the algorithm into the public domain in September 2000.

Like Diffie-Hellman, RSA uses the properties of modulo arithmetic applied to exponentiation of very large integers, where the modulus is also a very large prime number. Prior to the 1990s, the compute power needed to perform such operations (just to create the keys) was substantial, and the compute power necessary to break such algorithms was thought to be unaffordable by even the security services of major nation-states.

The founders of RSA did spend most of the 1980s and 1990s in what can only be called a pitched battle with the NSA and the White House. As this was during the heart of the Cold War and the Reagan-Bush defense buildup, it's not surprising that the government saw any widespread use of powerful encryption by *anybody* as a threat to national security. (They still see that threat, particularly since "anybody" can be a terrorist, while in the same breath they know how our modern digital economy cannot function without widespread public use of highly secure encryption.) This history in and of itself is worth your time and study, as an SSCP and as a citizen, but it is beyond the scope of this book.

ElGamal

First described by Taher ElGamal in 1985, this asymmetric encryption algorithm is based on the mathematical theory of cyclic groups and the inherent difficulties in computing discrete logarithms in such groups. Borrowing from Diffie-Hellman-Merkle key exchange concepts, ElGamal provides for asymmetric encryption of keys previously used in symmetric encryption schemes. ElGamal also proposed a digital signature mechanism that allows third parties to confirm the authenticity of a message signed with it; this signature mechanism is not widely used today, but it did lead the NSA to develop its Digital Signature Algorithm (DSA) as part of the Digital Signature Standard (DSS). DSS was adopted as FIPS 186 in 1996, and it has undergone four revisions since then. (Don't confuse DSA with ElGamal signature schemes.)

Some hybrid encryption systems use ElGamal to encrypt the symmetric keys used to encrypt message content. It is vulnerable to the chosen-ciphertext attack, in which the attacker somehow tricks or spoofs a legitimate user (an *oracle*) into decrypting an arbitrary message block and then sharing those results with the attacker. (Variations on this kind of attack were first known as *lunchtime attacks* since the user's machine was assumed to be available while they were at lunch.) ElGamal does provide padding and other means to limit this vulnerability.

ElGamal encryption is used in the GNU Privacy Guard system, which we'll look at in concert with PGP in the "Pretty Good Privacy" section.

Quantum Cryptography

Quantum mechanics has been a field of study and argument since 1905, when Albert Einstein published his now-famous paper on the photoelectric effect. One of the outcomes of that paper and the next few decades of incredible theoretical and practical research that flowed on from it was what some physicists called the "spooky side effects" of a universe made up of indivisible, small *quanta* or packets of force—packets that also behaved as if they were waves. Two of those side effects are at the heart of what may be the next revolution in computing and cryptography, based on quantum computing.

The first is what's known as the *observer effect*, which means that many of the properties of a quantum (such as its position, velocity, spin, etc.) cannot be known unless you *observe* it, and since observation is a kind of interaction, your observation *changes* the state of the quantum. (This is similar to our definition in Chapter 4 of an event in your information system: if something has changed its value or state, that's an indication that an event has occurred. The change of state is the relevant observation, whether you notice it or not.) Prior to observing such a quantum, or a system of quanta, its state is defined as being a set of probable outcomes all superimposed on each other. Observing the system *collapses* all of those probabilities into the right-now result. *Quantum computing* looks to have each of those probable outcomes be the outcome of a branch in a calculation; reading out that *qubit* (quantum bit) forces it to collapse into one result. Quantum computing may provide significant reductions in run time for massively parallel algorithms, which could give advantage both in computing new public and private keys, performing encryption and decryption, and in attacks against encryption systems.

The other spooky side effect is known as *entanglement*. Two particles created together are entangled, which means if you move one of them someplace else and then observe it, both it and its entangled twin will instantly take on the same state (the same spin, for example). Note that "instantly"—this change of state happens without any known message, energy, or force traveling the distance between the entangled twins. While that suggests science-fictional ideas such as faster-than-light communication, what it practically demonstrates is that an entangled quantum communications link is a tamper-proof way to ensure that no one has observed the content of your message or file once it was encrypted. In 2017, the Peoples' Republic of China launched its Micius satellite, which demonstrated this and other "action at a distance" effects across its 1,200-kilometer space-to-ground links.

Quantum key distribution is, at this writing, the only use of these spooky side effects in practical cryptologic systems. These systems generate large quantities of entangled particle pairs that are stored in some fashion and used as a keystream or one-time pad. Any attempts to interrogate the stored copy of the keystream would invalidate it. A variety of commercial products provide such one-time pads, and several different protocols based on these quantum effects are in use. Some of these are positioned at the executive communications market, for example, as they arguably provide greater than normal communications confidentiality and integrity protection. `https://en.wikipedia.org/wiki/ Quantum_key_distribution` provides a useful summary of work to date in this field.

In the meantime, researchers are working to develop algorithms that should be more resistant to quantum computing attacks. NIST plans to have proposals for post-quantum cryptography standards ready by 2025, and current estimates are that quantum computers capable of compromising today's algorithms will not become available until 2030 at the earliest. The European Union is also doing work in this direction with its PQCRYPTO project, which interestingly enough asserts (on its home page) that while RSA and similar uses of discrete logarithms, finite fields, or elliptic curves offer rich alternatives now, "these systems are all broken as soon as large quantum computers are built…[and] society needs to be prepared for the consequences, including cryptographic attacks accelerated by these computers." You might find "Post-quantum cryptography and dealing with the fallout of physics success," by Daniel Bernstein and Tanja Lange, 2017, an illuminating read; it's available at `https://eprint.iacr.org/2017/314.pdf`.

As costs come down through early adoption, and as hardware and systems capabilities continue to improve, you may find yourself dealing with spooky side effects on the job sooner than you might think. Watch this space…well, *that* space, please.

Hybrid Cryptosystems

Hybrid cryptosystems use multiple approaches to encrypt and decrypt the plaintext they are protecting. The most common hybrid systems are ones that combine asymmetric and symmetric algorithms. In most if not all of these systems, the cryptologic strength of the asymmetric algorithms are used to overcome potentially exploitable weaknesses in symmetric algorithms by means of computing a one-time session key, nonce, initialization vector, or other set of data that allows the far faster but weaker symmetric encryption process to handle the throughput needs of the systems' users. Marrying the two provides two new approaches you'll need to be familiar with.

- *Key encapsulation* processes, which are typically built with public key infrastructures (PKIs) to handle key exchange

- *Data (or payload) encapsulation* processes, which use more runtime-efficient symmetric-key algorithms

Most of the protocols we'll look at use some variation of this approach. As we examine these, keep the OSI protocol stack in mind. Somewhere in that stack, the user, an application, or a lower-level service must be able to initiate a secure exchange with a host, negotiate with that host, control the secure session's exchange of information, and then cleanly terminate the session. The protocols we'll examine in some detail support these tasks.

Elliptical Curve Cryptography

ECC seeks to find discrete logarithm problems that are even more difficult to work backward than those used by RSA or Diffie-Hellman-Merkle; these can be thought of as either providing far, far greater security for the same range of key sizes or equivalent security for smaller keys that require far less computation time to encrypt and decrypt messages via ECC.

There are two approaches to understanding and appreciating elliptical curve cryptography (ECC). One gets graphical and mathematical very quickly, and you'll find articles such as https://arstechnica.com/information-technology/2013/10/a-relatively-easy-to-understand-primer-on-elliptic-curve-cryptography/ quite helpful in explaining things without too much math. (The ArsTechnica article also animates this math, which is appealingly useful.) The other is to set the mathematics aside and look at the practicalities of EEC in action.

Applying ECC in a practical system is becoming easier all the time. It's become incredibly popular and is part of the TOR project (The Onion Relay, an anonymizing virtual private network, created by the U.S. Office of Naval Research in part to facilitate free speech and journalism); it's part of proof of ownership of BitCoins and is in Apple's iMessage Service. The Domain Name System uses it as part of DNSCurve to secure DNS information and is becoming a preferred member of cryptographic suites on many websites because it seems to provide perfect forward secrecy. You'll probably find it as a member of the encryption suites on your endpoints already.

There are some unknowns, or at least some things believed to be true but not proven so. In 2007, NSA released its Dual Elliptic Curve Deterministic Random Bit Generator, known as Dual_EC_DBRG. Despite some initial criticism and skepticism (users and cryptanalysts either trust or don't trust the NSA), it was one of the algorithms included in NIST's SP 800-90A standard. Researchers began to demonstrate the *potential* for such a backdoor, and documents that the *New York Times* had but never published appeared to demonstrate that NSA had in fact inserted such a backdoor into Dual_EC_DBRG. Supposedly, members of the American National Standards Institute group reviewing all of this had information that described how to disable such a backdoor *if* it existed but chose to do nothing with it. By 2014, after more details revealed by Edward Snowden, NIST withdrew its draft guidance supporting the use of Dual_EC_DBRG, recommending that users transition to other approved algorithms quickly. In addition, a presidential advisory panel confirmed that NSA had been spending $250 million per year to insert backdoors into software and hardware elements of encryption systems. RSA Security and others chose to withdraw certain products that had standardized on the use of this ill-fated random bit generator.

While none of this calls into question the underlying mathematical validity or power of ECC, it does shed quite an unfavorable light on the standards and review processes used to establish good working implementations of new encryption algorithms and technologies. Advocates of open source and alternative approaches, such as GnuPG, Open-PGP, and PGP/GPG, point to the Dual_EC_DBRG fracas as a case in point.

✔ The Modulus (Mod)

If math has never been your strong suit and you find this talk of using a modulus (mod) confusing, for the purposes of understanding the Diffie-Hellman Key Exchange, the concepts really aren't too difficult. Before jumping into why Diffie-Hellman works, let's first explain a few terms like *exponent*, *prime*, and *modulus*.

First, the exponent, which is written as a superscript value above another value. For example, in the formula $K = A^b \bmod p$, the exponent is the "b." When reading this, we say "A to the power of b."

CONTINUES

Using an exponent creates a large number quickly. For example, we know that 7 * 7 = 49. Using exponents, you could write 7 * 7 also as 7^2, which is to say "7 to the power of 2." So far, so good? Let's try 7^3 or 7 * 7 * 7. That is the same as 49 * 7, or 343, Last exponent example: how big is 7^7? That is 7*7*7*7*7*7*7, which comes to 823,543. Yes, with exponents, numbers get large very quickly.

On to prime numbers. Being prime is a trait of any whole number that can be divided only by itself, or 1, and get a whole number as a result. For example, the number 4 can be divisible by 4 (which equals 1) and by 2 (which equals 2). The number 49 is not a prime number, because it can divided by 7. But the number 7 is a prime because it is only divisible by itself and 1. Since there are so many ways to multiply any number of primes together to generate a non-prime, prime numbers become fewer and farther between as you look at larger and larger numbers. The Diffie-Hellmann Key Exchange makes use of this as it relies on using very large prime numbers as factors in its cogeneration of the session key.

Now onto the idea of modulus. The modulo operation divides any number by another number to get the remainder. It sounds complicated, but it really is as simple as getting the remainder after dividing. For example, if you divide 7 by 3, you get 2 plus 1 remaining. If you divide 21 by 4, then you get 5, plus 1 remaining. In both examples, the 1 remaining is called the *modulus*.

Remember the complicated-looking formula when Alice computed the key value *K*? The formula was $K = B^a \bmod p$. If you read that right, you take a number "B" to the power of "a" and then divide it by "p." Whatever remains as the remainder is now Alice's key value K. That's all there is to it..

Bob does something similar. Both have used large prime numbers in their calculations.

After walking through all this math, I imagine you're coming to a conclusion about the Diffie-Hellmann Key Exchange. It's not an exchange of keys at all, but rather two users mutually generating their key, together but separate. This way, no one could intercept the key being transmitted between them.

For a deeper explanation or answers to questions such as, "Why can't someone just derive the same secret key, knowing all the values?" or "How can Alice and Bob compute such large numbers?" take a look at:

```
http://pi.math.cornell.edu/~mec/2003-2004/cryptography/diffiehellman/
diffiehellman.html
```

Nonrepudiation

You often need to be able to thwart any attempts to deny that somebody took an action, sent a message, or agreed to something in a document. Virtually every transaction in business and many interpersonal transactions depend on being able to prove that both parties to the transaction actually participated in it. (Imagine trying to buy a house and having the seller claim that they never agreed to the signed offer and acceptance contract!) Nonrepudiation provides all the confidence that, having reached an agreement, one party or another cannot back away from the agreement by claiming that they never agreed to it. In most cases, this requires building a set of evidence that attests to the transaction or the agreement, the identity of the parties involved, and even the process they went through to reach agreement. In many nations, business and government agreements are literally bound up with special colored ribbons, riveted fasteners, and seals so that visibly and physically the agreement and all of its supporting evidence is in one package. This package can be audited, placed in protected storage (such as an official records office), and used as evidence if the parties have to seek enforcement or relief in a court of law.

Generalizing this, you can see that nonrepudiation requires that:

- The identity of all parties has been authenticated.
- All parties have proven that they have the authority or privilege to participate in the transaction.
- The terms and conditions of the transaction exist in a form that can be recorded.
- All of this information can be collectively or separately verified and validated to be true and correct, free from any attempts to tamper with or alter it.

Nonrepudiation and integrity of information are strongly linked. We believe that the bank notes or coins we spend are *legal tender*, able to be lawfully used to pay for goods and services, because we believe both in the integrity of the coins and paper notes themselves and that the issuing government won't turn around and say "Those are no longer valid."

Registered Email

Let's consider one of the most common examples of the failure to provide reliable nonrepudiation — the use of typical email systems. Although email protocols provide ways for senders and recipients to exchange delivery and read receipts, these fail in nearly all circumstances to provide any proof that what one party claims was sent in an email was received and opened by the intended recipients. Within an organization (that is, when on a single, unified email server), delivery and read receipts are somewhat reliable, but no one relies on them as legally acceptable evidence or proof. It's also trivially easy for senders or recipients to edit the email after it's been sent or received, falsifying address, delivery, or content information in the process. Recipients can easily claim that they never received the email in question, and this lack of verified receipt and viewing of an email can give rise to deception or fraud.

Postal mail systems have long used registered and certified mail delivery processes to provide legally acceptable proof that a letter or package sent by one party to another was in fact delivered to the recipient and received by them. These processes require proof of identification of sender and recipient, and in the case of certified mail they record every step along the delivery path. Courts of law have long recognized that these processes, and similar ones offered by private document or package courier companies, provide acceptable evidence of delivery and receipt. Of course, the U.S. Postal Service cannot prove that the envelope containing the letter was opened or that the letter was read or understood by the addressee—but by denying the opportunity to claim "I never received that letter," many contract disputes or simple misunderstandings can be quickly resolved.

There are several examples of commercial service providers who offer something conceptually similar to registered mail for email and e-documents. Many national postal authorities around the world have started to offer these "registered email" services to their individual, business, and government customers. The European Union set standards in place via the European Electronic Commerce Directive 2000/31/EC, for example, which specifies the technical standards such proof of receipt systems must meet so as to provide legally acceptable evidence of delivery and receipt. One of these systems, provided by RPost, uses multiple cryptographic techniques (many of which are patented) to provide these capabilities. The U.S. Department of Defense and other NATO nations have long used proprietary or closed government systems to ensure that when electronic messages are sent by one command to another, or to a subordinate unit, the recipient cannot ignore that message simply by claiming that "we never got that order." These systems, too, make extensive use of cryptographic techniques. Key to these systems is that strong identity verification, authentication, and information integrity protection measures must work together.

Digital Signatures and Nonrepudiation

Digital signatures use cryptographic techniques to authenticate the identity of the file, its contents, its originator or sender, or any combination of these assertions. Several important elements of a digital signature infrastructure are needed in order to be able to make these assertions hold true over time.

- **Authentication:** Some process must be able to validate that the person or entity signing the file, document, or message is who the signature is associated with.

- **Integrity:** Some process must be able to confirm that the file, document, or message has not been altered—in any way—from the state it was in at the moment it was signed.

- **Nonrepudiation:** Once signed, some process must exist that can defeat any claim by the signer that they did not actually sign the file, message, or document; the system must deny the possibility of a forged signature being affixed to a document, file, or message. This is a one-way declaration of nonrepudiation by the originator; it does not specifically bind an instance of the message, document, or file, to the identity of a specific recipient.

Note that digital signatures, by themselves, are *not* responsible for assuring the confidentiality of the content of the message, document, or file, nor of the identity of the person or entity that signed it. Privacy, too, is not protected (for either the sender/originator or the recipient).

From a practical perspective, such a digital signature system should be scalable; it should not require significant effort to add new signatories to it or for recipients of files or messages to validate the signatures attached to them. As with key management, there should also be mechanisms to expire a signature in ways that do not invalidate documents signed prior to that expiration date. In many respects this is building an infrastructure of *trust*, by providing the mechanisms to assert trust between two parties, extend it from them to a third, and so on.

With the publication of Diffie-Hellman and the RSA algorithms, efforts accelerated to develop a workable infrastructure concept to support digital signatures.

The basic digital signature process involves the use of a highly secure hash function and asymmetric encryption in the following way. Suppose our friend Carol wants to send a message to Bob, but in doing so, she needs to prove to Bob that the message is inarguably from her and not from some imposter. Carol and Bob agree to use the following digital signature protocol:

1. Carol produces a strong hash of the message content. This is known as the *secure message digest*.
2. Carol "encrypts" that hash value, using the trapdoor function and her private key. This new value is her digital signature.
3. Carol sends the message and her digital signature to Bob.
4. Bob "decrypts" Carol's digital signature, using the same trapdoor algorithm and Carol's public signature, to produce the signed hash value.
5. Bob uses the same hash function to produce a comparison hash of the message he received (not including the signature). If this matches the value he computed in step 4, he has proven that Carol (who is the only one who knows her private key) is the only one who could have sent that message.

Again, please note that *signing* the message does not require Carol to encrypt its content, nor Bob to decrypt it. They can, of course, agree to use an encryption process (ideally a hybrid one relying upon their public and private keys) if so required. Note, too, that if a hostile third party such as Ted or Alice attempts to spoof Carol's digital signature, they can succeed only if they already have Carol's private key—or have hacked it via a brute force, burglary, or other attack mechanism. Note, too, that digitally signing a file for *storage* provides the same mix of integrity, authentication, and nonrepudiation protection. (Digitally signing an entire storage backup medium or file set, for example, provides a powerful assertion that the backup *content* is what the signature block asserts it to be.)

In many ways this process is independent of the algorithms used for producing the message hash, public and private keys, or the encryption and decryption used in this process. The root of this all, of course, is in how and where those public and private keys come from, and *that* bit of the infrastructure became associated with digital certificates as the vehicles by which trust is bestowed, recognized, distributed, and managed.

Digital signatures have widespread application in almost every area of systems integrity, availability, safety, and overall trustworthiness. Digital signatures are used in validating that a software update package or distribution kit is authentic or that a database backup set is from the system, date, and time it claims to be. Systems health checks, configuration management and control, and other change control processes can also digitally sign a system (at the level of a file directory or a whole disk volume) at the time the approved change is completed and routinely check by computing the digest value and comparing it to the signature to detect any changes.

All of this, of course, relies upon the sender or originator keeping their secret key *secret* and that there is some process as described in this section that can authenticate the validity of that originator's public (and therefore their private) key.

Hashed Message Authentication Codes

Message authentication codes have long been used as a way of asserting that a particular message did in fact come from a properly authorized originator. Some messaging systems would sequentially number each message as part of formatting it for transmission, which when combined with sending date, time, originator ID, and other information, gave a reasonably unique and verifiable way to prevent attempts by third parties to spoof traffic into the system. Hashed message authentication codes (HMACs) perform this same function and were originally generated by noncryptographic hash functions. In use, HMACs are similar to generating a digital signature for the message contents. Senders and recipients then need to agree to a protocol for the exchange of an HMAC and its associated message content in ways that preserve message integrity and sender authenticity.

Depending upon the hash used to produce a digital signature, there may be exploitable weaknesses that leave the system open to attack. Replacing a standard hash with a cryptographic hash, using a strong cryptographic key, and using the HMAC algorithm allows systems to verify both the integrity of the message data and authenticate the sender of the message (or signer of the digital signature). HMAC first breaks the key into two halves (the *inner* and *outer* keys), then hashes the message first with the inner key, and then hashes that result with the outer key. This double-hash, using two different keys, leads to HMAC having greater immunity against *length-extension attacks*, which systems with only one pass through the hash function can be susceptible to. Similar to SHA-256 and other hash functions, HMAC breaks the message (or file) into fixed-length blocks and iteratively applies a compression function to them. It does not encrypt the message; as with all digital signature processes, the original version of the file or message used to generate the signature must accompany the signature so that the recipient (or later reader) can repeat the signature generation process and compare results to demonstrate authenticity.

Bellare, Canetti, and Krawczyk first published HMAC in a 1996 paper, and then in 1997 wrote RFC 2104 to bring it into the Internet community. It can make use of most any iterative hash function and is part of IPsec, TLS, and JSON Web Tokens. It was later included in FIPS 198 and in its later version FIPS 198-1, which specify the use of cryptographic hash functions to generate reliable message authentication codes for authenticating the information in the message.

Digital Signature Algorithm

The Digital Signature Algorithm (DSA) was first proposed by NIST in August 1991 as part of its Digital Signatures Standard (DSS) proposal. Although many software companies complained (having made significant investments in their own digital signature systems, many based on RSA's cryptosystem), NIST moved ahead with its efforts and adopted DSA as Federal Information Processing Standard 186 in 1994. As of this writing there have been four revisions to DSA, the latest in 2013. DSA was patented by the U.S. government, which has made it available royalty-free worldwide.

DSA uses a combination of modular exponentiation and discrete logarithms to generate a digital signature given a public and private key pair. It supports full verification of authentic signatures and thus provides authentication, integrity, and nonrepudiation. DSA uses a four-step process.

- Key generation, which consists of parameter generation and then computation of a per-user pair of public and private keys based on those parameters
- Key distribution
- Signing
- Signature verification

The algorithm has demonstrated extreme sensitivity to the entropy, secrecy, and uniqueness of the random signature value k that is used during the signing process. Violating any one of these three cryptologic requirements, even by revealing just a few bits of k, can end up revealing the entire private key to an attacker. Experience with and analysis of DSA shows that typical cryptologic hygiene functions—not reusing a key value or a portion of one, for example—must be followed to keep the system secure. This vulnerability is also present in ECDSA, the elliptic curve variant of DSA, and was famously exploited in 2010 by the *overflow* group's attack on Sony, which had been using ECDSA to sign software for its PlayStation 3 console. (Sony had failed to generate a new k for each pair of keys.)

DSA has been incorporated into multiple cryptographic libraries, such as Botan, Bouncy Castle, OpenSSL, and wolfCrypt.

Digital Certificates

Digital signatures—and the whole system of public key encryption—require some kind of authority, broker, or other function that can generate the public and private keys, authoritatively *bind* them to an identity, issue the keys to their owners, authenticate a public key as valid upon request (that is, that it is in fact associated with the identity as claimed), and manage key revocation and expiration. These issues gave rise to the need for special forms of digital signatures known as *digital certificates*. These are intrinsically bound up with public key infrastructures, webs and hierarchies of trust, and other related concepts, which will all be explored together in the "Understand Public Key Infrastructure Systems" section of this chapter.

Digital certificates are one of the lynch pins that hold the public key infrastructure together. It's best to think of these certificates as the result of the following process:

- **Private key generation:** A user requests that a server generate a private key for them. This can be a built-in service in the endpoint device's operating system, an additional server layered on top of that OS, or an application-provided service. The server does this private key generation in accordance with the standards that apply for the type of key needed. (Most keys and digital certificates comply with the X.509 Certificate standard.) The private key never leaves the server, unless the requesting user exports it (for archival purposes in an HSM, perhaps).

- **Public key generation:** The server also generates the corresponding public key for this user. (It's not published yet, of course.)

- **Certificate signing request (CSR):** The server issues a request to a complaint certificate authority selected by the user, containing required identification fields as well as the user-generated public key. The certificate signing request is digitally signed using the requestor's private key. The private key is not part of the CSR. (Note that these are sometimes referred to as *SSL CSRs*, even though SSL has largely been replaced by TLS if not completely retired by the time you read this.)

- **Certificate enrollment:** The server registers the identity information, public key, and digital signature in its records, and issues the certificate to the user.

The results of this process are a publicly registered, cryptographically secure binding or association of an identity and a public key; the strength of that binding, that is, its acceptability by the marketplace of users, is fundamentally tied to the trustworthiness of the certificate authority. The certificate authority (CA) is the one that issues certificates, sets their expiration dates, revokes them upon indications of compromise or for other legitimate reasons, and thereby facilitates the use of public-private key cryptography. (This is true whether the CA serves the general public or is a private CA internal to an organization.)

Public CAs include companies such as Comodo, Geotrust, Digicert, Thawte, Entrust, and many others. Symantec had been a major player in the public CA marketplace, but in 2018, Google had issues with Symantec over the latter's issuing of free certificates in an attempt to stimulate small and startup business use. These were quickly gobbled up by fraudsters and exploited in a number of ways. One result of this was that Symantec sold its CA business line to Digicert.

Various circumstances might invalidate a certificate, such as the following:

- Change of the subject's name (does not always invalidate the certificate, depending on policy and the implementing technology)

- Change of association between the subject and the certificate authority (such as when the subject is an employee leaving the company that acts as the certificate authority)

- Compromise of the private key that corresponds to the public key included in the certificate

In these circumstances, the CA must revoke the certificate. One common way is to put that certificate's serial number on a certificate revocation list (CRL) maintained and made public, perhaps on a website, by the CA.

Checking that a certificate you have received has not been revoked is an important step in *verifying* it. You can either download the latest CRL from the CA or check directly with the CA in real time using the Online Certificate Status Protocol (OCSP). If the certificate has not been revoked, the digital signature of the certificate authority is authentic, and you trust that CA, then the chain of logic is complete.

Once you have verified a certificate, you may consider the data contained in it as authentic. That choice, like others in our field, is a risk to be balanced. Because digital certificates are such an important part of modern security, it comes as no surprise that attackers have worked hard—and have often succeeded—at discovering and exploiting vulnerabilities associated with certificates. Dozens of flaws with digital certificates have been uncovered over the years.

Some attackers have focused their efforts on certificate authorities. One approach seeks to exploit weaknesses in the domain validation schemes a CA employs to authenticate the applicant for a new certificate. Another is to directly compromise the databases maintained by a certificate authority to cause the issuance of rogue certificates.

The potential use of rogue certificates has afflicted more than one mobile banking application, weakening their defense against man-in-the-middle (MITM) attacks. The MITM risk is that an attacker may intercept an encrypted connection, pose to each side as the other participant, copy the user's banking credentials, and steal their money. Recently, a defensive tactic known as *pinning*—associating a particular host with their expected certificate—has become popular. Pinning, however, fails to solve the problem if the application does not check to see whether it is connected to a trusted source (that is, authenticate the hostname) before using the certificate.

Critics have long pointed to cryptographic issues with digital certificates, as well. To make certificates more difficult to subvert, the *hash function* must provide unique values. The ability to generate two different files with identical hash values makes possible a so-called "collision attack," diluting the value of the digital signatures used in certificates. The National Institute of Standards and Technology warned in 2015 that advances in processing speed had rendered unsafe the use of the popular SHA-1 cryptographic algorithm, and in 2017 Google researchers demonstrated a hash collision attack against SHA-1.

Pure implementation issues not directly due to cryptographic issues have plagued certificate-based security in recent years as well, as the infamous "HeartBleed" and "POODLE" vulnerabilities of 2014 illustrated only too well.

Many of these certificate-based vulnerabilities have been addressed, over the years, with new designs and new implementation versions. Yet as long as clever attackers seek to undermine complex authentication systems, you can never be absolutely certain that a certificate is trustworthy.

The responsible management of digital certificates is so important because they are critical to modern authentication methods. Certificates have so many uses!

For example, a software developer may use a credential scheme to allow their application to log into a database without having to hard code the username and password into the source code. It is also possible to digitally sign software and patches upon release with credentials so that any tampering with the executable file can be detected. IPsec, a framework of open standards helping to secure communications over the Internet, relies on digital certificates, as do almost all virtual private network (VPN) technologies. Digital certificates also make possible the Secure/Multipurpose Internet Mail Extension (S/MIME) capabilities that can be used to encrypt electronic mail.

The place where the everyday user interacts with digital certificates most often, without question, is when they visit a "secure" website—that is, one with a URL that begins with "HTTPS" and not "HTTP."

When you connect to a website with an address that begins with "HTTPS," you are specifying that you want the browser session to use Transport Layer Security (TLS), a cryptographic protocol that provides communications security between computer networks. (TLS has largely supplanted the earlier protocol Secure Sockets Layer, which introduced this capability.)

TLS uses digital certificates. A peek at the National Institute for Standards and Technology guidance gives you a sense of the complexity of the configuration possibilities:

> *The TLS server shall be configured with one or more public key certificates and the associated private keys. TLS server implementations should support multiple server certificates with their associated private keys to support algorithm and key size agility.*
>
> *There are six options for TLS server certificates that can satisfy the requirement for Approved cryptography: an RSA key encipherment certificate; an RSA signature certificate; an Elliptic Curve Digital Signature Algorithm (ECDSA) signature certificate; a Digital Signature Algorithm (DSA) signature certificate; a Diffie-Hellman certificate; and an ECDH certificate...*
>
> *TLS servers shall be configured with certificates issued by a CA, rather than self-signed certificates. Furthermore, TLS server certificates shall be issued by a CA that publishes revocation information in either a Certificate Revocation List (CRL) [RFC5280] or in Online Certificate Status Protocol (OCSP) [RFC6960] responses.*
>
> *NIST Special Publication 800-52, Guidelines for the Selection, Configuration and Use of Transport Layer Security (TLS) Implementations, April 2014*
> `(https://doi.org/10.6028/NIST.SP.800-52r1)`

The full details, which extend for several additional pages, are beyond the scope of this chapter. The key concept is that your web browser and the website server use certificates to be sure of the identity of the other side of the transaction.

The most popular design for the content and format of digital certificates is defined by the standard X.509, provided by the Standardization sector of the International Telecommunications Union (ITU-T). Version 1 was defined in 1988, version 2 in 1993, and version 3 (the current version) in 1996.

An X.509 certificate consists of three required fields: *tbscertificate*, *signatureAlgorithm*, and *signatureValue*. Here is a quick look at the contents of each.

Inside the *tbscertificate* field, you will find the names of the *subject* and the *issuer*. This field also contains the public key associated with the subject and the "validity period" specifying the *notBefore* and *notAfter* times. The certificate authority generates and inserts a unique *serialNumber* for the certificate, too.

The *signatureAlgorithm* field contains an identifier for the cryptographic algorithm used by the certificate authority to sign the certificate.

The *signatureValue* field contains a digital signature computed for this certificate, encoded as a bit string.

NOTE   For more information about the X.509 certificate and its required fields, see RFC 5280, "Internet X.509 Public Key Infrastructure Certificate and Certificate Revocation List (CRL) Profile," from the Internet Engineering Task Force (https://doi.org/10.17487/RFC5280).

In addition to specifying the content of X.509 certificates, the standard lays out a certification *path validation algorithm*. Digital certificates build and rely upon a chain of trust, and a certificate chain carefully lists for examination each CA in the chain, conveying credence to the certificate.

A certificate can in fact be *self-signed* by the subject. Properly constructed self-signed certificates adhere to the format and satisfy the standard, leaving it up to the recipient to evaluate whether they are trustworthy. Self-certification limits, naturally, the sum of conveyed trust to the subject alone. On the other hand, self-signed certificates do eliminate the potential risk of third parties that may improperly sign certificates or have themselves been compromised by an attack.

Before leaving the subject of digital certificates, we must tackle the difference between a certificate and a *blockchain*. Blockchains have made cryptocurrencies possible (and increasingly popular) in recent years. They are based on a cryptographic message integrity scheme. A blockchain is a decentralized public record of transactions calculated by distributed computing systems across the Internet. The blockchain uses cryptographic encryption to ensure that any tampering with that record can be detected.

Briefly, the blocks keep batches of valid transactions that are hashed and encoded into something called a *Merkel tree*. Each block holds the cryptographic hash of the previous block. Hence, they are chained together, in a set of continuous links, all the way back to a *genesis block*. This distributed public chain of verifiable blocks ensures the integrity of the blockchain transaction records.

Encryption Algorithms

Cryptographic algorithms describe the process by which plaintext is encrypted and ciphertext decrypted back to its original plaintext. Those algorithms have to meet a number of mathematical and logical conditions if they are going to provide reliable, collision-free mapping of plaintext to ciphertext (for encryption or hashing) and then from ciphertext back to plaintext (in the case of decryption). Collisions would mean that any two plaintext strings could produce the same hash, which would invalidate any attempt to use hashes for digital signatures or message authentication codes. Collisions during encryption would also render any attempt to protect or obscure the meaning of plaintext for storage or transmission impossible, since upon decryption, there would be no reliable way to know which of the meanings had been intended.

Cryptographic algorithms also have to be sufficiently robust that they do not provide any easy mathematical or logical attacks that can defeat their protections; the section

"Cryptographic Attacks, Cryptanalysis, and Countermeasures" goes into some of these attacks in further detail. Perhaps the most successful strategy to defeat a target's use of encryption is not to attack it head-on, but to go around it via a *side-channel* attack, which attempts to find and exploit weaknesses in the operational procedures the target uses to implement cryptographic security. Mismanaged keys, passwords that are allowed to be of trivial length or complexity, vulnerability to social engineering, and even sufficiently poor physical security can make it laughably easy for an attacker to obtain information about keys that are in use.

It is difficult to separate algorithms from protocols, and protocols from systems. Public key encryption is a case in point. While almost any asymmetric algorithm can be used as part of session key generation and use, the notion that private keys and public keys depend upon an infrastructure of certificates being generated and distributed (either by a hierarchy or web of trust) ties two infrastructures to the algorithms. It is also difficult—and perhaps meaningless—to attempt to separate cryptographic systems and techniques from the operational processes by which you or any organization puts them to use, audits conformance to standards and procedures, maintains them, and updates, refreshes, or renews keys and other keying materials. *Cryptographic hygiene* offers a mental model or framework that can encourage a commonsense, disciplined approach to reducing these risks.

Key Strength

Cryptographic key strength was introduced in the first section of this chapter as being strongly related to the number of bits in the encryption key used by a given encryption algorithm. This bit depth actually defines the size of the *search space* that a brute-force attack would have to go through, checking each possible value, until it found one that matched the hash value or ciphertext being attacked. Such brute-force attacks can, of course, get lucky and strike a match on one of the first few attempts…or have to run almost forever until a winner turns up. Computer scientists refer to this as a *halting problem*, in that while you know the maximum number of iterations the search loop must perform, you have no way of knowing whether it will take one iteration, a handful, or a full 2^n times around the loop for an *n*-bit key. This search space size was the first practical way to estimate the *work factor* associated with cracking a particular cipher. Cryptanalysts could then estimate the number of CPU (or GPU) instruction cycles needed for each iteration, translate that into seconds (or microseconds), and then multiply to estimate the length of how long one's secrets might remain safe from an attacker in terms of hours, days, or weeks.

The search space argument regarding cryptographic strength started to fall apart as the cost of high-performance graphic processing units (GPUs) fell while their processing power soared. (Think about how many complex vector calculations have to be done each second to take a streaming HD video, uncompress it, render it into clusters of pixels of the right color and intensity, provide those pixels to the video driver circuits, and then send the information out to the display. One *frame* of video is about 6.221 MB of data; at 60 frames per second, one second of video involves about 374 MB of data total, all the result of parallel processing streams inside the GPU.) Software systems for designing massively parallel task streams, dispatching workloads to processors, and coordinating their efforts to produce a finished result have become far more commonplace and more powerful; the hypervisor contained in most modern desktop or laptop computers has many of these capabilities built right in. These factors all compound together to give cryptanalysts—hostile and friendly alike—entirely new and affordable ways to bring thousands or tens of thousands of CPUs (and GPUs) to a code-breaking task. Attempts have been made by cryptanalysts to express cryptographic strength in "MIP-years," that is, the number of millions of instructions per second a CPU executes, across a whole year, but this has proven challenging to translate across dissimilar architectures of GPUs, CPUs, and such.

Sometimes 256 May Not Be Greater Than 128

The search space argument suggests that it's reasonable to expect a longer key will be more secure than a shorter one. All else being equal, the longer the key, the larger the key space and therefore the longer it will take to brute-force a key. But with AES, it turns out that all else is not equal. Owing to problems with the design of AES-256, Alex Biryukov, Orr Dunkelman, Nathan Keller, Dmitry Khovratovich, and Adi Shamir reported in 2009 that there is an attack on AES-256 that requires only 2^{119} time (compared with 2^{128} time for AES-128, or the 2^{256} time one would expect from AES-256). Practically, this does not matter as a 2^{119} time attack is still completely infeasible using any technology available or likely to be available within the next decade or two. (Work that out in MIP-years to see why it's infeasible for the moment.) The attacks analyzed by Biryukov et al. are of a type known as *related-key* attacks that are impractical in properly implemented systems. Biryukov et al. also found a weakness in AES-192, but that attack takes 2^{176}, not 2^{192} as it ought to, if AES-192 had no flaws, but that's still much better than AES-128.

These and similar cryptanalyst findings demonstrate that as cryptographic algorithms become more complex, a measure of their strength (or weakness) needs to consider other factors than processing needs alone. The size of a data space associated with part of an algorithm, the number of rounds used, or other parameters may have a marked effect on the strength of an algorithm.

Cryptographic Safety Factor

Other cryptanalysts have also struggled with the difficulty in making a meaningful estimate of the strength of a cryptographic algorithm. One approach was taken in the selection process for the algorithm that became the Advanced Encryption Standard; for this, cryptographer Eli Biham introduced the concept of a safety factor.

Biham's safety factor notes that all modern ciphers are built as a series of rounds, each using a subkey derived from the main key. Cryptographers typically attempt to break ciphers by first attacking a simplified version of the cipher with a reduced number of rounds. For example, early cryptographic attacks on DES (before it fell to simple brute-force) revealed an attack on eight rounds (the full DES has 16 rounds). With AES-256, there is an attack that works on a simplified version of 10 rounds (the full AES has 14 rounds). This was developed after attacks on six-, seven-, and nine-round versions.

Biham's safety factor is the ratio of the number of rounds in the cipher, divided by the largest number of rounds that have been successfully attacked so far. While obviously dependent on the level of effort expended by cryptographers trying to undermine a cipher, it is still a useful metric, at least when comparing ciphers that have received sufficient attention from cryptographers.

Using this measure, AES-256 currently has a safety factor of 1.4. Other ciphers, such as Twofish, have greater safety factors, and it was for this reason that the team that developed the Twofish algorithm argued that it ought to have been selected as the Advanced Encryption Standard instead of the algorithm (Rijndael) that was selected.

In a somewhat tongue-in-cheek fashion, Lenstra, Kleinjung and Thomé have suggested that another, and possibly more useful, approach, would be to estimate the amount of energy (as heat) that each such attack process needs. In their paper titled "Universal Security, from bits and mips to pools, lakes, and beyond," they focus on how difficult it really is to usefully predict (or model) the strength of an encryption process in terms that are comparable to non-encryption-based ideas of work and time. For more food for thought you can head to `https://eprint.iacr.org/2013/635.pdf`.

The sad news is, however, that no matter what algorithm you choose and no matter how carefully you choose its cryptovariables, you are still in a race against time. Processing power in the hands of the attackers will continue to increase, especially as they become more adept at sharing the load around in their dark web bastion areas. You can stay a few steps ahead of them, however, if you are diligent in keeping your systems and their cryptologic components properly maintained and updated and operate them in ways that do not inadvertently lead to compromising them.

CRYPTOGRAPHIC ATTACKS, CRYPTANALYSIS, AND COUNTERMEASURES

As American cryptologist Bruce Schneier famously stated, "All cryptography can eventually be broken—the only question is how much effort is required." Many cryptographers, hostile and friendly alike, read these words and think that this is a two-variable inequality: what's the value to me (defender or attacker) of the information, and what's the value to me of the effort required to successfully attack that information asset (or protect it from compromise, damage, or loss)? This oversimplifies the *time* element of the problem and the inherent *asymmetry* in the way that attacker and defender view the time value of information and effort.

The defenders and their organization have invested substantially in obtaining, creating, and using their information assets to gain a temporary competitive advantage. They are also usually constrained by the ways that financial markets work—if they incur huge costs in the immediate term because of an incident, they may have to finance or carry those costs for years to come. Thus, the *future value* of their losses can be far greater than the actual costs incurred during an incident. As a security professional, you may already be accustomed to justifying investments in better information security systems, technologies, procedures, and workforce training on the basis of the time value of the costs you can avoid versus the revenues you can protect. You may also face one of those *tipping points* at which the long-term strategic value of a decision or action—and thereby the information assets that support that course of action—are just too significant to ignore; and yet, that tipping point won't last forever.

The attacker may or may not face similar time value propositions, depending upon their own agendas, goals, or objectives. Their objectives may be immediate profit from reselling the data that they exfiltrate, or they may see their attacks on your systems, facilitated by cracking their way past your cryptographic defenses, as just one step in a longer and more complex kill chain. Then, too, the attackers might view stealing (or disrupting) your information assets as an action that produces immediate competitive advantage *for them*, in ways we have no way to recognize.

You're in a race against time with all of your current and potential adversaries "out there" in the wild. You cannot stand still; your defensive cryptographic systems get weaker with time as your adversaries' abilities to analyze, assess, and circumvent them get stronger and stronger (and cheaper and cheaper to buy, build, rent, or use). That's the bad news regarding your cryptologic risk situation; it should also be a wake-up call.

It's also some good news for your proactive defense strategy, tactics, and operations. You need to gather and exploit the threat intelligence you have available to you and tune that to help you assess your current state of *cryptologic hygiene*.

Cryptologic Hygiene as Countermeasures

Cryptologic hygiene is an operational attitude and approach that takes planned, managed, and proactive steps to assess your cryptologic systems, and your use of them, across the entire face of your systems' cryptologic attack surfaces. This requires you to examine the following:

- Algorithm and protocol selection, such as in cryptologic suites.
- Algorithm and protocol implementation.

- Operational use of cryptographic systems as part of routine end user activities.

- Systems administration of cryptologic systems.

- Continuous vulnerability assessment, including CVE information regarding the systems, algorithms, cipher suites, and cryptologic management tools in use in your organization. This includes mitigation of those vulnerabilities.

- Key generation, management, and use, including verified backups as required.

- Identity, digital signature, and digital certificate management, backup, and use.

- Business continuity and disaster recovery cryptologic processes.

- End user education and training regarding cryptographic defenses.

- Education, training, and expectation management for all levels of management, leadership, and other stakeholders.

Your organization's unique risk situation and context, and its information security needs, may dictate that other cryptology-oriented elements be included in your cryptologic hygiene plans.

Each of these topic areas (and others you might need to add) *may* present a determined attacker with exploitable vulnerabilities. Many have been identified by the cryptanalyst communities and are written about in journals, blog posts, or other publications. Some are reported as Common Vulnerabilities and Exposures; others appear in white papers and conference proceedings posted on the websites of security systems vendors, information security associations such as (ISC)^2, ISACA, and the IEEE CS, to name a few.

Cryptologic hygiene is a subset of your overall security hygiene and posture, but it's also the same attitude and mind-set at work. It asks you to address the fundamental issues of the quality and maturity of your processes for using, managing, controlling, protecting, assessing, improving, and restoring your cryptographic defenses. It asks to be a subset of your overall information security process maturity modeling and measurement.

A Starter Set of Crypto-Hygiene Practices

Let's take a look at some starting points for putting a cryptologic hygiene program into action. There are any number of standards documents that address aspects of this hygiene process, many of which address information security processes across the board. Others are very intensely focused on what might be called the high-capacity, high-demand cryptologic user base, such as what you'd expect in a major financial institution, a credit card payment processor, or even at a certificate authority. The following rules of thumb should give you a simpler place to start, which may be enough to address the needs of a small office/home office (SOHO) or small to medium-sized organization infrastructure.

DIY Need Not Apply An important rule in cryptographic hygiene is to never invent your own cryptographic algorithm, process, or system, even if you think it's absolutely necessary to do so. Although technology professionals are generally smart people, it is entirely too common that we become overconfident in our abilities. In 1864, famed cryptographer Charles Babbage wrote, "One of the most singular characteristics of the art of deciphering is the strong conviction possessed by every person, even moderately acquainted with it, that he is able to construct a cipher which nobody else can decipher." This leads to a false sense of security. Simply because you have invented a system that you cannot defeat does not mean it cannot (or will not) be defeated by someone else.

Know Your System Baselines and How to Maintain Them Know what you've already got and how to use it. Your systems already have significant cryptologic components in them. Most web browsers, for example, already bring you the capabilities to manage the use of encryption suites, digital certificates, digital signatures, and other encryption-based security measures. Start with a very detailed inventory; discover and catalog every element. Make sure you have current vendor-supplied operational and maintenance information on hand, or at least know where to get it. Systems vendors, platform providers, and even your browser provider offer substantial libraries of how-to information—from simple procedures through in-depth knowledge base articles—which you should be familiar with. Use these support pages to identify active community support boards; join in the learning by joining the conversation.

Manage and Back Up Your Baselines You also need to put your cryptographic infrastructure under solid configuration management and control. Plan and schedule changes, whether those are certificate renewals, minor patches and updates, or major upgrades. Make and securely keep backups of certificates and private keys, especially for archived or backup datasets. Identify the human elements associated with each cryptographic configuration item (CCI, to coin an acronym); these are opportunities to keep end users engaged with security by building their awareness and their skills.

Stay Sharp It is crucial to stay current. Knowing and managing your baselines should point you to the communities of practice that directly apply to the systems and technologies your organization depends upon. Find the places you need to frequent to stay informed about new exploits or attacks or cryptanalysis results that suggest a vulnerability might exist in your systems.

Protect Across the Life Cycle It is also essential to practice good housekeeping. Your systems' baseline and configuration management processes should identify components of your systems that need special end-of-life treatment, so as not to compromise your cryptographic defenses. You may have little or no direct involvement in key management or the destruction of expired, revoked, or compromised keying materials, if you're like the majority of business and nonprofit organizations and are totally dependent upon commodity product systems, such as servers, workstations, and endpoints, and their built-in hybrid encryption systems. Nonetheless, it's good to have your hardware, software, firmware, and data baselines clearly identify cryptographically sensitive items that may need special protection while in use, when undergoing repairs, or when being disposed of.

If You Can't Update, Increase Your Watchfulness   Think about the CVE process and overlay its timeline onto the kill chain conceptual model. Chances are that many exploiters in the wild will learn about that vulnerability the same way you will, by means of notifications from the CVE database operators. Three time windows start clocking out starting on "zero day"—the time to develop a fix or patch, the time for you to validate that you can safely install the fix without causing *more* disruption to business processes, and the time for attackers to take advantage of that vulnerability and get into your systems. It's not hard to guess which one of those time windows runs out the fastest.

Prudent software and systems management dictates that you test and evaluate *any* change to your systems *before* putting it into production or operational use, no matter how urgent and compelling the need to update may seem to be. Security hygiene— and therefore cryptologic hygiene—dictates that between the time you *have* the fix in hand and the time you've finished testing it and declaring it the "new normal" that you increase your watchfulness. The larger your deployed architecture and the greater the mix of systems, versions, and endpoint technologies employed with it, the harder it becomes to baseline it and manage to that baseline. You should be doing this alone: the IT departments and the formal configuration management and control teams in your organization own the lion's share of this burden. Your role should focus on the cryptologic aspects of that architecture, particularly the procedural ones, to make sure that someone else's major change package doesn't demolish the crypto-walls that are relied upon today.

Your first response to seeing a new CVE announcement should be to ask yourself, "How would I spot that new exploit in action against my systems?" Think like the adversary; red team your current surveillance and monitoring processes and see whether you can detect this new exploit in action. Any new exploits you cannot detect, which might remotely allow an intruder into your systems, are crying out for changing something in your monitoring, analysis, detection, and reporting operations.

As you continue to apply a cryptographic hygiene mindset, you'll probably discover more rules to put into your cryptographic process maturity handbook. One way to do that is to look at common attack patterns; along the way, let's also look at some "famous fails" when it comes to design, implementation, and use cases gone wrong.

Cryptography Is Not a Standalone Answer

This may be a blinding flash of the obvious, but it's part of counteracting the "sprinkle a little crypto dust" fallacy, so you may have to keep this rule handy and use it often. For example, consider the *private keys* on your client endpoint systems. Where are they kept? How do *you* keep them safe and secure?

If you're working in a SOHO system or any systems infrastructure where you do not buy and manage your own certificates (and thereby generate and manage your users' private and public keys on your own), then you are vitally dependent upon the access control systems and policies on your in-house file servers, database servers, web servers, network control systems, and each and every one of your client endpoint devices. That means that *anybody* with superuser or systems administrative privileges, who has physical or logical access to *any* of these machines, has access to where its host operating system stores its certificates, public keys, private keys, and the tables that OS uses to associate each user identity with its keys (and possibly the password salts, hashed passwords, and other encryption-related parameters). Because we need systems that are easy to administer, it's easy for such a user to call up the right built-in utility functions and export those files.

So how do you stop a *lunchtime attack* from purloining a copy of those key caches?

Administratively, you teach your users what the risks might be and how each of them is a vital component in the overall security system. You motivate them to become true believers in the idle-lock settings; you work with them to eliminate the yellow stickies with the password cribs. You get them to be suspicious of the pizza delivery man wandering the hallways (one of my favorite force protection drills, after I received an unordered pizza box with a "boom!" note inside it).

Physically, you identify the right mix of protection mechanisms that keep both your on-site and your mobile devices protected; this may include mobile device managers and their capabilities to lock or brick such a device if it wanders off site.

Logically, you thoroughly understand what you need in the way of access control capabilities; use what's built into your OS and servers for all that it's worth. Understand what to log, and what to look for in those logs, as it might relate to attempted attacks on your key stores and caches.

Without every other trick in your information security playbook working like clockwork for you, you cannot protect the number-one set of secret ingredients in your competitive advantage: your users' and your company's private keys, and the cryptovariables, seeds, and salts that go with them.

The "Understand Public Key Infrastructure Systems" section in this chapter will go into more depth and detail on key and certificate management and the cryptologic hygiene measures to consider. This is enough, for now, to get you seeing your systems from the hostile cryptanalysts' perspective, cryptologically speaking.

Common Attack Patterns and Methods

It's now time to look outside of your cryptologic attack surface and think about the ways in which an attacker might attempt to circumvent your defenses. Start from the assumption that your attacker will know your system; the only thing that they won't know (right away) are the specifics about the user IDs, credentials, and keys that provide the real strength that your defenses need.

Along the way, we'll mention some attack-specific countermeasures for you to consider as part of the ways in which your organization chooses, installs, uses, and maintains its cryptologic defenses. Since you're not developing your own encryption or hashing algorithms, we won't address countermeasures that *designers* should take. These are, of course, in addition to all the normal, customary, and usual cryptographic hygiene elements regarding keeping systems up-to-date, under control, and protected. Keeping yourself "fully patched" and your knowledge up to date as well is, of course, part of that expected set of proactive measures.

Attacks Against the Human Element

The people in your organization are perhaps its greatest strength and its greatest opportunity for exploitation by a determined adversary. Too many businesses have suffered when an insider becomes susceptible to coercion, blackmail, or other "undue influences," as they say. Some have had employees kidnapped and pressured or otherwise influenced into revealing information that allows an attacker to defeat otherwise impregnable information defenses. Technical exploitation of lost or stolen endpoint devices is becoming commonplace. Burglary and other clandestine means of entering a facility to gain information are risks that should not be ignored.

You've addressed those risks to your organization with various physical, logical, and administrative mitigations and security controls. Be sure to extend that to the cryptologic elements of your systems. You may be safe in relying on system and data archives protected by encryption, if you've used strong hybrid systems to provide you assurances of the forward secrecy of those archives; but to read and use those archives when you need them, you've got to have those session keys *somewhere*. How do you protect them against the exploitable vulnerabilities in the human elements of your systems?

Algorithm Attacks

These are attack patterns that depend upon intercepting and collecting quantities of ciphertext and plaintext and then analyzing them to look for patterns. Traffic between multiple senders and recipients may reveal coincidental changes in message length or frequency when correlated to other observable activities, for example. Four main types of attack fall into this category.

- **Ciphertext-only attacks** occur when the attacker has access only to the encrypted traffic (ciphertext). In many cases, some information about the plaintext can be guessed (such as the language of the message, which can lead to knowledge of the character probability distribution or the format of the message, which can give clues to parts of the plaintext). Wired Equivalent Privacy (WEP), the original security algorithm for Wi-Fi™, is vulnerable to a number of ciphertext-only attacks. By capturing a sufficient number of packets (which typically can be gathered within minutes on a busy network), it is possible to derive the key used in the RC4 stream cipher. It is thought that the 45 million credit cards purloined from the American retail giant T.J. Maxx were obtained by exploiting WEP.

- **Known-plaintext attacks** can happen when the attacker knows some or all of the plaintext of one or more messages (as well as the ciphertext). This frequently happens when parts of the message tend to be fixed (such as protocol headers or other relatively invariant parts of the messages being communicated). An example of a known-plaintext attack is the famous German Enigma cipher machine, which was cracked in large part by relying upon known plaintexts. Many messages contained the same word in the same place or contained the same text (e.g., "Nothing to report."), making deciphering the messages possible.

- **Chosen-plaintext attacks** see the attacker is able to inject any plaintext the attacker chooses into the target's communications systems (or a copy of them) and thereby obtain the corresponding ciphertext. The classic example of a chosen-plaintext attack occurred during WWII when the United States intercepted messages indicating the Japanese were planning an attack on a location known as "AF" in code. The United States suspected this might be Midway Island, and to confirm their hypothesis, the United States arranged for a plaintext message to be sent from Midway Island indicating that the island's water purification plant had broken down. When the Japanese intercepted the message and then transmitted a coded message referring to AF, the United States had the confirmation they needed.

- **Chosen-ciphertext attacks** occur when the attacker is able to inject any ciphertext into the target's communications systems (or a copy of them) and thereby obtain the corresponding plaintext. An example of this was the attack on SSL 3.0 developed by Bleichenbacher of Bell Labs that could obtain the RSA private key of a website after trying between 300,000 and 2 million chosen ciphertexts.

As you might expect, different cryptographic systems and their algorithms have differing levels of vulnerability to these types of attacks.

✔ Heartbleed—An Implementation Flaw Case Study

Heartbleed was an implementation flaw in the implementation of the TLS protocol used to secure web traffic (HTTPS). Part of the protocol defined a "heartbeat" packet that contains a text message and a length field. The computer receiving the message is simply to send the message back. The defect was that the size of the message sent back was not based on the actual size of the received heartbeat packet, but on the length parameter sent by the requester. So, a malicious actor could send a heartbeat packet containing the message "Hello, world!" but with a length field of, say, 64,000. The reply would contain "Hello, world!" plus the next 63,987 bytes of whatever happened to be in memory beyond that message. That memory could contain the private key used to secure the website, or copies of previous messages containing confidential information. Access to a web server's private keys would enable an attacker to decrypt past and future web traffic, as well as spoof the identity of the website, enabling phishing attacks.

The flaw existed in the widely used library for two years before being reported and patched. At least half a million secure websites were estimated to have been affected, not to mention the hundreds of thousands of devices with an embedded web server used to manage the device. In one example, a curious computing science student used the flaw to exfiltrate 900 social insurance numbers from the Canada Revenue Agency, earning an 18-month conditional sentence to prison for his efforts. Cybersecurity columnist Joseph Steinberg wrote in *Forbes*: "Some might argue that Heartbleed is the worst vulnerability found (at least in terms of its potential impact) since commercial traffic began to flow on the Internet."

You can find more information at `https://heartbleed.com`.

Brute Force

A brute-force attack is one that simply steps through all possible values until one of them works (requiring little thought, planning, reconnaissance, or analysis). Typically, this involves building (or mathematically generating) a search space of all possible values, such as 2^{64} binary numbers for a 64-bit key space. If luck is with you (the defender), your key or hash value won't match in the first few (days or weeks) of an attacker's search of that space. Then again, luck may favor the *attacker*. Brute-force attacks against password hashes, ciphertext, digital signatures, or almost any element of your systems are possible. Brute-force attacks are commonly targeted against intercepted individual passwords or against exfiltrated password hash tables. Cryptanalytic attacks may also resort to brute-force attacks against ciphertext.

WEP, as a case study, reveals the value of a well-placed brute-force attack. Wired Equivalent Privacy (WEP) was the first approach to encryption used for Wi-Fi™ networks. One of its major design flaws was its reliance on the RC4 encryption algorithm, which was quickly shown to be susceptible to brute-force attacks. RC4 did not have an initialization vector built into its algorithm, so the WEP designers chose to use a 24-bit IV combined with the symmetric encryption key to feed to the keystream generator. Such a short IV repeats far too quickly; in typical usage, less than three minutes of Wi-Fi™ packet sniffing would provide more than enough samples to use to attack and break WEP's encryption as a result. (As a result, WEP should not be used, especially when the stronger WPA and WPA-2 are available.)

Modified or *optimized* brute-force attacks are ones in which a little knowledge on the attacker's part is used to drastically reduce their search time. This can involve any number of techniques, such as precomputing a dictionary or rainbow table.

Countermeasures to brute-force attacks include strong password and passphrase hygiene, using properly updated cryptographic hash, encryption and decryption suites, and effective, operational security procedures.

Man-in-the-Middle Attack

Man-in-the-middle (MiTM) attacks show up at almost every layer of the OSI protocol stack—including layer 8, the human-to-human layer. When they involve the attacker (imposter) attempting to sidestep, subvert, or otherwise attack the cryptographic processes used by the parties, it's worth considering them as a cryptologic attack. For example, a MiTM attacker (Mallory, let's say) attempts to insert herself into a conversation between Bob and Carol, who are using HTTPS as part of their processes. Bob and Carol are relying upon the digital certificates each provides to the other (via their browsers' use of them and their built-in encryption suites) to confirm Bob's assertion that he is in fact Bob, and Carol's that she actually is Carol. However, if one or more of these certificates were issues by a compromised certificate authority (such as the Dutch CA DigiNotar, which was compromised in 2011), Bob and Carol might *believe* they are talking to each other, when in fact they are talking *through* Mallory. (The DigiNotar compromise affected more than 300,000 Gmail users.)

Side-Channel Attacks

Side-channel attacks involve measuring observable characteristics of the cryptographic process to deduce information to assist with compromising encrypted information. This usually requires the attacker to have a copy of the system being attacked and the ability to open it up, capture internal or intermediate data, make measurements, or even take infrared high-speed images to observe changes in heat signatures. These can include the following:

- Timing
- Cache access
- Power consumption
- Electromagnetic emanations
- Error information

The time taken to encrypt or decrypt a block of data can vary depending on the key or plaintext, and a careful analysis of the time taken to encrypt or decrypt the data can reveal information. The time to perform a cryptographic operation can vary for a number of reasons.

- Conditional branches within the code, which can change the time of execution depending on the branches taken, which in turn depend on the value of the key or plaintext
- CPU instructions that take variable time to complete depending on the operands (e.g., multiplication and division)
- Memory access, which can vary depending on where the data is located (type of memory) or the access history (thus affecting the cache and thus the speed of memory access)

Cache attacks typically involve processes running on different virtual machines on the same physical processor. As the VM performing the encryption is time-sliced with the VM running the attacker's processes, the attacker can probe the processor's cache to deduce information about the plaintext and the key and thus compromise the encryption process. A cache-timing attack was at the heart of the Spectre and Meltdown attacks revealed in 2018 as methods of extracting data from protected regions of a processor's memory (e.g., keys or plaintext messages).

The power consumed by the device performing the cryptographic operation may vary depending on the instructions executed, which in turn depend on the key and data being encrypted. By carefully monitoring the power consumed by the device, it can sometimes be possible to extract information about the key or plaintext. This type of attack has been most successfully demonstrated against smartcards because of the relative ease with which the device's power consumption can be monitored, but the attack mechanism has wide applicability.

All electronic systems emit electromagnetic radiation, and it is possible to capture this, sometimes at some distance from the device. These radio signals can sometimes be analyzed to reveal information about the data being processed by the device. Early examples of this type of attack involved analyzing the emanations of cryptographic devices that printed the decrypted message on teletypewriters to determine which characters were being printed.

Error information provided (or leaked) by decryption software can provide useful information for attackers. In the Padding Oracle Attack, a system that can be sent any number of test messages and that generates a distinctive error for encrypted messages that are not properly padded can be used to decrypt messages without knowing the key. The defense is to report generic errors and not to distinguish between padding errors and other errors.

Countermeasures exist, but in some cases, they can be difficult to implement or can exact a considerable performance penalty. In the case of timing attacks, it is necessary to modify the algorithm so that it is isochronous, which is to say runs in constant time regardless of the key and data being processed.

The difficulty of implementing a secure algorithm that is secure against side-channel attacks is another reason for the "DIY need not apply" edict. Do not attempt to d write your own cryptographic implementation—use a tested and widely used cryptographic library instead.

Differential Fault Analysis

Differential fault analysis is a cryptographic attack in which faults are induced in the circuitry performing the cryptographic operation in the expectation that the device can be forced to reveal information on its internal state that can be used to deduce the key.

For example, in 2004 Christophe Giraud published an attack on AES-128 implemented on a smart card. By using a Xenon strobe and removing the cover of the smart card processor, his team was able to induce faults in the execution of the algorithm that enabled them, after multiple induced faults, to derive enough information to determine the full key value.

Birthday Attack

A birthday attack is a method of compromising cryptographic hashes, such as those used for digital signatures. The name is derived from the observation that while the odds that anyone in a group of 23 people has a specific date as their birthday is 23 out of 365, or 6 percent, the odds that there are two people in the group of 23 with the same birthday are 50 percent. Thus, any seemingly rare event might not be so rare when considering multiple possible occurrences.

A birthday attack against a digitally signed document would attempt to create a bogus document that somehow generates the same hash value as the original does, which would be a *hash collision*. Cryptographic hash functions are required to be free from collisions, and algorithm designers go to great length to design to prevent this and then test to verify their success. A birthday attack might attempt to have any type of file (a document or an executable binary) be mistaken as genuine.

The choice of a provably collision-free cryptographic hash is your best countermeasure for such attacks.

Related-Key Attack

A related-key attack is a form of known-ciphertext attack in which the attacker is able to observe the encryption of the same block of data using two keys, neither of which is known to the attacker but that have a known mathematical relationship.

While it is rare that the attacker can arrange for two mathematically related keys to be used, poor implementations of cryptography can lead to keys being generated that have a known relationship that can be exploited by the attacker. Short, poorly chosen keys can make it easier for attackers to identify possible related-key pairs; this was another means of successfully attacking WEP, for example.

Meet-in-the-Middle Attack

A meet-in-the-middle is a known-plaintext attack against block ciphers that perform two or more rounds of encryption. One might think double (or triple) encryption would increase the security in proportion to the combined length of the keys. However, the math behind this doesn't support the increased complexity.

By creating separate lookup tables that capture the intermediate result (that is, after each round of encryption) of the possible combinations of both plaintext and ciphertext, it is possible to find matches between values that will limit the possible keys that must be tested in order to find the correct key. This attack, which first came to prominence when it was used to defeat the 2DES algorithm, can be applied to a broad range of ciphers.

Unfortunately, chaining together cryptography algorithms by running them multiple times does not add as much additional security as one might think. With 2DES, the total impact of the second run was to increase complexity from 2^{56} to 2^{57}. This has a small overall impact compared to the work done.

Effective countermeasures may include choosing a stronger algorithm that uses longer keys and of course choosing those keys wisely. If this is not an option, your current algorithms may produce somewhat greater security by increasing the number of rounds they execute. 3DES, for example, does not get you all the way to a 168-bit key strength—but its 112-bit equivalent strength is much greater than that provided by 56-bit "single" DES.

Replay Attack

A replay attack is one in which the attacker does not decrypt the message. Instead, the attacker merely sends the same encrypted message. The attacker hopes that the receiving system will assume that the message originated with the authorized party because the information was encrypted.

Replay attacks can involve user or subject access request credentials, transaction replay, or almost any step or series of steps in one of your business processes. (A rather stealthy replay is the *invoice replay*, in which a "vendor" repeatedly bills a larger firm for the same small purchase, with the purchase amount carefully chosen to not trigger human authorizations.) Most of these are not cryptographic attacks, per se, but might need to bypass or sidestep parts of your cryptographic defenses. Replay attacks are also possible against systems that require multiple-factor authentication, such as online banking systems that require a separate authentication step as part of some transaction requests.

Most countermeasures to replay attacks via encrypted traffic involve using session keys, cryptographic nonces, timestamps, block sequence identifiers, or other means to prevent any two blocks or messages from being bit-for-bit identical to each other within the same session. (Since a different session key should be used for each session, the replay of blocks from one session should be rejected by a subsequent session.) Each of these tactics, of course, will have its own false positive and false negative error rates to contend with.

Cryptanalytic Attacks

These types of attacks tend to be more theoretical in nature, as they often require more knowledge and skill with the underlying mathematics used by the algorithms and systems being analyzed. In most cases, there are few countermeasures available to end users or administrators, other than selection of a different algorithm or process.

Linear Cryptanalysis

Linear cryptanalysis was first described by Mitsuru Matsui in 1992. It is a known-plaintext attack that involves a statistical analysis of the operation of the cipher to create linear equations that relate bits in the plaintext, key, and ciphertext.

For example, an examination of the cipher might suggest a linear equation that says the second bit of the plaintext XORed with the fourth and seventh bits of the ciphertext equals the fifth bit of the key.

$$P_2 \oplus C_4 \oplus C_7 = K_5$$

With a perfect cipher, this equation would be true only half of the time. If there is a significant bias (i.e., the equation is true significantly more, or significantly less, than half of the time), then this fact can be used to guess, with probability better than 50 percent, the values of some or all of the bits of the key.

By combining a series of such equations, it becomes possible to come up with guesses for the key that are far more likely to be correct than simple random guessing, with the result that finding the key is orders of magnitude faster than a simple exhaustive search.

Differential Cryptanalysis

Differential cryptanalysis is a chosen-plaintext attack that was originally developed by Eli Biham and Adi Shamir in the late 1980s and involves comparing the effect of changing bits in the plaintext on the ciphertext output. By submitting carefully chosen pairs of plaintext and comparing the differences between the plaintext pairs with the differences between the resulting ciphertext pairs, one can make probabilistic statements about the bits in the key, leading to a key search space that can be (for a cipher vulnerable to differential analysis) far smaller than an exhaustive search.

Since the development of these two methods, all newly proposed ciphers are tested exhaustively for resistance to these attacks before being approved for use. The Advanced Encryption Standard has been demonstrated to be resistant to such forms of analysis.

Quantum Cryptanalysis

With recent developments in quantum computing, there has been great interest in the ability of quantum computers to break ciphers considered highly resistant to traditional computing methods.

Symmetric ciphers are relatively resistant to quantum cryptanalysis, with the best algorithm able to reduce the key search for a 128-bit key from 2^{128} to 2^{64}, and a 256-bit key from 2^{256} to 2^{128}. While a 2^{64} key search is within the realm of current technology, 2^{128} is not and is not likely to be for decades to come, so the solution to defending against quantum cryptography for symmetric ciphers is merely to double the key length.

For asymmetric (i.e., public key ciphers), the problem is much more difficult. Asymmetric ciphers depend on difficult mathematical problems such as factoring very large integers. Unfortunately, these problems are hard only for classical computers. Using quantum computers, integer factorization becomes much easier.

That said, quantum computers have a long way to go before they can compromise currently used public key algorithms. Consider that as of 2018, the largest integer factored by a quantum computer was 291311 (e.g., six digits). The integers used in RSA public key systems are recommended to be 2,048 bits in length, or more than 600 integer digits.

Secure Cryptoprocessors, Hardware Security Modules, and Trusted Platform Modules

The challenge with standard microprocessors is that code running with the highest privilege can access any device and any memory location, meaning that the security of the system depends entirely on the security of all of the software operating at that privilege level. If that software is defective or can be compromised, then the fundamental security of everything done on that processor becomes suspect.

To address this problem, hardware modules called *secure cryptoprocessors* have been developed that are resistant to hardware tampering and that have a very limited interface (i.e., attack surface), making it easier to verify the integrity and secure operation of the (limited) code running on the cryptoprocessor.

Cryptoprocessors are used to provide services such as the following:

- Hardware-based true random number generators (TRNGs)
- Secure generation of keys using the embedded TRNG
- Secure storage of keys that are not externally accessible
- Encryption and digital signing using internally secured keys
- High-speed encryption, offloading the main processor from the computational burden of cryptographic operations

Features of cryptoprocessors that enhance their security over standard microprocessors (that could provide most of these services in software) can include the following:

- Tamper detection with automatic destruction of storage in the event of tampering, and a design that makes it difficult to tamper with the device without leaving obvious traces of the physical compromise. These protections can range from anti-tamper stickers that clearly show attempts to access the device's internal components to secure enclosures that detect unauthorized attempts to open the device and automatically erase or destroy sensitive key material.
- Chip design features such as shield layers to prevent eavesdropping on internal signals using ion probes or other microscopic devices
- A hardware-based cryptographic accelerator (i.e., specialized instructions or logic to increase the performance of standard cryptographic algorithms such as AES, SHA, RSA, ECC, DSA, ECDSA, etc.)
- A trusted boot process that validates the initial boot firmware and operating system load

There are many types of secure cryptoprocessors.

- Proprietary, such as Apple's Secure Enclave Processor (SEP), found in newer iPhones
- Open standard, such as the Trusted Platform Module as specified by ISO/IEC 11889 standard and used in some laptops and servers
- Standalone (e.g., separate standalone device with external communications ports)
- Smart cards

Trusted Platform Module

A Trusted Platform Module (TPM) is a separate processor that provides secure storage and cryptographic services as specified by ISO/IEC 11889. A TPM can be used by the operating system, processor BIOS, or application (if the OS provides access to the TPM) to provide a number of cryptographic and security services.

- Generate private/public key pairs such that the private key never leaves the TPM in plaintext, substantially increasing the security related to the private key. (Public/private keys are discussed later in this chapter.)

- Digitally sign data using a private key that is stored on the TPM and that never leaves the confines of the TPM, significantly decreasing the possibility that the key can become known by an attacker and used to forge identities and launch man-in-the-middle attacks. (Digital signatures are discussed later in this chapter.)

- Encrypt data such that it can only be decrypted using the same TPM.

- Verify the state of the machine the TPM is installed on to detect certain forms of tampering (i.e., with the BIOS).

The Private Endorsement Key is a fundamental component of a TPM's security. This key is generated by the TPM manufacturer and burned into the TPM hardware during the manufacturing process. Because of this, the user/system owner depends upon the security of the TPM manufacturer to ensure that the PEK remains confidential.

We also depend on the quality of the TPM manufacturer's processes. In 2017 it was revealed that a defect in the software library used by Infineon for its line of smartcards and TPMs contained a flaw that made it possible to deduce the private key stored internally. As a result, there were millions of cryptographic keys made unreliable and vulnerable. Attackers were able to calculate the private portion of an account holder's key from having access to only the public portion. What happened, unfortunately, is that hackers impersonated legitimate users with the assurance and nonrepudiation provided by having their private keys.

Cryptographic Module

A cryptographic module is typically a hardware device that implements key generation and other cryptographic functions and is embedded in a larger system.

The advantages of using a cryptographic module as opposed to obtaining the equivalent functionality from a cryptographic software library include the following:

- By performing critical cryptographic functions on a separate device that is dedicated to that purpose, it is much harder for malware or other software-based attacks to compromise the security of the cryptographic operation.

- By isolating security-sensitive functionality in an isolated device with limited interfaces and attack surfaces, it is easier to provide assurances about the secure operation of the device. It also makes it easier to provide secure functions to larger systems by embedding a cryptographic module within the larger system.

- Increased availability of noncryptographic dedicated resources.

- Most secure cryptographic modules contain physical security protections including tamper resistance and tamper detection, making it difficult to compromise the security of the device even if the device has been physically compromised.

- Some cryptographic modules can enforce separation of duties so that certain sensitive operations such as manipulating key storage can be done only with the cooperation of two different individuals who authenticate to the cryptographic module separately.

Some government organizations have issued standards related to the security of cryptographic modules and have established evaluation and certification processes so that manufacturers can have the security of their devices validated by an independent third party and users can have confidence in the security that using the module will provide their larger system.

For example, the U.S. government's FIPS 140-2, "Security Requirements for Cryptographic Modules," specifies the requirements for cryptographic hardware and software to meet four different levels of security. It also provides for certification of products to validate they meet the requirements.

Internationally, the "Common Criteria for Information Technology Security Evaluation," documented in the ISO/IEC 15408 standard, provides an alternate set of requirements and certification processes to validate information security products.

Hardware Security Module

A hardware security module is a physically separate device used to safely store and protect various sets of information, which may be cryptographic keys or other highly sensitive mission-critical data. They are typically designed to be tamper-resistant and visibly show (or alarm) if tampering has been attempted. Data centers, especially those serving financial institutions, may have HSMs clustered or racked together with redundant, separately serviceable power, cooling, and network access. HSMs can perform a variety of services via APIs to other network systems, such as:

- Onboard secure cryptographic key generation.

- Onboard secure cryptographic key storage, especially for highest-level or master keys.

- Key management.

- Encryption and digital signature services.

- Transparent Data Encryption (TDE) key generation and management. TDE is a database encryption technology used by Oracle, Microsoft, IBM, and others for protecting data at rest, at the file level.

HSMs can also offload asymmetric encryption and decryption from application servers; when specialized for this role, they may be referred to as *cryptographic accelerators*. While they may not achieve throughput rates that can match dedicated hardware encryption and decryption systems, they have been able to perform as many as 10,000 1024-bit RSA signs per second. To help meet NIST's recommendation, in 2010, to move to 2,048-bit keys for RSA use, there has been increasing emphasis in the HSM market to provide greater performance capability, as well as providing elliptic curve cryptographic support.

Some HSMs have the capability to host a full operating system, hypervisor, and suite of virtual machines within their physically and logically protected enclosure. This provides an enhanced degree of protection for an entire applications stack (the set of all components from the operating system on up through all layers of applications logic). Use cases that require this, particularly ones requiring a simple and reliable means to validate full stack integrity, can make use of HSM-provided remote attestation features.

Certificate authorities and registration authorities make extensive use of HSMs to have reliable, secure, high-performance capabilities to generate, store, manage, and control distribution of asymmetric key pairs and certificates. These applications call for HSMs to have very strong physical and logical security protection built in, quite often involving multipart user authentication such as the Blakley-Shamir secret sharing schema. Full audit and logging of all activities and secure key backup and recovery capabilities are must-have features in this application.

Banking applications often use specialized HSMs, using a nonstandard API, to support specific security requirements in the payment card industry. Protocols and processes involved with verifying a user's PINs, controlling ATMs and point of sales terminals, verifying card transaction attempts, generating and validating card magnetic stripe data and other card-related security codes, and supporting smart card transactions are some of the unique needs that HSMs need to support.

Domain name registrars are making increasing use of HSMs to store and protect information, such as to store key material used to sign zonefiles. The OpenDNSSEC suite supports the use of an HSM in this.

On a smaller note, HSMs are also available as a hardware cryptocurrency wallet.

UNDERSTAND THE REASONS AND REQUIREMENTS FOR CRYPTOGRAPHY

From a functional and performance requirements perspective, cryptography provides the security systems architect with a significant set of capabilities to address many different information security needs. Chapter 1, "Security Operations and Administration," examined these different information security needs in some depth; you'll recall CIANA, which embraces confidentiality, integrity, availability, nonrepudiation, and authentication. You'll also recall the growing demand, internationally as well as domestically, for organizations to provide greater degrees of transparency, auditability, safety, and privacy protection for the information entrusted to their care. We might call this CIANA+TAPS.

As part of your ongoing security assessments, you should be able to start with your organization's information classification guide in one hand and your systems architectural baselines in the other and demonstrate how each element of the set of CIANA+TAPS requirements set. Not every element of information in your organization must be kept confidential; in fact, much of it is finally published in customer-facing or public-facing documents (but the internal drafts of the *next* updated version of that information probably needs to enjoy confidentiality, as part of protecting your firm's competitive advantage).

Systems analysts would refer to what we're about to do as a requirements-to-design decomposition. Such an exercise may show you that some of your toolkit items—your basic capabilities—are much more important to your overall mission than you realized they were. These are things you have just *got* to get right and keep them working safely, efficiently, and correctly! They may also be opportunities for capacity or capability improvements. Another bucket of requirements may appear for which you have no immediately recognized technical capabilities that address them. These may be functional requirements that need further analysis and maybe a restatement (or negotiation if possible); failing that, get shopping and get creative!

When your systems already exist, you are not designing but *tracing* requirements down to the components of the system that deliver what that requirement needs. Traceability exercises can provide valuable insight into your currently deployed systems, especially when you need to demonstrate to management and leadership that their investment in cryptographic technologies and systems meets or exceeds the organization's information security needs.

With that in mind, let's start flowing and tracing!

Confidentiality

Confidentiality is the requirement to restrict access to information to only those people, organizations, systems, and processes that have been previously authorized to have such access. Confidentiality may selectively restrict the reading or viewing of that data, loading it into memory (as data or as an executable), copying it, viewing metadata about that information asset, or viewing a transaction history that reveals accesses to that data. Confidentiality can also place restrictions on accesses to previous versions of the data.

As Chapter 2 made clear, confidentiality as a concept broadly embraces the needs to control access to or disclosure of company proprietary data, intellectual property, trade secrets, preliminary business plans, concepts, or designs, and any other data that has been shared with the organization under an expectation that such data will not be disclosed to others without agreement or due process of law.

Declaring a piece of information as having *any* confidentiality restrictions splits the world into two populations: those who have your permission to read, view, or use that information, and those who do not. (We traditionally refer to these groups as those who are "cleared" or "not cleared" to handle that category of information.) This is fundamentally an access control and privilege management issue for data at rest and in use; by causing data to *move* from storage areas to processing or display endpoints (or to transit the Internet to other users or servers), it's also a data communications security issue. Fundamentally, confidentiality requirements invoke the *no-write-down* problem, as discussed in Chapter 2, "Access Controls," your systems cannot allow a process (paper, person-to-person, or computerized) that is cleared for that data to pass it to a process that is at a lower security level (one that is not cleared to handle that data).

Access control depends upon strong ways to authenticate subjects and authorize their specific access requests; most of this requires provably secure cryptographic hashing of credentials, protection of hashed credentials stored in the access control system, and strictly enforced privilege restrictions on those subjects which can modify the security parameters of other subjects or objects in the system.

Protection of the confidentiality of information at rest and in motion is done with a combination of the right storage and communications protocols, which (no doubt) make use of appropriate encryption technologies.

A growing number of applications and systems are now able to process sets of encrypted data without needing to decrypt them, doing so without revealing confidential information. These *pervasive encryption* architectures are making extensive use of *homomorphic encryption*, which is based on the theory of groups.

Integrity and Authenticity

Integrity asserts that a data set is whole, complete, and intact; further, it asserts that the life history of that data is fully known so that we can be confident that the data is exactly what we say it is, no more and no less. This is comparable to the chain of custody process and mind-set for evidence pertaining to an incident. Information integrity demands that we build an audit trail that clearly shows that the only people, processes, programs, or hardware that had access to that data were on our list of trusted, cleared, and verified subjects. This is an access control issue and one that must also enforce restrictions that prevent *read-down*, or the attempt by a cleared and trusted process operating at a higher security level to read data from a lower-level domain, process, or source, and thus potentially contaminate a higher-level data asset with unverified, unaudited, or otherwise potentially hazardous data. Downloading and installing executable files is an example of a read-down process, since in nearly all cases, you'd consider your systems as worthy of more protection than the great uncontrolled wilderness of the Internet.

In the context of data or systems integrity, *authenticity* refers to the sources from which we gathered or drew the data. The credit risk data for a customer, for example, typically consists of data from third-party commercial credit scoring agencies, from news and social media reporting, from interviews with the customer conducted by your organization's employees, and from documents, applications, and correspondence sent to your organization by that customer. Each of those data sources has a different degree of authenticity: the interview notes taken by your staff and the original applications submitted by the customer are principally taken at their face value (*prima fascia*) as authentic. Third-party credit scoring reports come from trusted sources, but you have no real insight into the sources of data they have used to develop their score.

Both the integrity and authenticity of your data are protected using cryptographic techniques in much the same ways that you've assured their confidentiality. Access control protects which subjects can access the data and what privileges they can exercise in doing so. Encrypted hash techniques provide for secure message or file digests, which when combined with digital signatures and encryption at rest (and in motion) protect the data from being tampered with (or a spoofed set of data substituted for it). These same techniques provide for continued assertion that a data set that claims to have come to one process from another one has, in fact, come along that auditable trail of events.

In other cases, you may need to use Hash-based Message Authentication Codes (HMAC) as part of the process by which one part of your system asserts the authenticity of a message (or file) to another. HMAC concatenates a secret key (which has been XORed with a string to pad it to a fixed length) and hashes that. It then takes that hash, combines it with the key again, and hashes it a second time producing the HMAC value. If an attacker (or malfunctioning process) attempts to change the message but it does not know the secret key K, the HMAC value will not match. This enables the recipient to verify both the integrity and origin (e.g., authentication or nonrepudiation) of the message. Among other uses, HMAC functions are found within the IPsec and TLS protocols. HMAC is a less complex method of ensuring message integrity and authentication but with the overhead of sharing a symmetric cipher key. Digital signatures eliminate the need to share a secret, but it requires the overhead of a shared key infrastructure such as PKI or IKE.

Systems integrity, and therefore the integrity of your information assets themselves, is also in part assured by the techniques you employ to protect and preserve event data, such as systems and applications logs, alarms, systems health telemetry, traffic monitoring data, and other information. In the event of an information security incident, these data sets not only help you determine what went wrong and how it happened; they can also be critical to your attempts to prove that your recovery and restoration of the systems to their required state is complete and correct. Without protected transaction logs, for example, you'd have no way to know if your database reflects reality or a morphed and incomplete view of it. The same cryptographic techniques you use to protect the integrity of your business information should also be applied to protect the information that keeps your systems infrastructure safely and reliably operating.

Data Sensitivity

Data sensitivity is the business world's way of describing what the military and government systems communities refer to as the *security classification* of information. Based on an overall risk assessment, organizations must categorize (or classify) information into related groups that reflect the types of harm that could come to the organization, its stakeholders, its people, or its constituents as a result of compromise, loss of integrity, misuse, or simply the failure to have it be available as and when it is needed. Such classifications might reflect the needs to protect:

- Safety-critical information, whose compromise, loss of integrity, or availability could lead systems to operate in ways that damage property, injure people, or cause death and destruction

- Emergency notification information, which may have far more urgent or demanding availability needs than other "routine" business information might

- Private information pertaining to individuals, such as personally identifying information, whether published or not

- Proprietary information, which would include anything the business did not want to disclose to competitors or others in the marketplace

- Trade secrets

- Other information requiring special protection, dictated by compliance regimes, regulations, contracts, or law

This last category — the *compliance-driven* information sensitivity classification — is taking on a far greater role in driving the design, operation, audit, verification, testing, and ongoing use of virtually every aspect of information security. Increasingly, legislatures and courts around the world are holding individual executive officers as well as division or line managers personally and sometimes criminally liable for the damages of a data breach or other information security incident.

Chapter 2 looks in greater depth and provides further guidance on information security classification processes and guidelines. Even the smallest, most local of businesses or nonprofit organizations needs to dedicate senior leader, manager, and security analyst time and effort to translate their overall risk posture into an effective information security classification process. Then, of course, leadership and management need to make sure that the organization *uses* that classification process.

Availability

Imagine a world without cryptography.

It's not customary to think of cryptography as having a strong role to play in systems or information availability; perhaps it's time to turn that paradigm on its head. Without extensive use of strong encryption, your access control systems cannot function reliably. You cannot authenticate incoming data or messages as being from recognized, legitimate sources. You have little way to validate that software updates and distribution kits are in fact from the vendor, or are complete and correct, with no malware snuck into them. Many of the handshakes that are necessary at the session, presentation, and application layers cannot effectively function, or if they do, they cannot provide automatic and prompt assurance of a trustworthy connection.

At a minimum, your business processes run slower, as if you've jumped back in time to the early days of the personal computer revolution. There is no HTTPS. You spend more time validating information and inspecting, checking, and reassuring yourself that no malware has taken over your machine.

When your systems crash or when you detect an intruder in your midst, you've got few options but to trust that the backups you made earlier have not already been tampered with. This may require that you reload with them anyway and spend more time manually validating that what you think should be the state of your systems and your data is, in fact, what you've reloaded and reinitialized them to be.

Access control; digital signatures; secure message and file digests; integrity-protecting, confidentiality-assuring storage encryption; automatic and auditable secure transaction processing—each of these encryption-powered processes and more set the pace by which your business or organization uses its information assets to get business done.

That's availability.

Nonrepudiation

For many reasons, organizations and individuals need to be able to prove that a message was originated and sent to them by the person or organization identified in that message. Nonrepudiation can work both ways, though.

- Recipients can disprove a sender's claim that they were the one who originated the message.

- Senders can disprove a recipient's claim that the message was never received or opened by the addressee.

The EU has established some fairly stringent requirements in the European Electronic Commerce Directive 2000/31/EC for messaging systems to meet in order to provide legally acceptable evidence that attests to sending, receiving, opening, and displaying a message. (Thus far, no one has any ideas about how to prove that the recipient actually read and understood the message, of course!) In the U.S. marketplaces, various U.S. Federal District Courts have established precedent law that lines up with the EU on this; many U.S. government agencies, large corporations, and industry vertical associations and channels are switching their fax, email, file exchange, and even paper-based correspondence, order processing, and non-real-time process control flows over to systems that provide such bidirectional nonrepudiation.

A variety of cryptographic techniques are used by the different commercial products that provide these services; as there are contentious patent infringement cases in the works on several of these, it's inappropriate to delve too deeply into their technical details. Suffice it to say that combinations of cryptographically secure message digests, digital signatures, full PKI-supported encryption of contents and attachments, and other means all track the flow of a message: from the sender hitting Send through the system; to the recipients' mail servers; from those servers to the recipient; and finally the actions taken by the recipient to open, delete, forward, or move the email or any of its attachments. In some systems, such as RMail and RSign, senders can validate that a cryptographically generated receipt itself and the files and message text it references have not been altered any time after it was originally sent. This proves to be vital in establishing a chain of custody argument for the content of such a message.

This may be another instance where the build-versus-buy decision can be greatly simplified for an organization. Many of these services are available from providers with field-proven APIs, and contracts for use of these services can be much cheaper than typical first-class letter postage rates in the West. This can transform paper-based, manually-intensive information tasks into smooth, automated, and more auditable processes while enhancing other aspects of information security in the bargain.

Another cryptographic approach to achieving nonrepudiation involves using blockchain technologies, which could provide a significant advantage when a sequence of transactions between multiple parties adds value and information to a file, message, or ledger. Blockchains (described in more detail later in the "Blockchains" section) cryptographically hash a new block of data in a chain using the hashes and content of previous blocks; thus, even a single bit changed in any one block invalidates the blockchain's end-to-end hash. Since a blockchain depends upon a loosely coupled, distributed web of trust, which does not have one central trust authority acting like a root CA, it would take a significant amount of collusion across the thousands of blockchain processing nodes and their owner/operators to convincingly fake a spoof blockchain instance.

All of these technologies, of course, rest on the trustworthiness and integrity of the public key infrastructure and the certificate authorities that enable it. For the vast majority of transactions and use cases, this trust is justified. However, constant vigilance is still necessary, not only because of events such as the DigiNotar compromise that affected more than 300,000 Gmail users but also 2017's reports that Symantec's issuance of more than 30,000 compromised HTTPS certificates, some of which were abused as part of phishing attacks.

Authentication

We commonly talk about *authentication* in CIANA-like terms to assert that the user, process, or node that has taken some action—such as sending a message or using an information asset—did in fact have proper authority to do so, at that date and time, and for the stated purpose. It refers to the back-and-forth loops of challenge and confirmation that are often needed so that both parties in a conversation can be 100.0000 percent certain that the right parties have had the right conversation and its meaning has been clearly and unambiguously understood. (This gets its roots in the weapons release authentication disciplines used by military forces, which all strive to remove any risk of misunderstanding before lethal force shoots down an unknown aircraft or sinks a ship, for example.) CIANA's use of authentication invokes nonrepudiation, but it also goes to the heart of the *identity* of the sender *and* recipient, as well as to the *integrity* of the content of the message or the file in question.

The first line of defense in a rock-solid authentication system is access control, and cryptographic technologies are essential to nearly every access control system in use today.

Access control systems use a two-part process to allow subjects (such as users, processes, or nodes on a network) to access and use objects (such as datafiles, storage subsystems, CPUs, or areas in memory). As you saw in Chapter 2, the first step is to *authenticate* that the subject is in fact the person, process, or node that it claims to be; it makes that claim by submitting a set of credentials, such as a user ID or process ID, along with other *factors* that attest to its authenticity. The access control service must then compare these submitted credentials with previously proofed credentials to validate that the claimed subject is who or what they claim to be.

Cryptographic techniques protect (or should protect) every step in this process. Identity proofing and provisioning stores cryptographically hashed versions of the credentials for each subject ID, thus protecting the credential information itself from compromise or alteration. Subjects should submit cryptographically hashed versions of their credentials, and it is these hashed forms that are compared.

The second step is to *authorize* what the now-authenticated subject wants to do to a specific object. This comparison of requested privileges versus previously approved privileges may involve significant constraint checking that involves the subject's role, current and temporary conditions, or other factors that support the organization's security needs. Once authorized, the subject can now make use of the object, perhaps by writing to a file or data set.

Protecting the data that drives the access control system requires the use of multiple cryptographic techniques (in effect, its host operating system's access control, file management and identity systems are "plussed up" with additional application-specific hashes, message or file digests, etc., to meet the CIANA+PS needs of your access control system).

Privacy

Privacy borrows heavily from our concepts of confidentiality, but it adds a significant portion of integrity to its mix. Unlike confidential data, which we believe will spend its life within its classification level (unless an authorized process down-writes it to a lower level), *private* data will usually need to change hands in controlled, auditable, and transparent ways. You give your bank PII about you when you apply for an account; their systems combine that with other data about you, which they've received from other trusted members of their community or marketplace to create a combination of PII and NPI. They use that in all of their decisions about what banking services to offer to you and how closely to manage your use of them. Government regulators and others will require various disclosures that may need elements from your PII and NPI. Those disclosures do not "publish" your NPI or make your PII lose its required privacy protection; rather, they require keeping a detailed chain of custody-style audit trail that ensures that your data, plus data from other sources, have only been accessed, used, shared, modified, retired, archived, or deleted by controlled and authorized use of trusted processes by trusted users.

Personal and private healthcare information is sometimes referred to as protected health information (PHI). Typically this information is focused on a specific individual person and includes PII or NPI along with information detailing current or historical medical treatment, care providers involved in such treatment, diagnoses, outcomes, prescriptions or other medical supplies and devices used in that treatment or after-care, and of course anything and everything associated with costs, billing, insurance coverages, and outstanding balances due by the patient.

Other sets of private information might include educational data, residential address history, employment history, and voter registration and voting history (which ideally only contains what elections you voted in and at what polling place and *not* how you voted on candidates or ballot initiatives!). Even your usage of public services, such as which books you've checked out at the county library, are potentially parts of records afforded some degree of privacy protection by law or by custom.

Most nations have separate and distinct legal regimes for defining, regulating, and enforcing the protection of each of these different sets of information. And as you might expect, each of *those* regulatory systems probably has different specific requirements as to how that data protection must be accomplished by you and be auditable and verifiable by the regulators.

Every step of such processes involves access control; each step benefits from high-integrity processes that log any attempts to access the data, tracks the nature of authorized actions taken with it, and even makes note of who viewed such logs.

Safety

Information systems safety requires that no harm is done by the *actions* taken as a result of the decisions made by our use of our information systems. The systems design must preclude, to the greatest extent possible, any failure modes of the system that might lead to such harmful actions being taken. These failure modes should include incorrect behavior on the part of the system's human operators as well as failures of the hardware, software, communications, or data elements.

Unsafe operation—the "do no harm" criterion—is something that each organization must evaluate, for each business process. Incorrectly transferring money out of a customer's account, for example, harms that customer; incorrectly crediting a customer's account as paid in full when in fact no payment has been received, accepted, and processed harms the business and its stakeholders. *Harm* does not have to strictly be interpreted as bodily injury, death, or physical damage to property, although these types of harm are of course your first priority to avoid.

(Note that many systems *must*, by their nature, take harmful actions; military weapons systems are perhaps the obvious case, but there are many others in daily use around the world. Safe operational use of such systems requires that *collateral damage*, or harm caused unintentionally, be minimized or avoided wherever possible. Deliberate misuse of such systems should also be prevented by appropriate safety interlocks, whether physical, logical, or administrative.)

Once a potentially harmful business process has been identified (as part of risk assessment) and the vulnerabilities in that process that could cause it to do harm in unauthorized ways have been identified, safety engineering principles can and should guide the process designers to include authorization checks, interlocks, fail-safe logic, redundancies, or other controls to mitigate the risk of deliberate but unauthorized action, component failure, or accidental misuse from causing harm.

Each of those high-risk steps ought to sound like something that needs the best access control, data integrity, and accountability processes that you can provide. As with other aspects of CIANA+PS, that will mean that cryptographic hashes, secure message and file digests, digital signatures, and encrypted data in motion, at rest, and in use, all play a part in assuring you—and innocent bystanders—that your systems can only operate in safe ways, even when they are failing or used incorrectly.

Regulatory and Compliance

Legal and regulatory requirements can directly specify that certain cryptologic standards of performance be met by your information systems, by citing a specific FIPS or ISO standard, for example. They can also implicitly require you to meet such standards as a result of their data protection, privacy, safety, transparency, or auditability requirements themselves. For example, any business involved in handling credit or debit card payments must make sure that those elements of their systems meet the security requirements of the Payment Card Industry Security Standards Council; failure to do so can result in a business being blocked from processing card payments. Depending upon the volume of your payment card business activities, you may even be required to implement a hardware security module (HSM) as part of attaining and maintaining compliance.

As part of baselining your cryptographic systems technology infrastructure, you should identify all the standards or specifications that your systems are required to meet as a result of such laws, regulations, or your organization's contractual obligations.

Transparency and Auditability

The legal and ethical requirements of due care and due diligence drive all organizations, public or private, to meet minimum acceptable standards of transparency and auditability.

Transparency provides stakeholders with appropriate oversight of the decisions that the organization's leaders, managers, and workers have made in the conduct of business activities. (Those stakeholders can be the organization's owners, investors, employees, customers, suppliers, others in its local business community, and of course bystanders who have no business relationship with the organization but are impacted by its activities.) Government regulators, tax authorities, law enforcement, health inspectors, and many other official functions also have legal and ethical responsibilities that require them to have some degree of oversight as well. In many societies, there is an expectation that the news media will exercise a degree of oversight over both public and private affairs as well.

Oversight includes insight. *Insight* grants you visibility of the data; you can see what led the managers to make certain decisions, such as by reading the minutes of their meetings or their internal communications, if you are authorized the right level (or depth) of insight. *Oversight* requires you to reach conclusions or make judgments as to the legal or ethical correctness of the decision or whether the decision process—including the gathering and processing of any information that informed that process—meets the generally accepted standards for that kind of decision, in that kind of business, for due care and due diligence.

Obviously, achieving transparency may require you to publish or otherwise disclose information that might otherwise have been kept confidential or private.

Almost every information system in use is subject to some kind of audit requirements (even your personal computer at home is subject to audit, by your nation's income tax or revenue agencies, for example). Audit requirements exist for financial, inventory, human resources, hazardous materials, systems safety, and information safety and security needs, to name just a few examples. Most audit requirements that organizations must adhere to also require that data that is subject to audit be suitably protected from unauthorized changes and that full records be kept of all *authorized* changes to that information. Confidentiality requirements may also be levied by audit requirements.

Transparency and auditability, therefore, boil down to access control, access accounting, data integrity, nonrepudiation, confidentiality, and privacy, all of which are difficult if not impossible to achieve without a solid cryptologic capability.

Competitive Edge

Increasingly, businesses, nonprofit organizations, and even government activities are finding that their marketplace of customers, suppliers, constituents, and stakeholders is demanding better information stewardship from them. These stakeholders all want to see visible, tangible evidence that your team takes your CIANA+TAPS responsibilities seriously and that you carry them to completion with due care and due diligence.

In some marketplaces, this is only a growing sense of expectation or a "mark of quality" that customers or other stakeholders will perceive as being associated with your business. In other markets, potential customers will just not do business with you if they cannot clearly see that you know how to keep information about that business with them safe, secure, private, and intact.

Either way you look at it, your organization's investments in more effective use of cryptography—and thereby better, stronger information security—makes a solid contribution to your overall reputation in your marketplace.

UNDERSTAND AND SUPPORT SECURE PROTOCOLS

Cryptographic protocols package one or more algorithms with a set of process descriptions and instructions that structure the use of those algorithms to get specific types of work done. Secure email, for example, is a class of protocols; S/MIME, DKIM, and other approaches are protocols that support organizational and individual email users in attaining some or all of their email-related information security needs.

Certain sets of protocols become so pervasive and important to information security that they've been designated as *infrastructures*. You can think of an infrastructure as the bedrock layer of support and capability; certain protocols layer onto that to build foundations. On top of those foundations, you build business processes that address the specific needs of your organization, and those business processes probably use many other protocols that are widely used throughout the digital and business worlds. In these terms, we might think of TCP/IP as a bedrock infrastructure, onto which key management (via IPsec, PKI, or other approaches) provides a secure infrastructure. That infrastructure supports identity management and access control (as sets of protocols, systems, and services); it also supports secure email, secure web browsing, virtual private networks, and just about everything else we need. That layer of protocols provides generic services to every user and organization; you choose *implementations* of them, as particular sets of hardware, software, and procedures, to meet the sweet spot of risk mitigation, cost, and regulatory and legal compliance needs.

This may suggest that there's an accepted, formal distinction between an infrastructure and a protocol—but there is not. It's really in the eyes of the users and the use cases that capture their needs for form, fit, function, and security. (It might also bring to mind the OSI model and the need to think beyond the Application Layer into the human and organizational layers.)

Let's first look at some of these services and protocols and then some common use cases. Then we'll wrap this section up with a look at some practical limitations and common vulnerabilities to keep in mind.

Services and Protocols

As with the difference between protocols and infrastructures, there's no real hard and fast rules as to whether a set of capabilities, data formats, processes, and procedures is a service, a protocol, or both at the same time. Arguably, IPsec, as a set of protocols and mechanisms, could be considered as a service; blockchain, by contrast, is a set of protocols on its way to becoming an infrastructure. PGP and the set of capabilities wrapped around it or springing from it represent an alternative set of capabilities to those whose design is dominated by major multinational corporations and the American national security state; even if you're not a believer in the more extreme conspiracy theories, being able to operate in an alternate set of protocols and services (and the infrastructures they use and provide) may be prudent.

One thing that's worth mentioning at an overview level is the *negotiation* processes that go on when using any of these protocols. It's similar to what happens at the Physical layer of the OSI 7-Layer or TCP/IP protocol stack: each party uses an established protocol of handshakes to signal what capabilities they want to use for the session, whether that is baud rate on a communications circuit or encryption algorithm and corresponding cryptovariables. Each party strives to push this negotiation to the highest quality settings that it can (since this will make service provision and use more effective and efficient); after some give and take, the two parties either agree and the session setup continues, or the connection attempt is dropped by one or both sides. (This can give the attacker the opportunity to force the negotiation to a lower-quality standard—or lower-grade encryption suite—if they believe their target has a vulnerability at that lower level that they can exploit.)

Please note that the encryption suites and algorithms discussed in the following sections as supported by a protocol or service are provided as illustrative only and are subject to change, as vulnerabilities are found by cryptanalysis, hostile exploitation, or other testing.

IPsec

Internet Protocol Security (IPsec) makes extensive use of asymmetric encryption algorithms (packaged as encryption suites), key exchange infrastructures, digital certificates, and bulk encryption protocols to deliver the security services that the original Internet Protocol could not. It was developed during the late 1980s and early 1990s to provide Internet layer (level 3) security functions, specifically the authentication and encryption of packets as they are transferred around the Internet. It needed to provide a variety of security benefits: peer authentication, sender (data origination) authentication, data integrity and confidentiality, and protection against replay attacks. IPsec can provide these services automatically, without needing application layer interaction or setup. IPsec introduced several new protocols to support these services.

- *Authentication headers (AH)* achieve connectionless data integrity for IP datagrams and support data origin authentication. These allow recipients to validate that messages have not been altered in transit and provides a degree of protection against replay attacks.

- *Encapsulating security payloads (ESP)* also provide a partial sequence integrity mechanism, which also adds to anti-replay protection. This also provides a limited degree of traffic flow confidentiality, while protecting the confidentiality and integrity of datagram content.

- *Internet Security Association and Key Management Protocol (ISAKAMP)* offers an overall process and framework for key exchange and authentication of parties. Keying material itself can be provided by manually configuring pre-shared keys or using the Internet Key Exchange protocols (IKE and IKEv2). Kerberized Internet Negotiation of Keys (KINK) or the IPSECKEY DNS record can also be used as ways for parties to exchange and manage keys.

IPsec also provides the mechanisms to form *security associations (SA)* that are created and used by two (or more) cooperating systems agreeing to sets of encryption suites, encryption and authentication keys, and all of the cryptovariables that go with that (such as key lifetimes). This allows those internetworked systems to then implement AH, ESP, or both, to meet their agreed-to needs. Implementing AH and ESP would require multiple SAs be created so that the sequence of steps be clearly established and well-regulated to provide the required security.

As you might expect, the list of current cryptographic algorithm suites that are supported by IPsec or recommended for use with it changes as new exploits or cryptanalytic attacks make such changes advisable.

IPsec provides two methods of operation, known as transport mode and tunnel mode.

- *Transport mode* encrypts only the payload (data content) of the IP packets being sent, which leaves all of the routing information intact. However, when transport mode uses the IPsec authentication header, services like NAT cannot operate because this will invalidate the hash value associated with the header and the routing information in it.

- *Tunnel mode* encrypts the entire IP packet, routing headers and all; it then encapsulates that encrypted payload into a new IP packet, with a new header. This can be used to build virtual private networks (VPNs) and can also be used for private host-to-host chat functions. Since the "as-built" packets from the sending system are encrypted and encapsulated for actual transmission through the network, any packet-centric services such as NAT can function correctly.

IPsec can be implemented in three different ways. It's normally built right into the operating system by including its functions within the *IP stack* (the set of operating systems service routines that implement the Internet Protocol in that environment). When such modification of the operating system is not desired, IPsec can be implemented as a separate set of functions that sit (in effect) between the device drivers and the operating system's IP stack, earning it the name *bump-in-the-stack*. If external cryptoprocessors are used (that is, not under the direct, integrated control of the operating system), it's also possible to do what's called a *bump-in-the-wire* implementation.

Originally developed for IPv4, work is in process to fully port IPsec over to IPv6.

TLS

Transport Layer Security (TLS) provides for secure connections, but it's hard to say exactly where in the TCP/IP or OSI protocol stacks it actually sits. It runs on top of the transport layer, and yet it is treated by many applications as if it *is* the transport layer. But applications that use TLS must actively take steps to initiate and control its use. It's also further confusing, since the presentation layer is normally thought to provide encryption services for higher layers (such as the application layer in the OSI model). Perhaps it's best to think of it as providing services at the transport layer and above, as required, and leave it at that. It has largely replaced its predecessor, Secure Sockets Layer, which was found to be vulnerable to attacks on SSL's block cipher algorithms. (SSL also had this "identity problem" in terms of which layer of the protocol stack it did or didn't belong to.) Nonetheless, many in the industry still talk of "SSL encryption certificates" when the actual protocol using them is TLS.

The TLS handshake dictates the process by which a secure session is established:

1. The handshake starts when the client requests a TLS connection to a server, typically on port 443, or uses a specific protocol like STARTTLS when using mail or news protocols.

2. Client and server negotiate what cipher suite (cryptographic algorithms and hash functions) will be used for the session.

3. The server authenticates its identity, usually by using a digital certificate (which identifies the server, the CA that authenticates that certificate), and provides the client with the server's public encryption key.

4. The client confirms the certificate's validity.

5. Session keys are generated, either by the client encrypting a random number or by using the Diffie-Hellman key exchange to securely generate and exchange this random number.

   If any of these steps fail, the secure connection is not created.

6. The session key is used to symmetrically encrypt and decrypt all subsequent data exchanges during this session, until the client or server signals the end of the session.

The process is shown in Figure 5.12.

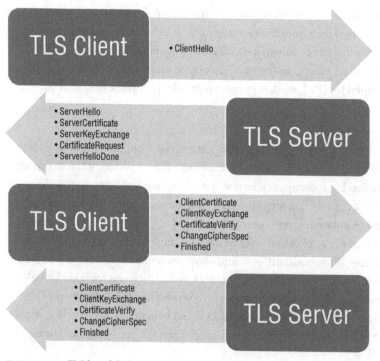

FIGURE 5.12 **TLS handshake**

The *TLS cipher suite* is the set of cryptographic algorithms used within TLS across its four major operational phases of key exchange and agreement, authentication, block and stream encryption, and message authentication. This suite is updated as older algorithms are shown to be too vulnerable and as new algorithms become adopted by the Internet Engineering Task Force (IETF) and the web community. As with all algorithms and protocols involving security, the two versions of TLS cipher suite now in common use, V1 and V1.2, are coming to their end of life. On June 30, 2018, SSL, TLS 1.1, and TLS 1.2 were declared obsolete by the IETF. The major browsers, such as Firefox, Chrome, and Bing, have been phasing them out in favor of their replacements. Be sure to check to see if your organization is using them anywhere else. Note that the Payment Card Industry Data Security Standard (PCI DSS) requires use of the new versions, so any credit, debit, or payment processing systems you support may need to be double-checked as well.

TLS has gone through two revisions since its first introduction, and in creating TLS 1.3, RFC 8446 in August 2018 added significant improvements to TLS. One key set of changes involved strengthening forward secrecy of TLS sessions. *Forward secrecy* (also known as *perfect forward secrecy*) provides for the protection of past sessions in the event that the server's private key has been compromised. This protection is ensured by requiring a unique session key for every session a client initiates; in doing so, it offers protection against the Heartbleed exploit that affected SSL and OpenSSL, first reported in 2014. TLS 1.3 also removes support for other cryptographic and hash functions that have proven weak.

TLS 1.3 implements the concept of *ephemeral key exchange*, supported by many algorithms and cryptographic suites. "Traditional" Diffie-Hellman-Merkle, for example, dictates mathematically that unless one of the parties changes their private key (or they agree to changing some other cryptovariable), then the same session key will result. Numerous workarounds have been attempted to avoid the risks that this introduces. How each key exchange generates this one-moment-in-time (that is, *ephemeral*) shared key is not germane to us right now; what *is* important to consider is that this can mean that Diffie-Hellman Ephemeral (DHE), Elliptic Curve D-H Ephemeral (ECDHE), and others weaken the authentication mechanism: if the key is different every time, so is the digital signature. Some other authentication process, such as RSA, PSK, or ECDHA, must then be used to complete the process.

However, TLS 1.3 also added some potential pitfalls that you should be aware of. TLS in its initial versions required at least two round-trip cycles to perform its initialization handshake, which involved using asymmetric encryption. This slowed down the loading of web pages, which impacts customer satisfaction and the business bottom line. TLS 1.3 cut this down to one round-trip time (RTT) and added a capability to allow servers to "remember" a previous session's handshakes and pick up, in effect, where the session left off. If that sounds to you like reusing a one-time session key, you'd be right to think so. This "zero RTT" option is fast, of course, but it opens the door to replay attacks. Some organizations are already planning on turning this feature off as they migrate to TLS 1.3.

Pretty Good Privacy

In much the same timeframe in which Rivest, Shamir and Adleman were battling with the U.S. government over making powerful encryption available to private citizens, businesses, and others, another battle started to rage over a software package called Pretty Good Privacy. PGP had been created by Phil Zimmerman, a long-time anti-nuclear activist, in 1991; he released it into the wild via a friend who posted it in Usenet and on Peacenet, which was an ISP that focused on supporting various grass-roots political and social movements around the world. Almost immediately, the government realized that PGP's use of 128-bit (and larger) encryption keys violated the 40-bit limit established for *export of munitions* as defined in the Militarily Critical Technologies List; the government began a criminal investigation of Zimmerman, his associates, and PGP. Zimmerman then published the source code of PGP and its underlying symmetric encryption algorithm (the Bassomatic) in book form (via MIT Press), which was protected as free speech under the First Amendment of the U.S. Constitution. By 1996, the government backed down and did not bring criminal charges against Zimmerman.

PGP uses a web of trust concept but does embody a concept of key servers that can act as a decentralized mesh of repositories and clearinghouses. Its design provides not only for encryption of data in motion but also for data at rest.

Initially, PGP as a software product allowed end users to encrypt any content, whether that was a file or the body of an email message. Various distributions used different encryption algorithms, such as ElGamal, DSA, and CAST-128. The designs and source code of PGP have moved through a variety of commercial products, including the z/OS encryption facility for the IBM z mainframe computer family.

PGP is described by some as being "as the closest you're likely to get to military-grade encryption." As of this writing, there do not seem to be known methods, computational or cryptographic, for breaking PGP encryption. Wikipedia and other sources cite a 2006 case in which U.S. Customs agents could not break PGP-encrypted content, suspected to be child pornography, on a laptop they had seized. A bug in certain implementations of PGP was discovered in May 2018, which under certain circumstances could lead to disclosing the plaintext associated with a given ciphertext of emails encrypted by these email variants.

Since inception, PGP has evolved in several directions. It still is available in various free software and open source distributions; it's also available in a variety of commercial product forms.

OpenPGP

A variety of efforts are underway to bring PGP and its use of different algorithms into an Internet set of standards. Some of these standards support the use of PGP by email clients; others look to specify the encryption suites used by PGP in different implementations. RFC 4880 is the main vehicle for change within the IETF for bringing PGP into the formally accepted Internet baseline. There is also work ongoing to develop a PGP-compliant open source library of JavaScript routines for use in web applications that want to use PGP when supported by browsers running the app.

GNU Privacy Guard GNU Privacy Guard (GPG) is part of the GNU project, which aims to provide users with what the project calls the four essential freedoms that software users should have and enjoy. GPG provides a free and open source implementation of the OpenPGP standard, consistent with RFC 4800. It provides key management and access modules, support for S/MIME and SSH, and tools for easy integration into a variety of applications. It's also available as Gpg4win, which provides GPG capabilities for Microsoft Windows systems, including a plugin for Outlook email.

GPG comes as a preinstalled component on many Linux distribution kits and is available in freeware, shareware, and commercial product forms for the Mac and for Windows platforms as well.

"Free," in the context of "free software, should be thought of in the same way as "free speech," rather than "free beer," as explained on `https://www.gnu.org/home.en.html`. Free software advocates assert that this conflux of corporate and government interests is far too willing to sacrifice individual freedom of choice, including the freedom to speak or to keep something private. Without freely available source code for important infrastructure elements such as GPG and the GNU variant of Linux, they argue, individuals have no real way to know what software to trust or what information and communications they can rely upon. Whether you agree or disagree with their politics, GPG and other free software systems are increasingly becoming common elements in the IT architectures that SSCPs need to support and defend.

It is interesting to note that the German government initially donated 250,000 Deutschmarks (about $132,000) to the development and support of GPG.

Hypertext Transfer Protocol Secure

Hypertext Transfer Protocol Secure (or HTTPS) is an application layer protocol in TCP/IP and the OSI model; it is simply Hypertext Transfer Protocol (HTTP) using TLS (now that SSL is deprecated) to provide secure, encrypted interactions between clients and servers using hypertext. HTTPS is commonly used by web browser applications programs. HTTPS provides important benefits to clients and servers alike.

- Authentication of identity, especially of the server's identity to the client
- Privacy and integrity of the data transferred during the session
- Protection against man-in-the-middle attacks that could attempt to hijack an HTTP session
- Simplicity

By building directly on TLS, HTTPS provides for strong encryption of the entire HTTPS session's data content or payload, using the CAs that were preinstalled in the browser by the browser application developer (Mozilla, Microsoft, DuckDuckGo, Apple, etc.). This leads to a hierarchy of trust, in which the end user should trust the security of the session only if the following conditions hold true:

- The browser software correctly implements HTTPS.
- Certificates are correctly installed in the browser.
- The CA vouches only for legitimate websites.
- The certificate correctly identifies the website.
- The negotiated encryption sufficiently protects the user's data.

Users should be aware that HTTPS use alone cannot protect everything about the user's web browsing activities. HTTPS still needs resolvable IP addresses at both ends of the session; even if the content of the session is kept safe, traffic analysis of captured packets may still reveal more than some users want. Metadata about individual page viewings may also be available for others to sniff and inspect.

Secure Multipurpose Internet Mail Extensions

Secure Multipurpose Internet Mail Extensions (S/MIME) provides presentation-layer authentication, message integrity, nonrepudiation, privacy, and data security benefits to users. Using PKI, it requires the user to obtain and install their own certificate, which is then used in forming a digital signature. It provides end-to-end encryption of the email payload and thus makes it difficult for organizations to implement outgoing and incoming email inspection for malware or other contraband without performing this inspection on each end-user workstation after receipt and decryption.

As an end-to-end security solution, S/MIME defeats—or complicates—attempts to have enterprise-wide or server-hosted antimalware scanning (or scanning for other banned content), since S/MIME has encrypted such malware or banned content by encrypting the message content and its attachments. S/MIME may also be difficult, or at least not well suited, to use with a webmail client, if the user's private key is not accessible from the webmail server. Workarounds, such as those used by PGP Desktop and some versions of GnuPG, will implement the signature process via the client system's clipboard, which does offer better protection of the private key.

SMIME has other issues, which may mean it is limited in the security it can offer to users of organizational email systems. Its signatures are "detached"—that is, they are not tied to the content of the message itself, so all that they authenticate is the sender's identity and not that the sender sent the message in question. In May 2018, the EFF announced that there were critical vulnerabilities in S/MIME, particularly when forms of OpenPGP are used. EFAIL, as this vulnerability is called, can allow attackers to hide unknown plaintext within the original message (using various HTML tags). EFAIL affects many email systems, and as such, it will require much coordination between vendors to fix.

DomainKeys Identified Mail

DomainKeys Identified Mail (DKIM) provides an infrastructure for authenticating that an email came from the domain its address information claims it did and was thus (presumably) authorized by that domain operator or owner. It can prevent or limit the vulnerability of an organization's email system to phishing and email spam attacks. It works by attaching a digital signature to the email message, and the receiving email service validates that signature. This confirms that the email itself (and possibly some of the attachments to it) was not tampered with during transmission, providing a degree of data integrity protection. As an infrastructure service, DKIM is not normally visible to the end users (senders or recipients), which means it does not function as an end-to-end email authentication service.

DKIM can provide some support to spam filtering, acting as an anti-phishing defense as well. Using the domain-based message authentication, reporting, and conformance (DMARC) protocol, mailing services that use DKIM can protect their domain from being spoofed as part of a phishing operation. Based on DNS records and a header field added to them by RFC 5322, DMARC and DKIM together offer a degree of nonrepudiation. This has proven useful to journalists investigating claims regarding the legitimacy of emails leaked during recent political campaigns, such as during the U.S. Presidential Election in 2016. This use of DNS records also makes DKIM compatible with S/MIME and OpenPGP for example; it is compatible with DNSSEC and with the Sender Policy Framework (SPF) as well.

Note that the use of cryptographic checksums by DKIM does impose a computational overhead not usually associated with sending email. Time will tell whether this burden will make bulk spamming too expensive or not.

Both the original RFC that proposed DKIM and work since then have identified a number of possible attack vectors and weaknesses. Some of these are related to the use of short (weak) encryption keys that can easily fall prey to a brute-force attack; others relate to ways that clever spammers can spoof, misroute, forward, or otherwise misuse the email infrastructure in ways DKIM cannot help secure. Note, too, that while DKIM use may help in authentication of senders, this is not the same as offering protection against arbitrary forwarding of emails (bulk or not). A malicious sender within a reputable domain could conceivably compose a bad message, have it DKIM-signed, and send it to themselves at some mailbox from which they can retrieve it as a file. From there, they can resend it to targets who will have no effective way to determine it is fraudulent. Including an expiration time on signatures or even periodically revoking a public key or doing so upon notice of an incident involving such emails remain as options for the domain owners. Filtering outgoing email from the domain may be of limited utility as well, without having clear rules to differentiate emails potentially being misused by spammers from legitimate outgoing ones.

Ongoing work in the IETF Standards Track is adding elliptic curve cryptography to the RSA, which should facilitate making more secure use of shorter keys, which are easier to publish via DNS. There are also some concerns with DKIM and content modification, in that centralized (enterprise) antivirus systems may break the DKIM signature process; workarounds to this may add incompatibilities with MIME messages. Attempts were made to initiate author domain signing practices (ADSP), but by 2013 these were declared historic, as no significant deployment or use took place. (If you have signs of ADSP lingering in your email systems, they may be worth a closer look as candidates for upgrade or replacement.)

Blockchain

Think about the message digest process; it produces a hash value of a message (or file) that demonstrates that the content of that message has not been changed since the message digest was computed. A *blockchain* is nothing more than a series of messages, each with its own message digest, that taken together represent a transaction history about an item of interest; the message digest for the first block is computed normally, and then this is used as an input into the message digest for the next block, and so on. Thus, any attempt to make a change to the content of a block will invalidate all subsequent block-level message digests.

Blockchain technology is poised to turn much of our digital world sideways, if not completely onto its head. It does this by transforming the way we think about data. Traditionally, data is created (written), read, updated, tweaked, made into "old" and "updated" versions, updated again, deleted, restored; in many real-world practical situations this endless life cycle of change causes more trouble than we recognize. Blockchain treats all data as write-once, read-forever. And it never throws data away.

Blockchain also encourages (if not enforces) a fully distributed data model: every user of any data set has a full and complete copy of it; as new blocks (records) are added to that set, all registered users receive the update, and when the majority have agreed it was a legitimate update, it gets posted to this fully distributed ledger. In fact, referring to a blockchain as a *ledger* reveals that it views data sets as something that just keep growing, one record or transaction or event at a time. Mistakes in data are dealt with in blockchains by leaving the original data as it was created and then adding additional records as required to reverse the effect of the mistake. This provides a full audit trail of such corrections; and since blockchains are a distributed ledger, all parties to the blockchain must approve such changes for them to take effect.

In its simplest form, a blockchain starts with that first transaction (sometimes called the *genesis block*) and digitally signs it. Adding on the next block means that it is appended to the first block plus the digital signature attached to it, and then this whole aggregate block is digitally signed by *its* originator. Clearly, no changes can be made to the data in either block without it invalidating the second digest. As each processing node (or holder of this distributed data set) receives it, it generates a separate secure message digest and compares it with the arriving signature. Figure 5.13 provides a somewhat simplified sketch of this concept in action.

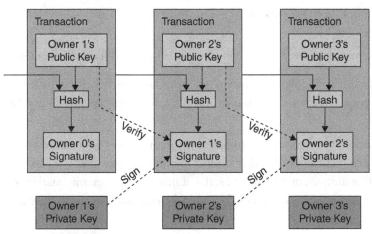

FIGURE 5.13 The blockchain concept

There are a lot more details to it than this simple sketch reveals. The basic concept, however, can be implemented using PKI, PGP/GPG, or a proprietary public/private key infrastructure. The contents of each block can be encrypted for storage, transmission, and use. Individual pairs or sets of users can and do use their own asymmetric encryption to keep their transactions private from others who are sharing the same ledger.

Bitcoin and many cryptocurrencies do something similar. *Every* Bitcoin user has the entire Bitcoin transaction history, for every Bitcoin ever mined, all in their individual copy of the database. But the only transactions they can read, and thereby extract data from and use in other ways, are the transactions (or blocks) that they can decrypt. The rest are as protected as anything else in this digital age is when it is using properly managed asymmetric encryption supported by a strong, trustworthy digital certificate infrastructure.

Note that blockchains are unforgiving of errors. If I authorize my Bitcoin wallet to pay you 378,456,223 Satoshis (or 3.78 Bitcoins), then as soon as I hit Send, those Satoshis are yours. If what I meant to do is send you only 2.0 Bitcoins, then I have to depend upon your goodwill (or other contractual arrangements that bind us together) to get you to send the difference back to me.

By providing strong nonrepudiation and data integrity for the transactions contained in the individual blocks, blockchains can implement digital provenance systems.

- Chain of custody control, auditing, and record-keeping for cyberforensics could use blockchains to irrefutably record who touched the evidence, when, how, and what they did to it.

- Parts or document provenance systems can prove the authenticity of the underlying data to help prove that safety-critical components (physical hardware, computer or network hardware, software, or firmware) are in fact what they claim to be.

- Representations of any kind of value can be made extremely difficult to counterfeit.

It is this last that explains the dramatic rise in the use of cryptocurrencies—the use of blockchains to represent money and to record and attest to the transactions done with that money.

- The cryptocurrency "miner" uses significant computing power to generate a new unique cryptocurrency identifier (similar to printing a new piece of paper currency with a unique combination of serial numbers, paper security markings, etc.). This "cryptodollar" is represented by a blockchain and is stored in the mining company's wallet.

- Bob buys that cryptodollar from the miner, and the underlying blockchain transfers to Bob's wallet; the new message digest reflects this transfer into Bob's wallet. The blockchain in the miner's wallet is updated to show this transaction.

- Later, Bob uses that cryptodollar to buy something from Ted's online store; the blockchain that is Bob's wallet is updated to reflect the "sell," and the blockchain that is Ted's wallet is updated to reflect the "buy."

If all we do is use strong message digest functions in the blockchain, we provide some very powerful nonrepudiation and data integrity to our cryptocurrency users. We must combine this with a suitable exchange of public and private keys to be able to protect the confidentiality of the data and to ensure that only people or processes Bob authorizes (for example) can see into Bob's wallet, read the transaction history that is there, or initiate a new transaction.

Finally, cryptocurrency systems need to address the issue of authority: who is it, exactly, that we trust as a "miner" of a cryptodollar? Bitcoin, for example, solves this problem by being a completely decentralized system with no "central bank" or authority involved. The "miners" are in fact the maintainers of copies of the total Bitcoin ledger, which records every Bitcoin owner's wallet information and its balance; voting algorithms provide for each distributed copy of the ledger to synchronize with the most correct copy. This maintenance function is computationally intensive, typically requiring many high-performance workstations running in parallel, so the Bitcoin system rewards or incentivizes its miners by letting them earn a fraction of a Bitcoin as they maintain the system's ledger.

One irony of the rise in popularity and widespread adoption of blockchains and cryptocurrencies is the false perception that since many money launderers, drug smugglers, and organized crime use these technologies, therefore anyone using them must also be a criminal. Of course, nearly all criminals use money, but that does not mean that all users of money are criminals!

Common Use Cases

Data at rest, in motion, and in use: that triplet defines our fundamental information security set of needs and is rapidly being addressed by *encryption* at rest, in motion, and in use. We're not quite yet at the point where the total life cycle of a data set is spent in encrypted form (although advocates of blockchain technologies suggest we are heading in that direction and for some very good reasons). That said, let's look at some common organizational uses of cryptographically powered information security.

Virtual Private Networks Virtual private networks (discussed in more detail in Chapter 6, "Network and Communications Security") can be and have been built in unencrypted forms; their first use was as logical tunneling under the Internetworking layer to provide ways to logically combine network segments that weren't physically in the same place. Nowadays, virtually every VPN implementation operates using PKI-enabled encryption processes.

A typical organization might unfortunately find itself hosting innumerable VPN connections and systems, if it cannot carefully manage what its end users can do at their endpoints. Some platform systems bring their own VPN capabilities built into them; others strongly encourage the use of a VPN to manage end-user connections to and use of the platform. Some of these may be needed for legitimate business purposes; others may not. Note that in many collaborative, creative environments, *gamification* has become a powerful way to engage team members in a complex, creative set of tasks, by associating symbolic "wins" with successfully accomplishing tasks or steps; such game platforms (such as the *Panoply* cybersecurity game engine at University of Texas at San Antonio's Center for Infrastructure Assurance and Security) could have important returns on investment that justify their use in your organization.

VPNs are also widely used by people to enjoy access to media sites in other geographic regions, whether to avoid copyright and marketing restrictions (such as sports broadcast blackouts) or to access news and information using what looks like a local area IP address to the content providing website. Anonymous browsing or connections via TOR, for example, may be required by some of your business processes. It's also worth considering that depending upon the nature of your business and applicable employment law, your organization may be somewhat constrained from *preventing* employees from using anonymous or secure connections for personal communications via employer-provided IT systems. Legitimately, an employee might need to communicate various forms of protected data, such as identity, health, education, with various other parties; whistleblower protection laws may also apply. While case law in this area is minimal as of this writing, caution—and good legal counsel—is advised.

It's possible, then, that any particular set of users could have multiple VPNs that they're using, only some of which might be directly in support of work-related tasks. Some of these VPNs might conflict with each other or with application platform settings or expectations (Microsoft Office 365 is known, for example, to sometimes need split tunneling setups to help better manage network bandwidth and traffic to avoid bottlenecks).

Proxy settings can also play hob with your ability to keep network services working effectively, with and without VPNs in action.

Federated Systems

Extending access to your IT infrastructure outside of your organization—and inviting outsiders to enjoy (hopefully limited) access to your systems and information assets— is made simpler and easier to manage and keep safe via a variety of federated access control strategies and mechanisms; Chapter 2 looks at these in some detail, including the use of mechanisms like Security Assertions Markup Language (SAML) to help automate and regulate such connections. Underneath all of these mechanisms is the encryption infrastructure that provides strong hash functions, point-to-point data integrity, confidentiality, and nonrepudiation, to name but a few. Your chosen access control systems should be your first port of call to understand how they negotiate the use of encryption with other systems in establishing connections such as single sign-on (SSO).

It's possible that in a fairly diverse federated environment, one of the partner organizations is far less adept and skillful at keeping its cryptographic systems up to date; it may also have inherent, systemic issues in the ways in which it manages its users, its keys, digital certificates, and everything else. Part of your threat-hunting skepticism might be to see if your systems can report on any connections that routinely negotiate to the weakest choices in your installed base of acceptable encryption suites and algorithms. (And you should certainly be hunting out and locking down *any* such connections that keep trying to use SSL, for example!)

Transaction and Workflow Processing

Many business processes—not just financial ones—are based on a transaction processing model. Inventory systems, for example, will receive a transaction from an assembly line system each time it allocates a part or subassembly to the flow at a workstation and thus reduce the number of such parts on hand. Students enrolling in a university course generate transactions that "sell" a seat in a particular class. Workflow processing systems build up sets of information related to a set of tasks and pass that information from workstation to workstation to control the actual work itself, model it, and provide a structure and framework to measure and assess it with. Patient care systems quite often model the flow of the *patient* from initial intake through post-discharge follow-up care by means of a workflow model.

Workflows depend upon data integrity; many also must protect the confidentiality and privacy of the data that they collect, process, route, and use. In many respects, this is a role-based access control problem that the workflow management system needs to help you solve. Depending upon the chosen platform, it may or may not integrate seamlessly with your existing access control system; lack of good integration means that each time a workflow is changed and worker roles are redefined, you may have to update your access control lists independently; similarly, as employees change jobs or depart the organization, you could have multiple systems to update. This is discussed in Chapter 1 as well.

Underneath that, your transaction and workflow processing systems may or may not be using their own encryption technologies to deliver on their promises of data protection and systems integrity. Some large database systems (which are underneath some of these applications platforms) do use encryption to implement record-level or even field-level access control capabilities. Whether these systems turn to the underlying server for encryption infrastructure support, or have their own baked-in encryption systems, may be an issue you need to investigate.

Many industries are beginning to adopt vertical applications systems that integrate transaction and workflow processing with email and communications management. Several vendors, such as Adobe and RPost, provide such capabilities. Adobe's approach tends to be focused around documents that flow between people and organizational units; RPost's does that too, but by replacing email and fax traffic as steps in transaction processing, it is showing interesting application in integrated logistics and process control environments. Blockchain technologies are being applied in this use case area quite successfully.

Regulatory and compliance requirements are driving organizations to have reliable nonrepudiation, safety, auditability, and transparency with respect to the fine-grained details of how products are assembled, how acceptance testing gets accomplished, and how customer orders are handled. These capabilities fundamentally depend upon the underlying cryptographic infrastructures and the cryptographic technologies your organization is using.

Integrated Logistics Support

Integrated logistics support (ILS) takes supply chain management several steps further by finding the most cost-effective ways to use information to improve and mature the organization's value chain. ILS extends that value chain far beyond the walls of the company or organization itself, by reaching as deep into the systems and information flows of its vendors, shippers, service providers, customers, and even their customers' customers, as there is value to be had in doing so.

From an information security perspective, that means that an ILS system crosses many organizational boundaries; it must meld together many different cultural perspectives on privacy, auditability, compliance, data and systems integrity, information quality, and protection. As an ILS may reach across many national borders, it must also face multiple legal, regulatory, and other compliance regimes. This is a federated systems problem writ large; this is transaction and workflow management taken across time zones, human languages and dialects, and organizational imperatives. This is also another problem domain that blockchain technologies are being put to use in, and they are already achieving some significant results.

One vexing question in ILS security is raised when the many different organizations in an extended ILS value chain do not have the same information security needs in common or if they have wildly different interpretations of what "confidentiality" means, for example. Your own organization might also find that some of its other customers or suppliers have their own unique perspectives on the risks that some of *your* value chains' members potentially expose their information and their systems to.

Keeping an ILS system safe and secure relies on much the same technical and managerial approaches to providing and maintaining the underlying cryptographic systems that support it.

Secure Collaboration

Collaboration suites and platforms are becoming essential in many businesses large and small. They provide much of the human-to-human activity that knits together complex project management teams, while being layer 8 of the integrated logistics support systems as well. They rely on the underlying access control systems, including SSO connections, to function effectively. Some collaboration platforms may provide separate encryption capabilities which users can invoke on a per-session basis or as part of their default settings. They may also provide the option to produce encrypted or plaintext recordings of sessions. Your organization may need to understand these capabilities if their use presents a data classification and management concern or if other compliance issues are associated with recordings of such collaboration sessions.

IoT, UAS, and ICS: The Untended Endpoints

These three different systems domains have two characteristics in common: they all have endpoint devices that generally are not directly tended to by people, and their technologies do not usually come with encrypted, secure links for data, commands, device health, and status information.

- *Internet of Things* (IoT) devices can range from the simplest of control devices, such as a home heating thermostat, to complex, semi-autonomous and mobile devices. Mobile freight and package handling devices used in warehouse and order fulfillment processing in warehouse operations, such as at Amazon, are but one example.

- *Industrial process control systems* (ICSs) interact directly on one side with physical manufacturing systems—furnaces, pumps, heavy machinery, or industrial robots—and an ICS-specific set of network protocols on the other.

- *Untended or uncrewed aerial systems* (UASs), and their cousins that move on land, water, or underwater, also have unique interfaces to the systems that control them.

UASs tend to have more complex mission management, dispatch, navigation planning, and safety requirements than the other two categories sometimes do. The UAS device itself may also have a "fail-safe" mission mode that causes the device to navigate to a predetermined safe point and come to rest, in the event of a protracted communications link failure or other conditions.

Many of these types of devices, in all three of these systems domains, tend to have limited onboard capacity to support sophisticated encryption of their uplinks and downlinks. Even if they do, the protocols used on those links may not always be compatible with TCP/IP-based protocols and services that the rest of your organization's networks and systems are using.

You may be lucky and find out that the IoT, UAS, ICS, or other robotics types of systems your organization is using or wants to begin using are directly supportable by your existing cryptographic systems and technologies. You may find that their systems, links, and operating procedures can hold to the same standards for key strength, key management, and use that you already have in place; they may also be compatible with your existing access control systems to the degree that this is an issue for your use of these untended endpoints. Then again, your organization has to either accept the potential for security compromise or plan to upgrade these systems and their interfaces to be more compatible with the rest of your cryptographic infrastructure.

For more about this, see the Appendix.

Deploying Cryptography: Some Challenging Scenarios

Thinking about those use cases as a starter set, let's superimpose them as a bundle across the sliding scale of organizational complexity and the IT architectures that result from (and often exacerbate) that complexity of interconnectedness.

Trusting SOHO

Taken altogether, small businesses (of less than 20 people) comprise the largest aggregate employer in most nations. This is the marketplace for small office/home office (SOHO) systems built with consumer-grade equipment and software and firmware installed and managed by the original equipment manufacturer (OEM) on their own schedule. It's the marketplace of little in-house cryptographic expertise (if any), and it's the never-ending consulting opportunity for the freelance or moonlighting security professional.

Such environments are anything but server-free, of course. Their router (typically provided by their ISP) provides DHCP services at a minimum; each endpoint has multiple servers built into it, and any network-attached storage devices provide even more. These environments are also prone to using many cloud-based storage solutions, particularly in the free end of the spectrum. Some of their uses may have set these up with encryption on some files, on some folders, or on a whole storage volume.

Many organizations in such circumstances do not get their own digital certificates; if they have a website, they may unknowingly rely on its hosting service (which might be WordPress or similar easy-entry web page development and hosting solutions) for HTTPS session support. User IDs, passwords, authorized devices (for MAC address filtering on routers), and even the use of built-in access controls can be unmanaged and disorganized. Document e-signing services may be used to provide digital signatures as part of some business processes, but the organization may not have any formal management process to control their use, maintain them, expire, or revoke them (as faces change at the company).

In such environments, some standard cryptographic hygiene measures are desperately needed. These organizations may have little or no procedural grasp of what to do when an employee quits, becomes disgruntled, or compromised. Dealing with lost or forgotten passwords or encryption keys can be a traumatic case study in learning on the fly every time it happens.

On-Premises Data Center

Once an organization has migrated to more of a structured data center as the power behind its IT infrastructure, it's also making the step toward more formalized information security measures. Greater awareness of compliance and regulatory demands for tighter security, even the use of encryption to protect sensitive information and restrict access to sensitive processes, may also be more common in such a setting. Most server systems come with certificate generation and management capabilities built right in; even consumer-grade NAS solutions often have these features although few SOHO architectures ever see them put into effective use. At this point, systems administrators can now generate and issue certificates, and the organization can digitally sign files, documents, archive copies of data sets, and so on.

Key management becomes an issue at this point; including HSM solutions as part of their IT architecture may be prudent.

Investment in a data center can be the tipping point at which management starts to seriously worry about data exfiltration, ransom attacks, and other high-impact threats to the company's survival and success. This brings two encryption-based worry beads to the table.

- **Weaponized and encrypted inbound content:** Their architecture's threat surface exposes them to many possible ways that weaponized content can make it into their systems, and if the connection being used by that attack vector has its encryption managed independently of the organization's control, there's no useful way to detect it or prevent it. Other means, such as tighter control of endpoint activities, software and even process-based allowed list control, endpoint and host-based intrusion detection and prevention, and behavior modeling and analysis can help but may not be enough.

- **Encrypted "east-west" internal traffic:** Almost every business process supported by your systems and architectures will move data internally, as different servers, operational locations, departments, and human beings get involved in the end-to-end of the business of doing business. This has to happen efficiently and reliably, of course. Some of those processes may have information security needs that dictate encryption be used to protect the data while in transit internally. How can you tell whether a particular stream of encrypted packets on your internal network is legitimate, is an exfiltration in process, or is some other part of an attacker's kill chain in action? Inspecting the unencrypted content of every packet might help, but doing this requires you to be your own MITM attacker. You have to ensure that every internal encrypted data flow path potentially carrying highly sensitive information must route itself through an encryption proxy service that provides you with opportunities for (automated) inspection, analysis, and logging. This has throughput performance penalties that can seriously affect your competitive advantage. It may also end up putting all of your most sensitive information into one high-value point of potential exploitation (the so-called "all eggs in one basket" problem).

High-Compliance Architectures

As an organization extends its business activities into areas that must meet stringent regulatory and other compliance requirements for data protection, safety, and reliability, the needs for encryption-based security solutions increase. By one count, more than 83 different types of business activities, from healthcare through gambling and from banking through medical care are subject to compliance regimes that dictate such architectures be put in place, managed effectively, used consistently, and be subject to verification testing, audit, inspection, and ongoing security assessment. All of the issues looked at throughout this chapter, and then some, require that the organization have some seriously capable in-house cryptologic talent—or trust its fate to its vendors and consultants.

These types of environments and architectures need powerful capabilities for monitoring the use of encryption by applications; this may require extensive analysis of behavioral norms to identify acceptable use versus usage worthy of further inspection and analysis. They also need to have a similar capability to monitor cloud-hosted service usage, in particular the ebb and flow of encrypted traffic and data via cloud-based application platforms, in order to be able to spot anomalous patterns of activity. These monitoring capabilities should be in-house, directly coupled to organizational management and leadership, to strengthen the sense that the "watchers" and the managers and leaders jointly own the challenges that maintaining such vigilance entails.

Limitations and Vulnerabilities

Probably the first real limitation I have to acknowledge is the flip side of the greatest strength we have going for us.

Common to almost all of the protocols and services discussed in this chapter is the fundamental assertion that the way our "crypto industry" works is effective at keeping our systems safe and secure. We depend upon its underlying business model for establishing encryption and decryption algorithms, choosing effective keys, and managing algorithms, keys, and protocols to stay a few steps ahead of well-funded attackers. We depend upon that community effort to grant us ways to stay months ahead of the attackers, perhaps even a few years ahead of them; we operate in that window of safety in time because we rely upon that ethical community of cryptographic practice. This community, as you know, is an incredibly large and complex system of individuals and organizations, including security agencies such as NSA or GCHQ; standards bodies like NIST, ISO, and the IEEE; the Internet engineering community (IETF and everyone who works with it); and the millions of defense-oriented cryptanalysts, hackers, ethical penetration testers, and end-user systems and security administrators. This system includes the CVE databases and the reporting channels, as well as the academic literature, blog sites, and conferences of all kinds.

We depend upon this human system to keep our window of security open for as many months as we can. We know it's a question of *when*, not *if* a particular key strength will fail to be sufficient. We know that all algorithms, processes, protocols, and systems will have vulnerabilities discovered in them.

In some respects, each of us in our end-user organizations can't do much to remedy the shortcomings of that defense-oriented community of practice. But we can and should recognize that it's not perfect. We cannot count on it to watch our backs; it only provides us the tools and techniques and shares common alarms with us when it finds them.

At a lower level of abstraction, there are some common limitations and vulnerabilities we can and should take ownership of.

Weak keys continue to be a source of vulnerabilities for almost every cryptologic process, procedure, protocol, or service. For example, consider the known vulnerability of IPsec to man-in-the-middle attacks when weak preshared keys are used. IKE in its original implementation and in IKEv1 had some flaws that might allow this to occur, which could then let an attacker capture and decrypt VPN traffic. When discovered, vendors such as Cisco Systems quickly developed and released patches to eliminate this vulnerability. Each end-user organization, however, had to correctly apply the patch and then correct other deficiencies (probably in their procedures) that were allowing weak keys to be generated and used in the first place. Somewhat later, IKEv2 was shown to be vulnerable to another variant on a MiTM attack that allowed session keys to be stolen; once in possession of these, the session is wide open to the attacker. This time, Bleichenbacher Oracles, a chosen-ciphertext attack against RSA, first published by Daniel Bleichenbacher in 1998, was the attack method of choice. The next section in this chapter will look at the overall key management problem, and some solutions to it, in more depth; but keep in mind that even the strongest key management process is held hostage by its algorithms and its end users.

Password vulnerability is also a never-ending issue. Complex passwords were thought to be the fix; those are out of favor, with longer, more user-friendly passphrases being today's preferred solution. It's not hard to believe that these, too, will fall prey to concerted GPU cluster attack machines that draw support from a Dark Web community of malpractice, long before quantum computing becomes commonplace and affordable.

Spurious content injection has also shown to be an Achilles' heel of a number of protocols, such as the EFAIL exploits found in S/MIME, which also seems to have affected

PGP/GPG email systems. Carnegie Mellon University's CERT recommendations included performing email decryption outside of the email client, disabling HTML rendering for email (as a way of blocking most exfiltration channels from being set up), and disabling remote content loading by email clients. (Do you disable these for your organization's email clients?)

The protocols and the services your organization depends upon may be rock solid in their design; however, common errors in their implementation into hardware, software, and procedures still reach up and bite the end users when attackers find and exploit such weaknesses. Buffer overflows continue to plague the industry, for example (one wonders how, these days, a product can get through design and testing and still have such classic flaws in it). Virtually every one of the algorithms and protocols discussed is available to you in many different implementation forms, from many different vendors or supply chain channels. Different implementations expose different vulnerabilities to exploitation than others do. This is as true for your cryptographic infrastructure as it is for the rest of your IT architecture and installed base of systems. We'll look more at these issues of IT supply chain security in Chapter 7, "Systems and Application Security."

UNDERSTAND PUBLIC KEY INFRASTRUCTURE SYSTEMS

Prior to the 1990s, the management of cryptologic keys, keying materials, and everything associated with encryption and decryption was monopolized by governments. A few commercial encryption systems, similar to the electromechanical rotor systems such as the Enigma, were in use before World War II, but these were the rare exception. The public competition that brought us the Data Encryption Standard in 1977 was driven in part by businesses that had started thinking about how and why they needed to start using encryption. By 1991, according to a NIST planning report published a decade later, the worldwide market for cryptographic *business* products had grown to an estimated $695 million USD (or about $1.3 billion, given inflation, in 2019). The market value of just the financial data protected by such use of DES was estimated to be between one and two *trillion* dollars in 1991, according to that same NIST Planning Report 01-2 published in 2001. (By 2018, the volume of funds transferred on Fedwire exceeded $716 *trillion* dollars, all of it protected by AES and other encryption technologies, of course.) Clearly, by 1991, quite a number of private businesses as well as the federal electronic funds clearinghouse system (or Fedwire) had learned much about the fine art of safely and securely managing cryptologic systems and their keys.

The principle challenges remain the same. Only the keys you are using *right now* to encrypt something are a secret that you can and should protect. You must share that key with the recipients or end users of the messages or data you encrypt it with. How you manage that sharing, without compromising that key, is the challenge. We've looked at that challenge earlier in this chapter in a number of ways. Let's review it all by way of leading up to a final look at key management in a public key world and how *that* problem boils down to how we create, maintain, and manage millions of trust relationships. In doing so, we'll look at the principle tasks that taken together comprise cryptologic key management as a discipline.

- Key generation, including determining the key size and key strength necessary to meet your information security requirements

- Key distribution, including trust relationships between key generator, distributor, and users

- Key expiration and revocation

- Scheduling and managing periodic key changes or key rotations across a network of subscribers or users

- Lost key recovery and key escrow to meet users' information security needs

- Key escrow and recovery to meet the needs of law enforcement or digital discovery

- Destruction or safe disposal of keys, keying materials, cryptovariables, and devices

- Coping with data remanence issues

Again, it's worth remembering that these tasks exist whether you're using purely symmetric encryption, purely asymmetric encryption, or a hybrid system, and whether you're using block ciphers, stream ciphers, or a mix of both technologies. We'll also see that many concepts from risk mitigation and control, such as separation of duties and shared responsibilities, have their place in the world of key management.

Fundamental Key Management Concepts

You'll recall that encryption systems consist of algorithms for encryption and decryption; the keys and control variables (or *cryptovariables*) that are used by those algorithms; and then the software, hardware, communications interfaces, and procedures that make that set of math-based manipulation of symbols into a working, useful cryptographic system. By definition:

- *Symmetric encryption* uses the same key for encryption and decryption (or in some cases a simple transformation of one key into the other). The encryption and decryption algorithms are logical inverses of each other. Symmetric encryption also implies that if an attacker can work out the *decryption* key (from intercepted ciphertext, or from known-plaintext attacks), then he can easily determine the corresponding *encryption* key, and vice versa. Symmetric encryption tends to be very efficient, in terms of CPU processing power or number of logic gates used in hardware encryption and decryption systems.

- *Asymmetric encryption* uses encryption algorithms that are fundamentally different from their corresponding decryption algorithms; the encryption and decryption keys themselves are also very different from each other, and the decryption key cannot readily be computed or estimated from the encryption key itself. The nature of the mathematics chosen for key generation, and the algorithms them- selves, make it *computationally infeasible* to be able to reverse calculate the decryption key from the ciphertext and the encryption key. Asymmetric encryp- tion and decryption use significantly more CPU cycles, hardware elements, or both to perform their operations, but this runtime performance penalty buys users a significantly greater degree of resulting resistance to attack.

This leads us to revisit three important types of cryptographic keys:

- A *session key* is used for encrypting a single session of data exchange or data encryption. That unit of work can be a message, a file, an entire disk drive or stor- age system image; it can be an HTTPS connection to a web page, a client-server connection of any kind, or any other set of information required. Once that session's worth of data has been encrypted, the session key is never used again. Furthermore, any future session keys generated by that system should not be easy to predict or precalculate by an attacker. For symmetric encryption, the same ses- sion key is used by the recipient to decrypt the session's information (be it a file or a stream of packets or bits); when through, the recipient must also not reuse the session key.

- A *public key* is part of an associated pair of keys that a user needs to operate an asymmetric cryptographic system. As its name implies, it can be and usually is made public. Unlike the session key (or a symmetric encryption key), it is not used in the encryption process directly; instead, it is used by the sender (its owner) and the recipient to co-generate a shared, secret session key. So long as sender and recipient obey the rules of session keys (and never reuse it, destroy it when no lon- ger needed, and protect it while it is in use), the ciphertext cannot be decrypted using the public key alone.

- A *private key* is the other part of that associated pair; it is known to the originator (the owner of the identity associated with the public and private key pair), and the originator never shares it with anybody or any other system. It is used by the sender, along with his public key, in a process of shared key cogeneration with the recipient.

You'll also hear two other terms associated with keys when various cryptographic encapsulation techniques are used:

- Key encryption keys (KEK), sometimes called *key wrapping keys*, are used when a cryptographic key itself must be protected by a surrounding wrapper or layer of encryption. For example, once a hybrid encryption system has successfully cogenerated a session key, it is usually put in a packet that is further encrypted using such a KEK.

- Data encryption keys (DEK) are the keys used to encrypt payload data only; session keys might also be called DEKs in some systems.

Key Strength and Key Generation

Key strength is the result of two principle factors: the size of the key itself (expressed as the number of bits to represent it) and the randomness associated with the key value and its generation process. Your choices about both of these factors should always be driven by your particular information security requirements, especially the *time period* over which you need the data you're about to encrypt to be kept safe from prying eyes or corrupting fingers.

Key Size   Generally, the longer the key, the more difficult it is to attack encrypted messages; it determines the *search space*, the set of all possible numeric values that fit within the number of bits in the key that a brute-force attack must attempt in order to find a match. What constitutes a secure key length changes with time as computer power increases and cryptanalysis techniques become more sophisticated. In 1977, the U.S. government selected a symmetric block cipher they dubbed the Data Encryption Standard (DES), which was considered secure for nonclassified use, with the intent that banking systems and other commercial business users could start to use it to protect their data. But by 1999, multiple cryptanalysts demonstrated that DES could be cracked in as little as 24 hours using large arrays of processors such as the EFF's DES Cracking Machine, for a cost of only $250,000. Governments' monopoly on powerful code-breaking hardware had crumbled with the birth and explosive growth of the personal computer market, especially its appetite for higher-performance single-chip CPUs, math co-processors, and graphics processors.

As DES was replaced with AES, key sizes grew from 56 bits (DES) to 128, then 192, and then 256 bits. A brute-force attack on a 128-bit key, using a single CPU, would take something on the order of 14 billion years of CPU time to try every possible value. Of course, the attacker could be lucky on their first handful of attempts. Any clues that the attacker can use to reduce the size of that search space, bit by bit, raises their chance of success. AES, for example, was described in a 1999 paper to be vulnerable to attack by precomputing intermediate values (the Bleichenbacher Oracles attack mentioned earlier). Such intelligent guesswork can cut the effective key size (and resultant search space) down to a much more manageable size, perhaps back to the DES 56-bit window of vulnerability. Various organizations such as NIST in the United States, ANSSI in France, or the BSI in the United Kingdom provide concrete recommendations such as disallowing the use of 80-bit symmetric keys after 2012, and 112-bit keys after 2030. A strong key should be random enough to make it unlikely that an attacker can predict any of the bits of the key. If the mechanism used to generate keys is even somewhat predictable, then the system becomes easier to crack.

The choice of algorithm has a profound effect on the strength of a given size key as well. By comparing the estimated run time or work factor necessary to backward solve the decryption algorithm without the decryption key, it's been shown for example that ECC demonstrates the same level of key strength at about one-fourth the key size of the RSA algorithm.

Randomness   The strength of a symmetric key also depends on its being unpredictable (both "unguessable" in the human sense and resistant to mathematical attempts to generate the next key in a sequence, given one such key). Even if only some of the bits can be guessed, that can significantly reduce the strength of the cipher. Using a mechanism that will generate high-quality (i.e., cryptographically secure) random numbers is essential for key generation. The best method is to use hardware-based true random number generators (HRNGs) that use very low-level physical phenomena, such as thermal noise, to generate sequences of numbers as outputs that are statistically highly random. Such devices are embedded in various cryptographic hardware devices such as Trusted Platform Modules and Hardware Security Modules, discussed earlier, as well as in some microprocessors themselves.

Software-based RNGs are very hard to get right. For example, from 2006 until 2008, a defect introduced into the OpenSSL package in the Debian and Ubuntu Linux distributions caused all keys generated to be weak because of a bug in the random number generator (CVE-2008-0166).

Key Generation   Keys should be generated in a manner appropriate for the cryptographic algorithm being used. The proper method to generate a symmetric key is different from a public/private key pair. NIST SP800-133 Rev 2, "Recommendation for Cryptographic Key Generation," provides specific guidance. The best approach for generating asymmetric keys, however, is to use a trusted digital certificate provider, which will generate a public/private key pair bound to a specific identity. At some point, however, your organization's need for multiple public/private key pairs will dictate that you become your own certificate authority and take on the management burden and expense of generating and issuing key pairs to users within the organization. (At this point, investing in an HSM as a secure storage and processing part of your CA capabilities makes sense.) Generating your own certificates should not be confused with self-signing certificates. Self-signing certificates actually authenticate nothing but the certificate itself; they are quite useful in software and systems test environments, where a working, fully functional certificate, private key, and public key might be needed but are not required to provide security. Do not attempt to use self-signing certificates to protect anything!

Secure Key Storage and Use

Once you have generated a nice long and random key, how do you keep it secret? Obviously the first step is to encrypt your data encryption key (DEK) with another key, the key encryption key (KEK). That solves the problem but creates another: how do you secure your KEK? This depends on the sensitivity of the underlying data being encrypted and the mechanisms that are appropriate for the system you are designing.

A hardware security module (HSM) is specifically designed to securely generate and store KEKs and is among the more secure method of protecting keys. HSMs also provide for secure ways of replicating the KEKs between redundant HSMs and for enforcing controls so that no one individual can use the KEK to decrypt a data encryption key.

For systems that are deployed in the public cloud, the major cloud providers offer cloud implementations of HSM technology. Numerous hardware security module as a service (HSMaaS) vendors are available in the marketplace, often as a service offering in conjunction with other cryptographic functionality such as key escrow and cryptographic acceleration.

For less demanding applications, the approach must be tailored to the specific requirements and risks. This might permit storage of master keys in a: hardware-encrypted USB key, a password management app, or a secrets management package. Another factor to consider is how your keys are (securely) backed up. Losing access to your keys can cause you to lose access to significant amounts of other data (and backups of that data).

Key Distribution, Exchange, and Trust

Even the smallest of systems using encryption—two nodes or even one node that writes encrypted data to storage to retrieve, decrypt, and use it later—has the issue of getting the keys from the generation function to each point of use. In the more general case of a network of multiple users, all of whom are cleared to the same level of information security classification and all of whom need to communicate with each other, the key generation function has to distribute a copy of the key (and any other required cryptovariables) to each node that will participate in a multiway sharing of information. For n users in a system, that's n different sets of messages going back and forth to send the key and verify its receipt. On the other hand, for systems that require each pair of those *n* users to have their own separate key so that pair-wise communication and data sharing remains secret from the others on the network that's $n(n - 1)$, or roughly n^2 key exchanges that need to be managed, confirmed, and kept track of. (Keeping track of which user nodes or systems have which key at what time is a major part of what keeps the encryption system synchronized across those users; it's also necessary to investigate lost or possibly compromised keys, and it's a major component in providing nonrepudiation of messages sent through the system as well.)

Three different trust relationships exist in a key distribution system:

- The key distributor has to trust that the recipients are who they claim they are (which requires that they are still using the same identities they had the *last* time keys were sent to them) and that their facility, local key storage, systems, and users have not been compromised without it being reported to the key distributor.

- The recipients have to trust that the key distributor has not been compromised without their knowledge.

- Individual user recipients have to trust that no other users on the network (whether they share keys with them or not) have been compromised without their knowledge.

The net effect of these trust relationships is that all parties can trust that the keys they've just been issued will provide the level of security protection that the system, with proper keys, is supposed to provide. The ultimate organizational owners of the network may be the anchor of all of these trust relationships (that is, the one whose assertions of trust the other nodes can depend upon), or it may be the key distributor that does this. (We'll look at this in more detail in the "Hierarchies of Trust" and "Web of Trust" sections.)

Keys are sent from the distributor to user nodes in one of two ways.

- *In-band* distribution uses the same communications channels and protocols that the parties use for normal message or data traffic between them.

- *Out-of-band* distribution uses a physically, electrically, logically, and administratively separate and distinct channel for key distribution and management. This may be a physical channel, such as a courier, a different VPN, or a dedicated circuit used solely for key distribution.

Part of the trust that all parties must repose in each other includes the fact that they share the protection responsibility for that distribution system, whether it is in-band or out-of-band.

Key exchange, which is used with hybrid encryption systems as part of a public key encryption infrastructure, is different than key distribution. It may still use in-band or out-of-band communication channels to support the exchange process; but by its nature, it does *not* depend upon the parties in the key exchange having a previously established trust relationship with each other.

Key Rotation, Expiration, and Revocation

As with everything in information security, your cryptographic keys are part of your race against time with your attacker. The longer you use any given key—the more packets, messages, or files you use it to encrypt—the greater the opportunity *you give your attackers* to possibly succeed in attacking your encryption processes. One time-tested countermeasure is to change your keys, early and often. Ideally, you'd use a new key every byte (which sounds like an infinitely long one-time pad key being put to use). Practically, you've got to find the balance between the costs and efforts involved in changing keys versus the risk that adversaries can break your encryption and get at your data or systems as a result.

Many organizations establish a *key rotation schedule*, by which they plan for the routine replacement of keys currently in use with newly minted keys. NIST, ISO, and the Payment Card Industry Security Standards Council recommend that keys be changed at least annually, and this includes public/private key pairs as well as symmetric keys generated with them and used to encrypt archival data backups. Other industries may require keys to be changed more frequently.

In practice, the keys used to encrypt new data are changed each year, and all of the previously encrypted data is decrypted using the retired keys and then re-encrypted using the new key within the year following the key rotation. Thus, by the end of a year after the key rotation, there is no data encrypted using the retired key, at which time it can be destroyed. In cases in which backups must be maintained for longer than one year, either a process for securely archiving retired keys must be instituted or backups will have to also be re-encrypted with the new key.

Key revocation is the process of formally notifying key users, and users of data encrypted with a key, that the key has been compromised or its safety and security is in doubt. If there is evidence or even suspicion that a key has been compromised, it ought to be rotated (that is, *replaced*) as soon as feasible. Best practice also dictates that keys be replaced when essential personnel with access to cryptographic material leave their position.

Key rotation, expiration, and revocation all reduce the likelihood that an attacker can break your encryption systems, or otherwise circumvent them, and then have unrestricted access to your information and information systems. By smartly rotating and expiring keys, you can also manage the amount of archival or backup data that is protected by any particular set of keys. (Think of this as *limiting your exposure* to losing that data, in the event the key is compromised without your knowledge.)

✔ "Rotate" Does *Not* Mean "Reuse"

Rotating your keys is not like rotating your tires: you do not take a key at the end of its scheduled usage lifetime for one application or pair of users and then assign it to another and continue using it. Early encryption systems did this, believing that their adversaries could not surreptitiously gather enough ciphertext messages between enough nodes in the system to make the system vulnerable to attack. This was a dangerous assumption to make, and experience usually proved it a foolish one as well.

Rotate by destroying the old keys and then generate and distribute a new key to take its place.

Key Destruction

Once a key has been retired and it has been determined that there is no data that has been encrypted using that key that will need to be decrypted, then it must be securely destroyed. This involves locating every copy of the key and deleting it in a manner appropriate for the media on which it was stored to ensure that it cannot be recovered.

Depending on the media and the risk of it becoming accessible to unauthorized individuals, this may require overwriting the storage, degaussing of the media, or physical destruction of the media or device containing the media.

Records must be kept documenting the locations of the destroyed keys and the means used to ensure secure destruction. In many regulatory and compliance regimes, these records are subject to audit.

Key Management Vulnerabilities

There are a number of vulnerabilities that can be introduced through the incorrect use, storage, and management of cryptographic keys.

There are potential trust concerns when dealing with some agencies. While NIST is highly regarded as operating with virtues in line with most cryptography users, agencies such as the NSA also possess both the expertise and responsibility to monitor electronic communications, and therefore it cannot be assumed that they will always prioritize protecting privacy over intelligence. They've also repeatedly stated that their national security duties *require* them to attempt to find ways to build in backdoors or otherwise weaken encryption processes, whether they acknowledge that they've done so or not. "Don't worry if your system crashes, because NSA has a backup copy of it" may be an apocryphal bit of gallows humor, but if the thought of NSA having a copy of your communications or data makes you or your company uncomfortable, consider using an alternative such as a PGP-based system that's outside of the NSA/NIST nexus of the cryptographic community.

Symmetric and private keys depend upon confidentiality to be effective. This means great care must be taken with how the keys are stored to reduce the possibility of their becoming known to unauthorized entities. There are a number of approaches to secure key storage, from key management software to key management services provided by cloud service providers to dedicated hardware devices that keep the keys stored internally in a tamper-resistant secure device.

Keys that have reached the end of their lifetime (and all properly managed keys should have a defined lifetime) must be securely destroyed to prevent their misuse in the future. Keys should not be reused and should be rotated (replaced) periodically to ensure that the amount of data encrypted using a single key is limited and that the lifetime of data encrypted using a given key is likewise limited.

Another vulnerability can arise from insider threats. A rogue employee with access to key material can use that access to defeat the security of encrypted material (or enable another to do the same). Dual control or segregation of duties can be employed to ensure that at least two people must be actively involved before any key management operation that might compromise the security of the system can be completed. Another popular method to mitigate the risk of a rogue employee exposing cryptographic material is to use a third party to safeguard keys. A key escrow agent is a trusted external party that ensures the cryptographic keys are safe from unintended abuse or leaks. As an analogy, this is similar to how an escrow agreement is used to safeguard a large sum of money when purchasing a home.

The final leg of the CIA triad must also be considered: availability. If the key management system cannot provide access to the key material to authorized processes when required, then access to the encrypted material will be denied, even if the encrypted data is readily accessible.

Key operations must be logged in a manner that ensures accountability and traceability, providing the forensic evidence essential to analysis of a suspected possible compromise, intrusion, or data breach.

Finally, where possible, key management functions ought to be automated. Manual processes are more prone to error (either by commission or omission), leading to weaknesses in the system that depends upon the keys for security.

Escrow and Key Recovery

During the 1980s and 1990s, the U.S. government (and some of its NATO allies) pushed hard to get legislative support for a concept they called *key escrow*. Key escrow would require any private person (corporate or individual) who created a cryptographic key to place a copy of it on deposit with the government, who would have to have legal authority, such as a search or surveillance (wiretap) warrant from a court before they could take the key out of escrow and use it to decrypt intercepted files or messages involving that party. Needless to say, the outcry across many communities was substantial. This was also still at a time when the U.S. government believed it could systematically restrict export of encryption technologies, and only allow downgraded, more easily breakable versions of American-made encryption products to be exported. Market economics quickly demonstrated that foreign systems vendors would dominate the world market, which would leave American technology and software firms with nothing but a domestic market. Eventually, key escrow as a government agenda item lost what luster it might have had. But it's not dead yet; periodically, governments protest that they need the ability to break *everybody's* encryption, just in case they find the nuggets of information they need to thwart a terrorist attack. Key escrow, alas, cannot force the criminal or terrorist—or a foreign intelligence agent—to submit their keys to a government escrow agency.

Lost Key Insurance   As the use of password managers, hardware security modules, and other such systems has grown, business and personal users are finding legitimate reasons to want some form of "lost or forgotten key insurance," so to speak. Key escrow and key recovery are often discussed as options to mitigate the risk of lost, corrupted, or forgotten keys and digital certificates.

Internally, key escrow processes can be useful, and solutions such as hardware security modules (or even HSMaaS approaches) may be worth considering. When an organization takes on the task of being its own CA and issues certificates (and therefore public-private key pairs) to users, it may want to look further at its needs for internal key escrow. There are also legitimate business continuity needs to identify ways to safely escrow (or archive) certificates and keys and then be able to quickly reinstall them as part of recovering from an incident or disaster. In most cases, recovering a private key associated with a digital certificate issued by a public-facing CA is not possible.

Hacking Back a Lost Key   *Key recovery* has become the collective, polite term for any capabilities, efforts, or attempts to reverse engineer or hack back the decryption keys associated with a set of ciphertext, such as account passwords, digital signatures, encrypted files or disk drives, smartphones, network traffic, or messages of any kind, for the purpose of making the key-protected content available and useful to its owners again. Presumably, these attacks are carried out by ethical hackers, whose actions are constrained and authorized by a suitable contract with the owners of the systems or accounts in question.

There are two difficulties with such concepts, one technical and the other legal.

The legal difficulty is that for any activity involving a U.S. person, the U.S. government can serve anyone even remotely involved with that person with a National Security Letter (NSL). An NSL is a warrant issued by the U.S. Foreign Intelligence Surveillance Court, and it requires the person it is served on to surrender or make available any information the NSL asks for, without informing anyone, even their attorney, about the NSL. Presumably, LastPass, Mozilla, Google, Microsoft, or any firm making a password manager service available could be served with such an NSL; they would have no legal recourse but to comply. If your password manager can reveal or recover your master password to *you*, it can do so when compelled by an NSL (or even a much weaker search warrant or subpoena. (The penalties for not complying are quite painful, as spelled out in the Uniting and Strengthening America by Providing Appropriate Tools Required to Intercept and Obstruct Terrorism Act of 2001, known as the USA PATRIOT Act.)

The technical difficulty goes to the heart of our widely held assumption that our whole public cryptography infrastructure, when used with strong keys and with proper cryptographic hygiene measures in place, will really keep our information and systems safe, secure, and reliable. If the encryption keys and algorithms used are as strong as we all *hope* they are, any attempts at key recovery should be expensive, time-consuming, and impossible to guarantee to be completed in any specific or reasonable amount of time. Such brute-force key recovery, aided by guesses, fragmentary memory, or other information provided by the owner to the key recovery service, may help speed the process up; but at the end of the day, either all of our secrets *are* safe and key recovery is a pipe dream or key recovery is real, affordable, and practical, and nothing is as safe as we hope and need it to be.

Separation of Duties, Dual Control, and Split Knowledge

It's fundamental to risk management and mitigation that any business process that involves a high-impact risk should be designed, implemented, monitored, and managed in such a way that no one person or system element has the opportunity to corrupt that process on their own. We add redundancy to such high-impact risk control processes in a variety of ways.

- **Majority voting:** Redundant, parallel processing elements (people or systems) each execute separately on the same inputs and previous system state; the results are compared, and differences beyond a tolerance value are flagged to supervisory functions for investigation and resolution. (Blockchain systems and other distributed, high-reliability systems use this technique.)

- **Split (or shared) knowledge:** Critical process knowledge is not granted to a sole individual person, node, or component; instead, multiple such people or nodes must bring their knowledge together to a trusted system component that combines them, and validates that result, before allowing the process to continue. This is similar to multifactor authentication; some hardware security modules use physically separate and distinct additional factors for each human interacting with the HSM, all of which (or a set majority of which) must be present in order to allow HSM critical maintenance or management functions to be performed. Using asymmetric encryption in a key exchange process to generate a session key is an example of a split knowledge process.

- **Dual (or multiple) control:** The process is designed with layers or sequences of approval and authorization steps, each of which is performed by a unique individual person or systems component; all process steps must be correctly completed in the proper sequence for the results to be valid. High-value financial transactions often require two or three different company officers to authorize before a check can be issued or an electronic payment can be processed. This can also include process steps where all parties must execute their part of the step simultaneously, if not also at the same location. Such locations are sometimes known as *no lone zones*, since policy and process design prohibit one person being in the area and attempting to perform the process task by themselves.

Each of these control techniques can play a part in applying a *separation of duties* control strategy. Separation of duties reduces the risk that one employee can take an action that can cause harm to the organization, its information, its systems, or its customers, without that action being detected and possibly prevented or remedied in a timely fashion. Separation of duties also protects the employees from potentially being falsely accused of negligence or willfully taking harmful action by helping to isolate where in the chain of business processes an error, misstep, or improper action actually took place.

Protecting your cryptographic systems, keying material, keys, and even the data remaining in the devices or system after an encryption session is completed may very well require some form of dual control or separation of duties. Compliance requirements in many business areas may also require that your systems have no "lone zones" or one-person tasks or functions in critical process flows.

Hierarchies of Trust

We've now got some of the major building blocks to provide for trustworthy distribution of the software (and hardware) elements of a public encryption system. Before we can start building an infrastructure with them, we first need to look more closely at what *trustworthy* means and how we establish, share and encourage strangers to trust each other—or at least, trust enough to communicate with them.

We first must recognize that a trust relationship between two parties is actually the sum of two one-way trust relationships: Bob *confers his trust* upon Carol, and Carol confers her trust upon Bob, which we observe by saying "Bob and Carol trust each other." (If you think that looks like a grant of privilege from Bob to Carol, you're right!) A *transitive trust relationship* occurs when Carol trusts Alice, and because Bob trusts Carol, he therefore also trusts Alice. And since Alice trusts Ted, Bob and Carol each trust Ted. Thus, a transitive chain of trust is created. (If Ted trusts Alice but chooses not to trust Bob, you can see that the web or mesh of trust relationships can get...murky.) Strictly speaking, these are peer-to-peer trust relationships, as no one person in this group is the designated or accepted authority regarding trustworthiness.

Conversationally, we talk about chains of trust, webs of trust, and hierarchies of trust. Implicit in each of these ideas is the notion that those trust architectures have some "coin of the realm," some agreed-to set of ideas, messages, data, or other things that are both the token of that trust and what is being exchanged in a trustworthy fashion. Money, for example, is exchanged both as a token (a representation) of value and of trust.

In information and communications systems terms, the foremost token of trust is a certificate that asserts that the identity of the certificate holder and the public key associated with that certificate are linked or bound with each other. This gives rise to two different concepts of how trust conferred by one node upon another can be scaled up to larger numbers of nodes.

- A hierarchy of trust exists when a single node is recognized as the authority for asserting or conferring trust. This conferring of trust can be delegated downward (made transitive) by that trust authority conferring a special status to a set of intermediate nodes, each of which can act as a trust authority for other intermediary nodes or end user nodes (recipients of trust), which (in tree structure terms) are the leaf nodes. The trust anchor is the trust authority, as the root of this tree of trust, conferring trust downward through any number of intermediaries, to the leaf nodes. Hierarchies of trust resemble forests of trees (in data structure terms!), with one root branching out to start many subtrees, which may further branch, until finally we reach the *leaf* nodes at the very tip of each twig.

- A certificate authority is the anchor node of a hierarchy of trust, issuing the certificates that bind individual identities with their corresponding public keys.
- A web of trust has no designated or accepted single authority for trust, and acts in peer-to-peer fashion to establish chains of trust.

NOTE In nature, of course, trees grow from their roots upward; information systems designers, out of habit, start drawing trees by putting the anchor node at the top of the page and thus grow their digital trees downward.

In both hierarchies of trust and webs of trust, any given node can be a member of one or more trust relationships and therefore be a member of one or more chains or webs of trust.

In hierarchies of trust, end users, seeking to validate the trustworthiness of a certificate, infer that a certificate from a trusted end (leaf) node is trustworthy if the intermediary who issued it is, on up to the anchor. Webs of trust, by contrast, involve peer-to-peer trust relationships that do not rely on central certificate authorities as the anchors. Hierarchies of trust are much more scalable (to billions of certificates in use) than webs of trust. Both systems have drawbacks and issues, particularly with respect to certificate revocation, expiration, or the failure of a node to maintain trustworthiness. (The details of those issues are beyond the scope of this chapter, but you do need to be aware that these issues exist and are not straightforward.)

TLS and secure HTTP (HTTPS) require the use of a certificate, granted by a certificate authority. SSL and TLS established what was called the *chain of trust*, shown in Figure 5.14. The chain of trust starts with the CA itself generating a self-signed certificate, called a *root certificate*, which anchors the chain of trust. This root certificate can be used to generate and authenticate any number of intermediate certificates, which can also be used to authenticate (sign) other intermediate certificates. The end-entity, or end-user certificate, is the distant end of the chain of trust; it authenticates the end user's identity and is signed by an intermediate certificate issuer (or, hypothetically, it could be signed by the root authority). End-entity or "leaf" certificates (borrowing from tree structure terminology) are terminal—they cannot be used to sign other certificates of any kind.

Certificates of this kind allow browsers or other client-side programs to use a certification path validation algorithm, which has to validate that (a) the subject of the certificate matches the host name being connected to, and (b) the certificate is signed by a trusted authority, has not been revoked, and has not expired. Figure 5.15 shows this in simplified form.

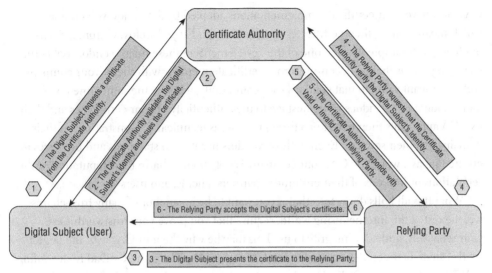

FIGURE 5.14 **Chains of trust**

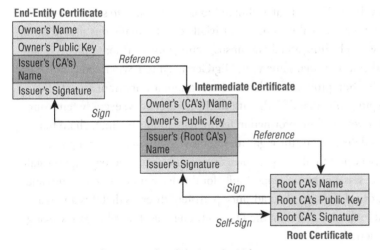

FIGURE 5.15 **Certification path validation algorithm**

In 2008, the IETF published updated versions of the X.509 standard, which defines these certificates and the protocols for their use.

As it turns out, *anyone* can become a self-authenticating certificate authority. This could be helpful if your organization requires an isolated LAN in which certificate-based services are necessary, but all use of those services stays within that LAN, for example. To become part of the world-spanning infrastructure, however, those wanting to become

CAs must have their certificate implementations adopted by the major web browsers, which means getting their certificates bundled in with Edge, Firefox, Chrome, Safari, or Opera, for example. In fact, one of the key elements of these major vendor root certificate programs is that by becoming a root certificate member with them, your company adds significant value to that vendor's user community, while at the same time potentially holding that vendor's value hostage to the authenticity of your certificates and their use. CA applicants then have to go through rigorous technical demonstrations of their domains and their services. Each of those vendors has its own standards and processes to ensure that as a would-be CA, your company is not about to harm their reputation or the reputations or interests of their customers, partners, clients, and users worldwide.

What this all boils down to is that if you want to be an anchor of many trust chains, we, the rest of the Internet-using world, require that you prove your trustworthiness, your reliability, and your integrity to us. This may be why the four CAs with the largest market share between them are IdenTrust, Comodo, DigiCert, and GoDaddy, according to W3Techs surveys. In 2017, Google and Mozilla rejected Symantec's certificates from their browser bundles, citing numerous repeated violations of trust—including incorrect or unjustified issuance of more than 30,000 HTTPS certificates. Some of this involved issuing free "domain-validated" certificates, thought to be a great way to stimulate further small business development; in reality, it made it trivially easy for malicious sites to spring into action, typically with phishing attacks on unsuspecting targets. Prior to this, Symantec had been the market leader; that same year, DigiCert acquired Symantec.

The certificate validation process also demonstrates another important aspect of cybersecurity and cryptography that SSCPs must deal with every day: every system your organization uses is the result of an information technology supply chain, a chain that runs from designers and developers, through subsystems vendors and parts suppliers to end-user sales and service and finally to your own organization's technology support staff. Every step of that process is a potential opportunity for threats to find vulnerabilities and exploit them. In fact, one definition of an advance persistent threat is that it is an organization or entity that looks at as much of the IT supply chain as it possibly can, seeking points of entry or influence.

Web of Trust

In the world of public key cryptography, a *web of trust* is a network of trust relationships built and maintained by the users or members of that network. It exists without needing a central, single root certificate authority or one single anchor for all trust chains. In human terms, it's how our relationships work; we look to someone we already trust as the source of transitive trust when they introduce us to someone else. Supply chains and business relationships work this way. Small webs of trust can be quite powerful protection to those who participate in them, since almost no participant would want to risk being ejected from the web (via a revocation of trust) because they have vouched for an unreliable and untrustworthy person as a candidate for membership and participation in that web.

The original advocates of a web of trust concept, such as Phil Zimmerman, believed that the hierarchy of trust concept places far too much dependence upon the root CA process and the government, industrial, and business processes that authenticate CAs as trustworthy. All human organizations make mistakes in judgment; some of those mistakes can put an organization out of business or cause a government to fall. Then, too, governments have legitimate motivations regarding the survival of their own societies and institutions that naturally conflict with just the *idea* of allowing individual people, businesses, and organizations to have too many secrets that governments are not privy to.

The problem with web of trust architectures is that they still depend upon some kind of authentication of trustworthiness. In the current PGP web of trust, this has notably been performed by having *certificate-signing parties*, which as social occasions bring together many people who are willing to attest to the validity of the certificate in question. A software developer might host such a party (with or without cocktails and hors d'oeuvres), inviting key customers, wholesalers, resellers, and OEMs to join in a web-based assertion of authenticity. Practically speaking, it's not likely that a software giant could depend upon certificate-signing parties so that it has an authenticated certificate it can digitally sign its next release with. It's also hard to see how a major wholesaler and distributor, such as Ingram Micro, could do business in such a fashion.

Hierarchies of trust and webs of trust have one structural aspect in common, and that is the need to facilitate the flow of trust across subtrees or subnets in their hierarchies or webs. In the hierarchy model, the one root node CA delegates authority to issue certificates in its name to tiers of intermediate nodes, many of whom may also delegate downward. Users underneath one intermediate node who need to verify a certificate issued by some other intermediate node, in another subtree, need to depend upon the hierarchy's navigation features as their verification request flows up the forest, then back down to the right issuing node to be verified. Webs of trust have the same need to pass a verification request along until some node, somewhere, can verify it. These same subtree and subnet challenges make revocation of trust a management challenge as well.

One measure of the success or uptake of the web of trust concept is the size of the set of users who have connectivity with each other; that is, all users of this set participate in trust relationships with all other users. This *strong set* as it is called numbered about 55,000 people as of 2015. That's not a lot. There have been some analyses published as to why PGP and the web of trust failed to come into more widespread use, and their arguments may be relevant to whether your organization should consider web of trust concepts in its own operations (and use of cryptographic security solutions).

Cryptocurrencies demonstrate a blend of both trust concepts. Their reliance on widespread PKI reflects their reliance on the hierarchy of CAs to establish trustworthy digital signatures and the public/private key pairs that those require; but their very nature as a fully distributed ledger embodies and establishes a web of trust among their subscribers and users. It is this duality, in part, that leads some blockchain enthusiasts, advocates, researchers, and practitioners to suggest that perhaps we are on the edge of another change in the way the digital social compact works. We've seen one such change as what might be called the *PKI revolution* built onto the computer revolution, which brought personal information security powered by pervasive encryption to billions of users worldwide. Blockchain technologies arguably present a comparable disruption to the ways in which we assert and verify trustworthiness. "A Declaration of Independence: Toward a New Social Contract for the Digital Economy," by Don Tapscott, cofounder of the Blockchain Research Institute, may help inform your thinking as you help not only secure your organization against the next wave of disruptive ideas and technologies but help secure their readiness to take advantage of them; it can be found at
https://www.blockchainresearchinstitute.org/socialcontract/.

SUMMARY

You'll probably need to be more of a systems engineer, and less of a mathematician, to successfully apply cryptography as part of your overall approach to meeting your organization's information security needs. You'll need to have a firm grasp on the procedural aspects of encrypting and decrypting data to protect your data while it's in storage, in transit, and in use; you'll need to pay especially close attention to the step-by-step of keeping that data secure as it sees greater use in collaborative business processes involving partners and other outside organizations. Getting to know the algorithms and their important characteristics, even on just a by-name basis, starts to help you know which of these cryptographic tools to reach for as you look to solve real problems or address real needs.

As with so many other aspects of information security, how you manage and maintain your cryptographic infrastructure is as important as how you've selected and installed those cryptosystems for your end users to make use of. Cryptographic hygiene, as a subset of more overall information security hygiene, can focus your attention on these management challenges and may give you some leverage in strengthening and maturing your organization's current cryptographic management processes.

Cryptography can give your organization a competitive advantage; it can help you stay a few steps ahead of the adversaries that might otherwise find your systems easy to penetrate and easy to take advantage of. It provides a comprehensive suite of capabilities, each of which has many significant roles to play in improving the efficiency, reliability, integrity, and safety of your organization's business processes. It's becoming a mandatory part of many of these business processes, as a growing body of law, regulation, and compliance requirements demonstrates. It is not the answer to every information security challenge.

One final thought about cryptography: it can also be the edge you need to keep your company from becoming another infamous "crypto-fail" case study, where your organization ends up being the subject of blogs, articles, and government inquiry reports for years to come.

Cryptography: it's more than just a growth industry. It's gone from being the stuff of secrets and spies to one of the fundamental drivers of change in our modern world.

And that modern world needs more people like you who can successfully apply it, as part of keeping their organization's information, systems, and processes safe.

Network and Communications Security

SECURING YOUR ORGANIZATION'S INTERNAL networks and its use of the Internet is a difficult and challenging task, and that's a major part of what this chapter will help you with. From its review of the fundamental architecture of the Internet, it will examine the commonly used protocols and services, always with an eye to the security issues involved. You'll be challenged to switch from your white-hat network defender perspective and take up the point of view of your attackers throughout.

But we as white hats must also grapple with the *convergence* of communications and computing technologies. People, their devices, and their ways of doing business no longer accept old-fashioned boundaries that used to exist between voice, video, TXT and SMS, data, or a myriad of other computer-enabled information services. This convergence transforms what we trust when we communicate and how we achieve that trust. As SSCPs, we need to know how to gauge the trustworthiness of a particular communications system, keep it operating at the required level of trust, and improve that trustworthiness if that's what our stakeholders need. Let's look in more detail at how communications security can be achieved and, based on that, get into the details of securing the network-based elements of our communications systems.

To do this, we'll be using the more comprehensive CIANA+PS mnemonic, as a way to keep all of these separate but related security concerns fresh in our minds. We'll also have to address the growing need for network security to achieve the information privacy and safety needs of the organization. This is just one way you'll start thinking in terms of protocol stacks—as system descriptors, as road maps for diagnosing problems, and as models of the threat and risk landscape.

UNDERSTAND AND APPLY FUNDAMENTAL CONCEPTS OF NETWORKING

As with most everything else in our digital world, a set of published standards define the layers upon layers by which we go from physical wires or radio waves to web-based, cloud-hosted services. This layered approach provides inherent scalability, versatility, and adaptability. Complete new sets of functional, physical, or performance requirements—including network and information security—can be added on either by adding new protocols and services at the right layers or by modifying existing ones to fix problems or implement new features. This helps the Internet architecture have a high degree of backward compatibility—not every computer attached to the Internet has to upgrade to a new version of a protocol, or even a wholly new internetworking model, at the same time. (With hundreds of billions of devices currently connected to the Internet, that could be a daunting if not impossible change management challenge.)

Layers of abstraction provide the mental agility that powers the frameworks we use to design, build, use, and secure our computer networks. We take a set of ideas, and we wrap them in a larger, more general, or more abstract concept; we give that concept a catchy name, and then we use that name as part of specifying, building, and testing the processes that use that "black box" along with many others to build up a system that does something purposeful. As a simple example, think about placing a phone call to a family member: you require that the call go to the right person (well, to their phone handset or device); you do *not* care about the details of how the phone companies make that call happen. You *abstract away* the details of signaling and switching systems, analog to digital voice (and video) conversion, compression, and all the rest of what makes that bit of infrastructure just plain *work* when you want it and need it.

As information systems security professionals and as digital natives of one kind or another, we've got a number of such stacks of layers of abstraction to deal with when it comes to computer networking.

- ISO's Open Systems Interconnect Reference Model, which goes from the Physical layer to the Application layer

- IETF's Transmission Control Protocol over Internet Protocol (TCP/IP) standard, which goes from the Physical layer to the Transport layer

- Design paradigms involving data, control, and management planes, which logically separate our views of these distinctly different but interrelated information flows through and over our networks

Many network and systems professionals use a variety of names to refer to one or both of these protocol stacks, and sometimes even confuse one with the other. For the sake of clarity, it's best to refer to ISO's model as the OSI Seven-Layer Reference Model (a proper name which differentiates it from other open systems interconnection models published by ISO); then, use TCP/IP to refer to the IETF's four-layer protocol standard. Both of these are called *protocol stacks* because as you build an implementation of them, you build the lowest-level functions first and then layer the next set onto that foundation; similarly, as you execute a function at a higher level, it has to request services from protocols further down the stack at lower levels (all the way down to the physical transmission of the signals themselves).

Many network engineers and technicians may thoroughly understand the TCP/IP model since they use it every day, but they have little or no understanding of the OSI Seven-Layer Reference Model. They often see it as too abstract or too conceptual to have any real utility in the day-to-day world of network administration or network security. Nothing could be further from the truth. As you'll see, the OSI's top three levels provide powerful ways for you to think about information systems security, beyond just keeping the networks secure. In fact, many of the most troublesome information security threats that SSCPs must deal with occur at the upper layers of the OSI Seven Layer Reference Model—beyond the scope of what TCP/IP concerns itself with. As an SSCP, you need a solid understanding of how TCP/IP works—how its protocols for device and port addressing and mapping, routing, and delivery, and network management all play together. You will also need an equally thorough understanding of the OSI Seven Layer Reference Model, how it contrasts with TCP/IP, and what happens in its top three layers. Taken together, these two protocols provide the infrastructure of all of our communications and computing systems. Understanding them is the key to understanding why and how networks can be vulnerable—and provides the clues you need to choose the best ways to secure those networks.

That third set of perspectives is also important to keep in mind and use alongside your OSI and TCP/IP thought models. At one level it might seem too abstract to reduce all computer networking to the three broad functions of handling data, controlling its flow, and managing the devices and the networks themselves. Yet this is how the actual devices themselves are designed and built and how the software stacks that implement these protocols are designed, coded, and work with each other. This viewpoint starts internally to every hardware device on our networks, as each device must receive a stream of 1s and 0s and sort them out into groups that convey their meaning as control functions, as management directives, or as data to process. Economy of function dictates that separate logical elements (in hardware and software) take on these logically distinct tasks.

One final set of layers to keep in mind—always—is that every function that makes our networks possible depends upon physical, logical, and administrative actions, processes, and control parameters used by them. That's four sets of frameworks, protocol stacks, or perspectives, all cross-cutting and interconnected, assisting and interfering with each other at the same time.

Complementary, Not Competing, Frameworks

Both the TCP/IP protocol stack and the OSI Seven Layer Reference Model grew out of efforts in the 1960s and 1970s to continue to evolve and expand both the capabilities of computer networks and their usefulness. *Transmission Control Protocol over Internet Protocol (TCP/IP)* was developed during the 1970s, based on original ARPANET protocols and a variety of competing (and in some cases conflicting) systems developed in private industry and in other countries. From 1978 to 1992, these ideas were merged together to become the published TCP/IP standard; ARPANET was officially migrated to this standard on January 1, 1993; since this protocol became known as "the Internet protocol," that date is as good a date to declare as the "birth of the Internet" as any. TCP/IP is defined as consisting of four basic layers. (You'll learn why that "over" is in the name in a moment.)

The decade of the 1970s also saw two different international organizations, the International Organization for Standardization (ISO) and the International Telegraph and Telephone Consultative Committee (CCITT), working on ways to expand the TCP/IP protocol stack to embrace higher-level functions that business, industry, and government felt were needed. By 1984, this led to the publication of the International Telecommunications Union (ITU, the renamed CCITT) Standard X.200 and ISO Standard 7498.

This new standard had two major components, and here is where some of the confusion among network engineers and IT professionals begins. The first component was the Basic Reference Model, which is an abstract (or conceptual) model of what computer networking is and how it works. This became known as the *Open Systems Interconnection (OSI) Reference Model*, sometimes known as the seven-layer OSI model or just the seven-layer network model. Since ISO subsequently developed more reference models in the open systems interconnection family, it's preferable to refer to this one as the OSI Seven Layer Reference Model to avoid confusion. This way, the name represents first the family of models (OSI), then the layers of network protocols used in that family. The other major component was a whole series of highly detailed technical standards.

In many respects, both TCP/IP and the OSI Seven-LayerReference Model largely agree on what happens in the first four layers of their model. But while TCP/IP doesn't address how things get done beyond its top layer, the OSI Reference Model does. Its three top layers are all dealing with information stored in computers as bits and bytes, representing both the data that needs to be sent over the network and the addressing and control information needed to make that happen. The bottommost layer has to transform computer representations of data and control into the actual signaling needed to transmit and receive across the network. (We'll look at each layer in greater depth in subsequent sections as we examine their potential vulnerabilities.)

✔ **Why Master Both Frameworks?**

While it's true that systems vendors, security professionals, network engineers, systems administrators, and the trade press all talk in terms of both the OSI 7-layer model and the TCP/IP protocol stack, the number-one best reason to know them both is *because your enemies know them better!*

Amateur attackers and the crews developing the kill chains that APTs will use to take down your systems know these frameworks inside and out. They study them; they model them; they build target and attack systems using them; they customize and reverse-engineer and hack out their own implementations of them.

Don't let your adversaries keep that monopoly of knowledge.

OSI and TCP/IP Models

All three of these sets of concepts—the two protocol stacks and the set of *planes* (data, control, and management)—have a number of important operational concepts in common. Let's first review these before diving into the details of how each protocol stack or the planes use these concepts to help you meet your needs. These common concepts include the following:

- **Datagrams** are groups of individual data symbols, such as bits or bytes, that are treated as one unit by a protocol.

- **Protocols** define the functions to be performed, the interfaces for requesting these functions as services, and the input, output, error, and control interfaces associated with using that protocol. (These will be discussed in detail in the "Commonly Used Ports and Protocols" section.)

- **Handshakes** provide a lower-level coordination and control function; most protocols define a set of handshakes for their use.

- **Packets and encapsulation** are how datagrams are packaged with routing and control information needed by the next layer of the protocol stack so that it can accommodate the requested function or routing.

- **Addressing, routing, and switching** functions provide ways for endpoints and users to identify themselves to the network, direct the flow of information to other endpoints by specifying logical or symbolic addresses, and specify how the network maps these symbolic addresses to specific network hardware and software elements.

- **Network segmentation** provides ways to logically and physically break up a large network into smaller subnetworks, providing some degree of isolation of subnets from each other, in order to better manage, provision, control, and protect the Internet and each subnet.

- **Uniform resource locators (URLs)** provide the symbolic addressing of files (or of content within those files) and the protocols that allow users and endpoints to access those files, information, or services. These resources can be on the Internet, on a local intranet, or even on a single system (such as links to elements of documents in the same directory subtree).

Each of the concepts discussed in the preceding list embodies its own layers of abstraction.

A protocol stack is a document—a set of ideas or design standards. Designers and builders *implement* the protocol stack into the right set of hardware, software, and procedural tasks (done by people or others). These implementations present the features of the protocol stack as *services* that can be requested by subjects (people or software tasks).

All computer networking protocol stacks provide well-defined processes for managing and controlling the sending and receiving of data. Both TCP/IP and the OSI Seven-Layer Reference Model refer to groups of data values as a *datagram*; just what a datagram *is* depends in large part on what layer of the protocol stack it is making use of in its journey across the network.

Datagrams and Protocol Data Units

First, let's introduce the concept of a datagram, which is a common term when talking about communications and network protocols. A *datagram* is the unit of information used by a protocol layer or a function within it. It's the unit of measure of information in each individual transfer. Each layer of the protocol stacks takes the datagram it receives from the layers above it and repackages it as necessary to achieve the desired results. Sending a message via flashlights (or an Aldiss lamp, for those of the sea services) illustrates the datagram concept:

- An on/off flash of the light, or a flash of a different duration, is one bit's worth of information; the datagrams at the lamp level are bits.

- If the message being sent is encoded in Morse code, then that code dictates a sequence of short and long pulses for each datagram that represents a letter, digit, or other symbol.

- Higher layers in the protocol would then define sequences of handshakes to verify sender and receiver, indicate what kind of data is about to be sent, and specify how to acknowledge or request retransmission. Each of those sequences might have one or more message in it, and each of those messages would be a datagram at that level of the protocol.

- Finally, the captain of one of those two ships dictated a particular message to be sent to the other ship, and *that* message, captain-to-captain, is itself a datagram.

Note, however, another usage of this word. The User Datagram Protocol (UDP) is an alternate data communications protocol to Transmission Control Protocol, and both of these are at the same level (layer 3, Internetworking) of the TCP/IP stack. And to add to the terminological confusion, the OSI Reference Model (as you'll see in a moment) uses a protocol data unit (PDU) to refer to the unit of measure of the data sent in a single protocol unit and datagram to UDP. Be careful not to confuse UDP and PDU!

Table 6.1 may help you avoid some of this confusion by placing the OSI and TCP/IP stacks and their datagram naming conventions side by side. We'll examine each layer in greater detail in a few moments.

TABLE 6.1 OSI and TCP/IP Datagram Naming

TYPES OF LAYERS	TYPICAL PROTOCOLS	OSI LAYER	OSI PROTOCOL DATA UNIT NAME	TCP/IP LAYER	TCP/IP DATAGRAM NAME
Host layers	HTTP, HTTPS, SMTP, IMAP, SNMP, POP3, FTP, and so on	7. Application	Data	*(Outside of TCP/ IP model scope)*	Data
	Characters, MPEG, SSL/ TLS, Compression, S/ MIME, and so on	6. Presentation			
	NetBIOS, SAP, Session handshaking connections	5. Session			
	TCP, UDP	4. Transport	Segment, except UDP Datagram	Transport	Segment

CONTINUES

TYPES OF LAYERS	TYPICAL PROTOCOLS	OSI LAYER	OSI PROTOCOL DATA UNIT NAME	TCP/IP LAYER	TCP/IP DATAGRAM NAME
Media layers	IPv4 / IPv6 IP address, ICMP, IPsec, ARP, MPLS, and so on	3. Network	Packet	Network (or Internet-working)	Packet
	Ethernet, 802.1, PPP, ATM, Fibre Channel, FDDI, MAC Address	2. Link	Frame	Data Link	Frame
	Cables, Connectors, 10BaseT, 802.11x, ISDN, T1, and so on	1. Physical	Symbol	Physical	Bits

Handshakes

In signaling and control systems terms, a *handshake* is a defined set of message exchanges between two elements that initiates, coordinates, and performs some function or service involving the two elements. It's a sequence of small, simple communications that we send and receive, such as hello and goodbye, ask and reply, or acknowledge or not-acknowledge, which control and carry out the communications we need. Handshakes are defined in the protocols we agree to use. Let's look at a simple file transfer to a server that I want to do via File Transfer Protocol (FTP)[1] to illustrate this:

1. I ask my laptop (by interacting with its operating system) to run the file transfer client app.

2. Now that it's running, my FTP client app asks the OS to connect to the FTP server.

3. The FTP server accepts my FTP client's connection request.

4. My FTP client requests to upload a file to a designated folder in the directory tree on that server.

5. The FTP server accepts the request and says "start sending" to my FTP client.

6. My client sends a chunk of data to the server; the server acknowledges receipt, or it requests a retransmission if it encounters an error.

7. My client signals the server that the file has been fully uploaded and asks the server to mark the received file as closed, updating its directories to reflect this new file.

[1] It's interesting to note that the Internet was first created to facilitate things like simple file transfers between computer centers; email was created as a higher-level protocol that used FTP to send and receive small files that were the email notes themselves.

8. My client informs me of successfully completing the upload.

9. With no more files to transfer, I exit the FTP app.

This sequence of steps is akin to a *business process*—it's designed to accomplish a specific logical function, and implicit in its flow are the handshakes that invoke lower-level functions or support services, pass data and control information to and from those services, and detect and handle any errors or exceptions involved in performing those services. Step 2, for example, may have to initiate both a physical and logical connection to the Internet via my laptop's Wi-Fi device, the Wi-Fi router/modem provided by my Internet service provider (ISP), and the ISP's connectivity to the Internet itself. Step 2 also has to perform any required connections with the FTP server, which might include authenticating me as a legitimate user, my laptop as an authorized device, and even the IP address or region I'm connecting from as an approved remote login locale. Each of those activities involves multiple sets of handshakes. The *physical* connections handle the electronic (or electro-optical) signaling that the devices themselves need to communicate with each other. The *logical* connections are how the right pair of endpoints—the user NIC and the server or other endpoint NIC—get connected with each other, rather than with some other device "out there" in the wilds of the Internet. This happens through *address resolution* and *name resolution*, which I'll cover in more detail in the "Addressing, Routing and Switching Concepts" section.

Packets and Encapsulation

Note in that FTP example earlier how the file I uploaded was broken into a series of chunks, or *packets*, rather than sent in one contiguous block of data. Each packet is sent across the Internet by itself (wrapped in header and trailer information that identifies the sender, recipient, and other important information). Breaking a large file into packets allows smarter trade-offs between actual throughput rate and error rates and recovery strategies. (Rather than resend the entire file because line noise corrupted one or two bytes, we might need to resend just the one corrupted packet.) However, since sending each packet requires a certain amount of handshake overhead to package, address, route, send, receive, unpack, and acknowledge, the smaller the packet size, the less efficient the overall communications system can be.

Sending a file by breaking it up into packets has an interesting consequence: if each packet has a unique serial number as part of its header, as long as the receiving application can put the packets back together in the proper order, we don't need to care what order they are sent in or arrive in. If the receiver requested a retransmission of packet number 41, it can still receive and process packet 42, or even several more, while waiting for the sender to retransmit it.

Right away we see a key feature of packet-based communications systems: we have to add information to each packet in order to tell both the recipient *and* the next layer in the protocol stack what to do with it! In our FTP example earlier, we start by breaking the file up into fixed-length chunks, or packets, of data—but we've got to wrap them with data that says where it's from, where it's going, and the packet sequence number. That data goes in a header (data preceding the actual segment data itself), and new end-to-end error correcting checksums are put into a new trailer. This creates a new datagram at this level of the protocol stack. That new, *longer* datagram is given to the first layer of the protocol stack. That layer probably has to do something to it; that means it will encapsulate the datagram it was given by adding another header and trailer. At the receiver, each layer of the protocol unwraps the datagram it receives from the lower layer (by processing the information in *its* header and trailer, and then removing them) and passes this *shorter* datagram up to the next layer. Sometimes, the datagram from a higher layer in a protocol stack will be referred to as the *payload* for the next layer down. Figure 6.1 shows this in action.

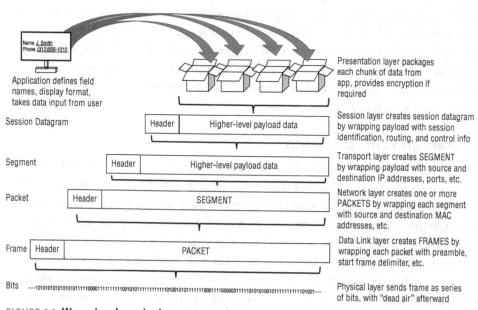

FIGURE 6.1 Wrapping: layer-by-layer encapsulation

The flow of wrapping, as shown in Figure 6.1, illustrates how a higher-layer protocol *logically* communicates with its opposite number in another system by having to first wrap and pass its datagrams to lower-layer protocols in its own stack. It's not until at the physical layer connections that signals actually move from one system to another. (Note that this even holds true for two virtual machines talking to each other over a software-defined network that connects them, even if they're running on the same bare-metal host!) In OSI Seven-Layer Reference Model terminology, this means that layer N of the

…U) it receives from layer N+1, processes and wraps it
…ter to produce the datagram at its layer, and passes
…n the stack.

…like, layer by layer, in the upcoming sections.

…witching Concepts

…ne, VoIP, web surfing, broadcast TV and radio, or
…ystems, they all have a common job to do and reflect
…level of abstraction, any communications system
must be able to:

- connect users and processes to each other and to the resources that they need to use, modify, or create to each other

- by making logical connections between services

- to endpoint devices that those users and processes can connect to and use

- and then terminate that logical service-to-service connection when the users no longer need it.

We see this in action every day. You use your smartphone to call your family; I use my laptop to access my bank account. The connections I use only need to be in service while I am using them; in fact, if the communications system needs to dynamically reroute that connection *during* the time I'm using it (or while you are speaking to your spouse or children), so long as the quality of the service I enjoy is not affected, I don't care. When you or I place a call, we usually have our device look up the name of the party we want to connect with and *resolve* that into a set of information that tells the routing and switching systems what endpoint device we want to connect with (assuming that the party to whom we wish to speak is collocated with that endpoint device, of course). This is *name resolution* in simple, human terms. As users, we don't care how the call is routed or what switching operations have to take place to make that happen.

In simple terms:

- *Name resolution* maps the name of an end user, service, or resource into a set of address information, which reflects the nature and design of the communications system being used. (Postal communications need mailing or physical addresses, phone systems need phone numbers, and TCP/IP traffic needs IP addresses.) Names are symbols, and typically the name of a person, device, resource, or service does not change throughout its lifetime unless there really is a fundamental change of the nature or identity of whom or what the name is linked to. (You get married and take your spouse's surname as yours; you are still you, and yet you are declaring you are *more* than "just" you in taking their name as part of your own.

Of course, not all cultures have this same tradition.) Names
people to remember and recall than their corresponding addre

- *Addresses* associated with a name may change quite frequently: my
  address (which is effectively its *name*) doesn't change when I travel fro
  work, but its IP address will change many times along that journey. Name
  tion, therefore, has to map my phone's MAC address to its *current* IP address,
  Internet session is to take place.

- *Routing* uses the address information for the users, services, or resources that need
  to communicate with each other to establish a pathway through the communications system, over which their information will be sent back and forth across.
  Routes may be predetermined, be determined once and kept static throughout
  a communications session, or be dynamically set up during a session. (Think of
  postal workers delivering the mail despite a road being blocked by trees damaged
  by a storm.)

- *Switching* provides the communications system itself with ways to identify alternate routes within its system, support efficient use of systems elements, support
  system or element maintenance, and provide alternate routing in the event of
  outages.

Let's look at addressing and routing with another generalization: with the exception of simple point-to-point systems using dedicated communication paths, you can
say that all communications systems use an underlying mesh network that connects
multiple devices. Some of these devices are endpoints, and some of them are network
routing, switching, and control devices. This mesh of connectedness allows the builders and owners of the system to increase the geographic or logical reach and span of
the system and bring on additional end users to meet their business needs. Most of
that network is common use; only an individual endpoint device and its connection to
the nearest switching and routing device on the mesh are dedicated to an individual
end user (or set of users and processes that share that endpoint). Because of our roots
in twisted-pair copper wire telephone systems, this connection from the last switching
node out to the end user's *point of presence* is often called *the last mile* regardless of
how long or short the length of the cable really is (or whether it's measured in Impe-
rial or metric units).

Wired communications systems (often known as *land-line* systems) depend upon the
network to be able to translate a logical device address into the commands to their switch-
gear to set up the connection to the proper pair of wires to the requested endpoint device.
This is true whether the endpoint is a telephone or a router/modem device. In phone
systems, it's the telephone number that is used to route the call; for Internet traffic, several different layers of address information are involved. At the lowest level is the *media*

access control or MAC address, associated with a specific network interface card (NIC) or NIC-equivalent circuit in a smartphone or other device. The MAC address is normally assigned by the device manufacturer and must be unique to ensure correct routing. The next layer up the protocol stacks deal with Internet Protocol (IP) addresses, which will often have a port number associated with them, to correctly connect software processes at both ends of the connection to each other. (This keeps your HTTPS sessions from getting into the middle of a VoIP call, for example.) Protocols dictate how MAC addresses get translated into IP addresses, how IP addresses are assigned (statically or dynamically) and how ports and services provided by other protocols are associated with each other, as you'll see later in this chapter.

Addressing is actually two protocols in one: it's the way we assign an address to an entity (a person, a mailbox, an apartment building, or a NIC), and it's the rules and data we use to translate or *resolve* one kind of address into another. Let's take a closer look at this by bringing in some TCP/IP (or OSI Seven-Layer) specifics.

Name Resolution in TCP/IP

The Internet Corporation for Assigned Numbers and Names (ICANN), the Internet Assigned Numbers Authority (IANA), and the six regional Internet registries (RIRs) manage the overall processes for assigning IP addresses, registering domain names, and resolving disputes about names and numbers. The RIRs manage the local Internet registries (LIR) in their allocation of IP addresses and domain names to customers in their regions. ISPs typically function as LIRs. In network systems, name resolution most often refers to resolving a host name into its corresponding IP address. The Domain Name System (DNS) was established to provide a worldwide, hierarchical, distributed directory system and the services that support this. RFCs 1034 and 1035 established the structure of the domain name space and naming conventions, giving us the familiar names which we use in email and web crawling. RFCs 1123, 2181, and 5892 specify the definitive rules for fully qualified domain names (FQDNs) such as www.bbc.co.uk, which consist of various *labels* separated by periods (or "dots" as people read them aloud). In this example, *bbc* is the host name, and *co.uk* is the top-level domain, indicating a commercial organization in the United Kingdom. As you move dot by dot to the left in a name, you move from domains (.com, .edu) through *subdomains*. Finally, you get to the leftmost label, in this example *www*. This is the *host* name.

A corresponding authoritative domain nameserver handles each layer of this process. This is shown in Figure 6.2, using www.wikipedia.org as an example FQDN. Without multiple levels of caching, this would quickly become a performance nightmare. DNS caches exist at the local machine level, or at various intermediate resolver hosts, to help provide faster name resolution and better traffic management.

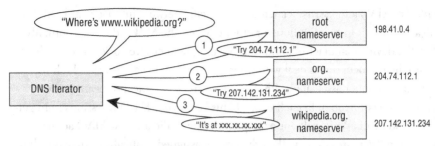

FIGURE 6.2 **DNS resolver in action**

DNS as a protocol uses UDP to communicate between its various nameservers and clients requesting name resolution services. Figure 6.3 shows how an individual application program may have its own local cache; if this does not successfully resolve a name (or a reverse name lookup), lookup next attempts to use the host operating system's cache and then that provided by the ISP. The ISP, in turn, may have to refer to other DNS name resolvers it knows about.

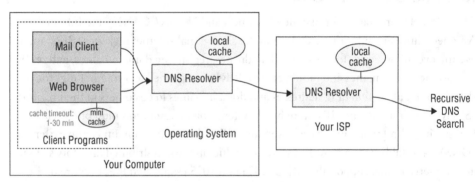

FIGURE 6.3 **DNS caching**

Name resolution query and test tools help administrators and users identify the source of traffic (genuine or suspicious) by providing easy web-based lookup capabilities. The authoritative tool is at `https://whois.icann.org` and is supported in multiple languages there. This is a forward resolver—domain name to IP address. Other *whois* functions hosted by web hosting companies will allow either a domain name or an IP address to be entered (thus doing a reverse name lookup). Note that multiple FQDNs may be associated with a single IP address.

NOTE   In Windows client environments, NetBIOS names may also be in use, which are used to support server message block (SMB) exchanges between systems as part of file and print service sharing. (SMB was previously known as Common Internet File System [CIFS].) Up to four different steps may be necessary for Windows to resolve a NetBIOS name. Windows also allows an IP host name to be substituted in SMB traffic for NetBIOS names, which can make it doubly difficult to diagnose why some devices, services, and applications are sharing and working together and others are not in a Windows networking environment.

DNS Security Extensions

As with much of the original Internet's design and implementation, DNS was not developed with security in mind. It became glaringly apparent, however, that extensions to DNS would have to be introduced to cope with the various threats that DNS faces. RFC 3833 detailed some of these threats, such as DNS cache poisoning, and established the basic DNS Security Extensions (DNSSEC). These extensions provide for authentication of DNS-stored data, but *not* its confidentiality, since the DNS must function as a publicly available but thoroughly reliable and *authoritative* source of information. DNSSEC can provide this level of authentication protection for more than just names and IP addresses, however, such as certificate records, SSH fingerprints, TLS trust anchors (TLSA), and public encryption keys (via IPsec).

In an interview in 2009,[2] Dan Kaminski commented on the reasons that widespread adoption of DNSSEC seemed to be hampered.

- No readily available backward-compatible standard that would be scalable to the entire Internet

- Disagreement between various implementations over ownership and control of top-level domain root keys

- Perceived complexity of DNSSEC

Since then, vendors, the IETF, and the RIRs have continued to look at threat mitigations and at ways to make DNSSEC more scalable and easier to implement. In 2018, the Réseaux IP Européens Network Coordination Centre (RIPE NCC), which serves Europe, Central Asia, Russia, and West Asia, posted its analysis of whether DNS over TLS (DoT, not to be confused with the U.S. Department of Transportation) or DNS-based Authentication of Named Entities (DANE) might mean that DNSSEC isn't as important to the overall security of the Internet as it was first believed to be.[3] The original vulnerabilities remain; the need for widespread if not universal use of effective and reliable countermeasures is just as urgent. It just may be, says RIPE NCC, that there may be other approaches worth considering.

[2] Michael Mimoso, TechTearget SearchSecurity, 25 June 2009.
`https://searchsecurity.techtarget.com/news/1360143/`
`Kaminsky-interview-DNSSEC-addresses-cross-organizational-trust-and-security`

[3] Willem Toorop, 23 Aug 2018. `https://labs.ripe.net/Members/willem_toorop/`
`sunrise-dns-over-tls-sunset-dnssec`

Address Resolution

Address resolution is the set of services, functions, and protocols that take one type of address and translate it or *resolve* it into another type of address. Phone numbers are resolved into last-mile wiring pair designators and connection points, IP addresses are resolved into MAC addresses, URLs are resolved into IP addresses, and so on. This usually involves lookup tables, but for sizable networks, it's more efficient to break these lookup tables into highly localized ones so that local changes can be updated quickly and easily. Address resolution is a simple process: my endpoint merely asks the mesh connection point (my "Internet on-ramp" so to speak) if it knows how to resolve the address I have, such as an IP address, into a MAC address. If it does, it gives me the resolved MAC address. If it does not, it asks all the other mesh points it is connected with to try to resolve the address for me. Eventually, the last-mile mesh connection point that services the endpoint that the IP address is assigned to provides an answer back, which trickles back, path by path, through the nodes that were asking for it and finally back to my endpoint device. If no mesh points know where that IP address is located (that is, what IP address corresponds to it), then I get an address not found error (or the address resolution request times out unsatisfied).

Routing

Address resolution is akin to knowing where your friend lives; routing is knowing how to give driving or walking directions from where you are to that friend's place of abode. Routing takes into account both the reasonably permanent nature of the transportation systems (the roads, bus lines, sidewalks, and so on) as well as the temporary ones like traffic congestion and weather. Google Maps, for example, presents users with options to avoid high-congestion routes, choose scenic journeys, walk, or take public transportation (if these options exist for a particular journey of point A to point B). Communications systems are designed to provide three different possible routing capabilities.

■ *Dynamically routed connections* depend upon the mesh choosing the right best path, moment by moment, across the network in order to provide the required service. Traffic congestion or signal quality problems detected by one node might dictate that better service quality or throughput can be had by routing the *next* packet to a different node. This ability to choose alternate routes enables networks to be *self-annealing*, meaning that they can automatically work around a broken connection or a failed node in the network. (At most, the endpoints directly affected by that failed node or connection suffer a loss of service.)

   In TCP/IP systems, routing is performed by a set of routers working together in an *autonomous system* (AS, also known as a *routing domain*) to provide routing services across a larger area or region. Routers in that AS that are connected to other network elements outside the AS are on the *exterior* or are known as *edge* routers; those that only connect to other member routers in the AS are *interior* routers. These routers use routing protocols that are generally classified into three groups, based on their purpose (interior or exterior gateway), behavior (classful or classless), and operation (distance-vector, path-vector, or link-state protocol). Figure 6.4 shows the most frequently encountered dynamic routing protocols arranged in a family tree to illustrate these concepts. Note that RIPv1, RIPv2, and IGRP are considered legacy or are obsolete.

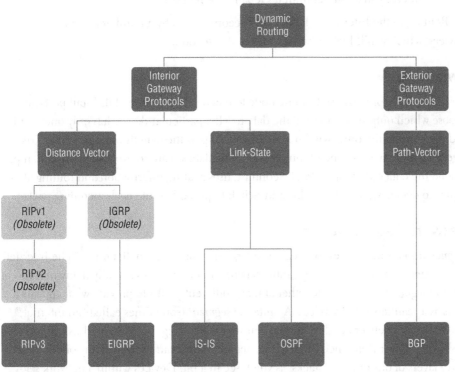

FIGURE 6.4 **Dynamic routing protocols family tree**

- *Static routing for connections* identifies each step in the path, from endpoint to endpoint, and then preserves that route in a table for use as the connection is established and used. Early telephone and data network operators could identify "hops" (the connection between two nodes and the nodes themselves) that had measurably higher availability, bandwidth, signal quality, or other aspects that affected overall quality of service (QoS); customers who needed such quality were offered the opportunity to pay for it. If circuits between nodes on a static route failed, or nodes themselves failed, then the "guaranteed" connection failed too. By the 1980s, most of the long-haul communications providers had quietly substituted dynamic routing underneath their "static" connections, albeit with some additional logic to attempt to preserve required QoS. Gradually, the network operators saw the business case for improving the QoS across most of their network, which almost completely did away with static routing as a useful premium service.

- *Hardwired* or *dedicated connections* are typified by the last mile of twisted pair, fiber optic, or coax cable that comes from the network to the service user's point of presence connection. Only those users at your endpoint (in your home or business) can use that connection. If it fails (or you sever it while digging in your garden), you're off net until it's repaired or replaced.

Routing in the Internet is defined and accomplished by a number of protocols and services, which you'll look at further later in this section.

Switching

Switching is the process used by one node to receive data on one of its input ports and choose which output port to send the data to. (If a particular device has only one input and one output, the only switching it can do is to pass the data through or deny it passage.) A simple switch depends on the incoming data stream to explicitly state which path to send the data out on; a router, by contrast, uses routing information and routing algorithms to decide what to tell its built-in switch to properly route each incoming packet.

Network Segmentation

Segmentation is the process of breaking a large network into smaller ones. "The Internet" (capitalized) acts as if it is one gigantic network, but it's not. It's actually many millions of *internet segments* that come together at many different points to provide what appears to users as a seamless set of services. An *internet segment* (sometimes called "an internet," lowercase) is a network of devices that communicate using TCP/IP and thus support the OSI Seven-Layer Reference Model. This segmentation can happen at any of the three lower layers of our protocol stacks, as you'll see in a bit. Devices within a network segment can communicate with each other, but which layer the segments connect on and what kind of device implements that connection can restrict the "outside world" to seeing the connection device (such as a router) and not the nodes on the subnet below it.

Segmentation of a large internet into multiple, smaller network segments provides a number of practical benefits, which affect that choice of how to join segments and at which layer of the protocol stack. The switch or router that runs the segment and its connection with the next higher segment are two single points of failure for the segment. If the device fails or the cable is damaged, no device on that segment can communicate with the other devices or the outside world. This can also help isolate other segments from failure of routers or switches, cables, or errors (or attacks) that are flooding a segment with traffic.

In the last decade, segmentation of an organization's networks for security, load balancing, and performance has increased in importance and visibility. In particular, segmentation to achieve a *zero-trust architecture* provides internal firewalls to monitor attempts by subjects in one part of the organization (and its network) to access information resources in other parts of the system. Zero-trust designs are often used in conjunction with very fine-grained attribute-based access control solutions in order to attain the desired degree of information security.

Subnets are different than network segments. We'll take a deep dive into the fine art of *subnetting* after we've looked at the overall protocol stacks, in the "IPv4 Addresses, DHCP, and Subnets" section.

URLs and the Web

In 1990, Tim Berners-Lee, a researcher at CERN in Switzerland, confronted the problem that CERN was having: they could not find and use what they already knew or discovered, because they could not effectively keep track of everything they wrote and where they put it. CERN was drowning in its own data. Berners-Lee wanted to take the much older idea of a hyperlinked or hypertext-based document one step further. Instead of just having links to points within the document, he wanted to have documents be able to point to other documents anywhere on the Internet. This required that several new ingredients be added to the Internet.

- A unique way of naming a document that included where it could be found on the Internet, which came to be called a *locator*
- Ways to embed those unique names into another document, where the document's creator wanted the *links* to be (rather than just in a list at the end, for example)
- A means of identifying a computer on the Internet as one that stored such documents and would make them available as a service
- Directory systems and tools that could collect the addresses or names of those document servers
- Keyword search capabilities that could identify what documents on a server contained which keywords
- Applications that an individual user could run that could query multiple servers to see if they had documents that the user might want, and then present those documents to the user to view, download, or use in other ways
- Protocols that could tie all of those moving parts together in sensible, scalable, and maintainable ways

By 1991, new words entered our vernacular: *web page*, *Hypertext Transfer Protocol* (*HTTP*), *web browser*, *web crawler*, and *URL*, to name a few. Today, all of that has become so commonplace, so ubiquitous, that it's easy to overlook just how many powerfully innovative ideas had to come together all at once. Knowing when to use the right *uniform resource locators (URLs)* became more important than understanding IP addresses. URLs provide an unambiguous way to identify a protocol, a server on the network, and a specific asset on that server. Additionally, a URL as a command line can contain values to be passed as variables to a process running on the server. By 1998, the business of growing and regulating both IP addresses and domain names grew to the point that a new non-profit, nongovernmental organization was created, the Internet Corporation for Assigned Names and Numbers (ICANN, pronounced "eye-can").

The rapid acceptance of the World Wide Web and the HTTP concepts and protocols that empowered it demonstrates a vital idea: the layered, keep-it-simple approach embodied in the TCP/IP protocol stack and the OSI Seven-Layer Reference Model *work*. Those stacks give us a strong but simple foundation on which we can build virtually any information service we can imagine.

OSI Reference Model

ISO's OSI Seven-Layer Reference Model is a conceptual model made up of seven layers that describes information flow from one computing asset to another over a network. Each layer of the this Reference Model performs or facilitates a specific network function. The layers are arranged in the bottom (most concrete or physical) to top (most abstract) order, as shown in Figure 6.5.

LAYER	DESCRIPTION	PROTOCOL DATA UNIT (PDU)	Applied Use
Application	— Coding and conversion functions on application layer data — Ensures information sent from one system's application layer is readable at destination system's application layer	Data	HTTP, HTTPS, DICOM, LDAP, MIME, SMTP, FTP, SFTP
Presentation	— Establishes, manages, and terminates communication sessions between presentation layer entities — Communication sessions consist of service requests and service responses between applications on different network devices	Data	In many references, no distinction between Presentation and Application layer protocols & TLS, SSL
Session	— Session management capabilities between hosts — Assists in synchronization, dialog control, and critical operation management — Remembers session information like password verification so a host does not have to repeatedly supply credentials on subsequent access requests	Data	RPC, SMB, SSH, NFS, NetBIOS, H.245, PAP, PPTP, SCP, ZIP
Transport	— Reliable internetwork data transport services transparent to upper layers — Functions include flow control, multiplexing, virtual circuit management, and error checking and recovery	Segment	TCP, UDP, BGP, DCCP, FCP, RDP
Network	— Provides routing and related functions that enable multiple data links to be combined into an internetwork — Uses logical addressing versus physical addressing of devices	Packet	ATM, Routers, IP, IPSec, ICMP, OPSF, IPv4, IPv6, IPX, DDP, SPB
Data Link	— Provides reliable transit of data across a physical network link	Frame	Ethernet, FDDI, Frame Relay, VLAN, MAC, Switches, SPB
Physical	— Bit-level transmission between different devices; electrical or mechanical interfaces; activates, maintains, and deactivates the physical link between communicating network systems	Bits	Volts, PINS, bit-rate, serial or parallel, USB, Ethernet 10Base varieties

FIGURE 6.5 **OSI Seven-Layer Reference Model**

This Reference Model, defined in ISO/IEC 7498-1, is a product of research and collaboration from the International Organization for Standardization (ISO). Known throughout the industry as the OSI Seven-Layer Reference Model, it is much more than just a conceptual model. Whether you see the Physical layer as the bottom of the stack or as the outer layer of your system depends upon whether you're *building* or *defending* your system. APT kill chains, for example, focus quite heavily on using Application layer protocols such as HTTP and HTTPS as potential ways to cross your threat surface; users will complain to your help desk about service interruptions that they first see at layer 7 but which may actually be caused by problems at lower layers in the protocol stack. Your business process designers will start at this more abstract layer of the stack and progressively decompose their designs of business processes into lower-level functions until they are finally able to tell the network engineers the types of servers and endpoints needed, their connections with each other, and where on the face of the planet (and on what desktop, on what floor, in which building) each endpoint or server will be. At that point, the network engineers can identify the layer 1 and 2 connections to tie them all together, and the layer 3 devices that bring it alive as a network.

As a network designer, diagnostician, and security enforcer, you'll need to effortlessly navigate across this stack, probably many times as you investigate and resolve any given information security incident.

One caveat: nothing in the discussion of these layers, here or even in the RFCs that defined them, should be taken to mean that functions or processes are confined to segregated layers when implemented. The lines between layers are useful to understand; they are powerful design and troubleshooting constructs. Feature by feature, function by function, each implementation stack of hardware, firmware, and software will do what its designers thought it needed to do. Even a layer 3 device has to work all the way down to the physical interconnection level, but you probably won't find an area on its schematics or logic diagram labeled "here there be layer 1 functions." It's at this level of implementation that the data, control, and management planes as design paradigms may be more obvious. One result of this is that you rarely will find the need to be a "model purist" since many real-world products and implementations blend features from every perspective on a particular layer of the protocol stacks.

With that said, let's get started at the Physical layer.

✔ Please Do Not Throw Sausage Pizza Away

You'll need to memorize the order of these layers, so a handy bottom-to-top mnemonic like this one may help. If you don't care for sausage pizza, try seafood pasta instead; or if you need one that flows from top to bottom, you can always remember that *All People Seem To Need Data Processing*.

Layer 1: The Physical Layer

The Physical layer defines the electrical, mechanical, procedural, and functional specifications for activating, maintaining, and deactivating the physical link between communicating network systems. The Physical layer consists of transmitting raw bits, rather than logical data packets, over a physical link that connects devices across a network. Typically, a physical connection between two NICs requires a pair of modulator/demodulator devices (modems) and the interconnecting medium itself. On the computer side of the NIC, digital signals travel very short distances and at very high speeds; pulse widths are measured in nanoseconds. Getting the same data flow to travel further than about 18 inches requires some kind of transmission line and its associated driver circuits, which is what it takes to get gigabit service to flow down 100 meters of Cat 6 unshielded twisted pair wiring, for example. (Those same voltages would be quite disruptive *inside* the computer.) Changing that internal bitstream into radio waves needs drivers that can use antennas for sending and receiving signals; optical interfaces require LEDs or lasers and very fast photodetectors.

Physical layer specifications further define how the bit stream is *modulated* onto a carrier signal such as a radio wave, electrical signal, audio signal, or a series of light pulses. Physical media can include twisted pair copper wire, coaxial cable, or fiber-optic cable, or be radiated through free space via radio waves or light pulses. Note that while grammarians use *media* as the plural form of *medium*, communications and network engineers tend to use both words interchangeably for the physical components that carry the modulated signal—but not the signal itself. These specifications also define the connectors to be used on the media side of the NIC. The most commonly used connector, for example, is a Bell System type RJ-45 jack and socket; the male end (the jack) is crimped onto an eight-conductor cable, with four pairs of wires twisted and wrapped around each other in various ways to limit crosstalk and external electromagnetic interference. Such cabling is referred to as either *unshielded twisted pair (UTP)* or *shielded twisted pair (STP)*; usually the shielded twisted pair is rated for higher bit rates for a specified service distance. These cable types can also be *plenum rated*, meaning that they can be run inside air conditioning and ventilation ducts or open return areas, because they will not give off toxic fumes as they are heated by a fire.

Physical layer protocols can be broadly classed by the interconnection needs of different industries—or by how different industries have borrowed good ideas from each other and propagated those technologies to meet their own needs. In many cases, those lines are blurring and will continue to blur. Long-haul telecommunications standards that started out at the circuit and multiplexing level find homes in many high-capacity data systems, which form the backbones for voice, video, multimedia, and Internet traffic. Here are some examples:

- Computer interconnection standards include Ethernet (the lioness' share of installed Internet technologies), Token Ring (largely obsolete now), and serial data connections such as the Electronics Industry Association (EIA) standards

RS-232, EIA-422, RS-449, and RS-485, which used to be the stock-in-trade of the computer hobbyist and hacker. Numerous wiring standards exist to support these physical interconnection standards.

- Communications systems standards include Frame Relay, ATM, SONET, SDH, PDH, CDMA, and GSM.

- Wireless protocols such as the IEEE 802.11.

- Aviation data bus standards are primarily published by Aeronautical Radio, Inc., known as ARINC; their ARINC 818 Avionics Digital Video Bus (ADVB) standard is an example of a Physical layer interface serving the aviation industry.

- Controller area network bus (CAN bus) standards define similar protocols for use in automotive and other vehicle control and diagnostic settings.

- Personal area network standards, such as Bluetooth.

- Modulated ultrasound and many near-field communications standards have protocols defined at the Physical layer as well.

- X10, devised by Pico Electronics, Glenrothes, Scotland, is a de facto standard for smart home control devices.

- And many more.

Multiple standards such as the IEEE 802 series define many of the important characteristics for wireless, wired, fiber, and optical physical connections. The newest connection to start to garner prominence in the marketplace is LiFi, the use of high-speed LEDs and photodetectors that are part of room or area lighting as an alternative to radio waves. Aircraft cabins, for example, could use LiFi to provide higher bandwidth connectivity to each passenger seat without the weight penalties of cabling and without the potential electromagnetic interference with flight control and navigation systems that Wi-Fi can sometimes cause.

The NIC also handles collision detection and avoidance so that its attempts to transmit bits on a shared medium are not interfered with by another NIC. It also interfaces with the Link layer by managing the flow of datagrams between the NIC's media control functions and the higher protocol layer's interfaces.

At layer 1, the datagram is the bit. The details of how different media turn bits (or handfuls of bits) into modulated signals to place onto wires, fibers, radio waves, or light waves are (thankfully!) beyond the scope of what SSCPs need to deal with. That said, it's worth considering that at layer 1, addresses don't really matter! For wired (or fibered) systems, it's that physical path from one device to the next that gets the bits where they need to go; that receiving device has to receive all of the bits, unwrap them, and use layer 2 logic to determine whether that set of bits was addressed to it.

This also demonstrates a powerful advantage of this layers-of-abstraction model: nearly everything interesting that needs to happen to turn the user's data (our payload) into transmittable, receivable physical signals can happen with absolutely zero knowledge of how that transmission or reception actually happens! This means that changing out a 10BaseT physical media with Cat 6 Ethernet gives your systems as much as a thousand-time increase in throughput, with no changes needed at the network address, protocol, or application layers. (At most, very low-level device driver settings might need to be configured via operating system functions, as part of such an upgrade, and only on the servers that actually interface with that part of your *physical plant*, the collection of network wiring and cabling that ties everything together.)

Network topologies are established at the Physical layer; this is where the wired, fibered, RF, or optical connections of multiple nodes first take form. For example, a ring network (one-way or bidirectional) requires a separate NIC for each direction around the ring; a star connection requires one NIC for each node being connected to. Each of these NICs brings its own MAC address to the table, although that MAC address lives at layer 2 (in its Media Access Control sublayer). Bus systems require a different type of NIC altogether. Wireless networks start as a mesh in the physical domain (since all radios can receive from any compatible transmitter that's within range) and then establish MAC-to-MAC connections via layer 2.

It's also worth pointing out that the physical domain defines both the collision domain and the physical segment. A collision domain is the physical or electronic space in which multiple devices are competing for each other's attention; if their signals outshout each other, some kind of collision detection and avoidance is needed to keep things working properly. For wired (or fiber-connected) networks, all of the nodes connected by the same cable or fiber are in the same collision domain; for wireless connections, all receivers that can detect a specific transmitter are in that transmitter's collision domain. (If you think that suggests that typical Wi-Fi usage means lots of overlapping collision domains, you'd be right!) At the physical level, that connection is also known as a *segment*. But don't get confused: you *segment* (chop into logical pieces) a network into logical subnetworks, which are properly called *subnets*, at either layer 2 or layer 3 but not at layer 1. (*Microsegmentation*, a strategy for zero-trust architectures, can happen at almost any layer your security needs require.)

Repeaters, hubs, modems, fiber media converters (which are a type of model), and other equipment that does not perform any address mapping, encapsulation, or framing of data are considered layer 1 devices, as are the cables and fibers themselves.

Layer 2: The Data Link Layer

The Data Link layer is the second layer in the OSI Reference Model, and it transfers data between network nodes on the physical link. This layer encodes bits into packets prior to transmission and then decodes the packets back into bits. The data link layer is where the protocols for the network specifications are established. It's also where the network topology, such as star, ring, or mesh, establishes the device-to-device connections. The Data Link layer provides reliability because it offers capabilities for synchronization, error control, alerting, and flow control. These services are important because if transmission or packet sequencing fails, errors and alerts are helpful in correcting the problems quickly. Flow control at the Data Link layer is vital so the devices send and receive data flows at a manageable rate.

There are two sublayers of the Data Link layer as established by the Institute of Electrical and Electronics Engineers (IEEE) per the IEEE 802 series of specifications:

- **The logical link control (LLC) sublayer** controls packet synchronization, flow control, and error checking. This upper sublayer provides the interface between the media access control (MAC) sublayer and the network layer. The LLC enables multiplexing protocols as they are transmitted over the MAC layer and demultiplexing the protocols as they are received. LLC also facilitates node-to-node flow control and error management, such as automatic repeat request (ARQ).

- **The media access control (MAC) sublayer** is the interface between the LLC and the Physical layer (layer 1). At this sublayer, there is transmission of data packets to and from the network-interface card (NIC) and another remotely shared channel. MAC provides an addressing mechanism and channel access so nodes on a network can communicate with each other. MAC addressing works at the data link layer (layer 2). It is similar to IP addressing except that IP addressing is applicable to networking and routing performed at the network layer (layer 3). MAC addressing is commonly referred to as *physical addressing*, while IP addressing (performed at the Network layer, layer 3) is referred to *logical addressing*. Network layer addressing is discussed in the next section.

A MAC address is unique and specific to each computing platform. It is a 12-digit hexadecimal number that is 48 bits long. There are two common MAC address formats,

MM:MM:MM:SS:SS:SS or MM-MM-MM-SS-SS-SS. The first half of a MAC address, called a *prefix*, contains the ID number of the adapter manufacturer. These IDs are regulated by the IEEE. For example, the prefixes 00:13:10, 00:25:9C, and 68:7F:74 (plus many others) all belong to Linksys (Cisco Systems). The second half of a MAC address represents the serial number assigned to the adapter by the manufacturer. It is possible for devices from separate manufacturers to have the same device portion, the rightmost 24-bit number. The prefixes will differ to accomplish uniqueness. Each 24-bit field represents more than 16.7 million possibilities, which for a time seemed to be more than enough addresses; not anymore. Part of IPv6 is the adoption of a larger, 64-bit MAC address, and the protocols to allow devices with 48-bit MAC addresses to participate in IPv6 networks successfully.

Note that one of the bits in the first octet (in the organizational unique identifier ([OUI]) flags whether that MAC address is universally or locally administered. Many NICs have features that allow the local systems administrator to overwrite the manufacturer-provided MAC address with one of their own choosing. This does provide the end-user organization with a great capability to manage devices by using their own internal MAC addressing schemes, but it can be misused to allow one NIC to impersonate another one (so-called MAC address spoofing).

Let's take a closer look at the structure of a frame. As mentioned, the payload is the set of bits given to layer 2 by layer 3 (or a layer-spanning protocol) to be sent to another device on the network. Conceptually, each frame consists of the following:

- A preamble, which is a 56-bit series of alternating 1s and 0s. This synchronization pattern helps serial data receivers ensure that they are receiving a frame and not a series of noise bits.

- The start frame delimiter (SFD), which signals to the receiver that the preamble is over and that the real frame data is about to start. Different media require different SFD patterns.

- The destination MAC address.

- The source MAC address.

- The Ether Type field, which indicates either the length of the payload in octets or the protocol type that is encapsulated in the frame's payload.

- The payload data, of variable length (depending on the Ether Type field).

- A frame check sequence, which provides a checksum across the entire frame, to support error detection.

The interpacket gap is a period of dead space on the media, which helps transmitters and receivers manage the link and helps signify the end of the previous frame and the start of the next. It is not, specifically, a part of either frame, and it can be of variable length. Layer 2 devices include bridges, modems, NICs, and switches that don't use IP addresses (thus called *layer 2 switches*). Firewalls make their first useful appearance at layer 2, performing rule-based and behavior-based packet scanning and filtering. Data center designs can make effective use of layer 2 firewalls.

Layer 3: The Network Layer

Layer 3, the Network layer, is defined in the OSI Seven-Layer Reference Model as the place where variable-length sequences of fixed-length packets (that make up what the user or higher protocols want sent and received) are transmitted (or received). Routing and switching happens at layer 3, as logical paths between two hosts are created. It is at layer 3 that Internet Protocol (IP) addresses are established and used; these are sometimes referred to as *logical addresses*, in contrast to the *physical* MAC addresses at layer 2. We'll look in detail at the assignment and resolution of IP addresses in the "IPv4 Addresses, DHCP, and Subnets" and "IPv4 vs. IPv6: Key Differences and Options" sections later in this chapter.

Layer 3 protocols route and forward data packets to destinations, while providing various quality of service capabilities such as packet sequencing, congestion control, and error handling. Layer 3's specification in RFC 1122 left a great deal of the implementation details to individual designers and builders to determine; it provides a best-efforts core of functionality that they can (and did) feel free to pick and choose from as they built their systems. For example, one implementation might do a robust job of handling errors detected by layer 2 or 1 services, while other implementations may not even notice such errors. (Many OSs and applicationsstill provide less than meaningful information to their users when such errors occur. Window's cryptic message that "a network cable may have become unplugged," for example, gives the user a place to start troubleshooting from. Contrast this with most browsers, which display an uninformative "cannot find server" message but offer little other information. The user doesn't know if this is a bad URL, a failure to find a DNS server, or that they've failed to properly log into the Wi-Fi provider's network, just to name a few possibilities.)

This *best-efforts basis* extends to security considerations as well: until IPsec was engineered and standardized, IPv4 had little in the way of native capabilities to provide protection against any number of possible attacks. IPsec was discussed in further detail in Chapter 5, "Cryptography."

ISO 7498/4 also defines a number of network management and administration functions that (conceptually) reside at layer 3. These protocols provide greater support to routing, managing multicast groups, address assignment (at the Network layer), and other status information and error handling capabilities. Note that it is the job of the payload—the datagrams being carried by the protocols—that make these functions belong to the Network layer, and not the protocol that carries or implements them.

The most common device you'll see at layer 3 is the router; combination bridge-routers, or *brouters*, are also in use (bridging together two or more Wi-Fi LAN segments, for example). Layer 3 switches are those that can deal with IP addresses. Firewalls also are part of the layer 3 landscape.

Layer 3 uses a *packet*. For now, let's focus on the IP version 4 format of its header, shown in Figure 6.6, which has been in use since the 1970s and thus is almost universally used: Key Differences and Options

- Both the source and destination address fields are 32-bit IPv4 addresses.

- The Identification, Flags, and Fragment Offset fields participate in error detection and reassembly of packet fragments.

- The Time To Live (TTL) field keeps a packet from floating around the Internet forever. Each router or gateway that processes the packet decrements the TTL field, and if its value hits zero, the packet is discarded rather than passed on. If that happens, the router or gateway is supposed to send an ICPM packet to the originator with fields set to indicate which packet didn't live long enough to get where it was supposed to go. (The tracert function uses TTL in order to determine what path packets are taking as they go from sender to receiver.)

- The Protocol field indicates whether the packet is using ICMP, TCP, Exterior Gateway, IPv6, or Interior Gateway Routing Protocol.

- Finally comes the data (or payload) portion.

Note that IPv6 uses a different header format, which you'll look at later in the "IPv4 vs. IPv6" section.

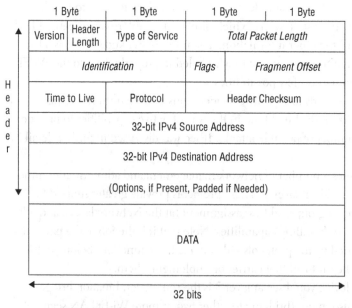

FIGURE 6.6 **IPv4 packet format**

You'll note that we went from MAC addresses at layer 2 to IP addresses at layer 3. This requires the use of Address Resolution Protocol (ARP), one of several protocols that span multiple layers. We'll look at those together after we examine layer 7.

Layer 3 supports both connection-oriented and connectionless protocols, and a simple way to keep these separate in your mind (and in use) is to think of the sequence of events involved in each.

- Connectionless protocols are used by devices that send their data immediately, without first using any type of handshake to establish a relationship with the receiving end. User Datagram Protocol (UDP) is perhaps the most well-known of these, and it finds widespread use in streaming media, voice over IP (VOIP), or other content delivery systems, where there are far too many endpoints authorized or intended as recipients to use a point-to-point or narrowcast protocol. Ethernet and IPX are other examples of connectionless protocols in widespread use.

- Connection-oriented protocols first use a handshake to establish a logical relationship with services at both sender and receiver ends of the connection; these protocols exist at the Transport layer and above in both OSI and TCP/IP protocol stacks. The most well-known of these protocols is of course the Transport Control Protocol (TCP). As a layer 4 or Transport layer protocol, it runs on top of the Internetworking Protocol (IP) defined at layer 3; thus, we call it TCP over IP.

- Routing protocols used by Internet backbone devices and services, such as Border Gateway Protocol (BGP), which functions as an inter-domain routing protocol. Open Shortest Path First (OSPF), an interior gateway protocol that uses a link state routing algorithm, is an important protocol in large, complex, high-capacity and high-speed networks, so it is found quite frequently in enterprise systems. Routing Information Protocol (RIP) was an early protocol that you may find still in use; it uses hop counts as its metric, also live in layer 3. Finally, the Internet Group Management Protocol (IGMP) provides for simultaneous transmission of video services to multiple recipients.

NOTE   BGP is often thought of as a Network layer or Transport layer protocol. However, it actually functions on top of TCP, which technically makes it a Session layer protocol in the OSI Seven-Layer Reference Model. Consequently, a security professional might encounter it being discussed at any of these layers.

Layer 4: The Transport Layer

Two main protocols are defined at this layer, which, as its name suggests, involves the transport or movement of variable-length streams of data from one endpoint service to

---

another. These streams are broken down for the sender by layer 4 protocols into fixed-length *packets*, which are then handed off to layer 3 to flow to the recipients.

Ports   Transport layer protocols primarily work with *ports*. Ports are software-defined labels for the connections between two processes, usually ones that are running on two different computers; ports are also used for many forms of interprocess communication on a single computer. The source and destination port, plus the protocol identification and other protocol-related information, is contained in that protocol's header. Each protocol defines what fields are needed in its header and prescribes required and optional actions that receiving nodes should take based on header information, errors in transmission, or other conditions. Ports are typically bidirectional, using the same port number on sender and receiver to establish the connection. Some protocols may use multiple port numbers simultaneously.

Connection-Oriented Protocols   The first and most important of these is the Transport Control Protocol (TCP), which seems to have given its name to the entire layer, but it is *not* all that happens at layer 4 of the OSI Reference Model, nor at the Transport layer in the TCP/IP model. TCP provides a connection-oriented flow of packets between *sockets* defined by the IP address and port number used by sender and recipient both, using the handshake shown in Figure 6.7. (The term *socket* hearkens back to operator-tended switchboards at which phone calls were set up, plug-into-socket, as operators routed calls.)

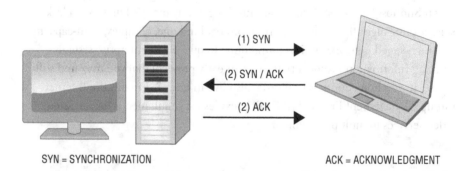

SYN = SYNCHRONIZATION   ACK = ACKNOWLEDGMENT

(1)   A client node sends a SYN data packet over an IP network to a destination node on the same or an external network. The SYN packet is asking if the destination is open for new connections.

(2)   The target node must have open ports that can accept and initiate new connections. When the destination target receives the SYN packet from the client node, it responds and returns a confirmation receipt, specifically the ACK packet or SYN/ACK packet.

(3)   The client node receives the SYN/ACK from the destination and responds with an ACK packet.

Upon completion of this process, the connection is created and the host and target can communicate.

FIGURE 6.7 **TCP three-way handshake**

Connection-oriented protocols provide quality of service and greater reliability by means of flow control, error checking, and error recovery by means of packet retransmission requests using packet sequence numbers. The OSI Reference Model defines four other connection-oriented protocols, known as TP0 through TP4, which build on each other to provide a comprehensive set of transport services.

- TP0 performs packet segmentation and reassembly, which may be useful in some systems to reduce latency. (This is referred to in TCP/IP as *fragmentation*.) TP0 figures out the smallest practicable protocol data unit (PDU) that the underlying networks can support and then establishes segmentation and reassembly accordingly.

- TP1 adds error recovery capabilities to TP0, assigning sequence numbers to each PDU. It can reinitiate a connection if too many PDUs are not acknowledged by recipients.

- TP2 adds multiplexing and demultiplexing services.

- TP3 combines all of the features of TP0, TP1, and TP2.

- TP4 is the full equivalent of TCP as a protocol.

Connectionless Protocols   Connectionless protocols do not use sockets, so there is no setup handshake prior to the sender starting to flow data toward the recipients. The most common example of a connectionless protocol at layer 4 is the User Datagram Protocol (UDP). UDP is most often used for broadcasting to large numbers of user destinations. Because it does not provide for any flow control, sequencing, or error recovery, it is also considered as less reliable and less secure. However, this means that UDP is a low-overhead protocol, which makes it admirably suited to transferring high data volumes where errors can be better tolerated. Streaming multimedia and VoIP, for example, can often tolerate dropped, corrupted, or lost packets, which might introduce noticeable image or audio artifacts that do not dramatically disrupt the end user's experience or use of the data being streamed.

TIP   The IP header protocol field value for UDP is 17 (0x11).

Layer 5: Session Layer

The *sessions* model covers a wide range of human and computer systems interconnections. Logging into an early time sharing or remote access system created a session, bounded by its login and logout (or exit) commands, typically by using a dumb terminal (one that only displayed what was received and typed, and sent what was typed, and supported no other applications). Uses of SSH and PuTTY mimic such sessions today, but they use an application on their client device to connect to a remote login protocol on the host. It's important to distinguish between the human concept of a session and the

---

protocol stack's use of it. This layer of the protocol stack supports applications in creating, managing, and terminating each logical session as a distinct entity; we humans may very well have multiple such sessions active as we accomplish one somewhat-integrated set of purposeful tasks in a "session" of Internet use.

At the Sessions layer, applications use remote procedure calls (RPCs) to make service requests and responses as the way to request services be performed by other networked devices participating in the session. RPCs provide mechanisms to synchronize services, as well as deal with service requests that go unanswered or cannot complete because of errors. Application design must consider the need for session checkpointing and restart, graceful degradation, error recovery, and additional authentication and verification that may be required by the business logic that the session is supporting. For example, online banking sessions quite frequently start with multifactor authentication at the start of the session but may demand additional authentication (via the same factors or by challenging for additional factors) before sensitive functions, such as a wire transfer to an external account, can be performed. Transactions often require several steps to input, verify, and assemble input data, and at any point the user may need to cancel the transaction safely. The design of this logic is in the application, of course; and the application has part of its logic executing on the client-side endpoint and part of it executing on the host. RPCs are one way to tie host and client together.

✔ RPC or API?

It turns out there are two styles or design paradigms for creating ways for applications running on one system to obtain services from applications running on another system. In web programming terms, such an *application programming interface* (API) provides definition of interface names and parameters that can be accessed by other programs. *Remote procedure calls (RPCs)* are one style of writing web APIs, while *representational state transfers* or RESTful programming is another. At the risk of oversimplifying, RPCs provide a very narrow view of the data objects being handed back and forth, while a REST *endpoint* is more like making a service call to a resource that owns (encapsulates) the data in question. RPCs get one job done; REST endpoints (or RESTful programming) decouple the business logic from the domain of the data objects.

Assuming that they are implemented correctly, neither approach is inherently more secure than the other. But experience suggests that can be a risky bet. Either way.

Sessions can be established in various ways to allow (or prevent) simultaneous sending and receiving of data by different systems participating in the session. A multiway VoIP call illustrates this: typically, if more than one person attempts to talk at a time, some recipients will hear a garbled and broken-up rendition of some parts of each, rather than hearing both voices clearly overlaid. Thus, sessions may need to be managed as follows:

- **Full duplex:** In these sessions, data is sent over a connection between two or more devices in both directions at the same time. Full-duplex channels can be constructed either as a pair of simplex links or using one channel designed to permit bidirectional simultaneous transmissions. If multiple devices need to be connected using full-duplex mode, many individual links are required because one full-duplex link can connect only two devices.

- **Half-duplex:** Half-duplex has the capability of sending data in both directions, but in only one direction at a time. While this may seem like a step down in capability from full duplex, it is widely used and successful across single network media like cable, radio frequency, and Ethernet, as examples. The communications work well when the devices take turns sending and receiving. A small bit of *turnaround time* may be needed to allow lower levels in the protocol stack (down to and including the physical) to perform the necessary switching of transmit and receive functions around.

- **Simplex operation:** The communication channels are a one-way street. An example of simplex construction is where a fiber optics run or a network cable as a single strand sends data and another separate channel receives data.

As an example, a media streaming service needs to use at least a half-duplex session model to manage user login and authentication, service, or product selection, and then start streaming the data to the user's device. Users may need or want to pause the streaming, replay part of it, skip ahead, or even terminate the streaming itself. UDP might be the protocol used to stream the video to the user, and it is a simplex protocol at heart. It does not notice nor acknowledge that the user went away or that the link dropped. This suggests that two sessions are in use when streaming from YouTube or MLB.TV: one that coordinates the client's player application, and its requests to pause, rewind, fast forward, or stop playing, and the other being the simplex UDP high data rate flow to that player app. At the server end, the other half of that player app needs to be able to interact with and control the UDP sending process. Since UDP has no way to detect that the receiver—or any one receiver in a UDP broadcast—has stopped listening or that the link has gone down, most services will implement some form of a periodic "still-alive" check as a way to prevent servers from wasting time streaming to nowhere. This would require the use of TCP or Stream Control Transmission Protocol (SCTP), which are the tools of choice for this task.

NOTE Many real-time systems have business or process control needs for right-now data and as such tolerate a few missed packets more easily than they can deal with retransmission delays.

Layer 6: Presentation Layer

Layer 6, the Presentation layer, supports the mapping of data in terms and formats used by applications into terms and formats needed by the lower-level protocols in the stack. It is sometimes referred to as the *syntax* layer (since it provides the structured rules by which the *semantics* or meaning of applications data fields are transferred). The Presentation layer handles protocol-level encryption and decryption of data (protecting data in motion), translates data from representational formats that applications use into formats better suited to protocol use, and can interpret semantical or metadata about applications data into terms and formats that can be sent via the Internet.

This layer was created to consolidate both the thinking and design of protocols to handle the wide differences in the ways that 1970s-era systems formatted, displayed, and used data. Different character sets, such as EBCDIC, ASCII, or FIELDATA, used different numbers of bits; they represented the same character, such as an uppercase A, by different sets of bits. Byte sizes were different on different manufacturers' minicomputers and mainframes. The "presentation" of data to the user and the interaction with the user could range from a simple chat, a batch input from a file and a printed report of the results, or a predefined on-screen form with specified fields for data display and edit. Such a form is one example of a data structure that "presentation" must consider; others would be a list of data items retrieved by a query, such as "all flights from San Diego to Minneapolis on Tuesday morning." Since its creation, the presentation layer has provided a place for many different protocols to handle newer information formats, such as voice, video, or animation formats.

Serializing and *deserializing* of complex data structures is handled by the presentation layer working in conjunction with application layer services. In that last example, each set of data about one particular flight—the airline, flight number, departure and arrival time, and other fields—must be transferred from sender to recipient in a predefined order; this process must repeat for each flight being displayed. (Note that these terms do not refer to taking bytes of data and flowing them out one bit after another in *serial* fashion.)

There are several sublayers and protocols that programmers can use to achieve an effective presentation-layer interface between applications on the one hand and the session layer and the rest of the protocol stack on the other. HTTP is an excellent example of such a protocol.

The Network Basic Input/Output System (NetBIOS) and Server Message Block (SMB) are also important to consider at the Presentation layer. NetBIOS is actually an API rather than a formal protocol per se. From its roots in IBM's initial development of the personal computer, NetBIOS now runs over TCP/IP (or NBT, if you can handle one more acronym!) or any other transport mechanism. Both NetBIOS and SMB allow programs to communicate with each other, whether they are on the same host or different hosts on a network.

Keep in mind that many of the cross-layer protocols, apps, and older protocols involved with file transfer, email, and network-attached filesystems and storage resources all "play through" layer 6 and may not make use of any features or protocols at this level if they don't need to. The Common Internet File System (CIFS) protocol is one such example.

TIP On the one hand, encryption and compression services are typically handled at the Presentation layer. But on the other hand, TLS encryption (and its predecessor SSL) spans multiple layers in the protocol stacks' views of the networking world, as shown in Chapter 5. TLS is one such example of a valuable cross-layer protocol.

Let the layers of abstraction aid your thinking, but do not feel duty-bound to stay within it. Real life on the Web and the Net don't, and neither do your adversaries.

Layer 7: Application Layer

It is at layer 7 that the end user is closest to accomplishing their purpose or intention for any particular Internet session or activity. This is the level where applications on host servers communicate with apps on the clients; users interact with these client-side apps via their endpoint devices to accomplish their online shopping or banking, check their email, or monitor and interact with a process control system and its supervisory control and data acquisition (SCADA) management functions. Many different protocols reside at this layer and reach down through the protocol stack to accomplish their assigned tasks:

- HTTP and HTTPS provide the hypertext transfer protocols that bring websites, their content, and the apps hosted on them to user endpoints.
- Email protocols such as SNMP, IMAP, and POP3 connect users to their email servers, and those servers to each other as they route email and attachments to addressees.
- TFTP, FTP, and SFTP provide file transfer services.
- SSH and Telnet provide command-line login and interaction capabilities.
- LDAP provides for the management of shared directory information to support integrated access control across multiple cooperating systems.

These protocols, and their commonly used ports, are looked at in more detail in the "Commonly Used Ports and Protocols" section later in this chapter.

TCP/IP Reference Model

The term *TCP/IP* can sometimes seem to be a generic concept to define everything—protocols, networking models, and even a synonym for the Internet itself. The concepts behind TCP/IP are central to understanding telecommunications and networking, but there are specific principles and processes that information security professionals must understand in depth. To start, TCP/IP is a set of rules (protocols) that provide a framework or governance for communications that enables interconnection of separate nodes across different network boundaries on the Internet. TCP/IP sets up the way processors package data into data packets, senders transfer the packets, and receivers accept the packets, as well as routing information to the destination.

The acronym often is used to refer to the entire protocol suite, which contains other protocols besides TCP and IP. The Transport layer of both the OSI and TCP/IP models is home to UDP in addition to TCP. Similarly, the OSI Seven-Layer Reference Model's network layer and the TCP/IP model's Internet layer each house the IP, ARP, IGMP, and ICMP protocols. Expanding further is when someone mentions the TCP/IP stack, which likely is referring to protocols and layers above and below the earlier two.

If strictly talking about IP and TCP as individual protocols and not the entire TCP/IP protocol suite, then TCP/IP consists of TCP layered on top of IP to determine the logistics of data in motion and establish virtual circuits. TCP and IP are long-standing pair of protocols, developed in 1978 by Bob Kahn and Vint Cerf. A description of TCP/IP methodology is that a data stream is split into IP packets that are then reassembled into the data stream at the destination. If the destination does not acknowledge receipt of a packet, TCP/IP supports retransmitting lost packets, a feature performed by TCP. In short, TCP/IP includes the destination and route with the packet while also ensuring the reliability by checking for errors and supporting requests for re-transmission.

TCP/IP as a protocol stack or reference model grew out of the ARPANET protocols that first launched the Internet Age. It was originally defined by IETF's RFC 1122 in October 1989, and its authors and working group drew two lines in the sand, metaphorically speaking, by focusing just on how the *internetworking* of computers would take place. Below the RFC's field of view (and its lowest layer) were the physical interconnection protocols and methods; a rich body of choices already existed there, and standards bodies had codified many of them while business and industry practice established other technologies as *de facto* standards. Above the span of the RFC's vision were the growing body of applications-specific needs and other systems support protocols, which were captured in RFC 1123. Get the core functions of internetworking defined and nailed down first, the authors of RFC 1122 seemed to be suggesting; then work on what comes next. This divide-and-conquer strategy was different than the omnibus approach taken by ISO and CCITT, but the end result was actually a harmonious agreement where it was most needed.

It's natural to ask if TCP/IP is a three-layer or four-layer model. RFC 1122 specifies *three* layers, which are Link, Internet, and Transport, and then goes on to reference the Application layer defined in RFC 1123. As a result, some books, courses, authors, analysts, and working network and security engineers see TCP/IP as a three-layer stack, while others include RFC 1123's services and applications as part of the "Internet Hosts—Communication Layer." In TCP/IP terms, the Application layer has a number of protocols in it that actually span into the layers below them, as you'll see in a bit. I'll take the four-layer perspective in this book, largely for practical reasons, and then look at the protocols that seem to span layers.

As we look at TCP/IP we cannot help but compare it to the OSI Seven-Layer Reference Model; in doing so, we might be well advised to keep Jon Postel's maxim, as paraphrased in RFC 1123, in mind:

"Be liberal in what you accept, and conservative in what you send."

Figure 6.8 helps put these two protocol stacks in context with each other.

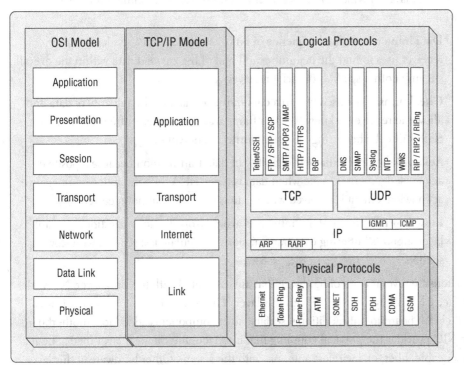

FIGURE 6.8 OSI and TCP/IP side-by-side comparison

The Link Layer

The Link layer is called by several other names, including the Network Interface layer or the Data Link layer (and, indeed, the TCP/IP model's Link layer includes some of the same functionality as the OSI model's Data Link layer). It is sometimes thought of as the Physical layer of the TCP/IP protocol stack, but this would not technically be correct as it does not contain nor directly reference the physical processes of turning data bits into signals and sending those signals out an antenna, a cable, or a light wave. Instead, look at the Link layer as the physical *interface* between the host system and the network hardware. The role of this layer is to facilitate TCP/IP data packets across the network transmission channel in a reliable manner. This layer can detect transmission errors. This layer determines how common data link standards like IEEE 802.2 and X.25 format data packets for transmission and routing. The way TCP/IP was designed allows the data format to be independent of the network access method, frame format, and medium which establishes TCP/IP to interconnect across disparate or different networks. It is this independence from any specific network technology that makes TCP/IP scalable to new networking technologies such as Asynchronous Transfer Mode (ATM). Similarly, this enables local area network services to flow over Ethernet connections or wide area network (WAN) technologies such as X.25 or Frame Relay.

The Link layer provides a number of important services by defining the use of the following:

- **Data frames:** A defined sequence of bits or symbols from a sender that the receiver uses to find the beginning and end of the payload data within the overall stream of other symbols or bits it receives.

- **Checksums:** Data used within a data frame to manage the integrity of data and allow the receiver to know the data frame was received error-free. These are especially critical when using almost all forms of encryption.

- **Acknowledgment:** Enables reliability in data transmission because a positive acknowledgement is made when data is received. A timeout notice or a negative acknowledgement is received when data is expected but not received.

- **Flow control:** To maintain traffic and avoid errors due to congestion, the Link layer supports buffering data transmissions to regulate fast senders with slow senders.

There are several types of hardware that are associated with the Link layer. Network interface cards are typically used with this layer. The NIC is hardware, ranging from a small circuit board to only additional surface layer components added to a motherboard. The NIC provides the physical coupling that interfaces the Physical layer media, be it a copper cable, fiber, or a wireless antenna, with the system. Other hardware at this layer would include the various networking hardware such as a switch, bridge, or hub. These three differentiate from each other by how they do or do not separate signals between ports. Switches are by far the most common layer hardware in terms of networking.

The Internet Layer

TCP/IP's Internet layer corresponds to the OSI reference model's Network layer and serves much the same purpose. Using core protocols like IP, ARP, ICMP, and IGMP, the Internet layer is responsible for addressing, packaging, and routing functions of data packets. Unlike the link layer, the Internet layer does not take advantage of data sequencing and acknowledgment services. The Internet layer performs several invaluable functions. To transmit packets from host to host, IP selects the next-hop or gateway for outgoing packets across the Link layer. It transfers data packets up to the Transport layer for incoming packets if the data meets transmission parameters. To that end, the Internet layer helps with error detection and diagnostic capability, providing a degree of data integrity protection during the transmission process. The Internet Protocol is the principal, routable communications protocol responsible for addressing, routing, and the fragmentation and reassembly of data packets. This was originally defined in RFC 791.

- The Internet Control Message Protocol (ICMP) provides diagnostic functions and error reporting when there is unsuccessful delivery of IP packets. RFC 792 defined ICMP, and although it operates by having its messages encapsulated within IP datagrams, it is nonetheless defined as an Internet Layer protocol.

- The Internet Group Management Protocol (IGMP) multicast groups or destination computers addressed for simultaneous broadcast are managed by this protocol. RFC 1112 defined this as a set of extensions to both hosts and the host-gateway interface, largely to support multicasting at the IP layer by means of access to Link layer multicasting services.

The Transport Layer

At the Transport layer, services are provided to the Application layer for session and datagram communication. You may also hear this layer referred to as the *host-to-host transport layer*. In the TCP/IP model, the Transport layer does not make use of the features of the Link layer. It assumes an unreliable connection at the Link layer. Therefore, at the Transport layer, session establishment, packet acknowledgment, and data sequencing are accomplished to enable reliable communications. The core protocols of the Transport layer are Transmission Control Protocol (TCP) and the User Datagram Protocol (UDP).

TCP communications are segments treated as a sequence of bytes with no record or field boundaries to provide a one-to-one, connection-oriented, reliable communications service. TCP is responsible for ensuring the connection stays reliable and all packets are accounted for. This is done by sequencing and acknowledging each packet sent. This helps with recovery in case packets get lost during transmission. This is accomplished in part by the recipient sending an acknowledgment (ACK) back to the sender for each segment successfully received. Recipients can request retransmission of segments that arrive with errors in them, and the sender will also resend segments that are not acknowledged after a pre-specified timeout period.

In the TCP header there is some important information contained in areas called *flag fields*. These fields are important because they can contain one or more control bits in the form of an 8-bit length flag field. The bits determine the function of that TCP packet and request a specific manner of response from the recipient. Multiple flags can be used in some conditions. In the TCP three-way handshake, for example, both the SYN and ACK flags are set. The bit positions correspond to a control setting per single flag. Each position can be set on with a value of 1 or off with a value of 0. Each of the eight flags is a byte presented in either hex or binary format. The hex representation of 00010010 is 0x12.

Of that 8-bit flag field, let's specify the last six flags: URG, ACK, PSH, RST, SYN, and FIN. A mnemonic phrase can be helpful, such as "Unskilled Attackers Pester Real Security Folks." Using the first letter of each flag, we refer to these handshake flags as UAPRSF; at any state in the handshake we replace a letter with a zero to indicate a flag not set as shown in Figure 6.9. Thus, the hex 0x12 represents the flags 00A00S0 (ACK and SYN are set).

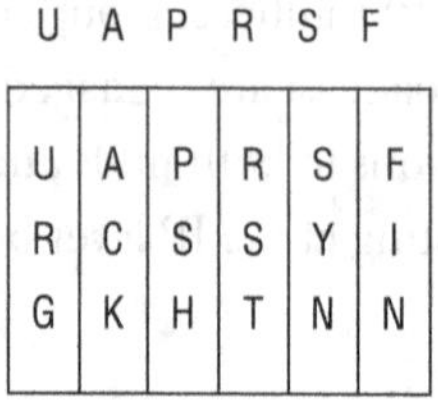

U	A	P	R	S	F
R	C	S	S	Y	I
G	K	H	T	N	N

URG =	Urgent	*Unskilled*
ACK =	Acknowledgment	*Attackers*
PSH =	Push	*Pester*
RST =	Reset	*Real*
SYN =	Syn	*Security*
FIN =	Finished	*Folks*

FIGURE 6.9 TCP flag fields

This layer encompasses the services performed by the OSI reference model's Transport layer and some of its Session layer functions.

NOTE UDP is used by services like NetBIOS name service, NetBIOS datagram service, and SNMP.

The Application Layer

RFC 1123 defined the Application layer as home for a set of services and support functions that are part of the basic Internet protocol stack. As with the OSI reference model, these services provide the APIs, such as Windows Sockets and NetBIOS, to allow applications to use protocol services such as datagrams, name resolution, and session definition, creation, and control. New protocols for the Application layer continue to be developed to meet new needs.

The most widely known Application layer protocols are those used for the exchange of user information.

- **Hypertext Transfer Protocol** (HTTP) is the foundation of file and data transfer on the World Wide Web, which comprises and supports websites. Secure HTTP (HTTPS) provides use of encryption services to provide a high degree of confidentiality, integrity, authentication, and nonrepudiation support to web services.

- **File Transfer Protocol** (FTP) enables file transfer in the client-server architecture. It uses TCP for a reliable connection. Trivial File Transfer Protocol, which uses UDP, is simpler and imposes less overhead and is suitable for applications that are less sensitive to data integrity impacts that can come from using UDP.

- **Simple Mail Transfer Protocol** (SMTP) email and associated attachments can be sent and received via this protocol. Other mail protocols that work at this layer include Post Office Protocol (POP3, its third version) and Internet Message Access Protocol (IMAP).

- **Remote login**. Telnet is a bidirectional interactive text-oriented communication protocol used to access or log on to networked computers remotely. Telnet has no built-in security, so it should be avoided in use over the public Internet or on any networks where eavesdropping, packet sniffing or other security risks exist. Use Secure Shell (SSH) instead if at all possible.

Application layer protocols can also be used to manage service on TCP/IP networks, as follows:

- The Domain Name System resolves a host name from human-readable language to an IP address. This protocol allows names such as www.isc2.org to be mapped to an IP address. As an application layer protocol, DNS arguably reaches across all layers in the TCP/IP stack and is thus more of a cross-layer protocol.

- The Routing Information Protocol (RIP) is used by routers to exchange routing information on an IP network.

- The Simple Network Management Protocol (SNMP) is used to manage network devices from a network management console. The network management console collects and exchanges network management information about routers, bridges, and intelligent hubs, for example.

Another example of an application-layer protocol is the Routing Information Protocol (RIP). Routers need to maintain internal routing tables that help them quickly contribute to resolving addresses and directing incoming traffic to their correct output port. Early networks relied on manual update of router tables, but this is not scalable and is quite prone to error. RIP was one of the earliest protocols adopted, and it uses a distance and time vector routing algorithm that counts the hops that a packet goes through on its way across the network. When RIP sees a maximum of 16 hops counted out, it considers that the distance is infinite and that the destination address is unreachable. This severely constrained the size of a network that could use RIP, but it also is how RIP prevents routing loops (with packets going around the net forever, looking for a place to get off, "just like Charlie on the M.T.A." in the song by the Kingston Trio). RIP also implemented controls to assure correct routing, with names such as *split horizon*, *route poisoning*, and *hold-down timers*, which also contribute to the overall network being self-annealing (when a router goes offline or otherwise becomes unreachable). In its original form, RIP sends out a fully updated router table every 30 seconds, but as networks grew in size, this started to create bursty high-volume traffic.

RIP versions 2 and 3 attempted to fix issues such as this, but RIP remains a difficult technology to scale up to very large networks and should probably be avoided in those settings. It can still be quite useful in smaller networks. RIP uses UDP and is assigned to port 520. RIPng, or RIP Next Generation, extends RIPv2 and moves it to port 521 for use in IPv6, where it will use multicast group FF02::9.

TIP   Unless you have strong reasons not to, you should actively secure everything you do. Secure Shell (SSH) uses encryption to protect login credentials, commands sent by the user, outputs from the host, and all file transfers conducted by SSH. It should be your default choice for remote logins, rather than Telnet, which should be used only if SSH is not available or not working properly. In the same vein, Secure File Transfer Protocol (SFTP) should be the first choice, rather than its unsecure (unencrypted) progenitor FTP.

Converged Protocols

Converged protocols differ from encapsulated, multilayer protocols. Converged protocols are what happens when you merge specialty or proprietary protocols with standard protocols, such TCP/IP suite protocols. With converged protocols, an organization can reduce reliance on distinct, costly proprietary hardware, as well as create variations of performance, depending on which converged protocol is being used.

Some common examples of converged protocols are described here:

- **Fibre Channel over Ethernet (FCoE):** Fibre Channel solutions usually need separate fiber-optic cabling infrastructure to deliver network data-storage options, such as a storage area network (SAN) or network-attached storage (NAS). Fibre Channel is useful because it allows for high-speed file transfers achieving 128Gbps and today reaching for 256Gbps. Fibre Channel over Ethernet was developed to facilitate Fibre Channel to work more efficiently, while using less expensive copper cables over Ethernet connections. Using 10Gbps Ethernet, FCoE uses Ethernet frames to support the Fibre Channel communications.

- **Internet Small Computer System Interface (iSCSI):** iSCSI is often viewed as a low-cost alternative to Fibre Channel. It is also a networking storage standard but is based on IP. It facilitates connection of a remote storage volume over a network as if the device were attached locally. The iSCSI transmits SCSI commands over IP networks and performs like a virtual SATA (or SCSI) cable.

- **Multiprotocol Label Switching (MPLS):** MPLS is a high-throughput, high-performance network technology that directs data across a network based on short path labels rather than longer network addresses. Compared with IP routing processes that are complex and take a longer time to navigate, MPLS saves significant time. Using encapsulation, MPLS is designed to handle a wide range of protocols. An MPLS network can handle T1/E1, ATM, Frame Relay, SONET, and DSL network technologies, not just TCP/IP and compatible protocols. MPLS is often used to create a virtual dedicated circuit between two stations.

Software-Defined Networks

Software-defined networking (SDN) is an emerging network administration approach to designing, building, and centrally managing a network. Settings to hardware can be changed through a central management interface. Some of the primary features are flexibility, vendor neutrality, and use of open standards. In a traditional network construct, routing and switching are primarily in the realm of hardware resources. In many cases, this reality creates a vendor reliance that limits the dynamic ability of an organization to anticipate or even react to change.

SDN separates hardware and hardware settings at the infrastructure layer from network services and data transmission at the network layer. The configuration is virtualized and managed in a control plane similar to managing virtual hosts through a hypervisor console. This also removes the need for applications and their hosts to deal with the lower-level networking concepts of IP addressing, subnets, routing, and so on.

TIP   Network virtualization, with data transmission paths, communication decision trees, and traffic flow control, is a good way to describe SDN.

IPV4 ADDRESSES, DHCP, AND SUBNETS

Now that you have an idea of how the layers fit together conceptually, let's look at some of the details of how IP addressing gets implemented within an organization's network and within the Internet as a whole. As it's still the dominant ecosystem or *monoculture* on almost all networks, let's use IPv4 addresses to illustrate. Recall that an IPv4 address field is a 32-bit number, represented as four octets (8-bit chunks) written usually as base 10 numbers.

Let's start "out there" in the Internet, where we see two kinds of addresses: static and dynamic. *Static IP addresses* are assigned once to a device, and they remain unchanged; thus, 8.8.8.8 has been the main IP address for Google since, well, *ever*, and it probably always will be. The advantage of a static IP address for a server or web page is that virtually every layer of ARP and DNS cache on the Internet will know it; it will be quicker and easier to find. By contrast, a *dynamic IP address is assigned each time that device connects to the network.* ISPs most often use dynamic assignment of IP addresses to subscriber equipment, since this allows them to manage a pool of addresses better. Your subscriber equipment (your modem, router, PC, or laptop) then needs a DHCP server to assign them an address.

It's this use of DHCP, by the way, that means that almost everybody's SOHO router can use the same IP address *on the LAN side*, such as 192.168.2.1 or 192.168.1.1. The router connects on one side (the wide area network) to the Internet by way of your ISP and on the other side to the devices on its local network segment. Devices on the LAN segment can see other devices on that segment, but they cannot see "out the WAN side," you might say, without using network address translation, which we'll look at in a moment.

IPv4 Address Classes

IPv4's addressing scheme was developed with classes of addresses in mind. These were originally designed to be able to split the octets so that one set represented a node within a network, while the other octets were used to define very large, large, and small networks. At the time (1970s), this was thought to make it easier for humans to manage IP addresses. Over time, this has proven impractical. Despite this, IPv4 address class nomenclature remains a fixed part of our network landscape, and SSCPs need to be familiar with the defined address classes.

- Class A addresses used the first octet to define such very large networks (at most 127 of them), using 0 in the first bit to signify a Class A address or some other address type. IBM, for example, might have required all 24 bits worth of the other octets to assign IP addresses to all of its nodes. Think of Class A addresses as looking like <net>.<node>.<node>.<node>.

- Class B addresses used two octets for the network identifier and two for the node, or <net>.<net>.<node>.<node>. The first 2 bits of the address would be 10.

- Class C addresses used the first three octets for the network identifier: <net>.<net>.<net>.node, giving smaller organizations networks of at most 256 addresses; the first 3 bits of the first octet are 110.

- Class D and Class E addresses were reserved for experimental and other purposes.

Table 6.2 summarizes these address classes.

TABLE 6.2 IPv4 Address Classes

CLASS	LEADING BITS	SIZE OF NETWORK NUMBER FIELD	SIZE OF NODE NUMBER FIELD	NUMBER OF NETWORKS	NUMBER OF NODES PER NETWORK	START ADDRESS	END ADDRESS
A	0	8	24	128	16,777,216	0.0.0.0	127.255.255.255
B	10	16	16	16,384	65,536	128.0.0.0	191. 255.255.255
C	110	24	8	2,097,152	256	192.0.0.0	223. 255.255.255

There are, as you might expect, some special cases to keep in mind:

- 127.0.0.1 is commonly known as the loopback address, which apps can use for testing the local IP protocol stack. Packets addressed to the local loopback are sent only from one part of the stack to another ("looped back" on the stack), rather than out onto the Physical layer of the network or to another virtual machine hosted on the same system. Note that this means that the entire range of the addresses starting with 127 are so reserved, so you could use any of them.

- 169.254.0.0 is called the link local address, which is used to auto-assign an IP address when there is no DHCP server that responds. In many cases, systems that are using the link local address suggest that the DHCP server has failed to connect with them, for some reason.

The node address of 255 is reserved for broadcast use. *Broadcast messages* go to all nodes on the specified network; thus, sending a message to 192.168.2.255 sends it to all nodes on the 192.168.2 network, and sending it to 192.168.255.255 sends it to a lot more nodes! Broadcast messages are blocked by routers from traveling out onto their WAN side. By contrast, multicasting can provide ways to allow a router to send messages to other nodes beyond a router, using the address range of 224. 255.255.255 to 239.255.255.255. *Unicasting* is what happens when you do not use 255 as part of the node address field — the message goes only to the specific address. Although the SSCP exam won't ask about the details of setting up and managing broadcasts and multicasts, you should be aware of what these terms mean and recognize the address ranges involved.

Subnetting in IPv4

Subnetting seems to confuse people easily, but in real life, we deal with sets and subsets of things all the time. We rent an apartment, and it has a street address, but the building is further broken down into individual subaddresses known as the apartment number. This makes postal mail delivery, emergency services, and just day-to-day navigation by the residents easier. Telephone area codes primarily divide a country into geographic regions, and the next few digits of a phone number (the city code or exchange) divide the area code's map further. This, too, is a convenience feature, but first for the designers and operators of early phone networks and switches. (Phone number portability is rapidly erasing this correspondence of phone number to location.)

Subnetting allows network designers and administrators ways to logically group a set of devices together in ways that make sense to the organization. Suppose your company's main Class B IP address is 163.241, meaning you have 16 bits' worth of node addresses to assign. If you use them all, you have *one* subgroup, 0.0 to 254.254. (Remember that broadcast address!) Conversely:

- Using the last two bits gives you three subgroups.
- Using the last octet gives you 127 subgroups.
- And so on.

Designing your company's network to support subgroups requires that you know three things: your address class, the number of subgroups you need, and the number of nodes in each subgroup. This lets you start to create your subnet masks. A subnet mask, written in IP address format, shows which bit positions (starting from the right or least significant bit) are allocated to the node number within a subnet. For example, a mask of 255.255.255.0 says that the last 8 bits are used for the node numbers within each of 254 possible subnets (if this were a Class B address). Another subnet mask might be 255.255.255.128, indicating two subnets on a Class C address, with up to 127 nodes on each subnet. (Subnets do not have to be defined on byte or octet boundaries after all.)

Subnets are defined using the full range of values available for the given number of bits (minus 2 for addresses 0 and 255). Thus, if you require 11 nodes on each subnet, you still need to use four bits for the subnet portion of the address, giving you address 0, node addresses 1 through 11, and 15 for all-bits-on; two addresses are therefore unused.

This did get cumbersome after a while, and in 1993, Classless Inter-Domain Routing (CIDR) was introduced to help simplify both the notation and the calculation of subnets. CIDR appends the number of subnet address bits to the main IP address. For example, 192.168.1.168/24 shows that 24 bits are assigned for the *network* address, and the remaining 8 bits are therefore available for the node-within-subnet address. (Caution: don't get those backward!) Table 6.3 shows some examples to illustrate.

TABLE 6.3 **Address Classes and CIDR**

CLASS	NUMBER OF NETWORK BITS	NUMBER OF NODE BITS	SUBNET MASK	CIDR NOTATION
A	9	23	255.128.0.0	/9
B	17	15	255.255.128.0	/17
C	28	4	255.255.255.240	/28

Unless you're designing the network, most of what you need to do with subnets is to *recognize* subnets when you see them and interpret both the subnet masks and the CIDR notation, if present, to help you figure things out. CIDR counts bits starting with the leftmost bit of the IP address; it counts left to right. What's left after you run out of CIDR are the number of bits to use to assign addresses to nodes on the subnet (minus 2).

Before we can look at subnetting in IPv6, we first have to deal with the key changes to the Internet that the new version 6 is bringing in.

NOTE   Permanent and temporary addresses in the context of MAC and IP addresses can be a bit misleading. MAC addresses are meant to be permanent, but they can be changed via some NICs and modern operating systems. A NIC change is truly a change on the hardware, but the operating system makes the change in memory. However, the operating system change is still effective, and the altered or assigned MAC address overrules the MAC issued by the NIC manufacturer. Additionally, with an increasing reliance on virtualization, the MAC address becomes much less permanent. With every new virtual machine created, the MAC address often is a new one as well. This can be of special concern when software packages enforce licensing according to the MAC address (presumed a physical asset and wouldn't change no matter how often the client reinstalls the server). IP addresses are changed often by manual intervention or via DHCP services. The IP address can be assigned to be static, but an administrator can relatively quickly change it.

Running Out of Addresses?

By the early 1990s, it was clear that the IP address system then in use would not be able to keep up with the anticipated explosive growth in the numbers of devices attempting to connect to the Internet. At that point, version 4 of the protocol (or IPv4 as it's known) used a 32-bit address field, represented in the familiar four-octet address notation (such as 192.168.2.). That could handle only about 4.3 billion unique addresses; by 2012, we already had eight billion devices connected to the Internet and had invented additional protocols such as NAT to help cope. IPv4 also had a number of other faults that needed to be resolved. Let's see what the road to that future looks like.

IPV4 VS. IPV6: KEY DIFFERENCES AND OPTIONS

Over the years it's been in use, network engineers and security professionals have noticed that the design of IPv4 has a number of shortcomings to it. It did not have security built into it; its address space was limited, and even with workarounds like NAT, it still doesn't have enough addresses to handle the explosive demand for IoT devices. (Another whole class of Internet users are *robots*, smart software agents, with or without their hardware that let them interact with the physical world. Robots are using the Internet to learn from each other's experiences in accomplishing different tasks, and are becoming more autonomous and self-directing in this learning with each passing day.)

IPv6 brings a number of much-needed improvements to our network infrastructures.

- Dramatic increase in the size of the IP address field, allowing over 18 quintillion (a billion billions[4]) nodes on each of 18 quintillion networks. Using 64-bit address fields each for network and node addresses provides for a billion networks of a billion nodes or hosts on each network.

- More efficient routing, since ISPs and backbone service providers can use hierarchical arrangements of routing tables, while reducing if not eliminating fragmentation by better use of information about maximum transmission unit size.

- More efficient packet processing by eliminating the IP-level checksum (which proved to be redundant given most transport layer protocols).

- Directed data flows, which is more of a multicast rather than a broadcast flow. This can make broad distribution of streaming multimedia (sports events, movies, etc.) much more efficient.

- Simplified network configuration, using new autoconfigure capabilities, which can eliminate the need for DHCP and NAT.

- Simplify end-to-end connectivity at the IP layer by eliminating NAT. This can make services such as VOIP and quality of service more capable.

- Security is greatly enhanced, which may allow for greater use of ICMP (since most firewalls block IPv4 ICMP traffic as a security precaution). IPsec as defined in IPv4 becomes a mandatory part of IPv6 as a result.

[4] Sometimes referred to as a *Sagan*, after noted astrophysicist Carl Sagan, who would talk about the "billions and billions of stars" in our galaxy.

IPv6 was published in draft in 1996 and became an official Internet standard in 2017. The problem is that IPv6 is not backward compatible with IPv4; you cannot just flow IPv4 packets onto a purely IPv6 network and expect anything useful to happen. Everything about IPv6 *packages* the user data differently and flows it differently, requiring different implementations of the basic layers of the TCP/IP protocol stack. Figure 6.10 shows how these differences affect both the size and structure of the IP network layer header. This giant leap of changes from IPv4 to IPv6 stands to make IPv6 the clear winner, over time, and is comparable to the leap from analog video on VHS to digital video. By way of analogy, to send a video recorded on a VHS tape over the Internet, you must first convert its analog audio, video, chroma, and synchronization information into bits, and package (encode) those bits into a file using any of a wide range of digital video encoders such as MP4. The resulting digital MP4 file can then transit the Internet.

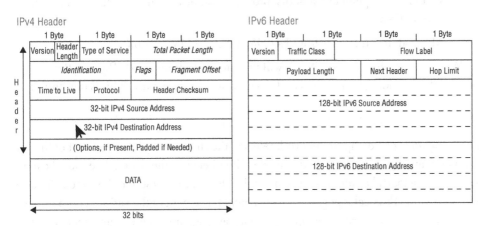

FIGURE 6.10 **Changes to packet header from IPv4 to IPv6**

Note that the 128-bit address field contains a 16-bit subnet prefix field. It's perhaps tempting to think that with a truly cosmic number of total possible addresses, there's no longer a reason to worry about subnetting once you've transitioned to an all-IPv6 architecture. This really isn't the case. Subnetting still gives the network administrator control over more than just broadcast traffic. By restricting user network nodes to well-defined connections, it can also provide a degree of security, as in a zero-trust (or near-zero-trust) architecture. Supernetting—the combination of unused addresses on multiple subnets into another distinct subnet—is also both supported by IPv6 and of benefit. As with everything else, it all depends upon your architecture, your needs, and your specific security requirements.

For organizations setting up new network infrastructures, there's a lot to be gained by going directly to an IPv6 implementation. Such systems may still have to deal with legacy devices that operate only in IPv4, such as "bring your own devices" users. Organizations trying to transition their existing IPv4 networks to IPv6 may find it worth the effort to use a variety of "dual-rail" approaches to effectively run both IPv4 and IPv6 at the same time on the same systems.

- Dual stack, in which your network hardware and management systems run both protocols simultaneously, over the same physical layer.

- Tunnel, by encapsulating one protocol's packets within the other's structure. Usually, this is done by encapsulating IPv6 packets inside IPv4 packets.

- Network Address Translation–Protocol Translation (NAT-PT), but this seems best done with application layer gateways.

- Dual-stack application layer gateways, supported by almost all major operating systems and equipment vendors, provide a somewhat smoother transition from IPv4 to IPv6.

- MAC address increases from EUI-48 to EUI-64 (48 to 64 bit).

With each passing month, SSCPs will need to know more about IPv6 and the changes it is heralding for personal and organizational Internet use. This is our future!

Network Topographies

The *topography* of a computer network refers to the structure and arrangement of the various nodes and their connections depicted as links between the nodes. The model can be described as a logical or physical design. Logical topography describes how the data flows on the network. Physical topography is the actual placement of the various components of a network. The physical topography is not always the same as the logical topography. The basic topologies are point to point, ring, bus, star, and mesh. Each has its place in most any organization's network architecture.

NOTE   You may sometimes see these referred to as *topologies*, but strictly speaking, *topology* is a mathematical study of surfaces and shapes, which looks at ways that a shape can be distorted (stretched, inverted, or rotated, for example) without changing its essential characteristics. A *topography* is a description or model of one specific type of arrangement, as if it is plotted out on a map, and the essential characteristics of that arrangement of elements.

Ring Topography   In a ring topography, devices are connected in a one-way circular loop pattern, with the connection going *through* each device. Figure 6.11 provides a basic illustration. Each node processes the data it receives and either keeps it or passes it along to the next node on the ring; if a node stops working, the entire ring stops working.

As a result, ring systems suffer from *collisions* when more than one device tries to send data at the same time, as competing signals interfere with each other on the physical transmission medium. Early *token ring networks* handled collision avoidance by having any device that detects a sufficiently long idle time on the ring transmit a special packet (the token) along the ring; the token is passed along until the first node that needs to transmit data appends its data to the token and then transmits that set (token plus data) along the ring. Once the data plus token reaches the intended recipient, it retains the data packet and releases the token by sending it out for use by another node.

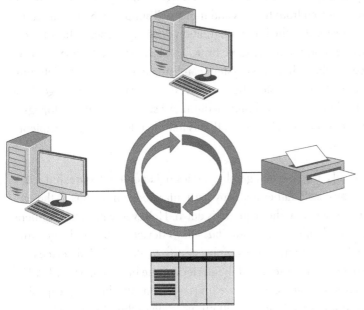

FIGURE 6.11 **A ring topography**

Token rings can work well in smaller networks over short distances, in situations that do not need other features that a central server could provide while it brokers and distributes traffic to user nodes. In such circumstances, using a bidirectional ring (two cables, two sets of NICs per node, transmitting in opposite directions around the circle) may offer greater reliability. Token rings have largely been abandoned because they just do not scale well to support larger organizations.

In the late 1980s, fiber distributed data interface (FDDI) ring networks were becoming very popular, as these could achieve 100MBps network speeds over distances up to 50km. As fast Ethernet technologies improved, FDDI fell out of favor for most business applications. FDDI is well suited to applications in industrial control, in energy generation and distribution, and in hazardous environments. These settings have very stressing requirements for reliability, fault tolerance, graceful degradation, and high immunity to RF or electromagnetic interference. They can also need communications systems that are totally free from electrical signals and hence cannot be possible ignition sources. FDDI architectures tend to be trees of interconnected rings.

Bus Topography   This topography gets its name from the arrays of parallel power and signal lines that make up power distribution *buses* and the internal backplanes inside a computer. Each node or system on a bus is connected by either a cable containing many parallel connections or a single-circuit cable. Unlike a ring topography, the bus does not go through each node; a node or device can be powered off, idle, in a fault state, or disconnected from the bus and traffic will simply go on past its connection point. This means that the bus configuration does experience data collisions as multiple systems can transmit at the same time. The bus topography does have a collision avoidance capability because a system can listen to the cabling to determine whether there is traffic. When a system hears traffic, it waits. When it no longer hears traffic, it releases the data onto the cabling medium. All systems on the bus topography can hear the network traffic. A system that is not intended to be the recipient simply ignores the data.

The bus topography, like the ring topography, has a single point of failure, but it is the interconnecting bus itself, rather than any particular node on the bus. If the bus is disconnected from a segment, the segment is down. However, within the segment, nodes can still reach each other. A *hot-swap bus* allows devices to be unplugged from the bus, both from data and from power supply circuits, to allow a failed device to be removed without disrupting the rest of the devices or the bus itself. Many RAID enclosures—even consumer-grade, two-drive units—provide this hot-swap capability so that business continues to function without needing to shut down a network attached storage system to swap out a failed drive or one that is sending up smart device alarms of an impending failure.

A bus topography is terminated at both ends of the network, and because of the nature of their signaling circuits, they rarely exceed 3 meters in overall length unless some type of bus extender is used to connect two bus segments together. Bus architectures have their use within many subsystems, such as within a storage subsystem rack, but become impractical when extended to larger architectures.

Star Topography   In a star topography, the connected devices are attached to a central traffic management device which can be a router, hub, or switch. Figure 6.12 shows how a dedicated line is run from each device to the central router, hub, or switch. A benefit of star topography is that there is segment resiliency; if a link to one endpoint device goes down, the rest of the network is still functional. Cabling is more efficiently used and damaged cable is easier to detect and remediate.

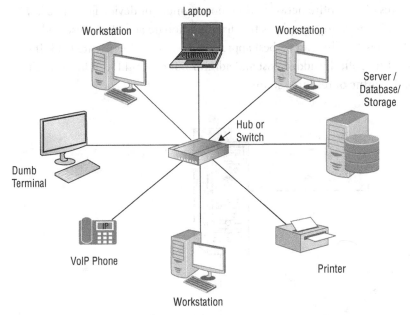

FIGURE 6.12 **A star topography**

Various logical configurations of a bus or ring topography can result in a star topography. An Ethernet network can be deployed as a physical star because it is based on a bus. The hub or switch device in this case is actually a logical bus connection device. A physical star pattern can be accomplished with a multistation access unit (MAU). An MAU allows for the cable segments to be deployed as a star while internally the device makes logical ring connections.

Note that a point-to-point topography is a degenerate case of a star, in which the star node has only one connection point. Your laptop or PC may have only one RJ45 jack on it, but with its Wi-Fi, Bluetooth, USB, and possibly other interfaces, it can easily be the central node in a star arrangement of connections to other devices. It's good to understand point to point, however, as it logically shows up in tunneling protocols and is an easy way to connect two computers or other devices together without having the overhead of a third device acting as a switch or router. It's also the model for peer-to-peer service relationships.

Mesh Topography   Putting it all together, a mesh topography is the interconnection of all of the systems on a network across a number of individual paths. The concept of a full mesh topography means that every system is connected to every other system. A partial mesh topography stops short of total connection but does connect many systems to many other systems. The key benefit of a mesh topography is the maximum levels of resiliency it provides as redundant connections prevent failures of the entire network when one segment or device fails. The key disadvantage of a mesh topography is the disproportionate added expense and administrative hassle. This can be best appreciated when seeing Figure 6.13. It's also worth noting both the added cost and administration could lead to a security implication by virtue of resource strain.

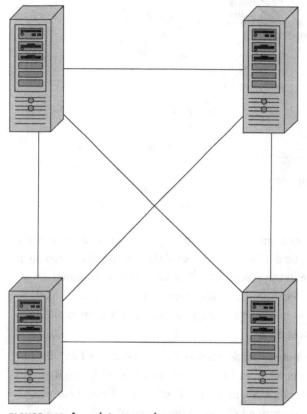

FIGURE 6.13 **A mesh topography**

Mesh systems can be either strongly connected or weakly connected, depending upon whether each node or device has a direct connection to every other device in the mesh. As the number of devices increases, such strongly connected meshes (all nodes talk directly with each other) can get complicated *and* expensive to build, configure, and manage. Data center designs often use mesh systems that may couple strongly connected meshes, as network segments, with other strongly connected mesh segments, via weakly connected meshes, as a way to balance performance, availability, and cost, while providing an ability to do load leveling across these clusters of devices.

Network Relationships

Almost every activity performed by elements of any computing system use a *service provision* model as its basic design and operational paradigm. Services define specific sets of operations that can be performed against a specific type of object, while providing an interface by which other processes can request that the service be executed on their behalf. Printing a file, for example, might involve many different service requests.

- The end user identifies and selects a file to be printed, using either an operating system utility (such as Windows Explorer) or another application.

- That application or utility requests that the operating system verify that the file exists and that access control restrictions allow it to be printed by this user and by the utility or application in question.

- The operating system sends a request to the print service, specifying the file to be printed.

- The print service asks the user to select any print controls, such as number of copies, desired printer, printer tray or paper, etc.

- The print manager service passes the file and the parameters to the printer's device driver, which verifies that it can print that type of file with those parameter settings.

- The printer device driver requests that the file and parameters be put on its print queue by the print queue manager service.

- The print queue manager service interrogates the printer and, if it is available to print a file, sends (or starts sending) the next file in the print queue for that printer. Eventually, it sends the file the user just requested to the printer.

- And so on.

Each service relationship has two parties involved in it: the *server* is the process that performs the requested service on behalf of the requesting *client* process. These client-server relationships can quickly become many layers deep, as you can see from this incomplete and simplified look at part of the trail of services that is invoked when you right-click a file and select Print from the context menu that appears.

Extending these service concepts to a system-of-systems or network context adds an important twist.

Client-Server

In a networking context, a *server* is a system that provides a set of well-defined services to a variety of other requesting subjects on the network or network segment as appropriate. Servers are best thought of in terms of the *workloads* or *job streams* that they can support. A network-attached storage system, for example, may be optimized to provide fast access to files and fast transfer of their contents to clients on the network, but it may not be optimized to support compute-intensive processing tasks. Servers usually run an operating system that is expressly tailored to managing many service job streams for many clients, rather than the typical endpoint operating systems (such as Windows, Android, or Linux) that you see on most endpoints. That operating system has either the server software built into it as a standard set of features (such as we see in Windows Server) or a server application such as Apache is installed, and it then handles all of the server interactions with clients.

Client-server relationships can also exist at some of the lowest levels in our systems. Almost every router provides DHCP, access list control, and other services, which support clients by assigning IP addresses, managing proxy relationships, and performing a wide variety of other functions.

But at any level of abstraction and at any level of your systems architecture, managing servers so that they work effectively with your access control servers, your intrusion detection and prevention services, your traffic monitoring and load balancing services, and many other servers and services that make up your network management and control planes is both complex and vital to keeping the entire infrastructure reliable, resilient, safe, secure, auditable, and recoverable.

Peer to Peer

Peer to peer (P2P) in any form or use attempts to decentralize network and systems operation; depending upon your point of view, it either makes a P2P system *unmanaged,* without any directive or controlling authority, or makes it *unmanageable,* and thus prone to misuse, abuse, and attacks. Since its early days, P2P computing has been a technical, social, and economic paradigm. Think of Grace Hopper's early desires to share idle computing power among government agencies, which in its inception was a distributed P2P unmanaged approach to solving economic and social problems. This vision gave rise to the ARPANET and was part of its initial *trusting* nature and design. A third point of view, of course, is that the management of a P2P system is distributed across its constituent nodes, with no one node having to be online, functioning, and in charge of the network in order to assure that services are available, and information flows as required.

P2P Implementations

P2P has since evolved in four basic types of implementations. The first relies on native operating systems features to provide serverless connections between computers on a LAN, and it facilitates file, resource, and service sharing. CPU sharing, particularly with distributed applications providing the task or workflow management, is part of this category. The second focuses strictly on content sharing and because of its widespread use for sharing pirated content has become rather notorious. The third type of implementation involves the use of blockchain technologies to implement distributed, shared ledgers and then use those ledgers to collaboratively perform tasks. The fourth involves ad hoc wireless networks, which you'll look at in greater detail in the "Operate and Configure Wireless Technologies" section in this chapter.

Native OS-Supported P2P   Native OS-supported P2P systems have been the backbone of the SOHO market almost since the start of personal computing. Each P2P client on the LAN uses its native capabilities to identify whether to share device-oriented services (such as Internet access or printing) to other systems on the LAN. File and storage volume access are also published as shared by each client. Network discovery features, also native in each client (to a greater or lesser degree), then provide ways for users and applications to search for, identify, select, and connect with such resources. P2P clients running Microsoft Windows OS will use NetBIOS, Server Message Block (SMB), and Windows Workgroups as part of managing that client's view of the shared environment. LANs with a mix of Windows and non-Windows clients can sometimes find it difficult to establish the right type of desired sharing.

Device sharing via P2P can also be done by a distributed application. Until Microsoft migrated it into Azure and transformed its service model, the personal use versions of Skype employed a P2P application sharing model as a way of providing access to the local PSTN; individual Skype users could configure their installed copy of Skype to permit remote users to access a local dial-out or dial-in connection, for example.

CPU sharing P2P arrangements have been used to create informal massively parallel processing systems. Early examples of this on a consensual basis included analysis of radio telescope and other data as part of the search for extraterrestrial intelligence. Cryptocurrency mining operations, for example, is sometimes conducted by a botnet of systems, each of which is performing its allocated piece of the computation; the use of the botnet's CPU may or may not be with the informed consent of its user or owner. Such distributed *cycle-stealing* is also used in many attacks on cryptographic systems.

In business settings, experience shows that at some point most SOHO users face information security and systems availability needs that dictate a more managed solution than P2P can provide; servers are introduced to govern access control, resource sharing, and backup and restore, and to provide accountability for systems and resource utilization.

Content Sharing P2P   File sharing services such as Napster and BitTorrent systems minimized the numbers of files that they stored on their own operators' central servers by looking to users who've downloaded a particular torrent to be willing to share pieces of it with other users. Ostensibly, this was for performance reasons, as it allowed users to download portions of a torrent from other users who may be closer to them on the Internet than they are to a higher-capacity, higher-speed main server site. In reality, most of this use of P2P for torrent and file sharing was seen by the courts in many countries as a thinly disguised attempt to dodge responsibility for violating the intellectual property rights, such as copyright, claimed by the original creator of the content; the torrent operator doesn't have the files in question, only pointers to people who *might* have pieces of the file in question.

To add insult to injury, P2P file sharing services are notorious for propagating malware payloads around the Internet, either via the applications that they require users to download, install, and use (to be able to then share content), by means of the shared content itself, or both.

✔ Before You P2P Content...

P2P content and file sharing service usage can subject an organization to considerable risk of malware infection, data exfiltration, and other types of inappropriate systems use; it can also expose the organization to the risks of civil or criminal liabilities as well as reputational damage. Organizations should subject any request to use P2P capabilities to intensive scrutiny to ensure that all legal and systems security risks are properly identified, managed, and controlled, before allowing any such programs to be installed or used. Experts in business operations, risk management, legal counsel, and information security should make this assessment and recommendation to senior management and leadership on a case-by-case basis.

Blockchain P2P Approaches   Blockchains work in essentially a peer-to-peer fashion, since they depend upon the users of the blockchain to add new blocks and to validate the integrity of the chain itself, rather than relying upon a central server architecture to do this in an authoritative manner. Blockchains are already being implemented as part of financial systems, public records and land title systems, logistics and supply chain management, parts and data pedigree, and many other applications and use cases. Work is underway to extend blockchain into certificate authentication and management approaches, which could lead to distributed, decentralized authentication for nodes in a P2P system.

Trusting the Endpoints

The other meaning of the acronym P2P is, of course, *point-to-point*, and it's somewhat ironic that point-to-point is the final connection from the network that serves the collection of peers to each of the peers itself. Securing that link is a vital part of keeping the whole peer-to-peer system secure. Many security systems vendors, such as Palo Alto Networks, Cisco Systems, and Symantec, advocate extensive use of policy-driven virtual private networks (VPNs) as part of a zero-trust approach to securing your networks. To what extent this could be part of peer-to-peer systems is unclear, but worth considering, and we'll examine this further in the "Zero-Trust Network Architectures" section later in this chapter.

Transmission Media Types

All networks need some kind of physical transmission media to be able to function, and that usually requires some kind of controlled and managed process of installation, maintenance, and protection. Most businesses and many families do not consider randomly festooning cables all over the place as a positive decorating statement. Besides being unattractive if not downright unsightly, badly managed wiring closets and cable plants present hazards to people working in and around them, which can lead to injury, damage to cables and equipment, and expensive downtime. The physical cabling of your network infrastructure also presents many meters or miles of targets of opportunity for would-be attackers, if they can get surreptitious access to it and clip in sniffers or monitoring devices. As part of managing the physical aspects of risk mitigation controls, as a security professional, you need to understand and appreciate the different types of transmission media used in modern network systems, their inherent risks, and what you can do about those risks.

The most commonly used LAN technologies you'll encounter are Ethernet and IEEE 802.11-based wireless systems. Since we'll look at wireless systems and their security issues in greater depth later in this chapter, let's just dive right into Ethernet-based LANs and the issues associated with their various physical media technologies. Most of what you'll need to be working with, as it pertains to transmission media safety and security, applies at the Link layer and below, of course.

Ethernet Basics

Ethernet is based on the IEEE 802.3 standard and is the most common LAN technology in use. It is so popular because it allows low-cost network implementation and is easy to understand, implement, and maintain. Ethernet is also applicable and flexible for use in a wide variety of network topologies. It is most commonly deployed with star or bus topologies. Another strength of Ethernet is that it can support two-way, full-duplex communications using twisted-pair cabling. Ethernet operates in two layers of the OSI model, the physical layer and the data link layer. A protocol data unit for Ethernet is a frame.

Ethernet is a shared-media, or broadcast, LAN technology. Ethernet as a broadcast technology allows numerous devices to communicate over the same medium. Ethernet supports collision detection and avoidance native to the attached networking devices. The design of an Ethernet LANs has network nodes and interconnecting media or links. The network nodes can be of two types.

- **Data Terminal Equipment (DTE):** These are basically the variety of endpoint devices employed to convert user information into signals or reconvert received signals. Examples of DTEs include personal computers, workstations, file servers, and print servers. The DTE can also be a terminal to be used by the end user. They can be the source or destination system.

- **Data Communication Equipment (DCE):** DCEs can be standalone devices like repeaters, network switches, and routers. These intermediate network devices receive and forward frames across the network. A DCE can be part of a DTE or connected to the DTE. Other examples of DCEs include interface cards, gateways, and modems.

Ethernet is categorized by data transfer rate and distance. Some data rates for operation over optical fibers and twisted-pair cables are as follows:

- **Fast Ethernet:** Fast Ethernet refers to an Ethernet network that can transfer data at a rate of 100Mbps.
- **Gigabit Ethernet:** Gigabit Ethernet delivers a data rate of 1,000Mbps (1Gbps).
- **10 Gigabit Ethernet:** 10 Gigabit Ethernet is the recent generation and delivers a data rate of 10Gbps (10,000Mbps). It is generally used for backbones in high-end applications requiring high data rates.

NOTE Data rates are often measured in Mbps (megabits per second, sometimes represented as Mbits/s). Note that Mbps as a rate differs from MBps (megabytes per second, sometimes represented as Mbytes/s). To convert data rates, know that there are 8 bits per byte, and thus 80 Mbps/s is equivalent to 10MBps.

There are various properties and components of LAN technologies that are complementary and should be understood within the context of how the different media configurations work. Of the examples discussed in this chapter, a security professional can expect to deal with combinations of all on the LAN. Ethernet and Wi-Fi LANs employ a variety of methods, including analog, digital, synchronous, and asynchronous communications and baseband, broadband, broadcast, multicast, and unicast technologies.

Network Cabling

Network cabling describes the connection of devices, hardware, or components via one or more types of physical data transmission media. There are many types that exist, and each has particular specifications and capabilities. For instance, some types of network cabling have distance or span limitations and may not provide sufficient reach and availability of data across wide geographical areas. Network throughput requirements, transmission distances, and site-specific physical layout characteristics, will influence or dictate what cabling and interconnection standards are selected for use. Cables can be damaged during installation, and stepping on cables, slamming a door shut on them, or rolling over them with a heavily loaded cart, dolly, or chair can pinch them and break one or more conductors in them. Selecting the wrong types of cables and not treating them properly during installation and use is a major cause of network performance issues that can be devilishly hard to diagnose and trace down to the one or more cables that need to be replaced. Network cables, whether copper or glass fiber, are not *fragile*, but they should not be treated as if they are made of steel.

Copper is one of the best materials to use for carrying electronic signals. It is easily shaped into very fine wires that can maintain a high degree of mechanical flexibility and performs well at room temperature. Even though copper can carry signals a far distance, there is some resistance in the metal, so the signal strength does eventually degrade. All in all, it is a very cost-effective choice for the conductor elements in any Ethernet cabling.

Fiber-optic cable provides an alternative to conductor-based network cabling over copper. Fiber-optic cables transmit pulses of light rather than electricity. This gives fiber-optic cable the advantage of being extremely fast and nearly impervious to tapping and interference. Fiber-optic cables can also transmit over a much longer distance before attenuation degrades the signal. The drawbacks are the relative difficultly to install and the initial expense of the line. The security and performance fiber optic offers comes at a steep price.

Network cables come in two conductor types—electrical and optical fiber. Most electrical interconnect cables use copper conductors, which can easily be spliced into by an intruder—sometimes without causing any break in the conductors and interruption or downtime on the connection. Most optical fiber is a bit more challenging to cut through, polish the ends of the glass fibers, and cap them to allow a tap to be put onto the fiber. It's not impossible, but it takes more time to do, and that greater downtime may be easier to detect, if you're monitoring for it.

✔ Fire Safety and Cable Types

Because regular PVC releases toxic fumes when it burns, many modern building codes and fire insurance policy conditions require a different material for sheathing network cables. A *plenum cable* is one that is covered with a special coating that does not give off toxic fumes when heated or burned. Plenum cable is so named because it can be run in air plenums or enclosed spaces in a building, many of which may be part of the heating, ventilation, and air conditioning (HVAC) systems. It is typically made up of several fire-retardant plastics, like either a low-smoke PVC or a fluorinated ethylene polymer (FEP). Non-plenum-rated cabling must usually be run inside steel conduit or in cableways that are not open to building air and ventilation and that can be sealed to prevent smoke and fumes from escaping during a fire.

Several different types of electrical signaling cabling are in common use for Ethernet installations.

Coaxial Cable   Coaxial cable, also called coax, was a popular networking cable type used throughout the 1970s and 1980s. In the early 1990s, its use quickly declined as a data cable because of the popularity and capabilities of twisted-pair wiring, although it is still widely employed for analog transmission. Coaxial cable has a center core of copper wire as an inner conductor surrounded by an insulating layer, surrounded by a conducting shield. There are some coaxial cables that have an additional insulating outer sheath or jacket.

Coax enables two-way communications because the center copper core and the braided shielding layer act as two independent conductors. The various shielding design of coaxial cable makes it fairly resistant to electromagnetic interference (EMI) and less susceptible to leakage. Coax handles weak signals very well, and it can carry a signal over longer distances than twisted-pair cabling can. It was quite popular for most of the 1970s and 1980s, as it supported relatively high bandwidth. Twisted-pair cabling is now preferred simply because it is less costly and easier to install. Coaxial cable requires the use of special *segment terminators*, which complete the electrical circuit between the center conductor and the shield to create the transmission line characteristics needed by the type of system being installed. Twisted-pair cabling does not require such terminators (although an unterminated long run of twisted-pair cable, plugged into a router or other device, may generate noise that the device's NIC and the attached computer may still have to spend some amount of overhead to ignore). Coaxial cable is bulkier and has a larger minimum arc radius than does twisted-pair cable. The arc radius is the smallest curve that the cable can be shaped into before damaging the internal conductors. Bending the coax beyond the minimum arc is thus a relatively common cause of coaxial cabling failures.

Baseband and Broadband Cables   There is a naming convention used to label most network cable technologies, and it follows the pattern XXyyyyZZ. XX represents the maximum speed the cable type offers, such as 10Mbps for a 10Base2 cable. The next series of letters, yyyy, represents whether it is baseband or broadband cable, such as baseband for a 10Base2 cable. Most networking cables are baseband cables. However, when used in specific configurations, coaxial cable can be used as a broadband connection, such as with cable modems. ZZ either represents the maximum distance the cable can be used or acts as shorthand to represent the technology of the cable, such as the approximately 200 meters for 10Base2 cable (actually 185 meters, but it's rounded up to 200) or T or TX for twisted-pair in 10Base-T or 100Base-TX.

Twisted-Pair   As mentioned before, twisted-pair cabling has become a preferred option because it is extremely thin and flexible versus the bulkiness of coaxial cable.

All types of twisted pair are made up of four pairs of wires that are twisted around each other and then sheathed in a PVC insulator. There are two types of twisted pair, shielded twisted pair (STP) and unshielded twisted pair (UTP). STP has a metal foil wrapper around the wires underneath the external sheath. The foil provides additional protection from external EMI. UTP lacks the foil around the sheath. UTP is most often used to refer to 10Base-T, 100Base-T, or 1000Base-T, which are now considered outdated and not used.

UTP and STP are both a collection of small copper wires that are twisted in pairs, which helps to guard against interference from external radio frequencies and electric and magnetic waves. The arrangement also reduces interference between the pairs themselves. The interference is called *crosstalk* and happens when data transmitted over one set of wires is pulled into another set of wires because the electric signal radiates electromagnetic waves that leak through the sheathing. To combat this, each twisted pair is twisted at a different rate, measured in twists per inch. The staggered twists prevent the signal or electromagnetic radiation from escaping from one pair of wires to another pair.

There are several classes of UTP cabling. The various categories are created through the use of tighter twists of the wire pairs, variations in the quality of the conductor, and variations in the quality of the external shielding. Note that UTP is susceptible to external EMI, so it may be prone to service interruption or significantly degraded throughput in environments with large EMI sources, such as electrical motors, near elevator hoist motors, pumps, or power transformers and conditioning equipment.

Table 6.4 shows the important characteristics for the most common network cabling types.

TABLE 6.4 **Important Characteristics for Common Network Cabling Types**

TYPE	MAX SPEED	DISTANCE	DIFFICULTY OF INSTALLATION	SUSCEPTIBILITY TO EMI	COST
10Base2	10Mbps	185 meters	Medium	Medium	Medium
10Base5	10Mbps	500 meters	High	Low	High
10Base-T (UTP)	10Mbps	100 meters	Low	High	Very Low
STP	155Mbps	100 meters	Medium	Medium	High
100Base-T/100Base-TX	100Mbps	100 meters	Low	High	Low
1000Base-T	1Gbps	100 meters	Low	High	Medium
Fiber-optic	2+Gbps	2+ kilometers	Very high	None	Very high

Extending a Cable's Reach with Repeaters While it is true that exceeding the maximum length of a cable type's capabilities will result in a degraded signal, this process of attenuation can be mitigated through the use of repeaters and concentrators. By way of quick review, a repeater connects two separate communications media. When the repeater receives an incoming transmission on one media, including both signal and noise, it regenerates only the signal and retransmits it across the second media. A concentrator does the same thing except it has more than two ports. Security professionals should recognize that using more than four repeaters in a row is discouraged. Using more than four repeaters in a row is discouraged. The 5-4-3 rule has been developed to guide proper use of repeaters and concentrators to maximize cable lengths and remove as much attenuation problems as possible.

The 5-4-3 rule outlines a deployment strategy for repeaters and concentrators in segments arranged in a tree topography with a central hub, or trunk, connecting the segments, like branches of a tree. In this configuration, between any two nodes on the network the following must be true:

- There can be a maximum of five segments.

- The segments can be connected by a maximum of four repeaters and concentrators.

- Only three of those five segments can have additional or other user, server, or networking device connections.

This 5-4-3 rule does *not* apply to switched networks or the use of bridges and routers in place of repeaters.

Commonly Used Ports and Protocols

Most if not all of the protocols used on the Internet have been defined in requests for change (RFCs) issued by committees of the IETF. If you haven't read any of these yet, start with RFC 1122 and 1123 as a way to gain some insight on just how many layers upon layers there are within the Internet's structures and processes. You'll note that the protocols themselves are usually not written as hard and fast requirements, each feature of which must be obeyed in order to claim that one has built a "compliant" system. The RFCs recognize that systems implementers will do what they need to do to get their particular jobs done.

Port assignments are an example of the built-in flexibility that is a hallmark of everything Internet. The Internet Assigned Numbers Authority (IANA) publishes a list of the officially assigned port numbers associated with all defined protocols, which you can find at `https://www.iana.org/assignments/service-names-port-numbers/service-names-port-numbers.xhtml`.

Port remapping is sometimes used by various service providers as a way to enhance security, hide services, or possibly to improve service delivery. Remapping of email-associated ports has been commonly done by some ISP-provided email services for these reasons; their subscribers have to make sure that they've remapped the protocol-port assignments the same way, or no connection takes place.

The following tables group the most commonly encountered ports and protocols into several broad functional groups: Table 6.5, security and access control; Table 6.6, network management; Table 6.7, email; Table 6.8, web services; and Table 6.9, utilities. These are somewhat arbitrary groupings, and they are sorted alphabetically on the protocol name, so try not to read too much into the arrangement of these tables. Note that a number of defined, standard protocols, such as ICMP, ARP, and its cousin RARP do not use ports.

TABLE 6.5 Commonly Used Security and Access Control Protocols and Port Numbers

PROTOCOL	TCP/UDP	PORT NUMBER	DESCRIPTION
IPsec	UDP ESP AH	500 (IKE) 50 51	Port 4500 for IPsec NAT-traversal mode. L2TP port 1701, set to allow inbound IPsec secured traffic only, ISAKMP 500 TCP, UDP. KINK 910 TCP, UDP. AH_ESP_encap 2070. ESP_encap 2797.
Lightweight Directory Access Protocol (LDAP)	TCP, UDP	389	LDAP provides a mechanism of accessing and maintaining distributed directory information. LDAP is based on the ITU-T X.500 standard but has been simplified and altered to work over TCP/IP networks.
Lightweight Directory Access Protocol over TLS/SSL (LDAPS)	TCP, UDP	636	LDAPS provides the same function as LDAP but over a secure connection that is provided by either SSL or TLS.

TABLE 6.6 Commonly Used Network Management Protocols and Port Numbers

PROTOCOL	TCP/UDP	PORT NUMBER	DESCRIPTION
Border Gateway Protocol (BGP)	TCP	179	BGP is used on the public Internet and by ISPs to maintain very large routing tables and traffic processing, which involve millions of entries to search, manage, and maintain every moment of the day.

CONTINUES

PROTOCOL	TCP/UDP	PORT NUMBER	DESCRIPTION
Common Management Information Protocol (CMIP)	TCP, UDP CMIP Agent	163 164	
Domain Name System (DNS)	TCP, UDP	53	Resolves domain names into IP addresses for network routing. Hierarchical, using top-level domain servers (.com, .org, etc.) that support lower-tier servers for public name resolution. DNS servers can also be set up in private networks.
Dynamic Host Configuration Protocol (DHCP)	UDP	67/68	DHCP is used on networks that do not use static IP address assignment (almost all of them).
NetBIOS	TCP, UDP	137/138/139	NetBIOS (more correctly, NETBIOS over TCP/IP, or NBT) has long been the central protocol used to interconnect Microsoft Windows machines.
Network Time Protocol (NTP)	UDP	123	One of the most overlooked protocols is NTP. NTP is used to synchronize the devices on the Internet. Most secure services simply will not support devices whose clocks are too far out of sync, for example.
Secure Shell (SSH)	TCP	22	Used to manage network devices securely at the command level; secure alternative to Telnet, which does not support secure connections.
Simple Network Management Protocol (SNMP)	TCP, UDP	161/162	SNMP is used by network administrators as a method of network management. SNMP can monitor, configure, and control network devices. SNMP traps can be set to notify a central server when specific actions are occurring.
Telnet	TCP	23	Teletype-like unsecure command-line interface used to manage network device. Use only when SSH unavailable.

TABLE 6.7 Commonly Used Email Protocols and Port Numbers

PROTOCOL	TCP/UDP	PORT NUMBER	DESCRIPTION
Internet Message Access Protocol (IMAP)	TCP	143	IMAP version 3 is the second of the main protocols used to retrieve mail from a server. While POP has wider support, IMAP supports a wider array of remote mailbox operations that can be helpful to users.
Post Office Protocol (POP) v3	TCP	110	POP version 3 provides client–server email services, including transfer of complete inbox (or other folder) contents to the client.
Simple Mail Transfer Protocol (SMTP)	TCP	25	Transfer mail (email) between mail servers and between end user (client) and mail server.

TABLE 6.8 Commonly Used Web Page Access Protocols and Port Numbers

PROTOCOL	TCP/UDP	PORT NUMBER	DESCRIPTION
Hypertext Transfer Protocol (HTTP)	TCP	80	HTTP is the main protocol that is used by web browsers and is thus used by any client that uses files located on these servers.
Hypertext Transfer Protocol over SSL/TLS (HTTPS)	TCP	443	HTTPS is used in conjunction with HTTP to provide the same services but doing it using a secure connection that is provided by either SSL or TLS.

TABLE 6.9 Commonly Used Utility Protocols and Port Numbers

PROTOCOL	TCP/UDP	PORT NUMBER	DESCRIPTION
File Transfer Protocol (FTP)	TCP	20/21	FTP control is handled on TCP port 21 and its data transfer can use TCP port 20 as well as dynamic ports depending on the specific configuration.
FTP over TLS/SSL (RFC 4217)	TCP	989/990	FTP over TLS/SSL uses the FTP protocol, which is then secured using either SSL or TLS.
Trivial File Transfer Protocol (TFTP)	UDP	69	TFTP offers a method of file transfer without the session establishment requirements that FTP has; using UDP instead of TCP, the receiving device must verify complete and correct transfer. TFTP is typically used by devices to upgrade software and firmware.

It's good to note at this point that as we move down the protocol stack, each successive layer adds additional addressing, routing, and control information to the data payload it received from the layer above it. This is done by *encapsulating* or wrapping its own header around what it's given by the layers of the protocol stack or the application-layer socket call that asks for its service. Thus, the datagram produced at the transport layer contains the protocol-specific header and the payload data. This is passed to the network layer, along with the required address information and other fields; the network layer puts that information into its IPv4 (or IPv6) header, sets the Protocol field accordingly, appends the datagram it just received from the transport layer, and passes that on to the link layer. (And so on.)

Most of the protocols that use layer 4 either use TCP/IP as a stateful or connection-oriented way of transferring data or use UDP, which is stateless and not connection-oriented. TCP bundles its data and headers into *segments* (not to be confused with "segments" at layer 1), whereas UDP and some other transport layer protocols call their bundles *datagrams*.

Stateful communications processes have the sender and receiver go through a sequence of steps, with each keeping track of which step the other has initiated, successfully completed, or asked for a retry on. Each of those steps is often called the *state* of the process at the sender or receiver. Stateful processes require an unambiguous identification of sender and recipient, each state that they might be in, and some kind of protocols for error detection and requests for retransmission, which a connection provides.

Stateless communication processes do not require the sender and receiver to know where the other is in the process. This means that the sender does not need a connection, does not need to service retransmission requests, and may not even need to validate who the listeners are. Broadcast traffic is typically both stateless and connectionless.

Layer 4 devices include gateways (which can bridge dissimilar network architectures together, and route traffic between them) and firewalls. Note that the function of a gateway is often performed at every layer where it is needed, up through layer 7. Layer 7 gateways often function as edge devices, such as at the edge of a cloud-hosted software defined network and an on-premise physical network. Firewalls can also be *multihomed*; that is, they are able to filter or screen traffic across multiple paths, which also makes them suitable as gateways in some situations.

From here on up, the two protocol stacks conceptually diverge. TCP/IP as a standard stops at layer 4 and allocates to users, applications, and other unspecified higher-order logic the tasks of managing what traffic to transport and how to make business or organizational sense of what's getting transported. The OSI Seven Layer Reference Model continues to add further layers of abstraction, and for one very good reason: because each layer adds clarity when taking business processes into the Internet or into the clouds (which you get to through the Internet, of course). That clarity aids the design process and the development of sound operational procedures; it is also a great help when trying to diagnose and debug problems.

You also see that from here on up, almost all functions except perhaps that of the firewall and the gateway are hosted either in operating systems or applications software, which of course is running on servers or endpoint devices. You'll find very little direct hardware implementation of protocols and services above the Transport layer without it having a significant embedded firmware component.

Cross-Layer Protocols and Services

Remember, both TCP/IP and the OSI reference model are *models*, models that define and describe in varying degrees of specificity and generality. OSI and TCP/IP both must support some important functions that cross layers, and without these, it's not clear if the Internet would work very well at all! The most important of these are as follows:

- *Dynamic Host Configuration Protocol (DHCP)* assigns IPv4 (and later IPv6) addresses to new devices as they join the network. This set of handshakes allows DHCP to accept or reject new devices based on a variety of rules and conditions that administrators can use to restrict a network. DHCP servers allow subscriber devices to lease an IP address, for a specific period of time (or indefinitely); as the expiration time reaches its half-life, the subscribing device requests a renewal.

- *Address Resolution Protocol (ARP)* is a discovery protocol, by which a network device determines the corresponding IP address for a given MAC address by (quite literally) asking other network devices for it. On each device, ARP maintains in its cache a list of IP address and MAC address pairs. Failing to find the address there, ARP seeks to find either the DHCP that assigned that IP address or some other network device whose ARP cache knows the desired address.

- *Domain Name Service (DNS)* works at layer 4 and layer 7 by attempting to resolve a domain name (such as isc2.org) into its IP address. The search starts with the requesting device's local DNS cache and then seeks "up the chain" to find either a device that knows of the requested domain or a domain name server that has that information. Layer 3 has no connection to DNS.

- *Network management functions* have to cut across every layer of the protocol stacks, providing configuration, inspection, and control functions. These functions provide the services that allow user programs like ipconfig to instantiate, initiate, terminate, or monitor communications devices and activities. Simple Network Management Protocol (SNMP) is quite prevalent in the TCP/IP community; Common Management Information Protocol (CMIP) and its associated Common Management Information Service (CMIS) are more recognized in OSI communities.

- *Cross MAC and PHY (or physical) scheduling* is vital when dealing with wireless networks. Since timing of wireless data exchanges can vary considerably (mobile devices are often moving!), being able to schedule packets and frames can help make such networks achieve better throughput and be more energy efficient. (Mobile customers and their device batteries appreciate that.)

■ *Network Address Translation (NAT)*, sometimes known as Port Address Translation (PAT), IP masquerading, NAT overload, and many-to-one NAT, all provide ways of allowing a routing function to edit a packet to change (translate) one set of IP addresses for another. Originally, this was thought to make it easier to move a device from one part of your network to another without having to change its IP address. As we became more aware of the IPv4 address space being exhausted, NAT became an incredibly popular workaround, a way to sidestep running out of IP addresses. Although it lives at layer 3, NAT won't work right if it cannot reach into the other layers of the stack (and the traffic) as it needs to.

IPsec

Although IPsec (originally known as Internet Protocol Security) was discussed in more depth in Chapter 5, it's worth noting here that IPsec is really more of a bundle of protocols rather than just a protocol by itself. Its open and extensible architecture provides IPv4 with a much stronger foundation of security features than it could originally support. Implementers can choose, for example, to use its defined key management system (IKE and IKEv2), Kerberized Internet Negotiation of Keys (KINK), or go directly to PKI, among other options. With the sheer size of the deployed base of systems running on IPv4, the rollout of IPsec made its initial adoption an option for implementers and users to choose as they needed. IPv6 makes IPsec a mandatory component.

UNDERSTAND NETWORK ATTACKS AND COUNTERMEASURES

Your adversaries may be using any strategy in the entire spectrum of attacks as they seek to gain their advantages at the expense of your organization and its systems. They might attempt to disrupt, degrade, deny, disable, or even destroy information and the services your systems use to get work done. They might also just be "borrowing" some network capacity, storage space, and CPU cycles from your systems to provide them a launch pad for attacks onto *other* systems. They might be conducting any of these types of operations to support any step of their kill chain. The only real limiting factor on such attacks, regardless of what network layer you think about, is the imagination of the attacker.

Attackers will seek your threat surface's weakest points. We often think that attackers see your threat surface as if it starts at the Application layer of the OSI Seven-Layer model, believing that it must be peeled back layer by layer to get to the targets of their choice. (Perhaps more realistically, they see your threat surface starting at "layer 8" and the human elements.) Experience suggests, however, that attackers will seek to probe your system for exploitable vulnerabilities across every layer of that protocol stack. Can they freely enter your business premises and conduct their own walk-around vulnerability assessment? They certainly might try, and if they *can* get in, you can be assured that their "exposure scanners" will be tuned to look across all eight layers nonstop.

Remember, too, that the network protocols our businesses, our organizations, and many of the tasks of daily life now depend upon all grew up in the days before we recognized the need for end-to-end, top-to-bottom information systems security. As our awareness has grown, our industry has redeveloped the protocols, re-architected the Internet (a few times), and rebuilt applications to achieve greater levels of safety, privacy, and security. Google Chrome's recent implementation of DNS over TLS is but one example of such changes. Your own organization cannot make every security change happen overnight, for many good reasons; thus, it relies on its security professionals to spot the unmitigated exposures, develop workarounds to control the risks they present, and maintain constant vigilance.

What should you do?

Beat them at their own game. Keep that seven-layer-plus-people view firmly in mind, while keeping your eyes wide open for the *cross-layer* exposures that are inherent in every aspect of your digital business processes and presence. Let the way this section is structured help you in that regard. Start thinking like an attacker; think, too, like a frustrated and disgruntled employee might, or a family member or significant other of a staff member who blames the organization for problems on their home front. Set possible motive aside and look for ways to *hurt* the organization.

▶▶ REAL WORLD EXAMPLE:
The Largest Financial Industry Data Breach: An Inside Job?

On July 29, 2019, Capitol One Financial Corporation disclosed that it had detected a significant data breach involving customer and applicant financial and personal data, possibly affecting over 106 million US and Canadian individuals and business customers. Within days, the FBI arrested Paige Thomson, a former Amazon Web Services employee, on suspicion of having committed the breach which exfiltrated data going back over 14 years. Initial details have been reported by many news and industry media and an initial report by Cyberint offers a quick look at the details. You can request a copy of it at https://1.cyberint.com/cyberint-on-capital-one-data-breach?hs_preview=cPCeyG1N-11737071327.

As this case unfolds, and ultimately goes to trial, we'll no doubt learn more as to what management decisions facilitated this inside job, rather than prevented it.

As a complement to the layer-by-layer view, this section also looks in a bit more depth at a variety of common network attacks. Be sure that you know how these attacks work and what to look for as indicators (or indicators of compromise) as part of your defensive measures. Know, too, how to isolate and contain such attacks.

So put on your gray hacker hat, walk around your organization's facilities—inside and out—and start thinking nefarious thoughts to help you hunt around your own systems looking for ways to cause trouble. Take your CIANA+PS with you, as you look for weaknesses in your systems' delivery of the confidentiality, integrity, availability, nonrepudiation, authentication, privacy, and safety that are your total information security needs.

CIANA+PS Layer by Layer

Let's now consider some of the security implications at each layer of the OSI Seven-Layer Reference Model, as well as one step beyond that model into the layers of human activities that give purpose and intent to our networks. In doing so, it's also useful to think about what might be called the commonsense computing hygiene standard:

- Physically protect information systems, their power and communications infrastructures, and all information storage facilities from loss, damage, or access by unauthorized persons or devices.
- Logically control access to information systems by all users, including visitors, guests, and repair technicians, preferably by more than just a username and password.
- Logically and administratively ensure that disclosure of private or confidential information must be done through approved procedures, methods, and channels.
- Physically, logically, and administratively ensure that information and equipment is properly rendered unreadable or otherwise destroyed when it reaches the end of its useful service life or legally required retention period.
- Administratively ensure that all staff and systems users have the right training, education, and threat awareness to take appropriate steps to keep the organization's information safe, secure, and available.

If you need a short set of rules to live by—or if you come into an organization and find no preexisting information security programs, procedures, or controls in place—these can be a great place to start while you're taking on a more thoroughgoing risk assessment.

In the meantime, let's look at the layers.

Layer 1: Physical

It's often said that there is no security without physical security, and for good reason. Physical layer attacks can be targeted at your people, their devices, their interconnecting media, their power distribution systems, or even as ports of entry for malware or reconnaissance tools. Clipping a passive tee or splitter/repeater into an Ethernet cable of almost any type—fiber optic included—is quite possible in almost all circumstances, if an attacker can physically gain access to any portion of your cable and wiring plant. Quite often, patch panels have unused jacks in them, which may provide very quick and easy physical and logical access to a "walk-by shoot-in" of most any kind of data or executable file. Wi-Fi and other wireless network layers are especially prone to hijack attacks that start at the physical layer.

With a bit of extra time and unhindered access, attackers who can physically trigger a factory reset button on almost any router, switch, hub, or gateway can flash their own firmware into it. This can be a significant risk when any member of the organization—or any visitor, authorized or not—can have even a minute's unguarded access to its infrastructure or endpoints.

The attacker's tools include everything needed for forced or surreptitious entry into your workspaces and premises—including a suitably innocuous wardrobe—and a small bag of hand tools, cable taps (passive or with active repeaters), patch cords, thumb drives, and a smartphone. Don't forget the most classic forms of physical intelligence gathering—shoulder surfing, binoculars, or just walking around and being nosy.

Wireless Attacks RF-based attacks can range from bluejacking, bluebugging, and bluesnarfing attacks (targeted against Bluetooth devices presumably authorized to be part of your systems or on your property), access point hijacking, and long-range surveillance using high-gain antennas. All of your wireless systems are exposed to the possibility of being jammed, spoofed, intercepted, or degraded by interference.

- **Jamming attacks** are when a stronger transmitter deliberately overrides your intended transmitters and prevents a physical *link closure* (the receiver can recognize the radio waves as a signal, demodulate it, and maintain a demodulation lock on that signal long enough to recognize it as a signal rather than dismiss it as noise).

- **Spoofing attacks** are when a transmitter acts in ways to get a receiver to mistake it as the anticipated sender. Jamming may or may not be part of a spoofing attack.

- **Interception** occurs when an unauthorized third party can also receive what your transmitters are sending, capture it, and break it out into frames, packets, etc., as used by layer 2 and above.

- **Electromagnetic interference (EMI)** can be caused by lightning strikes that are not properly grounded (or *earthed*, as those outside of North America often refer to this as). Large electrical motors, arc welders, or even the ignition systems on furnaces and boilers that can also radiate significant radio-frequency energy that can couple onto signal or power cables or directly into electronic equipment.

Troubleshooting possible Wi-Fi, Bluetooth, and other near-field security issues can be made simpler by using free or inexpensive signal mapping software on a smartphone. User complaints of intermittent problems with their wireless connections might be caused by interference, attackers, or by some other systems issue; a quick walk-around with a Wi-Fi mapper app on your smartphone might reveal saturated channels, while inspecting access control logs on the access points in question might also provide insight.

Countermeasures at the Physical Layer Start with Planning   It's important to consider that most modern intrusion detection and prevention systems cannot reach down into layer 1 elements as part of detecting and isolating a possible intrusion. You'll have to rely on the human elements of your network support or IT team, as well as the others on the security team with you, to periodically inspect and audit your layer 1.

Physically hardening your systems starts before you install them. Plan ahead; identify ways to secure cabling runs, wiring closets, racks full of routers, switches, hubs, and gateways. Plan on protecting your ISP's point of presence. Provide for power conditioning and strongly consider an uninterruptible power supply that can report out, as a network device, whenever it sees a power event. Select the physical locks and alarms you need to deny *any unauthorized person* from enjoying quick, easy, undetected, and uninterrupted access to your systems' vital underpinnings. Your network engineers, or the cable-pulling technicians that they use (or have on staff), should be fully aware of all of the safety and security needs to keep cables and equipment out of harm's way and people away from it; nonetheless, you start with a full baseline audit of your networks to identify and authenticate every device that is connected to them.

Layer 1 and layer 2 blur together in many ways; you'll need solid data from audits of your layer 2 configuration to spot anomalies in MAC addresses that are showing up on different parts of your system than where you were expecting them to be.

Use Wi-Fi mapping applications to help you routinely survey your physical offices and facilities, identify each access point you see, and ensure that it's one of your own. Look for changes; look for cables that have been moved around or equipment and endpoints you thought weren't mobile that are showing up on different network segments. Automate the mapping of your own networks and automate comparing today's map with the controlled baseline version of a validated, verified, and audited map.

It may seem outlandish to worry about whether any of the LED indicators on your network equipment are visible to a possible attacker. They blink with each bit flowing through, and an attacker who can see your router from across the street (even if they need a telescope) could be reading your traffic. Many devices now offer the option to turn the LEDs off in normal use (which also saves a tiny bit of power); turn them off when you're not diagnosing problems with the equipment or its use.

✔ Accidents as "Attackers"

Safety hazards, such as cabling that is not properly snugged down or equipment that's not properly secured in racks, can be a source of self-inflicted attacks as well. Terry, for example, shared with me an incident that happened when he had been stationed with a military unit at a forward-deployed location in Southwest Asia, where his duties included everything necessary to keep a small network, server, and communications node operational. A junior officer newly assigned to his location came to his trailer-mounted network operations center while the crew was reconfiguring most of it and insisted they let him in and give him an informal tour...while he was wearing casual clothes and flip-flops. Despite attempts to deny him entry, the officer "pulled rank," came in, promptly caught his flip-flop on a temporary patch cable, tripped, and in falling managed to yank several other cables out of their jacks, damaging the patch panel in the process.

Beware the risks of trying to remove what you think are unused cables from conduits, cableways, and plenum areas, as these well-intended hygiene efforts can also damage other cables if not done carefully.

Layer 2: Link

Attackers at this level have somehow found their way past your physical, logical, and administrative safeguards you've put in place, either to protect layer 1 or to preclude the attacker from reaching down through the protocol stack and attempting to take charge of your layer 2 devices and services on your internet. (Yes, that's "internet" in lowercase, signifying that it's a *network segment* running TCP/IP.) Perhaps they've recognized the value of the wealth of CVE data that's out there waiting to be learned from; perhaps they've found a device or two that still have the factory defaults of "admin" and "password" set on them.

Many attacks end up using layer-spanning protocols, but since they ultimately come to ground on layer 2, let's look at them here first. Know that they probably apply all the way up to beyond layer 7. Examples of such attacks can include:

- MAC address–related attacks, such as MAC spoofing (which can be done via command-line access in many systems) or causing a content addressable memory (CAM) table overflow on the device
- DHCP lease-based denial-of-service attack (also called IP pool starvation attack)

- ARP attacks, such as sending IP/MAC pairs to falsify an IP address for a known MAC, or vice versa
- VLAN attacks: VLAN hopping via falsified (spoofed) VLAN IDs in packets
- Denial of service by looping packets, as in a Spanning Tree Protocol (STP) attack
- Reconnaissance attacks against link layer discovery protocols
- SSID spoofing as part of man-in-the-middle attacks against your wireless infrastructure

An example attack vector unique to the data link layer would include forging the MAC address, otherwise known as ARP spoofing. By forging ARP requests or replies, an attacker can fool data link layer switching to redirect network traffic intended for a legitimate host to the attacker's machine. ARP spoofing is also a common precursor to man-in-the-middle (MitM) attacks and session hijacking attacks, both of which are further discussed later in the chapter.

Countermeasures at the Link Layer   This is where proper configuration of network and systems devices and services is paramount to attaining and maintaining a suitable level of security. Network-level devices such as IDS and IPS have a role here, of course; SIEMS can assist in data gathering and integration as well. If your organization has not invested in those type of systems yet, don't panic: you've got a tremendous number of built-in capabilities that you can and should master as part of your first line of defense, as pointed out by Leon Adato in his *Network Monitoring for Dummies*.[5] Command-line applications such as `ipconfig` (in Windows systems) get you access to a variety of tools and information; systems logs, performance monitoring counters, and built-in control capabilities (such as the Windows Management Instrumentation) provide some fairly powerful ways to exert greater visibility into the networks surrounding and supporting your systems. You will need better tools to manage all of the SNMP and ICMP data, the log files, and counters that you gather up, as well as the data you log and collect in the routers and other network devices themselves. But while you're doing that, consider the following as high-return-on-investment countermeasures:

- Secure your network against external sniffers via encryption.
- Use SSH instead of unsecure remote login, remote shell, etc.
- Ensure maximum use of SSL/TLS.
- Use secured versions of email protocols, such as S/MIME or PGP.
- Use network switching techniques, such as dynamic ARP inspection or rate limiting of ARP packets.

[5] Leon Adato, *Network Monitoring for Dummies, 2nd Solarwinds Special Edition*. Hoboken, NJ, 2019: John Wiley & Sons. ISBN 978-1-119-60303-0.

- Control when networks are operating in promiscuous mode.
- Use allowed listing of known, trusted MAC addresses.
- Use blocked listing of suspected hostile MAC addresses.
- Use honeynets to spot potential DNS snooping.
- Do latency checks, which may reveal that a potential or suspect attacker is in fact monitoring your network.
- Turn off or block services (on *all* devices) that are not necessary for any legitimate business process. Program access control rules to turn off services that should not be used outside of normal business hours.
- Monitor what processes and users are actually using network monitoring tools, such as Netmon, on your systems; when in doubt, one of those might be serving an intruder!

In Chapters 2 and 3, you saw that the *threat surface* is an imaginary boundary wrapped around your systems, with crossing points for every service, pathway, or connection that is made from inside that boundary to the outside world. The count of all of those crossing points, or the sum of all of the vulnerable spots on that surface, is a measure of the size of your system's threat surface. Each unneeded service that you shut off, each unnecessary port that you block, reduces that number of vulnerabilities in that particular threat surface. Threat surfaces can be meaningfully modeled at every layer of the OSI Seven-Layer Reference Model and around every separate segment or subnet of your networks.

Layer 3: Internetworking (IP)

Keep in mind that IP is a *connectionless* and therefore stateless protocol; the protocol stack itself remembers nothing about the series of events that senders and recipients have gone through; that has to happen at the Session layer if not at the Application layer if the business logic needs to be stateful. (An online shopping cart is stateful; but the storefront app and the client it loads onto your endpoint, via HTML and JavaScript files, are what implement that state-tracking, not the layer 3 operation of the Internet.) By itself, layer 3 does not provide any kind of authentication. It's also worthwhile to remember that just because an attack vector has become the child's play of the script kiddies doesn't mean that serious APT threat actors can't or won't use that same vector in attacking *your* systems.

ICMP, the other major protocol at this layer, is also simple and easy for attackers to use as they conduct reconnaissance probes against your systems. It can also facilitate other types of attacks. That said, be very cautious when thinking of shutting ICMP down completely. Services such as ping (not an acronym, but rather was named by its creator

Mike Muus after the sound a sonar makes[6]) are darned-near vital to keeping the Internet and your own networks working correctly. But there are ways to filter incoming ICMP traffic, allowing you to be somewhat more careful in what you let into your systems.

Attacks at any layer of the protocol stacks can be either hit-and-run or very persistent. The hit-and-run attacker may need to inject only a few bad packets to achieve their desired results. This can make them hard to detect. The persistent threat requires more continuous action be taken to accomplish the attack.

Typical attacks seen at this level, which exploit known common vulnerabilities or just the nature of IP networks, can include the following:

- IP spoofing, in which the attacker impersonates a known, trusted IP address (or masks their own known or suspected hostile IP address) by manipulation of IP packet headers.

- Routing (RIP) attacks, typically by repeatedly issuing falsified RIP Response messages, which then cause redirection of traffic to the attacker.

- ICMP attacks, which can include smurf attacks using ICMP packets to attempt a distributed denial-of-service (DDoS) attack against the spoofed IP address of the target system. (ICMP can also be misused by certain attack tools, transforming it into a command and control or data exfiltration tool, albeit a slow one. This does *not* mean you should turn off ICMP completely.)

- Ping flood, which overwhelms a target by sending it far more echo requests ("ping" packets) than it can respond to.

- Ping-of-death attacks, which use an ICMP datagram that exceeds maximum size; most modern operating systems have ensured that their network stacks are no longer vulnerable to these, but that doesn't mean that a fix to something in the stack won't undo this bit of hardening.

- Teardrop attacks, which place false offset information into fragmented packets, which causes empty or overlapping spots in the resultant data stream during reassembly. This can lead to applications that use those data streams to behave erratically or become unstable, which may reveal other exploitable vulnerabilities to other attacks.

- Packet sniffing reconnaissance, providing valuable target intelligence data for the attacker to exploit.

Countermeasures at the IP Layer   First on your list of countermeasure strategies should be to implement IPsec if you haven't already done so for your IPv4 networks. Whether you deploy IPsec in tunnel mode or transport mode (or both) should be

---

[6] Elizabeth D. Zwicky, Simon Cooper & D. Brent Chapman, *Building Internet Firewalls, 2nd Edition*. 2000. O'Reilly Media. ASIN B011DATOPM, see paragraph 22.4.1.

driven by your organization's impact assessment and CIANA+PS needs. Other options to consider include these:

- Securing ICMP
- Securing routers and routing protocols with packet filtering (and the ACLs this requires)
- Providing ACL protection against address spoofing

Layer 4: Transport

Layer 4 is where packet sniffers, protocol analyzers, and network mapping tools pay big dividends for the black hats. For the white hats, the same tools—and the skill and cunning needed to understand and exploit what those tools can reveal—are essential in vulnerability assessment, systems characterization and fingerprinting, active defense, and incident detection and response. Although it's beyond the scope of this book to make you a protocol wizard, it's *not* beyond the scope of the SSCP's ongoing duties to take on, understand, and master what happens at the transport layer.

Attack vectors unique to the transport layer would include attacks utilizing TCP and UDP. One specific example would be the SYN flood attack that drains a target's network memory resources by continuously initiating TCP-based connections but not allowing them to complete. Some common exploitations that focus on layer 4 can include the following:

- SYN floods, which can be defended against by implementing SYN cookies.
- Injection attacks, which involve the attackers guessing at the next packet sequence number, or forcing a reset of sequence numbers, to jump their packets in ahead of a legitimate one. This is also called TCP hijacking.
- Opt-Ack attack, which is in essence a self-inflicted denial-of-service attack, such as when the attacker convinces the target to send replies quickly.
- TLS attacks, which tend to be attacks on how compression, encryption, and key management are used in TLS.
- Bypass of proper certificate use for mobile apps.
- TCP port scans, host sweeps, or other network mapping as part of reconnaissance.
- OS and application fingerprinting, as part of reconnaissance.

Countermeasures at the Transport Layer   Most of your countermeasure options at layer 4 involve better identity management and access control, along with improved traffic inspection and filtering. Start by considering the following:

- TCP intercept and filtering (routers, firewalls)
- DoS prevention services (such as Cloudflare, Prolexic, and many others)

- Blocked listing of attackers' IP addresses
- Allowed listing of known, trusted IP addresses
- Better use of SSL/TLS and SSH
- Fingerprint scrubbing techniques
- Traffic monitoring
- Traffic analysis

It's at layer 4 that you may also need to conduct your own target reconnaissance or *threat hunting* activities. Automated scanning, geolocating, and collating IP addresses that are part of incoming traffic may reveal "dangerous waters" you do not want your systems and your end users swimming in; these become candidate addresses to blocklist for incoming *and* outgoing traffic. *Traffic monitoring* focuses your attention on which processes, connecting to which IP addresses, are using what fraction of your network capacity at any moment or across the day. Follow that trail of breadcrumbs, though: you'll need to be able to determine if the way in which traffic is being generated (by what kinds of processes), owned, forked, or launched on behalf of what user or subject identities in your systems, is using how much traffic, before you can determine if that's merely unusual or is a suspicious anomaly worthy of sounding the alarm.

Traffic analysis attempts to find meaning in the patterns of communications traffic across a set of senders and recipients, without relying upon knowledge of the content of the messages themselves. Traffic analysis was a major part of winning the Battles for the Atlantic—the Allied anti-submarine campaigns against Germany in both World Wars. It's a major part of market research, political campaigning, and a powerful tool used by APTs as they seek out webs of connections between possible targets of interest. Traffic analysis can help *you* determine if your East-West traffic (the data flowing *internally* on your networks) is within a sense of "business normal" or not. It can also help you look at how your people and the endpoints they use are flowing information into and out of your systems.

Layer 5: Session

Some security professionals believe that attacks at the Session layer (and the Presentation layer too) haven't been too prevalent. These are not layers that have a clean way to abstract and understand what they do and how they do it, in ways that separate out vulnerabilities in these layers from vulnerabilities in the applications above them. Application layer attacks are becoming more and more common, but of course, those aren't packet or routing attacks; one might even argue that they're not really even a *network* attack, only one that gets to its targets by way of the network connection. (Ironically, this viewpoint suggests the attacker needs the network to work reliably as much as the defenders do; in much the same vein, modern militaries have often decided that they gain more in intelligence and surveillance information by leaving their opponents' communications systems intact, than they gain by putting those systems out of action during the conflict.) Other security practitioners believe that we're seeing more attacks that try to take advantage of Session-level complexities. As defensive awareness and response has grown, so has the complexity of session hijacking and related session layer attacks. Many of the steps involved in a session hijack can generate other issues, such as "ACK storms," in which both the spoofed and attacking host are sending ACKs with correct sequence numbers and other information in the packet headers; this might require an attacker to take further steps to silence this storm so that it's not detectable as a symptom of a possible intrusion.

Attack approaches that do have Session layer implications, for example, include the following:

- Session hijacking attacks attempt to harvest and exploit a valid session key and reuse it, either to continue a session that has been terminated or to substitute the attacker for the legitimate client (or server) in the session. These are also sometimes known as cookie hijacking attacks.

- Man-in-the-middle attacks, similar to session hijacking, involve the attacker inserting themselves into the link between the two parties, either as part of covert surveillance (via packet sniffing) or by altering the packets themselves. In the extreme, each of the parties believes that they are still in contact with the other, as the MitM attacker successfully masquerades to each as the other.

- ARP poisoning attacks are conducted by spoofing ARP messages onto a local network, possibly by altering their own device's MAC address to gain access to the network. The attack seeks to alter the target's ARP cache, which causes the target to misroute packets to the attacker.

- DNS poisoning attempts to modify the target system's DNS resolver cache, which will result in the target misrouting traffic to the attacker.

- Local system hosts file corruption or poisoning are similar to ARP and DNS poisoning attacks in that they seek to subvert the target system's local cache of host names and addressing information, causing the target to misdirect traffic to the attacker instead.

- Blind hijacking is where the attacker injects commands into the communications stream but cannot see results, such as error messages or system response directly.

- Man-in-the-browser attacks are similar to other MitM attacks but rely on a Trojan horse that manipulates calls to/from stack and browser. Browser helper objects, extensions, API hooking, and Ajax worms can inadvertently facilitate these types of attacks.

- Session sniffing attacks can allow the attacker to gain a legitimate session ID and then spoof it.

- SSH downgrade attacks attempt to control the negotiation process by which systems choose cryptographic algorithms and control variables. This process exists to allow systems at different versions of algorithms and cryptographic software suites to negotiate to the highest mutually compatible level of encryption they can support. Attackers can misdirect this negotiation by refusing to accept higher-grade encryption choices by the target, hoping that the target will eventually settle on something the attacker already knows how to crack.

Countermeasures at the Session Layer   As with the Transport layer, most of the countermeasures available to you at the Session layer require some substantial sleuthing around in your system. Problems with inconsistent applications or systems behavior, such as being able to consistently connect to websites or hosts you frequently use, might be caused by errors in your local hosts file (containing your ARP and DNS cache). Finding and fixing those errors is one thing; investigating whether they were the result of user error, applications or systems errors, or deliberate enemy action is quite another set of investigative tasks to take on!

Also, remember that your threat modeling should have divided the world into those networks you can trust, and those that you cannot. Many of your DoS prevention strategies therefore need to focus on that outside, hostile world—or, rather, on its (ideally) limited connection points with your trusted networks.

Countermeasures to consider include the following:

- Replace weak password authentication protocols such as PAP, CHAP, and NT LAN Manager (NTLM), which are often enabled as a default to support backward compatibility, with much stronger authentication protocols.
- Migrate to strong systems for identity management and access control.
- Use PKI as part of your identity management, access control, and authentication systems.
- Verify correct settings of DNS servers on your network and disable known attack methods, such as allowing recursive DNS queries from external hosts.
- Use tools such as SNORT at the session layer as part of an active monitoring and alarm system.
- Implementation and use of more robust IDSs or IPSs.

Layer 6: Presentation

The Presentation layer marketplace is dominated by the use of NetBIOS and Server Message Block (SMB) technologies, thanks to the sheer number of Windows-based systems and servers deployed and on the Internet. Just as importantly, many of the cross-layer protocols, older protocols such as SNMP and FTP, and many apps all work through layer

6 or make use of its functionality. TLS functions here; as does its predecessor SSL and Apple Filing Protocol (AFP).

As a result, attacks tend to focus on three broad categories of capabilities and functionality.

- Encryption, decryption, key management, and related logic. In particular, "grow-your-own" encryption and hash algorithms may expose their vulnerabilities here in layer 6.

- Authentication methods, particularly in poorly implemented Kerberos systems, or systems with poorly configured or protected Active Directory services.

- Known NetBIOS or SMB vulnerabilities.

Countermeasures at the Presentation Layer In some cases, replacing an insecure app such as FTP with its more secure follow-on could be a practical countermeasure.

Layer 7: Applications

Applications represent the most visible and accessible portion of the threat surfaces your organization exposes to potential attack. Applications penetrate your security perimeters — deliberately — so that your people, your customers, or others you do business with can actually *do* business with you via your information systems. It's also those same applications that are how the real *information work* gets done by the organization — and don't forget that all of that value-creating work gets done at the endpoints and not on the servers or networks themselves. Chapter 7, "Systems and Application Security," addresses many of the ways you'll need to help your organization secure its applications and the data they use from attack, but let's take a moment to consider two specific cases a bit further.

- **Voice, POTS, and VOIP:** Plain old telephone service and voice-over IP all share a common security issue: how do you provide the "full CIANA+PS" of protection to what people *say* to each other, regardless of the channel or the technology they use?

- **Collaboration systems:** LinkedIn, Facebook Workspace, Microsoft Teams, and even VoIP systems like Skype provide many ways in which people can organize workflows, collaborate on developing information (such as books or software), and have conversations with each other. Each of these was designed with the goal of empowering users to build and evolve their own patterns of collaboration with each other.

Collaboration platforms and the process of collaborating itself should be guided by your organization's information security classification guidelines; in particular, your team needs to share portions of those classification guidelines with the external organizations and individual people that you welcome into your collaboration spaces and channels. Without their knowing, informed consent and cooperation, you cannot expect to keep any of your information confidential or otherwise safe for long.

Vulnerabilities and Assessment

Many of these attacks are often part of a protracted series of intrusions taken by more sophisticated attackers. Such *advanced persistent threats* may spend months, even a year or more, in their efforts to crack open and exploit the systems of a target business or organization in ways that will meet the attacker's needs. Your monitoring systems—no matter what technology you use, including the "carbon-based" ones (such as *people*)—should be tuned to help you be on the lookout for attack processes such as the following:

- SQL or other injection exploits built-in capabilities in many database systems and applications that allow a user to enter an arbitrary set of Structured Query Language (SQL) commands as they perform legitimate work. Entering arbitrarily long text into such a query input field can (as with most buffer overflow attacks) lead to arbitrary code execution. Attackers can also enter legitimate SQL commands that may misuse the application, such as by creating bogus suppliers in a logistics management database (as part of a false invoicing attack to be conducted later on).

- Cross-site scripting (XSS), which exploits the trust that a user has for a particular website; these typically involve code injection attacks that the user (and their browser) unwittingly facilitate.

- Cross-site request forgery (XSRF or CSRF), which exploits the trust that a website has in its user's browser, allowing it to issue commands (to other sites) not authorized or requested by the user.

- Remote code execution (RCE) attacks attempt to remotely (via a network) get the target to execute an arbitrary set of memory locations as if they are part of legitimate software code. Buffer overflows are common components of such arbitrary code execution and RCE attacks.

- Format string vulnerabilities have been exploited since 1989, when it was discovered that the string data in a program that specifies the formatting of data for input or output can, if badly constructed, cause an arbitrary code execution error to occur.

- Username enumeration as a reconnaissance technique seeks to capture the names, IDs, and other parameters associated with all users on a target system, as a prelude to an identity or username hijacking.

- HTTP flood attacks, also known as Get/Post floods, similar to ping floods and other distributed denial-of-service attacks, attempt to cause the target host to run out of resources and thus deny or degrade services to legitimate users.

- HTTP server resource pool exhaustion (Slowloris, for example) are another form of denial-of-service attack. By attempting to open as many connections as possible with the target, the attacker can cause the server to exhaust its maximum connection pool. Such attacks use far less bandwidth, do not require a botnet, and are far less disruptive on unrelated services and hosts at the target.

- Low-and-slow attacks have the attacker access the target system and using its built-in capabilities to accomplish steps in the attacker's kill chain. These steps are spread out over time, and kept small, so as to "fly under the radar" of the target's defenses. By not using malware, and by spreading their behavior out over a long time period, low-and-slow attacks also can avoid many behavioral analysis threat detection systems. Ransom attacks provide a compelling set of examples to learn from; strong, multifactor access authentication is thought to be the only defense against such attacks.

- DoS/DDoS attacks on known server vulnerabilities start by reconnaissance that identifies the specifics of the target's server systems, including revision and update levels if detectable, and then using published CVE data or other vulnerability sources to select and use appropriate exploits.

- NTP amplification attacks have the attacker repeatedly request that traffic monitoring service reports from a Network Time Protocol (NTP) provider be sent to the spoofed IP address of their chosen target. This attempts to overwhelm the target with large UDP data volumes, as a denial-of-service tactic.

- App-layer DoS/DDoS attacks target applications programs and platforms directly in attempts to overload or crash the app, its underlying database server(s), and its host if possible.

- Device or app, attacks are variations on a session hijacking, in that the attacker attempts to masquerade as a legitimate user or superuser of the device or application in question. Embedded control devices, medical systems (whether implanted or bedside), and the applications that interact with them, are all becoming targets of opportunity for a variety of attack patterns.

- User hijacking typically involves misusing a legitimate user's login credentials in order to enter a target's IT systems. Once inside, the attacker may start to install (and then hide) the command and control hooks they need to be able to return to the target, conduct additional reconnaissance, and carry out the rest of their attack plan, without the users whose identity has been hijacked being the wiser.

WARNING   Depending upon where in the world your business does business or where its team members may travel on for business or pleasure, the dire possibility exists that one or more of your people may be taken hostage or otherwise coerced into aiding and abetting unauthorized persons in their attacks on your organization's IT systems. If this might apply to your organization, work with your physical security and human resources teams to determine the need for your IT security to be able to protect against and assist employees under duress.

Countermeasures at the Applications Layer   Multiple parts of your total information security process have to come together to protect your information and information systems from being exploited via applications-layer vulnerabilities. Software development and test; business logic design and business process implementation; user training and skills development; network, IT systems, and communications security; all these plus the culture of your organization can help you succeed or fail at protecting against such threats. Practically speaking, it's nearly an all-hands, full-time job of watching, listening, and thinking about what your systems and your business rhythms—much less your technical monitoring and alarm systems—are trying to tell you, as you layer on additional Applications layer countermeasures:

- Monitor website visitor behavior as a part of gathering intelligence data about legitimate users and potential attackers alike.

- Block known bad bots.

- Challenge suspicious or unrecognized entities with a cross-platform JavaScript tester such as jstest (at `http://jstest.jcoglan.com/`).

- Run privacy-verifying cookie web test tools, such as `https://www.cookiebot.com/en/gdpr-cookies/`. Add challenges such as CAPTCHAs to determine whether the entity is a human or a robot trying to be one.

- Use two-factor/multifactor authentication.

- Use application-layer IDS and IPS.

- Provide more effective user training and education focused on attentiveness to unusual systems or applications behavior.

- Establish strong data quality programs and procedures (see Chapter 7).

Beyond Layer 7

Let's face it: the most prevalent attack vector is one involving phishing attempts to get end users to open an email or follow a link to a website. Phishing no longer is constrained to using downloadable files as its mode of operation. Many are using embedded scripts that use built-in features of the target system, allowing the attacker to "live off the land" as they skate past the anti-malware sentinels to achieve their inimical intentions.

Chapter 1 stressed the vital importance of engaging with your end users, their managers, and the organization's senior leadership; the more you can enlist their knowing, active cooperation with the security measures you've recommended and implemented, the more effective they can be at protecting everyone's information and livelihood. Chapters 3 and 4 also showed how important it is to share security assessment results— the findings and especially the *good findings*—with your end users. They'll actually learn more from seeing that things are working *right*, that everyone's security efforts are paying off, than they will from yet another incident report. But they will, of course, learn from both and *need* to learn from both.

Your end users have another important contribution to make to your security plans and programs: they can provide you with the hard data and the hard-one operational insights that *you* can use to make the business case for everything you do. Sometimes the right business answer is to live with a risk, if the cost of a fix (or the risk of a fix going wrong) is too high.

Common Network Attack Types

The following types of attack patterns are seen across the spectrum of attack vectors, as they're used by attackers from script kiddies to APTs alike. As a result, they are also powerful tools for you to use as part of your own ethical penetration testing and assessments of your own systems. We'll look at them in brief here; consider setting up some isolated testing cells using a few virtual servers and a software-defined net (suitably isolated from the real world *and* your production systems, of course), grab a copy of tools such as Metasploit, and start to study these types of attacks in greater depth.

You may also want to consider developing an ongoing workflow or process that supports your organization in learning more about such attacks and growing your team's ability to spot them if they are occurring and stop them in their tracks. Perhaps an "attack of the month club" as a lunchtime brown-bag session could be a useful way to stimulate end user interest.

Distributed Denial-of-Service Attacks

When an attacker does not have the skills or tools for a sophisticated attack, they may use a brute-force attack, which can be just as effective. Simply flooding the targeted system with UDP packets from infected machines has proven successful, especially as the Internet of Things (IoT) devices have been used, unwittingly, to help launch the distributed denial-of-service (DDoS) attacks. A typical DDoS attack consists of a large number of individual machines that are subverted to bombard a target with overwhelming traffic over a short period of time. With each compromised machine, be it a PC, IoT device, networking hardware, or server, their individual contribution would amount to no damage alone. But the collective sum of tens of thousands of attacking platforms creates a crushing amount of traffic to the end target. Such networks of systems, surreptitiously taken control of by an attacker, are often known as *botnets* or sometimes *zombie botnets*, because of the ways in which the botnet machines slavishly follow the commands of their secret master controller, often under the influence of a malware infection, and unbeknownst to the device's owner.

Although the term *botnet* has grown in popular media because of the use of the tactic in enlisting IoT devices such as baby monitors, TVs, webcams, and other network-aware wireless devices, botnets were weaponized almost 20 years ago. Medical devices were hacked when the FDA published guidance that any Unix-based machines were to have a standard, known configuration. These certified, special-purpose computing devices became targets because they inherited the weaknesses of the standard configurations. Once hackers discovered vulnerabilities to exploit, the weaknesses were applicable across an entire platform, and a medical device botnet was created. The number and varieties of devices used to create botnets has expanded. In 2016, large numbers of digital recording video (DVR) devices and other Internet-enabled systems were used to create the Mirai botnet. This botnet was used in a series of DDoS attacks against Dyn.com, one of the largest providers of DNS services. This attack disrupted major computing platforms operated by PayPal, Twitter, Reddit, GitHub, Amazon, Netflix, Spotify, and RuneScape. In sum, botnets are enslaving vast numbers of IoT devices and creating highly successful DDoS attacks.

DDoS and Spam   A working definition of spam is the electronic equivalent of junk mail in the physical world. In most cases, spam is a nuisance but not an attempted cybersecurity attack. However, spam can exist in the context of a DDoS attack. When an attacker sends a command to launch a spam campaign, the end result is an overwhelming volume of traffic. The spam traffic likely originates from a set of malicious botnets, with the outcome being spam. The receiving systems process the messages as legitimate, which is a mistake. The spam bots have spoofed the email addresses, which is a tactic unlike packet-level DDoS.

Normally, an individual spam message is just an unsolicited email message with unwanted advertising, perhaps even seeking to deliver a malicious payload. However, as part of a DDoS attack, spam can be used as an acceptable type of traffic to deliver an onslaught of data. The volume of data to be received could shut down a system or mail gateway.

Man-in-the-Middle Attacks

In one important sense, every Internet communication is between two parties, who take turns being sender and recipient. Even a broadcast event is nothing more than a series of one-on-one sends and receives, repeated with different recipients. The man-in-the-middle attack spoofs the identity of both sender and recipient and intercepts the traffic that flows between them. The attacker may simply be reading and copying the traffic via a passive listening device or tap; or they may be *impersonating* the credentials of one or both of the parties so that they can alter the traffic being exchanged to suit their own purposes. In successful MitM attacks, the entire session is overheard by the attacker, while the two parties are blissfully ignorant that anything has gone amiss. Figure 6.14 illustrates a typical MitM attack pattern, which can happen at almost any layer of any communications protocol in any system.

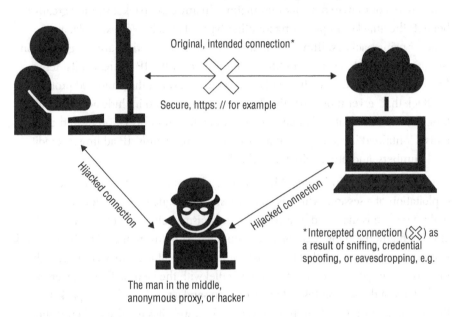

FIGURE 6.14 Man-in-the-middle attack

There are two main ways to prevent or detect MitM: authentication and tamper detection. Authentication provides some degree of certainty that a given message has come from a legitimate source. Tamper detection merely shows evidence that a message may have been altered.

- **Authentication:** To prevent MitM attacks, cryptographic protocols are used to authenticate the endpoints or transmission media. One such technique is to employ Transport Layer Security (TLS) server paired with X.509 certificates. The X.509 certificates are used by the mutually trusted certificate authority (CA) to authenticate one or more entities. The message and an exchange of public keys are employed to make the channel secure.

- **Tamper detection:** Another way to detect MitM is through examination of any latency in the transaction above baseline expectations. Response times are checked and normal factors like long calculations of hash functions are accounted for. If delay is not explained, there may be unwanted, malicious third-party interference in the communication.

- **Packet sniffing:** Administrators often use packet sniffing tools for legitimate purposes as part of troubleshooting. Attackers conduct passive MitM packet sniffing to gain information for adversarial purposes. Any unencrypted protocols are subject to passive attacks where an attacker has been able to place a packet sniffing tool to monitor traffic. The monitoring might be used to determine traffic types and patterns or to map network information. In any case, packet sniffing greatly benefits the attacker in preparing for other types of attacks. For example, an attacker using packet sniffing might discover that a prospective target organization still uses an outdated version of SSL; or they discover the IP address of its Active Directory controller. The attacker is now set up to exploit that outdated protocol or attack that server more directly. Packet sniffing can also include actually grabbing packets in transit and attempting to extract useful information from the contents. Contained in some packets are usernames, passwords, IP addresses, credit card numbers, and other valuable payload.

- **Hijacking attacks:** Similar to a MitM attack, a hijacking attack involves the exploitation of a session, which is an established dialogue between devices. Normally a session is managed by a control mechanism such as a cookie or token. An attacker might try to intercept or eavesdrop the session token or cookie. In the case where an attacker has sniffed the cookie or token, the attacker may connect with the server using the legitimate token in parallel with the victim. The attacker might also intercept the session token to use, or even send a specially formed packet to the victim to terminate their initial session. Many websites require authentication and use cookies to remember session tracking information. When the session is terminated as the user logs out, the cookie and credentials are typically cleared. Hijacking a session and stealing the token or cookie while the session is active can provide an attacker with valuable, sensitive information, such as unique details on what site was visited. Even worse, hijacking the session cookie may allow the attacker an opportunity to continue a session, posing at the victim.

TIP   *Promiscuous mode* is a setting that packet sniffers enable to stop a device from discarding or filtering data unintended for it. The packet sniffer can gain access to the additional traffic and data packets that otherwise would have been filtered.

DNS Cache Poisoning

DNS servers at all levels across the Internet and within your local internet segments cache the results of every address resolution that they request and receive. This allows the local machine's protocol stack to save significant time and resources to resolve a URL or IP address into a MAC address (or vice versa) that's already been searched for by the Internet and on the Internet once before. *Cache poisoning* occurs when one machine's DNS cache has incorrect data in it, which it provides to other devices requesting its resolution of an address. The bad data thus propagates to DNS caches at the endpoint, to the server, and even into backbone DNS servers across the Internet. *DNS spoofing* is a deliberate poisoning of cache data in an attempt to reroute traffic to an imposter site, or to block users from accessing the legitimate site or address. DNS spoofing is commonly used by governments to restrict what websites or IP addresses their citizens (or anyone in their jurisdiction) can visit or view. It's also used in private settings to reroute attempts to connect to undesirable or suspicious addresses.

In 2010, the Great Firewall of China inadvertently propagated to DNS servers in the United States by means of badly configured data in a DNS server located outside of both countries. This server copied address redirection information that would censor access to sites such as Facebook, Twitter, and YouTube, which then propagated into U.S.-based DNS servers large and small.

The long-term solution is to implement DNSSEC across your systems; note, too, that the Stop Online Policy Act, a piece of U.S. legislation, almost made DNSSEC illegal, since DNSSEC has no way to differentiate a permitted "good" website or address from a "bad" one.

DHCP Attacks

The Dynamic Host Configuration Protocol (DHCP) works at the application layer, which dynamically assigns an IP address and other network configuration parameters via a special-purpose server to each device on a network. DHCP also ensures each IP address is unique. This service enables networked nodes to communicate with other IP networks. The DHCP server removes the need for a network administrator or other person to manually assign and reassign IP addresses to endpoints on demand. As DHCP dynamically manages network address assignment, this protocol is actually an application layer protocol. Devices needing an IP address must handshake with a DHCP server to obtain a *lease* on an IP address via a broadcast message, which a DHCP server responds to.

Attacks on DHCP are plentiful and almost simple, given that the protocol's design is based on trusting the perceived source of the DHCP broadcast and handshake replies. DHCP can be exploited using a DHCP starvation attack, where forged requests continually request new IP addresses until the allotted pool of addresses is exhausted. Another attack is the DHCP spoof attack, where an untrusted client continues to spread DHCP messages throughout the network.

Attack vectors specific to the application layer are varied. To begin the list, consider the application layer protocols such as HTTP, FTP, SMTP, and SNMP. Attacks like SQL injection or cross-site scripting operate at the application layer. Every attack on the user interface falls into this category. So do HTTP-based attacks such as an HTTP flood or input validation attacks.

SYN Flooding

TCP initiates a connection by sending a SYN packet, which when received and accepted is replied to with a SYN-ACK packet. The SYN flooding DoS attack is executed by sending massive amounts of those SYN packets for which the sending nodes (typically zombie botnet systems) do not acknowledge any of the replies. SYN flooding is a form of denial-of-service attack, exploiting properties of the Transmission Control Protocol (TCP) at the transport layer (Layer 4). The SYN packets accumulate at the recipient system and the software crashes because it cannot handle the overflow. The attacker attempts to consume enough server resources to make the system unresponsive to legitimate traffic. Some refer to this attack as the half-open attack because of the partial three-way TCP/IP handshake that underlies the attack. Eventually, given enough connection attempts, the capacity of the network card and stack to maintain open connections is exhausted. The attack was imagined decades before it was actually performed. Until the source code and descriptions of the SYN flooding attacks were published in 1996 in the magazines *2600* and *Phrack*, attackers had not executed the attack successfully. That changed when the publicly available information was used in an attack against Panix, a New York ISP, for several days.

Even though these types of attacks have such a long history and the mitigations have been in existence for almost as long, SYN flooding is still a common attack. There are some ways to mitigate a SYN flood vulnerability. A few of the most prevalent approaches to consider are:

- **Increasing backlog queue:** This is an allowance or increase of half-open connections a system will sustain. It requires additional memory resources to increase the maximum backlog. Depending on the availability of memory resources, mitigating the SYN flooding threat can degrade system performance. A risk-benefit analysis is required against unwanted denial-of-service impact and slower performance.

- **Recycling the oldest half-open TCP connection:** This is a first-in, first-out queueing strategy where once the backlog queue limit is reached, the oldest half-open request is overwritten. The benefit is fully establishing legitimate connections faster than the backlog can be filled with malicious SYN packets. However, if the backlog queue is too small or the attack too voluminous, this mitigation can be insufficient.

- **SYN cookies:** The server responds to each connection request, SYN, with a SYN-ACK packet. The SYN request is dropped from the backlog. The port is open to new, ideally legitimate connections. If the initial connection is legitimate, the original sender will send its ACK packet. The initial recipient, which created the SYN cookie, will reconstruct the SYN backlog queue entry. Of course, there will be some limitations as some information about the TCP connection can be lost. This is more advantageous than the full denial-of-service outage.

Smurfing

Smurfing is a historical type of attack dating back to the 1990s that is categorized as a DDOS attack. The name comes from a popular children's TV cartoon show of the time and represents the concept of an overwhelming number of very small, almost identical attackers that successfully overtake a larger opponent.

The Internet Control Message Protocol (ICMP) uses ping packets to troubleshoot network connections by determining the reachability of a target host and a single system as the legitimate source. Smurfing exploits the functionality of the ICMP and broadcast subnets configured to magnify ICMP pings that will respond. These misconfigured networks are called *smurf amplifiers*. Using the IP broadcast, attackers send packets spoofing an intended victim source IP. The echo ICMP packet is used because ping checks to see systems are alive on the network. The result of the broadcast message, especially if exploiting the presence of smurf amplification, is that all the computers on the network will respond back to the targeted system. See Figure 6.15 for an illustration of the effect on the targeted system. In a large, distributed network, the volume of responses can overwhelm the target system.

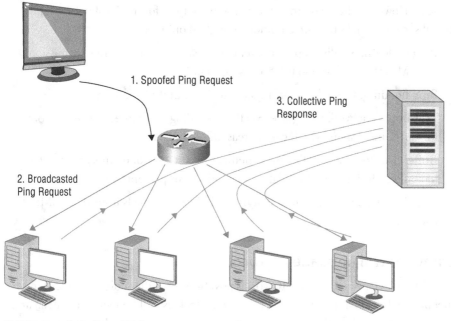

FIGURE 6.15 **Smurfing attack**

Today, techniques exist to mitigate the effects of DDOS attacks. However, the attack method still works well in multiple, effective forms. The famed Mirai attack that crippled several enterprise networks was a form of a DDoS attack, modeled after a smurf attack. Dozens of companies were affected including Dyn DNS, GitHub, CNN, Reddit, Visa, HBO, and the BBC.

NOTE Internet Relay Chat (IRC) servers were highly susceptible to these attacks. Script kiddies or younger hackers in general preferred smurf attacks through IRC servers to take down chat rooms.

Today, the smurf attack is uncommon. Prevention of an attack involves routine actions that administrators commonly use. External ping requests or broadcasts are typically ignored. The host or router is configured to be nonresponsive and the requests are not forwarded. The remediation of smurf attacks also had a social component as benevolent actors posted lists of smurf amplifiers. Administrators of systems would notice their IP addresses on the smurf amplifier list and take action to configure the systems correctly. Those administrators that did not would get feedback from business or community users in the network about performance degradation. That pressure persuaded them to take the appropriate actions.

Some of the other commands that are central to creating these types of attacks, like `ping` and `echo`, are now commonly blocked. These include `sourceroute` and `traceroute`. However, these commands can also be helpful for troubleshooting. There are several specific attacks that are common enough to outline:

- **Ping of death:** Sending a ping packet that violates the maximum transmission unit (MTU) size of 65,536 bytes, causing a crash.

- **Ping flooding:** Overwhelming a system with a multitude of pings.

- **Teardrop:** A network layer (layer 3) attack, sending malformed packets to confuse the operating system, which cannot reassemble the packet.

- **Buffer overflow:** Attacks that overwhelm a specific type of memory on a system—the buffers. Robust input validation in applications prevents this attack.

- **Fraggle:** A type of smurf attack that uses UDP Echo packets instead of ICMP packets.

Internet Control Message Protocol

Internet Control Message Protocol (ICMP) is possibly one of the more misunderstood Internet protocols from a security perspective. Yes, attackers will frequently use `ping` and `tracert` as key elements of their attempts to map your networks, and this sometimes scares management and leadership into asking that ICMP usage be shut off or locked down in some fashion. Since network administrators and security specialists *need* ICMP features as part of their day-to-day management and protection of the organization's systems and networks, following this dictum might cause more harm than good. You'll frequently hear or see advice in security blogs that caution against this, unless your use case *and* your network management skills can really keep your networks operating without it.

Attacks on Large (Enterprise) Networks

A number of protocols have been developed that are fundamental to the way that the Internet manages itself internally in order to optimize the flow of traffic. These protocols are also used by operators of large private networks, such as enterprise systems, for much the same purposes. As you might expect, high-capacity, high-volume internets attract the attention of a variety of attackers. Two key protocols used for managing very large *backbone* networks have shown certain exploitable vulnerabilities you may need to be aware of if you're working with enterprise-level systems or working with an ISP.

Border Gateway Protocol Attacks

Border Gateway Protocol (BGP) is the global routing protocol used by the Internet backbone and by large private internets to manage routing and control information across the network. BGP defines an *autonomous system (AS)* as a set of peer router nodes working together to manage routing information between nodes in the interior of this set of nodes (which form a logical subnet) and between the AS nodes at the edge or boundary of this set of AS nodes (thus the name *border gateway* is associated with these nodes). BGP operates by choosing the shortest path through the internet by navigating the least number of peer nodes along a particular route. The paths are stored in a routing information base (RIB). Only one route per destination is stored in the routing table, but the RIB is aware of multiple paths to a destination. Each router determines which routes to store from the RIB. As such, the RIB keeps track of possible routes. When routes are deleted, the RIB silently removes them without notification to peers. RIB entries never time out. BGP functions on top of TCP. Therefore, in the context of OSI model layers, BGP is technically a session layer protocol, even though its functions seem more associated with the Transport layer.

BGP's shortest path algorithms inherently grant a network in one region the ability to negatively influence the path that traffic takes far outside that region. Countries with an authoritarian view on controlling network traffic within their borders take advantage of that vulnerability. An example of this happened with China and Russia in 2018, when both countries abused how BGP operates to redirect traffic away from and through their borders. Western countries experienced availability outages for several minutes while the core Internet routers fought conflicting messages and converged path updates.

BGP was initially designed to carry Internet reachability information only, but it has expanded in capability to carry routes for Multicast, IPv6, VPNs, and a variety of other data. It is important to note that small corporate networks do not employ BGP but that very large, globe-spanning enterprise networks may need to.

Open Shortest Path First Versions 1 and 2

The Open Shortest Path First (OSPF) protocol is common in large enterprise networks because it provides fast convergence and scalability. *Convergence* refers to how routing tables get updated. OSPF is a link-state protocol, specifically one of the interior gateway protocols (IGPs) standardized by the Internet Engineering Task Force (IETF). Link-state protocols gather information from nearby routing devices and create a network topography, making the protocol very efficient. OSPF monitors the topography and when it detects a change, it automatically reroutes the topography. Within seconds, OSPF is able to reroute from link failures and create loop-free routing.

OSPF supports Internet Protocol version 4 (IPv4) and Internet Protocol version 6 (IPv6) networks. The updates for IPv6 are specified as OSPF version 3. OSPF computes traffic load and seek to balance it between routes. To do so, several variables are included, such as the round-trip distance in time of a router, data throughput of a link, or link availability and reliability. OSPF encapsulates data directly in IP packets and does not use a transport protocol like UDP or TCP. Part of the design of OSPF is its reliance on the network administrator to set key tuning parameters, such as *cost*, which after all can be somewhat arbitrarily determined to meet performance or other needs.

In a paper titled "Persistent OSPF Attacks" published through Stanford University (by Gabi Nakibly, Alex Kirshon, Dima Gonikman, and Dan Bonch 2012), the researchers share two new attack vectors made available by the OSPF standard. This interesting paper describes how the execution of the attacks relies on eavesdropping, requiring the attacker to be local to a networking device in the path.

SCADA, IoT, and the Implications of Multilayer Protocols

TCP/IP is an example of a multilayer protocol, in that it works because its dozens of individual component protocols are located across the various protocol stack layers that depend upon *encapsulation*, or the wrapping of one protocol's datagrams as the payload for the protocol at the next lower layer to use. For example, web servers provide data to web browser clients by encapsulating it via HTTP, which is then sent as packets via TCP. TCP is encapsulated in IP, and that packet is encapsulated in Ethernet. TCP/IP can also add additional layers of encapsulation. SSL/TLS encryption can be added to the communication to provide additional confidentiality. In turn, a network layer encryption can be achieved using IPsec.

TCP/IP encapsulation can be used for adversarial purposes. Some attack tools can hide or isolate an unauthorized protocol within an authorized one. Using a tool like HTTP tunnel, FTP can be hidden within an HTTP packet to get around egress restrictions.

Attackers can also use multilayer protocol encapsulation to provide an ability to fool interior switching devices to gain access to a virtual local area network (VLAN). VLANs are used to isolate network traffic to its own separate broadcast domain. The switch knows what VLAN to place that traffic on according to a tag identifying the VLAN ID. Those tags, per IEEE 802.1Q, encapsulate each packet. Where a VLAN is established through logical addressing, VLAN hopping is an attack using a double-encapsulated IEEE 802.1Q VLAN tag. To be clear, that's one VLAN tag encapsulating a packet already encapsulated with a different VLAN ID. The first VLAN tag is removed by the first switch it encounters. The next switch will inadvertently move traffic according to the second-layer VLAN-encapsulated tag.

Widespread use of multilayer protocols makes it possible for other communication protocols to move their data by using more ubiquitous transport protocols such as TCP/IP. Industrial control systems in the energy and utility industries do this to transfer supervisory control and data acquisition (SCADA) data between systems and user locations. Let's take a closer look at these two use cases.

SCADA and Industrial Control Systems Attacks

Proprietary technologies established the SCADA systems, but recently they have moved to more open and standardized solutions. With the evolution come security concerns. Initially, the systems were designed for decentralized facilities like power, oil, gas pipelines, water distribution, and wastewater collection systems. Connections were not a primary concern as the systems were designed to be open, robust, and easily operated and repaired. Any security was a secondary concern, which prior to 9/11 was often assumed to be provided by company security guards acting as tripwires by calling on local law enforcement responders to handle an intruder of any kind. In the United States, the President's Commission on Critical Infrastructure Protection sought to change this, and by the end of the 1990s there had already been considerable progress made in raising awareness within government and industry that SCADA and other ICS systems were a soft underbelly that presented a high-value strategic target to almost any type of attacker. Despite that heightened security awareness, business pressures drove operators to create numerous interconnections of SCADA and ICS systems via the Internet, data sharing with back-office and web-based corporate information systems, and email-enabled control of these.

The STUXNET attack on the Iranian nuclear fuels processing facilities was an attack on their SCADA systems. Late in 2018, attacks on SCADA and ICS systems in nickel smelting and processing industries, and at newspaper printing centers, were reported.

Thanks to the work of the PCCIP, there is almost unanimous recognition that attacks on the information systems that control public utilities, transportation, power and energy, communications, and almost every other aspect of a nation's economy are tantamount to strategic attacks on that nation itself. These are not privacy concerns; these are safety, security, systems integrity, and availability of service deliveries to their customers—many of whom are of course other industrial users. This means that security professionals who can speak both SCADA, ICS, and TCP/IP are in high demand and will be for quite a few years to come.

SCADA is a control system architecture that uses computers to gather data on processes and send control commands to connected devices that comprise the system. The connected devices, networked data communications, and graphical user interfaces perform high-level process supervisory management. Field sensors and actuators inform automatic processing through the SCADA system. However, manual operator interfaces are part of operations to enable monitoring and the issuing of process commands. Other peripheral devices, such as programmable logic controllers and discrete proportional integral derivative (PID) controllers, actually control industrial equipment or machinery. These controller devices, such as PIDs, are directly in the real-time feedback loops necessary for safe and effective operation of the machinery they control, such as furnaces, generators, hydraulic presses, or assembly lines—but they have zero security capabilities built into them, and (much like IPv4 before IPsec) their owners must implement required security measures externally to these controllers and SCADA systems elements. (You might say that the security process has to *encapsulate* the industrial control or SCADA system first in order to protect it.)

SCADA systems utilize a legacy protocol called Distributed Network Protocol (DNP3). DNP3 is found primarily in the electric and water utility and management industries. Data is transported across various components in the industrial controls systems like substation computers, remote terminal units (RTUs), and SCADA master stations (control centers). DNP3 is an open and public standard. There are many similarities between DNP3 and the TCP/IP suite, as they are both multilayer protocols that have link and transport functionality in their respective layers.

Ultimately, to provide some connectivity to these SCADA systems over public networks, there is the solution of encapsulating DNP3 over TCP/IP. This encapsulation, while obviously bridging a connection between disparate standards, does introduce great risk. Perhaps the more common exploitation of this risk is through man-in-the-middle attacks.

NOTE   Another protocol worth noting in industrial control systems is Modbus. It is a de facto standard of application layer protocol. It is used in several variations from plain Modbus to Modbus+ and Modbus/TCP. The protocol enables a Modbus client (or master) to send a request to a Modbus server (or slave) with a function code that specifies the action to be taken and a data field that provides the additional information.

DDoS and IoT Device Attacks

As an emerging technology, IoT devices deserve a little more attention in this chapter. From a security perspective, these devices offer a soft target for potential attackers. They are delivered with default settings that are easily guessed or, in fact, publicly well-known. Administrative credentials and management access are wide open to Internet-facing interfaces. Attackers can exploit the devices with relatively simple remote access code. What compounds the vulnerabilities are that users do not interact with the devices the same way as they do with office automation or other endpoint computing assets. The default settings are rarely changed, even if the end user has the ability to make changes. Vendors are typically slow to provide upgrades and patches, if they supply post-sale manufacturing support at all. For these reasons, the devices are easy prey, and users often have no idea the devices are hacked until it is too late.

The volume of IoT devices generates a lot of concern from security professionals. It is estimated that there are already tens of millions of vulnerable IoT devices. That number is growing. The interconnections are usually always on, left unprotected to ingress and egress unlike a typical LAN or WAN, but they enjoy high-speed connections. These variables explain why a botnet of huge groups of commandeered IoT devices presents a serious problem. Common attack sequences consist of compromising the device to send spam or broadcast messages. If spam filters block that attack, a tailored malware insert may be tried, like fast flux, which is a DNS technique to hide spamming attacks. If that does not accomplish the disruption, a brute-force type of DDoS might be launched. Increasingly, well-resourced websites have sufficient bandwidth and can expand capacity above baseline or normal usage levels to withstand most attacks. However, just the threat of launching an attack can be enough to convince website owners to pay a ransom to extortionists to avoid testing the limits of the targeted site's ability to remain responsive.

MANAGE NETWORK ACCESS CONTROLS

Access control is the process of ensuring that devices, people, or software processes can only read, write, move, use, or know about information assets within your systems if you permit them to do so. Access control, as explored in greater depth in Chapter 2, consists of the three big "AAA" functions.

- **Authentication** of a subject's identity, as they attempt to connect to your systems, that they are in fact someone or something you know and will approve to have access.

- **Authorization** of a subject's *specific requests* to take action with your systems' resources or information.

- **Accounting** for every access attempt, the results of authentication and authorization checks, and what resulted from the attempt.

Access control starts by applying the information security classification guidelines to your information architecture and in doing so must identify *subjects* (people, processes, or hardware devices) that can be granted access to your systems as well as the specific actions they are *privileged* to take with the *objects* within your systems. This is the "big picture" view of access control—it should apply to every aspect of your information systems and their security. Access control must be enforced via physical, logical, and administrative means:

- Physical controls would ensure that no one could access your server rooms or network wiring closets unless their identity was authenticated, and they were authorized to enter those areas to perform specific tasks.

- Logical controls would ensure that end users could access information assets they need to, as part of their jobs, but are prevented from accessing files or databases that they do not have a valid need-to-know privilege established.

- Administrative controls might establish that mobile devices cannot be brought into sensitive areas of the company's workspaces.

Network access control (NAC) can be seen as a somewhat smaller portion of this overall problem. It starts by recognizing that every asset shared on a network must be protected by some form of access control and that this be done in harmony with the organization's overall access control policies, procedures, and real-time decision-making processes. NAC focuses on the *logical* controls necessary to carry out management's decisions, as specified in administrative controls such as corporate policies, procedures, or guidelines. NAC systems must also depend upon someone else, such as the building architect and construction contractors, the security guards, or the IT security team, to ensure that the *physical* controls are in place to protect both NAC as a system and the networks as an infrastructure.

✔ Endpoint Security Is Not Enough

The endpoints you own and manage—or the endpoints owned by employees, visitors, or others that you allow access to your networks with—can be as secure as possible, but that cannot protect you from attacks coming in from the Internet via your ISP's point of presence and from attacks coming in from unknown (and therefore unauthorized) devices attempting to connect to your networks. An attacker bypassing your physical security controls could get into your systems in many ways, as shown in the "Layer 1: Physical" section earlier in this chapter. NAC is your *next* line of defense.

Hardening of your endpoints is covered in Chapter 7.

Figure 6.16 illustrates this concept, and we'll look at it step-by-step. Along the vertical network backbone are the DHCP server (needed even for networks using statically assigned IP addresses) and the two core service providers for access control: the AAA server itself, and the NAC Policy server.

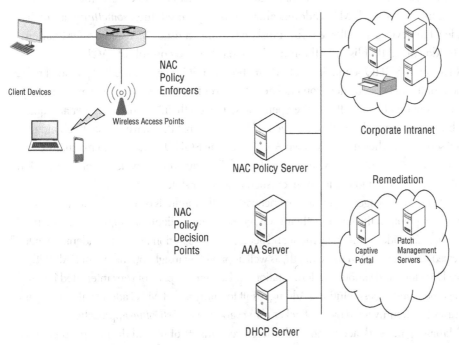

FIGURE 6.16 **Network access control in context**

Taken together, these three *policy decision points* – at the physical, logical, and administrative levels – must put the mechanisms and procedures in place so that you can systematically:

- Detect an attempt by a device to attach to the network, which almost always will end up requiring the device to request an IP address or present an IP address it already has.

- Authenticate that the device in question is known to the system; its identity has been previously established and it is approved to connect. (MAC addresses are often the first factor used in this process.)

- Determine what the device, as a *subject*, is permitted to do on the network, particularly in terms of access to other systems or assets.

- Keep accounting data (log files) that record the connection attempt and the access requests.

- Terminate the access at the request of the subject, or when conditions indicate the subject has attempted to violate an access constraint, or at systems administrator direction.

Now, let's take a closer look at that router. It's the first layer of enforcement for our access control system. If MAC address allowed listing is used, then *something* has to (a) decide what devices are allowed, (b) translate that into a list of MAC addresses to allow, and (c) download that list into the router's onboard access control list (ACL).

In a typical SOHO setup, the DHCP function is built into either the ISP-provided router/modem or the network owner's router. The AAA server function is handled by user account management functions built into the operating system on their "main" computer and quite possibly on any network-attached storage (NAS) devices that they have in use. Each cloud-hosted service that they use has its own AAA server; the SOHO owner has to manually coordinate updates to each of those systems in order to fully provision a new device or de-provision one that is no longer allowed to connect (such as a lost or stolen smartphone).

Scale this up to larger organizational networks, with hundreds of access points and thousands of endpoints in the hands of their users, guests, visiting clients or suppliers, and the need for an integrated identity management and access control solution becomes evident. Chapter 2 addressed access control in some depth, as well as providing insight on the use of RADIUS, Active Directory, and various implementations of Kerberos as parts of your integrated identity management and access solutions. Adding insult to injury is that MAC address filtering by itself can easily be circumvented by an attacker using various MAC *spoofing* approaches.

Managing network access control, therefore, consists of several distinct problem sets.

- *Monitoring* the network to detect attempts by new devices to connect or that might be attempting to connect to other network segments or resources

- *Admission* of a subject device to the network, which includes denying or otherwise restricting access in some circumstances

- *Remote access control* of devices attempting to connect to the network by way of the Internet, a VPN connection, or a dial-in telephone circuit

Let's look further at each of these in the following sections.

Network Access Control and Monitoring

As you might expect, there are multiple approaches to network access control that need to be considered. Key decisions that need to be made include the following:

- **Centralized versus distributed decision-making:** This considers whether to implement one AAA server system to serve the entire organization or whether to implement multiple AAA servers that provide access control over logical or physical subnets of the overall network infrastructure. Performance, scalability, and synchronization needs affect this choice.

- **Agent versus agentless designs:** The AAA servers will need to interrogate each endpoint to answer a number of important questions regarding its identity and configuration. This can be done either by requiring an access control agent to be loaded and running on each such endpoint, by the server using remote scanning and interrogation techniques, or by using a mix of approaches. Microsoft Windows, macOS, and many Linux implementations contain built-in access control agents that can be used by your overall AAA system.

- **Out-of-band versus inline:** Out-of-band devices separate the functions of deciding and enforcing and reports to a central server or console for management. This approach uses (or reuses) existing infrastructure switches, gateways, and firewalls to enforce policy. Some practitioners contend the out-of-band configuration can be disruptive. Inline devices sit in the middle of traffic flow, usually above the access switch level, and decide whether to admit or restrict traffic from each endpoint as it logs in. These can become bottlenecks if they become overloaded. Routers or gateways with built-in access control functions and capabilities are inline access control devices, as would a hardware firewall or inline intrusion detection and prevention system.

Chapter 2 goes into further detail about the implications of architectural choices.

Admission

Admission is the process that decides whether to allow (admit) a device to connect to the network, to deny its request for access, or to invoke other services to deal with the request. It's worth pointing out, however, that in almost all cases, we misspeak when we talk about a *device* attempting to access our networks: it's more than likely a *software process* onboard that device that is making the access attempt, probably in the service of other software processes. The device is just the *host endpoint*.

True, there can be *hardware-only* devices attempting to access your networks. These do not interact with any of the protocols or signals flowing on the network segment; but they may split or copy that signal for passive rerouting to a packet sniffer. Some layer 2 devices, such as switches, may have little firmware on board and thus might rightly be considered as a *device* rather than a *process hosted on a device*. But above layer 2, where all of the value is to be made by your business and stolen or corrupted by an attacker, connections are being made and managed by the software that rides on the device. Laptop computers, smartphones, and servers are all making a hardware connection at the Physical layer, but then useg software to interact with your network (whether with a connection or in connectionless fashion) at layer 2 and above.

Recognizing the software-intensive nature of a subject that is attempting to connect is important to understanding whether it is a threat or not. This is where the next choice regarding access control strategies comes into play.

Pre-Admission versus Post-Admission   This choice reflects whether a subject will be examined for compliance with appropriate policies prior to being granted access or whether it will be granted access but then have its behavior subject to monitoring for compliance. One such compliance policy might be to ensure that the subject has up-to-date anti-malware software and definitions loaded and active on it. Another compliance policy might check for specific revisions, updates, or patches to the operating systems, or critical applications (such as browsers). Other pre-admission checks might enforce the need for multifactor authentication by the human user of the device (and its processes) or the processes and the device itself. These are best implemented as a series of additional challenges; each additional factor is not challenged for if the preceding ones have failed to pass the test, to protect the existence of the additional factors.

Post-admission, by contrast, can be as simple as "allow all devices" access control settings on routers at the perimeter (edge) of your systems. This can allow limited access to some network segments, resources, or systems, with these further decisions being invoked by the behavior of the subject. Timeouts, violations of specific policy constraints, or other conditions might then lead the AAA server or the systems administrators to eject the subject from the system in whatever way is suitable.

Remediation

Pre-admission checks may determine that a device's onboard software, antivirus protection, or other characteristics are such that it cannot be allowed onto the network at all unless certain remedial (i.e., repair) actions are taken by the device's user. Such a device may, of course, be completely denied access. The system can, however, be configured to direct and enforce that remediation take place via one of two approaches.

- **Quarantine:** The endpoint is restricted to a specific IP network or assigned VLAN that provides users with routed access only to certain hosts and applications, like the patch management and update servers. Typically, these will use ARP or Neighbor Discovery Protocol (NDP) to aid in reducing the administrative burden of manually managing quarantine VLANs for larger organizational networks.

- **Captive portals:** User access to websites is intercepted and redirected to a web application that guides a user through system remediation. Access is limited to the captive portal until remediation is completed.

In either case, once the user and their device seem to have completed the required remediation, the user can re-attempt to access the network, where the pre-admission tests will again be applied.

Monitoring

Network monitoring in an access control context can refer to two broad categories of watchfulness: behavioral monitoring of endpoints and the processes running on them; and monitoring the health and status of endpoints to detect possible compromises of their integrity, safety, or security.

Indicators of Compromise (IoCs)   Health and status monitoring means being on the lookout for any possible *indicators of compromise*; these are events that suggest with high confidence that a system has been corrupted by some form of malware or detected an intrusion in progress. Your own organizational risk assessment process should identify your own working set of such IoCs, along with setting a maximum allowable time-to-detect for each type of IoC based in part upon what you think the compromise may actually mean to the confidentiality, integrity, availability, privacy, or safety of your data and your systems. Many such lists of possible IoCs have been published, such as one in 2013 by Ericka Chickowski at Darkreading.com.

- Unusual outbound network traffic
- Anomalies in privileged user account creation, use, elevation, or activity
- Anomalies in login behavior, such as logins from out-of-the-ordinary geographic areas, times of day, or devices
- Frequent, repeated, or otherwise suspicious attempts by a user or process to access systems, servers, or resources outside of the scope of their assigned duties, job, or function
- Significant and unusual increases in database read attempts or access attempts to specific files
- HTML response sizes are unusually large
- Mismatches in ports versus applications
- Suspicious, unplanned, or unrecognized changes to systems files, such as the Windows Registry hive
- Anomalies in DNS requests
- Unexpected patching, updating, or modification of systems or applications software
- Unexpected changes in mobile device profiles
- Unexpected blobs[7] of data showing up in unusual places in your storage systems

---

[7] Binary large objects or *blobs* are a unit of storage space allocation that is independent of the underlying or supporting disk or device technologies, which allows a blob to be almost arbitrarily large. Or small.

- Web traffic exhibiting possible bot-like behavior, such as opening dozens of web pages simultaneously
- Signs of DDoS, such as slowdowns in network performance, firewall failover, or back-end systems being heavily loaded[8]

Not all of those IoCs relate directly to access control monitoring, of course. But it's clear that your overall intrusion detection capabilities need to be *integrated* in ways that enable and enhance your ability to spot these kinds of events quickly.

Endpoint Behavioral Monitoring, Detection, and Response   The underlying assumption in most of systems security is that if a system element is behaving in "normal" ways, then it is probably still a trustworthy element of the system, since if the element had been somehow corrupted, this would show up in *some* kind of observable changes in its behavior. Humans, software processes, and devices are all assumed to give off some kind of "tells" that indicate a change in their trustworthiness, integrity, or reliability. Biometric analysis might detect a human end user is under unusual stress; larger patterns of behavior, such as logging in more on the weekends than was typical, might indicate a compromise or just might indicate a lot of additional work needs to be done.

The problem with behavioral modeling is that if it's going to work well at all, it needs to be based on *huge* amounts of data. Simple rule-based systems, such as the Boolean conditions in some attribute-based access control (ABAC) models, quickly get too complex for the human security staff to build, modify, or maintain confidence in. So-called *signature analysis* systems try to get past this by looking at far more parameters than the ABAC system might be able to handle, but someone or something has got to analyze the subject in question and develop that new signature.

Machine learning approaches are being used in a number of systems to deal with the complexities of behavioral modeling and analysis. ML, as it's known in our acronym-rich world, is a subset of the whole field of applied artificial intelligence (AI). Many security professionals and their managers are hesitant to place their trust and confidence in ML security solutions, however, since these systems often cannot explain their "reasoning" for why a particular series of events involving a set of subjects and objects is a *positive* or alarm-worthy indicator of possible compromise. Managers are also rightly cautious in trying to decide whether the *possible* cost of a security incident is greater than the *guaranteed* cost of disruption to business operations if a positive IoC alarm leads to a containment, shutdown, and possible eradication of an ongoing business activity and its information assets. False positives—alarms

---

[8] You can find this list at `https://www.darkreading.com/attacks-breaches/top-15-indicators-of-compromise/d/d-id/1140647?page_number=1`.

that needn't have happened—can often outweigh the anticipated losses if the risk event turned out to be real.

Endpoint detection and response (EDR) systems have become more popular in the security marketplace in recent years, as vendors strive to find more manageable solutions to sifting through terabytes of data per day (from even a medium-sized enterprise network) to spot potentially alarm-worthy events. This whole subject area, if you pardon the pun, is still quite unsettled.

Network Access Control Standards and Protocols

Several standards—some set by the IEEE or other standards bodies, and some set by widespread market adoption of a vendor technology—form the foundation of most access control systems.

X.500 Directory Access Protocol Standard   Developed by the International Telecommunications Union Technical Standardizations sector (which is known as ITU-T). X.500 bases its approach on an underlying *directory information tree* data model, which allows entities in the tree to be spread across (and managed by) one or more *directory service agents* that act as directory and storage servers. An X.500-compatible directory is thus distributed and independent of the underlying storage or server technology. X.500 was first published in the late 1980s and has continued to be the dominant directory standard. It provided a fully featured set of functionalities in its Directory Access Protocol (DAP), which fully integrated with the OSI Seven-Layer stack; some organizations found it to have too much overhead, and so the Lightweight Directory Access Protocol was born.

IEEE 802.1X Port-Based Access Control Standard   IEEE 802.1X provides an industry-recognized standard for port-based access control systems to follow. Well-known security frameworks such as ISO 27002, various NIST publications, and the standards required by the Payment Card Industry Data Security Standard all recommend appropriate access control systems be put in place and kept operational; one or more of these standards may also require that companies working in those industries or business areas comply with their requirements, and with the requirements of IEEE 802.1X. In many situations, these standards would require the use of X.509-compliant digital certificates, and the PKI infrastructure that makes those possible, as part of a robust access control implementation.

Kerberos   Kerberos is not an access control system; it is an authentication system that is often incorporated with LDAP as part of a full-feature access control system. Kerberos, named after the three-headed guard dog of Hades in Greek mythology (renamed "Fluffy" in *Harry Potter and the Philosopher's Stone*), uses PKI as part of its secure token generation and token-passing processes. This allows the Kerberos server to support the requesting subject and the authentication server (the first A in AAA) to validate each other's identity.

Microsoft Active Directory   Microsoft's Active Directory (AD) provides a fully featured AAA solution, complete with fully integrated identity provisioning, authentication, and management tools; because of Microsoft's market share, AD is almost everywhere. While it does require its own host to be running Microsoft's Windows Server as the native operating system, AD can manage access control for any operating system and network environment that supports LDAP versions 2 and 3. It is a proprietary technology, licensed to user organizations; nonetheless, it is a *de facto* standard in the marketplace.

OAuth and OpenID   These two open systems protocols provide systems designers and security architects with new standards that support identity authentication and access control. These are related to Security Assertion Markup Language in their approach but offer alternative systems for website and mobile applications support.

SAML   The Security Assertion Markup Language (SAML, pronounced "sam-el") provides an open standard markup language format that can be used to exchange authentication and authorization data between elements of a system, such as between servers in a distributed AAA architecture, or in federated systems. The most significant application of SAML is in supporting and facilitating single sign-on (SSO) without having to use cookies. SAML 2.0 became an OASIS [9] standard in 2005.

✔ Single Sign *Off?*

Single sign-off is not an access control issue or capability per se. It doesn't have to gain permission from the IAM systems to log off or shut down, but it also can't just hang up the phone and walk away, so to speak.

Single sign-off depends on the host operating system gathering information about all the applications, platforms, systems, and information assets that a user or subject has established access to, and at the click of the "sign off" button, it walks through that list, terminating applications, closing the files the apps had open, and releasing resources back to the system. As each task in the sign-off completes, the operating system that supports it notifies the access control accounting functions and makes notes in its own event logs as dictated by local policy settings.

In most cases, single sign-off is a local machine or local host activity. Active sessions created by the user or subject are usually not considered by single shut-off, and in most

[9] OASIS is the Organization for the Advancement of Structured Information Standards, which grew out of cooperation between standard generalized markup language (SGML) vendors in 1993.

cases, they are presumed to have a timeout feature that will close them down in an orderly fashion after a period of inactivity, regardless of the reason. In other cases, there may be powerful business reasons for keeping those sessions running even if the initiating subject has logged off and gone away on vacation!

Thus, single sign-*on* can enable far more connections to information assets than single sign-*off* will automatically disconnect and close down.

Remote Access Operation and Configuration

Remote access is the broad category of the ways in which users access your information systems without a direct connection via your Layer 1 infrastructure. They need this remote access to perform all sorts of business functions, which can all be grouped under the name *telework*, or working at a distance, enabled and empowered via telecommunications systems.

Such remote access to your endpoints, servers, network devices, or communications capabilities can be accomplished in a variety of ways:

- Command-line login through the Internet via endpoint client-side use of Telnet, SSH, or similar mechanisms

- Command-line login via dial-in connections through the Public Switched Phone Network (PSTN)

- Web-based login access via the Internet

- Fax machine connections for sending or receiving facsimile traffic, either via PSTN or IP connections

- VoIP or session initiation protocol (SIP) users, via the Internet

- PSTN connections supporting IP phone calls between external and internal subscribers

- Virtual private network (VPN) connections, tunneling under layers of your Internet infrastructure, may also provide external (remote) access

Figure 6.17 illustrates this important aspect of network access control, and that is the access to your network and systems, and their resources, from processes and devices that are not just TCP/IP-based endpoint devices coming in over the Internet. As this figure suggests, the universe of endpoints contains many other types of devices, each of which presents its own unique twists to the network access control problems and processes we've looked at elsewhere in this book.

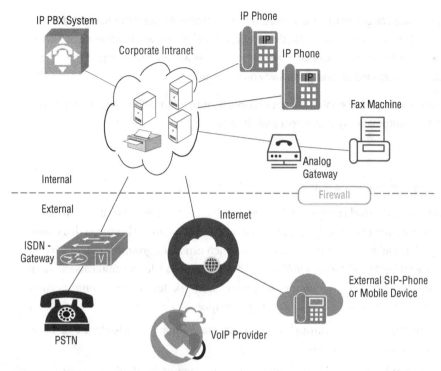

FIGURE 6.17 **Remote access in context**

- IP phone systems are becoming quite popular in many business and organizational contexts that have a "brick-and-mortar" physical set of facilities in which many of their employees have their workspaces, meet with clients or suppliers, and communicate with the outside world. These are usually hosted by a *private branch exchange* (PBX) system, which manages the assignment of phone numbers and IP addresses to endpoint telephone sets (the desktop or wall-mounted phones that people use), along with associating personal users' names, IDs, or other directory information with that phone number. IP phone systems may share the same physical cabling, routing, and switching infrastructure as your in-house data systems use, or they may ride out-of-band on separate interconnections and wiring.

- Fax machines are still in common use in many parts of the world (including the North American marketplace) and require analog gateway access. Many government agencies, for example, can receive official documents by fax but cannot do so via email attachments or online at their own website.

- Public Switched Telephone Network (PSTN) dial-in and dial-out connections provide the tie-in of the internal IP phone systems to the rest of the telephone system.

- External VoIP provider connections, via the organization's ISP connection to the Internet, provide collaboration environments in which voice, video, screen sharing, and file sharing are facilitated.

- SIP phones use the Session Initiation Protocol (SIP) to provide standardized ways to initiate, control, and terminate VoIP calls. External SIP devices may be able to connect to VoIP users within your organization (and on your networks) without a VoIP services provider such as Skype, if you've configured this type of support.

This figure, and those lists, suggest why the "Dial-In" part of RADIUS's name is still a problem set to be reckoned with for today's information systems security professionals. And there is no sign that the PSTN side of our systems will go away any time soon.

Many of these different use cases involve layering additional protocols on top of your TCP/IP infrastructure or using other protocols to tunnel past some of its layers. Each presents its own unique security challenges that must be addressed; looking into these is beyond the scope of this book unfortunately.

Thin Clients

Almost as soon as the client-server concept was introduced, industry and academia have had a devil of a time defining just what a *thin client* was—or for that matter what a *thick* client was. The terms *thin* and *thick* seem to relate to the number of functions that are performed by the client itself, more than anything else: a simple IoT thermostat would be a very thin client, whereas a home security control station might be a server to all of the thin client security sensors, alarms, and controls throughout the household while being a thicker client to the security company's servers itself. Another measure of thinness relates to how easily an end user can reconfigure the endpoint's onboard software or firmware, changing the installed functionality or introducing new capabilities and functions to the device. *Dumb* and *smart* are somewhat synonymous with *thin* and *thick*, although both sets of terms have a comparable lack of precision.

From a network access control perspective, your organization's business use cases and its information security needs should guide you in identifying strategies to control categories of client endpoint devices, be they thick or thin. The thinnest client one can imagine receives a set of data and transforms it into something in the real world—it prints it, it displays it, it commands a physical machine or device into action with it—while allowing input data from a simple device to be sent via its interface to its connection to your networks. Right away, this forces you to think about what type of connections you want to support and whether that pushes functionality back into the endpoint or not. Truly "dumb" serial terminals, for example, support asynchronous serial data exchange via an RS-232 style interface; they do not support any protocols above layer 1 and may not even answer to WRU ("who are you?") commands sent to them by the server.

Remote Access Security Management

Organizations that allow for remote access are extending their risk beyond the figurative corporate walls. With the expansion of risk come additional security requirements. The private network can be compromised by remote access attacks. Figure 6.18 illustrates some common areas of increased risk of remote access.

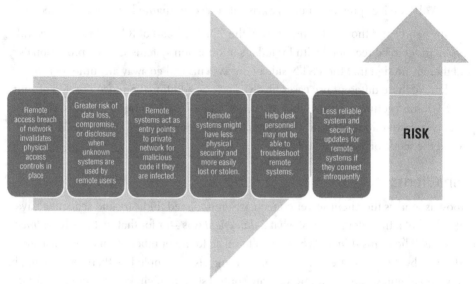

FIGURE 6.18 **Common areas of increased risk in remote access**

Because remote access expands the private network beyond the corporate environment, it invalidates many of the physical controls in place, which increases information risk for the organization. Taking extra precaution with authentication of remote access users is therefore a wise and prudent investment, addressing one's due diligence responsibilities. There are specific remote access protocols and services that an organization will use to strengthen credential management and permissions for remote clients and users. Most likely, the use of a centralized remote access authentication system should be in place. Some examples of remote authentication protocols are Password Authentication Protocol (PAP), Challenge Handshake Authentication Protocol (CHAP), Extensible Authentication Protocol (EAP, or its extensions PEAP or LEAP), Remote Authentication Dial-In User Service (RADIUS), and Terminal Access Controller Access Control System Plus (TACACS+).

Centralized Remote Authentication Services

Centralized remote authentication services add an extra layer of protection between the remote access clients and the private, internal network. Remote authentication and authorization services using a centralized server are different and separated from the similar services used for network clients locally. This is important because in the event a remote access server is compromised, the entire network's authentication and authorization services are unaffected. A few leading examples are RADIUS and TACACS+.

- **Remote Authentication Dial-In User Service (RADIUS):** Dial-up users pass logon credentials to a RADIUS server for authentication. Similar to the process used by domain clients sending logon credentials to a domain controller for authentication, although RADIUS is no longer limited to dial-up users.

- **Diameter:** Diameter is essentially the successor to RADIUS. One significant improvement Diameter provides is added reliability. However, it really has not developed much traction in the marketplace.

- **Terminal Access Controller Access-Control System (TACACS):** This provides an alternative to RADIUS. TACACS is available in three versions: original TACACS, Extended TACACS (XTACACS), and TACACS+. TACACS integrates the authentication and authorization processes. XTACACS keeps the authentication, authorization, and accounting processes separate. TACACS+ improves XTACACS by adding two-factor authentication. TACACS+ is the most current and relevant version of this product line.

Virtual Private Networks

A virtual private network (VPN) is a communication tunnel through an untrusted (or trusted) network that establishes a secure, point-to-point connection with authentication and protected data traffic. Most VPNs use encryption to protect the encapsulated traffic, but encryption is not necessary for the connection to be considered a VPN. Encryption is typically provided via an SSL or TLS connection.

The most common application of VPNs is to establish secure communications through the Internet between two distant networks. Business cases for the use of VPNs show many different needs that can be supported, if properly implemented.

- Inside a private network for added layers of data protection
- Between end-user systems connected to an ISP
- As a link between two separate and distinct private networks
- Provide security for legacy applications that rely on risky or vulnerable communication protocols or methodologies, especially when communication is across a network

Properly implemented, VPN solutions can clearly provide confidentiality, privacy, authentication, and integrity for the data that they protect as it transits other networks (which may be untrustworthy, such as the public Internet, or operate as trusted networks themselves). The business logic that uses VPNs as part of its data-in-motion protection may in turn address safety, nonrepudiation, and availability needs as well.

WARNING   Sophisticated attackers are becoming more skilled and cunning in their use of VPNs to tunnel into and out of their target's trusted and secured network infrastructures.

Tunneling

The concept of tunneling is fundamental to understanding how VPN works. Tunneling is a network communications process that encapsulates a packet of data with another protocol to protect the initial packet. The encapsulation is what creates the logical illusion of a communications tunnel over the untrusted intermediary network, since the encapsulated traffic is visible only to the systems on either end of the tunnel. At the ends of the tunnel, the initial protocol packet is encapsulated and de-encapsulated to accomplish communication.

Tunneling is demonstrated by commercial mail forwarding agents using national and international postal mail system. Normal (nontunneled) mail works by encapsulating your messages in envelopes or packages, which are externally marked with sender's and recipient's postal addresses. Laws and regulations prohibit other parties from opening postal mail without a court order or search warrant. If the recipient moves, they need to leave a change of address order with their servicing post office, and the postal system then handles the rerouting of the mail to the new address. Commercial mail forwarders, by contrast, receive mail sent to a recipient at the mail forwarder's address; they bundle these up into larger parcels and send those (via postal systems or parcel services such as UPS or DHL) to the recipient at their preferred service address. The forwarding agent provides a "landing address" in the city, state, or country it is physically operating in, and its national postal service has no business knowing what is in the bundles of mail that it ships to its customers, as envelopes inside other envelopes or packages.

In situations where bypassing a firewall, gateway, proxy, or other networking device is warranted, tunneling is used. The authorized data is encapsulated, and the transmission is permitted even though access inside the tunnel is restricted. An advantage of tunneling is that traffic control devices cannot block or drop the communications because they cannot interrogate the packet contents. This can be useful in streamlining important content and connections. However, this capability is also a potential security problem as security devices meant to protect the private network from malicious content cannot scan the packets as they arrive or leave. This is particularly true if tunneling involves encryption. The sensitive data will maintain confidentiality and integrity. However, again, the data is unreadable by networking devices. Tunneling can also provide a way to route traffic that is created using nonroutable protocols over the Internet.

VPN operations involve three distinct hops or segments that each operate somewhat differently.

- **Origin to VPN client:** This is usually within the endpoint itself, using a device driver, service set, and user interface loaded on the endpoint device. The user may have multiple web browser sessions or service connections via different protocols and their ports; all of them are bundled together via the VPN client for routing via the tunnel. Each individual service may or may not be separately encrypted; all share the user's origin IP address.

- **VPN client to VPN server:** This runs over your organizational IT infrastructure through the Internet to the server. This traffic is usually bulk encrypted and encapsulated so that externally only the VPN client and VPN server IP addresses are visible.

- **VPN server to user's requested servers**: At the landing point, the VPN server bulk decrypts the traffic, breaks it out into its separate streams for each connection with each service, and translates the user's endpoint IP addresses into ones based off of the local landing point's IP address. This creates the illusion that the user is originating the connections at that local IP address. The VPN server flows this traffic out via its ISP connection, through the Internet, to the intended recipients.

Surveillance or reconnaissance efforts that attempt to exploit the VPN landing point to server traffic will not be able to identify the sender's actual IP address (and thus country or geographic region of origin), as it's been translated into an address assigned to the VPN provider. Traffic analysis (whether for marketing or target reconnaissance) efforts will thus be frustrated.

Several concerns arise when using VPNs within or through your organization's networks:

- **Content inspection difficulties:** It can be difficult to impossible to inspect the content of VPN traffic, since many VPN processes provide encryption to prevent *any* party other than the VPN user from seeing into the packets. This can stymie efforts to detect data exfiltration or inappropriate use of organizational IT assets.

- **Network traffic loading and congestion:** Many VPN protocols attempt to use the largest frame or packet size they can, as a way of improving the overall transfer rate. This can often cause bandwidth on the internal network to suffer.

- **VPN misuse for broadcast traffic:** Since the protocols are really designed to support point-to-point communication, multicasting (even narrowcasting to a few users) can cause congestion problems.

The Proliferation of Tunneling

Normal use of Internet services and corporate networks permit daily use of tunneling that is almost transparent to regular end users. There are many common uses. Many websites resolve the connection over a Secure Sockets Layer (SSL) or Transport Layer Security (TLS) connection. That is an example of tunneling. The cleartext web communications are tunneled within an SSL or TLS session. With Internet telephone or VoIP systems, voice communication is being encapsulated inside a voice over IP protocol. Note that TLS (or SSL, if you must use it) can be used as a VPN protocol and not just as a session encryption process on top of TCP/IP.

VPN links provide a cost-effective and secure pathway through the Internet for the connection of two or more separated networks. This efficiency is measured against the higher costs of creating direct or leased point-to-point solutions. Additionally, the VPN links can be connected across multiple Internet Service Providers (ISPs).

Common VPN Protocols

VPNs can be implemented using software or hardware solutions. In either case, there are variations and combinations based on how the tunnel is implemented. There are four common VPN protocols that provide a foundational view of how VPNs are built.

- **PPTP:** Data link layer (layer 2) use on IP networks
- **L2TP:** Data link layer (layer 2) use on any LAN protocol
- **IPsec:** Network layer (layer 3) use on IP networks

Point-to-Point Tunneling Protocol (PPTP)

PTPP was developed from the dial-up protocol called Point-to-Point Protocol (PPP). It encapsulates traffic at the data link layer (layer 2) of the OSI model and is used on IP networks. It encapsulates the PPP packets and creates a point-to-point tunnel connecting two separate systems. PPTP protects the authentication traffic using the same authentication protocols supported by PPP:

- Microsoft Challenge Handshake Authentication Protocol (MS-CHAP)
- Challenge Handshake Authentication Protocol (CHAP)
- Password Authentication Protocol (PAP)
- Extensible Authentication Protocol (EAP)
- Shiva Password Authentication Protocol (SPAP)
- Microsoft Point to Point Encryption (MPPE)

NOTE   Don't confuse MPPE with PPTP in the RFC 2637 standard, as Microsoft did use proprietary modifications to PTP in its development of this protocol.

Be aware that the session establishment process for PTPP is not itself encrypted. The authentication process shares the IP addresses of sender and receiver in cleartext. The packets may even contain user IDs and hashed passwords, any of which could be intercepted by a MitM attack.

Layer 2 Tunneling Protocol

Layer 2 Tunneling Protocol (L2TP) was derived to create a point-to-point tunnel to connect disparate networks. This protocol does not employ encryption, so it does not provide confidentiality or strong authentication. In conjunction with IPsec, those services are possible. IPsec with L2TP is a common security structure. L2TP also supports TACACS+ and RADIUS. A most recent version, L2TPv3, improves upon security features to include improved encapsulation and the ability to use communication technologies like Frame Relay, Ethernet, and ATM, other than simply Point-to-Point Protocol (PPP) over an IP network.

IPsec VPN

IPsec provides the protocols by which internetworking computers can create *security associations (SAs)* and negotiate the details of key distribution. These are the perfect building blocks of a VPN, gathered into a *domain of interpretation (DOI)*. This IPsec construct contains all of the definitions for the various security parameters needed to negotiate, establish, and operate a secure VPN, such as SAs and IKE negotiation. (See RFC 2407 and 2408 for additional information.) In effect, inbound VPN traffic needs the destination IP address, the chosen security protocol (AH or Encapsulating Security Protocol, also an IPsec protocol), and a control value called the *security parameter index*. Outbound traffic is handled by invoking the SA that is associated with this VPN tunnel.

NOTE ESP actually operates at the network layer (layer 3). It has the added flexibility to operate in transport mode or tunnel mode. In transport mode, the IP packet data is encrypted, but the header of the packet is not. In tunnel mode, the entire IP packet is encrypted, and a new header is added to the packet to govern transmission through the tunnel. Each has its own benefits depending on the available network bandwidth and sensitivity of the information.

MANAGE NETWORK SECURITY

Managing network security, as a task, should suggest that key performance requirements have been translated into the physical, logical, and administrative features of your network security system and that each of these requirements has an associated key performance indicator or metric that you communicate to management and leadership. The list of indicators of compromise that your risk assessment and vulnerability assessments have identified provide an excellent starting point for such *key risk indicators* (KRIs, similar to KPIs for key performance indicators). Don't be confused, however: an *indicator* in security terms is a signal created by an event that could call your attention to that event; a *performance indicator* is usually expressed as a count, a rate (changes in counts over time), a trend, or a ratio. Performance indicators are *metrics*, not alarm bells, in and of themselves.

Vulnerability assessment and risk mitigation either drove your organization's initial network and systems specification, design, and build-out, or they have highlighted areas where the networks and systems need to be redesigned, reconfigured, or perhaps just tweaked a little to deliver better security performance (that is, to provide greater confidence that the CIANA+PS needs of the organization will be met or exceeded). At the tactical level of network implementation, three major sets of choices must be considered: placement of network security devices, network segmentation, and secure device management.

Let's look at a few use case examples to illustrate the context of these choices.

Intranet This type of network offers internal organizational users a specific set of information resources, services, systems, and telecommunications capabilities; but it restricts access to or use of these to an identifiable set of users. Intranets are logically segregated from other networks, such as the external Internet, by means of an appropriate set of network security devices and functions (such as a firewall). Intranets may host inward-facing websites and are often where back-end databases are found that support public-facing or customer-facing web applications. Usually, intranet use is restricted to an organization's employees or trusted outside parties only. Remote access to intranets can be securely provided.

Extranet An extranet is a controlled private network that allows partners, vendors, suppliers, and possibly an authorized set of customers to have access to a specific set of organizational information resources, servers, and websites. The access and information available are typically less controlled than on an intranet, but more constrained than a publicly facing website. An extranet is similar to a DMZ because it allows the required level of access without exposing the entire organization's network.

Intranets and extranets offer different mixes of capabilities to business users, while also providing a different mix of risk mitigation (or security) features; these are summarized in Figure 6.19.

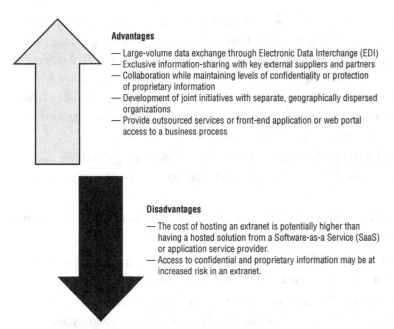

Advantages

— Large-volume data exchange through Electronic Data Interchange (EDI)
— Exclusive information-sharing with key external suppliers and partners
— Collaboration while maintaining levels of confidentiality or protection of proprietary information
— Development of joint initiatives with separate, geographically dispersed organizations
— Provide outsourced services or front-end application or web portal access to a business process

Disadvantages

— The cost of hosting an extranet is potentially higher than having a hosted solution from a Software-as-a Service (SaaS) or application service provider.
— Access to confidential and proprietary information may be at increased risk in an extranet.

FIGURE 6.19 **Extranet advantages and disadvantages**

Content Distribution Networks A content distribution network (CDN), also called a *content delivery network*, is a collection of resource services, proxy servers, and data centers deployed to provide low latency, high performance, and high availability of content, especially multimedia, e-commerce, and social networking sites, across a very large (often national or continental) area. The content itself may originate in one server system and then be replicated to multiple server sites for distribution; cloud-based distribution networks are also used in CDN implementations. This can provide a mix of cost, throughput, and reliability considerations that the CDN's owners and operators can balance against their business models and use cases. Sports programming, for example, is quite often distributed via CDN architectures to markets around the world. Some architectures use high-capacity links that can push live content to local area redistribution points, which buffer the content and push it out to subscribers, rather than attempting to have subscribers from around the globe get individual content feeds from servers at the content origination point. This may bring with it other issues with regard to copyright or intellectual property protection, marketing and distribution agreements with content providers, and even local market legal, regulatory, and cultural constraints on such content distribution. Akami, CloudFlare, Azure CDN, Amazon CloudFront, Verizon, and Level 3 Communications all offer a variety of CDN services that content distributors can use. These are all client-server models by design.

Some client-to-client or peer-to-peer (P2P) content distribution networks exist. The most widely recognized P2P CDN is BitTorrent, which does have a reputation for facilitating the pirating of content. There are significant concerns with P2P systems in that P2P systems usually expose each peer's systems internals to each other, which does not happen with client-server models. P2P CDN, by definition, requires a level of trust that participants will not abuse their access to other participants' machines or their data. Some specific P2P CDN threats to be aware of include:

- **DDoS attacks:** Unlike the traditional TCP SYN-ACK flooding of a server, the P2P network is disrupted when an overwhelming number of search requests are processed.

- **Poisoning of the network:** Inserting useless data that may not be malware, but the superfluous, useless information can degrade performance.

- **Privacy and identity:** Fellow peers may have access to data the sender did not intend to share, simply because of the nature of the P2P data stream.

- **Fairness in sharing:** The network depends on sharing and contribution, not hoarding or leeching by those who download content but rarely add content.

Logical and Physical Placement of Network Devices

Any type of network device can potentially contribute to the overall security of your networks, provided it's put in the right place and configured to work correctly where you put it. Monitoring can be performed by the native hardware and firmware within the device, by its operating system, or by applications loaded onto it. The *field of regard* that such monitoring can consider is suggested by the names for such systems:

- **Host-based monitoring** looks internally at the system it is installed and operating on in order to protect it from intrusion, malware, or other security problems that might directly affect that host. This monitoring usually can extend to any device connected to that host, such as a removable or network-attached storage device. It can monitor or inspect network traffic or other data that flows *through* the device, but not traffic on a network segment that the host is not connected to. Host-based monitoring can also interrogate the onboard health, status, and monitoring capabilities of routers, switches, other endpoints, or servers. However, with each segment of the network the monitoring transits to monitor a distant device, it can incur the risk that that interconnection has been compromised somehow or is under surveillance. A host-based intrusion detection or prevention system (HIDS and HIPS, for example) can protect its own host and in doing so can quarantine an incoming malware payload and prevent it from leaving the host to infect other systems. But they are typically not designed to be high-throughput traffic monitoring devices.

- **Network-based monitoring, also called inline,** narrows its scope to the data flowing along the network segment that it sits in. Hardware firewalls are examples of inline hardware monitoring solutions, which are designed to provide high throughput while using a variety of traffic inspection and behavior modeling capabilities to filter out incoming or outcoming traffic that does not conform to security policy expectations and requirements.

Network-based or inline monitoring devices are further characterized as *active* or *passive*:

- **Active security devices** inspect the incoming traffic's headers and content for violations of security policies and constraints; traffic that passes inspection is then returned to the network to be passed onto the intended recipient. Examples of active security devices include next-generation firewalls (NGFWs), Network-based Intrusion Detection or Prevention Systems (NIDS or NIPS), and *sandboxing solutions* which provide quarantine network segments and devices which traffic suspected of carrying malware can be routed to for analysis and testing. Attack or intrusion prevention systems are, in this sense, active security technologies.

- **Passive security devices** perform the same inspections, but they do not interrupt or sit in the flow of the data itself. Data loss prevention (DLP) appliances and intrusion detection systems (IDS) are examples of the passive class of inline monitoring systems.

Both active and passive security devices signal alarms to security operations reporting systems when suspect traffic is detected.

Network-based monitoring devices or appliances often work with another type of inline device known as a *visibility* appliance. SSL or TLS visibility appliances attempt to decrypt protected traffic to allow for content inspection; this of course would require that the appliance has access to the session keys used to encrypt the traffic in the first place. Networks that support centralized key management, perhaps with a hardware security manager (HSM) solution, may be able to support such decrypted inspection of content, but as we saw in Chapter 5, this can come with significant throughput penalties and cannot inspect content encrypted with nonmanaged session keys (such as the private keys of individual employees or the ones used by intruders).

Segmentation

Traditionally, network engineers would break a large organizational network into *segments* based on considerations such as traffic and load balancing, congestion, and geographic or physical dispersion of endpoints and servers. Segments by and large are not *subnets* in the IPv4 classless inter-domain routing (CIDR) sense of the term. Segments are joined together by active devices such as routers or gateways. And in many respects, a perimeter firewall segments the Internet into two segments: all of it *outside* your firewall and all of it inside your organization. We have looked to such perimeter firewalls to keep the interior network segment safe from intruders and malware, and to some degree, keep our data inside the perimeter. Further segmentation of an internal network into various zones for security purposes began to be popular as corporate networks grew in size and complexity, and as virtual LANs (VLANs) and VPNs became more common.

Virtual LANs

Using a defense-in-depth strategy, organizations often will create logical segments on the network without expensive and major physical topology changes to the infrastructure itself. With implementation of internal routers and switches, a number of VLANs can be configured for improved security and networking. On a port-by-port basis, the network administrator can configure the routing devices to group ports together and distinguish one group from another to establish the VLANs. Thus, multiple logical segments can coexist on one physical network. If permitted, communication between VLANs is unfettered. However, a security feature of the design is the ability to configure filtering and blocking for traffic, ports, and protocols that are not allowed. Routing can be provided by an external router or by the internal software of a switch if using a multilayer switch. In summary, VLANs are important in network and security design because they do the following:

- Isolate traffic between network segments. In the event of an attack, compromise can be contained within a specific VLAN or subset of VLANs.

- Reduce a network's vulnerability to sniffers as VLANs are configured by default to deny routable traffic unless explicitly allowed.

- Protect against broadcast storms or floods of unwanted multicast network traffic.

- Provide a tiering strategy for information protection of assets. Higher value assets can be grouped and provided maximum levels of safeguarding while lower value assets can be protected in a more efficient manner.

VLANs are managed through software configuration, which means the devices in the group do not have to be moved physically. The VLAN can be managed centrally efficiently and effectively.

TIP   VLANs have similarity to subnets. However, they are different. VLANs are created by configuring routing devices, like switches to allow traffic through ports. Subnets are created by IP address and subnet mask assignments.

Traditional segmentation approaches looked to physical segmentation, in which segment layer 1 connections joined at a device such as a router, as well as logical segmentation.

Logical segmentation is often done using VLANs and in effect is a software-defined network (rather than a network or its subnets and segments defined by which devices are plugged in via layer 1 to other devices). Layer 3 devices such as switches and routers could enforce this segmentation via their onboard access control lists (ACLs), which presumably are synchronized with the organizational access control and authorization servers.

Security-based network segmentation is also known as *domain-based network architecture*, which groups sets of information resources and systems into domains based upon security classification, risk, or other attributes important to the organization. Separating network traffic at the collision domain helps avoid network congestion. Separating network traffic into broadcast domains further limits an adversary's ability to sniff out valuable clues regarding the network topology. Going further, separating a network into segments isolates local network traffic from traveling across routes. This again mitigates the risk of a potential adversary learning about the network design, provided, of course, that something at that segment boundary enforces access control and data transit security policies. It finds its most common expression in the use of demilitarized zones at the perimeters of organizational systems.

Demilitarized Zones

A demilitarized zone (DMZ) is a perimeter network that separates or isolates the organization's internal local area networks (LANs) from the public, untrusted Internet. This is a separate physical or logical network segment apart from the organizational intranet or internal network. The goal for a DMZ is primarily security, achieved by limiting access, but it also improves overall network performance. The DMZ is outside of the perimeter corporate firewalls, so precautions and tailored security controls are used to enforce separation and privilege management. The organization's network is behind firewalls, and external network nodes can access only what is exposed in the DMZ.

One of the most common uses of a DMZ is the publicly facing corporate website. Customers and suppliers alike may need access to certain resources, and a group of web servers outside the corporate network can provide the appropriate access in a timely manner. The platform, as a publicly facing asset, is highly likely to be attacked. From a security perspective, the benefit is that the internal corporate network can remain safe if the machines in the DMZ are compromised. At the very least, properly designed DMZ segmentation allows the organization some extra time to identify and respond to an attack before the entire organizational network is also infected.

NOTE Ethical penetration attempts to enter the more secure corporate or enterprise environment can start from hosts in the DMZ; it's also a great place to host usability testing of new public-facing or customer-facing services before exposing them beyond the DMZ.

Segmentation: Not Secure Enough?

However, segmentation as a network security approach has failed to cope with what a growing number of security analysts and practitioners point out is the number one exploitable vulnerability in any system: our human concept of *trust*. In a short video hosted at Palo Alto Networks' website, John Kindervag points this out. "Trust is its own exploit. It is its own vulnerability," says Kindervag. He explains the built-in conflict by noting that "trust is this human emotion which we have injected into our digital system.[10]" The concept of systems being *trustworthy*, he says, is a broken model.

Defense in depth is perhaps the classic trust-based architecture. It presupposes that the most important secrets and the most valuable information can be identified and segregated off behind a perimeter (a *trust surface*); a layer of intrusion detection and prevention systems protects that trust surface, and the whole is surrounded by *another* perimeter. Layer upon layer of such security measures are often shown with a uniformed guard force patrolling the outermost perimeter, often with a moat surrounding the castle, and the crown jewels of the organization's information deep inside the castle protected by concentric barriers of machines, manpower, walls, and other hazards. The only real problem with this classical model, though, is that most real-world, practical organizational systems are anything but a concentric set of security zones. Instead, dozens, perhaps hundreds of security *fiefdoms* are scattered about the virtual and physical globe, but they are still protected by a set of concentric outer perimeters. The flawed assumption still is that the attacker will enter your systems at or near where their desired information targets are located, and that this intrusion will therefore be detected as it crosses the threat surfaces around those assets. For this reason (and others), a growing number of security professionals consider defense in depth as a broken model.

Unfortunately, most intrusions nowadays start out in some far, distant, and almost pedestrian corner of your systems *where the going-in is easy*. The intruder establishes reentry capabilities, often including false identities (or purloined copies of legitimate user credentials). They now roam laterally across the many-connected mesh of your systems, servers, databases, and endpoints, all of which live on a trusted internal network.

Before we look further at techniques for segmenting your network, let's look at a different design paradigm, one that exhorts us to "trust never, always verify."

Zero-Trust Network Architectures

Zero trust as a network and systems security concept was invented by analysts at Forrester Research in 2010. At their website, they challenge security professionals to change their

---

[10] Available at `https://www.paloaltonetworks.com/cyberpedia/what-is-a-zero-trust-architecture`; the rest of this page is a good four-minute read as well.

mind-set: assume your system is already compromised but you just don't know it yet, they advise. Forrester recognizes that the information security industry and the IT industry as a whole are "at the early stages of a new technology revolution."

Micro-segmentation is one of these new revolutionary concepts. Once you've assumed that you have intruders in your midst, you need to think laterally and identify the crossing-points between functional zones. By breaking your network up into finer-grained zones, you progressively introduce more hurdles for an insider threat (which is what an intruder *is*, once they're in your system!) to cross the virtual walls between compartments of information security. Major network systems vendors such as Cisco, Nuage, and VMware also point out that network virtualization makes micro-segmentation much easier, while providing a degree of dynamic micro-segmentation as workloads on different types of servers expand and contract with business rhythms.

Zero-trust architectures cannot reliably function without robust multifactor authentication (MFA); in fact, as was pointed out in Chapter 2, MFA is the primary defense we have against ransom attacks that live off the land by means of exploiting built-in systems capabilities against us. Since then, some major players in the IT market such as Google have announced their shift to zero-trust architectures on their internal systems; others, such as Duo and CloudFlare, have brought various multifactor authentication solutions to the market that may make implementing a zero-trust architecture easier for you to consider, plan, and achieve.

In his presentation at the March 2019 RSA Conference, Nico Popp, senior VP of Information Protection at Symantec, looked at the problems of dissimilar endpoint devices in a zero-trust context. The risks presented by unmanaged devices and external users, he suggested, may be best addressed by using various approaches to *web isolation technology*, which provides for execution and rendering of web sessions at the host/server end of the connection, rather than on the endpoint device. Endpoints then become agentless; only a visual stream of data flows to the endpoint, and all that flows from the endpoint are the keystrokes and gesture data itself. (This is very much a flashback to the dumb terminals used in the 1960s and 1970s with time-sharing or remote access systems.) The presentation itself makes for interesting and thought-provoking reading; it can be found at `https://www.rsaconference.com/writable/ presentations/file_upload/spo3-t08-how_to_apply_a_zero-trust_model_to_ cloud_data_and_identity.pdf`.

Secure Device Management

Network security management encompasses everything involved in architecting, installing, using, maintaining, assessing, and listening to the network security devices, databases, monitoring, and analytics capabilities necessary to *know* the security posture of your organization's networks. This encompasses configuration management and configuration control of your security devices and the coordinated update of access control information throughout your system as users legitimately join and depart your organization, as privileges are required to change, and as the business normal behavior of your systems evolves with time.

Larger enterprises sometimes turn to outside vendors to provide both network security products, such as firewalls, IDS and IPS, web proxies, load balancers, and VPNs, but also to provide the ongoing day-to-day management and operation of those systems. These managed security solutions as services are positioned to address the compliance and reporting requirements of a wide variety of legal, regulatory, and marketplace standards, such as PCI DSS, HIPAA, SOX,[11] GDPR, and many others.

Your organization can, of course, implement a full-function secure device management set of procedures on its own, and this may provide some cost savings and provide a greater degree of tailoring than you might get with a services and systems vendor. On the other hand, it holds your organization hostage to those few talented individuals who build and operate that system for you, and manage all of those devices; someday, *everybody* leaves the job they are in and moves on to something different. Going with a large vendor-provided management services contract provides a degree of depth to your security players' bench.

Unified Threat Management (UTM)   UTM is a concept that integrates the functionality described in this chapter in each type of network and security device into a minimum number of multifunction devices. The goal is to move away from numerous devices that provide singular or point solutions to a simplified architecture and management of combination devices. Another benefit is simplified administration of vendor relationships and proprietary interconnections. Some of the earliest adopters of UTM are firewall, IDS, and IPS integrated devices. Next-generation devices and solutions bring together capabilities like web proxy and content filtering, data loss prevention (DLP), virtual private network (VPN), and security information and event management (SIEM) to name a few. Some security professionals caution against UTM approaches as they may erode the benefits of a defense-in-depth security approach. Others would argue that the classical layered approach is the digital equivalent of a Maginot Line approach to defending against attackers who don't play by the rules that layered defenses are designed to work with.

---

[11] The Public Company Accounting Reform and Investor Protection Act of 2002, with the acronym SOX reflecting its two legislative sponsors, Senator Paul Sarbanes and Representative Michael Oxley.

OPERATE AND CONFIGURE NETWORK-BASED SECURITY DEVICES

The tools used to provide robust network security include a number of security device categories. These devices are found in all types of networks. You do not need all of the following devices in every network, but one or more types are commonly present. In fact, following a defense-in-depth approach, it is usually more advantageous for a full complement of these devices working together at different OSI layers and performing different services. A single device will almost never satisfy every security requirement. That said, improperly used, incorrectly configured, or unmanaged security devices implemented in excess can result in security failure too. You need to analyze requirements and provide tailored, risk-based solutions.

A range of network components exist across the spectrum of hardware, software, and services. Using the right ones and making sure they are configured or employed in ways that will increase security is essential. Earlier, we discussed some of these technologies, such as transmission media and content distribution networks (CDNs). The sections that follow will delve further into the security considerations of such network components as firewalls, intrusion detection systems (IDSs), Security Information and Event Management (SIEM), hardware devices, and endpoints.

Key to the way that many of these devices work is the concept of network address translation, which deserves an in-depth look before we proceed.

Network Address Translation

Network address translation (NAT) can be implemented on a variety of different devices such as firewalls, routers, gateways, and proxies. It can be used only on IP networks and operates at the network layer (layer 3). Originally, NAT was designed to extend the use of IPv4 since the pool of available addresses were quickly being exhausted. To that point, NAT is a legacy technology that comes with disadvantages and advantages.

First, consider its advantages. NAT is used to accomplish network and security objectives to hide the identity of internal clients, mask the routable design of your private network, and keep network addressing costs at a minimum by using the fewest public IP addresses as possible. Through NAT processes the organization assigns internal IP addresses, perhaps even a private addressing scheme. The NAT appliance catalogs the addresses and will convert them into public IP addresses for transmission over the Internet. On the internal network, NAT allows for any address to be used, and this does not cause collisions or conflict with public Internet hosts with the same IP addresses. In effect, NAT translates the IP addresses of the internal clients to leased addresses outside the environment. NAT offers numerous benefits, including the following:

- Connection of an entire private network to the Internet using only a single or just a few leased public IP addresses.

- Use of private IP addresses (10.0.0.0–10.255.255.255) in a private network and retaining the ability to communicate with the Internet as the NAT translates to a public, routable address. (It's worth recalling that millions—perhaps *billions*—of devices on internet segments in every corner of the globe share the same *private* IP addresses, hidden behind the NAT tables in the first-level router or device that connects that segment to the Internet.)

- Isolating the internal IP addressing scheme and network topography of an internal, private network from the Internet.

- Providing two-way connections from private IP addresses inside the NAT device to and from the Internet, so long as those connections originated from within the internal protected network.

NAT can also provide an easy solution to carry out changes on segments of an internal (on-premises) network that might otherwise involve having to reassign IP addresses to everything on the affected segments. This can facilitate temporary relocation of some staff members, for example, as part of coping with surges in workload or facilities issues such as a busted pipe that makes a work area unusable.

Public IP addresses are essentially all allocated, now that the pool of class A (see Table 6.3) addresses were exhausted years ago. This explains the upward trend in popularity of NAT. Security concerns also favor the use of NAT, which mitigates many intrusion types of attacks. With only roughly 4 billion addresses available in IPv4, the world has simply deployed more devices using IP than there are unique IP addresses available. The fact that early designers of the Internet and TCP/IP reserved a few blocks of addresses for private, unrestricted use is becoming a very good idea. These set aside IP addresses, known as private IP addresses, are defined in the standard, RFC 1918.

Now, consider some of NAT's disadvantages. Again, remember that NAT was developed to help deal with the fact IPv4 addressing was being exhausted. To that end, NAT was assumed to be a temporary solution. Because it was considered only temporary, the Internet Engineering Task Force (IETF) responsible for defining protocol standards didn't pursue creating an in-depth official standard for NAT. In fact, while the IETF recognized the benefits of NAT and published a general specification, they avoided developing a technical specification to discourage NAT's widespread adoption. For that reason alone, the biggest disadvantage to NAT is how inconsistent is its implementation in devices.

A few technical disadvantages of NAT have been recognized, but solutions to those problems were discovered or developed without needing to reinvent NAT. For example, consider how peer-to-peer communication is handled. Without NAT, an initiator communicates with a target. This works provided both the initiator and the target have routable addresses. With NAT implemented, an initiator on the Internet seeking to connect with a target behind NAT cannot connect with a nonroutable address. One way to solve this is for the peer-to-peer session to begin "backwards," with the target first connecting with the originator for the purpose of discovering NAT in place. Then, once NAT's outside public address is known, the originator can begin a new peer-to-peer session. Services such as Skype, which rely on peer-to-peer or VoIP protocols, needed to create innovative ways to sidestep how NAT would otherwise break their service. Skype, for example, employs "SuperNodes" on public addresses to permit a peer-to-peer connection, even if both the target and the initiator are behind NAT.

Another disadvantage is how IPsec checks integrity. IPsec computes a hash value for the purpose of ensuring the integrity of each packet. That hash value is computed using various parts of the packet, and since NAT changes the packet's values, that hash value is no longer valid. NAT-Traversal (NAT-T) was developed to resolve this, ensuring that IPsec isn't broken when one or both ends of the IPsec tunnel cross over a NAT device.

Moving from the network layer (layer 3) to the transport layer (layer 4), there is a variation of NAT called port address translation (PAT). Whereas NAT maps one internal IP address to one external IP address, PAT adds an external port number to the mapping of one internal IP address to an external IP address. Thus, PAT can theoretically support 65,536 (2^{16}) simultaneous communications from internal clients over a single external leased IP address. In contrast to NAT's requirement to lease as many public IP addresses as you want to have for simultaneous communications, PAT allows you to lease fewer IP addresses. With each leased IP address, you get a reasonable 100:1 ratio of internal clients to external leased IP addresses.

Additional Security Device Considerations

A few specific device types and use cases don't quite fit cleanly into any one functional bucket. They may present vulnerabilities, opportunities for better security and control, or a mix of both. These types of contradictory situations (they are not necessarily *problems* or issues to resolve) do seem to arise as user organizations and technology vendors push the edge of their comfort zones. You may already have some instances of these situations in your architecture already, and they may bear closer scrutiny.

Securing Cloud-Hosted "Devices"

Securing your organization's business processes and information assets that have been migrated to the cloud will be addressed in more depth in Chapter 7. It's worth noting, however, that the devices you're familiar with in your physical on-premises networks and data centers are fully virtualized in the cloud. Building a cloud-hosted software-defined network lets you define how services are used, and this will invoke services such as load balancing, virtual-to-physical interfaces to gateways, user-defined and distributed routing, and others. You'll be able to use scripts that use familiar concepts, such as IPv4-compatible addressing, subnetting, NAT, PAT, and IPsec to implement pools of virtual resources that support front-end and back-end applications components. Using distributed firewalls, for example, simplifies setting a set of rules applied to each new VM that is instanced on a given subnet or segment. The thought process for the design, device and service selection, placement, management, and monitoring of the security aspects of your network doesn't change—but it does require you to think about *managing services* rather than managing devices. And part of the task of managing services via the cloud is knowing your service level agreement with your cloud provider.

Endpoints as Security Devices

An *endpoint* is any physical device at which the virtual world of data and information gets transformed into action in the real world and where the real world is observed or sensed and that observation turned into data. Smartphones ultimately have their touch screen as a two-way endpoint device-within-a-device, you might say. Endpoints can be anything from the thinnest and dumbest of clients—such as a "smart" thermostat or a valve controller—all the way up through supercomputing-capable nodes on your network themselves. Endpoints are where the business value of information turns into human decision, into physical action, into tangible outputs; without endpoints, our systems have no purpose.

As such, endpoints represent both high-risk points on our threat surfaces, as well as highly capable security enforcement capabilities in our integrated security system.

Host-based security applications, such as anti-malware, HIDS, HIPS, and others can provide exceptional capabilities at the *edges* of your systems. *Edge computing* is an architectural concept that recognizes the huge volume of data that gets generated within very localized LAN segments of much larger systems; data volumes and the need for real-time action often dictate that processing of that data has to be pushed to the edge, as close to the endpoints as possible. *Security event information management* is a classic example of a problem that's calling out for edge computing solutions. The trends indicate that this is the direction that many organizations need to be moving in. Watch this space.

Jump Boxes and Servers

Borrowing from earlier traditions in electrical and electronic systems designs for maintainability, a jump box or jump server provides a (presumably) trusted backdoor into an otherwise secure environment such as a zero-trust network segment. This can also allow for geographically remote access into such secure environments. These backdoors may be intended to be only for temporary use, but as is often the case, both users and maintainers believe that the backdoor offers unique advantages and they become loath to give these up. As more organizations make greater use of virtual machines and software-defined networks, so too are they tempted to use jump boxes as a way of configuring, managing, diagnosing, and maintaining these systems.

The very *idea* of deliberately building in backdoors to access highly secure environments ought to set off alarm bells in your mind. Every designer who's built a backdoor into a system knew that *they*, after all, wouldn't go off on vacation and leave that backdoor unlocked, although history suggests otherwise.

There are any number of techniques that can be employed to improve the security of such jump server arrangements, including:

- More effective segmentation of subnets and VLANs involved
- Firewall use to secure VLANs and subnets
- Multifactor and other access control techniques to tightly control access via the jump server
- Blocking outbound access from the jump server to anywhere else in your systems or to the Internet
- Allowed listing and restrictions on software installed and used on the jump server
- Thorough logging and near-real-time analysis of jump server activities

If your organization has a compelling business need for such a jumper-cable approach, it might be worthwhile to look deeper into software-defined networks as a better, more manageable (and auditable) way of providing a tightly controlled remote access capability.

Firewalls and Proxies

Firewalls, gateways, and proxies provide a number of services, one of which is *filtering* of traffic attempting to cross through them. As such, they are inline, active security devices: blocked traffic can be discarded or rerouted to a quarantine area, such as a sandbox, honeypot, or padded room network segment, whether for threat analysis, device remediation, or a mix of both. Let's look at firewalls in some depth and then see how gateways and proxies provide complementary security capabilities for our networks.

Firewalls

A firewall is used to prevent unauthorized data flow from one area of the network to another. The boundary could be between trusted segments and the Internet or between other parts of a private network. In any case, a firewall creates a boundary and is employed to prevent or allow traffic from moving across that boundary. Network and communications systems firewalls prevent the spread of potentially hazardous *information*, whether in the form of malware payloads, unauthorized connection attempts, or exceptionally high volumes of traffic that might disrupt services behind the firewall.

It's important to stress right from the start that a *firewall* is a logical set of functions—and those functions do *not* have to live inside one piece of hardware, or one set of software running on one piece of hardware, in order to *be* a firewall. In fact, it's far more likely that your networks will use multiple devices, multiple pieces of software, to implement the firewall functionality your system needs, where and when you need it applied. You'll monitor, control, and manage that logical or virtual firewall, and all of its component parts, via connections you establish on the data, control, and management planes of your network and its security infrastructures.

TIP "A firewall is very rarely a single physical object. It is a logical choke point. Usually, it has multiple parts, and some of those parts may do other tasks besides act as a firewall."[12]

Smaller, simpler network systems (such as SOHO or slightly larger) may employ a single firewall at their perimeter—at the point on their threat surface where a connection to the external Internet comes into their network. The simplest of these is the firewall app contained within a router or router/modem combination device. Firewalls, however, can play only a limited role in an access control system, since they cannot authenticate connection attempts by subjects on the outside of the firewall.

---

[12] Zwicky, Cooper, and Chapman, 2000. *Building Internet Firewalls, 2nd Edition*. Sebastopol, CA: O'Reilly and Associates.

Some firewall products and literature will refer to the outer, unprotected and uncontrolled network side of the router as the WAN side, and the inner or protected side as the LAN side. This does make a typical firewall seem somewhat like a diode, since it won't do what you need it to if you plug it in backwards.

Firewalls are also used to *segment* a network into logical (and physical) zones, based on a variety of considerations including security. Software test systems and their subnets, for example, should probably be firewalled off from other organizational network segments to prevent malfunctioning software or test data from being mistakenly used as part of normal production operations. Malware quarantine and evaluation labs are another case where internal firewalls need to keep something inside a perimeter from getting out into the larger surrounding space. (Sometimes a threat surface *contains* rather than *excludes*.)

WARNING   Firewalls as perimeter control devices cannot prevent lateral movement within their protected interior subnet. Once intruders have made it past or around the firewall, they can go anywhere and do anything on the systems that are attached to that subnet. Preventing lateral movement by intruders requires network segmentation, using firewalls in tandem with other technologies, and the boundary points between those internal segments.

The capabilities of a firewall can be accomplished with software, hardware, or both. Data coming into and out of the private network or internal segments must pass through the firewall. The firewall examines and inspects each packet and blocks those that do not match specified security criteria. These activities and some other network events are captured on firewall logs. Review and auditing of logs are extremely valuable security tools that security professionals use for incident detection and response, forensic analysis, and improvement of the performance of the security assets.

Firewalls require configuration and human management, which is why security professionals must understand how best to use them. They do not automatically provide benefit. Security professionals have to configure filtering rules that define permitted traffic. These rules, be they to determine filtering or deny packets, make up the decision process of the firewall. For example, one firewall rule may say "For all inbound packets routed with an internal source address, drop those packets." Also important is how a firewall acts when it fails. If a firewall ceases to operate well, for example, it becomes overwhelmed, then the firewall optimally should fail "closed." This means the firewall should not allow *any* packets through. To make sure the rules remain in place, the firewall must be monitored against unauthorized change, and configurations must be kept current over time. Like any other device or endpoint, firewalls have vulnerabilities to be closed or patched, and security professionals also oversee the patching and upgrade procedures.

6

NETWORK AND COMMUNICATIONS SECURITY

Firewalls should be configured to log events of interest, and analysis of these logs both in real time and somewhat later are invaluable to identifying possible indicators of compromise. Of these possible IoCs, consider the following starter set as candidates for real-time alarms to the SOC:

- Reboot or restart of a firewall
- Failure to start or a device crashing
- Changes to the firewall configuration file
- A configuration or system error while the firewall is running
- Unusual probes for access on ports
- Unsuccessful login attempts on devices

Firewalls as functions are being embedded or integrated into many more products and service offerings. As they become more sophisticated, they also become more complex to use effectively. Taking vendor training courses on the firewall systems products that your organization uses would be money well spent, along with retraining when significant new revisions to your installed firewall systems are pushed out or offered by your vendors.

TIP Although the term can be used in other contexts about access control, the list of rules that govern a firewall is usually referred to as the access control list (ACL). An ACL contains specifications for authorized ports, protocols, list of permissions, IP addresses, URLs, and other variables to establish acceptable traffic.

Types of Firewalls

There are four basic types of firewalls: static packet filtering firewalls, application-level firewalls, stateful inspection firewalls, and circuit-level firewalls. The key differentiator between all four firewalls is the OSI model layer at which each operates.

- **Static packet filtering firewalls** are the earliest and the simplest of firewall designs. Also called a *screening router*, the packet-filtering firewall is the fastest design as well. Operating at the OSI Reference Model's Network layer, the packet-filtering firewall inspects each packet. If a packet breaks the rules put in place, the packet is dropped and/or logged. Able to work most quickly, a packet filtering firewall will mitigate the risk of a particular packet type. This type of firewall offers no authentication mechanism and can be vulnerable to spoofing.
- **Application-level firewalls** examine packets and network traffic with much more scrutiny than can be done with packet filtering firewalls. Operating at the higher OSI Reference Model's application layer, an application-level firewall seeks to

identify what kind of application traffic wants to cross the boundary. Often used as a separator between end users and the external network, the application-level firewall functions as a proxy. Deep inspection takes time, making this firewall the slowest of all types.

- **Stateful inspection firewalls** monitor the *state* of network connections. This firewall operates at the network and transport layers of the OSI model. The connection state is based on how TCP operates and how TCP establishes a session through the "three-way handshake," discussed earlier. That state, plus other connection attributes such as destination and source details, is kept track of and saved temporarily in memory. Over time, these details are used for smartly applying filters.

- **Circuit-level firewalls** are functionally simple and efficient, operating most like a stateful inspection firewall. The primary difference is this firewall works only at the session layer of the OSI Reference Model. For a circuit-level firewall, the only task is to ensure the TCP handshaking is complete. No actual packet is inspected, nor would any individual packet be dropped. Traffic coming through a circuit-level firewall will appear as if it originated from the gateway, since the circuit-level firewall's big benefit is to verify the session, while masking any details about the protected network.

In the early 2000s, firewall designers evolved products that could span multiple OSI levels. Such next-generation firewalls (NGFWs) oftentimes combined more traditional features of the four basic firewall types with IDS or IPS functions, sometimes referred to as *deep packet inspection*. Some NGFW products also used encryption and decryption appliances to attempt to inspect encrypted traffic on SSL or TLS connections flowing through the NGFW's connections. Signature-based and rule-based inspection processes are often used in NGFWs. As the complexity and capability of firewalls continues to develop, the nomenclature has shifted again: the newest stars on the firewall front line are the *unified threat management* (UTM) platforms and products. Sorting through the complexities of NGFW offerings versus UTM platforms is both beyond the scope of what we can do in this book, and a rapidly changing marketplace of ideas, product claims, and demonstrated successes. The threat actors, too, are watching this space closely.

Multihomed Firewalls

Firewalls normally have two NICs—one facing outward to the unprotected WAN side, the other facing inward to the protected LAN segment or subnet. Multihomed firewalls have three or more NICs, and their internal routing functions can be configured to use these multiple "home ports" in whatever way suits the network's security needs. One multihomed firewall might, for example, support a number of separate interior segments, each protected from the others, whether it has a connection to an outer or surrounding perimeter network or not.

Multihomed firewalls can be high-performance firewall devices, servers, or general-purpose computers pressed into service to provide special screening and management of traffic on a LAN segment. They can allow some traffic to flow through unmolested (so to speak), while shunting other traffic off for more detailed analysis and review.

Gateways

An important function of a gateway device is that it connects networks that are using different network protocols. They may be hardware devices or software applications, and they operate at the application layer (layer 7), but arguably also at the presentation layer (layer 6, where formats change). The gateway device transforms the format of one data stream from one network to a compatible format usable by the second network. Because of this functionality, gateways are also called *protocol translators*. Another distinction is that gateways connect systems that are on different broadcast and collision domains. There are many types of gateways, including data, mail, application, secure, and Internet.

Gateways are also used to interconnect IPv4 networks with IPv6 networks.

Proxies

A proxy is a form of gateway that performs as a mediator, filter, caching server, and even address translation server for a network. However, they do not translate across protocols. A proxy performs a function or requests a service on behalf of another system and connects network segments that use the same protocol. A common use of a proxy is to function as a NAT server. NAT provides access to the Internet to private network clients while protecting those clients' identities. When a response is received, the proxy server determines which client it is destined for by reviewing its mappings and then sends the packets on to the client. NAT allows one set of IP addresses to be used for traffic within a private network and another set of IP addresses for outside traffic. Systems on either side of a proxy are part of different broadcast domains and different collision domains.

NOTE   *Network tarpits*, also called *Teergrube*, the German word for tarpit, may be found on network technologies like a proxy server. Much like the famous ones in La Brea, California.

Tarpits can purposely delay incoming connections to deter spamming and broadcast storms.

Firewall Deployment Architectures

It's unfortunate, but many of the terms used in our industry about firewalls all have very loose meanings and are often used as if they are interchangeable; usually, they are not.

Screened subnet, DMZ, bastion hosts, perimeter networks, and many other similar-sounding terms quite often mean what their user says they mean, rather than what the listener assumes they do. When a vendor is telling you that their product or system can do one of these jobs or your boss is asking if the company's networks have one of these features, it's best to ask for clear, precise statements about what specific functions are intended.[13] With that in mind, we'll try to be clearer about how these terms are used here in this section and consistently throughout this book.

DMZ, Bastion, or Screened Hosts Let's start with the concept of a demilitarized zone. As you can imagine, this is a boundary area between two opposing military forces, with both parties limiting what their forces can do in this region. This term typically refers to a perimeter network that enjoys some protection on the external Internet-facing side and provides LAN connectivity for hosts that provide services that need to face the outside world. Public-facing web pages, customer-facing web pages and web apps, and external-facing email are some common applications that might run on servers on this *perimeter, DMZ,* or *screened* network. FTP or SFTP, DNS servers, proxy servers, and others may also be hosted in the DMZ. The hosts that support these apps are thus known as *screened hosts* or *bastion hosts* (this latter name referring to the doubly hardened defensive works on ancient castles). Figure 6.20 illustrates this concept. Note the use of several firewalls, along with two network intrusion prevention devices; if those NIPS and the firewalls all report into a SIEMs, we've got the makings of an integrated defense-in-depth architecture.

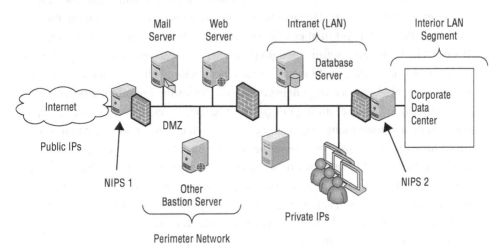

FIGURE 6.20 **Perimeter net and screened hosts**

[13] William S. Davis wrote this advice in September 2000, and it's still as relevant today. See it in his "Firewalls: What I Wish I'd Known When I Was Getting Started," at the SANS Penetration Testing Site, `https://cyber-defense.sans.org/resources/papers/gsec/firewalls-started-100289`

It's normally good practice to have one screened or bastion host support only one application; this minimizes cascading failures or disruptions if a vulnerability in one app is exploited or the app and its server crash from other nonhostile causes. Using virtual machines as the host environments for these app servers makes managing and securing these applications hosts more straightforward, whether you're running in a virtualized SDN in the cloud or on an on-site set of server hardware and networks.

Extranets   This separation of public-facing and internal-users-only segmentation of organizational networks also shows up in *extranets*, which were initially being created to support data-intensive business-to-business electronic commerce. These business processes might involve significant volumes of highly structured traffic flowing from apps running on customers', partners', or suppliers' servers. The extranet firewalled off other business processes to enhance security and integrity (on all sides of the firewalls). Extranets, or any screened perimeter architecture, can also allow an organization to distinguish highly trusted external participants from less-than-fully trusted ones—or the ones that require far more strenuous compliance requirements from the ones that don't.

Another application of a bastion server is to perform additional traffic screening, filtering, inspection, or verification. In these circumstances, the bastion server acts more like a firewall and less like a host for an application. Be cautious, though, since the deeper and more thorough the inspection and analysis, the lower the overall throughput rate is probably going to be.

Multitier Firewalls and Segmentation   As network infrastructures become larger and more complex, the need to layer tiers upon tiers of firewalls—or segment the networks into smaller and smaller subsegments and subnets—brings with it some trade-offs that must be carefully thought through. *Microsegmentation*, as suggested by the zero-trust advocates, could see a firewall-type function being inserted in hundreds or thousands of places in a large network system. Each such firewall function can increase security, while requiring integration into your access control architecture, configuration management system, and configuration control processes. Such additional firewalls are going to be generating new streams of alarm and indicator data, health and status data, downstream monitoring reporting, and log files. None of this comes to you for free or without risk of misconfiguration and error. Without effective management, end to end, cradle to grave, the new protections you're adding with each new firewall and each new layer of complexity could turn out to introduce more exploitable vulnerabilities than the protection is worth.

Disruptions to Firewalled Thinking

As with everything in IT, thinking about firewalls has to start with the basics, but it does us no good to stay with those basics as if they cover all situations well. William Davis' lament about what he wished he knew about firewalls when he was getting started is still true today. With that foundational knowledge in place, thinking *conceptually* about filtering, inspecting, stateful inspection, microsegmentation, endpoint behavioral modeling, and a dozen other firewall-like thoughts can be successful.

But the marketplace will disrupt that thinking, in part because the threat is constantly changing and in part because analysts, designers, and vendors come up with new and possibly better ideas. Your employers or clients may already be adopting and adapting these or other disruptive influences:

- Cloud hosting services providers have their own approaches to dynamic, distributed firewall-like services. Amazon Web Services (AWS) calls these *security groups*, which provide a type of virtual firewall instance per virtual private cloud or virtual networking space.

- Firewall as a service (FWaaS) is being provided by some cloud systems. This sounds simple—it moves all of that inspection, filtering, and screening into the cloud for you—but it may place a greater burden on what *you* need to do to ensure that all of your connections into that cloud that you and your customers use are properly secured. It also places perhaps a greater than normal burden of trustworthiness upon your cloud services provider. You might recall the Corporate Partner Access program that the NSA was operating, which invited and encouraged major telecoms and IT companies to *voluntarily* provide information to the NSA that the companies thought might be "in the national interest." No law prohibits this; this is not *search* or *seizure* by government. But the possibility that your cloud provider might think they should (as an ethical, business, or political imperative) "blow the whistle" on you might have a chilling effect upon your relationship with them.

- Software-defined networks and virtual networking are also disrupting our traditional thought models about firewall architectures and deployment. The inherent flexibility they bring can provide a competitive advantage, but it shifts the configuration control points from being boxes, racks, patch panels, and cables to scripts that engage and direct virtually dispatched instances of firewall apps and their host containers.

Each of these disruptive technologies requires a fundamental shift in attitudes and behaviors on the human elements in your systems, and in the relationships your system and organization have with others. Gaining the best return on investing in such disruptions will require thoughtful change leadership, at all levels, including your own.

Network Intrusion Detection/Prevention Systems

Intrusion detection systems (IDSs) and intrusion prevention systems (IPSs) both perform the same core function: they identify events that might be indicators of an attempted intrusion, collect additional data, characterize it, and present alerts or indicators of compromise to higher levels of network and systems security management. Host-based IPS or IDS (that is, HIPS or HIDS) protect that host from possible intrusion; anti-malware systems, or built-in security features in the host operating system, are often components of a HIPS or HIDS implementation. Network-based IDS and IPS (NIDS and NIPS) look at network traffic attempting to flow past them, and much as a firewall does, they inspect that traffic to determine whether it may be suggestive of a security incident (such as an intrusion) in progress.

NIDS and NIPS inspection and filtering can be driven by simple parameter-based rule sets (such as MAC address filtering, or access to certain ports or applications in various time of day windows) or use more complex signature patterns. Both blocked and allowed listing (negative and positive security) approaches can be used by intrusion *prevention* systems to separate friend from foe. More advanced firewalls, such as next-generation firewalls (NGFWs) or unified threat management (UTM) systems incorporate a variety of intrusion detection and prevention mechanisms, further blurring the line between IDS/IPS products and firewalls as systems approaches to security. Realistically, many new products and security solutions come with built-in capabilities to detect, decide, and block traffic or connection attempts (if you turn these features on).

An intrusion detection system can be a standalone device or, as is often the case, can exist in the form of additional functionality within a firewall. The main purpose of an IDS is to monitor network traffic and/or compare file hashes. If something is deemed suspicious, the IDS will alert on that traffic. This brings up the primary "weakness" of an IDS: they will alert about suspicious traffic, but an IDS traditionally will not actively act to prevent the threat. Acting to prevent traffic falls under the definition of an intrusion prevention system.

Another weakness of IDSs is their difficulty to "tune" or customize according to the unique traffic patterns of your network. Invariably, a newly placed IDS will alert unnecessarily on suspect traffic that turns out to be benign. In short, there is a strong tendency to alert on false positives. Similarly, some malicious traffic, positively identified by well-tuned countermeasures, will be missed by the IDS. In that case, the IDS must be adjusted or updated to avoid further false negatives.

IDSs help reduce the blocking of traffic and port access as false positive by efficiently detecting abnormal or undesirable events on the network. IDS functionality is often built into next-generation firewall, likely labeled as a module. In the scope of secure network components, the relevant concern is how the IDS and firewall might interoperate together. The integrated device might additionally provide extensive logging, auditing, and monitoring capabilities. When the abnormal or undesirable traffic is detected, the IDS might then perform a few actions. First, it would alert security personnel. Also, the IDS might put a temporary firewall rule in place.

Security Information and Event Management Systems

If there are three laws of security incidents and events, they might be as follows:

- Perfect protection of the environment is not possible. Therefore, detection and response capabilities are fundamental to continued business survival and success.

- It is not a question of if the environment will be breached, but of when. And it probably already has been breached.

- Even the smallest of networks and IT architectures can produce millions of log events, monitoring results, and indicators every day; unless you automate the vast majority of your analysis and correlation workflows, you will drown in the data while the intruders plunder your system behind your back.

Security information and event management is both a process, a set of systems, and a mind-set. If you follow the first law stated previously, you're investing in significant data collection capabilities, but the third law dictates that you'll need substantial machine help to sort that data into the alarms that are worthy of urgent response. SIEM as a process is defining a workflow, a rhythm, and a set of procedures that help you learn from the day-to-day; this can guide you into translating yesterday's "business normal" into today's tuning of the filter parameters, signatures, rules, or other control settings that your intrusion detection, prevention, and incident response capabilities need. And that second law points out that with an intruder already in your midst, you've got a lot of yesterdays' worth of data—weeks or months' worth, perhaps—to be combing through looking to find evidence of who it is and how they got in, in order to suggest what they might be after.

Two key factors make investing in a SIEM process and system a worthwhile payoff. First, your SIEMs need a diverse set of sources of information. The sources can and should vary as much as possible. It's little value to gather "relatable" information from the same type of source, e.g., several hosts or all the networking gear. A narrow range of source types provides a narrow scope of information and potential insight into the cause (or potential threat). Instead, sources should cover the full range from endpoint sources and applications hosts, through middleware and network devices, and to perimeter and boundary sources.

Second, correlating the collected information must be done using a thoughtful, intentional process, informed by both broad and deep knowledge of the systems, the architecture, and the business processes in use. If not, any correlation between event and triggered alerts amounts only to a simple "if…then" analysis. SIEM (as a process and as a tool set) needs to have a strong familiarity of the monitored environment. Raw data gathered from disparate sources will need to be normalized against what value would be expected versus what value should be considered an extreme or outlier piece of data. This helps to sift meaningful data from the noise.

SIEM tools encompass data inspection tools, machine learning practices, and automated risk evaluations. The security devices include firewalls, IPS/IDS, DLP, and even endpoint clients. The security devices provide data about machine and user activity that the SIEM analyzes and alerts on in real-time. The alerts are acted upon by the SIEM service vendor, specifically by security incident response personnel. The amounts of data are impossible for human or manual processing as logs are harvested from outputs from a variety of sources. The end goal of SIEM is to reduce signal to noise for the organization's staff. If SIEM operations are not managed internally, the customer organization requires a strong SIEM provider relationship as these systems are not automatic. Alerts and incidents have to be analyzed for false positives, meaning the SIEM sends an alert, which is later determined to not be a security incident. The vendor must communicate to make the SIEM effective and an extension of the information security team.

The SIEM is informed by other streams of security intelligence from outside the organization as well. In some cases, threat intelligence is gained from searching the dark web for instances of data that correlate to previous or potential attacks. For instance, an alert may come from a discussion board containing identifying information about a company or from individuals who are customers of the company. Such alerts might trigger remediation actions, including contacting law enforcement or customers. Or an alert might only be forwarded and archived for later correlation.

The community of SIEM users, systems developers, and researchers have developed several ways of formalizing the modeling of threat data so that different SIEM systems and users can readily exchange threat data with each other. The Structured Thread Information eXpression (STIX) language, which has incorporated another language called Cyber Observable eXPression (CybOX), focus on defining the threat; another language, the Trusted Automated eXchange of Indicator Information, provides format and flow control for exchanging STIX (and thereby CybOX) data between SIEMs environments. In many ways, these are data markup languages rather than procedurally focused programming languages. As you deepen your learning about security information and event management, you may find it useful to learn more about these languages. The U.S. Homeland Security (HS) Systems Engineering and Development Institute (SEDI) acts as moderator for these community-led efforts.

Routers and Switches

The concepts of broadcast domains and collision domains are pivotal to the ways in which switches and routers can improve both network performance and security. A *broadcast domain* is a logical division of a computer network, in which all nodes can reach each other by broadcast at the data link layer. The broadcast originates from one system in the group to all other systems within that group. A *collision domain* consists of all the devices connected using a shared media where a collision can happen between devices at any time. A data collision occurs if two systems transmit simultaneously, attempting to use the network medium at the same time, with the effect that one or both of the messages may be corrupted.

The operation of network security devices will be impacted by many circumstances of data transfer across media. Security professionals design and manage networks with consideration of forces that help or hinder the signal. Collisions and broadcasts must be managed as they are significant influencers of data transfer success. With respect to the OSI model, collision domains are divided by using any data link layer (layer 2) or higher device, and broadcast domains are divided by using any network layer (layer 3) or higher device. When a domain is divided, it means that systems on opposite sides of the deployed device are members of different domains.

Routers, as layer 3 devices, and switches, working at layer 2, provide complementary security functions for networks. They both look into the traffic being sent through them, and as they make decisions about where to send it, they also provide layers of masking (such as NAT and PAT) that can obscure the architecture of the LAN segment that they provide services to.

Switches Switches can create separate broadcast domains when used to create VLANs. The switch segments the network into VLANs, with broadcasts being handled within the individual VLANs. To permit traffic across VLANs, a router would have to be implemented. Switches cannot accomplish this distribution. Switches provide security services that other devices cannot. They look deeper into packets and can make granular traffic distribution decisions. By establishing and governing the VLANs, switches help to make it harder for attackers to sniff network traffic. Broadcast and collision information is contained; the valuable network traffic is not continually traveling through the network.

LAN Extenders   This is a multilayer switch used to extend network segment beyond the distance limitation specified in the IEEE 802.3 standard for a particular cable type. WAN switches, WAN routers, repeaters, or amplifiers can also be used as LAN extenders.

Routers   Routers are network layer (layer 3) devices. A router connects discrete networks using the same protocol, whereby a data packet comes in from one host on the first network, and the router inspects the IP address information in the packet header and determines the destination and best path. The router is able to decide the best logical path for the transmission of packets based on a calculation of speed, hops, preference, and other metrics. A router has programmed routing tables or routing policies. These tables can be statically defined or manually configured. The other way the routing tables can be created and managed is dynamically through adaptive routing. A router has the ability to determine as it processes data how to best forward data. The router can select and use different routes or given destinations based on the up-to-date conditions of the communication pathways within the interconnections. When a temporary outage of a node is present, the router can direct around the failed node and use other paths.

There are numerous dynamic routing protocols, such as Border Gateway Protocol (BGP), Open Shortest Path First (OSPF), and Routing Information Protocol (RIP). It should be noted that static routing and dynamic routing are best used together. Sometimes dynamic routing information fails to be exchanged, and static routes are used as a backup. Systems on either side of a router are part of different broadcast domains and different collision domains.

Network Security from Other Hardware Devices

Other network devices also have a role to play in creating and maintaining an effective, efficient, and secure network. Let's take a closer look at some of them.

Repeaters, Concentrators, and Amplifiers   Repeaters, concentrators, and amplifiers operate at the physical layer (layer 1). These simple devices serve to extend the maximum length a signal can travel over a specific media type. They connect network segments that use the same protocol and are used to connect systems that are part of the same collision domain and broadcast domain.

Hubs Hubs, also known as multiport repeaters, are a physical layer (layer 1) technology. They work only with interconnected systems using the same protocol, in the same domain. They simply repeat inbound traffic over all outbound ports to make the devices act like a single network segment. Because they offer very little security-related capability, they are typically prohibited in organizations and are replaced with switches. Hubs are mainly a legacy technology that have little modern use.

TIP Connecting network segments via repeaters or hubs goes against the recommendations of IEEE 802.3.

Modems Modems, or *modulator-demodulator units*, provide an essential service in every data communications system of any kind. They work *below* the Physical layer, where they transform the low-voltage digital pulse trains that are the data flows *inside* a computer, a router, switch, or an endpoint, into signals that can be driven great distances down a cable, down a fiber, or out an antenna and radiated through free space. When transforming those signals to go the distance requires using some kind of carrier signal (be that a radio wave, a light wave, or anything else), that requires modulation at the sending end and demodulation at the receiving end. Even the simplest fiber optic connection does this (even if the modulator is a light emitting diode). Without modems, your networks would have to have every device no further away than about 3 feet, and even then, it couldn't work very fast.

There are two bits of computer lore that do seem to be easily forgotten when it comes to modems.

- Every NIC has a modem in it; that's the part that drives the data stream down a 100-meter length of Cat 5 or Cat 6 cable, down a fiber, or out a Wi-Fi antenna. The modem pulls the bits out of the signals that *other* NIC modems have put on that cable, fiber, or out into the surrounding radio wave environment. On the *other* side of the NIC, facing into the computer, are the low-voltage, low-current, high-speed digital signals that the computer's bus, memory, CPU, and everything else work with.

- Every interconnection to an Internet service provider requires another modem to transform the computer-domain digital signals into voltages and currents that can flow along the "last mile" connection from your ISP's point of presence and into their edge gateway. Since that last mile might actually be *several* miles, that cannot be done over a Cat 5 or Cat 6 cable.

What confuses some practitioners is that at the start of the personal computer revolution, modems were separate pieces of equipment; they sat on the phone line or your cable TV wire as it entered your home or office and provided a digital connection to your LAN, usually via an RJ45 connection. Very quickly, modems were combined with switches, then with routers, and finally with Wi-Fi capabilities. Many service providers using fiber distribution systems provide a single set-top box that combines the fiber modem on one side, a router in the middle, NIC modems that drive the hardline RJ45 connections, another NIC modem that provides RJ11 telephone service points, and yet one more modem to drive the Wi-Fi signals in and out the antennas. The control systems embedded in these more complex modem/router combinations provide both router-level security services as well as authentication, authorization, and quality-of-service controls.

Modems are devices that can and do protect your systems, but they cannot do it all; they are also targets that attackers may attempt to penetrate and take control over. Even that ISP-provided SOHO modem/router has a user ID and a password associated with it and a hardware reset button on the back or the bottom somewhere. An intruder with physical access to that button can easily flash their own firmware update into the device and in doing so have a first-level hack into your systems.

Bridges   This technology operates at the data link layer (layer 2). A bridge forwards traffic from one network to another. Unlike repeaters, which just forward received signals, bridges direct signals based on knowledge of MAC addressing. If a network uses the same protocol, a bridge can be used even if the networks differ in topologies, cabling types, and speeds. A buffer is used to store packets, using a store-and-forward capability until the packets can be released if the networks have differing speeds. Systems on either side of a bridge are part of the same broadcast domain but are in different collision domains. Some bridges use a Spanning Tree Algorithm (STA) to prevent bridges from forwarding traffic in endless loops that can result in broadcast storms. STAs are an intelligent capability for bridges to prevent looping, establish redundant paths in case of a single bridge failure, uniquely identify bridges, assign bridge priority, and calculate the administrative costs of each pathway.

NOTE   Watch for broadcast storms on bridges, which can degrade network bandwidth and performance. The broadcast storms can happen when bridges are forwarding all traffic and become overwhelmed.

Wireless Access Points   These operate at the data link layer (layer 2). A wireless router is similar to a wired router in a network in that it also interrogates and determines the pathway and destination for a packet it receives. The wireless router also acts as an access point into the wireless (or wired) network in integrated networks. However, the utility in wireless routers is in the ability to allow portable endpoints to access the network, for example notebooks, laptops, and smartphones. Wireless routers can operate on the 2.4GHz and 5GHz bands simultaneously in a multiband configuration and provide data transfer rates of more than 300Mbps on the 2.4GHz band and 450Mbps on the 5GHz band. Wireless access points are discussed further in the "Wireless Access Points" section.

IP-Based Private Branch Exchange   A private branch exchange (PBX) is a special-purpose telephone switch that is used as a private telephone network within a company or organization. The PBX can interface with multiple devices. Not long ago, the PBX was always a physical switch, but today most PBX functionality is software-based, often hosted on a system with connections to the company's internal LAN and the Internet. Users of the PBX phone system can communicate internally within their company or organization. Equally, they can access external users. The PBX expands capacity for more phones than what would be possible using physical phone lines that use the public switched telephone network (PTSN). Voice data is multiplexed onto a dedicated line connected to other telephone switching devices. The PBX is able to control analog and digital signals using different communication channels like VoIP, ISDN, or POTS. There are several security concerns with PBX implementation that security professionals need to assess. For instance, many PBX implementations still have modems attached to enable dial-in access for services like remote maintenance.

Traffic-Shaping Devices

Network administrators often have to take actions to provide the most optimal flow of traffic within their systems and through its interconnections to the Internet. "Optimization," of course, is a judgment call, and it usually must reflect business priorities as well as cultural, legal, regulatory, or other marketplace expectations. Typically, optimization looks to balance such parameters as throughput, bandwidth requirements, latency, protocol performance, and congestion at critical points or links within the system. Organizations that run their own WAN services as extended private networks, for example, might need to optimize these services between their main headquarters and their branch offices or subordinate locations worldwide, or between data centers within the company. Another aspect of WAN and overall systems performance optimization is *load balancing*, which (as the name suggests) looks to how workloads and network traffic are assigned to servers, connecting links, and control nodes in ways that prevent any one element from becoming saturated. Heavily loaded elements on a network have a marked tendency to fail in sometimes unexpected ways, and sometimes these cause a cascade of failures as well as interruptions to the workflows they were supporting when they failed.

Many techniques can be used for network optimization and load balancing, such as:

- **Deduplication:** This reduces the data transferred by identifying data that is repeated in multiple files and replacing it essentially with a highly compressed replacement token (or a hashed pointer into a table); the processing time needed at both ends to identify duplicate portions, compress them, and then uncompress the data upon receipt can often produce substantial data transmission savings. (This is why Windows spends a few minutes "estimating" what to move when you tell it to copy or move files over a network connection.) Deduplication applies to large collections of files.

- **Compression:** This is applied as the file is prepared for transmission and applied to a single file; large reductions in file sizes (and transmission costs) can be obtained.

- **Latency optimization:** A number of strategies can help reduce layer 3 congestion and delays, including smarter choices about where to locate host systems that support specific applications processing, with respect to their data sources or sinks. *Edge computing* is in part a latency optimization approach.

- **Caching via local proxies:** This can recognize when humans tend to look for the same data as part of repetitive task flows.

- **Forward error correction:** This adds additional packets of loss-recovery information for every *n* packets sent. This can reduce retransmission requests on highly congested links.

- **Protocol spoofing:** This type of spoofing tries to recognize chatty or verbose applications and bundle multiple outputs from them into one set of packets which are unbundled at the other end.

- **Traffic shaping:** This allows administrators to set relative traffic throughput priorities based on applications. A near-real-time security monitoring application, for example, might need to have its traffic prioritized over an e-commerce billing and payments app: both are important to the business, but the mission need for one can tolerate arbitrary but manageable delays better than the other can.

- **Equalizing:** This makes assumptions about data usage, as a way to balance or even out traffic flow through the connection.

- **Simple rate limits:** These limits can also be set, on a per-user, per device, or even a per-application basis, as a way of throttling back the usage of the link. This might be useful as a stop-gap response when trying to alleviate congestion, before you've had time to investigate its root causes further.

While it's clear that network administrators need to use these (and other) optimization strategies and tactics to assure the availability and reliability of the networks, it may not be so obvious how these relate to *network security*. At first glance, each of these optimization techniques is driven to provide the best mix of throughput, latency, and other quality of service measures that meet the *business normal* mix of performance needs. This might mean that abnormal traffic, which doesn't fit in with these optimization strategies, is a new and different but legitimate business process meeting a transient need—such as responding to an important customer's emergency needs for assistance from your organization, and hence its information resources. But that abnormal traffic might also be a rogue user, such as an intruder, trying to perform some other tasks *not* part of your business logic, in ways that are trying to "fly under your radar" and not be noticeable. For example, exfiltrating a very large database (measured in terabytes) in one transfer would clearly upset most of these optimization strategies tuned to business normal; letting it sneak out a megabyte at a time might not, unless there's a lot of common data (such as data record structural information) that deduplication might attempt to optimize. If that deduplication service is handling a significantly larger volume of files than it usually does, that might be an indicator of compromise.

Without diving into more details than we have scope to investigate, it might be worthwhile to have a good chat with your network optimization gurus on your IT team to see what ideas they might have about instrumenting the traffic shaping and network optimization services to provide data your SIEMs might find worth looking into.

OPERATE AND CONFIGURE WIRELESS TECHNOLOGIES

Wireless communications technologies are everywhere, supporting use cases that go far beyond what most business logic imagined a decade or two ago. These technologies enable rapid adoption of incredibly small, ultra-portable devices, many of which bring little or no built-in security-friendly features or capabilities. Consistent with the history of the Internet, we do tend to develop newer and flashier wireless voice, video, data, process control, and other information transfer mechanisms; see them go through widespread adoption in the marketplaces; and only then start to realize that there might be some serious security problems in their design and use that need to be addressed. Quickly.

Unfortunately, there don't seem to be clear boundaries that separate one type of wireless (or cable-less, or fiber-less) technology, its uses, and its security issues from another. We can define *wireless* to mean that its digital data, control, and management signals do not go from one device to another over a wire, cable, or optical fiber; this leaves us with three primary sets of wireless methods.

The primary wireless technologies used by business and organizational networks include the following:

- Wi-Fi radio networks
- Bluetooth radio connections
- Near-field communications

- LiFi (visible or near-visible light signaling)
- Mobile phone connections

As businesses expand their use of IoTs, highly mobile remote devices such as unmanned aerial or mini-vehicle systems, and industrial process control also are using systems such as:

- Air to ground commercial aircraft data links.
- Business band radio.
- Unlicensed (typically low power) radio systems for voice or data.
- Personal area network low power systems, especially IPv6-compatible ones (known as 6LoWPAN technologies).
- Wireless *backhaul* networks, which tend to be special-purpose UHF radio. Some of these systems are evolving toward greater use of Ka-band very small aperture antenna (VSAT) systems and other microwave technologies.
- Radio control systems for hobbyists, modelers, IoT, UASs, and so on.

Your company or your clients may use only a few of these technologies; visitors to your facilities may bring others of these types of links in with them and (it is hoped, if not required)take them home again when they leave. As the on-site security team, however, you need to recognize that sophisticated threat actors are growing in their understanding of these technologies and their utility in getting into your systems.

It would take another book to cover all of these wireless capabilities, their intrinsic vulnerabilities, known exploits, and known hardening techniques to apply. Such books are desperately needed in the security marketplace today, but for now, we'll have to content ourselves with more of a look at the "big five" wireless ways we can lose control of our threat surfaces. First, we'll look at what they all have in common in terms of security concerns and opportunities for hardening; then, we'll look at some specific wireless standard interfaces.

Wireless: Common Characteristics

On the one hand, we could say that other than sound wave systems, everything wireless is done with electromagnetic radiation—light waves or radio waves are just slices of the same continuous *spectrum* of such radiation, including X-rays, gamma rays, and many more. Visible light, and the nearby infrared and ultraviolet parts are just one particular slice out of that spectrum. We talk about such radiation as being in *bands*, measured in either its wavelength (distance between peaks of the waves) or its frequency (which is the number of peaks passing a measurement point in one second of time). Given that c is the speed of light in a vacuum, the wavelength multiplied by the frequency equals c. Visible light is one band, infrared another, ultraviolet a third;

these together are a far larger band than all of the radio bands we use in our communications systems put together.

To a greater or lesser degree, communication systems in any of these bands have some physical limits to take into account in their design and use.

- Light, microwave, and even higher frequency radio signals are easily blocked by physical objects such as walls, hills, or bodies of water. Other bands can travel through walls or other material objects, but their signal strength is *attenuated* (reduced) depending upon the materials the barrier is made of.

- In most cases, these signals travel in straight lines from the emitting antenna or light source.

- Those straight-line signals spread out with distance and lose power as the square of the distance (known as the *inverse square loss*). Eventually, this loss is so great that no signal can be detected out of the surrounding *noise floor*, the radiation given off or reflected by physical objects.

- Air, water, and other materials can scatter light and radio waves, which greatly reduces the effective incoming signal strength at the receiver.

- No signal emitter is perfectly "clean"—they may send out their light or radio wave energy (the signal) in one fairly narrow set of wavelengths, but they all have "shoulders" alongside these where a little bit of energy bleeds out of the system. The cleanest or most *coherent* of lasers and LEDs emit the vast bulk of their energy on one very narrow set of wavelengths, but as with all physical systems, there's a tiny bit of noise on the shoulders.

- *Noise sources* are natural or man-made objects that give off energy across many bands in the spectrum, with no regard to who might be using that band for communications. Lightning and natural electrostatic buildup, solar flares, and cosmic radiation are some of the natural sources of electromagnetic noise. Electric arc lights, arc welders, switching power supplies, electric motors, electromagnets, and every electrical and electronic circuit give off such noise. Well-designed equipment has built-in features to limit noise being generated or leaking out from the equipment itself; poorly designed equipment (especially after-market replacement external power supply units for nearly every piece of electronic equipment) often broadcast noise across large swaths of the RF spectrum—often right in the middle of our Wi-Fi and Bluetooth bands.

What that all adds up to is that the overall CIANA+PS of your information systems will depend greatly upon the reliability and integrity of their wireless links. Those factors, combined with the power of your transmitters, the sensitivity of your receivers, and your antennae all determine your *link closure*, that is, the probability or confidence that the receiver will detect the right transmitter, lock onto its signal, decode it, and produce a steady stream of data as its output.

Those links, if implemented poorly, can be vulnerable to interference, deliberate jamming, eavesdropping, and hijacking. Physics will dictate the rules of this game: an attacker is not constrained by the types of antennas your equipment uses and thus can quite easily use higher-gain antennae and receivers to detect your signals from farther away, while using higher-power transmitters to jam or spoof your own transmitters.

Let's see this in action in the two big bands we deal with the most: light wave systems and the RF bands used for Wi-Fi, Bluetooth, Near Field Communications, and cell phones.

LIGHT and LiFi

In a TEDGlobal talk in 2011, Harald Haas used the term Li-Fi (rhymes with "why-why" and Wi-Fi) to the world. The widespread use of LED lighting provides an incredible installed base of data transmitters, if only we add a small integrated circuit chip to each LED light bulb or fixture. In lighting use, LED bulbs flash at twice the frequency of the mains electrical supply (by transforming the incoming AC power into a DC pulse train, 60Hz North American power becomes a 120Hz light pulse output). Changing that power supply slightly to allow a higher-frequency pulse train to go direct to the LEDs in the lamp won't change the human-perceivable lighting one bit; but a photodetector built into a smartphone, laptop, or other device will see the data stream.

For one-way streaming of data, this provides a nearly-built-in, ready-made capability to deliver high data rates to almost every nook and cranny of a work area, home, office, airplane cabin, or vehicle interior. Large indoor spaces, such as airport lobbies, stadiums, or concert halls, could take advantage of this. Demonstration systems have already used LED lighting in supermarkets to assist customers with light-compatible smartphones: by locating where the customer is in the store, the system can answer queries, point out special sale offers, or provide other targeted information to the individual customer. (Note, too, that the lighting power pulses to the LED can be shut off completely, and the high-frequency data pulses can be at power levels too low to be sensible by the human eye; the room can be dark, but the light—for the data—can stay on.)

Adding a photodetector to the light bulb itself allows each LED light bulb to become a data transceiver, and these types of systems are also seeing increasing use in the market-place. Work with avalanche photodiode technologies have demonstrated data detection at rates supporting 1.6GBps transfer rates.

Two sets of standards apply to light wave data systems. Li-Fi designers and developers are working toward the IEEE 802.11 set of standards, while other visible light communications (VLC) system houses are working with the IEEE 802.15.7r1 standards committee to provide an updated standard to use.

Li-Fi has some inherent advantages that are fueling its rise in adoption.

- It cannot ignite flammable vapors or substances in the area it's being used in. This makes it far safer than many radio frequency systems in hazardous environments such as poorly ventilated environments that might contain inflammable gases. This also makes it much safer to use in oxygen-rich environments such as medical intensive-care units, surgical suites, or emergency rooms.

- Visible light can be easily kept from leaking out of a workspace or room, since it doesn't travel through walls, and opaque window coverings are easy enough to install. (Compare this to RF shielding measures necessary to "TEMPEST-proof" a computer, or a room with computer equipment in it, to prevent the RF radiation that equipment gives off from being leaked out to potential eavesdroppers. TEMPEST is the name given by U.S. government agencies to programs, plans, standards, and testing necessary to deal with this security concern.)

- Virtually all human workspaces—and therefore places you would need to have human-serving endpoints—have rich and varied needs for lighting and data sharing. Using an already installed base of lighting power and control systems as part of a data distribution network is an opportunity waiting to happen.

- Visible light bounces off of walls and the surfaces of furnishings (this is why walls appear "light" in color); direct line of sight from the LED to the receiver is not required to have a *link closure* that can support up to 70MBps sustained data rates via IEEE 802.11-compliant TCP/IP.

Li-Fi technologies are somewhat limited to short range uses. LEDs used for illumination purposes have not yet demonstrated the reliability the market may demand for their use in data transmission, while retrofitting a building's lighting systems and their power distribution and control elements to be digital-data-friendly can be costly. Roaming across Li-Fi units also needs further development. The marketplace will shape whether these are characteristics that dictate ideal deployment and use cases or deter its widespread adoption. 2018 saw Li-Fi systems achieve about an $8 billion USD market share.

Thus far, there seem to be no practical limits to how much data can be poured over the infrared, visible, and ultraviolet spectrum than can be done via the useful radio frequency spectrum (which is 10,000 times smaller than that of visible light and its nearby cousins). Li-Fi and other VLC systems might not be on your inventory today, but you may find the use case for them soon.

Wireless Radio as a Medium

Wi-Fi, Bluetooth, near-field communications, and other digital data links use a variety of bands in the radio frequency spectrum. These bands are commonly referred to by their base frequency: the 2.4GHz Wi-Fi band is defined as all frequencies between 2.4GHz and 2.5GHz and has within it 14 channels (not all of which are authorized for use in certain countries), each channel being 22MHz wide, overlapping each other significantly. This does mean that in most cases, users can find at least three nonoverlapping channels, with at least one of them lightly loaded enough to provide for good link closure.

Table 6.10 offers a quick overview or summary of the different wireless uses common in our network environments today. Today's smartphone demonstrates the convergence of all of these communications systems and technologies into one bundle of information security risks.

TABLE 6.10 **Wireless Connections Overview**

TYPE	INTERNET PROTOCOL USE	WIRELESS EFFECTIVE DISTANCE (MAX)	SECURITY CONCERNS
Mobile phone	Via PSTN, Wi-Fi, or USB connection	1-10 kilometers	Calls, SMS, other services unsecured
Wi-Fi	Primary wireless connection to Internet via access points	10–100 meters	Access point security, connection metadata protection, content (if not TLS protected)
Bluetooth	Via endpoint extension devices (mice, keyboards)	1–3 meters	Minimal security built in; can provide covert channel to IP services
Near-field communications	Via endpoint extension for data sharing and acquisition	300 centimeters	Link security; FTP-like usage as insecure vector for access to endpoint, thence to wider network

TIP   Wi-Fi devices are designed to freely negotiate with each other which channel in their chosen band gives them the strongest, clearest signal. You'll rarely encounter a situation where the use of a different channel will prevent a deliberate attack, other than perhaps a jamming attack.

Unlicensed Radios

It's important to stress that, legally, almost without exception users in most countries are not required to have radio transmitter licenses to use Wi-Fi, Bluetooth, near-field communications, cell phones, and similar technologies. Governments license the use of the RF spectrum as a way to manage its use and prevent too many powerful transmitters from interfering with each other. Agencies such as the Federal Communications Commission

(FCC) in the United States may require manufacturers to *type certify* their transmitter designs and their implementations, which is an assurance to purchasers that a particular device meets the standards set for that class of device by that agency: it stays within its band, it does not produce unacceptable noise outside of its band, and so forth. (The International Telecommunications Union performs a similar function, coordinating the efforts of national telecommunications and radio regulatory agencies around the world.) Since there are so many unlicensed, low-power transmitters in use today (including garage door openers, baby monitors, home security systems, and toys), the chances are good that your data links will suffer some interference from them at one time or another.

Higher-capacity, longer-range systems, such as microwave or small aperture terminals (VSATs) do, however, require their operators to be licensed due to the much greater power levels that they operate at.

Wireless Endpoints: Are All of These Part of the Network?

It used to be that we could divide that "top five" set of wireless technologies into two main sets: those that were TCP/IP compatible systems, coming in at the Physical layer of our protocol stacks; and those that are not. Bluetooth, for example, is traditionally not a *network* technology; it was designed for personal area network use as a point-to-point pairwise interface to support wireless data sources such as mice, keyboards, or microphones, and wireless data sinks, such as earphones, speakers, or printers. The network purists might say that such PAN devices (Bluetooth or other) are *not* part of the network. They tend not to be discoverable by network discovery protocols, port sniffers, and such. They are supported *by* an endpoint, "beyond" the security boundary inside that endpoint that has the network on one side and the physical world and the end user on the other side.

From a security perspective, however, data in motion is still data in motion; end-to-end data security has to protect that data all the way out to where it is displayed, turned into sound or motion, or used to control other physical devices. Data in motion that is sent over a non-network connection via a wireless interface to a remote (untethered, unattached, mobile, and therefore vulnerable) endpoint *should* be part of the overall network security issue.

Broadly speaking, though, no matter what protocol stack or interface (or interfaces, plural!) they are using, the same risk management and mitigation processes should be engaged to protect the organization's information infrastructures.

Key considerations should include the following:

- Access control and identity management, both for the device and the users via that device.
- Location tracking and management; it might be too risky, for example, to allow an otherwise authorized user to access company systems from a heretofore unknown or not-yet-approved location.

- Link protection, from the physical connection on up, including appropriate use of secure protocols to protect authentication and payload data.

- Congestion and traffic management.

- Software and hardware configuration management and control, both for the mobile device's operating system and any installed applications.

Wireless endpoint devices present special security challenges for all of the same reasons that they offer such tantalizing and useful capabilities. They pack incredible compute power, data manipulation, and data storage into a tiny, portable package; their use of Wi-Fi, cell telephone, Bluetooth, near-field communications, and soon Li-Fi makes them incredible *connectible*. They are easily lost, stolen, or surreptitiously borrowed long enough to clone. And they keep getting smaller, more powerful, and *cheaper*.

Mobile Device Management and Endpoint Security

We've always had to deal with removable storage media for our computers—be it reels of tape, disk packs, floppy disks, or thumb drives. Data library solutions have struggled to cope with that, and most have been only marginally successful. In one very real sense, these types of mobile devices have resisted coming under management. At about the same time, mobile device technologies proved their worth to *attackers*, who would find ways to use them to spread malware, provide surveillance and reconnaissance capabilities, exfiltrate data, or for other roles in their kill chains.

The rapid expansion of smartphone use in the workplace has forced many businesses, nonprofit organizations, and government employers to develop and institute a wide range of solutions, all referred to as *mobile device management (MDM)*. Mobile devices can be any personal electronic device (PED), personal mobile device (PMD), or other such devices owned or leased by the company itself. MDM solutions attempt to make this more manageable by offering various ways to do the following:

- Uniquely identify each device, catalog it, and track its owner or assigned users.

- Associate an information security classification level with a device.

- Correlate or integrate MDM data with overall access control and identity management systems.

- Integrate a mobile device into multifactor authentication processes and systems.

- Provide for varying levels of configuration management and configuration control over the device's hardware, firmware, and software.

- Manage the device's anti-malware or other intrusion detection and prevention capabilities.

- Provide for ways to lock (or "brick") a device when it has been reported lost or stolen.

- Provide for onboard data management, including data retention, data configuration management and control.

- Integrate device-level encryption into organizational end-to-end data security.

- Manage the acceptable use of the device for nonbusiness purposes, or its use by other than the employee or staff member.

- Audit the use of the device, and the ebb and flow of data to and from the device.

- Implement restrictions on roaming for the device, if required by organizational policies.

These and other functional needs in the MDM marketplace find expression in several usage models, such as:

- **Bring your own device (BYOD):** The employee owns the device and is required to work with the organization's IT department to get it into the MDM system, keep it compliant with it, and keep their device usage compliant as well.

- **Choose your own device (CYOD):** The company identifies a limited set of device alternatives (such as a choice of three different makes and models of smartphones), which the company's MDM solution can effectively manage. The employee chooses which one they want; the company retains ownership and full management of the device.

- **Company owned personally enabled (COPE):** This is a variation on CYOD but may permit the employee as user greater latitude (and take more responsibility for) keeping the device configuration properly managed and updated.

As if that's not complicated enough, bring-your-own models also come in two additional forms, which also impact network security planning and operations.

- **Bring your own cloud (BYOC):** This refers to individual staff members using their personal cloud storage, SaaS, or even PaaS systems as part of what they use to accomplish work-related tasks.

- **Bring your own infrastructure (BYOI):** This starts with employees bringing in their own Wi-Fi hot spots and other connectivity solutions and grows from there.

All of these usage models, and others still no doubt being invented, need to come under administrative control—the organization's leadership and management has to set clear directives, policies, and guidelines in place, and couple them with appropriate training and human resources management processes to ensure that all users know what the mobile device usage expectations and requirements are. NIST SP 800-124r2 offers concrete guidance for dealing with the less-than-laptop size range of mobile devices; even if your organization does not have to comply with NIST publications, it's a worthwhile read as you're reviewing your company's administrative controls—or helping to write them if the company doesn't have any in force yet.

Data Retention Policies   The risks involved with having company data on a mobile device should draw attention to the *time value* of information. Your organizational information security classification guidelines should set hard limits on how long an individual employee can maintain a copy of each different type of classified or sensitive data. The need to know should have a time component, and this time component should drive the administrative policies and logical controls used by your MDM solutions to prevent "data hoarding" on anyone's mobile device. This will limit exposure to data loss if the device is lost or stolen.

An onboard *secure container* strategy can also help prevent data loss if a device falls into the wrong hands. Secure container systems keep the data in encrypted form and require a regular "keep-alive" contact with the device's designated server if they are to keep the data available on the device; failure to make contact within a required interval (weekly, perhaps) causes the container to lock the data, and then after another interval, destroy it.

Coping with Jailbreaks   Almost any mobile device can have its consumer-friendly access controls defeated and any factory-installed limitations removed or nullified. Lost or stolen devices are often *jailbroken* or *rooted*, as it's called, in attempts to unlock any MDM or user-imposed locks, security restrictions, or even encryption on data stored on the device. This ever-present risk dictates that every connection attempt by *any* mobile device should undergo integrity checks that can ascertain whether a jailbreak or root unlock has been attempted or has been successful; this should be done as part of checking if the device's firmware and software are all at the minimum required update levels. NIST SP 800-124r2 goes into this in some depth as well.

Wi-Fi

Wi-Fi, which actually does *not* mean "wireless fidelity,"[14] is probably the most prevalent and pervasive wireless radio technology currently in use. Let's focus a moment longer on protecting the data link between the endpoint device (such as a user's smartphone, laptop, smartwatch, etc.) and the wireless access point, which manages how, when, and which wireless subscriber devices can connect at layer 1 and above. (Note that a wireless access point can also be a wireless device itself!) Let's look at wireless security protocols.

- Wired Equivalency Protocol (WEP) was the first attempt at securing Wi-Fi. As the name suggests, it was a compromise intended to make some security easier to

[14]*Wi-Fi* is a registered but somewhat unenforced trademark of the Wi-Fi Alliance, the industry association which created the initial designs and related certifications. It is also written as *WiFi*, *wifi* or *wi-fi*.

achieve, but it proved to have far too many security flaws and was easily circumvented by attackers. Avoid its use altogether if you can.

- Wi-Fi Protected Access (WPA) was an interim replacement while the IEEE 802.11i standard was in development. It used preshared encryption keys (PSKs, sometimes called "WPA Personal") while providing Temporal Key Integrity Protocol (TKIP) for encryption. WPA Enterprise uses more robust encryption, an authentication server, or PKI certificates in the process.

- Wi-Fi Protected Access Version 2 (WPA2) took this the next step when IEEE 802.11i was released in 2004. Among other improvements, WPA2 brings Advanced Encryption Standard (AES) algorithms into use.

WARNING Cable or fiber-connected LAN segments might not need to have their links encrypted to protect the data traveling on them—if you can be confident that other physical controls prevent attackers from tapping the cables or fibers themselves, of course. But with wireless links, you don't have any option for protecting the bits being transmitted *except* to encrypt them.

Deploying a wireless network is relatively easy and has become the preference in many corporate environments large and small; it is in keeping with the tremendous change in mobile work ethics and habits as well as the social acceptance (if not dependence) upon being always connected while on the go. SOHO networks and even those for medium-sized organizations are increasingly turning to wireless solutions first because of their flexibility, agility, and speed of deployment; they are also customer-friendly and invite and encourage collaboration with visitors, such as vendors, suppliers, and partners, much more easily than a wired network does. Wi-Fi connections are almost *expected*, even in what might seem the most austere of locations. Your job, then, is to make those ubiquitous Wi-Fi connections available, reliable, and *secure*.

Let's take a closer look under the hood.

Wireless Standards and Protocols

Wireless network communications are governed by the IEEE 802.11 standard. As technologies and use cases have evolved, this standard has evolved as well, as shown in Table 6.11. Note that each version or amendment to the 802.11 standard offered improved maximum data rates. 802.11x is often used to indicate all of the specific implementations as a collective whole, but that is not preferred over a general reference to 802.11.

TABLE 6.11 **IEEE 802.11 Standard Amendments**

STANDARD	FREQUENCY	BANDWIDTH	MODULATION	MAX DATA RATE
802.11	2.4GHz	20MHz	DSSS, FHSS	2Mbps
802.11a	5GHz	20MHz	DSSS	54Mbps
802.11b	2.4GHz	20MHz	OFDM	11Mbps
802.11g	2.4GHz	20MHz	OFDM	54Mbps
802.11n	2.4 and 5GHz	20MHz, 40MHz	OFDM	600Mbps
802.11 ac	2.4 and 5GHz	20, 40, 80, 80+80, 160MHz	OFDM	6.93Gbps

DSSS: Direct Sequence Spread Spectrum
FHSS: Frequency Hopping Spread Spectrum
OFDM: Orthogonal Frequency Division Multiplexing

TIP   Do not confuse 802.11x with 802.1x; 11 is the Wi-Fi standard, while 1 relates to authentication and authorization.

Wired Equivalent Privacy and Wi-Fi Protected Access

The IEEE 802.11 standard defines two methods that wireless clients can use to authenticate to wireless access points (WAPs) before normal network communications can occur across the wireless link. These two methods are open system authentication (OSA) and shared key authentication (SKA).

- OSA provides no confidentiality or security because no real authentication is required. Communication happens if the radio signal is strong enough to reach a compatible receiver. All OSA transmissions are unencrypted.

- SKA enforces some form of authentication, and if the authentication isn't provided, the communication is blocked. The 802.11 standard defines one optional technique for SKA known as Wired Equivalent Privacy (WEP) with subsequent amendments to the original 802.11 standard adding WPA, WPA2, WPA3, and others. WPA3 is the current standard.

WEP was designed to protect against eavesdropping for wireless communications. The initial aim of WEP was to provide an equivalent level of protection against MitM types of attacks as wired networks have. WEP implemented encryption of data in wireless transmissions using a Rivest Cipher 4 (RC4) symmetric stream cipher. Message integrity verification is possible because a hash value is used to verify that received packets weren't modified or corrupted while in transit. It also can be configured to prevent unauthorized access. Incidentally, the knowledge or possession of the encryption key helps as a basic form of authentication. Without the key, access to the network itself is denied. WEP is used at the two lowest layers of the OSI Seven-Layer Reference Model: the data link and physical layers. It therefore does not offer end-to-end security. Over time, WEP has been shown to have weaknesses. For instance, WEP uses static encryption keys, which means the same key is used by every device on a wireless network. WEP was cracked via known-ciphertext (intercepted traffic) based attacks almost as soon as it was released. It takes less than a minute to hack through WEP protection using the simplest of brute-force methods.

Dissatisfied with the security provided by WEP, a group of industry and cryptographic researchers formed the Wi-Fi Alliance to develop a new encryption standard for use in these types of wireless connection. They called their first design the Wi-Fi Protected Access (WPA). As a replacement for WEP, WPA could be retrofitted to WEP firmware on wireless network interface cards designed for WEP already in the computing environment. That feature proved to be more problematic than it was worth. The changes to the wireless access points were extensive and hardware replacement was a better option.

WPA was intended as an interim solution until the IEEE published the promised 802.11i standard. That process lingered for years, so WPA was implemented independent of the 802.11 amendment. The WPA protocol implemented the Lightweight Extensible Authentication Protocol (LEAP) and Temporal Key Integrity Protocol (TKIP), which together support a per-packet key that dynamically generates a new 128-bit key for each packet. WPA negotiates a unique key set with each host. It improves upon the WEP 64-bit or 128-bit encryption key that had to be manually entered on wireless access points and devices and was not subject to change. WPA uses LEAP and TKIP to perform a Message Integrity Check, which is designed to prevent an attacker from altering and resending data packets. This replaces the cyclic redundancy check (CRC) that was used by the WEP standard. CRC's main flaw was that it did not provide a sufficiently strong data integrity guarantee for the packets it handled.

In 2008, researchers demonstrated that the encryption used in WPA could be broken in less than a minute using a known-ciphertext approach. This prompted further development, which led to the IEEE 802.11i standard finally being released, and with it the arrival of WPA2 as the replacement—not the next version—of Wi-Fi Protected Access.

IEE 802.11i and WPA2, and then WPA3

The next evolution was WPA2, which replaced WPA. Originally, it was meant to replace WEP, but as mentioned, the 802.11i standard lingered, and WPA was implemented independently. This amendment deals with the security issues of the original 802.11 standard. It was backward compatible to WPA. WPA2 provided U.S. government-grade security by implementing the National Institute of Standards and Technology (NIST) FIPS 140-2 compliant AES encryption algorithm and 802.1x-based authentications, and Counter Mode Cipher Block Chaining Message Authentication Code Protocol (CCMP). There are two versions of WPA2: WPA2-Personal and WPA2-Enterprise. WPA2-Personal protects unauthorized network access by utilizing a setup password. WPA2-Enterprise verifies network users through a server using Network Access Control (NAC).

The selection of the name WPA2 was needed because WPA was already published and in widespread use. However, WPA2 is not the second version of WPA. They are distinct and different. IEEE 802.11i, or WPA2, implemented concepts similar to IPsec to improve encryption and security within the wireless networks.

Up until 2017, there had not been any demonstrated attacks against WPA2; however, in October of that year, Mathy Vanhoef of imec-DistriNet at the Katholieke Universiteit Leuven, Belgium, showed how it could be done with key reinstallation attacks he named KRACK. Devices running the Android, Linux, Apple, Windows, and OpenBSD operating systems, as well as MediaTek Linksys, and other types of devices, are all vulnerable. Shortly after he published, patches were made available. In 2018, more attacks were demonstrated against WPA2, adding further impetus to the development and fielding of WPA3, which was finally released later that year. However, in April 2019, reports showed that even WPA3 is prone to attacks. Its *Dragonfly* algorithm replaces the four-way handshake used in WPA2 with a simultaneous authentication of equals (SAE) approach. This, too, has been shown to have vulnerabilities in it, in a paper titled *Dragonblood*, by Mathy Vanhoef (again) and Eyal Ronen. Their paper also criticizes the process used by Wi-Fi Alliance during development, testing, and roll-out of the new standard. Further enhancements to WPA3, including the hash-to-element (H2E) cryptographic technique, provide for greater protection from side-channel attacks. This and other continued improvements still make WPA3 the best choice.

NOTE   ArsTechnical has a lucid and rather scary analysis of WPA3 that draws heavily on Vanhoef's and Ronen's work; you can read it at https://arstechnica.com/ information-technology/2019/04/ serious-flaws-leave-wpa3-vulnerable-to-hacks-that-steal-wi-fi-passwords/.

WPA Authentication and Encryption

Several different components make up the encryption and authentication mechanisms used in WPA, WPA2, and WPA3.

- **IEEE 802.1X enterprise authentication:** Both WPA and WPA2 support the enterprise authentication known as 802.1X/EAP, a standard network access control that is port-based to ensure client access control to network resources. Effectively, 802.1X is a checking system that allows the wireless network to leverage the existing network infrastructure's authentication services. Through the use of 802.1X, other techniques and solutions such as RADIUS, TACACS, certificates, smart cards, token devices, and biometrics can be integrated into wireless networks providing techniques for multifactor authentication.

■ **Extensible Authentication Protocol (EAP):** EAP is an authentication framework versus a specific mechanism of authentication. EAP facilitates compatibility with new authentication technologies for existing wireless or point-to-point connection technologies. More than 40 different EAP methods of authentication are widely supported. These include the wireless methods of LEAP, EAP-TLS, EAP-SIM, EAP-AKA, and EAP-TTLS. Two significant EAP methods that bear a closer look are PEAP and LEAP.

TIP   EAP is not an assurance of security. For example, EAP-MD5 and a prerelease EAP known as LEAP are known to be vulnerable.

■ **Protected Extensible Authentication Protocol (PEAP):** PEAP provides a "PEAP tunnel" as it encapsulates EAP methods to provide authentication and, potentially, encryption. Since EAP was originally designed for use over physically isolated channels and hence assumed secured pathways, EAP is usually not encrypted. So, PEAP can provide encryption for EAP methods.

■ **Lightweight Extensible Authentication Protocol (LEAP):** LEAP is a Cisco proprietary alternative to TKIP for WPA, but it should not be used. An attack tool known as Asleap was released in 2004 that could exploit the ultimately weak protection provided by LEAP. Use of EAP-TLS is preferred. If LEAP is used, a complex password is an imperative. LEAP served the purpose of addressing deficiencies in TKIP before the advent of 802.11i/ WPA2.

■ **Temporal Key Integrity Protocol (TKIP):** TKIP was designed as the replacement for WEP without requiring replacement of legacy wireless hardware. TKIP was implemented into the 802.11 wireless networking standards within the guidelines of WPA. TKIP improvements start with a key-mixing function that combines the initialization vector (IV) (i.e., a random number) with the secret root key before using that key to perform encryption. Sequence counters and strong message integrity check (MIC) were also added to prevent packet replay attacks.

■ **Counter Mode with Cipher Block Chaining Message Authentication Code Protocol (CCMP):** CCMP was created to replace WEP and TKIP/WPA. CCMP uses Advanced Encryption Standard (AES) with a 128-bit key. CCMP is the preferred standard security protocol of 802.11 wireless networking indicated by 802.11i. To date, no attacks have yet been successful against the AES/CCMP encryption. CCMP is the standard encryption mechanism used in WPA2.

Wireless Access Points

Many cellular or mobile devices can potentially act as bridges that may be unsecured access into your network. Understanding the way the devices are exploited requires a brief introduction to Wireless Application Protocol (WAP). Where the devices or transmissions are not secure, e.g., access controlled or encrypted, the attacker can hijack the session and gain access to the private network. WAP had proved problematic in the marketplace, and the advent of more powerful smartphones with onboard browsers (which were capable of using PKI for session security) spelled the death knell of WAP as a protocol and an architecture. However, the acronym WAP lives on, representing *wireless access points* instead.

✔ Which WAP?

The easiest way to tell whether this acronym refers to a device or a protocol is in the context of its use. You connect *to* a device like a WAP, *using* a protocol like WAP. Of course, if you do, you're still not very secure, no matter how you *use* WAP. Use other protocols to secure a WAP.

Wireless access points (WAPs) are the devices within a physical environment that receive radio signals and then permit devices to connect to the network (based on the network's established access control parameters, of course). Even so, a security issue can result from a wireless access point that has a broadcast beacon that is set too powerfully and sends its beacon far beyond the necessary range. Whether broadcasting the beacon far away is seen as an advantage, say to roaming users, is a decision left to the company. This allows an unwanted wireless device the ability to connect even if the end user is prohibited from accessing the physical area where the wireless access point is installed. In short, securing the wireless access point requires attention to proper placement of the device, shielding it, and limiting noise transmission while satisfying customer need to connect.

Wireless access point security can best be thought of in terms of the three sets of devices you need to worry about: own, neighbors, and rogues.

- **Own devices** are, as the name suggests, *your* devices—the wireless endpoint devices you want to be authorized to connect to your network.

- **Neighbor devices** are those that do not belong to you and are not attempting to connect to your access points and thence to your network; they are simply in the same radio wave neighborhood as your access points are in. They may be legitimate users of other wireless networks you do not own and manage, or they may be rogues who haven't tried to connect to your systems. Neighbors might even be legitimate users of your own system who've just not attempted to connect yet.

- **Rogue devices** are ones that you do not allow to connect to your systems. These may be devices owned or being used by authorized employees, visitors, or guests, but the devices themselves are unknown to your access control and mobile device management processes. If that's the case, then *first* get the device's owner or operator to get that device suitably registered. Then it's no longer a rogue.

WAP security thus boils down to reliably identifying whether a signal that is trying to connect is from an own (or known) device or not. If it is, let it connect; if it is not, *ignore it*. Prevent it. But don't attempt to disconnect it from other neighboring WAPs that are not yours to manage, such as by attempting to jam it somehow. (That might be tantamount to hacking that neighboring system and could land you in a legal mess.)

That same three-part view applies to *access points* as well. There are the access points you own, operate, and are responsible for. There are the ones your neighbors own and operate (and which are none of your concern, unless they are inadvertently interfering with your wireless operations). And then there are access points that you *don't* own but that are trying to entice some of your *own wireless endpoints* to connect to them instead, in a classic MitM attack using access points. (Such attacks might be for harvesting credentials, as part of a DDOS attack, or some other tactic.)

Providing a secure wireless network needs to focus on using the right access point hardware for the environment you're operating in.

Conducting a Wi-Fi Site Survey   This type of site survey maps out your physical operating environment to find any Wi-Fi access points that are currently broadcasting into your workspaces, support areas (such as utility spaces, loading docks, and storage areas), reception areas, and the surrounding exterior landscape. A simple, informal survey can be conducted with a smartphone or laptop with a Wi-Fi analyzer or mapper application loaded on it. These mapper or analyzer apps collect any transmissions from Wi-Fi devices they can pick up and then display them as instantaneous signal strength or as plots of strength over time. (Many such apps can be downloaded for free or for minimal cost.) Simply walking about the area with a smartphone displaying such a map will indicate "hot zones" in which many nearby access points can be detected. By plotting these out along a floor plan, you'll have some ideas where your needs for solid, reliable connectivity versus the current ambient RF environment may give you some challenges to overcome. Putting your own access point (or its antennae) in a spot where other neighboring access points show strong signals may be all that it takes to overcome the potential for interference, jamming, or exposure to interception and misconnection.

You may need to make a more thorough site survey to properly identify potential interference, jamming, or other issues that would influence where you put what type of access points in to meet your needs. Professional Wi-Fi mapping and surveying tools make it easier to correlate highly accurate survey instrument location data with received signal strength (which can be a problem with a walkaround smartphone approach).

A site survey may also identify potential rogue access points. It will be good to know if any are in your RF neighborhood, but again, all you need to do is prevent your devices from talking to them.

Access Point Placement and Testing   Based on your site survey results and choices of equipment, it's time to put the access points into their recommended locations, turn them on, and evaluate how well your new Wi-Fi network performs. Multiple walk-throughs with Wi-Fi devices—both as mappers and running throughput-gobbling apps—will help you identify any possible dead zones or areas with poor signal strength. When you've moved devices about and changed settings to resolve these issues, lock the devices down, both physically and administratively—bring their location and configuration data under configuration management and control. Document this important part of your IT architectural baseline.

Antenna positioning and pointing, for example, can become something of a fine art in this adjustment process. Most antennae do not radiate their energy (or receive signals) with a uniform, spherical pattern of power or sensitivity—they have a "beam" effect, with a main lobe of energy distribution (or receive sensitivity) in one set of directions, and some near-to-blind spots (or *nulls*) in others. The wrong type of antenna pointed the wrong way can be your undoing.

Some commonsense placement issues pertaining to wireless access points worth considering include:

- Centrally locate the access point, rather than put it on one side of the room, to provide more uniform signal strength and coverage.
- Avoid putting the access point on top of metal cabinets or shelves.
- Place the access point as far away from large electric motors, or other EMI sources, as possible.
- Omnidirectional antennae should be vertically aligned; directional antennas should point toward the area you want to provide greatest signal strength toward.

TIP   For best signal strength, set up any access points that are located near each other with a maximum channel separation. For instance, for four access points located within close proximity, channel settings could be 1, 11, 1, and 11 if the arrangement was linear, like along a hallway across the length of a building. However, if the building is square and an access point is in each corner, the channel settings may need to be 1, 4, 8, and 11. The access points and the endpoints will still hunt for as clear a channel as they can find, but this may help you balance channel loading to improve availability.

Infrastructure Mode and Ad Hoc Mode   Wireless access points can be deployed in one of two modes known as *ad hoc* or *infrastructure*. As the names suggest, each mode is best suited for a particular type of network installation. *Ad hoc* (also known as peer to peer) requires less management and setup initially, and if you are changing your access point locations frequently, or the wireless endpoints move around a lot during the day, it may be a good place to start. It's well suited for SOHO or somewhat larger networks. *Infrastructure mode* provides a more scalable, manageable wireless network and can better manage security features across the network. It prevents a device's wireless NIC from attempting to directly connect to the network without the assistance of the access point. Many consumer-grade wireless router products, especially ones aimed at the gaming market, are often built with the capability of operating as infrastructure or ad hoc network access points. Note, too, that some printers, some Android devices, and systems such as Google Chromecast may not work well over ad hoc networks. Most business and organizational uses of access points benefit from having them in infrastructure mode; if you find some in ad hoc mode on your network, they might bear further investigation.

Infrastructure mode access points can operate in four different modes:

- **Standalone:** A wireless access point connects multiple wireless clients to each other but not to any wired resources.

- **Wired extension:** The wireless access point acts as a connection point, or hub, to link the wireless clients to the wired network.

- **Enterprise extended:** Multiple wireless access points (WAPs) all with the same extended service set identifier (ESSID) are used to connect a large physical area to the same wired network. Allows for physical device movement without losing connection to the ESSID.

- **Bridge:** A wireless connection is used to link two wired networks, often used between floors or buildings when running cables or wires is infeasible or inconvenient.

Service Set Identifiers (SSIDs)   Wireless networks are known by their Service Set Identifier (SSID), which is established by the access point's configuration and setup. Most access points come shipped from the vendor with default administrator user IDs, passwords, and SSIDs preconfigured—*change these immediately* to start to provide your wireless network some degree of improved security! The factory default SSIDs almost always clearly identify the manufacturer's name, the model number, and sometimes even the product revision level, which are important clues an attacker would love to have; it makes their job of researching your exploitable vulnerabilities so much easier. The SSID is a logical name for the wireless network, please note—it is *not* the logical name for the entire wireless network it is on. Thus, two access points that provide overlapping coverage areas would be configured to have the same SSID so that users can configure their endpoints to join *one* network, not hop back and forth between them. Some further fine points on SSIDs you should consider include:

- SSIDs used for infrastructure mode networks are called extended service set identifiers (ESSIDs).

- SSIDs used for ad hoc access points are known as basic service set identifiers (BSSIDs).

- Multiple access points operating in infrastructure mode will use their hardware MAC addresses as their individual BSSIDs, with the ESSID being the logical network name.

✔ Five Myths About Wi-Fi Security

According to a 2013 article by Eric Geier in PCWORLD, these false myths still are held to be good security hygiene when configuring and managing wireless networks. Abandon your belief, Geier says, in the following:

Myth #1: Don't broadcast your SSID. False. This doesn't add any appreciable security, since (a) most devices since the days of Windows 7 can still find all access points that are beaconing (inviting devices to know about them), and from there, determining their SSID is trivially easy; and (b) a "silent SSID" device might attract the attention of someone looking to figure out what you have got to hide.

Myth #2: Enable MAC address filtering. False. The downside of this is that with a wireless analyzer, a hacker can find all of those MAC addresses anyway (each time a device transmits to the access point) and then spoof their own to match.

Myth #3: Limit the router's IP address pool. False. Unfortunately, if the hacker has been inside your network once, a quick IP scan has revealed all of the addresses in use and can spoof one to enter through your access point.

> **Myth #4:** Disable DHCP on your wireless router. False. This has the same exploitable vulnerability as Myth #3.
>
> **Myth #5:** Small networks are harder to penetrate; therefore, set the broadcast power of your access point as low as you can to reduce effective range and exposure to attackers. False. Since attackers are more than happy to use high-gain antennas (even cheap *cantennas*, which are highly directional antennas made from old foil-lined cardboard potato chip cans, such as Pringles come in), they'll get in while your legitimate users may not be able to.

Captive Wireless Portals

Access points can be configured to allow devices to connect to only one specific portal, such as a single IP address or URL. This address or page then enforces other access control functions by forcing the device and its user to go through any required authentication steps, including multifactor authentication (which *should* be a foundational element of your network security architecture). Captive portals are frequently used in public Wi-Fi hotspots in airports, restaurants, hotels, and public parks and other spaces. They can collect a significant amount of information about the device that is attempting to connect, which can contribute to multifactor authentication, authorization for specific services, and as part of endpoint device integrity and health status. Failing a required software or hardware integrity check can force the device to route to a quarantine portal, for example.

As authentication and authorization measures, captive portals are also useful on wired connections as well as on wireless ones. Forcing the newly connecting device to go through such processes provides a *stateless* authentication, not dependent upon the access point being pre-programmed with the device's credentials—the network-level access control system can and should handle that. The portal may require input of credentials, payment, or an access code. Portals can also provide end users with banner announcements regarding appropriate use policies, and notice that users may be disconnected, and even prosecuted, for failing to abide by them. If end-user consent for tracking and information collection is required, the captive portal allows for that as well. Once the end user satisfies the conditions required by the starting page, only then can they communicate across the network.

Wireless Attacks

Attacks against the wireless elements of network systems can be against the access point, an endpoint, or both; the attacks themselves typically are part of a longer, more complex kill chain, and are but the first few steps in a process of gaining entry into the target IT systems and then taking control of portions of it. All of the attack types discussed with respect to wired networks can be launched at the access point and the wireless endpoint. Two particular types of attack are unique to wireless systems, however: war driving (and now war *droning*) and jamming as a form of denial of service.

Signal jamming is the malicious activity of overwhelming a wireless access point to the extent where legitimate traffic can no longer be processed. Even though this is illegal in most places, there are inexpensive jamming products, like a TV jammer, available for sale online.

War driving is a bit of a play on words. The term has roots back into a form of attack in the 1980s called *war dialing*, where computers would be used to make large number of phone calls searching for modems to exploit. War driving, in contrast, is when someone, usually in a moving vehicle, actively searches for Wi-Fi wireless networks using wireless network scanning tools. These scanning tools and software are readily available and, far too often, free. When a wireless network appears to be present, the attacker uses the tools to interrogate the wireless interface or a wireless detector to locate wireless network signals. Once an attacker knows a wireless network is present, they can use sniffers to gather wireless packets for investigation. The next steps in the attack are to discover hidden SSIDs, active IP addresses, valid MAC addresses, and even the authentication mechanism the clients use. MitM types of attacks may progress or the attackers may conduct advanced attacks with specialized tools, like AirCrack, AirSnort, and WireShark to attempt to break into the connection and attempt to gather additional important information. Using older security protocols such as WEP and WPA (or no security at all) almost guarantees that attackers will succeed at gaining entry into your system.

War driving has now moved to the skies, as private citizens can own and operate fairly sophisticated UAVs and other semi-autonomous mobile platforms. Equipping such a hobbyist-quality drone or radio-controlled car with a Wi-Fi repeater is fairly easy to do. This *war droning* brings our insecurities to new heights, and its remote pilot no longer can be some distance away from the scene.

War drivers often share the information they gather. Not all war driving attacks are meant to disrupt or be particularly malicious. It is very likely the attackers are trying to simply get Internet access for free. Using the data that they obtain from their own tools they combine data with GPS information about location. Then they publish the information to websites like WiGLE, openBmap, or Geomena. Other people access the maps of various networks to find locations where they can hijack the wireless and access the Internet or conduct additional attacks.

There are no laws that prohibit war driving, although nothing specifically allows it either. Some consider it ethically wrong, but at a high level it is somewhat analogous to neighborhood mapping in the physical world with house numbers and phone numbers publicly listed. In fact, the reporting of war driving information on the Web could be considered an expanded version of what wireless access points are meant to do by broadcasting and beaconing.

Bluetooth

Bluetooth is a short-range wireless radio interface standard, designed to support wireless mice, keyboards, or other devices, typically within 1 to 10 meters of the host computer they are being used with. Bluetooth is also used to support data synchronization between smart watches and fitness trackers with smartphones. Bluetooth has its own protocol stack, with one set of protocols for the controller (the time-critical radio elements) and another set for the host. There are 15 protocols altogether. Bluetooth does not operate over Internet protocol networks. NIST SP 800-121r2 provides a deeper understanding of Bluetooth, its operating modes, and security considerations for its use.

In contrast with Wi-Fi, Bluetooth has four security modes.

- Mode 1, unsecure, bypasses any built-in authentication and encryption (at host or device). This does not provide other nearby Bluetooth devices from pairing up with a host. This mode is supported only through Bluetooth Version 2.0 plus Enhanced Data Rate (EDR) and should not be used with later versions of Bluetooth.

- Mode 2, centralized security management, which provides some degree of authorization, authentication, and encryption of traffic between the devices.

- Mode 3, device pairing, looks to the remote device to initiate encryption-based security using a separate secret link (secret to the paired devices). This too is supported only by version 2.0 + EDR systems.

- Mode 4, key exchange, supports more advanced encryption algorithms, such as elliptic-curve Diffie-Hellman.

Bluetooth is prone to a number of security concerns, such as these:

- Bluejacking, which is the hijacking of a Bluetooth link to get the attacker's data onto an otherwise trusted device

- Bluebugging, by which attackers can remotely access a smartphone's unprotected Bluetooth link and use it as an eavesdropping platform, collect data from it, or operate it remotely

- Bluesnarfing, which is the theft of information from a wireless device through a Bluetooth connection

- Car whispering, which uses software to allow hackers to send and receive audio from a Bluetooth-enabled car entertainment system

Given these concerns, it's probably best that your mobile device management solution understand the vulnerabilities inherent in Bluetooth and ensure that each mobile device you allow onto your networks (or your business premises!) can be secured against exploitations targeted at its Bluetooth link.

Although Bluetooth does not actually provide a wireless Ethernet network standard, the technology does support wireless transmissions point to point over a short distance. In general use, the maximum effective distance is about 30 feet. However, there are industrial or advanced versions of Bluetooth that can reach 300 feet. Many types of endpoint devices support Bluetooth, such as mobile phones, laptops, printers, radios, and digital personal assistants, along with an increasing number of other IoT devices.

The benefits of Bluetooth are that it does not require base stations as it is a direct connection between devices. It also requires little power, which is good for use with the battery-operated end devices that typically feature Bluetooth.

There are also a few downsides. The transmission speed is slower than the 802.11b wireless standard. It conflicts and interferes with existing 802.11b and 802.11g networks as it uses the 2.4GHz broadcasting spectrum, causing problems for endpoint devices relying on the transmissions. Another significant downside is Bluetooth's inherent weakness due to its lack of encryption. Using Bluetooth to create a personal area network carries security implications, too, since a PAN most likely has vulnerabilities, but those vulnerabilities are not easily identified by corporate sweeps. The reason is that a PAN is a nonroutable section or extension of an existing LAN or WAN, making it not easily assessed.

Near-Field Communications

Near-field communications (NFC) provides a secure radio-frequency communications channel that works for devices within about 4cm (1.6in) of each other. Designed to meet the needs of contactless, card-less payment and debit authorizations, NFC uses secure on-device data storage and existing radio frequency identification (RFID) standards to carry out data transfers (such as phone-to-phone file sharing) or payment processing transactions.

Multiple standards organizations work on different aspects of NFC and its application to problems within the purview of each body.

NFC is susceptible to man-in-the-middle attacks at the physical link layer and is also susceptible to high-gain antenna interception. Relay attacks, similar to man-in-the-middle, are also possible. NFC as a standard does not include encryption, but like TCP/IP, it will allow for applications to layer on encrypted protection for data and routing information.

Cellular/Mobile Phone Networks

Today's mobile phone systems (or *cell phone systems* as they were originally called) provide end users with the ability to place or receive voice or video calls, connect to the Internet, and send and receive text or SMS messages from almost anywhere, and while moving on the ground or in the air. The systems consist of mobile endpoints, base stations, and connections into the public switched telephone system (PSTN) to provide links between base stations and to connect users' calls to other phones and to the Internet. The mobile endpoint device can be a laptop, smartphone, or any device that can accept a subscriber identity module or SIM card and use it to connect to and authenticate with a mobile services provider. Endpoints connect via radio to a *base station*, which provides for authentication and authorization, session or call origination, interfacing with the PSTN and other base stations as required to maintain the session while the mobile endpoint moves from the coverage pattern of one base station to another. These *coverage cells* or cells gave the system its original name—*cellular phone service*, with the endpoints being known as *cell phones*, long before they were terribly smart. As those first-generation devices grew in capability and the market's demand for them grew exponentially, these endpoints have become smaller, lighter, and far more capable. Table 6.12 summarizes these first four generations of mobile (or cell) phone systems.

TABLE 6.12 Basic Overview of Cellular Wireless Technologies

GENERATION	3G	4G	5G
Timeline	2002 to 2005	2010 to present	2018 to present
Messaging features	Graphics and formatted text	Full unified messaging	Full unified messaging
Data support	Packet switched	Native IPv6	Native IPv6
Target data rate	2 Mbps	1 Gpbs	20 Gbps

NOTE Systems that combine features from two generations are often named with half-generation numbers, such as 2.5G or 3.5G.

While many cellular technologies are labeled and sold as 4G, they may not actually reach the standards established for 4G by the International Telecommunications Union-Radio communications sector (ITU-R). The ITU-R set the standard for 4G in 2008. In

2010, the group decided that as long as a cellular carrier organization would be able to reach 4G-compliant services in the near future, the company could label the technology as 4G. Standards for 5G have been in development since 2014. However, the 5G network and compatible devices are expected to be commercially available worldwide in 2020. There have been localized deployments, like at the 2018 Winter Olympics in South Korea.

Mobile phone systems are not inherently secure; as of this writing, none offers built-in encryption or other security protection for the voice, video, SMS, or text messaging capabilities that are part of the package provided by the carrier network operator that is providing the services to the end user. Individual smartphone apps running as clients may establish TLS connections with servers and provide secure and encrypted Internet browsing, transaction processing, and e-commerce, and VoIP providers may provide security features, such as encryption, for their services when used via a mobile smartphone on a cell phone network. Many third parties are providing add-on apps to provide greater levels of security for voice, video, text, email, and other smartphone services that business and personal users want and are demanding. All of these represent both a challenge and an opportunity to organizational security managers and architects who need to extend the organization's security policies to include many different types of mobile smartphone devices. The challenge is that as of summer 2019, there are no clear market leaders as products, technologies, or standards for mobile phone security; the opportunity is that with a wide-open market, attackers have a larger target set to try to learn about and understand as well. For the time being, you may have to look at meeting mobile phone user security requirements on a business process by business process basis and then looking to what apps, features, channels, or forms of communications each business process needs and how to secure them effectively.

Ad Hoc Wireless Networks

Most wired and wireless networks are centralized, managed systems to one degree or another; they use clearly defined client-server relationships to provide critical services (such as DHCP), and they physically define communications links as a set of point-to-point links between endpoints and the network's switching fabric. As mobile telephony and computer networking blended into each other in the 1970s and 1980s, it was clear that a set of sufficiently smart wireless endpoints could dynamically configure and manage a LAN on an ad hoc, peer-to-peer (P2P) basis, without the need for a centralized server and controller. This research gave birth to wireless ad hoc networks (WANETs), also known as mobile ad hoc networks (MANET, pronounced with a hard *t* at the end, unlike the French modernist painter). There may be more than a dozen use cases for MANETs in such diverse applications as:

- Vehicular roadside networks
- Smart phone ad hoc networks (SPANs)

- Military tactical networks
- Ad hoc networks of mobile robots
- Disaster and rescue operational networks
- Hospital and clinical ad hoc networks
- Street lighting control networks
- Home automation and control networks

These all show varying levels of successful implementation and adoption in their respective markets. Ad hoc wireless networks can achieve high levels of performance and throughput, along with high resiliency in the face of intermittent services from the local public switched network, cellular phone networks, or other infrastructures. They can easily make use of lower-power radios in unlicensed portions of the RF spectrum (or be light wave based), which lowers implementation cost and time to market. No centralized control node means no single point of failure. Even so, smart algorithms for collision detection and contention management can actually make an ad hoc network more immune to interference than a similar managed wireless network might be.

There are, however, some challenges to having a system in which all elements are highly mobile. A few elements of the mesh could become isolated or suffer extremely poor connection to the exterior of their local area, if most other mobile elements have moved out of range of their various links. The network control and administration functions must be highly adaptive and self-annealing to allow the system to operate without a central supervisory or management function.

There are still a number of issues with wireless ad hoc networks that need further development (and in some cases, further research),such as:

- System reinitialization can be complicated if some (or many) devices on the ad hoc network are autonomous and require manual intervention to properly restart.

- Software and configuration update, management, and control can be more complex and time-consuming, especially if the network consists of many different device types (each with its own update process).

- Network access control capabilities are usually not implemented or are difficult to implement and manage with currently marketed technologies. This leaves them vulnerable to resource consumption denial of services attacks (or self-inflicted resource consumption choking).

- Packets can also be dropped or delayed by an intermediate node (either through malfunction or attack) on the network, which on a sparsely connected subtree could effectively disrupt services beyond that node.

Blockchain technologies and concepts may be a natural fit here, since most blockchain ledger systems are distributed P2P architectures that self-authenticate their ledgers and may or may not rely upon an external trust chain or web to bootstrap their internal certificate use. Identity management systems for IoT environments are also seeing a great deal of focused research and development on scalable, maintainable, adaptive, and affordable solutions to these problems. Watch this space.

That said, many organizations may find that there are substantial parts of business processes that can be safely and effectively supported by MANETs or WANETS tailored to their needs.

Transmission Security

Transmission security (or TRANSEC in military parlance) is the use of procedures and techniques *other than cryptography* to secure the content, meaning, and intention of information transmitted by any means or physical medium. Many of these techniques were developed to take fairly lengthy communications and break them apart into smaller pieces, and the loss of any one piece would make it difficult to impossible to deduce the correct meaning of the message. This early form of *packetized transmission* for security purposes predates electronic communications by centuries. From a security perspective, this forces your potential (or already known) adversaries to have to expand their real-time efforts to search for pieces of your message traffic; the more distinct pieces you can break your messages into, and the greater the number and types of transmission channels you can use, the greater the odds that your adversaries will miss one or more of them.

Transmission security measures can, of course, contribute to all aspects of our CIANA+PS paradigm by enhancing confidentiality and privacy, message and systems integrity, and the availability of message content. Nonrepudiation and authentication can also be enhanced by proper TRANSEC procedures and systems architectures, which also can make overall systems operation safer. In a curious irony, they can also somewhat *undo* nonrepudiation by providing a layer of *anonymity* for senders and recipients, much as a VPN can, by masking their identities, IP and MAC addresses, and physical location to a greater or lesser degree.

TRANSEC, if used effectively, can protect both the message content and its metadata. It can also thwart efforts by adversaries to use traffic analysis techniques to try to reverse-engineer the connectivity map of your organization, and correlate specific channel usage with other observable events. Be advised, though, that with sufficient time and sufficient interception of protected traffic, your adversaries will break your systems, uncrack your protected traffic, and start exploiting its content for their own purposes.

Your organization's security needs should dictate whether and how you use TRAN-SEC measures as part of your information systems, networks, and communications systems design. News media and organizations involved in humanitarian relief operations, for example, may have urgent and compelling needs to protect the identity and location of their on-scene reporters, coordinators, operations team members, or others in a local area. Companies involved in highly speculative, cutting-edge development projects might also need to provide additional layers of protection.

But that's not enough; put your gray hacker hat back on and think like your opponents in this never-ending struggle to maintain information security. APT threat actors may very well be using these techniques to protect their outward flow of exfiltrated data from your systems, while simultaneously using them to protect their inward flow of command and control directives. APTs are already well versed in using multiple user IDs in a complex, coordinated attack; this is a form of TRANSEC, too.

If we as white hats are always pitted against the black hats in a race against time, fragmentation of messaging across diverse channels and methods adds on a race across space component. Every such edge you can use is at best a temporary advantage, of course; and as more and more of the black hats are becoming more effective at sharing what they learn about the many, many targets all across the world, we white hats need every bit of edge we can get.

Anonymity Networks and Privacy-Enhancing Systems

Let's look at one form of Internet-based TRANSEC, and a handful of signaling modulation techniques, as food for thought. You'll need to dig deep into the details of any of these to see if they might be useful tools to meet your security needs—as well as how to detect if they are being used against you.

Probably the most well-known example of this in the Internet Age are anonymity networks such as TOR, Riffle, or Mix Networks, each of which use different techniques with much the same purpose in mind. Most of these do employ encryption (even in layers), so they are really hybrid approaches to security and anonymity. One way of thinking about these anonymity networks is to take the permutation and substitution functions used *inside* your encryption systems and scatter them about onto other proxy servers across the Internet.

TOR, along with Mixmaster and onion routing in other forms, are examples of mix networks. Other approaches are seen in systems like Freenet (`https://freenetproject.org`), Tails (`https://tails.boum.org`), and The Invisible Internet Project (I2P, at `https://geti2p.net`). I2P provides a fully encrypted private network layer that operates in a peer-to-peer fashion on top of the normal Internet. Freenet is also a P2P approach, providing a community of services including private, secure websites for a variety of topics; it also supports user development of apps to run on Freenet. Tails provides for a totally secure, removable operating system and anonymous Internet capability, which would boot from and run completely on a removable USB drive.

TOR and other onion relay systems and concepts are powerful and often necessary tools for organizations and individuals who need to provide the greatest possible security and privacy protection. Journalists, civil liberties advocates, and law enforcement often have to protect the anonymity of their sources, including the locations they may be sending from. Onion relays provide this.

To learn more about preserving and protecting anonymity and privacy on the Internet, visit `https://www.freehaven.net/anonbib/full/topic.html`, which provides hundreds of links to journal articles, websites, and other resources.

> ## ✔ Malicious Use of Anonymous Services
>
> Unfortunately, onion relays and other anonymity-assuring and privacy-enhancing tools can be put to malicious use, either by intruders or insider threats. When organizations have no legitimate business need for such anonymous communications, then blocking these services is recommended.
>
> The Australian Cyber Security Centre offers useful advice regarding when and how to block TOR or monitor its use on your systems. Find this and other useful guidance at `https://www.cyber.gov.au/acsc/view-all-content/publications/defending-against-malicious-use-tor-network`.

Frequency-Hopping Spread Spectrum

Frequency-hopping spread spectrum (FHSS) uses a pseudorandom sequencing of radio signals that the sender and receiver know. Early implementations relied on rapidly switching the signal across many frequency channels. The data is transmitted in a series, not in parallel. The frequency changes constantly. One frequency is used at a time, but over time, the entire band of available frequencies is used. The sender and receiver follow a hopping pattern in a synchronized way across the frequencies to communicate. Interference is minimized because reliance on a single frequency is not present. As with any system, the strength or weakness of FHSS as a security measure depends upon the strength of the pseudorandom number generator process and its salt; the size of the hop space (the number of channels available for use) will also affect how easily the system can be intercepted, analyzed, and attacked.

Direct Sequence Spread Spectrum

With direct sequence spread spectrum (DSSS), the stream of data is divided according to a spreading ratio into small pieces and assigned a frequency channel in a parallel form across the entire spectrum. The data signals are combined with a higher data bit rate at transmission points. DSSS has higher throughput than FHSS. Where interference still causes signal problems, DSSS has a special encoding mechanism known as chipping code that, along with redundancy of signal, enables a receiver to reconstruct any distorted data.

Orthogonal Frequency-Division Multiplexing

Orthogonal frequency-division multiplexing (OFDM) allows for tightly compacted transmissions due to using many closely spaced digital subcarriers. The multicarrier modulation scheme sends signals as perpendicular (orthogonal), which do not cause interference with each other. Ultimately, OFDM requires a smaller frequency set or channel band. It also offers greater data throughput than the other frequency use options.

Wireless Security Devices

WIPS and WIDS do for Wi-Fi what IPS and IDS do for wired networks: they focus on radio spectrum use within the area of a network's access points, detecting any signals that might indicate an attempt to intrude into or disrupt an organization's wireless networks. WIDS and WIPS are an important element of providing wireless access point security (which is explored in the "Wireless Access Points" section earlier in this chapter). Such threats might include the following:

- Rogue access points
- Misconfigured access points
- Client misassociation
- Unauthorized association
- MitM attacks
- Ad hoc networks
- MAC spoofing via wireless
- Honeypot or *evil twin* attack
- Denial of service attacks

WIDS detect and notify; WIPS have automatic capabilities to take action to block an offending transmission, deny a device access, shut down a link, etc. SOHO LANs may use a single hardware device with onboard antennae to provide WIPS coverage. Larger organizations may need a Multi Network Controller to direct the activities of multiple WIPS or WIDS throughout the premises.

As WIDS and WIPS products and systems developed, they relied heavily on rule-based or parameter-based techniques to identify those endpoints that would be allowed to connect from those that would not. These techniques included MAC address filtering, RF fingerprinting of known, authorized devices, and other signature-based methods. As with access control issues throughout our networks, though, this has proven over time to be unwieldy; somebody has to spend a great deal of time and effort developing those signatures, and dealing with both the false positive errors that allow a rogue device to connect and the false negative errors that block a legitimate user and their endpoint from getting work done via those networks.

WIPS and WIDS can be network devices or hosted, single boxes or sensors, reporting via inline IP to the control console. Network sensors will look for the control host via TLS, so implementing such systems is fairly straightforward are becoming more prevalent in the marketplace, providing business and organizational customers with subscription-based access control and accounting, anti-malware and antivirus, intrusion detection and pene-tration, and more. At present, many of these SECaaS offerings are aimed at larger corpo-rations. Opportunity exists to scale these downwards to the smaller organizations—which after all have been the hunting grounds for APTs looking to build their next zombie bot-net, harvest exploitable contact and customer lists, or use as stepping stones to conduct an intrusion into targets that serve their overall objectives directly.

Some compliance regimes such as PCI DSS are setting minimum standards for wire-less security scanning, detection, and prevention.

SUMMARY

Throughout this chapter, we looked at how we build trust and confidence into the globe-spanning communications that our businesses, our fortunes, and our very lives depend on. Whether by in-person conversation, videoconferencing, or the World Wide Web, people and businesses *communicate*. Communications, as we saw in earlier chap-ters, involves exchanging ideas to achieve a common pool of understanding—it is *not* just about data or information. Effective communication requires three basic ingredients: a system of symbols and protocols, a medium or a channel in which those protocols exchange symbols on behalf of senders and receivers, and *trust*—not that we always trust every communications process 100 percent nor do we need to!

We also have to grapple with the *convergence* of communications and computing technologies. People, their devices, and their ways of doing business no longer accept old-fashioned boundaries that used to exist between voice, video, TXT and SMS, data, or a myriad of other computer-enabled information services. This convergence transforms what we trust when we communicate and how we achieve that trust. As SSCPs, we need to know how to gauge the trustworthiness of a particular communications system, keep it operating at the required level of trust, and improve that trustworthiness if that's what our stakeholders need. Let's look in more detail at how communications security can be achieved and, based on that, get into the details of securing the network-based elements of our communications systems.

Finally, we saw that our CIA mnemonic for the three pillars of information security is probably not enough. We need to remember that confidentiality doesn't cover the needs for privacy and that information integrity does not build confidence that systems will operate safely, whether with complete and accurate information or in the face of misinformation or distorted, incomplete, or missing data. Nonrepudiation and anonymity have important and vital roles to play in our security architecture, and at the heart of everything we find the need to authenticate. Transparency and auditability provide the closure that makes our due care and due diligence responsibilities complete.

Systems and Application Security

WHICH VIEWPOINT IS THE best one to use when looking at your information security architecture, programs, policies, and procedures? If you're the end user, you might think it's the endpoints and apps that matter most. Senior managers and leaders might think it's the data that inform decisions in business processes from the strategic to operational levels and from long-range planning down to the transaction-by-transaction details of getting business done. Operations managers might emphasize core business processes as the right focal points for your security planning and attentiveness. Your chief finance officer, the purchasing and supply group, or your logistics support teams may see IT security as being parceled out across the different players in your IT supply chain. Other perspectives look more at deployment issues, especially if your organization has moved into the clouds (plural) or is planning such a major migration.

You, as the SSCP on scene, get to look at all of those views at the same time; you have to see it from the ground up.

This chapter is about keeping the installed base of hardware, systems software, apps, data, endpoints, infrastructure, and services all safe and sound, regardless of how these systems and elements are deployed and used. Virtualization of processing, storage, and networks can actually bring more security-enhancing capabilities to your systems and architectures than it does challenges and pitfalls, if you do your homework thoroughly. And as attackers are becoming more proficient at living off the land and not depending upon malware as part of their kill chain activities, it becomes harder to detect or suspect that something not quite normal is going on in your systems or endpoints.

It's time to go back to thinking about the many layers of security that need to be planned for, built in, exercised, and used to mutually support each other.

SYSTEMS AND SOFTWARE INSECURITY

Let's set the context for this chapter by borrowing from the spirit of the OSI seven-layer Reference Model. This can give us a holistic view of everything you need to assess, as you make sure that your organization can do its business reliably by counting on its IT systems and data to be there when they need them to be. We'll also invite our friend CIANA back to visit with us; confidentiality, integrity, availability, nonrepudiation, and authentication are primary characteristics of any information security program and posture, along with safety and privacy. Auditability and transparency are also taking on greater emphasis in many marketplaces and legal systems, so we'll need to keep them in mind as part of our information security planning as well. From the bottom of the stack, let's look at the kinds of questions or issues that need to be addressed as you assess your overall systems security and identify what actions you need to take to remedy any urgent deficiencies.

- **Physical:** How do you protect the hardware elements of your systems throughout their lifecycle? Is your supply chain secure? Does your organization have proper administrative controls in place to ensure that those who provide spare parts, consumables, and repair and maintenance services are trusted and reliable? How are physical security needs addressed via maintenance agreements or warranty service plans? Are adequate records kept regarding repair and replacement actions? Is all of your hardware under configuration management and control? Do you know where all of it is, at any given time? What about equipment disposal, particularly the disposal of storage media or any hardware where *data remanence* may be a concern? Much of this was covered in Chapter 1, "Security Operations and Administration."

- **Operating systems:** Do all of your systems—endpoints, servers, network control and management devices, and security systems properly maintained and kept up-to-date? What about your access control systems—are they kept up-to-date as well? Is your systems software supply chain secure? Do you receive update files or patch kits that are digitally signed by the vendor, and are those signatures validated before the organization applies the updates? How well does your organization exert configuration management and control of these software components? This, too, was covered in some depth in Chapter 1.

- **Network and systems management:** Significant effort is required to design and implement your network architectures so that they meet the security needs as established by administrative policy and guidance. Once you've established a secure network baseline, you need to bring it under configuration management and control in order to keep it secure. In most larger network architectures, it's wise to invest in automated systems and endpoint inventory workflows as part of configuration control as well. Chapter 6, "Network and Communications Security," in conjunction with Chapter 1, "Security Operations and Administration," addresses these important topics and provide valuable information and advice.

- **Data availability and integrity:** Think about CIANA+PS for a moment: every one of those attributes addresses the need to have reliable data available, where it's needed, when it's needed, and in the form that people need to get work done with it. If the data isn't there—or if the reliability of the system is so poor that workers at all levels of the organization cannot count on it—they will improvise, and they will make stuff up if they have to, to keep the production line flowing or to make a sale or to pay a bill. If they can. If they cannot—if the business logic simply cannot operate that way and there are no contingency procedures—then your business stops working. What is the process maturity of your organization's approach to data quality? Do you have procedures to deal with faulty or missing data that maintain systems integrity and operational safety in spite of missing, incomplete, or just plain wrong data as input?

- **Data protection, privacy, and confidentiality:** It's one thing to have the high-quality data your organization needs ready and available when it's needed to get the job done. It's quite another to let that data slip away, through either inadvertent disclosure, small data leaks, or wholesale data exfiltration. Legal, regulatory, and market compliance regimes are becoming more demanding every day; many are now specifying that company officers can be held *personally* responsible for data breaches, and that responsibility can mean substantial fines and even imprisonment.

- **Applications:** Applications can range from fully featured platforms with their own built-in database management capabilities to small, lightweight apps on individual smartphones. These may be commercial products, freeware or shareware; they may even be programs, script files, or other stored procedures and queries written by individual end users in your organization. Your risk management process should have identified these baselines, and identified which ones needed to be under what degree of formal configuration management and control. Chapter 3, "Risk Identification, Monitoring, and Analysis" showed you how to plan and account for all updates and patches, while Chapter 2 demonstrated ways for the information security team to know which systems and endpoints are hosting or using which apps and whether they are fully and properly updated or not.

- **Connections and sessions:** From the security viewpoint, this layer is out here on top of the applications layer, since your users are the ones that use sessions to make connections to your applications and data. It's at this layer that appropriate use policies, business process logic, partnerships and collaboration, and a wealth of other administrative decisions should come together to provide a strong procedural foundation for day-to-day, moment-by-moment use of your IT systems and the data they contain. It's also at this layer where many organizations are still doing things in very ad hoc ways, with spur-of-the-moment decision-making either maintaining and enhancing information security or putting it at risk. From a process or capabilities maturity modeling perspective, is your organization using well-understood, repeatable, auditable, and effective business logic, processes, and operational procedures? Or are you still all learning it as you go? Chapter 3, with its focus on risk management, should provide ways to drive down to the level of individual processes and, in doing so, help the organization know how well it is managing its information risk by way of how it does business day to day.

- **Endpoints:** This is where the data (which is abstract) gets transformed into action in the physical world and where real-world actions get modeled as data. Endpoints can be smartphones, workstations, laptops, point of sales terminals, Supervisory Control and Data Acquisition (SCADA) or industrial process control devices, or IoT devices. How well does your organization maintain and manage these? Which ones are subject to formal configuration management and control, and which ones are not? Can the organization quickly locate where each such device is, with respect to your networks and IT systems, and validate whether it is being used appropriately? What about the maintenance and update of the hardware, software, firmware, and control parameters and data onboard each endpoint, and also the effective configuration management and control of these endpoints?

- **Access management, authentication, authorization, and accounting:** This is probably the most critical layer of your security protocol stack! Everything that an attacker wants to achieve requires access to some part of your systems. Chapter 2 looked in detail at how to flow information security classification and risk management policies into the details of configuring your AAA systems (named for the critical functions of authentication, authorization, and accounting) and setting the details in place to restrict each subject and protect each object. Are your access control processes well-managed, mature, and under configuration management themselves? Do your audit capabilities help reveal potentially suspicious activities that might be an intruder in your midst?

- **Audit:** Every aspect of your organization's use of its IT infrastructures, its software, and its data is going to be subject to some kind of audit, by somebody, and on a continuing basis. From an information security perspective, any audit can find exploitable vulnerabilities in your systems or processes, and that's an opportunity to make urgently needed repairs or improvements. Failing to have those problems fixed on a subsequent audit can result in penalties, fines, or even being denied the ability to continue business operations. Audit requirements force us to make sure that our systems can maintain the *pedigree* of every audit-critical data item, showing its entire life history from first acquisition through every change made to it. Maintaining these *audit trails* throughout your systems is both a design issue and an operations and administration issue (Chapter 1), as well as providing the foundation for any security incident investigations and analysis (Chapter 4); here, we'll do a roundup of those issues and offer some specific advice and details.

- **Business Continuity:** Many different information security issues and control strategies come together to assure the continued survivability and operability of your organization's business functions; in the extreme, information security architectures such as backup and restore capabilities provide for recovery and restart from disruptions caused by attacks, natural disasters, or accidents.

Two major categories of concerns might seem to be missing from that list—and yet, each layer in that "security maturity model" cannot function if they are not properly taken into account.

- **Weaponized malware:** Although many new attack patterns are "living off the land" and using their target's own installed software and systems against them, malware still is a significant and pernicious threat. More than 350,000 new species of malware are observed in the wild *every day*. The old ways of keeping your systems and your organization safe from malware won't work anymore. This applies at every step: imagine, for example, receiving new motherboards for PCs, new endpoints, or new software that has been tampered with by attackers; how would your organization detect this when it happens? We'll look at different approaches later in this chapter, in the section titled "Identify and Analyze Malicious Code and Activity."

- **The security awareness and preparedness of your people:** It's time to junk that idea that your people are your weakest link—that's only the case if you let them be ignorant of the threat and if you fail to equip them with the attitude, the skills, and the tools to *help defend their own jobs* by being part of the active defense of the organization's information and its systems. As with *any* vulnerability, grab this one and turn it around. Start by looking at how your organization onboards new members of staff; look at position-specific training and acculturation. Use the risk management process (as in Chapter 3) to identify the critical business processes that have people-powered procedures that *should be* part of maintaining information security. From the "C-suite" senior leaders through to each knowledge worker at every level in the team, how well are you harnessing that talent and energy to improve and mature the overall information security posture and culture of the organization?

Let's apply this layered perspective starting with software—which we find in every layer of this model, or the OSI seven-layer Reference Model stack, from above the physical to below the people. From there, we'll take a closer look at information quality, information integrity, and information security, which are all intimately related to each other.

Software Vulnerabilities Across the Lifecycle

All software is imperfect, full of flaws. Everything in it, every step across its lifecycle of development, test, use, and support, is the result of compromise. Users never have enough time to step away from their business long enough to thoroughly understand their business logic; analysts cannot spend enough time on working with users to translate that business process logic into functional requirements. Designers are up against the schedule deadlines, as are the programmers, and the testers; even with the best in automated large-scale testing workflows, there is just no way to know that every stretch of code has been realistically tested. Competitive advantage goes to the business or organization that can get *enough* new functionality, that is *working correctly enough*, into production use faster than the others in their marketplace. Perfect isn't a requirement, nor is it achievable.

From the lowliest bit of firmware on up, every bit of device control logic, the operating systems, and the applications have flaws. Some of those flaws have been identified already. Some have not. Some of the identified flaws have been categorized as exploitable vulnerabilities; others may still be exploitable, but so far no one's imagination has been spent to figure out how to turn those flaws into opportunities to do something new and different (and maybe malicious). Even the tools that organizations use to manage software development, such as their integrated development environments (IDEs) and their configuration management systems, are flawed. In some respects, having a software-dependent world reminds us of what Winston Churchill said about the English language: with all those flaws, those logic traps, and those bugs just waiting to bite us, this must be the worst possible way to run a business or a planet-spanning civilization, except for all the others.

That might seem overwhelming, almost unmanageable. And for organizations that do *not* manage their systems, it can quickly become a security expert's worst nightmare waiting to happen. One approach to managing this mountain of possible bad news is to use a software development lifecycle model to think about fault detection, analysis, characterization, prioritization, mitigation, and remediation. You've probably run into software development lifecycle (SDLC) models such as Agile, Scrum, or the classic Waterfall before; as a security specialist, you're not writing code or designing a graphical user interface (GUI). You're not designing algorithms, nor are you implementing data structures or workflows by translating all of that into different programming languages. Let's look at these SDLCs in a more generic way.

Software Development as a Networked Sport

In almost all situations, software is developed *on* a network-based system. Even an individual end user writing their own Excel formulas or a Visual Basic (VBA) macro, strictly for their own use, is probably using resources on some organization's network. They're doing this on a PC, Mac, or other device, which as an endpoint is a full-blown OSI 7-layer stack in its own right. They're drawing upon resources and ideas they see out on the Web, and they're using development tools that are designed and marketed to support collaborative creation and use of data—and sometimes, that data can be *code* as well. An Excel formula is a procedural set of instructions, as is a VBA macro. When these user-defined bits become part of business processes the company depends upon, they've become part of your *shadow IT* system—unknown to the IT team, outside of configuration management, invisible to risk assessment and information security planning.

Larger, more formalized software development is done with a team of developers using a network-enabled IDE, such as Microsoft's Visual Studio; in the Linux world, NetBeans, Code:app:Blocks, or Eclipse CDT provide IDE capabilities. All support teams using networked systems to collaborate in their development activities.

Software development as a networked team sport starts with all of those gaps in analysis, assumptions about requirements, and compromises with schedule and resources that can introduce errors in understanding which lead to designed-in flaws. Now, put your team of developers onto a LAN segment, isolated off from the rest of the organization's systems, and have them use their chosen IDE and methodologies to start transforming user stories and use cases into requirements, requirements into designs, and designs into software and data structures. The *additional* vulnerabilities the company is exposed to in such an approach can include the following:

- Underlying vulnerabilities in the individual server or endpoint devices, their hardware, firmware, OS, and runtime support for applications.

- Vulnerabilities in the supporting LAN and its hardware, firmware, and software.

- Access control and user or subject privilege management errors, as reflected in the synchronization of network and systems management configuration settings such as access control lists, user groups and privileges, and applications allowed or blocked list management.

- Anti-malware and intrusion detection systems that have known vulnerabilities, are not patched or up-to-date, and are using outdated definition or signature data.

- Gaps in coverage of the configuration management and configuration control systems, such that shadow IT or other unauthorized changes can and have taken place; these may or may not introduce exploitable vulnerabilities. Many development teams, with their systems administrators' support, add their own tools, whether homemade, third-party commercial products, or shareware, into their development environments; these can increase the threat surface in poorly understood ways.

- Known vulnerabilities, reported in CVE databases, for which vendors have not supplied patches, updates, or procedural workarounds.

- Process or procedural vulnerabilities in the ways in which the team uses the IDE.

Vulnerabilities also get *built in* by your designers due to some all-too-common shortcomings in the ways that many programmers develop their code.

- **Poor design practices:** Applications are complex programs that designers build up from hundreds, perhaps thousands, of much smaller, simpler units of code. This decomposition of higher-level, more abstract functions into simpler, well-bounded lower-level functions is the heart of any good design process. When designers consistently use proven and well-understood design rules, the designs are more robust and resilient—that is, their required functions work well together and handle problems or errors in well-planned ways.

- **Inconsistent use of design patterns:** A *design pattern* is a recommended method, procedure, or definition of a way to accomplish a task. Experience and analysis have shown us that such design patterns can be built successfully and used safely to achieve correct results. Yet many programs are developed as if "from scratch," as if they are the first-ever attempt to solve that problem or perform that task. Assembling hundreds or thousands of such "first-time" sets of designs can be fraught with peril—and getting them to work can be a never-ending struggle.

- **Poor coding practices:** Since the 1940s, we've known that about 20 classes of bad programming practice can lead to all-too-familiar runtime errors and exploitable vulnerabilities. Universities, schools, and on-the-job training teaches programmers these "thou shalt nots" of programming; still, they keep showing up in business applications and systems software.

- **Inconsistent use (or no use at all) of proven, tested design and code libraries:** Software reuse is the process of building new software from modules of code that have been previously inspected, tested, and verified for correct and safe execution. Such design and code libraries, when published by reputable development teams, are a boon to any software development effort—as long as the right library elements are chosen for the tasks at hand and then used correctly in the program being developed. High-quality libraries can bring a wealth of security-related features built into their designs and code; in many cases, the library developer provides ongoing technical support and participates in common vulnerability reporting with the information systems security community. Sadly, many software teams succumb to schedule and budget pressures and use the first bit of cheap (or free) code that they find on the Internet that seems to fit their needs. Sometimes, too, application programmers speed-read the high-level documentation of a library or a library routine and accept what they read as proof that they've found what they need. Then they just plug it into their application and pray that it works right, never taking the time to read the code itself or verify that it will correctly and safely do what they need it to do *and do nothing else* in the process. There is a growing body of research data that suggests that commercial code libraries are being developed with better security practices in mind, and hence are producing lower rates of vulnerabilities (per thousand lines of source code, for example) than comparable open source libraries are achieving. Open source libraries may also be targets of opportunity for malicious parties to sponsor their own bug hunts, as they seek currently unrecognized vulnerabilities to exploit.

- **Weak enforcement of data typing and data modeling during software development:** A major business platform application, such as an enterprise resource planning (ERP) system, might have tens of thousands of identifiers—names for fields in records, for record types, for variables used in the software internally, and the like.

  - *Data modeling* is a formal process that translates the business logic into named data elements. It formalizes the constraints for initialization of each data item; how new values are input, calculated, produced, and checked against logical constraints; and how to handle errors in data elements. For example, one constraint on a credit card number field might specify the rules for validating it as part of a data set (including cardholder name, expiration date, and so forth); related constraints would dictate how to handle specific validation problems or issues.

- *Data typing* involves the rules by which the programmer can write code that works on a data item. Adding dollars to dates, for example, makes no sense, yet preventing a programming error from doing this requires data typing rules that define how the computer stores calendar dates and monetary amounts, *and* the rules regarding allowable operations on both types taken together. Organizations that manage their information systems with robust data dictionaries and use rigorously enforced data typing in their software development *tend* to see fewer exploitable errors due to data format, type or usage errors.

Every one of those vulnerabilities is an opportunity for an adversary to poison the well by introducing malformed code fragments into libraries being developed or to distort test procedures so that the results mask a vulnerability's existence. Automated testing can produce thousands of pages of output, if one were to actually print it out; more automated tools are used to summarize it, analyze it, and look for tell-tale flags of problems.

But wait, there's more bad news. Once your developers have finished building and testing a new release of a system, an application, or a web app, they've now got to bundle it up as a distribution kit and push it out to all of the servers and endpoints that need to install that update. This process can have its own errors of omission and commission that can lead to an exploitable opportunity for things to go wrong, or to be *made* to go wrong by an intruder in your midst.

Are those vulnerabilities under management? And even if they are, are they easy for an attacker to find and exploit?

Vulnerability Management: Another Network Team Sport

It's commonly accepted wisdom that responding to newly discovered vulnerabilities is important; we must urgently take action to develop and implement a fix, and update all of our affected systems; and while we're waiting for that fix, we must develop a workaround, a procedural way to avoid or contain the risk associated with that vulnerability, as quickly as possible. Yet experience shows us that in almost every business or organizational environment, prudence has to prevail. Businesses cannot operate if faced with a constant stream of updates, patches, and procedural tweaks. For one thing, such nonstop change makes it almost impossible to do any form of regression testing to verify that fixing one problem didn't create three more in some other areas of the organization's IT systems and its business logic. Most organizations, too, do not have the resources to be constantly updating their systems—whether those patches are needed at the infrastructure level, in major applications platforms that internal users depend upon, or in customer-facing web apps. Planned, orderly, intentional change management gives the teams a way to choose which vulnerabilities matter right now, and which ones can and should wait until the next planned build of an update package to the systems as a whole.

The larger your organization and the more diverse and complex its IT and OT architectures are, the greater the benefit to the organization of such a planned and managed process. By bringing all functional area voices together—including those from information security, manufacturing, and operations—the organization can make a more informed plan that spells out which known vulnerabilities will get fixed immediately, which can wait until the next planned release or update cycle, and which ones will just have to continue to wait even longer. This decision process, for example, must decide when to fix which vulnerabilities in the production IT systems and applications and when to do which fixes in the development support systems. (Should you disrupt an ongoing development for an urgent-seeming security fix and possibly delay a planned release of urgently needed capabilities into production use? Or is the potential risk of an exploit too great and the release must be held back until it can be fixed?)

Vulnerability management needs to embrace all of the disciplines and communities of practice across the organization. Business operations departments, customer service organizations, finance, legal, logistics, and many other internal end user constituencies may all have some powerful insights to offer, and skills to apply, as your organization takes on information risk management in a significant way. As your vulnerability management processes mature, you may also find great value in selectively including strategic partners or members of your most important collaboration networks.

✔ Cybersecurity Bill of Materials and Open Source Risk

The Heartbleed SSL vulnerability demonstrated how the widespread adoption of open source code can expose all of us to vulnerabilities. In response, the EU and several US agencies are pushing for all products to have a cybersecurity bill of materials (BOM), which would list each component of the product and its provenance. The details of adopting BOM processes across different industries and markets are still being worked out; watch this space.

Data-Driven Risk: The SDLC Perspective

Any software program—whether it's part of the operating system, an element of a major cloud-hosted applications platform, or a small utility program used during software distribution and update—can be driven to behave badly by the input data it reads in and works on. The classic buffer overflow flaw is, of course, a logic and design flaw at its heart, but it allows user-entered data to cause the program to behave in unanticipated ways, and some of that bad behavior may lead to exploitable situations for the attacker. This is not using malware to hack into our systems—this is using malformed data as input to cause our own systems to misbehave. A traditional database-based attack—the fictional employee who nonetheless gets a paycheck every pay period—has been updated to become the *false invoice* attack, in which the attacker sends a bill (an invoice) to a large company's accounts receivables department. In many cases, small invoices for a few tens of dollars will get paid almost automatically (some human action will be necessary to enter the source of the invoice as if they are a new supplier). The amount of each false invoice can vary and slowly increase. In the United Kingdom alone (not a large marketplace), false invoicing cost businesses upward of £92 million in 2020, according to UKFinance.org. By 2023, Juniper Research predicts, businesses will face up to USD $130 billion in online payment fraud by 2023.

Is false invoicing a human problem or a software problem? Both, actually; failing to identify the proper controls in the overall business process led to software that seemed to *trust* that a new supplier and a small-value invoice was…routine. Safe. (False invoicing is just one of hundreds of examples of the so-called *living off the land* attack patterns.)

Data quality programs should prevent exploits such as false invoicing by instituting the right level of review before creating a new business relationship. Data quality, as a discipline, asks that something be done to verify that the identity claimed on the face of that invoice is actually a real business, with a real presence in the marketplace; furthermore, data quality controls should be validating that this business that just sent in a bill for us to pay is one that we actually *do business with* in the first place.

Those may seem commonsense questions; they are. Yet, they go unasked thousands of times every day.

Coping with SDLC Risks

The good news in all of this is that there's a proven method for keeping these types of risks under control. You already know how to keep the exploitable vulnerabilities inherent in your SDLC systems, processes, and procedures from being turned against you. It takes a series of failures of your preexisting security measures, however, to let that happen and not detect its occurrence.

Access Control

Once inside your systems, intruders can and do have almost a free hand at exploiting any and every imaginable vulnerability, taking advantage of each step in your software development, test, deployment, and support processes to put in their own command and control logic. Multifactor authentication has become a must-have part of any access control system. Controlling and monitoring the lateral movement of users and subjects across your internal network segments must be part of your strategy.

Lateral Data and Code Movement Control

We've already heard more than enough horror stories of operational systems that were inadvertently loaded with test versions of data and software. Your IDE and the LAN segments that support it need stringent *two-way* controls on movement of code and data — to protect bad data and malware moving into the development shop as well as escaping out from it and into your production environments or the Internet at large. This should prevent the movement of code and data out of the test environment and into production unless it's part of a planned and managed "push" of a release into the update distribution process. This will also prevent malware, or maliciously formed bad data, from being exported into production, or the exfiltration of requirements, designs, and entire software libraries out into the wild or the hands of your competitors or adversaries.

Hardware and Software Supply Chain Security

At one level, your hardware, your operating systems, and even the IDE systems as applications themselves are probably coming into your organization via trusted or trustworthy suppliers. You have strong reason to believe, for example, that a major hardware or software vendor who publishes the digital signatures of their software distribution kits (for initial load as well as update of your systems) is worthy of trust — once, of course, you've verified the digital signatures on the items you've just taken delivery of from them. But your software developers may be using open source code libraries, or code snippets they've found on the Internet, which *may* actually do the job that needs to be done…but they may also have some hidden side effects, such as having a trap door or a Trojan horse feature built into them. It might be illuminating to have a conversation with someone in your development teams to gain insight as to how much of such unpedigreed software they incorporate into your organization's systems, services, and products.

Applications Designed with Security in Mind

Strange as it may seem, most applications software is specified, designed, written, and tested by people who rather innocently assume that the world is not a dangerous place. So, how do you, as a non-code-bending, non-software-trained SSCP help your company or organization get more defensive in the ways that it builds and maintains its software? A blog post by the editorial team at Synopsys, in their Software Architecture and Design

blog at www.synopsys.com/blogs/software-security/
principles-secure-software-design/, highlights four key points to ponder.

- Be paranoid. Know that somebodies, somewhere, are out to get you. Lots of them.

- Pay attention to abuse cases, instead of just the "business normal" use cases, as sources of your functional and nonfunctional requirements. Put on your gray hat and think like an attacker would; look at ways of deliberately trying to mislead or misuse your systems. This helps inoculate you (somewhat) against what the Synopsys team calls the three fallacies that lead to complacency about information security needs among software developers.

- Understand that small vulnerabilities cascade together to become just as disruptive as a few large vulnerabilities can be.

- Build things securely so that they last. Build for posterity.

One major problem has been that for decades, the software industry and academia have assumed that managers and senior designers are responsible for secure software design and development. It's no good teaching brand-new programmers about it, because they don't manage software projects, according to this view. As a result, an awful lot of insecure software gets written, as bad habits get engrained by use.

A great resource to learn with is the Open Web Application Security Project (OWASP), at www.owasp.org. OWASP is a nonprofit source of unbiased, vendor-neutral and platform-agnostic information and provides advice and ideas about the right ways to "bake in" security when designing web apps.

As the SSCP, you are the security specialist who can help your organization's software developers better appreciate the threat, recognize the abuse cases, and advocate for penetration-style security testing during development—not just after deployment!

Baking the security in from the start of software development requires turning a classic programmer's paradigm inside-out. Programmers are trusting souls; they trust that others will do their jobs correctly. They trust that users will "do the right thing," that network and systems security will validate the user, or that access control "done by someone else" will prevent any abuses. (Managers like this paradigm, too, because it shifts costs and efforts to other departments while making their jobs simpler and easier.) Instead, it's more than high time to borrow a page from the zero-trust school of thought for networks:

Trust no one, trust no input data, ever, and verify everything before you use it.

Listen to the Voice of the User

Too many organizations make it difficult for end users to call attention to problems encountered when they're using the IT systems and applications on the job. Help desks can often seem unfriendly, even downright condescending, when their first response to a frustrated user's call for help seems to be "Did you flush your cookies and browser cache yet?" And yes, it's true that the more details that can be captured during the trouble ticket creation process, the greater the likelihood that the problem can be investigated and resolved.

As an SSCP, you're asking the end users to maintain heightened awareness, and be on guard for any signs that their systems, applications, hardware, or even the flow of business around them seems…abnormal. You need to hear about phishing and vishing attempts; you need to multiply the numbers of eyes and ears and minds that are watching out for anomalies.

Do you have processes that truly invite end-user engagement and reporting? Do those processes provide useful feedback to users, individually, as groups, and to the entire organization, that demonstrates the value of the problem reports or security questions they submit? Do you provide them with positive affirmation that they're getting it right when security assessments or ethical penetration testing produces good findings?

If not, you've got some opportunities here. Take advantage of them.

Risks of Poorly Merged Systems

The rapid pace of corporate mergers and acquisitions and the equally rapid pace at which business units get spun off to become their own separate entities mean that many organizations end up with a poorly integrated smash-up of IT architectures. Often these are badly documented to begin with; in the process of the corporate reorganization, much of the tacit knowledge of where things are, how they work, and what vulnerabilities still exist and need attention disappeared with the key employees in IT, information security, or operational business units when they left the company.

If you've inherited such a hodge-podge of systems, in all likelihood you do not have anything remotely close to a well-understood, clean, and secure environment. The chances could be very high that somewhere in that mess is a poorly implemented and highly vulnerable community outreach or charity event web page, started as a pet project of a former employee or manager. Such web pages, or other shadow IT systems, could easily allow an intruder to gain access to everything in your new merged corporate environment. Kate Fazzini, in her book *Kingdom of Lies: Unnerving Adventures in the World of Cybercrime*,[1] illustrates one such example at a major financial institution, showing just how difficult it can be for even a well-equipped and highly trained security operations center team to find such gaping holes in their organization's cyber-armor.

In such circumstances, your first best bet might be to do some gray-box ethical penetration testing, possibly using a purple team strategy (in which the attacking red team and the defending blue team coordinate their efforts, share their findings, and work hand-in-glove every day) to gain the best understanding of the overall architecture and its weaknesses. From there, you can start to prioritize.

[1] Fazzini, Kate. 2019. Kingdom of Lies: Unnerving Adventures in the World of Cybercrime. ISBN 978-1250201348. St. Martin's Press.

Remember that your company's own value chains are coupled into larger value streams as they connect with both upstream and downstream relationships. The suppliers, vendors, and partners that help your organization build and deliver its products and services may face this same mergers and acquisitions systems integrity and security risks. Many of your strategic customers may also be facing similar issues. It's prudent to identify those upstream and downstream players who *might* be significant sources of risk or vulnerability to your own value chain and actively engage with them to seek ways to collaborate on reducing everybody's joint risk exposure and threat surfaces.

Hard to Design It Right, Easy to Fix It?

This is perhaps the most pernicious thought that troubles every software development team and every user of the software that they depend on in their jobs and in their private lives. Hardware, after all, is made of metal, plastic, glass, rubber, and dozens of other physical substances. Changing the hardware is hard work, we believe. A design error that says that our SOHO router overheats and burns out quickly, because we didn't provide enough ventilation, might require a larger plastic enclosure. That design change means new injection molds are needed to cast that enclosure's parts; new assembly line processes are needed, maybe requiring changes to the fixtures and tooling; and new shipping and packing materials for the empty enclosure and the finished product will be needed. That's a lot of work, and a lot of change to manage! But changing a few lines of code in something that exists only as a series of characters in a source code file seems *easy* by comparison.

This false logic leads many managers, users, and programmers to think that it's easy and simple to add in a missing feature or change the way a function works to better suit the end user's needs or preferences. It's just a simple matter of programming, isn't it, if we need to fix a bug we discovered after we deployed the application to our end users?

Right?

In fact, we see that software development is a constant exercise in balancing trade-offs.

- Can we really build all of the requirements our users say they need?
- Can we really test and validate everything we built and show that it meets the requirements?
- Can we do that for a price that we quoted or contracted for and with the people and development resources we have?
- Can we get it all done *before* the marketplace or the real world forces us to change the build-to requirements?

As with any project, software development managers constantly trade off risks versus resources versus time. Some of the risks involve dissatisfied customers when the product is finally delivered; some risks involve undetected but exploitable vulnerabilities in that product system. And all projects face a degree of uncertainty that the people, money, time, and other resources needed for development and acceptance testing won't be as available as was assumed when the project was started—or that those resources will be there to support the maintenance phase once the project goes operational.

How much security is enough to keep what sort of applications secure? As with anything else in the IT world, the information security aspects of any app should be a requirements-driven process.

✔ Security Requirements: Functional or Nonfunctional?

In systems analysis, a *functional requirement* is one that specifies a task that must be done; the requirement may also specify how users can verify that the task has completed successfully or if one of many error conditions have occurred. For example, the requirement might state that pressing the "start engine" button causes prerequisite safety conditions to be checked and then activate various subsystems, step-by-step, to start the engine; failure of any step aborts the start process, returns all subsystems to their safe pre-start condition, and sends alerts to the operator for resolution. By contrast, a *nonfunctional requirement* states a general characteristic that applies to the system or subsystem as a whole but is not obviously present in any particular feature or function. Security requirements are often considered nonfunctional. This can be confusing, as a few requirements examples can suggest.

- *Safety requirements* in a factory process control system might state that "the system will require two-factor authentication and two-step manual selection and authorization prior to allowing any function designated as safety-critical to be executed." As a broad statement, this is hard to test for; yet, when allocated down to specific subfunctions, either these specific verification steps are present in the module-level requirements, then built into the design, and observable under test, or they are not. Any as-built system element that *should* do such safety checks that does not is in violation of the requirements. So, is such a safety requirement functional or nonfunctional?

- *Confidentiality requirements* in a knowledge bank system might state that "no unauthorized users can view, access, download or use data in the system." This (and other) requirements might drive the specification, design, implementation, and use of the identity management and access control systems elements. But does the flow-down of this requirement stop there? Or do individual applications inherit a user authentication and authorization burden from this one high-level requirement?

- *Nonrepudiation requirements* for a clinical care system could dictate that there must be positive control for orders given by a physician, nurse practitioner, or other authorized caregiver, both as record of care decisions and as ways to prevent an order being unfilled or not carried out. The log of orders given is a functional requirement (somebody has to build the software that builds the log each time an order is entered). But is the nonrepudiation part functional or nonfunctional?

Many systems analysts will consider any requirement allocated to the human elements of the system as nonfunctional, since (they would argue) if the software or hardware isn't built to execute that function, that function isn't really a deliverable capability of the system. This also is the case, they'd argue, for functions "properly" allocated to the operating system or other IT infrastructure elements. Access control, for example, is rarely built into specific apps or platform systems, because it is far more efficient and effective to centralize the development and management of that function at the infrastructure level. Be careful—this train of thought leads to apps that have zero secure functions built into them, even the most trivial of input data validation!

Performance requirements, those analysts would say, are by nature functional requirements in this sense. The "-ilities"—the capabilities, availabilities, reliabilities, and all of the characteristics of the system stated in words that end in -ilities or -ility—are (they say) nonfunctional requirements.

As an SSCP, you'll probably not be asked to adjudicate this functional versus nonfunctional argument. You may, however, have the opportunity to take statements from the users about what they need the system to do, and how they need to see it done, and see where CIANA+PS-related concerns need to be assessed, analyzed, designed, built, tested, and then put to use. That includes monitoring, too, of course; there's no sense building something if you do not keep an eye on how it's being used and how well it's working.

We live and work in a highly imperfect world, of course; it's almost a certainty that a number of CIANA+PS-driven functional and nonfunctional requirements did not get captured in the high-level systems requirements documentation. Even if they did, chances are good that not all of them were properly implemented in the right subsystems, elements, or components of the overall application system. The two-view look as described earlier (from requirements downward and from on-the-floor operational use upward) should help SSCPs make their working list of possible vulnerabilities.

Possible vulnerabilities, we caution. These are places to start a more in-depth investigation; these are things to ask others on the IT staff or information security team about. Maybe you'll be pleasantly surprised and find that many of them are already on the known vulnerabilities or issues watch lists, with resolution plans in the works.

But maybe not.

Hardware and Software Supply Chain Security

Your organization's IT supply chain provides all of the hardware, firmware, software, default initialization data, operators' manuals, installation kits, and all of the spares and consumables that become the systems the organization depends upon. That chain doesn't start with the vendor who sends in the invoice to your accounts receivables or purchasing department—it reaches back through each vendor you deal with and through the suppliers who provide them with the subassemblies, parts, and software elements they bundle together into a system or product they lease or sell to your company. It reaches even further back to the chip manufacturers and to the designers *they* used to translate complex logic functions into the circuit designs and the firmware that drives them. (Every instruction your smartphone's CPU executes is performed by *microcode*, that is, firmware inside the CPU, that figures out what that instruction means and how to perform it. And that microcode…well, at some point it does turn into circuits that do simple things, many layers further down.)

Chapter 1 laid the foundations for operating a secure IT supply chain by stressing the importance of having a well-controlled and well-managed baseline. That baseline has to capture every element—every hardware item and every separate piece of software and firmware—so that your configuration management and control systems can know each instance of it by its revision level and update date and version ID. Effective baseline management requires that you know where each item in that inventory is and who its authorized users or subjects are. It requires that you be able to detect when a configuration item (as each of these manageable units of hardware, software, and data are known) goes missing. Security policies should then kick in almost automatically to prevent CIs that have "gone walkabouts" from reconnecting to your systems until they've gone through a variety of health, status, use, and integrity checks—if you let them reconnect at all. (There's a valid business case to be made to say that you just go ahead and "brick" or destructively lock out a device that's been reported as lost or stolen, rather than spend the effort to evaluate and rehabilitate it and run the risk that you've missed something in the process.)

It's been mentioned several times already, but it bears repeating. Software and firmware updates should not be allowed to be performed if they're not digitally signed and those signatures verified, all as part of your change control process. Change *management* should also be involved, as a way of mitigating the risk of an unexpected update being not what it seems to be on its surface.

Positive and Negative Models for Software Security

Ancient concepts of law, safety, and governance give us the idea that there are two ways to control the behavior of complex systems. *Positive control*, or *allowed listing*, lists by name those behaviors that are allowed, and thus everything else is prohibited. *Negative control*, or *blocked listing*, lists by name those behaviors that are prohibited, and thus everything else is allowed. (These are sometimes referred to as German and English common law, respectively.)

Antivirus or anti-malware tools demonstrate both of these approaches to systems security. Software allowed listing, port forwarding rules, or parameters in machine learning behavioral monitoring systems all aim to let previously identified and authorized software be run or installed, connections be established, or other network or system behavior be considered as "normal" and hence authorized. Malware signature recognition and (again) machine learning behavioral monitoring systems look for things known to be harmful to the system or similar enough to known malware that additional human authorization steps must be taken to allow the activity to continue.

A quick look at some numbers suggest why each model has its place. It's been estimated that in 2018, more than a million new pieces of malware were created every month "in the wild." As of this writing, AV-TEST GmbH notes on its website that it observes and categorizes more than 350,000 new malicious or potentially unwanted programs (PUPs) or applications (PUAs) every day, with a current total exceeding 875 million species. Although many are simple variations on exploits already in use, that's a lot of new signatures to keep track of! By contrast, a typical medium to large-sized corporation might have to deal with authenticating from 1,000 to 10,000 new applications, or new versions of applications, that it considers authenticated to be used on its systems and endpoints.

Positive control models, if properly implemented, can also be a major component of managing system and applications updates. The details of this are beyond the scope of this book; that said, using an allowed list system as part of how your organization manages all of its endpoints, all of its servers, and all of its devices in between can have several key advantages.

- As new versions of apps (or new apps) are authorized for use, a "push" of the approved allowed list to all devices can help ensure that old versions can no longer run without intervention or authorization.

- While new versions of apps are still being tested (for compatibility with existing systems or for operability considerations), the IT managers can prevent the inadvertent update of endpoints or servers.

Individual users and departments may have legitimate business needs for unique software, not used by others in the company; allowed list systems can keep this under control, down to the by-name individual who is requesting exceptions or overriding (or attempting to override) the allowed list system.

- Whitelisting can be an active part of separation of duties and functions, preventing the execution of otherwise authorized apps by otherwise authorized users when not accessing the system from the proper set of endpoints.

- Whitelisting can be an active part in license and seat management if a particular app is licensed only to a fixed number of users.

Is Blocked Listing Dead? Or Dying?

SSCPs ought to ask this about *every* aspect of information systems security. Fundamentally, this question is asking whether a positive or negative security model provides the best approach to information risk management and control. Both blocked and allowed listing have their place in access control, identity management, network connectivity, and traffic routing and control, as well as with operating systems and application software installation, update, and use. Some business processes (and their underlying information infrastructures) simply cannot work with allowed listing but can achieve effective levels of security with blocked listing instead. Crowdsourcing for data (such as crowd-science approaches like Zooniverse) are impractical to operate if all users and data they provide must be subject to positive security control, for example. Anti-malware and advanced threat detection systems, on the other hand, are increasingly becoming more reliant on allowed listing. SSCPs need to appreciate the basic concepts of both control models (positive and negative) and choose the right approach for each risk context they face.

Let's narrow down the question for now to application software only. NIST and many other authorities and pundits argue that allowed listing is the best (if not the only sensible) approach when dealing with highly secure environments. These environments are characterized by the willingness to spend money, time, and effort in having strong, positive configuration management and control of all aspects of their systems. User-written code, for example, just isn't allowed in such environments, and attempts to introduce it can get one fired (or even prosecuted!). Positive control is *trust-centric*—for it to work, you have to trust your software logistics, support, and supply chain to provide you with software that meets or exceeds both your performance requirements *and* your information security needs across the lifecycle of that software's use in your organization. Making positive security software control work requires administrative effort; the amount of effort is strongly related to the number of applications programs you need to allow, the frequency of their updates, and the numbers of systems (servers, endpoints, or both) that need to be under positive control.

Blocked listing is of course *threat-centric*. It's been the bedrock of anti-malware and antivirus software and hybrid solutions for decades. It relies on being able to define or describe the behavior signatures or other aspects of potentially harmful software. If a behavior, a digital signature, a file's hash, or other parameters aren't on the blocked list, the potential threat wins access to your system. The administrative burden here is shifted to the threat monitoring and intelligence community that supports the blocked list system vendor (that is, we transfer part of this risk to the anti-malware provider, rather than address it ourselves locally).

Positive security control is sometimes described as requiring a strong authoritarian culture and mind-set in the organization; it's argued that if users feel that they have an "inalienable right" to load and use any software that they want to, any time, then whitelisting stands in the way of them getting their job done. Yet blocked listing approaches work well (so far) when one central clearinghouse (such as an anti-malware provider) can push signature updates out to thousands if not millions of systems, almost all of them running different mixes of operating systems, applications, vendor-supplied updates and security patches, and locally grown code.

Software development shops probably need isolated "workbench" or lab systems on which their ongoing development software can evolve without the administrative burdens of an allowed list system. (Containerized virtual machines are probably safer and easier to administer and control for such purposes.) Academic or ethical hacking environments may also need to operate in a blocked, allowed, or no-list manner, depending on the task at hand. Ideally, other risk mitigation and control strategies can keep anything harmful in such labs from escaping (or being exfiltrated) out into the wild.

While the death certificate for negative control hasn't been signed yet, there does seem to be a strong trend in the marketplace. Until it is, and until all of the legacy systems that use such approaches are retired from the field, SSCPs will still need to understand how they work and be able to appreciate when they still might be the right choice for a specific set of information risk mitigation and control needs.

INFORMATION SECURITY = INFORMATION QUALITY + INFORMATION INTEGRITY

There's a simple maxim that ought to guide the way we build, protect, and use every element of our IT systems: if the data isn't correct, the system cannot behave correctly and may in fact misbehave in harmful, unsafe, or dangerous ways.

Whether you think about information systems security in terms of the CIA triplet, CIANA, or even CIANA+PS, every one of those attributes is about the information that our information systems are creating, storing, retrieving, and using. Whether we call it information or data doesn't really matter; its quality ought to be the cornerstone of our foundational approach to systems security and integrity. Yet it's somewhat frightening to realize how many systems security books, courses, practitioners, and programs ignore it; or at best, have delegated it to the database administrators or the end users to worry about.

Let's go a step further: audit requirements force us to keep a change log of every piece of data that might be subject to analysis, verification, and review by the many different auditors that modern organizations must contend with. That audit trail or pedigree is the evidence that the auditors are looking for, when they're trying to validate that the systems have been being used correctly and that they've produced the correct, required results, in order to stamp their seal of compliance approval upon the system and the organization. That audit trail also provides a powerful source of insight during investigations when things go wrong; it can provide the indications and even the evidence that proves who was at fault, as well as exonerating those who were not responsible. Auditable data can be your "get out of jail free" card—and as a member of the security team, you may need one if the organization gets itself into a serious legal situation over a data breach, information security incident, or a systems failure of any kind.

> ## ✔ Be Prepared for Ransom Attacks!
>
> Ransom attacks (with and without malware) have fast become big business worldwide for APTs large and small. When (not *if*) your systems are targeted by a ransom or ransomware attack, your senior leadership and managers will have a very stark and painful choice among three options: (1) pay up, and hope they deliver an unlock code that works; (2) don't pay up, and reload your systems from backup images and data (so long as you're 100 percent sure that they are 100 percent free of the ransom intruder or their malware) (3) don't pay up, reload what you can, and rebuild everything else from scratch. Norsk Hydro demonstrates the pitfalls and the costs—$60 million overall, with insurance paying barely 10% of that. See William Turton's analysis at `https://www.bloomberg.com/news/features/2020-07-23/how-to-survive-ransomware-attack-without-paying-ransom` for an insightful after-action analysis.
>
> No matter which choice your leadership may make, you have to do the most thorough job you can to ensure that the new systems you rebuild do not have that same ransom intruder or their ransomware inside and that you've plugged the holes that they snuck in through.

Data Modeling

Data quality starts with *data modeling*, which is the process of taking each type of information that the business uses and defining the constraints that go with it. Purchase amounts, prices, and costs, for example, are defined in a specific currency; if the business needs to deal with foreign exchange, then that relationship (how many U.S. dollars is a Mexican peso or Swiss franc worth) is not tied to an inventory item or an individual payment. The business logic defines how the business *should* (emphasis on the imperative) know whether the *value* for that field for that item makes sense or does not. Almost all data that organizations deal with comes in groups or sets—consider all of the different types of information on your driver's license, or in your passport, for example—and those sets of data are grouped or structured together into larger sets. Employee records all have certain items in common, but employees hired under one kind of contract may have different *types* of information associated with them than other employees do. (Salaried employees won't have an hourly rate or overtime factor, for example.)

Data dictionaries provide centralized repositories for such business rules, and in well-managed applications development and support environments, the organization works hard to ensure that the rules in the metadata in the data dictionary are built into the logic of the application used by the business.

Without a data dictionary as a driving force in the IT infrastructure, the organization resorts to old-fashioned people-facing procedures to capture those business logic rules. That procedural knowledge might be part of initial onboarding and training of employees; it might only exist in the user manual for a particular application or the desk-side "cheat sheet" used by an individual worker.

All organizations face a dilemma when it comes to procedural knowledge. Procedural knowledge is what workers in your organization use to produce value, at the point of work; this knowledge (and experience) guides them in shaping raw input materials and data into products and services. Quality management calls this point the *gemba* (a term borrowed from the Japanese), and as a result, many quality management and process maturity programs will advise "taking a *gemba walk*" through the organization as a way to gain first-hand insight into current practice within the organization. The smarter your people at the gemba, where the real value-producing work gets done in any organization, the more that those people know about their job. The more they understand the meaning of the data that they retrieve, use, create, receive, and process, the greater their ability to protect your organization when something surprising or abnormal happens. But the more we depend on smart and savvy people, the more likely it is that we do not understand all of our own business logic. This data about "how to do things" is really data about how to use data; we call it procedural metadata. (Think about taking a gemba walk of your own through your IT and information security workspaces throughout the organization; what might you learn?)

What can happen when that procedural metadata is not kept sufficiently secure? Loss or corruption of this procedural and business logic knowledge could cause critical business processes to fail to work correctly. At best, this might mean missed business opportunities (similar to suffering a denial-of-service [DOS] attack); at worst, this could lead to death or injury to staff, customers or bystanders, damage to property, and expenses and exposure to liability that could kill the business.

What can the SSCP do? In most cases, the SSCP is not, after all, a knowledge manager or a business process engineer by training and experience. In organizations where a lot of the business logic and procedural knowledge exists in personal notebooks, on yellow stickies on physical desktops, or in human experience and memory, the SSCP can help reduce information risk and decision risk by letting the business impact analysis (BIA) and the vulnerability assessment provide guidance and direction. Management and leadership need to set the priorities—which processes, outcomes, or assets need the most security attention and risk management, and which can wait for another day. And when the SSCP is assessing those high-priority processes and finds evidence that much of the business logic is in tacit form, inside the heads of the staff, or in soft, unmanageable and unprotected paper notes and crib sheets, that ought to signal an area for process *and* security improvement.

✔ Zero Trust and Data Protection: Encrypt, Tokenize, or Isolate?

Zero trust architectures plan for data protection by assuming that adversaries will get at your data, one way or another; they'll either steal copies of it, destroy it, or both, as part of their attack. Encryption and tokenization are both methods of making any stolen data worthless to an attacker (presuming of course that your cryptographic systems are fully updated and strong enough). Encryption may provide excellent protection at the file or disk volume level, and of course pays off well for protecting data in motion; but it may impose significant overhead when trying to separately encrypt each field in a record of a database or data warehouse. Tokenization, by contrast, replaces sensitive information with a placeholder token (usually produced with a cryptographic hash), with tokens being generated at database load and by input fields on user views, forms, and interfaces. This preserves the form and structure of data without the overhead of trying to encrypt each field.

Tokenizing approaches may prove more affordable and effective than encryption-based solutions, but as with all things, there are tradeoffs. Higher granularity (i.e., fields, not records) for data protection may be more secure, but will have implementation and runtime costs.

One further strategy is to focus on isolating data of like classification and categorization to separate domains, regions, or segments of your overall IT/OT architecture; this also helps reduce the exposure to lateral movement risks.

Preserving Data Across the Lifecycle

When we talk about data protection across its lifecycle, we actually refer to two distinct timeframes: from creation through use to disposal, and the more immediate cycle of data being at rest, in motion, and in use. In both cases, systems and security architects need to consider how the data might be corrupted, lost, disclosed to unauthorized parties, or not available in an authoritative and reliable form where authorized users and subjects need it, when they need it. Here are some examples:

- Error correction and retransmission in protocols such as TLS are actually providing protection against data loss (while UDP does not).

- Digital signatures provide protection against data loss and corruption.

- HTTPS (and TLS underneath it) provide layers of protection against inadvertent disclosure or misrouting of data to the wrong party.

- Other protocol measures that prevent MITM or session hijacking attacks protect data integrity, confidentiality, and assure that it only flows to known, authenticated recipients.

- Encrypted backup copies of data sets, databases, or entire storage volumes provide forward security in time—when read back and decrypted at a future date, the file content, signatures, secure file digests, etc., all can attest to its integrity.

- Access control systems should be accounting for all attempts to access data, whether it is stored in primary use locations (on production servers, for example), in hot backup servers in alternate locations, on load-balancing servers (whether in the cloud or in an on-premises data center), or in archival offline backup storage.

Today, most cloud storage providers (even free Dropbox or OneDrive accounts) bulk encrypt individual customer files and folder trees and then stripe them across multiple physical storage devices, as a way of eliminating or drastically reducing the risks of inadvertent disclosure. This does mean that on any given physical device at your cloud hosting company's data center, multiple customers' data is commingled (or cohabitating) on the same device. The encryption prevents disclosure of any data if the device is salvaged or pulled for maintenance or if one customer or the cloud hosting company is served with digital discovery orders. Cloud providers know that providing this type of security is all but expected by the marketplace today; nonetheless, check your SLA or TOR to make sure, and if in doubt, ask.

Business continuity and disaster recovery planning have a vital role to play in being the drivers for establishing your organization's data backup and recovery policies, plans, and procedures. Those plans, as Chapter 3 points out, are driven in large part by the business impact assessment (BIA), which was the output of the risk assessment process. The BIA also drove the creation of the information security classification guide and its procedures (your firm does *have* and *use* one of those, doesn't it?). Taken together these spell out what data needs to be made available *how quickly* in the event of a device failure, a catastrophic crash of one or more of your systems or applications platforms, or a ransom attack or malware infestation. Chapter 4 showed that as part of incident response, systems restoration and recovery needs to not only get the hardware, OS, and applications back up and running again but also must get databases, files, and other instances of important data back to the state it needs to be so that business activities can be started up again.

✔ Preventing a Blast from the Past

There's always the risk that the data, software, or systems images you write to backing storage is infected with malware that your current anti-malware scanners cannot detect. Protect against being infected by the sins of the past by reloading such backup data into isolated sandbox systems and thoroughly scanning it with the most up-to-date anti-malware signatures and definitions before using that data or software to reload into your production systems.

Two potential weaknesses in most systems architectures are data moving laterally within the organization—but still in transit—and data as it is processed for display and use in an endpoint device. (Remember that data that never goes to an endpoint is of questionable value to the organization; if the data dictionary defines no business logic for using it, it's probably worth asking why do you have it in the first place, and keep it secure and backed up in the second place.)

East-West (Internal) Data Movement   Chapter 5, "Cryptography," looked at some of the issues in so-called *east-west* or internal data flows, particularly if the organization routinely encrypts such data for internal movements.[2] These internal flows can occur in many ways depending upon your overall architecture.

- Between physical servers in different organizational units or locations
- Between virtual servers (which may support different applications or business processes)
- Across system and network segmentation boundaries
- From production servers to archival or backup servers
- As content push from headquarters environments to field locations

[2] Note that *north-south* data flows are the ones between servers and external clients or users.

- As part of load balancing and service delivery tuning across an enterprise system spanning multiple time zones or continents
- Between virtual servers, data warehouses, or data lakes maintained in separate cloud provider environments, but as part of a hybrid cloud system
- To and from cloud servers and on-premise physical servers or data centers

A simple example is the movement of data from a regional office's Dropbox or Google Docs cloud storage services into a SharePoint environment used at the organization's headquarters. A more complex example might involve record or transaction-level movement of customer-related data around in your system. In either case, you need to be able to determine whether a particular data movement is part of an authorized activity or not. When application logic and access control tightly control and monitor the use of sensitive data, then you are reasonably assured that the data has been under surveillance—that is, subject to full monitoring—regardless of where and how it is at rest, in use, or in transit. In the absence of such strong application logic, logging, and access control, however, you may be facing some significant CIANA+PS security concerns.

Keep in mind that data movement east-west can be at any level of granularity or volume; it can be a single record, a file, a database, or an entire storage subsystem's content that is in motion and therefore potentially a security concern. Real-time monitoring of such movement can be done in a number of ways, which all boil down to becoming your own man-in-the-middle on almost every connection within your systems. Fingerprinting techniques, such as generating a digital signature on any data flow that meets or exceeds certain security thresholds for sensitivity, can be used as part of enhanced logging. Each step you add takes time which impacts throughput, while each piece of metadata (such as a tag or signature) to each data flow adds to your overall storage needs.

At the heart of the east-west data movement problem is the risk that your efforts to monitor and control this traffic put you in the role of being your own man-in-the-middle attacker. This can have ethical and legal consequences of its own. Most companies and organizations allow for some personal use of the organization's IT systems and its Internet connection. This means that even the most innocent of HTTPS sessions—such as making reservations for an evening out with one's family—can involve personal use of encrypted traffic. Employee VoIP calls to medical practitioners or educational services providers are (in most jurisdictions) protected conversations, and if your acceptable use policies allow them to occur from the workplace or over employer-provided IT systems, you run the risk of violating the protections required for such data.

At some point, if most of your internal network traffic is encrypted, you have no practical way of knowing whether any given data stream is legitimately serving the business needs of the organization or if it is actually data being exfiltrated by an attacker without having some way of inspecting the encrypted contents itself or by adding another layer of encapsulation that can authoritatively show that a transfer is legitimate. Some approaches to this dilemma include the addition of hardware security modules (HSMs), which provide high-integrity storage of encryption keys and certificates, and then using so-called *TLS inspection* capabilities to act as a decrypting/inspecting/re-encrypting firewall at critical east-west data flow junctions. The throughput penalties on this can be substantial, without significant investment.

Data in Use at the Endpoint   Imagine that your user has queried data from a corporate server via an authorized app installed on their smartphone or other endpoint. That app has been configured to retrieve that data via an encrypted channel, and thus a set of encrypted data arrives in that smartphone. Should the data be decrypted at the endpoint for use? If so, several possible use cases need to be carefully considered regarding how to protect this data in use at the endpoint.

- **Data display and output:** The human user probably cannot make use of encrypted data; but while it's being displayed for them, another person (or another device) might be able to shoulder-surf that display surface and capture the data in its unencrypted form. Malware, screen capture tools, or built-in diagnostic capabilities on the endpoint itself might also be able to capture the data as it is displayed or output.

- **Data download or copy to another device:** The endpoint may be able to copy the now-decrypted data to an external storage device, or send it via Bluetooth, NFC, or another Wi-Fi or network connection to another device; this can happen with or without the end user's knowledge or action.

- **Data remanence:** Once the use of that decrypted data is complete, data still remains on the device. As shown in Chapter 5, special care must be taken to ensure that all copies of the decrypted data, including temporary, modified versions of it, are destroyed, wherever they might be on the endpoint. Endpoint management can provide significant levels of protection against loss or exposure of sensitive data in the event an endpoint (under management) is lost or stolen, as Chapter 6 examined.

- **Human covert paths:** The human end user of this endpoint may deliberately or inadvertently commingle knowledge and information, exposing one set of sensitive data to the wrong set of users, for example. This can be as innocent as a consultant who "technically levels" what two clients are asking him to do into a proposal for a third (and might violate contracts, ethics, or both in doing so). It can also happen when endpoints are used for personal as well as work-related information processing.

Note that some data, and some encryption processes, can provide for ways to keep the data encrypted while it is being used and yet not have its meaning revealed by such use. This sounds like some kind of alchemy or magic going on—as if we are adding two secret numbers together and getting a third, the meaning of which we can use immediately but without revealing anything about the two numbers we started with. (Hmm. Said that way, it's not so hard to imagine. There are an infinite number of pairs of numbers x, y that add together to the same result. Knowing that result doesn't tell you anything about x or y, except perhaps that if one of them is larger than the sum, the other must be smaller. That's not a lot to go on as a codebreaker.) Such *homomorphic encryption* systems are starting to see application in a variety of use cases.

Your chosen threat modeling methodology may help you gain additional insight into and leverage over these issues and others. (See Chapter 3's "Threat Modeling" section for details.) It's also worth discussing with your cloud services provider, if your organization has concerns about internal lateral movements of information, even if all of those information assets are hosted within the same cloud system. You may also find it useful to investigate (ISC)²'s Certified Cloud Security Professional (CCSP) program, as a way to sharpen your knowledge and skills in dealing with issues like these.

IDENTIFY AND ANALYZE MALICIOUS CODE AND ACTIVITY

It's well beyond the scope of this book to look at how to analyze and understand what any particular strain of malware might be trying to do. The *Grey Hat Hacker* series of books provides an effective introduction to the whole field of *reverse engineering* of software, malware or not, and if you've an interest or a need to become that kind of ethical hacker, they are a great place to start. (It does require a good sense of what software engineering is all about, and although you do not need an advanced degree to reverse engineer software, it might help.)

It's also becoming harder to separate the effects that malware may have on your systems, servers, and endpoints from the effects of malicious activity that is *not* using malformed code at all. That said, with millions of new types of malware appearing in the wild every week, your users are bound to encounter it. As new malware types proliferate and become part of any number of kill chains, it's probably more useful to characterize them by broader characteristics such as:

- **End-user interaction:** Scareware, ransomware, and many phishing payloads may display screens, prompts, or other content that attempt to get end users to take some kind of action. In doing so, the user unwittingly provides the malware with the opportunity to take other steps, such as download or install more of its payload, copy files, or even start up a ransom-related file encryption process.

- **End-user or endpoint passive monitoring:** Keystroke loggers, screen capture, web-cam and microphone access, and other tools can gather data about the system, its surroundings, and even its geographic location, as well as gather data about its end user, all without needing the end user to take any enabling actions. These tools are often used as part of reconnaissance and surveillance activities by attackers.

- **Command-and-control functions:** These payloads seek to install or create processes and subject (user) IDs that have elevated privileges or otherwise grant capabilities that allow them to take greater control of the system.

Malicious *activities*, by stark contrast, do not require the installation of any new software capabilities into your servers or endpoints. A disgruntled employee, for example—or the spouse, roommate, or significant other of an otherwise happy and productive employee—might abuse their login privileges to find ways in which they can perform tasks that are detrimental to the organization. Users, for example, are supposed to be able to delete their own files and make backup copies of them—but not delete everyone else's files or make their own backup copies of everything in the company's databases or systems files.

Let's take a closer look.

Malware

Malware, or software that is malicious in intent and effect, is the general name for any type of software that comes into your system without your full knowledge and consent, performs some functions you would not knowingly authorize it to, and in doing so diverts compute resources from your organization. It may also damage your data, your installed software, or even your computer hardware in the process. Cleaning up after a malware infestation can also be expensive, requiring thoroughly scanning many systems, thoroughly decontaminating them, reloading them from known clean backup copies, and then re-accomplishing all of the productive work lost during the infection and its cleanup. Malware has its origins in hacking attempts by various programmers and computer scientists to experiment with software and its interactions with hardware, operating systems, and other computing technologies. The earliest and most famous example of this was the "Morris worm," which Robert Tappan Morris released onto the Internet in 1988. Its spreading mechanism heralded the new era of massive replication of malware, leading to estimates as high as ten million dollars' worth of damaged and disrupted systems. Among other things, it also led to the first felony conviction for computer crime under U.S. law.

Malware is best classified not by type of malware but by the discrete functions that an attacker want to accomplish. For example, attackers might use malware as one way of:

- Providing undetected or "backdoor" access into a system

- Creating new users, including privileged users, surreptitiously

- Gathering data about the target system and its installed hardware, firmware and software, and peripherals
- Using the target system to perform reconnaissance, eavesdropping, or other activities against other computers on the same LAN or network segment with it
- Installing new services, device drivers, or other functions into operating systems, applications, or utility programs
- Elevating the privilege of a task or a user login beyond what normal system controls would allow
- Elevating a user or task to "root" or full, unrestricted systems administrative privilege levels
- Bypassing data integrity controls so as to provide undetected ability to modify files
- Altering or erasing data from log files associated with system events, resource access, security events, hardware status changes, or applications events
- Copying, moving, or deleting files without being detected, logged, or restricted
- Bypassing digital signatures, installing phony certificates, or otherwise nullifying cryptographic protections
- Changing hardware settings, either to change device behavior or to cause it to damage or destroy itself (such as shutting off a CPU fan and associated over-temperature alarm events)
- Surreptitiously collecting user-entered data, either during login events or during other activities
- Recording and later transmitting records of system, user, or application activities
- Allocating CPU, GPU, and other resources to support surreptitious execution of hacker-desired tasks
- Generating and sending network or system traffic to other devices or to tasks on other systems
- Launching malware-based or other attacks against other systems
- Propagating itself or other malware payloads to other hosts on any networks it can reach
- Harvesting contact information from documents, email systems, or other assets on the target system to use in propagating itself or other malware payloads to additional targets
- Establishing web page connections and transacting activity at websites of the hacker's choice
- Encrypting files (data or program code) as part of ransomware attacks

- Establishing hidden peer-to-peer or virtual private network connections with other systems, some of which may possibly be under the hacker's control

- Running tasks that disrupt, degrade, or otherwise impact normal work on that system

- Controlling multimedia devices, such as webcams, microphones, and so forth, to eavesdrop on users themselves or others in the immediate area of the target computer

- Monitoring a mobile device's location and tracking its movement as part of stalking or tracking the human user or the vehicle they are using

- Using a variety of multimedia or other systems functions to attempt to frighten, intimidate, coerce, or induce desired behavior in the humans using it or nearby it

In general, malware consists of a vehicle or package that gets introduced into the target system; it may then release or install a payload that functions separately from the vehicle. Trojan horse malware (classically named) disguises its nefarious payload within a wrapper or delivery "gift" that seems attractive, such as a useful program, a video or music file, or a purported update to another program. Other types of malware, such as viruses and worms, got their names from their similarities with the way such disease vectors can transmit sickness in animal or plant populations. Viruses, for example, infect one target machine and then launch out to attack others; worms look to find many instances within the target to infect, making their eradication from the host problematic.

The payloads that malware can bring with them have evolved as much as the "carrier" codes have. These payloads can provide hidden, unauthorized entry points into the system (such as a trapdoor or backdoor), facilitate the exfiltration of sensitive data, modify data (such as system event logs) to hide the malware's presence and activities, destroy or corrupt user data, or even encrypt it to hold it for ransom. Malware payloads also form a part of target reconnaissance and characterization activities carried out by some advanced persistent threats, such as by installing keyloggers, spyware of various types, or scareware. Malware payloads can also transform your system into a launch platform from which attacks on other systems can be originated. Payloads can also just steal CPU cycles by performing parts of a distributed computation by means of your system's CPUs and GPUs; other than slowing down your own work, such cycle-stealing usually does not harm the host system. Codebreaking and cryptocurrency mining are but two of the common uses of such cycle-stealing. Rootkits are a special class of malware that use a variety of privilege elevation techniques to insert themselves into the lowest-level (or kernel) functions in the operating system, which upon bootup get loaded and enabled before most anti-malware or antivirus systems get loaded and enabled. Rootkits, in essence, can give complete and almost undetectable control of your system to attackers and are a favorite of advanced persistent threats.

It's interesting to note that many of the behaviors of common malware can resemble the behavior of otherwise legitimate software. This can lead to two kinds of errors. False negative errors are when the malware detection system marks a legitimate program as if it were malware or quarantines or blocks attempts to connect to a web page mistakenly "known" to be a malware source. False positive errors occur when actual malware is not detected as such and is allowed to pass unreported.

Malware can be introduced into a system by direct use of operating systems functions, such as mounting a removable disk drive; just as often, malware enters a system by users interacting with "applications" that are more than what they seem and that come with hidden side effects. Malware often needs to target operating systems functions in order to be part of a successful attack. Most of what you have to do as an SSCP to protect your infrastructure from malware intrusions must take place inside the infrastructure, even if the path into the system starts with or makes use of the application layer. (Some applications, such as office productivity suites, do have features that must be tightly controlled to prevent them from being misused to introduce malware into a system; this can be another undesirable side effect of enabling tools that can create otherwise useful *shadow IT* apps.)

Malicious Code Countermeasures

One way to think about employing malware countermeasures is to break the problem into its separate parts.

- **Whitelisting**, providing control over what can be installed and executed on your systems in the first place
- **Protecting the software supply chain**, by using strong configuration management and controls that enforce policies about using digitally signed code from known sources
- **Prevention measures** that attempt to keep malware of any sort from entering your systems
- **Access control enforcement of device and subject health and integrity**, by means of quarantine and remediation subnets

Many different strategies and techniques exist for dealing with each part of this active anti-malware countermeasure strategy shown here. For example, software and applications allowed or blocked listing can be enforced by scanners that examine all incoming email; other similar approaches can restrict some classes of end users or subjects from browsing to or establishing connections (especially VPN connections) to sites that are not on the trusted-sites list maintained organizationally.

Most anti-malware applications are designed as host intrusion detection and prevention systems, and they tend to use signature and rule-based definitions as they attempt to determine whether a file contains suspect malware. Active anti-malware defenses running continuously on a host (whether that host is a server or an endpoint) can also detect behavior by an active process that seems suspect and then alert the security team, the end user, or both that something may be rotten in the state of the system, so to speak. Anti-malware scanners can be programmed to automatically examine every new file that is trying to come into the system, as well as periodically (or on demand) scan every file on any attached storage devices. These scanners can routinely be searching through high capacity network storage systems (so long as they're not encrypted, of course), and should be:

- Scanning your system to check for files that may be malware-infected or malware in disguise

- Inspecting the digital signatures of specific directories, such as boot sectors and operating system kernels to check for possible surreptitious changes that might indicate malware

- Inspecting processes, services, and tasks in main memory (or in virtual page swap areas) to detect any infected executable code

- Inspecting macros, templates, or other such files for suspicious or malicious code or values

- Moving suspect files or objects to special quarantine areas, and preventing further movement or execution of them

- Inspecting operating systems control parameter sets, such as the Windows Registry hives, for signatures or elements suggestive of known malware

- Monitoring system behavior to detect possible anomalies, suggestive of malware in action

- Monitoring incoming email or web traffic for possible malware

- Monitoring connection requests against lists of blocked sites

Where this concept breaks down is that those hundreds of thousands of new species of malware that appear every day probably are not defined by the rule sets or recognized by the signature analysis capabilities of your anti-malware systems. There's a great deal of interest in the marketplace for automated machine learning approaches that can generate new signatures—but these approaches tend to need dedicated software reverse engineering and test environments in which a suspect file can be subjected to hundreds of thousands of test cases, while the machine learning algorithm trains itself to separate friendly software from foe, if it can.

It's probably wise to see anti-malware solutions as just one part in your overall defensive strategy. Your access control system, for example, cannot by itself recognize a piece of malware for what it is. Inspecting encrypted traffic moving laterally on your internal networks can defeat the best of anti-malware inspection and detection systems. The danger always exists, of course, that *today*'s malware definitions and signatures won't recognize something *as* malware, and you'll copy it into an encrypted backup or archive of a database, software library, or system image. It's vitally important, therefore, to scan those images in an isolated sandbox, quarantine, or other clean system with the newest such malware signatures and definition files *before* you reload your systems from that data. This will reduce your risk of your systems being infected by something from the past; nothing, of course, can take that risk to zero (other than not plugging them in and turning them on in the first place).

✔ Anti-Malware Under Another Name?

A growing number of security systems vendors are offering products with capabilities known as *endpoint detection and response, advanced threat detection,* and others. As Chapter 6 points out, many of these incorporate next generation anti-malware approaches. Some may even use machine learning techniques to rapidly generate new signatures to use in behavioral analysis–based allowed or blocked list approaches. At its most basic level, detecting, preventing, and responding to attempted intrusion of malware into your systems is a fundamental requirement. The architecture of your systems should then help you determine the right solution for your organization's needs, including what mix of capabilities you need, hosted on what hardware elements, and where those elements are in your systems.

Malicious Activity

Setting aside our malware sensitivities for a moment, let's consider malicious activity, which at a minimum is by definition a violation of your organization's policies regarding acceptable use of its information systems, its information assets, and its IT infrastructure. This is an important point: if the organization has not defined these limits of acceptable use in writing, it may find its hands are tied when it tries to deal with systems usage that disrupts normal business operations, compromises private or proprietary data, or otherwise leads to safety or security concerns. By definition, malicious activity is a set of tasks, processes, or actions invoked by a person or people with the intention of satisfying their own agenda or interests without regard to any potential harm their actions may cause to the organization, its employees, customers, or other stakeholders. There does not have to be intent to harm in order for an action to be malicious; nor does there have to be intent to profit or gain from the activity, if it in fact does cause harm to the organization. While this may sound like a two-edged legal argument, it also causes some problems when trying to detect such activity.

What Kinds of Activities?

Almost any action that users might be able to take as part of their normal, everyday, *authorized and permitted* work tasks can become harmful or self-serving (and therefore malicious) if they are performed in a different context. Built-in capabilities to generate surveys and mass email them out to subscribers, for example, can be misused to support an employee's private business, personal, or political agendas. In doing so, the organization's email address, IP address, URL, or other recognizable marks on such outgoing email may be misconstrued by recipients to mean that the organization endorses the content of that email. This can lead to significant loss of business and damage to the organization's reputation if the email's content is significantly at odds with the way the organization positions itself in the marketplace. The unauthorized copying of private or proprietary data and removing the copy from the organization's systems, or *exfiltrating* it, is defined in many jurisdictions as a crime of theft. The damages to the organization can be severe enough that its directors face time in prison and the company can go out of business.

One factor in common is that in each instance management might recognize (in the breach) that the activity in question was a violation of privilege: the user (whoever they were) did not have permission to conduct the tasks in question. Whether the organization's access control systems implemented such privilege restrictions and effectively enforced them, however, is the other, more technical, side of the story.

Actual attacks on your systems, such as distributed denial-of-service attacks via zombie botnets, are of course malicious in nature and intent; but they're covered in greater depth in the section "Understand Network Attacks and Countermeasures" in Chapter 6.

✔ Beware Attackers Living Off the Land

In July 2017, Symantec's research showed an increasing number of ransom attacks—*not* ransomware!—in which the attackers used social engineering and other surreptitious, non-malware-based means to gain initial entry into target systems; they then used built-in systems functions to prepare target file systems for encryption at their command. In many cases, these attacks create few if any files at all on the target system, making it extremely difficult for most anti-malware, software allowed or blocked listing or intrusion detection and prevention technologies to recognize them for what they are. The attackers can also use the same systems functions to cover their tracks.

Symantec's bottom-line recommendation: multifactor user identification, combined with strong access control, is still the foundation of any well-managed IT security program.

Who's Doing It?

Although this may be one of the last questions that gets answered during an incident response and investigation, as a categorical, it helps us look at *how* we might detect such malicious activity in the first place. Several options exist and are in use today.

- **User behavioral modeling:** Typically using machine learning approaches, these systems attempt to understand each authorized user's *business normal* behavior, such as what apps they use, with data from which parts of the system, and how that pattern varies by hour, day, week, or even across a longer time span. For example, a user who normally works in accounts receivables or in purchasing probably has no legitimate need to be copying numerous payroll records (data outside of their normal span of duties), but their after-hours extensive use of purchasing records could be legitimate overtime activity or an attempt to mask their own role in a false invoicing or other fraud.

- **Endpoint behavior modeling:** Similar techniques can be applied to endpoint devices, in an attempt to identify when an endpoint's activities are potentially suspicious. Endpoints that characteristically show at most a handful of HTTPS sessions, that suddenly attempt to open hundreds of them, might be doing something worthy of investigation.

- **Access control:** Access control accounting data may reveal patterns in attempts to access certain data objects by certain subjects, which may or may not reveal behavior that is of concern.

- **Security logs:** These might indicate that a user ID is attempting to elevate its privilege too far or is attempting to modify the privilege constraints associated with objects in ways that may be suspicious.

The Insider Threat

People who are already granted access privileges to your systems, who then abuse those privileges in some deliberate way, are known as the *insider threat*. It's also unfortunately true that many cases of insider-triggered malicious activity are done so via accident or mistake—the user simply did not perform the right action, or attempted to perform it but did it incorrectly, without a malicious intention. Nonetheless, your trusted insiders can and do get things wrong from time to time. Without trying to go too deep into possible motivations, it may be possible in some circumstances to exploit user behavioral modeling in conjunction with biometric data to determine whether a particular member of your team is behaving in ways that you should view with caution if not outright alarm. (It's not just apocryphal humor that warns us to look closely if our systems administrators are driving Lamborghinis or otherwise living a lifestyle far beyond the salary and benefits they're earning from your organization.)

User and entity behavioral analytics (UEBA) refers to the use of statistical and machine learning approaches to aid in detecting a possible security risk involving a specific employee or other end user, or other hardware or software entity. Analytics algorithms seek patterns in the data collected about a modeled behavior, while looking for data that signals changes in behavior that diverge from a known and understood pattern. Different types of analytics approaches represent the different timeframes that management might need to appreciate as they consider potential security implications.

- Descriptive analytics looks at what happened, using behavioral profiles or signatures of past (or other current) events for comparison.

- Inquisitive analytics looks for the proximate causes of an event or series of events.

- Predictive analytics models the behavior of a system (or a person) and seeks to forecast likely or possible courses of action that system or person will take during a specified future time period.

- Prescriptive analytics combines these (and other) analytics approaches to synthesize recommended courses of action to deal with forecasts (from predictive analytics).

At certain gross levels, UEBA might seem to be quite similar to role-based access control: both ought to be able to detect in real time when a user makes repeated attempts to access resources beyond what their assigned roles allow them to use. UEBA, it is argued, can look at longer dwell times than RBAC can: if user 6079SmithW attempts several such access in the space of a few minutes, to the same objects, RBAC can probably detect it and alert the SOC. If, however, 6079SmithW spreads those access attempts across several days, interspersed with many other accesses (legitimate and perhaps also outside his realm of privilege), they may all be natural mistakes or a low and slow reconnaissance probe. UEBA promises to be able to look deep across the recent past history (in descriptive analytic terms) to identify possible patterns of behaviors of interest ("this user is getting too inquisitive for their own good").

UEBA and related approaches are also being developed to *generate* the data needed to configure RBAC systems, which can be notoriously difficult to configure and maintain for very large organizations, especially if fine-grained definition of roles and objects is required for enhanced security.

UEBA data monitoring can go beyond just the surveillance and recording of a user's interactions with your IT systems and include "off-board" data from third-party systems, social media sites, and traffic. It's not yet clear that the UEBA algorithms and tools are reliable enough to detect that a user's personal life is about to cause them to become a "disgruntled employee" who might strike out at the company via its information systems. Before you think that implementing a military-style personnel reliability program is advisable, talk with your organization's experts in human resources and employment law.

Many sources of stress that employees can be affected by are beyond what employers can rightly ask about or attempt to intervene in. In most cases, all that the organization can do is make sure that the required and permitted behavior is clearly defined and that unacceptable behavior (or inappropriate or prohibited information systems use) is communicated in writing. All employees need to be familiarized with these as general standards, as well as being trained on the standards that apply to their particular tasks. Consistent deviations from those standards present many different human resources and management challenges, only some of which might involve an insider threat to your information systems security.

Malicious Activity Countermeasures

Let's take a moment to quickly review the "top ten" countermeasures you'll need as you attempt to limit the occurrence of malicious activities and the damage that they can inflict upon your information systems and your organization. Hearken back to that holistic framework, inspired by the OSI 7-Layer Reference model, that I shared earlier in this chapter (and have shared in different ways throughout this book).

- **Physical controls** can mitigate introduction of malware, exfiltration of data or the entry of unauthorized persons into your premises and thereby into contact with your information systems infrastructure.

- **Logical controls** implement the lioness' share of the security policy decisions that the organization has made; these configure hardware, operating systems, network, and applications-level security features.

- **Administrative controls** ensure that risk management decisions—and therefore information security decisions—that management and leadership have made are effectively pushed out to everyone in the organization and that they are used to drive how physical and logical security controls are put into effect.

- **Hardening strategies** for systems, servers, applications, networks, and endpoints have been translated into procedures, and those procedures create the right mix of controls to ensure that identified vulnerabilities get fixed as and when prudent risk management dictates that they should be fixed.

- **Isolation, quarantine, and sandbox techniques** are used when individual user, subject, or endpoint behavior suggests that something may be happening that deserves more in-depth investigation. Quarantine or isolation of an entire LAN segment and all systems on it may be tremendously disruptive to normal business operations and activities, but indicators of compromise may make that the least unpalatable of choices.

Last but definitely not least on your list should be to engage with your end users; motivate, educate, and train them to be as much a part of your information defensive posture as possible. Most of your teammates and co-workers do not want to live their lives as if they are suspicious of everything around them; they do not want to be the "Big Brother" eyes of the state (or the C-suite) and watch over their co-workers' every move or utterance. Even so, you can go a long way toward creating a more effective security culture by properly inviting, welcoming, and receiving reports of potential security concerns from end users throughout the organization. In almost all cases, the majority of the end users of your systems do not work for you—you are not their boss, you do not write their performance evaluations—yet as part of "the establishment," as part of the supervisory and control structure, you may still be perceived as part of the *enforcement* of cultural norms and expectations within the organization. Use that two-edged sword wisely.

IMPLEMENT AND OPERATE ENDPOINT DEVICE SECURITY

It's at the endpoints of our systems that information inside those systems gets turned into human decisions and actions in the physical, real world; it's also at the endpoints that data is captured by sensors (such as mice, touchpads or keyboards, transducers, cameras, and microphones) and turned into data that our systems then use to model or represent that real world. Endpoints are where users access our systems and where data flows into and out of our systems. Endpoints can be the modem/router where our LAN joins the ISP's service drop to the Internet; endpoints are the laptop or desktop computers, the smartphones, and the IoT devices that we use for SCADA and industrial process control. An ATM is an endpoint, which outputs both data and cash, and in some cases receives deposits of cash or checks.

The full spectrum of security measures must be thoughtfully applied to endpoints across your systems.

- **Physical:** Are they protected from being tampered with? Can removable media or memory devices (such as USB drives) be plugged into them, and if so, what logical controls are in place to prevent unauthorized uploading or downloading of content or executable files?

- **Logical:** Does your access control and network management capability know when a device is turned on, rebooted, and attempts to connect to your networks or systems? If it's a mobile device, can you ascertain its location as part of the authentication process? Can you verify that its onboard firmware, software, and anti-malware protection (if applicable) are up-to-date? Can you remotely inventory all endpoints that are registered to be part of your systems and profile or inventory their current hardware, software, and data configuration?

- **Administrative:** Does your organization have policies, guidelines, and procedures published and in force that identify acceptable use of company-owned or managed endpoints, employee-owned endpoints, and endpoints belonging to or in the control of visitors, guests, or others? How are these policies enforced?

- **Monitoring and analysis:** What security, systems, application, and hardware information is captured in log files by your networks and systems as it pertains to endpoints, their access attempts to the networks and systems, and their usage?

- **Data movement:** Are you able to track or log the movement of data, particularly from sensitive or restricted-access files or data sets and to and from endpoints? Can you enforce whether data moved to and from an endpoint is encrypted in transit, or in use or at rest on the endpoint? Can you remotely manage storage facilities on the endpoint and delete data on it that is no longer required to be there, or is otherwise at risk of loss or compromise?

- **Data commingling:** Does your organization have acceptable use or other policies that set limits or constraints on the commingling of personal data and data belonging to the organization on the same endpoint, regardless of whether it is company-owned or employee-owned? How are these policies implemented and monitored for compliance?

- **Configuration management and control:** Is each endpoint under configuration management and control? Can you validate that the only hardware, firmware, or software changes made to the device were authorized by the configuration management decision process and were properly implemented?

- **Backups:** What requirements for providing backups of endpoint software and onboard data does your organization have? How are these backups carried out, verified to be correct and complete, stored, and then made available for use if and when an endpoint needs to be restored (or a replacement endpoint brought up to the same configuration)?

✔ When Is "The Cloud" an Endpoint?

It's easy to see that a USB removable storage device (or a hacking device disguised as a USB storage device) can be a data exfiltration avenue, one that endpoint management can and should be able to exert control over. When bring-your-own-infrastructure (BYOI) approaches encourage or allow users to store company data in their own privately managed cloud storage areas, the risk of exfiltration skyrockets. Containing that risk requires carefully managed security policies applied to those shared infrastructures as well as to the source data itself; you should also closely examine the business logic and processes that seem to require what could be a complex web of contracts, agreements, and services.

Mobile device management (MDM) systems can support many of these needs for laptops, smartphones, and some other mobile devices. Other IT asset management systems can be used to control, manage, and validate the configuration, health, and integrity of fixed-base systems such as desktop or workstation endpoints, regardless of whether they are connected via wireless, cable, or fiber links to your networks.

Printers and multifunction printer/copier/fax/scanner units represent a special class of endpoint security challenges. If sensitive data can be sent to a printer, it can leave your control in many ways. Some organizations find it useful to take advantage of steganographic watermarking capabilities built into many printers and multifunction units; this can make it easier to determine whether a file came into the system or was printed off or sent out by a particular device. Sometimes, just the fact that such steganographic watermarking is being used may deter someone from using the device to exfiltrate sensitive data.

Endpoints act as clients as far as network-provided services are concerned; but even the thinnest of clients needs an onboard operating system that hosts whatever applications are installed on that device. Many endpoints have significant processing and memory capacities, which makes it practical to install various integrated security applications on them. As the threats evolve and the defensive technologies evolve as well, the boundary lines between different types of products blur. As we see with network-based systems, intrusion detection, prevention, and firewall capabilities are showing up as integrated product offerings.

Let's look at a few, in a bit more detail.

HIDS

Host-based intrusion detection or prevention systems (HIDS or HIPS) fall into two broad classes: malware protection systems and access control systems. If the endpoint's onboard operating system is capable of defining multiple user roles and managing users by ID and by group, it already has the makings of a robust onboard access control system. Your security needs may dictate that you install a more rigorous client-side access control application as part of your overall organizational access control approach as a way of detecting and alerting security control personnel that unauthorized local device access attempts or user privilege elevations are being attempted.

Anti-malware systems have long been available as host-based installations. They are not truly applications, in that they don't really run on top of the host operating system but rather integrate with it to make it more difficult for malware to take hold of the host. The anti-malware system is installed so that parts of it load along with the operating system kernel, almost immediately after the hardware bootstrap loader has turned control over to the boot software on the system disk or other boot device. In theory, those areas of a disk or boot device can be updated only by trusted installer user IDs or other superuser/systems administrator–controlled processes. Of course, if malware is already *on* the endpoint and installed in those boot or *root* areas of the boot device, the anti-malware installation probably cannot detect it.

Our trust in our anti-malware systems providers goes right to the very core of our information security posture. You may recall the near hysteria that resulted when some U.S. government sources started to allege in 2017 that Kaspersky Lab's anti-malware products had backdoors built into them that allowed Russian intelligence agencies to insert malware of their choice onto systems supposedly under its protection. Even the European Union claimed, nearly a year later, that it had confirmed Kaspersky's products were malicious. As of this writing, it's not yet clear if these allegations have any basis in fact or not; regardless, it strongly suggests that having more than one way to scan all of your systems, servers, and endpoints—using more than one vendor's products and more than one set of signature and rule data to drive them with—is a prudent if not necessary precaution.

Host-Based Firewalls

In a fully layered defensive system, each server and endpoint should be running its own host-based defenses, including its own firewall. Windows and Mac systems ship with a factory-installed firewall, which in the absence of anything else you should enable, configure, and use. Other Linux distributions may or may not come with a built-in firewall, but there are many reputable apps to choose from to add this to a server or endpoint. Android systems are left something in a bit of a lurch: Google considers a firewall unnecessary for Android, especially if you restrict your computing to only those trusted apps on the Google Play store. This is similar to having a trusted software supply chain as part of your overall risk management process. The argument is also made that mobile smartphones (the marketplace for Android OS) are not intended to be used as always-on servers or even as peers in a P2P relationship and that therefore you still don't need a firewall. As a quick perusal of the Play store reveals, there are hundreds of firewall apps to choose from, many from well-known firewall providers.

Regardless of device type and its native OS, configuring your chosen host firewall's ACLs needs to harmonize with your overall approach to access control and privilege management. You'll also need to ensure that any MDM solutions that are managing the host device are also working compatibly with the host firewall and that both are working together seamlessly.

This suggests that your overall access control systems approach should ideally give you a one-stop-shopping experience: you use one management console interface to establish the constraints to check and the rules to use and then push that through to the MDM as well as to network and host-based systems such as firewalls, IPS and IDS, and even uniform threat management and Security Information and Event Management (SIEM) systems.

Allowed Lists: Positive Control for App Execution

Allowed list management defensive technologies work at the level of an individual executable file; if the file is on the *allowed list*, the list of known programs that are permitted to run on a given endpoint, then that program file is loaded and executed. If the file is not on the allowed list, the tool can be configured to block it completely or ask the user to input a justification. The justification (and the attempted execution) are sent to security personnel, who evaluate the request and the justification. In some environments, the allowed list system can be configured to allow the user to grant permission to install or run an otherwise unknown piece of software.

In principle, this would keep any unauthorized program from being loaded and executed on any endpoint so configured. This can certainly prevent many malware processes from being installed and run. Malware that might arrive as part of an encrypted file attached to an email or downloaded from a network resource, for example, might not have been detected by anti-malware systems scanning those interfaces. It also can defend a host against new malware threats that are completely unknown to the malware community. This in and of itself is worth its weight in gold!

In practice, however, there are some issues to consider. PowerShell, for example, is installed on every Windows machine; yet, it can give an individual user (or a script file that tries to access it) unparalleled capability to make mischief. Positive security control for applications can also fail to provide solid management of systems where the user (or a group of users) has a legitimate need to be building and running new programs, even as shadow IT apps. Psychologically conditioning the user to hit "authorize" dozens of times a day can lead to pushing that button one too many times in the wrong circumstances.

There's also the risk that a series of executions of known, recognized, and permitted programs could still invite disaster; this crosses over into endpoint and end-user behavioral modeling and requires that you identify business normal patterns of applications use. Endpoint and end user behavior modeling is seeing a resurgence of interest as machine learning techniques are making it more approachable and scalable. In most such cases, the machine learning is performed in an offline environment to generate and test new signatures, rule sets, or both; then those are loaded into production protective systems such as blocked or allowed list apps. Depending upon circumstances, that process can take as little as a day to generate a new signature.

It's worthwhile investigating whether your organization's security needs can identify policies that can be used to directly drive the ways in which an application allowed or blocked system can be put to use. Any such system you choose should be something you can integrate into your existing configuration management and control practices, particularly as they pertain to how your organization generates and uses endpoint golden images. You'll also need to investigate whether you need a server-based approach or need this deployed to each endpoint (and each mobile endpoint).

Endpoint Encryption

There are strong arguments that can be made that all endpoints, regardless of type, should have strong encryption methods used to completely lock down their internal or onboard storage. Some Windows- and Linux-based devices can in fact do this, using technologies such as Microsoft's BitLocker to encrypt the end user's data partition on an endpoint's hard drive, while allowing Windows itself to boot from an unencrypted space. Laptops, desktops, and other workstation-type endpoints with significant storage, processing, and RAM are prime candidates to have encryption applied to their hard drives.

Mobile phones, regardless of the operating system that they use, are also prime candidates for such encryption. It's beyond our scope to survey the different encryption options available, but suffice it to say that headline news of a few years ago had Manhattan District Attorney Cyrus Vance Jr. adding his voice to the choir attempting to convince everyone that putting encryption on smartphones protects more criminals than it protects law-abiding citizens. The numbers seem to show differently, as *Wired*'s Kevin Bankston pointed out in August 2015: millions of mobile phones and smartphones are stolen every year in the North American and European markets alone, while at best one or two headline-grabbing criminal cases involve encrypted smartphones that law enforcement cannot jailbreak.

There are some caveats, of course. If your MDM solutions or other device management approaches involve substantial device customization, such as flashing your own versions of ROMs in these devices, you may find that updated versions of the OS (such as Android) won't support device-level encryption. You should also thoroughly investigate what type of encryption is used and what that suggests for organizational policies about passcodes or other authentication factors users will have to use to access encrypted data on the endpoint or use it via encrypted services with company systems. (A four-digit passcode does not strong security make after all.)

Data remanence is an issue with endpoints, as data unencrypted for use, display, or output to another device can still remain accessible in some form even if the device is powered off and its battery or power supply removed.

MDM systems vendors have increasingly added encryption management, password management, and other security features into their product and service offerings. Some of these provide a corporate server-based encryption system that will not allow the endpoint to access, display, or use company data without the server and the endpoint being in a managed session together; this prevents offline use of confidential data, which is either a business impact or a security blessing. Others look to full device encryption and locking, which may be appropriate for company-owned, company-managed devices.

If you have a personal smartphone and you're not encrypting it, perhaps it's time to learn more about how to do that.

Trusted Platform Module

Trusted platform modules (TPMs) are specialized hardware devices, incorporated into the motherboard of the computer, phone, or tablet, that provide enhanced cryptographic-based device and process security services. A TPM is provided in a sealed, tamper-resistant hardware package that combines cryptographic services, host computer state descriptor information, and other data. TPMs are embedded into the computer's motherboard (so as to be nonremovable) and, in combination with device drivers and other software, achieve greater levels of security for that system. The Trusted Computing Group (TCG), a consortium of more than 120 manufacturers, software houses, and cybersecurity companies from around the world, develops and publishes standards that describe what TPMs should do and what they should not. The TCG defines trust in simple terms: a trusted device behaves in a particular, specified manner for a specified purpose. By storing key parameters about the host computer itself (chip-level serial numbers, for example), a TPM provides an extra measure of assurance that the computer system it is a part of is still behaving in the ways that its manufacturer intended. TPMs typically contain their own special-purpose, reduced instruction set computer; read-only memory for the control program; key, hash, and random number generators; and storage locations for configuration information, platform identity keys, and other data. TPMs are being incorporated into laptops, phones, and tablet systems, providing a world-class solution that is not strongly tied to or dominated by one manufacturer's chip set, operating system, or hierarchy of trust implementation.

TPMs protect the hardware itself by making it less attractive to steal or less useful (easier to lock) when the host computer or phone is lost or mislaid. Although the TPM does not control any software tasks (system or application) running on the host, it can add to the security of processes designed to make use of it. It's probably fair to consider a TPM as an additional hardware countermeasure to help make software and communications more secure.

In 2016, TCG published the latest edition of its standard, calling it TPM Main Specification 2.0; it was updated into the ISO/IEC 11889 standard later that year. TPM 2.0 was built with a "library approach" to allow greater flexibility, especially in implementing TPMs to serve the rapidly expanding world of IoT devices. TCG provided a brief overview of this in June 2019, `https://trustedcomputinggroup.org/wp-content/uploads/2019_TCG_TPM2_BriefOverview_DR02web.pdf`, which highlights the five key trust elements of TPM 2.0 and briefly sketches out the security features they can provide. Note that the first application suggested for the Discrete TPM is in control logic for automotive braking systems. Virtual TPMs can provide a cloud-based TPM element as part of a larger virtual systems design.

Mobile Device Management

Although mobile device management (MDM) was discussed in Chapter 6 as part of wireless network access control and security, it's worth expanding on a few key points.

- Regardless of whether the mobile endpoint is company-owned and managed, your users will complicate things greatly. Users may become excessively slow or uncooperative with keeping it fully updated and patched, for example. Windows 10 does allow end users to put off—sometimes for months—what otherwise might be an urgent push of an update. And in some instances, they are right to do so. Users who travel excessively may find that leaving a laptop powered up and operating while racing to an airport or a meeting is just too inconvenient; and if those users are senior managers or leaders, it's really up to you and the IT department to make the *user's* experience more effective, simpler, and even enjoyable. Horror stories abound of very senior officials whose government-issued smartphones, for example, went for more than a year without being patched or updated. At some point, that seems to cry out for an "office visit" by a technician who can completely swap out one device for a new one, with all of the user's data already ported over. Support for your security measures by the powerful users (as opposed to the notion of *power users*) in the organization is vital to getting everyone on board with them.

- Many factors are driving companies and organizations to deal with variations on the bring-your-own schemes, and as devices become more powerful, take on different form factors, and have personalization that appeals to individual end-user desires, more companies are finding that BYO variations are the approach that they need to take. MDM vendors clearly advertise and promote that their solutions can cope with an ever-increasing and bewildering array of smartphones, phablets, and laptops; at some point, smart watches and other device types will move out of the PAN and into broader use—presenting even more mobile devices to manage.

Already, many fitness watches can receive, display, store, and allow limited responses to emails, SMS, and other messaging; at some point, you may need to worry about whether the data flowing to such devices is potentially creating a data leak situation. It doesn't always have to be gigabytes of data being exfiltrated that an adversary is after.

✔ Avoiding Covert Channels of the Mind

Mobile endpoint security considerations put another classic security problem in stark relief: in almost every organization, there are people who have to deal with sensitive or security-classified information that comes from multiple compartments. Consultants, for example, must take great pains to ensure that they do not reveal Client A's significant challenges or new strategies to Client B, even by way of discussing those sensitive ideas or concerns with people within the consultant's own organization. These unplanned cross-connects between sets of secure information are known as *covert channels*, since the flow of ideas and information tends to happen in ways that the responsible managers or owners of those sets of information are not aware of.

As more and more BYO-style mobile device situations arise, you may need to pay particular attention to how your mobile users are made aware of these types of concerns and to what extent familiarization, training, or even formal nondisclosure agreements (NDAs) are required.

Secure Browsing

Because our use of web browsers is such an integral part of the hierarchies of trust that we rely upon for secure e-commerce, e-business, and e-personal use of the Web and the Net, it's important to consider two sides of the same coin: how well do our browsers protect our privacy while they purportedly are keeping us secure? The majority of web browser software is made freely available to users and systems builders alike; they come preinstalled by the original equipment manufacturers (OEMs) on many computer products for consumer or enterprise use. The development and support costs of these browsers are paid for by advertising (ads placed within web pages displayed to users), by analytics derived from users' browsing history, or by other demographic data that browser providers, search engines, and websites can gather during their contact with users. Browsers support a variety of add-on functions, many of which can be used by websites to gather information about you and your system, leave session-specific or site-related information on your computer for later use, or otherwise gain more insight about what you're doing while you are browsing than you might think possible or desirable.

Browsers, like many modern software packages, also gather telemetry data—data that supports analysis of the behavior and functioning of the browser while the user is interacting with it—and makes that telemetry available to its vendor. (Many products say that users opt into this to "improve the user experience," whether the user feels such improvement or not.) Whether we recognize this or not, this paradigm has transformed the web surfer from user-as-customer into user-as-product. In some circumstances, that can be of benefit to the user—it certainly provides the revenue stream that developers and infrastructure builders and maintainers need, at no additional direct cost to the user. But it can also be of potential harm to the user, be that user an individual or a business enterprise, if that aggregation of user-entered data, action history, and analytics violates the user's reasonable expectation of privacy, for example.

Let's start with a closer look at each side of that coin.

Private browsing is defined as using a web browser in such a way that the user's identity, browsing history, and user-entered data when interacting with web pages is kept confidential. Browsers such as Mozilla Firefox or Microsoft Edge provide ways for users to open a new window (supported by a separate task and process stream) for private browsing, in which location tracking, identification, cookie handling, and various add-ons may change the way that they provide information back to websites or leave session-tracking information on the user's computer. For most mainline browsers, telemetry is still gathered and made available to the browser's authors. To put "private browsing" into perspective, consider one data point: the unique identification of the system you're browsing from. Fully nonrepudiable identification of your system would require every device on the Internet to have a unique key or ID assigned to it that was an amalgam of IP address, hardware identifiers, software identifiers, and even your user ID on that system. A suitable cryptographic hash of all of this data would produce such a unique ID, which could not be de-hashed (decrypted) to get back to your specific username, for example. But if the search engine or web page keeps a history of activity tagged to that system identification, then every time you browse, your unique history continues to be updated. If that concerns you, can't you just avoid this by opening up a new *private* browser window, tab, or session? According to tests by the Electronic Frontier Foundation and others, no; so-called private browsing still generates an ID of your hardware, software, and session that is unique to one of a billion or more such addresses. And, of course, the browser telemetry is still going back "home" to its developers. In the meantime, private browsing usually does not prevent ads from being displayed or block pop-up windows from occurring, and some ad blockers and pop-up blockers are incompatible with private browsing modes.

Secure browsing is defined as using a web browser in such a way that it actively helps keep the user's system secure, while more assertively or aggressively protecting the user's privacy, data about the user's system, and data about the user's browsing history. Competition between the mainstream browsers as products (that is, as platforms for revenue generation for advertisers or for search engine providers) has driven some of them to incorporate more of these features, and so the line between "highly secure and safe" and "private" browsing continues to blur. Some of the more well-respected secure browsers, such as Waterfox or Pale Moon, are offshoots (or forks) from earlier points in the development of Mozilla Firefox. By eliminating many of the data-intensive add-in capabilities, telemetry gathering, and other features, these secure browsers are also relatively lightweight as compared to native Firefox (that is, they run faster and use fewer system resources to do so).

If you truly need private and secure browsing, consider using add-ons such as HTTPS-Everywhere, which go a step further by using HTTPS for all of your browsing and then routing it through The Onion Router (TOR). TOR, incidentally, was designed by the U.S. Naval Research Laboratory as a way to provide anonymous communication and web use for social advocates, journalists, and ordinary people living or working in repressive or totalitarian countries. TOR takes every packet exchange and routes it to different members of its peer-to-peer backbone infrastructure; by the time the connection leaves TOR and goes to the requested URL, the only thing the distant server can see is that last TOR node's IP address. This is very similar to using a VPN to hide your pathway, but with a serious twist: most VPNs bulk encrypt from your entry node to the landing node, providing anonymity and security, but try to minimize dynamic rerouting of your path for improved performance. TOR, on the other hand, dynamically reroutes to further mask your path and your identity, at the cost of sometimes significantly slower browsing.

In August 2021, Restore Privacy LLC updated its review and round-up of current secure browser offerings in the marketplace; `https://restoreprivacy.com/secure-browser/` provides useful comparisons while also illuminating some of the issues and concerns that might bring people in your organization to need secure browsing as part of their business processes. Other privacy-enhancing research and resources are also at this site.

One final approach to secure and private browsing is a sandbox system—a separate computer, outside of your organization's demilitarized zone (DMZ), that has no organizational or individual identifying data on it. The system is wiped (the disk is hard reformatted and re-imaged from a pristine image copy) after each session of use. Most businesses and many individuals do not have need of such a sandbox approach, but when the occasion warrants it, it works. Strict data hygiene practices must be in force when using such a sandbox; ensure that the bare minimum of information is put in by users as they interact with external systems and either prevent or thoroughly scan, test, and validate any data or program brought in via the sandbox from outside before introducing it into any other system in your infrastructure. (This is an excellent opportunity to consider the "write-down" and "read-up" restrictions in some of the classical access control models, as they apply to systems integrity and data confidentiality protection.)

✔ The Downside of a VPN

VPNs can do a marvelous job of keeping not only your data but the fact of your connection to a specific web page totally confidential; it's only on that "last hop" from the VPN's landing site in the country of your choice to the website of interest that actual IP addresses get used as packets flow to and from. Whether cookies make it back to your system or whether browser telemetry makes it from your system to the browser's home may require additional tweaking of the VPN and browser settings.

CONTINUES

If your connection requires some rigorous security verification, however, you may need to turn off the VPN. This is particularly true if the server in question blocks IP addresses originating in certain regions or countries. I discovered this some time ago as I spent a ten-minute Skype conversation with PayPal security without using a VPN. PayPal security noted that my previous login and transaction attempts, moments before, seemed to move around between six different countries on four continents, including Iran and Chechnya, in as few as five minutes. This caused PayPal's security algorithms to block the transaction attempts. Turning off the VPN allowed a "static" IP address (assigned by my ISP) to be used for the next entire session, which was successful. I cannot blame PayPal for being overly protective of my bank information in that regard.

IoT Endpoint Security

Since early 2019, quite a number of publications, vendor white papers, and products that address the growing need to secure Internet of Things devices and the networks that they interface with have hit the marketplace. The GSM Association, the trade body that represents more than 800 mobile phone systems operators and more than 300 other companies in this ecosystem, has continued to expand its IoT security - specific resources of guidelines, case studies, development kits, and other services to members. Find it at `https://www.gsma.com/iot/mobile-iot-resources/`, where you can gain insights regarding many threats and risks such as:

- Device cloning
- Securing the Internet of Things (IoT) endpoint's identity
- Attacks against the trust anchor
- Endpoint impersonation
- Service or peer impersonation
- Tampering with onboard firmware or software
- Remote code execution
- Unauthorized debugging or instrumentation of the device or the system it's a part of
- Side-channel attacks
- Compromised endpoints as threat vectors
- Securely deploying devices which lack back-end connections
- User safety, privacy, and security

Endpoint Security: EDR, MDR, XDR, UEM, and Others

From 2019 to 2021 a number of companies introduced or dramatically strengthened their service offerings for managing all of the enterprise's endpoints as swarms of semi-autonomous entities, rather than dealing with them individually. Previously, endpoint detection and reporting (EDR) tended to look at each detected endpoint on the network without regard to what other endpoints are doing. The biggest problem with this is that the identities behind a distributed, loosely-coupled, long dwell time attack are probably using a large set of entities, whether via botnets, misused credentials, or other means, to carry out their malicious actions. To address this a virtual alphabet soup of service offerings provide various extensions to the basic EDR model:

- XDR extends the detection and response to larger sets of endpoints, presuming that some may be working in collusion with each other

- MDR provides greater management and coordination of the enterprise's response to an incident or set of incidents

- UEM unifies or brings together the management of all endpoint security issues to one management console

The acronym itself doesn't really matter; what is important is whether a particular vendor or managed security services provider can effectively match your enterprise's needs with their capabilities in cost-effective ways.

OPERATE AND CONFIGURE CLOUD SECURITY

In many respects, configuring cloud-hosted business processes and the virtualized, scalable resources that support them is technically and operationally similar to what you'd be doing to secure an on-premises data center system. The same risk management and mitigation planning processes would lead to comparable choices about risk controls; overall security needs would still dictate monitoring, analysis, and alarm needs. The same compliance regimes in law, regulation, contract, and marketplace expectations will still dictate how your organization must maintain data and metadata about its use, both for inspection and for analysis during routine audits as well as in support of e-discovery orders from a court of law.

One key difference, of course, is administrative: your organization has an entirely different sort of *supply chain relationship* with a cloud services provider than it would have with suppliers, vendors, original equipment manufacturers, and maintenance organizations if it was running its own local data center. That contractual relationship is typically spelled out in service level agreements (SLAs), sometimes called *terms of reference* (TORs, not to be confused with The Onion Relay). SLAs and TORs should establish with great clarity where the dividing lines are with respect to privacy, security, systems integrity, data integrity, backup and restore capabilities, business continuity and disaster recovery support, and support for investigations, audits, and e-discovery. SLAs should also lay out specific constraints on *ethical penetration testing* that their customer organizations can do; pen testing can sometimes get out of hand, and your cloud provider understandably has many other customers to protect from *your* pen test activities.

(ISC)² and the Cloud Security Alliance have combined the knowledge and experience of their memberships to create the Certified Cloud Security Professional (CCSP) credential, as a way of growing the common core of skills that business and industry need as they move further into the cloud. This may be a logical path for you to consider as part of your ongoing professional growth and development.

With all of that in mind, let's take a brief look at the basic concepts of migrating your business processes to the cloud from the standpoint of keeping them safe, secure, private, and compliant.

Deployment Models

Cloud services are the data storage, processing, applications hosting, network connectivity, user experience, and security management services that corporate or individual end users would normally engage with on a local physical data center, but with a difference. Data center designs look to having specific hardware servers running copies or instances of applications, such as web apps that access a database. By contrast, cloud-hosted services use virtual machines—software-created instances of a complete operating system and application environment—that are created and run on shared computing hardware to meet moment-by-moment demand. In the traditional on-premises data center design, the customer organization had to buy or lease servers, storage units, connectivity, and everything else; if they sized that set of "bare metal" too small, they limited their overall throughput; if they sized it too large, they had a lot of expensive excess capacity sitting around idle. In the cloud service model, the owner or operator of the cloud provides all of the bare-metal servers, storage, networks, and interconnection, and they lease it out as virtual machines moment by moment to a wide variety of customers. Each customer pays for what they use, and no more. Maintenance, engineering support, environmental and physical infrastructure, and security of that cluster of processing and storage equipment are handled by the cloud services provider.

This concept started in the 1960s with a business model known as the *service bureau*; in fact, a book written at that time about the problems with the service bureau defined the business models of today's cloud services in some detail. Several ownership and use cases are now in common use.

- Private clouds operate on hardware owned or leased by one organization; they are used only to support the processing needs of that organization.

- Public clouds are operated by a cloud services provider organization, which leases time to any and all customers who want to migrate their business processes into their cloud. Government customers, private businesses, nonprofits, and individuals can all lease resources in the same private cloud data center, without having to worry about who else is sharing the machines with them. Isolation between customers, their processing, and their storage is the responsibility of the cloud services company, and they're usually quite diligent in how they do this.

- Hybrid clouds can be a combination of private cloud services (owned or operated by the customer) and public cloud services. Increasingly, hybrid deployments are involving multiple cloud hosting service providers. Geographic diversity in data center locations, communications capabilities, and services can often mean that public cloud customers cannot get exactly what they want and need from one supplier alone.

- Community clouds provide for affiliations and associations of local government or civic groups, and businesses that they work with, to operate in a somewhat federated fashion in a shared cloud services environment.

- *Govcloud* is a highly secure cloud hosting environment, which meets stringent U.S. and Canadian government security standards; Govcloud users can be businesses working with government agencies on classified projects or projects that have an unusually demanding information security set of needs.

In cloud parlance, *deployment* and *migration* are terms for the whole set of managerial, technical, and physical tasks necessary to take existing or planned business processes, including all of their data, software, and people-facing procedural elements, and move them into an appropriate cloud environment. Deployment or migration should also include well-defined test and evaluation plans and of course very thoroughgoing security planning. Logistic support should also consider how existing employees or staff members will be trained on using the new cloud-hosted business systems. Backup and restore capabilities must also be planned, and business continuity and disaster recovery planning need to reflect this migration as well.

Service Models

For more than two decades there have been three main *service models* that define in general terms the architecture of what your organization is leasing from its cloud services provider. These models are considered "classical" since they derive from the mainframe-computer-based service bureaus that were the infrastructure of affordable computing from the 1960s through the 1980s. They also facilitate straightforward migrations of existing business logic, systems, and data into public and hybrid cloud environments as a result. Figure 7.1 illustrates these three hierarchies of services; above the stair-step line across the middle are the services and data that the customer organization provides and that have direct configuration management, control, and information security responsibilities for. Below the stair-step line across the middle of Figure 7.1 is the land of the cloud services provider; these providers own or lease, manage, maintain, and keep secure all of the hardware, systems software, cabling, power, air conditioning and environmental controls, and of course the physical, administrative, and logical security for these elements.

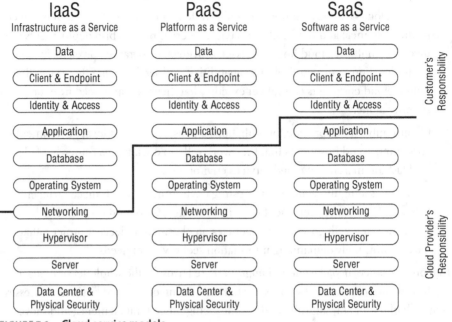

FIGURE 7.1   **Cloud service models**

Scaling up from the bare-iron server boards to greater levels of integrated functionality, we find the following:

- **Infrastructure as a service (IaaS):** This is equivalent to leasing or renting a room full of computers but with nothing installed on them. Basic networking services (in all cases, software-defined networks) are available, as these provide the only way that one VM can talk to another or to the outside world. The underlying server architecture provides CPU and GPU core processors, RAM, and channel connectivity to the network and to storage subsystems. The servers run what is called a *bare-metal* hypervisor, and the user then specifies (and either provides or leases rights to) the operating systems to be loaded into each virtual machine definition. If, for example, they need Windows Server 2016 scalable across up to 100 VMs, then, as workload expands, the cloud resource balancing and dispatch functions will instance more copies of the same Windows Server–based VM, including its predefined applications, database connections, and user identities. IaaS is well suited when the customer organization has significant investment tied up in fully functional systems, from the operating system on up through user-facing data manipulation interfaces, that they just want to move to a more scalable, durable, and perhaps more affordable hosting environment.

- **Platform as a service (PaaS):** This generally provides everything up through a database engine. The customer organization brings in its database definitions, back-end applications, stored queries, and other apps that they need to fully host their business processes. Most web app systems that are built around a back-end database-facing application will migrate to PaaS to gain much greater scalability; this shifts the database back-end load balancing, for example, more to the underlying PaaS environment's scheduling and control services.

- **Software as a service (SaaS):** This provides the customer organization with a fully integrated and supported application environment. Office 365 is a well-known example of this; the same user experience and the same manner of using files, integrating local endpoint and cloud-hosted storage, and inter-applications communication and data sharing are all supported and maintained via the SaaS application and the supporting platform and infrastructure underneath it. Salesforce is another example of a SaaS environment. In SaaS, the customer's business logic is built into procedures, scripts, macros, forms, or other application-dependent structures and definitions.

It's important to emphasize that in many respects, nothing technical changes from what you're used to in your on-premises data center or LAN environment as you move business logic into the clouds or as you move from IaaS to PaaS to SaaS. The same security considerations you would use to segment your organizational networks on hardware you own and manage are what you should do as you define the virtual machines you want to deploy to get work done with. You still write a technical specification: what can Machine X talk to, what should *not* be allowed to talk to it, query it, or attempt to connect to it, for example, is a dialogue you have about each machine on your network now, and will still need to work through when you migrate to the cloud. It's not mysterious.

However, much as each vendor's network hardware, management tools, SIEMs or unified threat management systems, firewalls, and access control systems have their own quirks, special features, and traps for the unwary, so do the tools and capabilities that each cloud services provider can make available for you to use. The number-one cause of cloud hosted services suffering data breaches, according to Amazon Web Services in 2018, were *user errors in configuring storage resources*.

As your organization plans to migrate to the cloud—or if it's already out there—get with your IT department and learn with them about how the chosen cloud hosting provider's security services need to be configured. Cloud service providers offer many training options, starting with free courses (and after all, the better trained their customers are, the more services they safely use; so free training pays for itself quickly). Take as much as you can; learn everything about this new world.

Before we look at the new concepts in cloud computing—*serverless services delivery*—let's take a deeper look at several key aspects of life in the cloud and at what you need to keep in mind as you secure what your organization has moved out there or is migrating out there.

Virtualization

Virtualization is a set of techniques that allow for far more efficient utilization of computing resources. Since the 1960s, many computer systems have been designed with *virtual memory*, which allows each program, task, or process to run as if it had the entire address space that the CPU could reach available to it. If the CPU had a 4GB address space, then every program would be built as if it had that entire space available to it. When loaded into memory, a combination of hardware and operating systems features would let the system assign blocks of RAM (called *pages*) to each task or process as it needed them. Since most processes do a tremendous amount of I/O to disk drives, networks, or people-facing input and output devices and these devices run much more slowly than the CPU does, many different processes can get a time slice of the CPU while others are waiting on their disks, mice, keyboards, or networks to respond.

Virtual Machines

A *virtual machine* is taking that concept one giant step further: instead of just virtualizing one process or program, take a copy of the operating system, its virtual memory management, its network and disk subsystem managers and device drivers, *and* the applications you want to run on it, and make one complete image file of it, which you can reload into RAM and start executing any time you want. *Hibernation* does this in many OS environments today; it takes very little time to load an 8GB hibernation file into RAM, as compared to bootstrap loading the operating system, then the runtime environments, then the applications, and then initializing everything again. Each VM is defined by what you build into its virtual hard disk (VHD) image file. The *hypervisor* then loads as many copies of the VM as you want, onto as many CPUs as your runtime performance needs and load balancing controls tell it you will need; each VM is its own separate world and its own separate address space and connection to a virtual network. Each copy of a VM that gets started up is an *instance* of that VM. Each instance can be separately stopped, restarted, shut down, hibernated, saved for later use, or deleted, without impacting other instances of the same VM and without altering the definition (or template) of that VM.

The *hypervisor* is a slimmed-down operating system, which specializes in building VHDs of VMs, loading them upon request, supervising their use of the baremetal processor, RAM, and system resources, and then shuts the VMs down and cleans up after them as required. Hypervisors can run directly on the bare metal server itself, as the booted-in operating system; or they can run as a special class of application on top of an installed and bootstrapped operating system.

Security for Virtual Machines

At their initial definition and creation, a VM cannot communicate with anything outside of itself and the devices it is logically attached to, such as the endpoint associated with the user running that VM and whatever virtual disk drives the VM's definition declares to be a part of it. The hypervisor can allow it to see LAN segments that you define, by means of virtual firewalls, virtual or distributed routers, or most any other type of network architecture and device imaginable. But the VM cannot just reach out and find these. VMs cannot share memory, unless you've defined ways in which the VMs can do that by means of services. Much as you'd do for physical machines, you'll need to take steps to allow each instance of a VM to have access to the outer world or to be visible to other VMs or to users on the Internet.

As a result, VMs are often *containerized* in sets of VMs related to a particular use. One container could contain a definition of a front-end web server, a back-end database application, and their supporting servers for DNS, networks, firewalls, email, and access control. That complete system has all the same functionality that the "real" deployed set of VMs would if they were connected to the Internet; but as a separate container, it can be run in isolation for software testing, for malware reverse engineering, for incident investigation and analysis, or for user or maintainer training. Containerizing VMs allows the system architects to choose what exactly they need in that environment and what they don't need. What runs inside that container stays inside that container, unless steps are taken to connect it to other networks or to the Internet. Ethical penetration testing often starts small and local by testing against containerized, scaled-down segments of your overall systems architecture.

In sum, all of the security and performance options that you would normally select and configure for on-site hardware, software, and network systems are available to you via the cloud. The same range of flexibility, responsiveness, scalability, security, risk and reward are all there. The only real difference is that the wait time to take delivery of a new instance of a VM or a container full of VMs might be just a few minutes; instancing new copies of a container as processing demands increase is also a matter of just a minute or so, especially if automatic load balancing has been set up to manage this for you. If you only need 128 CPUs worth of web server for two very busy hours every week, you don't need to buy or lease them for the other 166 hours and let them sit idle. And that's really the only difference.

This is a two-edged sword: you can vastly increase the resources available to support your organization's business needs in a handful of minutes—and increase its threat surface proportionately in the same few minutes. Achieving the same scale of expansion with real, physical systems takes longer; you have more capital tied up in it, so perhaps you work more deliberately. Perhaps you're also under greater schedule pressure to turn them on and get them producing revenues. On the other hand, by letting the hypervisor do the repetitive work for you, you've got more time to be more thorough in your analysis, inspection and verification of configuration settings, and your testing. This is just one aspect of your organization's choice to migrate to or expand their presence in the cloud.

Serverless Services

The classical cloud services model reflects the batch-mode, file-focused data processing models that were developed in the early days of computing. Those models gave birth to the concept of a database as a structured, centralized repository for information—the flow of data through the organization's business processes all centered around that database. Typical of such applications environments might be a major airline ticketing and reservations systems such as Apollo or Sabre, in which substantial portions of the business logic are implemented as individual applications programs that work around that database. The database was bundled with a server application, which provided the programming interfaces to the business applications (such as "will you quote" or "book now") that embodied the business logic. As these applications grew and demanded higher capacity, faster throughput, and greater levels of global access, the apps themselves would migrate from one operating system to another, from one set of hardware to another. Migrating such apps to the cloud continues to require focus by the end-user organization on the underlying infrastructure issues.

Serverless architectures break the thought model in two important ways. First, they challenge designers to think about data as *events*. A customer calls to request a flight; treat this as an *event*, rather than merely as a source of new data that needs to be put in a file (or a database) someplace. Instead of designing an integrated application that enters into the dialogue with the customer, the sales agent, and the database, the designer identifies *functions* or *services* that need to be performed on the new data as it comes in. By chaining a series of functions together, new business logic can be developed, hosted, and put into use more easily and more quickly. Because of this emphasis on small, lightweight functions, these cloud models are often referred to as *functions as a service* (FaaS). The second major change introduced by the serverless concept is that these smaller, lighter bits of applications logic do not need to be hosted and running in a VM *while waiting* for an event to give them new data to process. The functions take up storage space (in libraries) while not in use, but they are not running up RAM or CPU costs while idle.

Major cloud services providers have been offering functional or serverless architecture components and services for about ten years now.

Because they are so inexpensive to create and use, it is tempting for customer organizations to set up user accounts with default settings and then dive right in and start making work happen. This happens all too frequently in *greenfield* or startup entrepreneurial settings, which can be long on enthusiasm and short on in-depth, focused risk management. As with any default settings, most of these serverless architectures make early entry and exploration simple but inherently insecure. Default accounts and user IDs often have unrestricted privileges; users must actively set security restrictions, such as establishing access controls for data storage, function invocation (calls to execute them), and the redirection of function outputs to storage, to display, or to other functions. Because it is so easy to get up and running in a serverless architecture, naïve users can be lulled into thinking that they have "nothing to worry about" from a security perspective. Nothing, of course, is further from the truth. As with "classical" cloud computing, serverless architectures are nothing new in terms of security fundamentals. Yes, they each have different knobs and levers to activate the controls needed to establish vitally needed information security measures. But they don't require us to rethink what security is or what the organizational information security requirements are, just how to carry them out.

TIP   If you'd like to learn more about serverless architectures and security, check out Lynn Langit's course at `https://www.lynda.com/Developer-tutorials/ Serverless-Architectures/774902-2.html`.

Legal and Regulatory Concerns

Chapter 1 detailed many of the most significant legal and regulatory frameworks that apply to the use of information by businesses, nonprofit organizations, and public or government agencies. That chapter also examined how these laws drive us to develop and use our information systems in ways that assure the confidentiality, integrity, availability, nonrepudiation, authentication, privacy, and safety of the information in those systems and the actions our organizations take because of that information. These CIANA+PS imperatives apply whether our systems are on-premise hardware with no external network connections or are serverless processing frameworks hosted in hybrid public clouds. These legal, regulatory, and ethical requirements are *platform-agnostic*, not tied to any particular technology. Increasingly, they also apply in most jurisdictions worldwide.

These legal and regulatory frameworks focus on the following sets of issues and concerns:

- **Privacy-related data must be protected:** It's referred to by many names and acronyms—PII, NPI, personal data, and probably more. Used correctly, it provides verifiable ways to relate data about events or activities to a specific person or group of people, and in doing so, it creates value for those who hold that data. It adds value *to* the data in the process. Legal and ethical principles have already established rules governing how such data can be gathered, aggregated, stored, used, shared, moved, displayed, and disposed of. These same principles also dictate what rights (in law and ethics) the individual at the heart of that data has over the use of that data, and whether they have rights in reviewing it. Laws also define procedures (in some jurisdictions) to allow such individuals rights to appeal for such data to be corrected or even expunged (witness the EU's "right to be forgotten" concept, which is part of the GDPR).

- **Failure to apply known and recognized lessons-learned is no excuse:** In law and ethics, the burdens of due care and due diligence *require* senior executives, directors, and owners of information systems to apply both common sense and current wisdom to *all* of their responsibilities. If a managing director had the *opportunity* to learn that their systems were compromised and yet failed to learn this and act to mitigate the harm, that managing director failed in their duties. We accept this for the captains of our ships of business and commerce; what we as SSCPs need to appreciate is that we, too, have the opportunity to *act better* based on what we know. That's part of being a *professional* after all.

- **Recordkeeping systems—in fact, *any* information system, automated or paper-based—must be auditable:** Senior executives and directors of organizations are held accountable for the decisions they've made regarding the assets, information, people, and objectives that have been entrusted to their care. Think of this as applying "trust nothing, verify everything" to the social decision-making networks that run your organization—this is *zero-trust architecture* applied to the total organization, not just to its IT infrastructure. Every decision needs its audit trail; audit trails depend upon maintaining the pedigree of the data in custody, the data that is used, and even the data that was *not* used in making certain decisions. Those needs for transparency, auditability, and accountability combine to produce strict requirements for information security and risk mitigation controls.

- **E-discovery is becoming the norm:** Three trends are pushing us toward a future of more e-discovery, rather than less. The first is the growing complexity of collaborative business relationships and the intermeshing value chains and streams by which business gets done. The second is the more vigorous enforcement of the ever-increasing complexity of the legal and regulatory environment that surround them. The third trend is the increasing sophistication, reach, and impact of cyberattacks on businesses, nonprofits, and government activities. Whether it's to better resolve a risk situation or properly identify the responsible parties, the use of digital discovery continues to grow.

The key to successfully navigating these legal and regulatory waters is *administrative*: written policy directives, implemented into operational procedures, must exist and be used to respond to situations involving these issues. These policies and procedures should be reviewed by the organization's legal advisors, their compliance officers, or other professionals. Those procedures are also a great situational awareness checklist for you when you're challenged by a situation or an issue that seems new and different. This is especially true when dealing with technologies that are new to the organization—or poorly understood by its information security specialists.

Jurisdiction and Electronic Discovery in the Cloud

Before we can address anything about legal and regulatory concerns, we must first consider what *jurisdictions*, plural, your organization may fall under. A purely local business in a town in Idaho, for example, is already answerable to at least three layers of U.S. government at the city, state, and federal levels. If your organization has customers, vendors, partners, or investors in other countries, those countries may have legal claims of jurisdiction over your organization's activities. Shipping goods or information across state or national borders also exposes the organization to the legal, regulatory, cultural, and in some cases religious authorities of another country. In any given case, such as an employee whose inappropriate use of company-owned IT resources, it may not be immediately clear which country's laws or other constraints may have the most power to dictate to the organization. Legal and social concepts about privacy, data ownership, data protection, and due diligence, for example, can take on entirely different meanings in different societies. As a member of the information security team, you cannot sort these issues out yourself—you must depend upon senior leadership and management to sort them out for the benefit of the organization as a whole.

Once your organization migrates any of its business processes and hence its information into the cloud, you must now contend with additional jurisdictional concerns. What jurisdictions are your cloud service providers' data centers located in? What other countries might those data centers' connections to the Internet transit through, on their way into the great public switched network? What cultural or religious authorities might believe that they, too, have an interest in controlling or constraining your information activities?

If your SLA provides you with geographically dispersed data center support from your cloud services provider, your data could be moving from country to country or continent to continent quite frequently. This could be as part of optimizing service delivery to your customers, for routine operational backups, or as part of your business continuity planning. Such movements of information may also bring with them jurisdictional constraints and considerations.

E-discovery (electronic discovery) orders encompass any kind of legal document, such as a search warrant or subpoena, which has legal authority to demand that information be retrieved, removed, or copied from IT systems and made available to the courts, investigators, or other officials. These legal orders can take many forms, and in some countries and societies, written court orders are not needed for government officials to search, collect, copy, or just remove information from your organization's workplace, its computers, and computers it may be connected to that are located elsewhere. If you're the information security person on watch when such a digital discover order is served on the company and it and the officer of the law come to your workspaces, you cannot and should not attempt to block, resist, or deter them in their efforts to get what they've come for. However, *unless your organization's attorneys have advised you to the contrary*, you should try to do the following:

- Ask if you can notify your supervisor or manager and the organization's compliance officer or legal advisor of the e-discovery order being served. If the officials say no, do not argue with them.

- Ask to see identification, and make note of names, badge numbers, and the organization the officers are from.

- Ask for a copy of the order.

- Ask to remain in the area during the search, as an observer.

- Make notes, if you can, of what they search and what they take with them.

- Ask for an inventory of what they copy or take with them.

In almost all circumstances, it will do no good and in fact may cause grave damage if you attempt to argue with the officers serving the e-discovery orders; you may think that they are exceeding their authority, but your opinion won't prevail in court (or keep *you* out of jail if worst comes to worst).

E-discovery orders might be served on your organization or on a cloud services provider that hosts your business processes and data. Such discovery orders served on the cloud hosting service could end up taking copies of portions of your data, even though your data was not the subject of the order, if it is on the same physical devices that are being seized under the order. Suitable use of encryption, by you and by your cloud hosting service, should protect you in this instance.

✔ Beware the Constraints on Discussing E-Discovery Processes

There are a number of circumstances in which you might be the on-scene organizational representative who is served with an order that says you are prohibited from discussing the discovery order or search warrant with anyone. In U.S. law, a *national security letter (NSL)* is a much more powerful form of a search warrant, and it carries with it severe penalties if you violate its prohibition of disclosure, especially if you discuss even the fact that you've been served with an NSL with company officials or lawyers. NSLs are issued by the Foreign Intelligence Surveillance Court in classified, closed-door sessions.

Other constraints are less dramatic and perhaps seem obvious: discovery orders about a particular customer, client, or employee (even a senior officer of the organization) should *not* be disclosed to the subject of that discovery order, nor to anyone who might reasonably be expected to inform that subject. Penalties for such *tipping off* can be severe as well.

Talk with your company's compliance officer, or its legal team, to seek any advice or information they think you should have *before* such a discovery process happens.

Cooperative E-Discovery for Regulatory, Audit, and Insurance Purposes

E-discovery (or even the old-fashioned request for paper or printed records) may come from many sources other than a court of law. Many of these result from processes that your organization willingly chooses to comply with and participate in, as part of doing a particular type of business. Many different regulatory, insurance, and contractual requirements will subject your organization to audits; those audits require that the auditors be granted access to information and your information systems, and you and other staff members may have to assist in making that information available to them. Civil litigation, such as claims for damages being made to the company by an aggrieved party, may need to have e-discovery done to support attorneys, auditors, or investigators for both sides.

Such *cooperative* e-discovery processes shouldn't come to you, as one of the information security team, as surprises; your managers should be well aware that the audit or investigation is ongoing and that the organization has agreed to support it. Nonetheless, be careful, and be diligent: if such a surprise auditor comes to your work area and is asking for information for whatever purpose, take a moment and check with management to make sure that this is not something to be alarmed about. It might be an ethical penetration tester, or an intruder, or a disgruntled fellow employee who's about to take a wrong turn.

Ownership, Control, and Custody of Data

Many different legal and cultural systems have tried to establish the meaning of these terms in clear and unambiguous ways. The EU General Data Protection Regulation (GDPR), for example, specifies that the person (or organization) that actually has the data in their possession is its *custodian*; custodians have responsibilities to protect such information from unlawful disclosure, or disclosure in violation of contracts that they are a party to. *Data controllers* are the ones who can dictate what processing must be done to the data, including its dissemination or destruction. The *owner* of the data is the one who had a legal right to require others to pay for using the data or otherwise has a *right* in that data that others must respect. Your company may create vast quantities of data, some of which they have an ownership interest or claim on; they may then contract with or direct others to do processing with it or sell it or pass it on to third parties in the course of doing business. E-discovery will ultimately require the custodian to grant access to the requested data, regardless of whether the data's owners or controllers are tasked by that discovery order or process as well.

Privacy Considerations

Private data, whether personally identifying information (PII) or nonpublic personal information (NPI), may be a major component of your organization's various databases and systems.

- PII may be more familiar to you; it's generally accepted that this means the set of information necessary and sufficient to identify, locate, or contact a specific, individual person. PII is therefore generally the basis of a claim of identity, such as by showing a government-issued passport, identity card, or driver's license. Compromised or stolen PII is generally the starting point for identity theft.

- NPI is a superset of PII. Defined in U.S. law by the Financial Services Modernization Act of 1999, also known as the Gramm-Leach-Bliley Act (GBLA), NPI is all of the information associated with an individual that is held by financial institutions or businesses as a part of their business records. This can include residential address histories, employment histories, financial transaction and account details, and more. Internationally, multiple regulatory frameworks such as GDPR, the Second Accord of the Basel Committee on Banking Supervision (commonly referred to as Basel II), and the EU Privacy Directive extend the protection requirements of *privacy* over what seems to be a never-ending list of information about any specific person.

You may have personally experienced this extension of NPI into your private *history*, if you deal with a bank or financial institution that asks you questions about the current balance, the last few transactions over a certain amount, or other authentication challenges that substantiate your claim to be the knowledgeable owner or user of the account in question.

As you might expect, different jurisdictions may have significantly different terms and conditions that apply to such data and its use, retention, and proper disposal procedures. The most common mistake businesses make in this regard is to assume that if they do not have an operating location in a jurisdiction, then that jurisdiction's laws do not apply to the business. This impression is mistaken: the presence of even *one* customer or supplier in a city, state, or country is sufficient to apply that jurisdiction's laws to the business. As private data from your systems transits national borders and enters or leaves data centers on foreign soil, your organization faces more potential legal complexities. Chapter 1 provides an in-depth examination of the legal and regulatory frameworks for protection of privacy-related information; those principles should guide you in your choices of access control methodologies (as covered in Chapter 2) to minimize the risks of compromise, loss, or theft of this class of sensitive data.

Blockchain, Immutable Ledgers, and the Right to Be Forgotten

Adoption of blockchain technologies, particularly the use of private blockchains for internal enterprise applications, continues to grow. An October 2020 forecast by Price Waterhouse Coopers indicates that overall, blockchain will add $1.76 trillion USD to the global economy.[3] This is one of many technologies that has the potential to upset the classical paradigm of data processing focused around huge databases. Blockchain technologies are being applied to more than 200 different business use cases ranging from financial transaction processing, citizens services, asset management, payment processing, supply chain management, digital identity, healthcare, and many other activities. There are even recent patents on making *editable* blockchains, which does seem to be a contradiction in terms; yet, there is a real need for a systematic way to allow all parties to a blockchain to agree to fix errors in data stored in that blockchain. (The current paradigm is to record the corrections in the blockchain as *edit transactions* that add entries to the blockchain's ledger, rather than go back and change data in a particular transaction or ledger entry.)

What may be missing around the use of this technology is the cultural, process-oriented thinking that helps customers, individuals, systems users, and systems builders know how to use a "never forgets" technology in ways that protect rights of privacy, rights to appeal incorrect or damaging data, and a right to be forgiven or forgotten. Law and regulation are still struggling with the implications of this technology's widespread adoption.

Surveillance Data and the Cloud

Many organizations operate a growing variety of surveillance systems in and around their workplaces; these can be part of meeting safety or security needs or as part of monitoring workplace behavior and conduct of their employees. Different legal jurisdictions have very different interpretations as to when and how surveillance violates a person's privacy, while also imposing different constraints as to how that data can be used, shared with others, how long it can be retained, and how it must be disposed of. If your perimeter security surveillance system, for example, is storing its data in the cloud, which jurisdiction that cloud is in may have impact on your plans for using that data in the course of doing business.

[3] https://www.pwc.com/gx/en/industries/technology/publications/ blockchain-report-transform-business-economy.html, cited in https://tadviser.com/ index.php/Article:Blockchain_(world_market); check out TADVISER's insights into many blockchain use cases.

Data Storage and Transmission

Possibly the greatest benefit that organizations can gain from migrating into the cloud is how easily the cloud can support the need for *resilience* in both processing power and data availability. Three major characteristics inherent to cloud structures contribute to this. Compared to a fixed-size traditional on-premises data center, cloud-hosted systems provide the following:

- Extensive use of virtualization creates the flexibility and scalability to meet dynamically changing demands for throughput, data transfer rates, and service delivery.

- Virtual networking allows for rapid rehosting of data and business logic, whether across the hardware in one cloud service data center or to data centers anywhere on the Internet.

- Virtual storage definition and management allows for many different data migration, backup, restore, mirrored or parallel processing, and archiving to meet users' operational, continuity, or disaster recovery needs.

- Extensive use of encryption of data at rest and in motion within the cloud data center, and to and from user locations, provides for very high isolation of one customer organization's data from all other customers' data at that center.

Taken all together, this means that your organization can tailor its needs for availability, continuity, security, throughput, and processing power to meet a continually changing mix of needs.

Third-Party/Outsourcing Requirements

Unless your organization is running a private or hybrid cloud, your cloud services are all being outsourced to third parties; and through them, no doubt, other layers of outsourcing are taking place. A typical cloud hosting data center might be operated by one corporate structure, in terms of whom you as customer contract with and interact with directly; that structure may only lease the underlying data center hardware, networks, operating systems, security, and communications capabilities, and have their maintenance and support subcontracted out to multiple providers. In a very real sense, your SLA—the service level agreement—provides the contractual "air gap" that insulates you from the management and contractual responsibilities of making that data center into an effective cloud for customers to use. In some cases, the cloud services provider may not actually own or operate a physical data center at all but instead are reselling someone else's cloud services. Application platforms as integrated service models can often be provided this way. Educational and training organizations that use products such as Instructure's Canvas system are paying for the integration of Instructure's application design and functionality, layered on top of *somebody's* cloud services. The customer doesn't care whose cloud it is; their SLA with Instructure specifies their needs for geographic dispersion of data and processing to achieve their school's needs for availability, access, throughput, reliability, and recovery. Instructure, as a business, has to translate the hundreds or thousands of SLAs it has with its customers into a master SLA with its actual cloud hosting services provider (although in reality, they start *from* their master SLA and parcel it out into productized service offerings to their customers).

Lifecycles in the Cloud

Applying a lifecycle model to your organization's data, metadata, and business logic (as embodied in software, scripts, and people-facing procedures) leads to identifying two critical tasks that must be done in order to have the levels of information security (on all attributes, from confidentiality through safety) that you need.

- Your needs must be documented in the SLA, clearly identifying which tasks or measures of merit are the service provider's responsibilities and which ones are yours. This includes specifying how the service provider gives you visibility into their security services as they apply to your presence in their cloud and how they support you with monitoring data, alarms, and response capabilities.

- Your IT and information security team must know how to configure, manage, monitor, and assess the effectiveness of *all* of the tasks that are your own responsibility, with respect to their deployment into the cloud, including all security-related monitoring, inspection, alert, and incident response functions.

Both of those are very tall orders for most organizations. Your organization is the one paying the bills to the cloud services provider; your own due care and due diligence responsibilities dictate that your organization must clearly and completely specify what it needs done, what standards will be used to measure how well that service is provided, what provisions allow and support you in auditing that service delivery and performance, and how misunderstandings, miscommunications, mistakes, and disputes will be settled between the two parties. This has to happen throughout the contractual life span of your agreement with that cloud provider, as well as across the lifecycle of the individual data sets, software, and service bundles that make up the business logic that is migrated into the cloud. This includes the following:

- **Audit support for your systems, data, and processing:** You need to identify any special provisions that your SLA must incorporate so that your organization can comply with audits you have to respond to. This involves data and processes hosted in the cloud provider's systems.

- **Audits of the cloud provider's systems and processes:** You need to determine what roles your organization will have, if any, when the cloud provider is audited. Know the audit requirements (standing and ad hoc or special) that they have to comply with and how frequently they are audited. Check if the SLA states whether these are guaranteed to be zero impact to your business operations or whether they specify a level of tolerable disruption or downtime. (In many respects, this is parallel to how your organization needs to have a working understanding with its own customers when *they* are subject to audits that might require involvement or support from your side of the relationship.)

- **Data and software disposal needs:** These must be clearly specified, and the roles that other third-party service providers fulfill should be identified and understood. All software and data systems reach an end-of-useful-life point. Data retention in many instances is limited in law—companies must destroy such data after a certain number of years have passed, for example. Software and user-facing procedural scripting becomes obsolete and are ultimately retired (either the business function is no longer required, or something new has taken its place). Measures of merit or standards of performance should be specified via the SLA, and the SLA should also lay out how your organization can verify that such third-party services have been correctly and completely performed.

- **Nondisclosure agreements (NDAs):** Most cloud services providers have nondisclosure terms in their standard SLAs or TORs that set limits on both parties as to what they can disclose to others about the business or technical operations of the two parties, as well as restricting the disclosure of information belonging to each party. This needs to be carefully reviewed as part of negotiating your SLA or TOR with such service providers, for it is a two-edged sword: it restricts your organization as well as the service provider, by requiring both of you to protect each other's information, business practices, and many other types of information.

Shared Responsibility Model

That lifecycle perspective is known as the *shared responsibility model*. Look back at Figure 7.1; as you peel the layers off of each large grouping of functionality, it's not hard to see that as a customer, your organization has a vital and abiding interest in knowing not only *how things work* in the cloud service provider's domains of responsibility but also *how well they work*. Your organization's due diligence responsibilities make it answerable to its external and internal auditors, to its stakeholders, to its employees, and to those whom it does business with. The more that your business moves into the cloud, the more that your cloud services provider becomes your *strategic partner*. By definition, a strategic partner is one that enables and empowers you to have the flexibility, depth, breadth, resilience, power, and presence to take on the objectives that keep your organization growing, thriving, and competitive. *Treat it like one.*

Or, if your organization uses a hybrid cloud deployment that marries you up with two or more cloud hosting service providers, treat them all as part of one big happy family. While there may be sound business reasons to play one services supplier off of another; at the end of the day, it may be a greater win for your organization to find ways to grow those pairwise shared responsibility models into a multiway *modus vivendi*, a way of living and working together to everyone's mutual benefit. Such public hybrids do impose a burden on the customer organization to be mindful of keeping within the nondisclosure aspects of their agreements with each provider.

Layered Redundancy as a Survival Strategy

The advocates of *zero-trust architectures* advise us to trust nothing and always verify. Migrating your organization's business logic and information assets to a cloud services provider may be taking all of your most valuable eggs out of one basket—the one you hold—and moving them into another, solitary basket, managed and operated by that single cloud services provider. Once again, apply the OSI seven-layer thought model, but with an extra added dose of *redundancy*. Redundancy can be at the same layer of the stack or at different layers, of course.

Backup and archival storage of important information assets vital to your business survival are a case in point. Consider the following two headline news stories from the same week in June 2019 that indicate the need to have diversity, distribution, and useful, verifiable retrieval and re-activation tactics for the "secret sauce" that makes your organization stay alive and thrive:

- Norsk Hydro, struck by a ransomware attack, has spent more than £45 million (about $60 million USD) in recovering its business operations using archived paper copies of sales orders and processing manifests, which relied on bringing retired workers back to work to help them understand these documents and use them to get Norsk Hydro's 170 operating locations worldwide back into business.

- Universal Studios' archive vault fire in 2008, according to articles in the *New York Times*, destroyed not only the primary copies of studio recording sessions by many Universal artists but also the "safety backups" of those archive recordings, which had been kept in the same vault. Lawsuits filed shortly thereafter claim breach of contract and are seeking hundreds of millions of dollars in damages. Artist Sheryl Crow commented to the BBC that this "feels like we're slowly erasing things that matter."

It is, of course, too early to jump to too many conclusions about either of these incidents. Even so, they strongly suggest a possible frame of mind to use. Let's start thinking about how alternate approaches can help us ensure the safety and security of what we value most. For example:

- If you currently protect high-value business processes by having them deployed to a public cloud environment, are they important enough that keeping the paper-based, human-driven process knowledge safe in a fire-proof off-site vault is worthwhile?

- If your organization is using an email-enabled transaction process, complete with strong nonrepudiation features built right in, are there some transactions, with some customers or clients, that are so important that an additional form of verification and validation helps protect both parties *and* enhances the relationship?

In many cases, it may not make sense to spread the risk by using alternative processing, storage, or reuse tactics in a loosely parallel fashion this way. Not everything is that critical to your most important organizational goals. But in a few cases, it might be worthwhile.

And the smaller and more entrepreneurial your organization is—and the more dependent upon the creative energy of its people it is—the greater the potential return on a little parallel or alternate investment such as these might become.

OPERATE AND SECURE VIRTUAL ENVIRONMENTS

It's good to start with NIST Special Publication 800-125, which was released in January 2011. You might think that this means it is somewhat outdated, but you might want to think again. In its short 35 pages, it provides a succinct roundup of the key topics that every virtual systems user should pay attention to as they consider their information security and business continuity needs. These recommendations focus on the five primary functions that the hypervisor provides to make a cloud what you need it to become.

- Execution isolation and monitoring of virtual machines
- Device emulation, and access control of devices and to devices on your virtual systems and networks
- Privileged mode execution by processes on VMs or on the hypervisor on behalf of those VMs, as well as privilege escalation and de-escalation by processes, tasks, or subjects
- Overall management strategies for VMs, including mechanisms for creation, dispatch, termination, and resource sanitization and release after termination
- Administration, including configuration and change management, of hypervisors and host operating systems and other virtual environment software, firmware, and hardware

Let's look at some of these areas from NIST 800-125 in further detail:

Isolation and Monitoring of Guest Operating Systems   Guest operating systems (those that are loaded and executing in virtual machines) need to be isolated from each other, and closely monitored, if security is to be achieved and maintained. A number of strategies should be examined.

- **Partitioning:** This can include how you control the mix of physical and logical assets that are partitioned and made available to VMs to use during execution, as well as protecting virtual machines from *break-out* or *escape* attacks. Rogue tasks running on a VM should be prevented from affecting the execution of other VMs or from accessing or contaminating resources that are not allocated directly to them by the hypervisor; such escapes, if not controlled, could result in malicious code or data spreading across a whole fleet of VMs in a matter of minutes.

- **Covert channel isolation:** When the hypervisor is run on top of a *host operating system* that controls the underlying hardware, it often provides access to *guest tools* that allow instances of other OSs, running in the VMs it is hosting, to share overhead and resources when accessing file systems, directories, the system clipboard, and many others. If not properly controlled, these can provide attack vectors or information leaks to hostile processes running in other VMs or across the virtual-to-real network connection. Bare-metal hypervisors eliminate the opportunity for guest tools by eliminating this type of sharing.

- **Side-channel attacks:** These seek to determine characteristics of the underlying hardware, hypervisor, and the guest OS itself, with an eye to finding exploitable vulnerabilities.

System Image and Snapshot Management   A system image or snapshot file captures the contents of a VM's memory, CPU state, and other information regarding its connections to virtual and physical resources. Similar to the hibernation file on a modern endpoint, these images can be quickly reloaded into virtual memory and then activated, as well as replicated to create other instances of that VM as many times as are required. While this makes for resilient systems, it also means that security-sensitive data in that image can be easily exported from your systems by exfiltrating a copy of that image file.

Managing and securing these images is becoming an acute problem, as the number of endpoint devices capable of supporting multiple virtual machines continues to grow. As images proliferate (or *sprawl*, in NIST's colorful terminology), your security risks spread almost without limit. One VM on one workstation or phablet might contain an app with an exploitable vulnerability, and an image of that app can quickly be spread to other similar devices throughout your organization in short order. Since the VM is running under the control of a hypervisor, there's nothing for an application's allowed list utility to discover or send up alarms about; the vulnerability itself may not have malware installed with it, so HIPS or HIDS may not be able to detect and prevent its sprawling across other devices either.

Containerize for Improved Security   Containerized VMs are becoming much more necessary (not just desirable) in software development and test activities. This adds even more images to the management challenges you're facing. Software testing, ethical penetration testing, security assessment, internal user training, and even customer or external partner training are just some of the business activities that are benefiting from shared use of VM images. While it's simple to say "Bring each VM image or snapshot under configuration management and control," there are *thousands* of such images to control, if not more, across a typical organizational IT architecture.

There is some good news in all of this, however. Since VM system images are an encapsulated copy of the system, those images can easily be further quarantined or isolated for malware scanning or forensic analysis if necessary. Scanning an image file with anti-malware tools can often spot rootkits or other malware that can otherwise obscure its existence when it is running. Stopping a VM and capturing a complete image of it is also a lot easier than capturing a systems image from a bare-metal server or endpoint system since the hypervisor can halt the VM's CPU without causing any data or processor state information to be lost.

Endpoint and Desktop Virtualization Security Endpoint devices are becoming more and more capable and useful as VM hosts in many business use cases; in many respects, host-based hypervisors make using preconfigured VHD images or snapshots as easy as mounting a DVD and double-clicking a program. A common use case involves supporting special-purpose hardware that has been orphaned by its vendor and is no longer compatible with modern operating systems. The United Kingdom's National Health Service, for example, got hit hard by the WannaCry ransomware attack in part because NHS as a system could not afford the costs to upgrade printers, fax machines, and clinical systems in tens of thousands of healthcare providers' clinics across the country to bring them off of Windows XP or Windows 7 and onto Windows 10. Running one Windows 10 system in such a clinic and using a hosted hypervisor as the controller for these orphaned devices might have been a workable solution, but it was not explored in a timely way.

Everything said previously regarding image and snapshot management applies for each endpoint that is hypervisor-capable in your system. This includes guest devices, mobile devices, and employee-owned endpoints (whether they are under MDM or not). Each hypervisor-capable endpoint and each user who has access to that endpoint dramatically increases your threat surface. This may put a significant burden onto your preexisting access control, network security, monitoring, and analysis capabilities; yet, if you do not step up to the security management challenge of dealing with widespread virtualization use on your endpoints, you may be leaving your systems wide open to a surreptitious entry and attack (or an outright obvious one, such as a ransom attack).

Software-Defined Networking

Stop and think a moment about *software-defined networks*. Once you rise up from the hard realities of the physical layer, everything you do in configuring, testing, managing, securing, and repairing your networks takes place via software. The GUIs in the routers, switches, HIPS and HIDS, and SIEMs that you use to manage these devices are implemented via software. More sophisticated network and systems management, configuration control, and security systems have you using additional software to define the network. All of the tools you use at the touch-the-box level of networking, such as NAT, PAT, and even DHCP and DNS, are all ways of taking a *logical* or *administrative* definition of your connectivity needs and mapping that onto the underlying hardware. The software you use to define your networks is, in effect, taking your picture of the network at the control, management, and data planes, and commanding the hardware elements to configure themselves to match. The software doesn't move cables around at a patch panel, of course, and segmentation of networks that requires physically inserting a device between two segments will require some "hardware-defined" action (carried out by one of your carbon-based network and security assets).

Virtual networks take this a bit further, and while we don't have the scope here to look at them in greater depth or detail, let's look at the basics:

- The *physical substrate* is the layer of physical routers, cables, switches, and servers that provide the interconnections. This substrate provides a full OSI 7-layer stack (unless you tailor things out of it). It provides the connection to physical gateway devices, such as your ISP's point of presence or another on-site set of physically separate LAN segments. This layer has physical NICs talking to physical connections.

- Each *virtual network* is defined on top of that substrate but not necessarily on top of each other. Each virtual network has to define its IP addressing scheme and its subnets and supply all of the capabilities that virtual machines that users of that virtual network will need. Virtual routing and switching functions, virtual NIDS or NIPS, are all provided as software services that get invoked as the network stack on each virtual machine makes service requests of the virtual network (all via our old friends in the TCP/IP and OSI 7-Layer protocols). These definitions live as data sets, not as switch settings or physical connections between devices; much as NAT, PAT, or DHCP help map your internal LAN addressing and port structures into what the outside world interacts with. The NICs (and other hardware elements) are now reduced to software virtualizations of what they'd do in the real world.

Once again, you're starting from the same information security requirements, and you may have already mapped them onto your current physical network infrastructure. Mapping them onto a new virtual network involves the same choices and the same issues; it's just that you can replicate and expand a dynamically adjustable firewall or router capability in a VLAN by using a well-debugged script file, rather than having to finally go and buy equipment, install it, run cables, and *then* interact with its internal firmware and GUIs or web pages to configure it.

It's important to stay focused: keeping your entire virtualized infrastructure safe and secure is really no different than keeping a physical infrastructure of servers, applications, networks, endpoints, and ISP connections secure. The same best practices apply, but with one important caution added: for some reason, many organizations that migrate to the clouds *assume* that their cloud services provider will handle all of their security needs, or certainly the toughest ones; they then go about the business of building and running their own virtual data center as if it was completely isolated from the outside world and has no need for special security measures to be put in place. This is akin to believing that if only we use enough cryptography, we can solve all of our security problems. Both are false and dangerous myths.

Hypervisor

This is another area that is naturally high on NIST SP 800-125's recommended focus areas for virtual systems security. Bare-metal hypervisors and hosted hypervisors have dramatically different security profiles, and it's probably not overgeneralizing to say that unless you have a specific use case for hosted hypervisor use, don't. (One reasonable use case would be in teaching and training situations, wherein students are developing their own knowledge and skills in using hypervisors and building virtual machines. A bare-metal hypervisor doesn't provide enough of a user-friendly environment that other learning tasks and resources might require. On the other hand, you ought to be able to keep such machines isolated more easily.) If you must run hosted hypervisors, take a hard look at severely limiting the number and types of applications you install and use in each VM type that you run on that hypervisor; this will also help limit or reduce your threat surface.

Key recommendations from NIST include the following:

- Maintain the hypervisor as fully patched and updated using vendor-provided distribution kits. Most hypervisors contain features that let them hunt for updates and notify your systems administrator about them, and then install them automatically. If that doesn't fit with your configuration management and builds and control processes, then implementing a centralized, managed push process is called for.

- Tightly restrict and audit all access to the management interface of the hypervisor. This is the interface used to create, configure, and set control parameters for new VM types that you define, as well as editing existing machines and controlling the ways in which they get instantiated and are executed. NIST recommends that either a dedicated (out-of-band) communications interface be used to access hypervisor management interfaces or that a FIPS 140-2 validated authentication and encryption process is used to secure and protect in-band use of the management interface. Log all attempts at using the management interfaces, and audit those logs for anomalies that might indicate an intrusion attempt or attack.

- Synchronize all hypervisors to a trusted, authoritative time source, ideally the same source you use to synchronize clocks on all machines in your system.

- Disconnect unused physical hardware from the bare-metal server supporting the hypervisor; in particular, remove or disable unused network interfaces, USB ports, or other storage devices. External devices used for periodic backup or update should be attached and connected for that task and then disconnected from the system to reduce the threat surface.

- Disable all sharing services between guest and host OSs unless they are mandatory for your use case and situation. If they are, ensure that they can be tightly controlled and closely monitored.

- Use hypervisor-based security services to monitor the security of each guest OS that is launched under the hypervisor's control.

- Carefully monitor the hypervisor for any signs of compromise, and thoroughly assess all hypervisor activity logs on an ongoing basis.

Peel the cloud layer back far enough and all of that virtualization encounters the raw physicality of servers, memory, real NICs, and storage subsystems, all cabled together; they all eat power and generate heat as well as revenue. Even the smallest of virtualization labs in your software development or security testing work areas needs to be physically protected from all of the hazards of accident, sabotage, intrusion, theft, or misuse. These servers and everything that supports and interfaces with them need to be part of your overall information systems security plans, programs, and procedures. If all of your hypervisor use is via your cloud services providers, then double-check your SLA to make sure you understand what it commits your provider to do. Review, too, how that provider subjects itself to independent audit of its security measures, as well as how you as a customer can verify that they are living up to their end of the SLA.

Virtual Appliances

As *applications* have slimmed down into *apps*, so have applications and apps been further transformed into *appliances*. These are not the washing machine or vacuum cleaner type of appliances but software packaged into a form factor that simplifies its use in a very narrow way. Handheld point of sales devices epitomize this trend: a small box, not much bigger than a smart phone, that allows a retail salesperson to enter details of a customer purchase, swipe a credit or debit card for payment, and provide a receipt, with the order or purchase details dispatched to a fulfillment process that picks the items from inventory or prepares the customer's meal for them. A *virtual appliance* (VA) is a virtual machine preconfigured with its guest OS, applications, and interfaces, tailored to do its specific set of functions. Whether the virtual appliance is then loaded onto a hardware platform for direct execution or onto a cloud-hosted hypervisor for rapid deployment at scale is dictated by the underlying business need.

As with all software and machine images or snapshots, configuration management and control, user and device access control, and intrusion detection and prevention capabilities are a must. The onboard applications should be tailored to as limited a set of function points as are absolutely necessary to meet the need for the appliance; every extra function widens the threat surface of the appliance.

Another use of VAs is to preconfigure and deploy more feature-rich applications for end users to interact with from their endpoints. This can simplify software maintenance and configuration control: if you have 200 end users needing to frequently use a financial modeling application, you can either install it on every endpoint, install it once in a VA and let end users access and run instances of that VA (cloud hosted or locally hosted on their endpoint), or look to the software vendor for a platform solution. Each has its sweet spot as you balance cost, complexity, and management effort.

Continuity and Resilience

To some systems planners, managers, and security specialists, *continuity* and *resilience* are two sides of the same coin. They both measure or express how well your systems can continue to survive and function correctly in the face of rapid and potentially disruptive change, but while continuity describes your ability to recover from upsets, accidents, attacks, or disasters, resilience measures your systems' ability to cope with *too much good news*. Book publishing provides a case in point: printing, binding, and shipping books to retailers who stock their bookshelves with them and wait for customers to buy them can end up with a lot of unsold books if you print too many but can also result in many unhappy customers who still don't buy the book if you print far too few. E-publishing or other print-on-demand strategies trade off some of that risk for the immediacy of a download.

Cloud systems and their inherent virtualization provides both of these capacities, as we've seen from several perspectives throughout this chapter. Your organization's SLA with your cloud provider can give your business processes the geographic dispersion to survive most any natural disaster, terrorist action, or political upheaval, while providing the resiliency to scale dynamically to meet your needs.

Attacks and Countermeasures

Throughout this chapter—and in other places throughout this book—we've seen that our systems are exposed to attacks simply because they are connected to a public-facing Internet. Whether those systems run the seven-layer OSI stack on our private in-house data center or in a cloud hybrid of services from multiple cloud hosting providers doesn't really make much difference. Your threat surface is overwhelmingly defined by what you specify, select, include, enable, configure, and use; your choices in systems hardening, your prioritization of which vulnerabilities to fix today and which ones can wait a while are really not affected by where your organization hosts its business logic.

So, what *is* different about being in the cloud versus in your own in-house systems, from an attack and defense perspective?

- Shared responsibilities via your SLA, as a service model itself, can provide you with a far greater pool of experience and technology than your organization can generate, field, and afford to pay for by itself. The big ten cloud services providers spend billions of dollars in providing the best suite of security capabilities, tools, services, monitoring and alarm facilities, data isolation, and support that they can. These are core capabilities that are also the razor's edge of their competitiveness; if the marketplace did not fundamentally see these companies as providing services that can be fully secured, by the customers, to meet their various needs and use cases, these companies would not be as profitable as cloud providers as they are.

- Shared *constraints* are defined by your SLA. If you own and operate your own data centers and networks, you have a greater degree of inherent flexibility and freedom to bring in the ethical penetration testers and have them go at your systems and your organization, be that as white-box, black-box, or gray-box testing. You will still need to do security assessment testing, including penetration testing; first, though, *check with your cloud services provider.*

Your SLA and your relationship with your cloud services provider (or providers, plural, if you're doing a hybrid approach) is your most powerful tool when it comes to keeping your cloud-hosted, cloud-entangled business logic, processes, and information safe, secure, available, confidential, and private. You will pay for extra services that you ask for, such as the provider's assistance in tailoring security controls or assisting you in investigating an incident. But you would probably have to pay to bring in outside expert help anyway.

As a roundup, consider some of the various "top ten" lists of security issues related to cloud deployments; they commonly list insider threat, malware injections, use of insecure APIs, abuse of cloud services, denial-of-service attacks, data loss, shared vulnerabilities, and failure of the user's own due diligence processes. Account hijacking, privilege escalation, and catastrophic failure of backup and disaster recovery procedures add to these lists. Nothing is new there, just because your business has migrated into the clouds (plural, as more of you go hybrid in doing so).

The list of top countermeasures remains much the same:

- Multifactor access control.
- Rigorous management and auditing of privileged account use.
- Enforcing access control protection mechanisms on data storage.

- Intrusion detection and prevention for networks, hosts, and servers.
- Thorough, effective configuration management and control for all hardware, firmware, software, and interconnections.
- Engaging, informing, and involving all of your end users to be part of your active defenses.
- Anti-malware and application allowed and blocked list management.
- Secure business logic and process design, such as with separation of duties for critical or high-risk tasks.
- Audit, inspect, review, log, analyze, and monitor.
- Screen and filter against spam, phishing, and vishing attacks.
- Trust nothing; verify and authenticate everything.
- Endpoint security is paramount.

Shared Storage

Questions about shared storage in the cloud tend to reflect two broad sets of concerns.

- Physical storage devices and subsystems at the cloud services provider almost always contain data for multiple customers. This is probably the most common concern raised and the most common situation at major cloud services provider data centers. From the service provider's perspective, they simply cannot afford the legal complexities of allowing multiple customers' data to be freely commingled on a single disk drive, with no protections, barriers, or isolating technologies used to keep it separate. What most providers do is to encrypt individual user data files, encrypt the logical storage volumes that they create for that user or customer, and then stripe those storage volume extents or granules out onto individual disk drives in their storage subsystems. Each drive will no doubt have multiple such stripes of data from multiple customers on it, but since the storage volume's logical structure is separately encrypted for each customer, as well as each file being encrypted, someone who had access to the drive itself would need all of those decryption keys to start trying to read the data off of the disk drive. With proper key management security in place (such as a hardware security module being used to manage the keys), the likelihood of such cracking becoming successful is very, very low. Drives that are pulled from service due to malfunction or incipient fault are sanitized prior to being turned over to repair, salvage, or disposal. (If you're dealing with a cloud services provider who does *not* provide this type of security, you are strongly cautioned to start shopping around. Quickly.)

- Sharing of data with other users, such as external partners, vendors, or customers, which is stored in your cloud-hosted systems environment. This might involve a hybrid cloud system as well, if (for example) your main business processes and data are hosted in an Azure-based or AWS cloud environment, but you have groups of end users who routinely use Google Drive or Dropbox to share files with other parties. Your security requirements, in terms of function and performance, have not changed; this is no different than if you were hosting all of that data on an in-house server on your networks and providing these other users access to the data via SSO, perhaps mediated by specific applications.

In both cases, your organization's existing information security classification guides and policies, and your security requirements, plans, and programs, should already be driving you to implement safeguards for your existing on-premises servers, networks, end-points, and SSO or federated shared access. The shared responsibility model and your SLA may move some of these concerns (especially the first group) to your cloud services provider; *you* still need to own the responsibility to see that your security needs are being met, especially by transferring these risks to your cloud host.

SUMMARY

We've come full circle in this chapter, starting from looking at what makes software so insecure through what is or is not different about your information security needs and posture when you migrate your business processes and data into the cloud. We've tested the notion of using the OSI 7-layer reference model as a paradigm, not so much as just a protocol stack; we let it teach us to think about implementing and validating our systems security in layers from the physical to the personal. One clear observation is that it's becoming impossible—or perhaps not terribly useful—to try to separate systems security from network security, or software and applications security from people, procedural, and communications security. Convergence has welded these together, and therein we can find what we need to keep our businesses, our personal information, and our societies a bit safer, one day at a time.

Appendix: Cross-Domain Challenges

YOU'VE SEEN BY NOW that many of the protocols and design aspects of IT and OT systems (and security for those systems) do not cleanly fit within one layer of the ISO 7-Layer protocol stack; nor do they necessarily fit cleanly within a single SSCP domain. The nature and sophistication of the cyberattacks committed during the years 2019 to 2021 demonstrate that security professionals do need to sometimes step back from the particulars they are specialists in and take a more holistic view of certain strategic, tactical, and operational choices their organization has to make. This holistic view can help frame specific issues in a larger organizational context, while providing the insight an SSCP might need to put the right priorities or emphasis on the right details.

To help you as the on-scene SSCP make that holistic shift in viewpoint, this chapter rounds up a selection of these cross-domain challenges—which are of course cross-domain *opportunities* as well. We'll do this by pivoting selected topics and subtopics, a few from one domain, a handful from another, to bring them together in an integrated, more cohesive view of an issue, problem, or opportunity. This may approach some topics with more of a mission-oriented checklist, while others may require a closer look at the detailed interactions of elements in a security system (and how they may fail under duress).

Several "pivot strategies" appear as we look at information security from this perspective:

- **Pivot 1**: Turn the attackers' playbooks against them.
- **Pivot 2**: Cybersecurity hygiene: think small, act small.
- **Pivot 3**: Flip the "data-driven value function."
- **Pivot 4**: Operationalize security across the immediate and longer term.
- **Pivot 5**: Zero-trust architectures and operations.

PARADIGM SHIFTS IN INFORMATION SECURITY?

What's driving us to need to pivot our thinking in these and other ways? Several aspects of the attacks seen across cyberspace in the last few years argue that it's time to shift the security focus from prevention to detection and response:

- *Calling a cyberattack an "act of terror" doesn't help deal with it.* Identifying (or alleging) that attackers are state-sponsored agents or terrorists voids most business and cybersecurity liability insurance.

- *High-value federated systems of organizations are also high-value targets.* Interconnecting organizations via IT, OT, and people-based processes brings together previously isolated sets of data and processes, while exposing all players to greater M&A security risk. Regardless of what their motivations are, attackers are demonstrating that such lucrative integrated supply and value chain federations, partnerships, and consortia provide tempting targets for social engineering, data exfiltration, and process disruption.

- *Infrastructure attacks are more pervasive and more disruptive than previously anticipated.* Organizations are finding that previous assumptions regarding what it takes to "survive to operate" are no longer valid.

- *Disruption of manufacturing, transportation, and other physical systems by cyberattacks occurs more frequently and with greater impact.* Securing the IT-OT boundaries is thus becoming vital to organizational survival.

- *Individuals are at as great if not greater risk of attack than organizations are.* Individuals, rather than corporations or governments, are targeted by the vast majority of cyberattacks of all kinds, but it's unclear what fraction of these attacks end up producing useful data for subsequent social engineering or other components in larger, more sophisticated attacks against organizational targets.

- *Misinformation attacks are becoming more prevalent and disruptive.* Attackers have long used malformed data attacks to manipulate, mislead, defraud, or disrupt business and organizational processes and the systems they run on. This tactic has expanded to include fraudulent manipulation of indicators and sources of public or market opinion, such as astroturfing (as the next generation of "false likes" to manipulate perceptions of product, service, or business value).

- *Greater emphasis on safety and privacy* are changing the ways in which we think about managing projects. The traditional trio of cost, schedule, and performance still apply, of course, but in many ways, we're starting to see a greater emphasis on product and system safety, as well as on protecting privacy-related information that will be part of the resulting system.

Organizations, too, are rapidly changing the ways in which they and their people get work accomplished—or expose the organization to new and more challenging information security risks:

- *Human security behaviors are continuing to change.* Finding anomalous behaviors as part of intrusion or attack detection increasingly relies on modeling the expected normal behavior of legitimate users performing authorized work. This approach risks becoming another signature-based detection paradigm, which invites unpleasant surprises.

- *Transformational communication paradigms are changing the topologies of the organization and its systems.* Many organizations see continuous change in the ways that their workforce, customers, prospective customers, partners, suppliers, and stakeholders all come together to achieve their joint and several objectives. Social media technologies are not the issue here—it's the changes in the ways people think about finding, using, and sharing observations, insights, and data that are. This embraces more change, and more types of channels and collaborative networks, than most mobile device management (MDM) strategies, policies, and services can cope with.

- *Collaborative connectivity with digital nomads brings its own security challenges, which start with information classification and categorization policies.* As classical models of organizational control of employees continue to break down, different strategies are needed to help such highly mobile talent keep safe the secrets each organization they deal with has entrusted to them. This also places greater challenges on those organizations to ensure the right balance of information security and effective use of their information assets via collaboration with these nomads.

- *"Need to know" is expanding to include "need to appreciate the wisdom derived from what you (may or may not) need to know."* Metadata, semantic tags, and even the lessons learned from data that are embodied in the parameters of machine learning systems are increasingly becoming strategic information assets to many organizations. This means it may be time to rethink both policy and procedure for protecting these assets.

These and other, similar mini-trends are driven by—or are driving—the ways in which people and organizations incorporate apps, technologies, and changes in connectivity into their business logic and their collaboration with each other. These types of shifts in thinking are changing the face of competition in many ways as well. Taken altogether, they present challenges to information security professionals; coping with those challenges may be best served by changing the ways in which we think, starting with the ways we choose to frame and perceive these as problems, situations, or opportunities.

PIVOT 1: TURN THE ATTACKERS' PLAYBOOKS AGAINST THEM

Many existing defensive postures have been designed, deployed, and put to use as a collection of point defenses. These types of architectures often are a mix of top-down analyses that drove to a selection of security controls, or a bottoms-up inclusion of specific security controls dictated by various compliance mandates the organization has to meet. Coordinating the behavior of those point defenses with SIEM, SDS, or SOAR[1] systems is of course a logical and oftentimes necessary step to take. (Larger enterprise architectures probably could not function securely without such layered-on command, control, and communication capabilities as these technologies provide.)

One way to put this pivot strategy into action involves *security assessment*, which can make these assessments more holistic. Ideally, this would use scenarios drawn from real-world attacks as its starting points for planning, conducting, and evaluating assessment activities of all types. This requires the SSCP to be reading the vulnerability exposure and exploit insights within the context of a variety of persistent attack scenarios, rather than in an exploit-by-exploit, point-by-point fashion. In short, this is using the kill chains of various attackers as your plan of patrol, inspection, and assessment. You do, of course, need to ensure that over time, every control undergoes the right mix of security and operational assessment, just as every critical process should.

A variety of techniques, approaches, or resources can be helpful when working through this pivot strategy. Let's take a look.

ATT&CK: Pivoting Threat Intelligence

Typically, the various common vulnerabilities and exposures (CVE) databases, such as that maintained by MITRE or the national vulnerability databases (NVDs) published by a number of governments, are all arranged around each individual vulnerability, with search terms providing access via systems, applications, time, or other keywords. These real-world databases (which are kept very current by their providers) are of course valuable if not necessary elements of any vulnerability identification and management program. MITRE has pivoted its CVE data around real-world threat behaviors, as demonstrated in numerous advanced persistent threat attacks. This groups the use of different exploits into the broad phases of the cyber kill chain, expanded to as many as 17 major possible phases of a cyberattack as a military-style campaign plan. These are further

---

[1] Security incident and event monitoring (SIEM), software-defined security (SDS), and security orchestration, automation and response (SOAR) are complementary technologies and strategies for network, systems, and information security.

broken down into types of tactics, with each tactic linked to exploits, and the exploits linked to vulnerabilities and exposure data.

The real power of the ATT&CK framework, however, lies in the way in which MITRE has enabled any user to define their own frameworks for organizing attack-related scenarios to suit their own needs. Currently, MITRE offers three broad frameworks based on enterprise architectures, mobile services providers, and industrial process control environments. Tools are provided to let users make their own private copies of any of these templates and then tailor them to reflect their own systems, risks, and choices of threat scenarios. These private templates can be shared with others at their creators' discretion.

These templates can then form the basis of your security assessment planning and conduct or be used as thematic drivers throughout the organization's cybersecurity education, training, and awareness programs and activities.

Analysis: Real-Time and Retrospective

Pivoting our perspective on analysis and monitoring can be done by focusing on detecting an ongoing attack or intrusion, or the near-real time but retrospective detection that such a security compromise may have already occurred. This is akin to how the NIST cybersecurity framework CSF tries to shift attention and emphasis more onto the detection and response steps of the incident response cycle, rather than starting with planning and prevention. (There seems an implicit assumption in this: While the organization may or may not have done enough to prevent an intrusion, this rapidly becomes academic if the organization can't survive an ongoing attack and recover from its aftermath.) This leads one to think that in moderate-sized organizations with a SOC or SOC-like team, there may need to be three different types of analysis activities taking place, all of which look at precursors, indicators, and other security data but in different timeframes:

- Real-time analysis focuses on triggering alarms to initiate incident response activities; more often than not, this is done algorithmically. This happens around the clock, seven days a week, all year long. Because this is an analyst-intensive activity, most organizations use it only for the most urgent and compelling threat situations, ones involving very high-value information assets. This might be when other precursors and indicators have suggested an imminent insider threat action is about to take place.

- Near real-time analysis is performed or more actively guided with human SOC analysts working through indicators, security data, and their analytic results. The primary focus is to determine whether a security compromise may have started in the very recent past (hours or days ago) as a way to alert other investigators to determine if that incident is still underway. In more process-oriented shops, this might be done on a cyclic basis, system by system, or even security domain by domain. This, too, generally happens around the clock, every day throughout the year.

- Retrospective analysis is usually performed by normal office staff analysts, rather than around the clock. It seeks to determine if an intrusion or other security compromise occurred or began to happen at any time within the depth of time covered by the security data on hand. This, too, can become very analyst-intensive, particularly when the data that must be evaluated does not lend itself to machine learning-based analytic assessment. The depth of this backward view in time may be days, weeks, or months, and varies considerably across organizations. Such retrospective analysis may be triggered by events, such as the discovery of a previously unknown set of vulnerabilities in the organization's systems or security processes, or as an evidentiary process in a forensic investigation.

All of these types of analyses lend themselves to a degree of workflow and playbook management, whether the organization is using SOAR systems and tools or not. Some of those workflows and playbooks might benefit from being informed by, if not modeled after, some of the real-world attack scenarios captured in ATT&CK and other threat intelligence sources.

It's worth noting that a lot of the after-action analysis of real-world attacks on process control infrastructures and systems, such as Dragos and other security services vendors have published, emphasize that these real-world events are not tripping any predetermined indicators of compromise (IoCs); they're not fitting any signatures that the organization already had on hand and in use. Caution is advised, therefore: Don't let your own analysis processes become signature-driven. Many state-of-the-shelf machine learning systems can use generative adversarial networks (GANs) to generate thousands of potential signatures in minutes; this does not mean that you nor your analysts can easily and quickly assess those candidate signatures, explain them to management, and build enough trust in them quickly enough to empower the machines to make real-time alarm decisions for you.

As of this writing, there's no clear-cut advice regarding how much of your intuition and experience must come into real-time use, when one of your UEBA, ABAC, XDR,[2] or other risk-based access control tools raise the flag and proclaim that they've spotted something that might be suspicious or even hostile. Organizations facing high-value or

---

[2] User and entity behavior analytics (UEBA), attribute-based access control (ABAC), and extended detection and response (XDR) are becoming core elements of access control and security monitoring for devices, entities, and both human and nonhuman users and entities.

high-risk threats may find this involves creating hundreds of their own unique potential risk indicators (sometimes known as PRIs) that their models and human analytic processes must generate, trend, and monitor. Vendors and end-user organizations alike are expanding the field of regard of these tools, in an effort to be on the lookout for multiple entities, working at different times to collaboratively stage a complex, persistent attack. The best advice is to pivot your own perspective a bit; stand in the shoes of multiple sets of attackers, and see your systems, processes, and assets from their point of view.

At the end of the day, your organization may get a greater return on its budgets for analytics-driven monitoring and alarm capabilities by investing more in its human analysts, technicians, and on-shift SOC personnel. Keep your teammates' skills sharp, focused, and applied to the job; this will probably pay off sooner and more effectively than buying into hardware, software, or models that no one in the SOC team really knows how to use or bothers to use very much if at all.

The SOC as a Fusion Center

Fusion centers provide a powerful capability to bring the many different operational, planning, and support activities of a modern organization together into a real-time, focused environment for detecting and responding to surprises. PayPal, for example brings its customer service, order fulfillment, information security, fraud detection and response, and compliance monitoring, assessment, and reporting activities together into a fusion center. This stimulates rapid cross talk and collaboration across these different business operational groups. Adding their change management, suggestions and complaints processing, and internal help desk to the fusion center rounds out its 360-degree, full-circle visibility into every aspect of the company's business activities in real time.

Such fusion centers also act as an all-source intelligence capability, by combining data from sources traditionally used by security processes with very nontraditional sources. Outside sources might include third-party threat intelligence feeds, news services, and partner organizations; internal sources might also include departments such as HR, finance, and shareholder relations, as well as sources throughout the organization's entire product value chain. This breadth and depth of intelligence data can enable the fusion center to detect both external and internal threat situations or to flag events that seem unusual and therefore bear closer watching or investigation by the SOC.

Growing a fusion center can and probably should be an incremental process, which allows the organization as a whole and the SOC or fusion center team specifically to learn by doing. This simple strategy can also go a long way to defuse fear of change. And it's part of pivoting the SOC's point of view from being focused on "just security matters" to taking in the larger context that the organization lives and works in.

All-Source, Proactive Intelligence: Part of the Fusion Center

Many different business pressures drive organizations to structure their people, processes, and resources into functionally related groups. At their best, these provide a pipeline-like focus and efficiency on their activities, inputs, outputs, and outcomes. As with an integrated process team (IPT) or integrated process and product team (IPPT), these functionally aligned pipelines can develop deep knowledge and expertise on their areas of activities. An *intelligence fusion center* is a similar approach, aligned with advising real-time risk management and business *operational* decisions, rather than being oriented toward the longer-term developmental processes that the organization may use.

A fusion center is an operations center that uses all-source intelligence data to inform the organization in real time about its ongoing operations and other matters of interest. As an operations center, it generally operates 24 hours per day, throughout the year; people who represent each functional area of interest within the organization work together in the fusion center to bring together both the wide range of data sources and the equally broad range of business, process, or technical perspectives, expertise, and concerns within the organization.

In a business setting, an intelligence fusion center brings together people from across the organization to monitor, assess, and take actions based on events in real time. Intelligence sources would include data and insights drawn from a wide variety of channels, people, and functions, such as:

- News media, both of general and specialized market or business news
- Sales, customer service, and other business operational systems indicators
- Technical systems operational indicators from the industrial control or SCADA systems
- Threat intelligence feeds, in a variety of forms
- Billing and financial systems operational indicators
- Labor, human relations, or other workforce-related data
- Physical and cybersecurity system indicators
- Help desk, maintenance, or other problem reporting, analysis, and repair service indicators
- And others

A growing number of financial services and retail businesses put this fusion center process into action by combining their fraud detection, IT and cyber security, physical security, and customer-facing applications traffic and performance monitoring and control systems together. They also bring in their help desk, complaints processes (internal or external), customer service functions, compliance reporting, and even investor relations activities, and enable and empower these seemingly separate business processes and people to talk with each other and to collaborate with each other on a real-time basis. Manufacturing, transportation, materials handling, and medical services organizations are also using the all-source intelligence fusion center approach, bringing the additional and necessary safety voices to the conversation.

One way to think about the fusion center is to consider systems approaches, such as SEIM and SOAR, as providing some parts of the eyes, ears, and analytical horsepower that the team of people who are the fusion center need to do their jobs more effectively. A swarm-based attack conducted over a long dwell time is very difficult to detect; UEBA and other machine-learning-intensive approaches can only go so far in flagging events for human analytical consideration. The fusion center can be your organization's best last hope for detecting when many seemingly unrelated actions, being taken by many entities and identities, are affecting many different elements of your systems and architecture across a long span of days or weeks. As another example, the fusion center might be able to notice the effects of lateral movement that many attackers (and internal threat actors) enjoy in systems lacking a sound zero-trust approach.

Fusion centers are also great career-broadening and professional development opportunities for the people assigned to them. Many organizations that are using such fusion centers find it easier to teach security skills and mindsets to their business operations employees, rather than teaching their security specialists how to think and communicate in business-oriented ways. Yet even the most business-oriented fusion center needs its security experts. Finding and maintaining the right mix of attitudes and skills is a leadership and management challenge.

PIVOT 2: CYBERSECURITY HYGIENE: THINK SMALL, ACT SMALL

As of October 2021, it's estimated by a number of analysts in the United States, United Kingdom, and Australia, for example, that between one-quarter and one-third of all small and medium businesses and enterprises (SMBs and SMEs) that suffer a cyberattack will cease to function as a result. Many such organizations, along with small or home office (SOHO) operations, may rely on consumer-level technologies, and some of these can quickly become technical orphans when their manufacturers no longer generate software or firmware updates for them.

Gartner, Forrester, and other researchers report that the SMB market for managed security services is growing more than 10 percent per year. Yet even the best advice to such small and medium operators that managed security services providers (MSSPs) and analysts can give starts with the same simple truth: the organization and its leaders first need to know themselves and their information assets.

CIS IG 1 for the SMB and SME

The Center for Internet Security (CIS) has for several years grouped their hundreds of recommended security controls into what are termed *implementation groups* (IGs). The first of these is aimed at organizations with little or no in-house security knowledge or experience, and it provides a roadmap for achieving a sensible information security posture.

One good reference to use is Alan B. Watkin's book *Creating a Small Business Cybersecurity Program*. Published in 2020 by CISO DRG, it focuses first on bringing systems and information assets under management. Find them, identify them, evaluate and characterize them, and then bring them under control; these are Watkin's recommendations for how the smaller organizations, new to information security, should deal with securing their valuable, vulnerable information assets. These familiar touchstones of cybersecurity risk management may be old news to many SSCPs working with large-scale enterprise systems, whose owners are only too well aware of the compliance burdens they face; yet they are often new news to the SOHO and SMB systems owners and operators.

Hardening Individual Cybersecurity

Smaller-scale organizations provide yet another opportunity to flip a commonly held but largely incorrect (and harmful) meme around. Instead of seeing the individual human being—the employee or customer—as the weakest link in security, the SMB or SOHO environment often shows that the human element is the most necessary link in the value chain and thus the one worth investing in. A combination of tactics can help provide an affordable, manageable approach to hardening the human elements in any small organization; the same approach can scale well into larger organizations as well. This approach might include but not be limited to tactics such as:

- **Classify and categorize** the most visible, frequently used, and potentially valuable information assets and resources that the organization uses. As time permits, expand this process to include all such assets.

- Develop a *just-in-time security training, education, and awareness* mindset and approach. Every user needs the best security awareness and skills possible—but they need it *right now*, when they are doing a security-critical step in a workflow or process; being trained months before on the security implications of that step or task will probably have little pay-off in real time. *Microtraining*, which focuses the learning activity into a very short-duration event (perhaps less than a minute or two in length), can build on initial orientation training and awareness and eliminate or significantly reduce the need for routine classroom-based lecture-style security training events.

■ Deploy *just-in-time security assistance* as part of tasks, workflows, user procedures, and exception handling routines. Detecting situations in which workers are about to make a security blunder, such as sending classified information in an email, document, or process flow to an unauthorized recipient whose address popped up via auto-suggest, may require the use of an AI or machine learning system. These are becoming widely available, and at affordable per-use or per-seat costs, as add-ons for most email and document processing systems, and are being built into many industry vertical applications platforms such as Salesforce.

These and similar measures can help security be perceived as the critical enabler it can and must be—rather than being thought of only as a naysayer and an obstacle.

Many of the information security risk management frameworks, guides, and standards seem to be written and positioned for the benefit of very large enterprises (and their large and complex information architectures). Along the way, these documents might mention "cybersecurity hygiene," but at most they will point their reader to a variety of published lists of frequent or common recommendations.

This is not a bad thing.

In many respects, the hundreds of millions of small and medium-sized businesses (SMBs, often defined as ones with fewer than 500 full-time equivalent employees) represent a soft underbelly of the global information infrastructure. These, along with SOHO and individual end users, represent a high-leverage opportunity for improving the overall information security posture of our societies, communities, and marketplaces. SSCPs who have such very small organizations as their employers or clients already face this opportunity, where a little bit of sound security practice can go a long way; those who work in larger enterprises have equal opportunity to learn from focusing on first securing and protecting the individual user and then scale up through their local nets and the assets that they use, until arriving at the enterprise-level view of systems security.

This is not saying that an enterprise SSCP should attempt to invert the priority order of items on the vulnerability management list, or somehow attempt to pivot the classification and categorization structure that is in place (and presumably working well). Instead, it's an alternate pathway or journey through the enterprise's existing security systems, controls, and practices. Data-centric defense starts, after all, with the highest-value information assets and works outward; attackers, however, often start with the undervalued, oft-overlooked elements and users out at the undernourished edges of the organization and its systems.

Assume the Breach

Perhaps the highest-payoff thought experiment an SSCP can do for their small to medium-sized organization or SOHO client is to start with an assumption that an intrusion has occurred and work forward from there. Working through a hypothetical attack allows the defender(s) the chance to think critically about the in-place response plans, procedures, tools, and services.

Attitude is critically important to the success of such a review. Managers in the organization (including in the security or IT departments) may get the wrong impression and think that this is a fault-finding, finger-pointing exercise, looking to scapegoat or shift blame; it should never be done in that spirit. Instead, the on-scene SSCPs should approach this by looking for the unstated assumptions and getting these recognized and then logically challenged or tested.

An hour spent in a tabletop discussion or workshop can't, of course, cover everything exhaustively. Yet if it finds one untested assumption, which could lead to a disaster for the organization if proven false during an actual security incident, that kind of insight can more than pay for the modest investment of time. It may also help management better calibrate their risk thresholds and clarify some of their thinking about managing the organization's information security risks.

PIVOT 3: FLIP THE "DATA-DRIVEN VALUE FUNCTION"

Fundamental to data-centric resiliency and security is that the primary objective of any attack is your data. Attackers can steal it, deny you your own use of it, and destroy or degrade it to disrupt or misdirect your operations. Don't forget that your inbound (and outbound) software supply chains are treating the software that's being moved as data; it is the payload of your own data transportation management systems (the networks, servers, and services that make up the IT and OT systems that support these supply chains you're using).

From the attackers' perspective, they have two value functions, you might say, regarding your data: the first exploits your reliance on your own data and its inherent meaning, while the second requires attackers to make use of the meaning of your data themselves. Sabotage or ransom attacks that encrypt or hash your data are examples of the first value function; exfiltration for intelligence gathering or resale of your data are the second. Breaking this down further shows us that attackers have six basic methods they can use in generating value from their attacks on your data. Five of those six tactics—disrupting, degrading, denying, destroying, or delaying—rely on the impacts to your organization's activities as the source of value to the attacker. The last d— taking unauthorized delivery themselves of your data—involves downstream exploitation of the content or meaning of the data, by the attacker or those on the data exfiltration resale markets throughout the Dark Web.

Turning each d around, so that the attacker gains far less (if not zero) advantage from our data via those tactics, is the heart of data-centric defensive thinking:

- **Delivery (or *exfiltration*)** of your data to the attacker is routinely defeated when data is strongly encrypted or cryptographically tokenized. Presumably, the data will have a vanishingly small value to the attacker in its encrypted form and to anyone after the years it might take to break its encryption (or tokenization) have gone by. This should demotivate the attacker to continue probing your system for other assets, while it protects you, your customers, and stakeholders from having private or sensitive data misused against them.

- **Delaying attacks** (which target the data's availability to *you* and to your authorized users and business processes) are defeated, or their impacts minimized, when alternate processing paths and procedures enable decision-making and business tasks to continue. Risk-based criteria could be used to allow some processes to continue despite certain constraints not being met, as is illustrated by overdraft protection on checking or current accounts.

- **Destruction of data**, either by wholesale encryption of it or by widespread destruction of the storage systems it is kept on, is generally an act of sabotage. Mitigating this risk may also be done with alternate and backup processing capabilities, which could even include outsourcing some process activities.

- **Denial of access to (or use of) your data** is, of course, an attack on the availability of that data. As with data delaying attacks, mitigation strategies need to protect both the data itself and the processing systems, as a pipeline or a value chain, from disruption.

- **Degradation of data** can take many forms, from false invoicing to unauthorized changes to individual, critical data items. Access control, data quality, and effective, timely backup, restore, and rollback capabilities improve your chances of surviving through such attacks.

- **Disruption via data attacks** attempts to divert larger-scale organizational behaviors by means of manipulating the quality, integrity, timeliness, completeness, or availability of data. Misrouting an urgently needed shipment of replacement parts or subsystems, for example, can cause part of your organization's mission to go awry. If your organization is a supplier to a critical infrastructure organization, these knock-on impacts could even lead to injury, death, or property damage.

Data-Centric Defense and Resiliency

Systems like Microsoft SharePoint, Atlassian's Confluence, Google's G Suite, or others provide powerful "as a service" capabilities for groups to dynamically form, collaborate, and create and manage their own content. Whether the vendor (and your organization) calls it a content management service, a collaboration suite, a web-based app, or a content-enriched internal network doesn't really describe the security challenges of these systems. In many instances, these systems are managed with discretionary access control policies (or what used to be called *nondiscretionary* policies), since a default set of policies determine initial settings, property inheritance, and separation of groups and their data. As organizations grow, these systems can become overwhelming, producing vast forests upon forests of trees full of content.

From an attacker's perspective, being able to subvert a legitimate user's credentials to gain access (usually via SSO) to the organization's SharePoint clouds, or to its federated G Suite areas, is the textbook example of the risks of unrestricted or poorly controlled lateral movement. Many organizations operate far too large an extent of their shared content management as if it is a "system-high" security domain, with nearly everyone in the organization having "view" capabilities as a default. Such organizations leave to the individual content tree's creator-owner(s) to determine the need for more restrictive access and then carry out the enforcement of that decision.

This is quite possibly the first and most important place to start applying zero-trust architectural thinking. In almost every organization, there really is no compelling business need to have everyone be able to read (and hence copy) every bit of data or software that others in the organization must create, use, and manage. That's the key: *where no compelling need exists, no access should be granted.*

Some of these types of systems are ISO 27001/27018 and DoD Cloud SRG compliant with respect to data protection. Many are also fully compliant with a wide variety of data protection standards established by various laws. In the United States, the Family Educational Records Privacy Act (FERPA) regulates all educational providers, financial aid, and services organizations; the healthcare sector is regulated by the Health Insurance Portability and Accountability Act (HIPAA) and the Health Information Technology for Economic and Clinical Health (HITECH) Act. The financial services sector is regulated by a variety of US laws at the federal and state levels, with the Financial Industry Regulatory Authority (FINRA) being a private corporation created by law to implement and carry out these laws. In the European Union, the General Data Protection Regulation (GDPR) drives states member of the EU to implement GDPR's requirements in their national laws. Many nations beyond the European Union have created their own financial data protection laws and regulations patterned on GDPR as well. When they are used as the infrastructure for a properly managed and controlled applications platform *and* that platform's design and implementation enforces the right granularity of controls, then the organization's use of that platform-over-content-system, to coin a phrase, can also be compliant and secure.

Even so, many of these systems and the apps that are built on top of them have their fair share of exploitable vulnerabilities.

Ransomware as a Service

Cyberattacks during 2020 and 2021 showed an increasing use of weaponized patterns of attacks, particularly those involving ransomware. This gave rise to the term *ransomware as a service (RaaS)*, based around the concept of full-function sets of ransomware-based attack toolkits being developed and tested by one or more APTs and then released as products for other attack groups (APTs or otherwise) to put into action. (RaaS is not the first package or set of related exploits and attack strategies developed, weaponized, and shared across the ecosystem of cyber attackers as a community, although it's arguably the first to scale into widespread, highly visible use.) One current example of this, as of this writing, is the BlackMatter ransomware, which came to light via attacks starting in July

2021. Analysts have found many design similarities between BlackMatter attacks and previous malware-intensive ransom attacks. This suggests that it's the business model of providing RaaS capabilities to other attackers that is becoming the greater concern. REvil, a Russia-based APT, has become quite infamous as a purportedly private RaaS provider, which in October 2021 was forced offline via counterattacks conducted by a multinational law enforcement operation.

Perhaps not surprisingly, even the most recent official advice reemphasizes the same basic elements of cybersecurity hygiene:

- Implement, validate, enforce, and use effective backup, rollback, restoration, and business process continuity and recovery procedures.

- Enforce the use of unique, strong passphrases, coupled with effective multifactor authentication (MFA) throughout all levels of users and across all systems elements.

- Implement zero-trust architectural concepts, such as architectural segmentation by security domain, to prevent, control, and monitor attempts at lateral traversal across networks and systems.

Supply Chains, Security, and the SSCP

Supply chain attacks involve using the flow of products, services, data, or software as part of the attack mechanism themselves. More importantly, supply chain attacks by their nature provide rapid scaling effects, in which an attack on one element of the supply chain is automatically replicated onto thousands of unsuspecting client systems of that supply chain. Supply chain attacks have long been feared in the semiconductor and systems marketplaces, but it is only recently that the majority of businesses and other organizations have become aware enough of them to be worried about them.

The SUNBURST attacks during 2020, which used SolarWinds' own software update mechanisms to push ransomware to SolarWinds' clients, illustrate this. The clients had every reason to place trust and confidence in that (largely automated) update process. The attacks on Kayesa and Accellion, which we also learned about in 2021, were further wake-up calls to organizations and information security professionals.

In many cases, these attacks make use of zero-day exploits, both within the systems that provide initial entry into the supply chain, the software, and data that is the nominal, normally trustworthy payload of that supply chain, and within the target systems' environments themselves.

> ### The Uncontrollable Marketplaces for Zero-Day Exploits
>
> In her 2021 book, *New York Times* cybersecurity reporter Nicole Perloth shows how governments around the world lost control of their own exploits as a service channels, through which they discovered (and later weaponized) untold thousands of zero-day vulnerabilities. It makes for a sobering, if not frightening, must-read for information security professionals. (*This is how they tell me the world ends*, Bloomsbury. ISBN 9781635576061.)

This psychological aspect to supply chain attacks should not be underestimated. Supply chain attacks can impact organizations of any size. By targeting service provider systems, these attacks may also have a chilling effect on the adoption of managed security services by SMBs, who by themselves may not have the depth of technical knowledge or security insight to assess their own exposure to such supply chain attacks.

ICS, IoT, and SCADA: More Than SUNBURST

In some respects, 2021 was a "perfect storm" year for supply chain attacks, heightening the awareness of the risks of interconnection of organizational IT systems with their physical control systems. Significantly greater numbers of organizations of all sizes and types rely on edge, fog, IoT, and related operational technologies (OT) to manage many aspects of their business processes; more often than not, they do this with what seems to be a lack of due care and due diligence for what should be the synergisms of safety and security needs. For various reasons, these two communities of practice—safety and security—have long existed as if in separate worlds. Different government agencies establish the mandates they operate by and regulate the activities within their domains. Different standards, best practices, research, and teaching methods and materials are used. At heart, it is firmly believed that they have rightly different agendas, with different priorities, driving how they think, act, solve problems, and measure their successes.

From a policy perspective, safety and security actually have a number of common touch points. Both look to segregate assets into categories in ways that can be used to encapsulate systems elements for various control, supervisory, safety, or security reasons. Safety engineering has traditionally used physical proximity of different elements, such as machinery and its control systems, as a primary way of defining and delineating its *zones* of control. Elements that had a direct, immediate, and local bearing on the safe operation of the equipment would be in the *safety-critical zone*, for example, with nearby and related zones grouped together into *cells* or *regions* for overall direction, supervision, and management. Cells would be connected into *manufacturing zones* that reflect the sequence of processes in an assembly line or materials processing plant. Quality assurance analytics would then be pushed further back to the organization's *enterprise zone*.

Each of these zones is similar in concept to the IT security domains that are identified and managed via information asset classification and categorization processes. The boundaries between zones identify threat surfaces. Keeping these boundaries secure such that no unauthorized traffic can flow in either direction requires different security models than are classically used in IT security. One such model is the *data diode* approach, which as its name suggests, allows for data to flow in only one direction[3]; since no signals of any kind can flow in the reverse direction, this prevents the backward flow of potentially corrupted data, code, or hostile access attempts from systems elements on the receive side of the data diode. This also means that the data diode prevents the reverse flow of handshake data that IT systems rely upon to make use of layered protocols (such as the OSI 7-Layer or TCP/IP stacks). Data diodes provide a Layer 1 security solution, which of course means that they are hardware devices that must be properly placed within an enterprise's conjoined IT/OT architecture.

Eliminating the backward flow of protocol handshakes eliminates attack vectors that might abuse a protocol as a process, or use malformed data in the backward packet flow itself, as part of the attack. This requires proxy services to be used on either side of the one-way LED data path—the heart of the data diode—to handle the handshakes and unpackaging of data on the uplink side and then generate the handshakes and encapsulation necessary on the downlink side.

In effect, this makes the data diode into a protocol-transforming and isolating gateway. An industrial control safety-critical zone, for example, might see its inward flow of commands, sent via TCP or SNMP flows from its regional control center, being buffered, isolated, unpacked, and then repackaged into *common industrial protocol* (CIP) flows to enter into the safety-critical zone of the equipment and its programmable logic controllers (PLCs) themselves.

---

[3] In electrical systems, a *diode* is a device that only allows electrical current to flow in one direction (forward); it blocks any attempts to push current through in the other (reverse) direction. To be absolutely correct, however, electrical diodes do have a tiny bit of reverse leakage current, which in digital systems cannot cause a 1 bit to flip to a 0 bit. LEDs and photodiodes, as the send and receive elements of a data diode, can be physically forced to flow data in the reverse direction – the photodiode emitting light, the LED turning it into electricity—but this would be a sophisticated side-channel attack, tampering with the circuits themselves, and not something one can do with stolen credentials, malware, or malformed data.

In the US marketplace, NIST has set formal accreditation standards for data diodes; other products such as *unidirectional gateways* provide varying subsets of the data diode's full range of capabilities, but without meeting the rigorous testing (nor carrying the assurance) of the formally accredited data diodes. Both types of products are finding widespread application in hospitals, manufacturing, oil well and refinery, transportation, and other markets. As these markets continue to grow, the commoditization of data diodes, unidirectional gateways, and other related products is making them become more commonplace.

NIST SP 800-82, Guide to Industrial Control Systems (ICS) Security, was published in 2015; its reference architecture and other models are useful jumping-off points as you look to develop or improve your organization's ICS, SCADA, IoT, or robot-interconnected information architectures. As of this writing, a number of other ideas and proposals have been put forth by universities, government agencies, and systems houses.

Extending Physical Security: More Than Just Badges and Locks

This pivot asks us to reflect on the overarching purpose of all physical security thought, policies, procedures, and controls. These exist and are used to ensure the CIANA+PS characteristics of the data and the systems that our organizations need and use, while also protecting the people who use those data and systems as part of their work with the organization. Let's view this from a data-centric perspective but put it in combined IT-OT terms. Primarily, physical security of data as part of an IT-OT system focuses on assuring its availability for authorized use, its integrity, and its confidentiality; the other attributes of CIANA+PS can then be allocated to process elements using the other layers in the 7-Layer model, or to the 8th layer of administrative and people processes.

Physical threats may have more tangible, actionable precursors, which if recognized in time, can be used to inform risk-based access control and other security processes. Physical threats are characterized by movement toward a physical part of your systems—the valves that control water treatment or wastewater flow, for example, or the process controllers that run the HVAC of your smart building systems. Think of this as similar to a collision avoidance process for vehicles (or people) in motion: OT systems and their interfaces to IT environments add urgency to detecting the abnormal, erroneous, or unexpected movements or actions of robots, automated equipment, vehicles, people, packages, or anything else within security's area of regard. Any movement within a controlled or sensitive area, or movement toward such an area from outside it, needs to be immediately recognized. The SOC should quickly characterize this movement, identify the object(s) involved, and characterize or determine their intent or potential for harm.

Most organizations must depend upon various support services from public infra-structures, such as transportation, energy, communications, and emergency responders. In almost all areas of the world, these infrastructures become more overloaded and thus more fragile with each passing day, leading to service interruptions or quality of service issues. Start with your SOC's ability to monitor the health and status of your organiza-tion's own systems; can you continue to do that when commercial or public infrastructure support fails? A variety of physical security assessment techniques can help you identify and prioritize any vulnerabilities in systems such as:

- On-premises electrical power conditioning and backup, including its fail-over con-trols, alternative suppliers, fuel supplies, and critical spare parts, all require proper physical security controls. Controls should also include maintenance equipment and personnel necessary to operate and maintain these systems, as well as the SCADA and service delivery links into the organization's operational areas.

- Internet and public switched communications networks, including redundant or hybrid connections (such as multihomed routers).

- Communications and Internet connectivity for mobile or work-from-home employees.

- Physical security for mobile and work-from-home employees, as well as for their IT equipment and for information assets in their possession or immediate environment.

- Physical area access control and monitoring systems, including contactless iden-tity technologies, mechanical interlocks, alarms, and sensors. Many of these use different types of low-capacity IoT devices, which may be difficult to secure in the first place and keep operating reliably during a disruption (of almost any kind) in the second.

The IoRT: Robots Learning via the Net

The *Internet of Robotic Things (IoRT)* refers to the combination of robot devices and their web-based support, supervisory, and control systems. What differentiates IoRT systems from IoT systems is the degree of task-intensive learning that IoRT systems may provide. IoT devices typically have very significant limitations as to data processing, storage, and communications capabilities; they generally do not upload nor download large datasets at high speeds. Robot devices tend to have more local or on-board CPU and memory capac-ity. Self-navigating vehicles, for example, need to be able to take safety-related decisions rapidly, in real time, without being dependent upon their upstream supervisory nodes intervening in their local processes and situation. A self-navigating vehicle will probably not have on-board storage and computation capabilities to deal with all possible routes between all possible points in its service area, nor have the ability to digest real-time traffic advisories or other information to make intelligent decisions about altering its chosen path. To some extent, then, the vehicle can do on-board learning as it consults with its supervisory node and receives guidance updates from it.

Smart warehouse systems are another example, in which the robots that pick and pack merchandise items for shipment may need real-time help in determining an optimum movement to make with their appendages. An industrial robot on an assembly line has the benefits of being in a precisely calibrated environment, and it largely executes precalculated moves (within constraints measured in real time by its local sensors). The pick-and-pack robot does not have that luxury, and onboard processing to calculate such an optimal move to pick *this* object from the bin, rather than *that* one, may take minutes or even hours of local CPU and GPU time to run. Instead, it elevates the problem to its supervisor node, which engages a deep AI learning system to compute the right move, which is then passed to the robot on the warehouse floor, all in a fraction of a second. Many of these learning systems are built using function as a service (FaaS) cloud capabilities.

Each of these types of scenarios involves local, semi-autonomous processing elements—the robots—becoming dependent upon other levels of the organizational IT and OT systems, as well as on cloud services. Dealing with the availability, integrity, and reliability concerns of your organizations nonhuman users—its robots—puts a somewhat different perspective onto an SSCP's normal considerations regarding their organization's CIANA+PS needs. (Thus far, such robots do not have the capability to submit help desk tickets. Yet.)

PIVOT 4: OPERATIONALIZE SECURITY ACROSS THE IMMEDIATE AND LONGER TERM

Operationalizing security shifts our perspective by putting us in the position of each end user of the organization's information assets, its IT and OT systems, and their interfaces. This viewpoint emphasizes an in-the-moment or just-in-time identification of security risks, which become opportunities for the security professionals to assist or intervene. Let's look at some of the major opportunities to make this happen.

- **Email:** One example now becoming commonplace is the scanning of emails as they are being drafted to detect any possible breach of security. Simple pattern recognition, smart machine learning scanning, or tags associated with attachments (if any) may indicate the need for greater security measures to be applied. More common is the natural human tendency to rely upon autosuggestions for addressees (direct, .cc or .bcc); recent surveys show that more than 60 percent of law firms have suffered breach of confidentiality requirements by such autosuggestion mistakes.

- **Document and forms processing workflows:** Many business processes are now being orchestrated and automated with workflow and playbook systems, some of which use machine learning to recognize patterns in a user's work activities to custom-build workflows for those patterns. These workflows provide ample opportunity to scan work in progress (much as email can be scanned), as well as blocking the sending of a workflow package on to the next recipient (be that a human or nonhuman user) unless security conditions have been checked and met.

- **Compliance tracking:** A growing number of compliance regimes for safety, privacy, financial, and other needs are shifting their assessments to an ongoing or continuous process, rather than an annual or other periodic basis. Telemetry data can be gathered from workflows, email systems, and other processes that can then be used by an ongoing compliance monitoring and alerting system.

These and other related capabilities can be incorporated via add-ons for major email and office productivity suites and may be optionally available in applications platforms that serve your organization's market. They can be configured to provide assistance (in the form of suggestions or reminders), barriers and control points, or active intercessions that directly carry out security policies without user involvement. Automated redaction or encryption of sensitive information, such as PII, or generating an alert or alarm to supervisors or to security operations personnel, can also be done.

Continuous Assessment and Continuous Compliance

The central premise of risk-based access control points out the need and the opportunity to bring aspects of risk management, security assessment, and compliance activities together in an operationally sensitive manner. One of the clear lessons from the small and medium-sized organizations' experiences with risk management is to use a combination of bottom-up, first-fit approaches and top-down, full-spectrum, framework-based processes for risk identification, assessment, management, and mitigation. Central to all of these combination or tailored approaches is (or should be) the need for a risk register as a one-stop information bank.

With a risk register in hand, the routine tasks of the organization's security team have a common integrating point for their ongoing risk management activities, such as:

- Monitoring and analysis of data generated by security controls, both in real time and retrospectively, provides intrusion detection while enabling insights into ongoing adjustment, calibration, and assessment of security controls. SIEM systems, dashboards, and other analytic capabilities can enhance this.

- Active review of proposed changes to software, hardware, applications, workflows, or procedures should be informed by the insights from near real-time risk monitoring and controls assessment and calibration.

- Active review of help desk, trouble tickets, complaints, and other issues raised by users may also reveal precursors of risks, threats, and hazards. This can also signal opportunities for corrective or preventative security action.

Each of these is a learning opportunity for the organization, and some simple knowledge management stratagems can be applied to capture that knowledge and make it reusable. Centered about the risk register, these bits of knowledge and insight can be captured in checklists and workflows and the overall security education, awareness, and training program. Just-in-time security assistance and training efforts are also important ways to make use of ongoing security learning.

Connecting these larger processes together and operationalizing their knowledge and know-how in these ways may require both cultural and procedural changes within the organization. Fears of change, or resistance to sharing of knowledge, are common barriers to formalized knowledge management programs, and adding an active, real-time "security assistant" to end users' workflows and processes may run into similar resistance.

Taking the next step toward continuous compliance, for example, may require that many levels of management and leadership take on and embrace an attitude of being continuously accountable to compliance standards and authorities. To some leaders and managers, this is a natural, small step; they already view their due care and due diligence responsibilities in a nonstop, 24/7/365 light.

With an existing and operationalized continuous risk monitoring and assessment process in place, it should be a small step to extend these systems to the data gathering, analysis, and reporting processes used by formal and informal compliance assessment and audit. Compliance assessments often require the use of specific tests and evaluation activities, such as stress tests, simulated transactions, or other ethical penetration test activities, as ways of generating artifacts for audit. Planning these activities to be done on a continuous, rather than on a per-audit cycle basis, provides additional threat warning and security controls performance insight on a continuing basis as a bonus.

SDNs and SDS

In the vast majority of cases, modern network hardware elements provide a web-enabled means to configure, inspect, and control each device in a network. The physical connection fabric still must be dealt with by hand, of course; cables must be laid, Wi-Fi access points positioned, and routers, switches, and other devices must be mounted in racks or cabinets. Physical security for these elements is a must! Controlling that physical connection fabric requires that network and security administrators log on to each device and interact with its vendor-specific built-in capabilities. For even a modest-sized SMB architecture, dealing with each device individually is tedious, if not error-prone. Integrated software systems, fortunately, provide the means to bring all of those devices under centralized visibility, management, and control. Most organizations will quickly find that the licensing costs for such software-defined network (SDN) or security (SDS) systems quickly pay for themselves in many ways.

Software-Defined Networks

Software-defined networks (SDNs) are the combination of physical and virtual network elements into a centrally managed, configured, and controlled network. Their underlying physical connection fabric can be very general-purpose in design, such as is seen in a large data center environment. One or more *virtual connection fabrics* or *virtualized networks* can be defined and created by commands issued at the SDN app's command line or via its script management system, which then provides connectivity for virtual machines created to host applications and end-user tools.

SDNs provide their using organization with the capability to rapidly create, deploy, use, and then tear down new virtual networks to meet changing needs. In this respect, using an SDN is part of creating a private cloud infrastructure. (Other features, such as resource utilization and chargeback, would be needed to completely take this to an IaaS cloud architecture.)

SDNs usually require the use of gateway servers that specialize in connecting the virtual and physical connection fabrics to external networks, to ISP points of presence, or to other systems operating with other than IP protocol stacks.

It's important to extend the reach and span of the organization's access control policies and systems so that they include the physical connection fabric (and gateway elements) and all virtualized elements. Even when SDNs are used on a purely private, internal basis, this aspect of security policy and control should not be over.

Software-Defined Security

Software-defined security (SDS) builds upon the SDN concepts and systems by bringing together all the security-related configuration and management settings for the virtual and physical connection fabrics created and managed by the SDN systems. This brings all security-related controls, telemetry, and alarm data to a centralized, unified management console. The real power of the SDS, however, comes from its users having the tools to build and use scripts that directly carry out operational security changes to all of the SDN devices or to specific subsets or groups of such devices (real or virtual).

Using an SDS system in this way can actually transform the organization's view of risk tolerance from being a strategic to an operational one. Effective implementation of a risk-based access control strategy, for example, all but requires the ability to make near real-time changes to the security settings of network and system devices, real or virtual.

SOAR: Strategies for Focused Security Effort

For decades, quality management has taught that by making a process repeatable and measurable an organization can continually learn how to improve that process. Measurement and monitoring help identify variation, which may need to be removed or damped down to more acceptable levels; exception-handling branches in a process (or its workflow) become more visible, which makes it easier to verify that the right level of security and process control, such as dual control, is in place and functioning correctly. This is little more than carrying due care and due diligence responsibilities to a more granular, process flow by process flow degree.

Security orchestration, automation, and response (SOAR) systems provide integrated tool suites that can help an organization to better describe, define, manage, and learn from its security processes. SOAR systems are a recent addition to the security marketplace, and as of October 2021, none was sufficiently established to be presenting a de facto standard set of capabilities; different vendors and different organizations that use SOAR are still in the process of learning how to use what SOAR can offer.

Taking a closer look at its acronym reveals further insights about SOAR and its application:

- **Security** in this context shows that SOAR is applicable to any and every source of telemetry, monitoring, analysis, or assessment data. Its span of control ideally can include automation of test and assessment activities, while bringing together all of the process steps for incident detection and response.

- **Orchestration** is used by SOAR vendors and users to refer to the planned, deliberate bringing together of everything that a SOAR system will control and direct. This has to start at the policy level so that SOAR can be implemented correctly, step-by-step, as security systems, information assets, and people-driven procedures are brought under its purview.

- **Automation** refers to the use of scripting facilities to enable users to define and group procedures and checklists into workflows and then group workflows into playbooks. Thus, a playbook could be defined for managing the operational deployment of a new production system, with SOAR using the workflows from that playbook to control the execution of software tasks, coordinating actions by security or network administrators as these processes unfold.

- **Response** focuses on SOAR's positioning as a powerful addition to the incident response and recovery capabilities of an organization. SOAR systems can be used to integrate full event logging of every step taken, and every decision made at a checkpoint or milestone in a workflow.

Whether as a system, a service, or an in-house methodology and approach, SOAR can also make vulnerability management simpler and more effective. This may help the organization determine which vulnerabilities are proving to be more susceptible to high-impact exploitations by attackers, which can inform subsequent risk mitigation decisions.

A "DevSecOps" Culture: SOAR for Software Development

In the beginning, software was developed using lengthy, complex management processes that could take months to transform user or organizational needs into properly functioning software. Many organizations found this waiting intolerable; a variety of other management processes, such as rapid prototyping, have been tried in response. One approach, known as DevOps, compresses the cycle time of identifying the change, designing it, modifying and testing the software in question, and delivering it to the operational end user, all in a matter of days or weeks. For many software-intensive businesses and organizations, such as those with large web-based processes, DevOps can deliver multiple sets of software fixes across a 24-hour cycle, with each incremental delivery bringing a specific set of changes and fixes. Service-oriented architectures, in particular, can benefit from such a continuous, rolling update of their software components.

To coordinate, control, and lend automation support to DevOps, many internal IT organizations use continuous integration and continuous delivery (CI/CD) systems. As with SOAR, these provide playbook and workflow-oriented tools that define, control, and automate the ways in which planners, designers, developers, testers, and configuration managers work together throughout the flow of new features (or fixes to existing ones) to the operational or production system.

However, DevOps tended to sidestep many of the security considerations and processes, as if to say that these need only be performed when planning a major systems upgrade or in response to a significant and very disruptive set of problems. In response, many organizations have put security back into the DevOps cycle of activity; this cultural, managerial, and technical movement is known as *DevSecOps*. As cyberattacks became even more lucrative business opportunities for the attackers, and as infrastructure and OT systems attacks became more numerous, impactful, and notorious, the shift to DevSecOps by other organizations is making even more sense.

Security professionals should see strong parallels between SOAR and DevSecOps. Both aim to augment human-to-human coordination and hand-off of interim work products, assisted and enabled by executable, manageable workflows and playbooks. Both have the capability, as systems of systems, of being interconnected with risk management and mitigation, risk registers, vulnerability management, and change management and control systems. Both provide strong capabilities for collecting telemetry data along the way, while enforcing security policies at each step.

Bringing all of these systems together in manageable, measurable, and reliably repeatable ways can provide a major step change in the ways in which an organization builds more secure software, delivers it to users in more secure ways, and protects those users, their data, and the system as a whole.

PIVOT 5: ZERO-TRUST ARCHITECTURES AND OPERATIONS

The *zero-trust architecture* (ZTA) concept was developed to provide a unifying framework for the design and operation of agile, responsive, and secure systems. It is not a product, a service, or a specific set of technologies; nor is it safe to assume that one solution is the best-of-breed answer for every organization. Rather, it is a set of architectural principles that are then applied to an organization's specific operational and security needs; this drives the selection, adaptation, and use of specific technology components.

NIST SP 800-207, released in August 2020, provides a baseline view of the consensus of the IT industry, security professionals, and government on the guiding principles of a ZTA. Its definitions of core and supporting ZTA systems elements, and their interrelationships, make for important reading.

NOTE   ISO and ZTA?

It's worth noting that while ISO has not published a standard, handbook, or guideline specific to ZTA, nor for data-centric security, both of these concepts and many of their tenets, concepts, and supporting arguments can be found throughout the ISO 27000 family. To some extent, this may reflect the rapidly evolving nature of the thinking and the practice of putting such a game-changing idea into use.

Seven basic *tenets of zero-trust architectures*, as NIST refers to them, establish the general purpose and intent of a ZTA:

- All data and computing assets are treated as resources.
- All communications within the system, regardless of location, are secured.
- All access is granted on a per-session basis, using a least privilege test for each requested access to any and all resources.
- Dynamic, attribute-based policies are used to grant or deny each access request.

- No asset, device, or service is inherently trusted. Continuous diagnostics and monitoring (CDM) of the health, security posture, and integrity of all organization-owned and associated assets supports enforcement of update/patch levels and other security certifications (such as user training).

- All resource authentication and authorization processes are dynamic and must be strictly enforced prior to granting of any access capabilities. This is a constant cycle supported with continuous monitoring, which includes reauthentication and reauthorization based on policy requirements.

- Continuous monitoring of the state of systems, assets, network infrastructures, and communications systems provides context for access decisions, policy improvement, and policy enforcement.

Related to ZTA is the concept of a zero-trust *network* architecture (ZTNA), which is a term being used by many network and systems vendors, security services providers, and others. ZTNA may be thought of as a network-centric view of the overall ZTA model; not all ZTNA concepts (or service offerings) expressly address data-centric security, for example.

NIST SP 800-207 does not explicitly use the term ZTNA, but does provide six key points regarding a zero trust view of networks:

- **No implicit trust zones.** By assuming that an attacker is always present, assets (and services that make assets available) must use this assumption to strictly enforce authentication and authorization at the least privileges level.

- **Not all devices on the network are owned, configured, or controlled by the organization.** This embraces the BYOD reality of a highly mobile workforce, customer base, or other users that is now business as usual for most if not all organizations. Note too that even for bastion or isolated systems, this assumption should also dictate using a strict *device* authentication and authorization process.

- **No resource is inherently assumed to be trusted.** Assets and resources must be able to certify their security posture and health to the system's policy enforcement point (PEP) prior to an access request being granted; this protects users or clients as well as other systems assets and resources from possible harm.

- **Not all enterprise resources and assets are hosted on infrastructure owned, operated, or controlled by the organization.** Many may be cloud-hosted, with the organization sharing security responsibilities with the CSP(s) involved.

- **Remote subjects and assets cannot assume that their local network can be fully trusted.** Instead, subjects must assume that any communications channels, their access points, and services that are not directly owned, operated, and controlled by the organization may be compromised. Subjects should assume all traffic is subject to monitoring and possible interception.

- **Workflows and assets moving or shared between organization-controlled infrastructure and other systems should operate with a consistent security policy and posture.** This includes both temporary relocation of assets and devices as well as in-session collaboration between processes in each environment.

Figure A.1 illustrates these principles and concepts at work, in what NIST refers to as the core zero-trust architecture logical component view. It splits the core process into a control plane and data plane, as shown in the diagram. This core is supported by the elements shown on the diagram, which may be a combination of services or technologies provided (or hosted) by the organization itself and those of third-party providers. This is a technology-neutral, conceptual diagram; the specifics as to UEBA, authentication and authorization technologies, or SIEM versus SOAR choices, are left to the implementing organization.

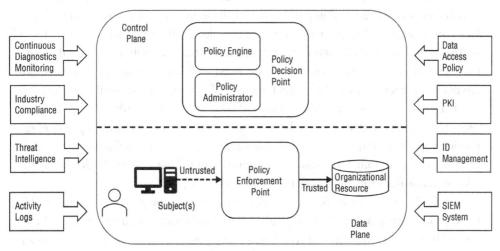

FIGURE A.1 **Zero-trust architecture logical core**

Many variations on a ZTA are of course possible, with each placing more or less emphasis on some aspects of the core set of principles and concepts. These alternatives include but are not limited to:

- Using enhanced identity governance techniques.
- Microsegmentation of the networks and resources.

- Software-defined perimeters (SDPs).[4] SDP aims to provide an integrated security architecture using standards-based, proven components that provide encryption, remote attestation, SAML, and mutual transport layer security, all within an X.509 certificate process.

- Intent-based networking (IBN). IBN uses machine learning–based approaches to provide intelligent, real-time control of network workflows in a highly secure fashion.

Note that both SDP and IBN exploit the capabilities of an SDN architecture but otherwise work to provide a network infrastructure–agnostic view of security. Both are strategies to avoid the problems and limitations of point-based defensive technologies, which many network access control (NAC) and anti-malware systems are prone to.

FIDO and Passwordless Authentication

The ignoble password has proven itself to be the bane of most systems users, administrators, and security professionals. For many reasons, passwords—and even lengthy passphrases—are too easily compromised, hacked, or circumvented. Dual and multiple factor authentication techniques have evolved to alleviate the risks that come with the use of passwords. Password managers offer one approach, but even with the best of these, a naïve user can end up using the same password on multiple accounts. Leets of passwords are rarely more secure than the original, memorable, human-user-friendly password was.

For more than a decade, an association of IT systems and security vendors, end-user organizations, and others have been working to develop standards and practices to provide a scalable, standards-based, vendor-agnostic approach for authentication that requires no user-supplied password. This industry group, known as the FIDO Alliance, takes its name from the initial concept of *fast ID online* (FIDO).

FIDO eliminates the weakest "what you know" factor—the password—from the initial sign-on process. Authentication involves digital certificate–based confirmation that the public key used when initially creating and provisioning the identity is in fact associated with the user (and their device) submitting the sign-on request. This does require the end user to obtain a digital certificate, have its private key stored securely in their device, and then use that device during the FIDO authentication process. Additional factors can involve biometrics, security tokens, or additional devices. Implementing organizations

---

[4] Also called a "black cloud," referring to its origins in defense circles where "black" systems elements are only acknowledged to exist if the requesting party has a validated need to know. This is related to cryptographic terminology that defines all plaintext elements of a system as "red," and all ciphertext elements as "black," again with strict need to know required to even acknowledge or divulge the existence of the cipher text.

may choose to allow the use of PINs, challenge questions, or similar techniques. FIDO has native support across Windows 10 and Android platforms, with browser support built in to Chrome, Firefox, Edge, and (currently the preview version of) Safari.

FIDO is an open standards–based authentication system, which means that organizations choosing to transition to FIDO can depend with confidence on a wide range of vendor solutions to meet their needs, with equal confidence that the vast majority of their end users will either already have or can affordably upgrade to a FIDO-compliant identity authentication process. These standards are available via `https://fidoalliance.org`.

FIDO also provides enhanced user privacy, which is particularly important when the user is connecting (and authenticating) to multiple organizations using the same device. Each such organization has no way to determine if such an authenticating device is acceptable or actively authenticated to another system, for example. FIDO neither keeps nor exchanges geolocation information about the user's device.

One of the challenges to consider with FIDO or any authentication system and approach is that of the highly mobile entity, such as a human user who does not always or routinely log on using the same device. Roving technical support or security team members, quality control analysts, other supervisory personnel, and outside customer support, sales, and consulting teams may present legitimate use cases needing a degree of device-independent but fully secure sign-on to your systems.

FIDO has also developed the FIDO Device Onboard (FDO) protocol, which migrates the FIDO interface to IoT and other devices.

Threat Hunting, Indicators, and Signature Dependence

Broadly speaking, four categories of signals present different types of warnings (and calls to action) that risk managers, security administrators, and end users alike need to be on the lookout for. Each category can be thought of as having a lifecycle of utility, starting with first awareness of the warning or signal, and ending when it is no longer useful and may even be distracting or disruptive to attempt to deal with.

Two of these categories of warning signals are *proactive*, or *leading edge* signals. They are observable before any action has been taken by an adversary:

- **Indicators of risks (IoRs)** should be identified as part of organizational and systems risk and vulnerability assessment. As recent events have demonstrated, it's quite possible for attackers to develop new ways of exploiting very old vulnerabilities, long since thought to have been patched, closed off, or avoided.

- **Precursors,** such as news items regarding events or trends in the marketplace, may help alert a risk-based security control process that the likelihood of threats or hazards acting on vulnerabilities may be increasing.

Two of these categories are *reactive*, or *trailing edge* signals. They are only observable after a hostile action has taken place:

- **Indicators of attack (IoAs)** are the behavior-based signals that an entity is behaving in ways that are probably hostile or harmful to your systems, assets, or people.
- **Indicators of compromise (IoCs)** are the changes in the behavior or security characteristics of the systems elements that have just been acted upon by an attacker.

One frequently used example of an IoA illustrates this difference. *Lateral movement* is the behavior of an entity within an organization's systems. This movement may or may not be hostile in nature. Most security technologies find it extremely difficult to unambiguously identify that lateral behavior is occurring in real time, much less interpret its intent. In many cases, such movement is using built-in systems capabilities, such as software on an allowed list, within the privilege set available to the user ID in question. This is why lateral movement is not on most lists of IoCs.

Guarav Banga, in his blog post at Balbix.com,[5] refers to this reactive nature of IoAs and IoCs alike as the "big lie in threat hunting." Melodrama aside, it's worth recognizing that virtually all of the security technologies available to organizations is based on a three-step process:

- First, defining what "business normal" is;
- Next, using that definition to try to spot abnormal, unusual, or unexpected events; and then
- Last, determining the cause or intent of the abnormal action, as part of choosing which type of incident response (i.e., security, maintenance, or disaster recovery) is most appropriate.

IoAs may, as Banga suggests, provide the context of the event, particularly when viewed in sequence; IoCs are often generated by various security technologies (such as anti-malware solutions and intrusion detection systems).

Signature dependence can result when the organization becomes overly reliant on templating, profiling, pattern-matching and similar techniques to generate real-time warnings that a security incident is in progress (or has recently finished without being detected soon enough). So far, the only known remedy or preventative for becoming so overly dependent is to rely on a mix of automated and human awareness, sensitivity, and judgment.

[5] https://www.balbix.com/blog/big-lie-in-threat-hunting/

OTHER DANGERS ON THE WEB AND NET

The terms *deep web* and *Dark Web* sometimes are used to refer to shady, suspect, or downright criminal activities; they bring to mind black markets dealing in contraband goods and unlawful services. Sometimes this view is correct; many times, it is not. If the *surface web* is content published to the world at large, the *deep web* is content that is not; it may merely be behind a paywall or restricted to internal users of that organization. The *Dark Web*, by contrast, is where those more unsavory activities and operators dwell.

Let's take a closer look.

Surface, Deep, and Dark Webs

It's important to keep these three slices or views of the web and the net separate from each other:

- **The surface web** consists of web pages that are open and exposed to web crawlers and search engines. Their IP addresses are thus resolvable by the Domain Name System (DNS). It's estimated that about 10 percent of the content of the Internet is on the surface web.

- **The deep web:** The vast majority of legitimate organizations have valid information security needs, starting from a need to know perspective and working through the full set of CIANA+PS information security characteristics. This leads to their use of the *deep web*, that set of web pages that are not publicly accessible (and whose names and addresses are not part of the global DNS). These pages may be behind a pay wall, for example, or require some form of user identity to be established and provisioned by the website's organization prior to allowing access. Nearly 90 percent of the web's content is estimated to be in this legitimate deep web.

- **The Dark Web:** This term refers to those websites and networks that generally are operated by threat actors, organized crime, and a variety of other groups and individuals. This subset of the Internet is where marketplaces for stolen data, new exploits and hacker tools, and related services are on offer. This may at best represent about 1 percent of the Web. It's also patrolled quite often by law enforcement and national security organizations, as well as by private threat hunting and threat intelligence services. Researchers of all kinds, from sociologists to cybersecurity, are known to peruse the pages of the Dark Web as well, in support of their legitimate tasks.

One way to think about the Dark Web and the risks that it poses to your organization is the notion that the worst way possible to detect an intrusion is to discover (or be told by someone) that your sensitive, proprietary data is for sale in a Dark Web marketplace.

Related to these terms is the concept of a *black net* or *black web,* which (borrowing from the cryptographic "red/black" terminology) refers to subnets and sets of web pages that "officially" don't exist. Web searches for their URLs or IP addresses simply get a 404 type of error; nothing acknowledges their existence, unless the access attempt is via a proven, reliable, and secure channel established by the builders and users of that black net or web. Legitimate use cases include providing safe, secure communications with political dissidents, refugees, whistleblowers, and those in the field that attempt to provide support, shelter, assistance, and protection to them.

The Dark Web: Many Dynamic Marketplaces

Trend Micro's Threat Intelligence Center has been providing insights into many different national or regional cybercriminal marketplaces within the Dark Web. To learn more, browse their reports, white papers, and other openly available threat intelligence reports at `https://www.trendmicro.com/vinfo/us/security/threat-intelligence-center/deep-web/`. Another good source is Mandiant's Threat Intelligence services, at `https://www.mandiant.com/threat/intelligence`. These and other threat intelligence services often provide free subscriptions to their news and information services, which can be quite illuminating.

Deep and Dark: Risks and Countermeasures

For most organizations with a well-established and supported set of security programs and processes, the risks of unauthorized crossings to and from your systems and the deep and the dark should already be well understood and defended against. Broad-spectrum access control, strong identity and entity management, and segmentation of data, compute, and other resources go a long way to protecting against these risks. Going any further into a more proactive defense against threats from the Dark Web, or from deep webs that are beyond your visibility or span of control, may represent an *edge case* for your organization. You should first try to determine if the potential gains in security are going to be worth the costs and the risks involved.

As with cryptographic systems and solutions, be very, very wary of trying to create a do-it-yourself Dark Web threat intelligence and warning capability. In many respects, such threat intelligence gathering is actually human intelligence—HUMINT—at its heart. Conducting this HUMINT by trolling through the digital back alleyways and marketplaces exposes the analyst to being traced back, hacked back, and targeted by many different organizations and individuals; it can also bring the analyst to the attention of many different law enforcement and national security intelligence activities that may be working the same part of the Dark Web, for reasons of their own.

Dealing with risks from the deep and dark present a classic build-or-buy type of choice for the organization, and for the vast majority, it's more straightforward and less risky to transfer or share some of these risks with a third-party threat intelligence service. That service may be working directly with the organization, through its existing MSSP, or with other third parties that are part of its IT and OT systems inward supply chains. Note too that the organization's legal and financial services elements can and should be engaging with threat intelligence services as well. For example, organizations that are involved with mergers and acquisitions activities (or ones presumed by their marketplaces to be contemplating such actions) are becoming prime targets of ransomware, disruption, and data exfiltration as espionage attacks.

DNS and Namespace Exploit Risks

Every Internet user is dependent upon the DNS and thus is exposed to two different possible sets of risks. You might think of these risks as *misrouting* and *masquerading* attacks:

- **Misrouting** attacks rely on the corruption of the DNS as a service infrastructure. Attackers look to willfully misdirect user traffic away from legitimate websites toward imposter sites, which provides opportunities for fraud, MITM attacks, malware propagation, and other risks.

- **Masquerading** attacks via DNS occur when the content of DNS message traffic to (and from) your systems is altered or misused for other purposes.

Internal to your organization, you'll need to apply greater levels of DNS service filtering, such as deep packet inspection. Firewalls, including web application firewalls, may be able to handle some of this for you. Further restrictions on inbound and outbound attempts to establish connections with your systems, such as with blocked and allowed lists, may also help prevent known or suspected hostile URLs, URIs, IP regions, or domains from making such connections.

If your organization operates its own internal DNS infrastructure, you should look closely at implementing DNS security extensions (DNSSEC). These are measures that must be applied across DNS as an infrastructure, from the root-level and top-level domain servers on down.

Cloud Security: Edgier and Foggier

Two seemingly different architectures—the hybrid IT/OT and cloud computing using edge or fog strategies—may actually have security lessons to learn from each other. Hybrid IT-OT architectures, as noted earlier, can be particularly difficult to secure and monitor. Zero-trust solutions often look at architectural changes based on rethinking some of the IT and cloud "business as usual" thinking, such as:

- Assuring that only fully trusted, tested, and validated software and data updates are flowed down to OT enclaves, systems, and devices

- Fragmenting bidirectional data flows, both within the OT enclave and across the IT-OT security perimeter, into unidirectional flows, which can be hardened via data diodes or unidirectional gateways

- Providing protocol isolation across the IT-OT perimeter

As the organization's virtual architectures shift more toward edge and fog systems, they may also make greater use of service-oriented architectures, hybrid cloud models, or other cloud deployment and service models.

One approach that is finding growing acceptance with organizations is to use *firewall as a service* (FWaaS) as part of their secure cloud computing strategy. These systems are also known as *secure access service edge* (SASE), a term coined by Gartner in 2019. They offer users a simpler and more tightly controlled direct access pathway to the resources, applications, and systems, based on defined privileges and any risk-based access control criteria in use. SASE and FWaaS offerings provide a wide range of capabilities, which are constantly evolving as this part of the security marketplace develops and matures.

Borrowing from the OT side of the security experience, it may be time for the organization and its security team to challenge some of the implicit assumptions that may be driving the edge and fog side of their cloud systems use. One example of this may be in the choice of software and systems development and support management processes currently in use. If these can be segregated by risk levels (for example), then those with lower-risk thresholds may do well with a CI/CD-style, rapid update approach, while more risk-intolerant processes and workflows may require a process geared to more formal security assessment throughout.

CURIOSITY AS COUNTERMEASURE

When asked what one personality trait or characteristic, more than any other, is so important for an information security specialist to have, many senior risk managers, CISOs, and seasoned cybersecurity professionals say *curiosity*. That probably sums up this appendix better than any other idea could.

Get curious. Stay curious. The daily grind of plowing through alerts and logs or monitoring the dashboards in a watch center can sometimes blunt the sharp edge of your curiosity. Keep this from happening by simply asking questions. Question what the data or the report seems to be suggesting; find its assumptions and challenge them, or better still, make your own educated guesses as to its unstated assumptions, and challenge these as well.

Every day, more than half a million new malware specimens are observed in the wild. None of the state of the shelf anti-malware, antivirus, or firewall systems and services can keep up with that rate of change. As the attackers continue to scale up with the as-a-service organizational and business model, so too will we see an increase in the numbers and kinds of probes, intrusion attempts, penetrations, and actions against the assets of legitimate businesses and organizations.

Your curiosity can't stop all of that, of course. But it's the one place you can choose to start from.

Get curious.

Index

industrial espionage, 13–15
intellectual property, 10–13
requirements, 665–666
security and, 6
confidentiality, integrity, availability (CIA), 7, 84
confidentiality, integrity, availability, nonrepudiation, authorization (CIANA)
    about, 8
    log files, 229
    OSI reference model and, 328–333
configuration control, 218–219
configuration control board (CCB), 68
configuration enumeration, 69
configuration item (CI), 68
configuration management (CM), 66–68, 218–219
configuration management and configuration control (CM/CC), 66–67
connectionless protocols, 497
connection-oriented protocols, 496–497
connections, 652
containerization
    virtual environments, 722–723
    VMs, 707
containment, 275–277
content distribution networks (CDNs), 585
contingency operations planning, 308
continuity, virtual environments, 727
continuous assessment, 752–753
continuous compliance, 752–753
continuous integration and continuous delivery (CI/CD) systems, 756
Control Objectives for Information and Related Technologies (COBIT), 192–193
controlled egress system, 60
controlled entry system, 60
controls
    administrative, 61–66
    compensating controls, 41–42
    corrective, 40
    detective controls, 39–40
    deterrent controls, 37–39
    dual control, 33
    implementing, 56–66
    least privilege, 30–31
    lifecycle, 42–43
    need to know, 30, 34–35
    physical, 58–60
    preventative, 39
    risk treatment, 200–202
    security and, 6
    separation of duties, 31–34
    technical, 57–58
    two-person integrity, 33
converged protocols
    Fibre Channel over Ethernet (FCoE), 508
    Internet Small Computer System Interface (iSCSI), 509
    Multiprotocol Label Switching (MPLS), 509

    network-attached storage (NAS), 509
    storage area network (SAN), 509
copyleft, 13
copyright, 12–13
CORAS, 183
corrective controls, 40
correlation, 270–271
cost centers, risk management and, 165–168
Cost Optimized Parallel COdeBreaker (COPACABANA), 361
Counter Mode with Cipher Block Chaining Message Authentication Code Protocol (CCMP), 629–630
countermeasures, implementation, 283–284
covert channels
    about, 696–697
    isolating, guest operating system, 721–722
credentials, 94
critical asset protection planning, 309
cross-layer protocols, 535–536
crossover error rate (CER), 96–97
cross-site request forgery (XSRF), 550
cross-site scripting (XSS), 550
cryptanalysis, 347
cryptanalytic attacks, 408–409
crypto family tree, 342
cryptocurrencies, 435–437
cryptographic accelerators, 413
cryptographic hygiene, 393, 396–400
cryptographic module, 411–412
Cryptographic Module Validation Program (CMVP), 345
cryptographic system, 345
cryptography. *See also* decryption; encryption
    about, 336, 425–437
    Advanced Encryption Standard (AES), 361–362
    algorithms
        about, 339–340
        Blowfish, 362–363
        encryption, 392–393
        IDEA, 363
        path validation algorithm, 392
        Twofish, 362–363
    attacks, 401–409
    auditability and, 423–424
    authentication and, 420–421
    authenticity, 415–417
    availability and, 418
    AZTEC, 371
    block ciphers, 353–358
    blockchain, 434–437
    CAST, 364
    cipher systems
        about, 353
        CAST, 364
        CryptoCypher, 365
        stream ciphers, 365–371
    collaboration security, 440
    competitive edge and, 424
    compliance-driven information, 417

risk mitigation controls, 56–57
risk register, 160–161
risk reporting
    CVSS, 163–164
    risk register, 160–161
    threats, intelligence sharing, 161–162
risk treatment
    about, 195–196
    acceptance, 196–197
    avoidance, 199
    controls, 200–202
    elimination, 199
    mitigation, 198
    recast, 199
    remediation, 198
    residual risk, 200
    share, 197
    transfer, 197
RiskIT, 192–193
Rivest, Ron, 370
Rivest-Shamir-Adleman (RSA), 374, 377–378
role-based access control (RBAC), 142–143
root certificate, 460
route poisoning, 508
routing
    about, 472, 478
    autonomous system (AS), 482
    dedicated connections, 484
    dynamically routed connections, 482–483
    hardwired, 484
    hold-down timers, 508
    route poisoning, 508
    split horizon, 508
    static routing, 483–484
Routing Information Protocol (RIP), 495, 507, 508, 544, 610
rude awakenings, 249–250
RUMINT, 104

S

safeguard value, 175
safety
    about, 263–264
    cryptography and, 422
    requirements, 665
    security and, 7
Salsa20 cipher, 370–371
salting, 351–353
sandboxing, malicious activity and, 688
Schneier, Bruce, 362–363, 395–396
scoping guidance, 64
search space, key strength, 393–394
secure access service edge (SASE), 766
secure browsing, endpoint device security and, 697–700
secure cryptoprocessors, 410–413
secure development lifecycle (SDL), threat modeling, 181–182
Secure Hash Algorithm-1 (SHA-1), 299

secure message digest, 385
Secure Shell (SSH), 507, 548
Secure Sockets Layer (SSL), 427
Secure/Multipurpose Internet Mail Extension (S/MIME), 390, 432–433
security. *See also* incident response
    accountability, 18
    authentication, 27–28
    authenticity, 6
    availability, 6, 17–18
    confidentiality
        about, 6, 8–9
        corporate espionage, 13–15
        industrial espionage, 13–15
        intellectual property, 10–13
        requirements, 665
    controls
        about, 6
        compensating controls, 41–42
        corrective, 40
        detective controls, 39–40
        deterrent controls, 37–39
        dual control, 33
        implementation, 56–66
        least privilege, 30–31
        lifecycle, 42–43
        need to know, 30, 34–35, 143
        preventative, 39
        separation of duties, 31–34
        two-person integrity, 33
    functional requirements, 665
    integrity, 6, 15–17
    job rotation, 35–36
    nonfunctional requirements, 665
    nonrepudiation, 7, 26–27
    operationalizing, 751–757
    physical, 650
    possession, 6
    privacy
        about, 7, 18–19, 25–26
        in information systems, 19–22
        in law, 19–22
        NPI, 22–23
        PII, 22–23
        in practice, 19–22
    privilege creep, 35–36
    ransom attacks, 249
    safety, 7, 28–29
    safety requirements, 665
    supply chain, 667
    transparency, 7
    utility, 6
Security Assertion Markup Language (SAML), 118–120, 574
security assessment
    assessment strategies, 213–215
    assessment-driven training, 212–213
    asset management, 218–219